This Thing Called Music

EUROPEA: ETHNOMUSICOLOGIES AND MODERNITIES

Series Editors: Philip V. Bohlman and Martin Stokes

The new millennium challenges ethnomusicologists, dedicated to studying the music of the world, to examine anew the Western musics they have treated as "traditional," and to forge new approaches to world musics that are often overlooked because of their deceptive familiarity. As the modern discipline of ethnomusicology expanded during the second half of the twentieth century, influenced significantly by ethnographic methods in the social sciences, ethnomusicology's "field" increasingly shifted to the exoticized Other. The comparative methodologies previously generated by Europeanist scholars to study and privilege Western musics were deliberately discarded. Europe as a cultural area was banished to historical musicology, and European vernacular musics became the spoils left to folk-music and, later, popular-music studies.

Europea challenges ethnomusicology to return to Europe and to encounter its disciplinary past afresh, and the present is a timely moment to do so. European unity nervously but insistently asserts itself through the political and cultural agendas of the European Union, causing Europeans to reflect on a bitterly and violently fragmented past and its ongoing repercussions in the present, and to confront new challenges and opportunities for integration. There is also an intellectual moment to be seized as Europeans reformulate the history of the present, an opportunity to move beyond the fragmentation and atomism the later twentieth century has bequeathed and to enter into broader social, cultural, and political relationships.

Europea is not simply a reflection of and on the current state of research. Rather, the volumes in this series move in new directions and experiment with diverse approaches. The series establishes a forum that can engage scholars, musicians, and other interlocutors in debates and discussions crucial to understanding the present historical juncture. This dialogue, grounded in ethnomusicology's interdisciplinarity, will be animated by reflexive attention to the specific social configurations of knowledge of and scholarship on the musics of Europe. Such knowledge and its circulation as ethnomusicological scholarship are by no means dependent on professional academics, but rather are conditioned, as elsewhere, by complex interactions between universities, museums, amateur organizations, state agencies, and markets. Both the broader view to which ethnomusicology aspires and the critical edge necessary to understanding the present moment are served by broadening the base on which "academic" discussion proceeds.

"Europe" will emerge from the volumes as a space for critical dialogue, embracing competing and often antagonistic voices from across the continent, across the Atlantic, across the Mediterranean and the Black Sea, and across a world altered ineluctably by European colonialism and globalization. The diverse subjects and interdisciplinary approaches in individual volumes capture something of—and, in a small way, become part of—the jangling polyphony through which the "New Europe" has explosively taken musical shape in public discourse, in expressive culture, and, increasingly, in political form. Europea: Ethnomusicologies and Modernities aims to provide a critical framework necessary to capture something of the turbulent dynamics of music performance, engaging the forces that inform and deform, contest and mediate the senses of identity, selfhood, belonging, and progress that shape "European" musical experience in Europe and across the world.

1. *Celtic Modern: Music at the Global Fringe*, edited by Martin Stokes and Philip V. Bohlman, 2003.
2. *Albanian Urban Lyric Song in the 1930s*, by Eno Koço, 2004.
3. *The Mediterranean in Music: Critical Perspectives, Common Concerns, Cultural Differences*, edited by David Cooper and Kevin Dawe, 2005.
4. *On a Rock in the Middle of the Ocean: Songs and Singers in Tory Island, Ireland*, by Lillis Ó Laoire, 2005.
5. *Transported by Song: Corsican Voices from Oral Tradition to World Stage*, by Caroline Bithell, 2007.
6. *Balkan Popular Culture and the Ottoman Ecumene: Music, Image, and Regional Political Discourse*, edited by Donna A. Buchanan, 2007.
7. *Music and Musicians in Crete: Performance and Ethnography in a Mediterranean Island Society*, by Kevin Dawe, 2007.
8. *The New (Ethno)musicologies*, edited by Henry Stobart, 2008.
9. *Balkan Refrain: Form and Tradition in European Folk Song*, by Dimitrije O. Golemović, 2010.
10. *Music and Displacement: Diasporas, Mobilities, and Dislocations in Europe and Beyond*, edited by Erik Levi and Florian Scheding, 2010.
11. *Balkan Epic: Song, History, Modernity*, edited by Philip V. Bohlman and Nada Petković, 2012.
12. *What Makes Music European: Looking beyond Sound*, by Marcello Sorce Keller, 2012.
13. *The Past Is Always Present: The Revival of the Byzantine Musical Tradition at Mount Athos*, Tore Tvarnø Lind, 2012.

14. *Becoming an Ethnomusicologist: A Miscellany of Influences*, by Bruno Nettl, 2013.
15. *Empire of Song: Europe and Nation in the Eurovision Song Contest*, by Dafni Tragaki, 2013.
16. *Revival and Reconciliation: Sacred Music in the Making of European Modernity*, by Philip V. Bohlman, 2013.
17. *Sámi Musical Performance and the Politics of Indigeneity in Northern Europe*, by Thomas R. Hilder, 2014.
18. *This Thing Called Music: Essays in Honor of Bruno Nettl*, edited by Victoria Lindsay Levine and Philip V. Bohlman, 2015.

This Thing Called Music

Essays in Honor of Bruno Nettl

Edited by
Victoria Lindsay Levine
Philip V. Bohlman

ROWMAN & LITTLEFIELD
Lanham • Boulder • New York • London

Published by Rowman & Littlefield
A wholly owned subsidiary of The Rowman & Littlefield Publishing Group, Inc.
4501 Forbes Boulevard, Suite 200, Lanham, Maryland 20706
www.rowman.com

Unit A, Whitacre Mews, 26-34 Stannary Street, London SE11 4AB

British Library Cataloguing in Publication Information Available

Library of Congress Cataloging-in-Publication Data

This thing called music : essays in honor of Bruno Nettl / edited by Victoria Lindsay Levine, Philip V. Bohlman.
pages cm. — (Europea : ethnomusicologies and modernities ; 18)
Includes bibliographical references and index.
ISBN 978-1-4422-4207-4 (cloth : alk. paper) — ISBN 978-1-4422-4208-1 (ebook) 1. Ethnomusicology. 2. Music—History and criticism. 3. Music—Social aspects. I. Levine, Victoria Lindsay, 1954—editor. II. Bohlman, Philip Vilas, editor. III. Nettl, Bruno, 1930—honoree.
ML3798.T56 2015
780.89–dc23 2014047223

™ The paper used in this publication meets the minimum requirements of American National Standard for Information Sciences—Permanence of Paper for Printed Library Materials, ANSI/NISO Z39.48-1992.

Printed in the United States of America

For Bruno Nettl
teacher, colleague, friend
on the occasion of his eighty-fifth birthday

Contents

List of Figures

List of Tables

Acknowledgments

The Festschrift is perhaps the academic literary genre most indebted to the accumulation of acknowledgments. The volume as a whole acknowledges the lifework of a colleague and friend, a teacher and inspiration. Each chapter expresses the more individual acknowledgment of a student or collaborator. The subjects that distinguish each chapter and the themes that link multiple sections together acknowledge the ways in which lessons in the classroom have been transformed into the influences that shape entire disciplines. There can be little question that the present Festschrift for Bruno Nettl, *This Thing Called Music*, exemplifies the finest qualities of the Festschrift to gather the voices of many to acknowledge the contributions of Bruno Nettl to modern ethnomusicology and his role in shaping the intellectual history of music in our day.

There is so much to acknowledge here, and within a matter of pages we turn over much of the task of acknowledging the many intellectual debts owed Bruno Nettl to the contributors who bring their own perspectives to the thing called music. There are many other individuals, nonetheless, whose roles in making this book possible—some smaller, others larger, all critical—deserve acknowledgment at this point. We are particularly grateful to the many students and colleagues who, from the very first queries about a Festschrift for Bruno Nettl, responded with enthusiasm and were quick to offer suggestions about the ways to make the volume really happen. As the list of distinguished contributors fully demonstrates, invitations were accepted with enthusiasm, and our contributors turned to their most thoughtful and significant research to honor Bruno Nettl. We are also grateful for the abundance of practical suggestions we received, above all from those who worked with us to make this book a Festschrift and to transform it as a Festschrift into a volume whose individual chapters cohere as a much larger chapter in the history of ethnomusicology.

Even as the scholarship in this volume stretches across disciplines and geographical boundaries, the editors are indebted to the support they received close to their own academic homes. At Colorado College, Vicki Levine's research and editorial work were supported by the Christine S. Johnson Professorship in music (Susan Ashley, dean), a Mellon Faculty-Student Collaborative Research Grant in the humanities (Sandra Wong, dean), and a Jackson Fellowship in Southwestern studies (Eric Leonard, director). She received invaluable help with manuscript preparation from research assistant Emily Kohut, music copyist Connor Rice, and Help Desk student worker Caitlin Taber. Felix Sanchez, creative director of the Colorado College Communications unit, kindly designed the book cover, using a photograph of Wanda Nettl's untitled paper collage provided by Natalie Fiol, the Nettls' granddaughter. Vicki also thanks her writing partner, Professor Tamara Bentley (art history), for ongoing encouragement. At the University of Chicago Phil Bohlman expresses his gratitude for research funding from the Department of Music (Anne W. Robertson, chair) and from the Division of Humanities (Martha T. Roth, dean). His research assistants never fail to enhance his writing and editorial work, and for this project Phil especially thanks Michael Figueroa. At the University of Illinois at Urbana-Champaign, Philip Yampolsky helped us with the final stages of production, particularly the preparation of the index for the book. We also wish to thank the School of Music at the University of Illinois, and its director, Jeffrey Magee, for financial support for the Festschrift itself and for logistical support as the book becomes a springboard for celebrating Bruno Nettl's half-century of teaching and scholarship at Illinois.

From the first stages devoted to planning this book, we were fortunate to have the support of many who recognized that its potential as a Festschrift would be considerable. Bennett Graff, senior editor at Rowman & Littlefield, sought not to dissuade us from publishing the book as a Festschrift; rather, he began to explore just what needed to be done to realize the potential of a Festschrift. We extend our thanks to Bennett, and to Martin Stokes, who, as co-editor of Europea: Ethnomusicologies and Modernities, enthusiastically supported inclusion of the Festschrift in that series. It was a pleasure to work with the editorial and production staff at Rowman & Littlefield, and we thank them for the many ways in which they worked with us as publication drew closer, especially Lara Graham and Monica Savaglia.

No project with or about Bruno Nettl would be complete without acknowledging the role of those who shared the sojourn of ethnomusicological scholarship with him and with us. To know Bruno as a teacher and scholar is to know him as a husband and father in his own family. This Festschrift, too, acknowledges the special intimacy of family, for it would have been impossible without our conversations with his wife, Wanda, and daughters Becky and Gloria. At home in Colorado Springs and Oak Park, our own spouses, Mark Levine and Christine Bohlman, were present from the start as we listened to and learned from our teacher, Bruno Nettl, and we close by thanking them for standing by us over the decades to which this Festschrift ultimately bears witness.

~

Introduction

Bruno Nettl's Lifetime in Search of Music

Victoria Lindsay Levine and Philip V. Bohlman

Who was in the audience that night [at the University of Illinois]? . . . An ethnomusicologist who'd spend the next forty years proving that music evaded every definition.

—Richard Powers, *Orfeo* (2014)

But to the central question, I have no answer and no theory.

—Bruno Nettl, *A Lifetime of Learning* (2014)

How remarkable it is to devote a lifetime of learning, writing, and teaching to this thing called music! It is the search for music's thingness—its materiality, its ontology, its tangibility and presence in human history—that defines Bruno Nettl's career. It is a search that inspired so many to join him—as students, colleagues, listeners, and learners—and it is a search that provides the substance of *This Thing Called Music*, the Festschrift with which Bruno's fellow sojourners honor him on the occasion of his eighty-fifth birthday.

The passion of a lifetime pursuit notwithstanding, Bruno is only too well aware that music's thingness is paradoxical. Whenever given the chance to focus on this thing called music—his lengthy essay on "Music" in the 2001 *New Grove Dictionary of Music and Musicians* was the first-ever entry on the central subject of the most venerable of all reference works devoted to music, indeed, an entry still not superseded—Bruno struck out along the pathway of potential plurals. If musics proliferated, especially across the intellectual history of ethnomusicology, this is for Bruno no ground for equivocating. In his 2014 novel, *Orfeo*, Richard Powers captures Bruno, not quite fictionally, as a concert-going ethnomusicologist at the University of Illinois's Smith Hall in the early 1960s, already determined to seek definitions for the indefinable. Critically important for his search is that the singularity of music's thingness actually resists the dismissal that could otherwise be reduced to non-definition. Quite the contrary, it is the singularity of the plurals that established music's primacy in Bruno's enjoinder to his students always to "think big!" Surely, we witness here one more motto befitting Bruno's lifetime in search of music, and it is hardly surprising that he emphasizes that message in the ACLS *Lifetime of Learning* Haskins Lecture in May 2014. Each new monograph and each new editorial endeavor expands the boundaries of ethnomusicology, enhancing the field in the many ways that project the big ideas while capturing the minute differences in the ways all humans and societies think about music.

It was our challenge as editors, one we enthusiastically embraced, to ensure that this Festschrift contributes to Bruno Nettl's lifetime in search of music that all the contributors here have followed so closely. As we responded to the challenge, we learned much, once again, about how complex this thing called music really is. As the editors initially sought structure for the different sections, for example, we thought we might tease out a group of themes that best characterized Bruno's scholarship and teaching. Identifying individual themes—the concentration on certain regions, music cultures, or repertories, for instance—proved to be difficult, and then impossible. A cluster of former students that might represent a Bruno Nettl school once again failed to materialize. Disciplinary boundaries did not parse conveniently into discrete academic allegiances. Even determining the core subject for the book—this thing called music—did not succeed in checking the influx of big ideas.

We freely confess to the obvious fact that the titles we have given to the individual sections evoke titles from some of Bruno's most influential publications, as well as his penchant for big ideas rather than staking the boundaries of specialized research. Quite deliberately, we chose these titles because they refer to the many rather than the few, hence the plurality of music's singularity. "Communities of Music" are notable for the ways they embody "Issues and Concepts" and afford the multiplication of "Change, Adaptation, and Survival." "Historical Studies" emerge from "Analytical Studies" to yield the "Intellectual History of Ethnomusicology."

Critical to all these sections and the chapters they contain, moreover, is the explicit connectivity and collectivity they reflect. It is together, as a collective, that we have joined with Bruno to experience this thing called music. The concept of the collective surely anchors the ideas that flood in upon Bruno's most ambitious writing about music and musics, for it is the collective that makes the singular plural. Drawing his *New Grove* entry on "Music" to a close, he writes: "The purpose of this article is, indeed, to show that, in its conception of music, the world is a pastiche of diversity" (Nettl 2001:436). We could not be more pleased that the collective of music scholars who contributed their voices and ideas to this Festschrift have captured precisely such a pastiche of diversity.

Many of the scholars who contributed to this Festschrift are Bruno's former students and doctoral advisees from the University of Illinois at Urbana-Champaign, including the editors. Although Bruno has retired from teaching, we remember him in his role as a professor, with high expectations tempered by encouragement, sociability, and engagement with all things musical at the university. Among his most popular courses were those focused on geographic regions, which were offered under the rubric "Music 317." These courses were among the few musicology offerings open to both undergraduate and graduate students, and we flocked to them from the School of Music, the Anthropology Department, and other departments across campus. Bruno provided lengthy reading and listening lists, and we studied those materials in depth because we knew we would be called upon for cogent synthesis and incisive discussion. Although the literature in the field has grown exponentially, the materials on those bibliographies and discographies have become classics that still constitute the core of required reading for any aspiring ethnomusicologist. Among the outstanding features of Bruno's course design was his openness to various analytical approaches and theoretical models. There was nothing dogmatic in the shape or content of his reading and listening lists, or in his lectures; no evidence of professional rivalries through omissions or obvious bias. Bruno consistently modeled an appreciation for the boundless curiosity, tempered by intellectual balance, he so richly demonstrates in his publications.

Fully aware of the long hours we worked preparing for seminars and exams, Bruno often stopped by our offices or library carrels with an invitation to coffee, lunch, Friday happy hour, or a party. To receive a photocopied installment from Bruno's *Chacun* papers, which began with "*Chacun à son goût*, or *de gustibus . . .* ?: A New Approach to the Determinants of Music" (1981), signaled an invitation to dessert at the Nettls' home. These hilariously clever epistles propounded Bruno's theory of just desserts, poking fun at academic polemic with the argument that the best music comes from cultures with the best desserts. He assigned a fictionalized name, inspired by particular sweets or pastries, to everyone invited to the party, and part of the fun of receiving the invitation was decoding the names and the invented publications attributed to them. The Nettls' home was always open to students, and during Bruno's teaching career it was the scene of spontaneous dance parties, marzipan-making sessions, riotous limerick readings, and, of course, dessert parties. Bruno taught us to be serious music scholars, but not to take ourselves too seriously.

Bruno wanted all of his former advisees to succeed, and therefore his guidance did not end when we finished our dissertations and received our diplomas. He mentored us during job searches and throughout our professional careers, writing countless letters of support for promotions and grant applications. Bruno's role as adviser has gradually transitioned to that of helpful colleague. He recommends us for research and publication opportunities and collaborates with us when our interests coincide. He is often the first to read our new publications and to send a congratulatory note, and he stays in touch through frequent phone calls and e-mail messages. Bruno celebrates our milestones, such as marriages, babies, and significant birthdays, and is particularly attentive as we weather the vicissitudes of aging. As an adviser, Bruno preferred to be perceived as avuncular rather than as a father figure; in actuality, he has always nurtured and maintained deep and abiding friendships with his former students.

Bruno's vocation for teaching extends beyond the University of Illinois and continues to inform new generations of music students and aspiring ethnomusicologists around the world. His magisterial volume, *The Study of Ethnomusicology: Thirty-one Issues and Concepts* (1983, 2005), is the most comprehensive introduction to our discipline and stands as a pinnacle in the history of music scholarship; its third edition went to press as this Festschrift was being completed. Prior to the publication of *The Study of Ethnomusicology*, Bruno introduced generations of students to our discipline through *Theory and Method in Ethnomusicology* (1964); the practice exercises and problems he presented in the appendix are just as applicable in 2015 as they were fifty years ago. In addition, thousands of students experiencing world music for the first time have received an introduction to the topic through the textbook *Excursions in World Music* (1992), now entering its seventh edition, the foundations for which were laid by Bruno and his co-authors from the University of Illinois and elsewhere.

Bruno is an intensely social person, and as such, he has established collegial relationships throughout the world, including with many of the contributors to this Festschrift. The essays presented here attest to his fruitful collaborations with colleagues in North America, Europe, the Middle East, and Asia. Bruno's appreciation of diverse topics, methodological approaches, and theoretical models is reflected in these pages. The contributors hail from ten countries; their terminology draws upon twelve languages other than English; and their primary disciplinary orientations include historical musicology, systematic musicology, music education, history, medical humanities, linguistic anthropology, and, of course, ethnomusicology. The collection itself evokes the myriad intellectual paths Bruno has traveled alongside many companions.

With this Festschrift, then, we celebrate listening and thinking, learning and writing, connectivity and collectivity, complexity and diversity, the singularity of plurals, boundary crossings, thinking big, and serious music scholarship, all imbued with a sense of wonder at this thing called music, and with gratitude for Bruno Nettl.

References

Nettl, Bruno. 1964. *Theory and Method in Ethnomusicology*. New York: Free Press of Glencoe.

———. 2001. "Music." In *The New Grove Dictionary of Music and Musicians*, revised edition, edited by Stanley Sadie, Volume 17, 425–37. London: Macmillan.

———. 2005. *The Study of Ethnomusicology: Thirty-one Issues and Concepts*, second edition. Urbana: University of Illinois Press.

———. 2014. *A Lifetime of Learning*. Philadelphia: American Council of Learned Societies.

Nettl, Bruno, Charles Capwell, Philip V. Bohlman, Isabel K. F. Wong, and Thomas Turino. 1992. *Excursions in World Music*, first edition. Englewood Cliffs, NJ: Prentice-Hall.

Powers, Richard. 2014. *Orfeo*. New York: W. W. Norton.

PART I

COMMUNITIES OF MUSIC

CHAPTER ONE

~

Recording the Life Review

A Case Study from the Medical Humanities

Theresa Allison

Bruno Nettl accepted me as a graduate student in 1992, the year after he retired from the University of Illinois. He thought it might be interesting to see what happened if a medical student also trained in ethnomusicology. Twenty-some years later, he remains active as a writer, a researcher, a teacher, and an advocate within the Society for Ethnomusicology and without. He continues to challenge his former students, now tenured faculty, music publishing professionals, and administrators, to grow and develop. With this in mind, it seems fitting that the only physician he mentored should try to bring together theories from medicine and ethnomusicology, in a case study about eighty- and ninety-year-old men and women who continued to learn, to grow, and to make music together.

Over the past sixty years, ethnomusicologists have examined and adapted theoretical models from fields such as cultural anthropology, social theory, philosophy, history, and political science. Gerontology, by contrast, has remained largely ignored in our discipline, despite the fact that many ethnomusicologists study with local elders and examine intergenerational differences. Similarly, while a growing number of gerontologists have become interested in the performing arts, few have considered the work of ethnomusicologists. This chapter integrates the two discourses using a single case study, the production of a CD and DVD in a uniquely geriatric setting, a nursing home.

In gerontology, we have long accepted Robert Butler's concept of the life review and the ways in which reminiscence can create meaning in later life (cf. Butler 1963; Butler 1974a; Butler 1974b; Haber 2006). In his seminal 1963 article, Butler contradicted prevailing medical theory, which associated reminiscence with senility, asserting instead that life review was a natural and universal occurrence, one important to the resolution of unresolved psychological conflicts (Butler 1963). His approach continues to be used in clinical practice and refined in theory (cf. Haber 2006; Webster, Bohlmeijer, and Westerhof 2010). But the life review holds within itself a tacit assumption that the process of integrating one's life is inherently narrative. In ethnomusicology we recognize that people do not merely talk about their lives, they enact their lives through daily routines and creative performances. The life review, I assert, may take place through performance as well as narrative, through music as well as words.

The narrative properties of reminiscence therapy and the life review in late life development have been well studied; however, little has been written about the performative and presentational aspects of the process. This is now changing. With the development of the National Center for Creative Aging,[1] researchers and advocates alike are gaining access to the wide variety of artistic products created by elders. We have seen successful grassroots interventions to enhance creativity among people with dementia, such as the iPod project[2] and Meet Me at MoMA.[3] Tool kits such as the TimeSlips[4] improvisational theater are being disseminated widely throughout skilled nursing facilities. Scholars are working not only to promote the role of the arts in aging, but also to promote the careful intellectual scrutiny of those arts. A new study of the health effects of singing in community choirs[5] has brought to the academic table questions of methodology and analytic goals as well as questions about humanity in relation to science.

I approach aging and the arts by looking at music as a performance medium through which elders not only create meaning, but present their lives through performance. Through concerts and music recordings, elders have the opportunity to create a permanent legacy for their families and their communities. I learned of the potential for songs to serve as life review from a group of older, self-identified non-musicians in a collaborative Songwriting Works workshop.[6] For example, their lilting waltz, "I'm 100 Years Old," includes the following lyrics:

Chorus:
I'm 100 years old or so I've been told
But I don't feel my age at all
I'll live and find out what this life is all about
And I hope and I pray it's a ball!

Verse 1 (soli, spoken by the elders):
When we were eighteen we had different lives
Some had husbands, some had wives
Did we ever carry on!
We graduated high school, went to college for a time
Some had children, went to work
And then the war was on

We went into the service: the Army, the Navy, the Shipyards
The Air Force, the Coast Guard saved hundreds of lives
The $64,000 question: Will we ever really have peace?
We watched while in that war so many, many died

Chorus (repeated)

Verse 2 (soli, spoken):
They say "Life begins at 40"—I can tell you it's true
Our 40s and 50s were sensational times
Just looking back on them—Oh boy, I can't tell you—
We were traveling gypsies
On the road all the time

Chorus (repeated)

Verse 3 (soli, spoken):
Sixty is like a diamond—to see your children all grown up
I'm happy, content—
We're still carrying on!
Keep your mind and body active
I can tell you that's a must!
To go through the stages, it's healthier to love
With peace in your heart
Life will agree with you
It sounds like a dream—but it's true
It's true!

Chorus (repeated)[7]

The composers and performers, whose average age was eighty-seven, wrote this song in a small group process, facilitated by the singer-songwriter Judith-Kate Friedman. Although not all songs written in this process fit the concept of a life review, "I'm 100 Years Old" certainly does. In a decade-by-decade overview of a lifetime, the singer-songwriters created an integrated story of vibrant adulthood. I could appreciate intuitively that it was written by a group of eighty- and ninety-year-olds from the World War II generation. My surprise was in learning that the composers were frail, chronically ill, self-identified non-musicians, some of whom had dementia, and all of whom were living in a nursing home.

To be fair, this music was not written at a stereotypical, for-profit skilled nursing facility. The Jewish Home, San Francisco, is a 430-bed, not-for-profit skilled nursing facility in San Francisco that was founded upon a philanthropic mission to serve the Jewish community more than 140 years ago. When the CD and DVD were produced, elders had already been writing songs for four years with Friedman. In 2003, after the production of the CD, some of them began a psalms study group with Friedman and the Jewish Home's Rabbi Sheldon Marder, in which they wrote psalm-inspired musical responses (Allison 2008; Friedman 2011; Marder 2005). Although I worked with Friedman, Rabbi Marder, and many of the elders who wrote and recorded the songs during two years of participant-observation research, and provided medical care at the Home for four years, the locus of this chapter is a specific, historical moment in the Home's seventeen-year-long songwriting history, two years prior to my first visit to the Home, and five years prior to the ethnographic research study.[8]

How Do You Produce a CD in a Nursing Home? Background and Method

In 1997, elders began weekly songwriting sessions with Friedman, one group including cognitively intact elders and a few cognitively impaired elders, the other including people who all had moderate to severe dementia who resided in a "wandering" or "egress-controlled" unit. Initially supported by the California Arts Council (1997–2000; 2001–2002), the Songwriting Works program was affirmed as a line item in the activities budget by the Home in 2000.

Between 1997 and 2001, more than two hundred elders at the Home participated in weekly groups facilitated by Friedman using the Songwriting Works approach. In 2001, they received a unique opportunity, philanthropic support to produce a commercial recording, and then funding to make a video documentary of the process. Through a strange twist of fate, the recording took place during the events and aftermath of the World Trade Center attack, causing their particular performance of life review to be silhouetted against a contemporary tragedy.

This performance of culture involved multiple steps. To create their CD, elders participated in much more than the processes of choosing topics and writing the songs. They were involved in the selection of those twelve songs that would represent their legacy; aesthetic decisions about orchestration (in particular what instruments would accompany the singers and who would get each solo); decisions about the ordering and presentation of songs, for concert performance and for the CD recording; production and selection of paintings and artwork used in the CD cover and booklet; rehearsals; concert preparation; public performance; professional recording; and finally, the careful process of editing and production. Friedman notes that "the elders were even involved in decisions about production values and aesthetics such as the ratio of reverb on a given mix or the layering and degree of stereo panning of voices in choral pieces at a portable studio brought into the Home's synagogue" (personal communication, May 2014). Because of the unique needs of the songwriters, this performance of life review involved staff members in supportive roles at the Home, including assistance with makeup, hair, and in some cases, bathing, dressing, and transportation via wheelchair. This is the process that the ethnomusicologist Chris Scales refers to as the interface between recording *culture* and *recording* culture (Scales 2012:3). They were learning how to make a record and, simultaneously, were presenting themselves for that permanent record. One of Scales's critical points involves the negotiation of autonomy between musicians and their producer, and in this aspect, *Island on a Hill* (2002) is unusual. The musicians themselves were almost completely naïve of the steps required to record their music and yet were given extraordinary degrees of autonomy in decision making vis-à-vis the recording company.

The essential prerequisites to CD production listed above are largely invisible to consumers of music, and were invisible to the songwriters themselves until special funding became available for the production of the recording. At that point Friedman, serving as project director, professional songwriter, and CD producer, began a weekly CD production class in collaboration with the Home's art and media director. Several, although not all, of the songwriters and one other elder, a skilled musician, joined the class and engaged in a nine-month process of learning how to produce a recording by producing their own, *Island on a Hill*. Friedman described this process to me in detail. She explained, "The first thing we did was to listen through every single song. There were forty songs, and the elders chose the songs [that they wanted to record and share]. I would play the songs for the group and we would all see their reaction, their and our own aesthetic sensibilities in the moment" (personal communication, April 2014). When asked about the unusual degree of decision making given to the elders, she agreed that the intent was to provide the elders with as much agency as possible in each part of the process. She explained, "We collaborated on production in the same inclusive way as in the songwriting process itself" (personal communication, May 2014). In this group of men and women who had been stripped of much of their independence through institutionalization in a nursing facility, CD production became an extraordinary opportunity not only to make music, but also to engage in decision making, to exercise control, and to present their legacy in musical form.

This process also differed from conventional psychology and the narrative form of reminiscence therapy. Friedman observed that "when the life review happens creatively, it doesn't matter if they are telling the truth or not" (personal communication, April 2014). The highly metaphoric nature of songwriting enables the composers to weave together dreams with fact, leading to a very different artistic output than the memoir that may result from a conventional life review. This may be one of the reasons why songwriting enables groups of cognitively intact men and women to interact with those who have dementia and succeed in the creation of what Friedman considers a good song.

Self-Presentation through Compact Disc Production

So, what is a good song? The audio recording, *Island on a Hill*, represented the twelve best songs out of forty compositions, selected by a jury of the composers themselves. Five of the twelve songs chosen for the CD, "Gefilte Fish," "Let the Fire Fall," "Chanukah Tonight," "Beautiful Hawaii," and "Island on a Hill," were prefaced by reminiscences spoken by some of the songwriters. Friedman notes that this was a production decision intended to provide more context and to include new participants in the project (e-mail communication, May 2014). The concluding cut, "Serenity," was not a Songwriting Works composition at all. Instead, "Serenity" presented a musical setting of a popular prayer by Reinhold Niebuhr (cf. Brown 1986: xxiv) recorded before the singer's death and included posthumously.

Reviewing the titles, a few topics stand out from the perspective of life review: there are multiple sonic, cultural, and religious references to Jewish culture, from the klezmer opening of the "Yiddishe Polka"; to songs about food such as "Gefilte Fish" and "Jewish Penicillin," a recipe for chicken soup; to the song about Chanukah. Other pieces, such as "*Esther, Mayn Schwester*" (Esther, My Sister), invoke Yiddish language to express a more universal concept, in this case the joy of a new grandchild. Still others recall family holidays in Yosemite National Park and in Hawaii. One of the more poignant songs, "Don't Forget Me," brings home the fears of being lost in a nursing home and of the deep-seated need for human relationships. Nearly half of the songs were written in groups in which some people had intact cognition and some had dementia. Two of the songs were written on a residential unit that is specially designed to house people who have moderate to severe dementia and who wander, or get lost.

The choice of the title track, "Island on a Hill," is significant for a different reason. The island on the hill can be seen on the CD jacket, also painted and designed by the songwriters. The island is the Home itself, and the song represents a thank you to the institution that houses the songwriters. Friedman has noted on multiple occasions that it is fairly common for new Songwriting Works groups to choose a tribute to a beloved place or group of

Figure 1.1. CD Cover, *Island on a Hill*. Courtesy of The Jewish Home, San Francisco

people as the theme of their first collectively composed song. New songwriting groups across the country have asked her if they could write their first song in honor of the institution or organization that provided the songwriting workshops. It is a classic form of musical reciprocity, a way of giving back when it is not possible to reciprocate through money or goods. In music more generally, the use of song to give back to a patron is a concept that stretches back many centuries, and across many cultures.

We should be attentive to the choice of songs because they were selected by a jury composed of the songwriters, based upon their own criteria. It is the same process I observed the songwriters to use when they selected songs to accompany the dedication of their new synagogue in 2007, and it provides the musicians with an almost unheard-of level of autonomy vis-à-vis a recording studio. In this process, musical beauty is only one criterion, balanced against issues of identity, memory, and personal history. Above all, Friedman says that the songs needed to resonate with the jury. It appears that they chose the songs they loved the most.

In essence, the songs in *Island on a Hill* can be treated as the products of life review activities, based upon vignettes that have been carefully mediated and selected for presentation in concert and for audio recording. The CD itself is a representation of their collective lives, one that can be given to their families as a legacy and played again in further reminiscence.

Life Review through Documentary Filming

The songs are further modified for presentation in the video documentary, *A 'Specially Wonderful Affair* (2002). For example, one scene in the video begins with a woman who lives at the Home talking about how to make gefilte fish and is then interspersed, line by line, with a man reciting the haiku poem that led to the song "Chanukah Tonight." The phrases are mixed out of sequence for artistic effect, creating what in musicology we might consider a hocket, a line-by-line interspersing of voices that, together, create an intact whole. Following the filming, the decision was made to include these spontaneous statements as cuts on the CD. The woman's statements were included as the "Recipe" followed by the song "Gefilte Fish." The man's recitation was included as the "Haiku" that preceded "Chanukah Tonight." This scene in the video segues to a rehearsal, showing the augmentation of the chorus by a klezmer band consisting of clarinet, violin, guitar, and piano. The decision to orchestrate with klezmer instruments was, according to Friedman, also a decision made by the group in conversation about their goals for the final musical sound. Accordion, bass, and drums were later added in the studio.

The klezmer band was chosen for the majority of songs that were intended to be klezmer tunes or to have a Yiddish or folk reference, but not for all of the songs. For example, "Jewish Penicillin" is a song about chicken soup, recited as a beat poem and accompanied only by fretless bass and drums, with judicious use of silence for emphasis by the woman who won that particular solo audition for the recording. The songs that have Hawaiian themes also include ukulele and slack key guitar in their accompaniment.

Reminiscence in the Context of Contemporary Events

Generally speaking, the medical literature treats the life review and reminiscence therapy as if they occur in a politico-historical vacuum. Effectiveness is predicated upon the timing of the life review within the life span of the individual who is reminiscing and the outcomes of the therapy. But, for older people who still possess all of their faculties, reminiscence occurs in the context of current events. The impact of current events was brought into sharp relief when the funding became available for the documentary film production in early September 2001. Prior to September, plans had been made to record the tracks professionally for the CD in two settings. The songs would be recorded in the synagogue, which was intended to function as a somewhat controlled, studio-like setting, using multiple tracks and takes. The songs would also be recorded in the Main Lounge, the Home's proscenium-style hall, during a concert for the community. Because of the new funding opportunity, a film crew was engaged to spend several days filming at the Home and to videotape both the on-site studio session and the live concert. On September 5, 2001, the singer-songwriters began final rehearsals and filming commenced. Then, on the day prior to the concert, the World Trade Center collapsed under the September 11 terrorist attacks. This tragic event led not only to a visceral reaction by the elders, but an artistic one. The response of the elders in the video was insightful and immediate, including statements such as "they killed so many thousands of people" and "I hope it doesn't lead to war" (*A 'Specially Wonderful Affair* 2002). The statements mirror the lines in "I'm 100 Years Old" about their World War II experiences. Despite the trauma of the events, the elders made it clear to the nursing home administration that they desired to continue, and this drove the decision to have the concert in the immediate wake of the World Trade Center's collapse. Another administrator noted that this approach of coming together as a community during tragedy was part of a long-standing tradition, and that being able to have the concert was empowering for the singers. Speaking with me years later, the songwriters still stood by their decision to finish the recording.

Although it is difficult to reconstruct the events more than a decade later, a few key program changes seem to have been made in response to the terrorist attacks. Prefatory remarks about the bombings were given by the director of resident life, who framed the concert as a supportive event in the context of a tragedy. Then the rabbi offered a prayer for peace. In the documentary itself, further changes are included that enhance the view of the concert as a supportive event. The film reflexively examined the circumstances under which it was made, interviewing musicians, elders, and administrators about the decision to proceed despite their grief. In the film, the concert appears to begin with the slow, nurturing, hopeful "*Esther, Mayn Schwester*," a song about a new grandchild, sung by the grandmother to a sister named Esther. The song is accompanied by images of an older woman holding a baby. Accompanied by images of a great-aunt holding her grand-niece, the song presents an intimate, caring event against the backdrop of violence. At the film's conclusion, even the credits serve as legacy moments, accompanied by one of Friedman's own compositions, "Things We Keep." The final credits include each elder's name, a current photographic still, and a portrait from the past. In this way, the elders are able to leave the audience with a visual representation both of who they are now and who they have been, bringing the two together in a unified self. The concept for the closing credits was that of the filmmaker, Nathan Friedkin.

In gerontology, we can speak of creating meaning through reminiscence therapy and life review in later life, but we enrich that conversation when we include artistic expression. We should look not only to narrative approaches, but also to performative approaches to the life review. Songwriting, singing, recording, and filming can all function as performances of life review. Moreover, when they express the culture and lives of their performers, the resulting music provides a permanent legacy for future generations.

Notes

1. The National Center for Creative Aging has multiple resources available on its website, www.creativeaging.org (accessed 21 February 2014).

2. Popularized through the documentary film *Alive Inside*, the iPod project, which aims to give an iPod MP3 player with personalized music to every institutionalized person with dementia, can be accessed through its website, musicandmemory.org (accessed 21 February 2014).

3. The Museum of Modern Art (New York) has a special program intended to enable people with Alzheimer's disease to come to the museum, enjoy the art, and have meaningful interactions with their loved ones and with docents. Information

on this project and its offshoots around the United States is available at www.moma.org/meetme (accessed 21 February 2014).

4. Online training for TimeSlips, including the storykit and resources for training certification, is available through the website www.timeslips.org (accessed 21 February 2014).

5. The Community of Voices project, led by the neuroscientist Julene Johnson at the University of California, San Francisco, is a partnership between community organizations and health sciences researchers, funded by the National Institutes for Health and the National Institute on Aging. It is a randomized, wait-list controlled trial of a one-year choral program that uses validated scientific measures to examine the effects of choral singing on health and well-being. The intervention and recruitment are ongoing, and more can be learned about the project at the website www.communityofvoices.org (accessed 21 February 2014).

6. Information about Songwriting Works programs, including trainings, can be found at www.songwritingworks.org (accessed 1 July 2014). A recording of "I'm 100 Years Old" is also available on the website.

7. © 1998–1999 Composing Together Works and Jewish Home, San Francisco. Words and music by Singers and Songwriters of the Jewish Home in San Francisco with Judith-Kate Friedman, California Arts Council artist-in-residence. Performed by the Singers and Songwriters on their debut CD *Island on a Hill* (2002). Distributed by cdbaby.com. A project of Songwriting Works, www.songwritingworks.org. For more information, contact: 360-385-1160.

8. The original ethnographic research was conducted in part with the resources of the Jewish Home, San Francisco, and with the support of a Health Resources Service Administration training grant. IRB research approval for the human subjects research study (2006–2008) was obtained through full committee review by the Committee on Human Research at the University of California, San Francisco (H11533-27356), and with the support of the research committee at the Jewish Home, San Francisco. Both Judith-Kate Friedman and Rabbi Sheldon Marder are published authors who waived their right to confidentiality in writing so that they could be credited appropriately. Portions of this chapter were presented at the November 2012 meetings of the Gerontological Society of America and at the University of California, San Francisco Geriatrics Grand Rounds in January 2014.

References

A 'Specially Wonderful Affair. 2002. (DVD). San Francisco: Friedkin Digital and Jewish Home.

Allison, Theresa A. 2008. "Songwriting and Transcending Institutional Boundaries in the Nursing Home." In *The Oxford Handbook of Medical Ethnomusicology*, edited by Benjamin Koen, Jacqueline Lloyd, Gregory Barz, and Karen Brummel-Smith, 218–45. New York: Oxford University Press.

Brown, Robert McAfee, ed. 1986. *The Essential Reinhold Niebuhr: Selected Essays*. Binghamton, NY: Vail-Ballou Press.

Butler, Robert N. 1963. "The Life Review: An Interpretation of Reminiscence in the Aged." *Psychiatry* 26: 65–76.

———. 1974a. "Life-review Therapy: Putting Memories to Work in Individual and Group Psychotherapy." *Geriatrics* 29(11): 165–73.

———. 1974b. "Successful Aging and the Role of the Life Review." *Journal of the American Geriatrics Society* 22(12): 529–35.

Friedman, Judith-Kate. 2011. "The Songwriting Works Model: Enhancing Brain Health and Fitness through Collaborative Musical Composition and Performance." In *Enhancing Cognitive Fitness in Adults: A Guidebook to the Use and Development of Community-Based Programs*, edited by Paula E. Hartman-Stein and Asenath LaRue, 325–58. New York: Springer.

Haber, David. 2006. "Life Review: Implementation, Theory, Research, and Therapy." *International Journal of Aging and Human Development* 63(2): 153–71.

Island on a Hill. 2002. (CD). San Francisco: Jewish Home and Composing Together Works.

Marder, Sheldon. 2005. "God Is in the Text: Using Sacred Text and Teaching in Jewish Pastoral Care." In *Jewish Pastoral Care: A Practical Handbook from Traditional and Contemporary Sources*, second edition, edited by Dayle A. Friedman, 183–210. Woodstock, VT: Jewish Lights Publishing.

Scales, Christopher. 2012. *Recording Culture: Powwow Music and the Aboriginal Recording Industry on the Northern Plains*. Durham, NC: Duke University Press.

Webster, Jeffrey Dean, Ernst T. Bohlmeijer, and Gerben J. Westerhof. 2010. "Mapping the Future of Reminiscence: A Conceptual Guide for Research and Practice." *Research on Aging* 32: 527–64.

CHAPTER TWO

Music in the Culture of Children

Patricia Shehan Campbell

The study of children's musical expressions, interests, and inclinations, especially outside the reach of direct adult influence, is a recent phenomenon. In music education, children are at the core of the teaching-learning enterprise, yet historically the accent has been on their role as passive receptacles of musical skill and knowledge, the nature and extent of which are determined by professional musician-educators. Still, children express and engage musically of their own accord, with and without an interest in matching, or even sounding remotely like, the adults who surround them. The study of children's musical lives—including their repertories, uses of music, musical values, song acquisition, learning music informally, and creating music—informs understandings of music as sound, behavior, and values. Bruno Nettl's early interest in the origins of music drew him to examine developmental phases of children's musical and spoken communication (1956), including characteristic traits of children's songs. He later recommended the inclusive study of *all* of a society's musical subcultures, including those of children (2005). Nettl's work prompted others to study children's musical cultures, generating the current movement, which attends to children's clear sense of agency such that the culture they know is their own, rather than one inherited intact from their elders. Drawing from work by ethnomusicologists, educators, sociologists, and psychologists, this chapter assesses the current state of research on children's musical culture, including the meaning of music in children's lives, the music of very young children, musical genres created by and for children, music and children's social networks, and the role of music technology and mediated music in childhood. My purpose is to explore some of the ways in which children conceptualize music, musical development among children, and how children acquire, discard, and invent musical traditions through the influence of family, friends, and music educators.

What Music Means to Children

Music matters to children, and they show their understanding of it in the way they use it in their lives. It lulls them to sleep and mediates their amusements (favorite TV shows, movies, video games, and child-friendly Internet sites). It figures in their singing games and their spontaneous songs while at play. Yet children do not typically define and describe music, for they value musical engagement over talking about it, and their world is blanketed in the music they make and to which they listen (Campbell 2010). For children, music just *is*, and the songs and sounds of their surroundings bring them joy, solace, safety, and a sense of identity. Music for them is an experience that is "in the air" they breathe, and it needs no explanation, since words cannot suffice to explain its meaning and value to them.

When they do talk about music, it becomes clear that children conceptualize music differently from adults. For adults, music is a contested domain. Scholars have described music in many ways, including sonic perspectives (organized sound within a temporal framework), euphonic perspectives (non-adaptive pleasure-seeking behavior), as adaptive behavior, as a harmonizing influence, as an act, and as a meaning-making system (Cross 2005; Levitin 2006; Pinker 1997; Small 1998). Adults attempt to implant their definitions of music in children, for example, in classes where music is presented according to its sonic elements (melody, rhythm, texture, timbre, form). The music that teachers select for curricular lessons, and the ways in which they direct children to experience it, reflect adult perceptions of its definition and meaning. Likewise, adults in the media select, compose, and arrange the music that they see as fit for children. Children's voices are noticeably absent, even though research suggests that children should be valued as co-constructors of their own rich musical cultures (Boynton and Kok 2006; Campbell 2010).

Research on children's conceptualizations of music indicates that they focus on the sonic and functional aspects of music. Sonic aspects encompass instruments, voices, natural sounds, and technology (devices that record, store, and play back sound), whereas functional aspects emerge in children's association of music with birthday parties, church services, family gatherings, weddings, and various rituals of life within a family (Whiteman and

Campbell 2011). As children mature, they develop greater vocabularies and the potential for articulating their impressions, although often only when pressed, since such definitions continue to be expressed indirectly or behaviorally. By middle childhood, they complicate their understanding of music to include an emphasis on music as a component of social life (Turino 2008), in which both making music and the sonic product are important to them, so long as it involves them with their peers (Small 1998). Mood is another realm children describe in explaining music's role for them. In the words of one ten-year-old boy, "music makes me feel good," and the shaping of mood that comes from listening, playing his keyboard, or singing loudly while walking his dog, gives music his value and meaning (Campbell 2010).

Music of the Very Young

Children's earliest musical experiences are up-close and personal, delivered by their parents and caretakers who inflect spoken communications with pitch, rhythm, and sometimes full-fledged musical expressions (Trehub 2006). Around the world, infant-directed singing is pervasive, referred to as "motherese" or "parentese." The undulant, often high-pitched and breathy voices of women (and men) are both gentle and playful (Dissanayake 2000). Characteristic of these vocal expressions are changes in dynamics, tempo, and timbre, with episodes of squeals, whispers, coos, and murmurs. Preverbal infants develop pitch and rhythmic awareness, as proto-conversational vocalization flows musically from adult to child (Trehub 2006). With the continuous parental flow of musical speech and song in a child's first year, the production of single words emerges, which leads to the development of two- and three-word communications and then full sentences. Whether they are growing up in Canada, Cambodia, or Kenya, children's early speech is as musical as that of their parents and caretakers (Trainor, Austin, and Desjardins 2000).

Educators, ethnomusicologists, and psychologists agree that the music young children can perceive is the music they may eventually learn to produce (Blacking 1995; Campbell 2010; Deliege and Sloboda 1996); what children absorb and how they process it influences their musical production in songs and rhythms. Infants can perceive time and temporal sequence, and their own rhythmic movement grows increasingly regular and patterned. By the age of three, children typically find the rhythms of speech and song easy to reproduce and develop the ability to keep a steady pulse, even as they learn to perform clapping and patting rhythmic patterns. Newborns can detect differences between high and low pitches. They hear melodic changes as small as a semitone before the age of one, and can group pitches of the music they hear based upon register, contour, and interval size. Pitch and time discrimination are acute among children entering school, and derive from the musical sounds that enter their young lives (Campbell and Scott-Kassner 2013).

Children's Musical Genres

Musical genres for children include adult-generated lullabies, the musical utterances and spontaneous songs of children at play, and children's songs and singing games, including those that are traditional and those that are newly created by children or for children by adults (Campbell 2010; Marsh 2008; Nettl 2005). There are also heritage songs, many of them on the school-music menu, including patriotic songs, seasonal songs, and songs containing texts that refer to historical events and figures, socially acceptable etiquette, and moral lessons. Teachers often deliver these genres live to children and many of the songs remain in school, although children embrace some and carry them intact into their play and leisure activities, or with intentional variation as parodies. Finally, media and technology deliver the music of entertainment to children (Bickford 2013; Emberly 2009; Lum 2007).

Of these genres, lullabies emerge earliest in the child's musical life. Across many cultures, mothers, fathers, other family members, and caregivers sing lullabies to children. Lullabies are soft, slow in tempo, and intended to calm, soothe, and lull infants and young children to sleep (Trehub 2006). Lullabies may consist of words or vocables and typically involve a gentle, pulsive movement as little ones are gently swung or rocked. Whereas some lullabies are transmitted orally generation by generation, such as the Anglo-American "Hush Little Baby," the Irish "Einini," the Serbian "Sviraj," or the Shongana "Yo Mamana Yo," many arise spontaneously.

Musical utterances and spontaneous songs emerge among children prior to school age, especially during play (Campbell 2010). These genres are typically open-ended and original, with beginnings and endings unpredictably developing from, and returning to, their playful interaction with toys and other children. These expressions are intermediary between speaking and singing, consisting of phrases of words or syllables that are sung or rhythmically chanted. Their melodies tend to be narrow in range, restricted to an interval of a third or a fourth, mostly stepwise in motion, and repetitive. Alongside spontaneous melodies are rhythmically chanted words and phrases that fluctuate between pulsive and more rapid, syncopated patterns. Around the world, children's vocal practices often resemble one another more than they sound like the adult music of a particular region (Campbell and Wiggins 2013; Lum and Whiteman 2012).

As children build their repertory of songs, spontaneous singing tends to decline. Children's physiological development, including greater lung capacity, well-exercised vocal folds, and a sharpened set of articulatory techniques, enables them to gain control of their voices and to use them expressively in controlling pitch, rhythm, dynamics, tempo, and quality. By school age and as a result of adult influences within the family, through the child-oriented media, and in child care and preschool, English-speaking children tend to know folk songs from the oral tradition, such as "Twinkle, Twinkle Little Star" and "Mary Had a Little Lamb." They experience an array of singing games (Opie and Opie 1985), including classics such as "Bluebird" and "Skip to My Lou" and interactive chants including "My Mama Told Me" or "My Sailor" (Campbell 2010), which involve children standing in pairs, circles, or lines as they clap, pat, stamp, snap fingers, and move their bodies in complex patterns that complement the music. Singing games include jump-rope and ball-bouncing chants, rhymes, hand-clapping and street games, and even an array of chanted cheers associated with organized sports, with musical and movement content and game rules transmitted among children informally and holistically.

Heritage songs appear in school music classes; the repertory includes standards that generations of curriculum specialists considered important to raising citizens of a common culture or nation-state. In the United States, "America the Beautiful," "This Land Is Your Land," and "De colores" exemplify heritage songs. The North American heritage repertory tends to concentrate on strophic form songs, often with verse-chorus arrangements, or narrative songs with multiple stanzas. The songs tend toward pentatonic, six-tone, or diatonic melodies, most often set in major rather than minor or modal keys. The presence of pentachordal (sol-fa-mi-re-do) patterns, and the three-tone mi-re-do final cadences from Anglo-, Latin-, and many African American songs, may indicate the value adults place upon asserting tonality, even when children themselves may tend toward the descending minor third.

Another adult-to-child genre, emanating from mediated sources, is music from children's entertainment. Music of classic and contemporary children's or family films reflects popular genres of the period, from concert music to songs from Broadway musicals, hip-hop, techno, and country. Comparisons of *Peter Pan* (1953), *Mary Poppins* (1964), *The Lion King* (1995), and *High School Musical* (2006) reveal more than a half-century gap between the lush predominance of strings to the fusion of instruments and electronic sampling techniques. Even as children are influenced by the sounds that surround them, so too are film composers, who reflect the sounds of their times in the scores they write for children's entertainment.

Music and Children's Social Networks

Children's social networks may be examined from several disciplinary perspectives, and recent work by Bickford (2012, 2013), Emberly (2009), and Minks (2006) reveals a growing interest among ethnomusicologists in the social functions of children's musical practices. Children live in multiple contexts, and work in cultural pedagogy recognizes that children learn in school as well as in other social and cultural settings (Campbell 2010; Katsuri 2002; Marsh 2008). Educators must understand the knowledge that children bring to school and turn to children's in-school and out-of-school experiences to convert knowledge from one context to another (Kertz-Welzel 2013).

In one theory of child development, Urie Bronfenbrenner posited that an ecological environment is a powerful influence on children's thought and action. He described a "set of nested structures, each inside the other like a set of Russian dolls" (1979) as proximal environments that nestle within systems that are increasingly distant from the child. These include the school system, local economy, and national policies and infrastructures for children's health, education, and welfare (Bronfenbrenner and Morris 1998). The microsystem, encompassing home and family, is the child's most immediate environment, followed by the neighborhood school. A child develops his or her social and cultural reality through interactions with parents, siblings, neighbors, teachers, and friends within this microsystem. Time spent in school, in after-school programs, on the playground, at the mall, and in religious institutions helps to shape identity. Bronfenbrenner refers to the relationship between the child's contexts of home, school, and neighborhood as the mesosytem, the influences of government policy and media as the exosystem, and the dominant beliefs of a culture as the macrosystem. His model offers an ecological perspective on the forces both near and far that influence the developing child in understanding self and others.

Arjun Appadurai's theory of "-scapes" (1996) is also relevant for understanding children's musical influences. For Appadurai, human life involves a web of interconnections, which are changing conceptions of self and other and re-shaping local identities. He recognized the impact of globalization on societal change and asserted that the world is no longer a collection of autonomous and monadic spaces. Thinking is now a more complex task, requiring consideration of nuances, hybrids, and resultant products of many mixed influences. In formulating a framework of five "-scapes" that influence the folkways of adults and children alike, Appadurai describes ethnoscapes (the people of our world, including immigrants, refugees, and tourists), technoscapes (the technological developments that deliver worldwide information), finanscapes (the movement of money, goods, and trade across cultures), mediascapes (the electronic distribution of cultural information, images, and attitudes), and ideoscapes (the floating images of political positions on constructs of freedom, welfare, citizens' rights, and democracy). These strands of influence encircle children, adding colorful pieces to their complex, mosaic-like identities.

Ethnomusicologists have applied Appadurai's and Bronfenbrenner's theories of social networks to understanding the contexts of children's musical lives. Lew (2006) studied Malay, Chinese, and Indian children in a Malaysian preschool and at home. She found that Bronfenbrenner's nested structures operate within the realm of children's musical utterances, rhythmic play, and heritage songs. All were traceable to musical sources in the home or school, including parents, entertainment by mediated sources, teachers, and peers. Young children's mediascapes were particularly influential in the music they spontaneously made at play. Lum (2007) applied Bronfenbrenner's micro-macro model in tandem with the techno-, media-, and ethno-scapes proposed by Appadurai in a study of first graders at an elementary school in Singapore. He noted that not only did home and school figure prominently in children's musical activities, larger social systems, driven by politics and cultural identity, also figured in the school music curriculum and the teacher's personal choices. Appadurai's concepts also applied to three Singaporean children selected as subjects for case studies, in their free play on various electronics and media sources, including portable karaoke machines, DVDs, CDs, and TV. These studies demonstrate the influence of children's social networks on their musical lives and validate the relevance of social network theory to children's musical development.

Children are born and bred within the intimacy of families, and in this closest and most constant of social units, they first learn the cultural patterns that define them. The structure of the family involves the distribution of status, authority, and responsibility within the nucleus of parents and children, and encompasses the network of kin relationships that link members of the extended family (Fomby and Cherlin 2007; McAdoo 2007). Children learn their current and eventual roles, rights, and responsibilities within the family and acquire family values and preferences that shape their decisions (Freeman 2000). Issues that concern individual achievement, lifestyle, and educational or occupational aspirations spring from the family, and the family's ethnicity, race, and religious beliefs are usually central in the mediation of children's values. As a result of family upbringing, children know a cultural reservoir of motivations, skills, attitudes, and behaviors that follow them through childhood, youth, and into adulthood.

From infancy onward, and even in utero, children are enveloped in the music of the family that is linked to the larger cultural community that shapes children's musical sensibilities. Various family demographic characteristics may influence children's exposure to and experience in culture and the arts, including music (Berrios-Miranda 2013; MacKinlay 2013). Marriage patterns, family size, and roles assumed by members of the nuclear family all influence children's musical behaviors, inclinations, and tastes. Even more relevant to children's musical development may be the parents' socioeconomic status and employment, the influence of religious beliefs and practices, and the presence of elders within the family circle, especially grandparents. Other considerations are the behaviors of families related to heritage, assimilation, or rediscovery of cultural identities. Finally, child-rearing practices naturally affect children's family experiences in music.

Families implant in children the subconscious foundation of reality within the scope of acceptable, valued behaviors. A web of attitudes, created through attunement over time within a family, community, and the larger culture, are called into play as children and youth make decisions. Children receive massive amounts of information both circumstantially and actively, and they turn that data into generalizations, stereotypes, and theories that they use to navigate life. Children of families who value music are often taught by example that musical choices concern not whether one will make music, but which instrument(s) they will learn. As Edward T. Hall postulated, the acquisition of culture begins with birth and is a "process [that] is automatic" (1992:225); it is "learned but not taught" (Rice 1994:65). Hall argued that "acquired information is so basic and so fundamental" (1992:225) as to be a part of the self, with behavior patterns that are automatic and not dissectible. Since behaviors are linked to subconscious and communal values, a family's behaviors and attitudes continuously project themselves to children, whose individual perceptions, attitudes, and choices are deeply affected by the behaviors they internalize from their home surroundings.

Children's musical repertory and musical values are more a matter of informal processes, in school and at home. Of these processes, enculturation is more informal, in which children achieve cultural competence by absorbing many facets of their home environments, learning by virtue of living within a family, community, or culture. Melville Herskovits described musical enculturation (1949) as so informal as to appear as ambient sounds such as singing and pitch-inflected speech. Alan P. Merriam defined a second and related phenomenon, socialization, as "the process of social learning as it is carried on in the early years of life" (1964:162). Children are socialized musically in ways that overlap with enculturative processes, through music intended by parents to entertain children, generate social interactivity and language development, and teach concepts such as numbers, body parts, and friends (Minks 2006). In both enculturation and socialization, the role of the family is certain and strong in the formation of children's musical behaviors and identities.

Children and Mediated Music

Children's musical development is enhanced through the media-produced surrounds of home, school, and other spheres of activity. Even young children are keen to join with the preferences of their peers and share a common culture in the preferred music on TV, radio, Internet, and electronic playback devices. They eat, do homework, fall asleep, and wake up to mediated music. It comes to them in stores, shops, markets, cars, buses, and even at school recess and leisure time. Teachers deliver active listening engagements and singing, and in more privileged sequential programs, children can play rhythm instruments, xylophones, recorders, and band and orchestral instruments. Yet beyond this limited exposure, and the possibility of private music lessons for some children, the musical enculturation and socialization of children increasingly comes from friends and the mediated music they share (Bickford 2013).

The most constant source of music piped into children's lives is television, while video-gaming devices come in at a close second in their continuous presence and influence. Programs such as *Sesame Street* have exposed North American children for well over a generation to social and cultural issues, as well as activities that support children's acquisition of basic skills in identifying numbers, colors, letters, social roles, and relationships. As edutainment, these programs combine elements from the entertainment industry with theories of child development and education to teach children about cognitive process, symbolic representation, and social environments (Campbell 2010; Campbell and Scott-Kassner 2013). In short segments, audiences of young children hear nursery songs and popular music forms, see dance images, and are introduced to diverse musical styles from guest artists such as Ladysmith Black Mambazo and Bobby McFerrin (Lury 2002).

Children are often attracted to, and intrigued by, music for older audiences. There are eager audiences of children for the music of child-stars Justin Bieber and Miley Cyrus, as once was the case for an earlier generation who followed NSync and the Backstreet Boys. Children are also captivated by the music and moves of adult artists such as Beyoncé and Lady Gaga (Campbell 2010). It appears that "in the new childhood, the distinction between the lived worlds of adults and children begins to blur. While certainly childhood and adulthood are not one and the same, the experiences of adults and children are more similar now than they were before" (Kincheloe 2002:79). Increasingly, children learn from popular culture's "cultural pedagogy,"[1] from radio and television programs, or by observing their elder siblings and parents engaged in music technology, imitating and emulating the next popular tune and advertisement jingle.

At home, on the Web, and at the arcade, video gaming has become increasingly prominent in children's mediated landscape. *Dance Dance Revolution*, a dance-simulation arcade game featuring popular music; *Mad Maestro*, where the player conducts classical music with the ability to control tempo, balance, and volume; *BeatMania*, where players scratch hip-hop turntables in time to the beat; and *Taiko no Tatsujin*, which features two Japanese *taiko* drums, are just a few music-based video games that have a global fan following. Jacob Smith suggests that "playing these games can feel like a genuinely musical experience: the controller is no longer a trigger but a percussion instrument, and the player stops thinking in terms of locking on targets and instead tries to feel the groove" (2004:65). Children playing Xboxes and PlayStations, or playing games on transportable hand-held devices, are bombarded by popular music that blasts in the background. MTV channels foreground popular music, as do action and adventure films that are accessed by children on their personal laptops and table-top computers, thus influencing their tastes. Karaoke singing is a global pastime in private and public spaces, as solo or group expression, suitable for all ages. Clearly, mediated music is pervasive and has a wide-ranging impact on children's musical intake, and they are often in control of the music they choose and discard, too. As Kincheloe explains, "driven by information technologies and media, these social changes have helped provide children with new degrees of control over the information on their own time schedules in isolation from adult supervision" (2002:78).

Conclusions

The ethnomusicological study of children's musical cultures continues to develop. Ethnomusicologists, anthropologists, folklorists, child development specialists, and educators are attending to the musical content of children's songs and the social and cultural significance of music in children's lives.

Children will always be drawn to music for its power and ability to bridle their energy, captivate their thoughts and feelings, and provide a safe haven from their worries. Music enhances their play and is an important means for learning their world. Ethnomusicologists' recognition of the presence of children's music in the cultures they study enriches and expands our understanding of the full spectrum of habits, heritage, mores, and values of a people writ large. Likewise, ethnomusicologists are developing an awareness of children as individuals and members of collective culture, with particular capacities, worldviews, and social identities all their own. Future ethnomusicological research on children has the potential to provide a more integrated view of human life through examination of the sounds, behaviors, and values of their musically expressive lives.

Note

1. Katsuri explains that "cultural pedagogy is the recognition that learning occurs not only in school, but also takes place in many other social and cultural sites/contexts (such as the mass media)" (2002:54).

References

Appadurai, A. 1996. *Modernity at Large: Cultural Dimensions of Globalization*. Minneapolis: University of Minnesota Press.

Berrios-Miranda, Marisol. 2013. "Musical Childhoods across Three Generations, from Puerto Rico to the USA." In *Oxford Handbook of Children's Musical Cultures*, edited by Patricia Shehan Campbell and Trevor Wiggins, 301–14. New York: Oxford University Press.

Bickford, Tyler. 2012. "The New 'Tween' Music Industry: The Disney Channel, Kidz Bop, and an Emerging Childhood Counterpublic." *Popular Music* 31(3): 417–36.

———. 2013. "Tinkering and Tethering in the Material Culture of Children's MP3 Players." In *Oxford Handbook of Children's Musical Cultures*, edited by Patricia Shehan Campbell and Trevor Wiggins, 527 42. New York: Oxford University Press.

Blacking John. 1995[1967]. *Venda Children's Songs: A Study in Ethnomusicological Analysis*. Chicago: University of Chicago.

Boynton, Susan, and Roe-Min Kok, eds. 2006. *Musical Childhoods and the Cultures of Youth*. Middletown, CT: Wesleyan University Press.

Bronfenbrenner, Urie. 1979. *The Ecology of Human Development: Experiments by Nature and Design*. Cambridge, MA: Harvard University Press.

———. 1995. "Developmental Ecology through Space and Time: A Future Perspective." In *Examining Lives in Context: Perspectives on the Ecology of Human Development*, edited by Phyllis Moen, Glenn H. Elder Jr., and Kurt Luscher, 619–47. Washington, DC: American Psychological Association.

Bronfenbrenner, Urie, and P. A. Morris, 1998. "The Ecology of Developmental Processes." In *Handbook of Child Psychology*, Vol. 1, edited by William Damon and Richard M. Lerner, 993–1028. New York: John Wiley and Sons.

Campbell, Patricia Shehan. 2010. *Songs in Their Heads: Music and Its Meaning in Children's Lives*, second edition. New York: Oxford University Press.

Campbell, Patricia Shehan, and Carol Scott-Kassner. 2013. *Music in Childhood*. Belmont, CA: Cengage.

Campbell, Patricia Shehan, and Trevor Wiggins, eds. 2013. *The Oxford Handbook of Children's Musical Cultures*. New York: Oxford University Press.

Cross, Ian. 2005. "Music and Meaning, Ambiguity, and Evolution." In *Musical Communication*, edited by Dorothy Miell, Raymond MacDonald, and David J. Hargreaves, 27–43. Oxford: Oxford University Press.

Deliege, Irene, and John Sloboda. 1996. *Musical Beginnings*. New York: Oxford University Press.

Dissanayake, Ellen. 2000. *Art and Intimacy: How the Arts Began*. Seattle: University of Washington Press.

Emberly, Andrea. 2009. "Mandela Went to China . . . and India Too": Musical Cultures of Childhood in South Africa." Ph.D. dissertation, University of Washington.

Fomby, Paula, and Andrew J. Cherlen. 2007. "Family Instability and Children's Well-Being." *American Sociological Review* 72(2): 181–204.

Freeman, J. 2000. "Families: The Essential Content for Gifts and Talents." In *International Handbook of Giftedness and Talent*, edited by Kurt A. Heller, Franz J. Monks, Robert J. Sternberg, and Rena F. Subotnik, 573–85. New York: Elsevier.

Hall, Edward T. 1992. "Improvisation as an Acquired, Multilevel Process." *Ethnomusicology* 36: 151–69.

Herskovits, Melville. 1949. *Man and His Works*. Evanston, IL: Northwestern University Press.

Katsuri, Sumana. 2002. "Constructing Childhood in a Corporate World: Cultural Studies, Childhood, and Disney." In *Kidworld: Childhood Studies, Global Perspectives, and Education*, edited by Gaile S. Cannella and Joe L. Kincheloe, 39–58. New York: Peter Lang.

Kertz-Welzel, Alexandra. 2013. "Children's and Adolescents' Musical Needs and Music Education in Germany." In *Oxford Handbook of Children's Musical Cultures*, edited by Patricia Shehan Campbell and Trevor Wiggins, 371–86. New York: Oxford University Press.

Kincheloe, Joe L. 2002. "The Complex Politics of McDonald's and the New Childhood: Colonizing Kidworld." In *Kidworld: Childhood Studies, Global Perspectives, and Education*, edited by Gaile S. Cannella and Joe L. Kincheloe, 75–121. New York: Peter Lang.

Levitin, Daniel. 2006. *This Is Your Brain on Music*. New York: Dutton.

Lew, Jackie Chooi Theng. 2006. "The Musical Lives of Young Malaysian Children: In School and at Home." Ph.D. dissertation, University of Washington.

Lum, Chee Hoo. 2007. "Musical Networks of Children: An Ethnography of Elementary School of Children in Singapore." Ph.D. dissertation, University of Washington.

Lum, Chee Hoo, and Peter Whiteman, eds. 2012. *Musical Childhoods of Asia and the Pacific*. New York: Information Age Publishing.

Lury, Keith. 2002. "Chewing Gum for the Ears: Children's Television and Popular Music." *Popular Music* 21(3): 291–311.

MacKinlay, Elizabeth. 2013. "The Musical Worlds of Aboriginal Children at Burrulula and Darwin in the Northern Territory of Australia." In *Oxford Handbook of Children's Musical Cultures*, edited by Patricia Shehan Campbell and Trevor Wiggins, 315–31. New York: Oxford University Press.

Marsh, Katherine. 2008. *The Musical Playground: Global Tradition and Change in Children's Songs and Games*. New York: Oxford University Press.

McAdoo, Harriette Pipes, ed. 2007. *Black Families*, fourth edition. Thousand Oaks, CA: Sage.

Merriam, Alan P. 1964. *The Anthropology of Music*. Evanston, IL: Northwestern University Press.

Minks, Amanda. 2006. "Afterword." In *Musical Childhoods and the Cultures of Youth*, edited by Susan Boynton and Roe-Hok Min, 209–18. Middletown, CT: Wesleyan University Press.

Nettl, Bruno. 1956. "Infant Musical Development and Primitive Music." *Southwestern Journal of Anthropology* 12(1): 87–91.

———. 2005[1983]. *The Study of Ethnomusicology: Thirty-one Issues and Concepts*. Urbana: University of Illinois Press.

Opie, Iona, and Peter Opie. 1985. *The Singing Game*. New York: Oxford University Press.

Pinker, Steven. 1997. *How the Mind Works*. New York: W. W. Norton.

Rice, Timothy. 1994. *May It Fill Your Soul: Experiencing Bulgarian Music*. Chicago: University of Chicago Press.

Small, Christopher. 1998. *Musicking: The Meanings of Performing and Listening*. Hanover, NH: University Press of New England.

Smith, J. 2004. "I Can See Tomorrow in Your Dance: A Study of *Dance Dance Revolution* and Music Video Games." *Journal of Popular Music Studies* 16(1): 58–84.

Trainor, Laurel J., Caren M. Austin, and Renee N. Desjardins. 2000. "Is Infant-Directed Speech Prosody a Result of the Vocal Expression of Emotion?" *Psychological Science* 11: 188–95.

Trehub, Sandra E. 2006. "Infants as Musical Connoisseurs." In *The Child as Musician*, edited by Gary McPherson, 33–49. Oxford: Oxford University Press.

Turino, Thomas. 2008. *Music as Social Life*. Chicago: University of Chicago Press.

Whiteman, Peter, and Patricia Shehan Campbell. 2011. "Picture It! Young Children Conceptualizing Music." In *Musical Childhoods of Asia and the Pacific*, edited by Chee-Hoo Lum and Peter Whiteman, 161–89. New York: Information Age Publishing.

CHAPTER THREE

~

The Mississippi Choctaw Fair and Veteran's Day Powwow

Music, Dance, and Layers of Identity

Chris Goertzen

One morning during the Mississippi Choctaw Veteran's Day Powwow, a parade bisects the Pearl River community. Pearl River is the largest of the tribe's eight small communities, which include about ten thousand enrolled members (www.choctaw.org/). Though a short, homespun parade, it's an impressive effort for a small, working-class populace. In 2012, a flashy convertible transporting an imperially waving Choctaw Indian Princess[1] and a Choctaw Transit bus carrying older veterans preceded seven decorated flatbed trailers towed by pickup trucks, some marchers, and a few men on horseback. Most of the floats bore children in Choctaw traditional clothing; one instead transported a powwow drum. I watched from a folding chair next to the road. My interest in powwows, and in Native music generally, was sparked by reading Bruno Nettl's descriptions of his early fieldwork at powwows, and reinforced over the years by how hospitable powwows are to my students and by how comfortable I feel at these events. On this day, Choctaw kids were rolling down the gentle hill opposite where I sat. My neighbors among the adult spectators on my side of the road were friendly—we were calling greetings to many of the same people in the parade, and so got acquainted and shared snacks.

Music issuing from the floats and vehicles touched several bases. An old, small double-headed drum repeated the rhythm that customarily announces the arrival of a Choctaw Social Dance group (a rapidly tapped pattern of an eighth note followed by two sixteenth notes), and the Choctaw powwow drum—named Southern Pine after its home community—performed a favorite tune (the Forty-Nine song the group plays for their Choctaw Two-Step Dance). Recordings blared from other floats: a country song, a boot camp chant, "The Star-Spangled Banner" sung in Choctaw, and Sousa's "Stars and Stripes Forever." In sum, patriotic tunes appropriate to the day flanked repertories limning three layers of identity: tribal Social Dance rhythms represented the specifically Choctaw layer, the powwow drum the broader Indian layer, and the country song the general rural layer.

When witnessing this celebration, it is easy to forget how young the attitudes, leisure, and financial wherewithal allowing a public display of Mississippi Choctaw pride are. Just two generations ago, these Indians were—as many elders now put it—"hiding in plain sight," avoiding drawing attention to their ethnicity in order to prevent new injuries resulting from enduring prejudice. When whites began taking Choctaw land early in U.S. history, the "tribe" was a loose confederation of thriving farming communities in and near central Mississippi. American presidents, starting with Jefferson but climaxing infamously with Jackson, appropriated most Choctaw land through a series of treaties from 1801 to 1839. Most Choctaw were forced to resettle in Oklahoma, and the minority that received parcels of land as part of a bargain allowing them to remain in Mississippi were cheated out of that land within a few generations. By the turn of the twentieth century, most of the roughly one thousand remaining Mississippi Choctaw were impoverished sharecroppers, with no tribal government. Tardy legislative remedies allowed gradual economic improvement later in the century. The Mississippi Band of Choctaw Indians received federal recognition in 1945, but only in the mid-1970s was a Choctaw government similar to that of today in place. Tax advantages encouraged businesses to locate on Choctaw land; a construction company arrived in 1969 and an automobile wiring harness plant in 1979, with other businesses trickling in subsequently. The Silver Star Resort and Casino opened in 1994. Today, although most jobs in and near the reservation are not particularly high-paying, the rate of employment exceeds that in surrounding counties (see Boykin 2002).

Today's tribal elders spent their formative years in hand-to-mouth sharecropping culture. One valuable result of the rapid improvement of the tribe's finances in the late twentieth century is that these elders, now experiencing the mixed blessings of American mass culture, can still ground tribal identity on detailed recollections of practices and beliefs that reach back centuries. But that inherited culture had become increasingly fragile during the first two-thirds of the twentieth century, since it survived on the socioeconomic margins: parents exhausted themselves just providing for their families. Also, the decades without any secular tribal government placed much community leadership in the hands of church authorities who looked down on Choctaw music and dance, which they considered to be pagan.

The Choctaw elder Thallis Lewis recently retired as director of the tribal Cultural Affairs Program after working forty-three years for the tribe. She had joined her sharecropping family in the fields near Bogue Chitto when she was six years old, and labored there through the remainder of her childhood whenever she was not in a classroom—she was in the first graduating class of Choctaw Central High School in 1964. Her father danced in one of the first three community-based troupes that regularly participated in the Choctaw Indian Fair during the 1960s. This event, conjoining inheritances from the ancient Green Corn ceremony with typical ingredients of Southern U.S. county and state fairs, was first held in 1949. But she didn't learn Choctaw Social Dances from him—long hours of work stood in the way of most recreational activities, and he died young. Later, when she began her own professional life as a student teacher, a blind singer and dancer named Ida Frazier began to teach Choctaw Social Dance at the Bogue Chitto Elementary School. At about this time—the late 1960s and early 1970s—a white music teacher at the tribal high school named Minnie Hand was incorporating Choctaw Social Dances and their music into her choral programs (interview, Pearl River, MS, May 2010).[2]

The early 1970s were pivotal for the Mississippi Choctaw. A brochure praising Choctaw culture went out as part of the tribal leaders' energetic courting of outside businesses: *Mississippi Band of Choctaw Indians: An Era of Change* (1972). One page described the scattered tribal communities. Then the authors devoted a page of laudatory prose and photos to these topics in turn: Choctaw Social Dances, three representative dances (the Wedding Dance, Fast War Dance, and Duck Dance), the ancient and still thriving sport of stickball, blowguns, traditional clothing, swamp cane basketry, the annual Choctaw Indian Fair, and the hill sacred to the Mississippi Choctaw, Nanih Waiya (the mother mound critical for Choctaw origin and migration myths, located near Noxapater, Mississippi). A few pages on Choctaw history close the pamphlet.

Choctaw Social Dance didn't just lead off the longest section of this publication, it featured in pictures of the Choctaw Fair. But those photographs also include a small one of young men wearing powwow regalia. I have seen no documentation of powwows in Choctaw Mississippi that early, but the idea was gaining traction. While many older Choctaw recall Minnie Hand's role bringing Choctaw Social Dance into the curricula of the tribal schools, a few also remember that she took her student choirs to powwows in several states,[3] and Levine witnessed a display of intertribal dancing at the 1985 Choctaw Fair (1990:79).

Many older Choctaw remain wary of powwow culture, including individuals with enduring influence on official policy such as Thallis Lewis. Nevertheless, the Tribal Council charily sponsors two or three powwows annually; it's taken for granted that they will allot much more money to support Social Dance. In sum, the vigorous resurgence and wholesale repurposing of Choctaw Social Dance and the introduction of powwow culture to the Mississippi Choctaw happened at about the same time, and involved some of the same people, though Social Dance remains favored.

Social Dances at the Choctaw Fair: Tribal Culture with Regional and National Accents

Howard and Levine have described the individual Choctaw Social Dances (1990) and Levine went on to demonstrate that these dances were once an important part of ceremonies centered on the stickball game (1997). Their work focused on Oklahoma Choctaw traditional culture; the picture in Mississippi evolved differently. The dance steps and songs match closely overall, though when Oklahoma Choctaw dancers get together with Mississippi Choctaw or members of either group with dancers belonging to Alabama's MoWa Choctaw (a state-recognized tribe of about three thousand based an hour's drive north of Mobile), all concerned note and enjoy small differences between their local forms of the dances and songs. Also, the historical connection with stickball has faded in Mississippi, where Choctaw dance authorities see dancing and stickball as coexisting rather than interdependent traditions. A few links remain: women's dance outfits, while emphasizing the diamonds representing the rattlesnake (respected for limiting rodents' depredations of crops) and undulating lines echoing the sacred mound (Nanih Waiya), also include dots and crosses representing stickballs and sticks (see figure 3.1). Second, while the main instrument accompanying the songs of Mississippi Choctaw Social Dances is a pair of claves, some chanters employ the longer stickball sticks. Last, the same small barrel drums that accompany stickball play—a team's drummers play while running along the sidelines, with volume and tempo reflecting the pace of the game and encouraging team members—also accompany the entrance and departure of a few dance groups from the tribal dance grounds and, very rarely, are also played between or during dances.

The steps of Choctaw Social Dances, the broad impressions conveyed by the music, and the clothes worn by the dancers are overall less flashy than

Figure 3.1. Women backing the Drum, Southern Pine, at the 2012 Choctaw Veteran's Day Powwow, wearing respectively powwow garb, a traditional Social Dance dress, and a university T-shirt. The membership of this drum overlaps with that of the Mystic Wind Choctaw Social Dancers. This is the most-traveled Mississippi Choctaw Drum and Social Dance group; the overlapping ensembles are frequently hired as a pair to perform at powwows or other festivals. For pictures of the complete ensemble, see their Facebook pages. ***Photo by Chris Goertzen***

parallel elements of powwow culture. In the Walk Dance, which in Mississippi begins most dance sets and ends all of them, the line of twenty or more dancers slowly enters or exits the dance grounds (men first), with steps synchronized. Some of the other dances are couple dances, often with the men and women in parallel lines. Kids catch on easily to the simpler numbers; teaching them begins in Head Start programs. Studying the dances further—a favorite part of elementary school classes in Choctaw culture—culminates in annual performances. The tribe's website asserts that "the entire community turns out for school spring festivals to watch children dance and enjoy a traditional meal of hominy, frybread, and fried chicken" (www.choctaw.org/

culture/index.html). This reflects the strongest Mississippi Choctaw social imperative: community solidarity. Throngs of enthusiastic relatives of the young dancers attend; the large sizes and interrelatedness of families means that these crowds really do include virtually everyone in a given community. As Thallis Lewis explained, "If I knew that my grandkids would be dancing, we'd be there. . . . Supporting the family and the community, people's going to be there. . . . A kid will turn around and look at you and smile" (interview, Pearl River, MS, May 2010).

The main public performance venue where outsiders can enjoy the Mississippi Choctaw Social Dances is the annual Choctaw Fair; there's room for eighteen troupes in the schedule as constituted in the late twentieth and early twenty-first century. Some ensembles are family or friendship group-based, but more bear the names of their communities (some locales support several troupes). Four or five times during each of the four days of the fair, ensembles enter the tribal dance ground on the hour (that venue being a concrete slab, roofed, replete with ceiling fans, located behind the tribal museum and across from the tribal offices in the Pearl River community). The audiences aren't large; this is, after all, a normal fair with a sizeable midway, with the cultural component interesting just a few outsiders. Fourteen troupes perform sets of seven to ten dances during the days; four favored troupes reach larger audiences when they perform shorter sets integrated into the first ("Chief's") hour of the evening entertainment in a neighboring amphitheater.

The Mississippi Choctaw officially categorize each Social Dance as a war, social, or animal dance.[4] When these clubs plan their dance sets, they also take into account an overlapping tacit classification by complexity of steps. Insider vocabularies for this don't yet exist; I would propose the following informal and fluid troika: stately, lively, and both lively and fun. Most of the social and animal dances fit also into my category of stately, whereas the war dances are lively without also being amusing. A few dances don't fit neatly into my classification, such as the Duck Dance, which is somewhat lively and fun (when tall pairs of girls slip under bridges made by the hands of short boys), though fitting overall into the stately group.

Most dance sets have the Walk Dance frame, with the other numbers including representatives of all three types of dances within both the Mississippi Choctaw and my classification. Nearly every dance set includes the longest and most fun dance, Stealing Partners, at about two-thirds of the way through the set, plus, almost as surely, the almost as amusing Snake Dance. The Raccoon Dance, in which individual boys (or men) and girls (or women) play tag among the line of dancers, and the House Dance, which draws on Anglo-American square dancing, are also fun dances. However, neither is as common as the main two in that group: the Raccoon Dance because it's less exciting than the similar Stealing Partners, and the House Dance because it requires the help of the septuagenarian Choctaw fiddler R. J. Willis or a tape of Choctaw fiddling. In any case, dances of varying levels of complexity, such as the Corn Dance and Friendship Dance, plus a War Dance and perhaps a Duck Dance, fill in the spaces in each set between the flanking iterations of the Walk Dance and the popular pair of Stealing Partners and Snake Dance. I will list two representative sets from the 2008 Choctaw Fair: the Choctaw Tribal Social Dancers performed the Walk, Snake, Corn, Quail, Fast War, Stealing Partners, Wedding, Four-Step War, and Walk dances. The Pearl River Social Dancers did the Jump, Quail, Friendship, Corn, Drunk, Snake, Stealing Partners, Fast War, and Walk dances.[5]

The morning and afternoon Social Dance sets don't completely fill their allotted hours, so the emcees improvise fillers. The default insertion is a blow gun demonstration, often shaped as a competition between fair staff. Alternatively, an emcee recites a Choctaw tale. The favorite in recent years has been "'Possum and Raccoon," about how the opossum got a hairless tail, but containing a lesson about overgrown egos (Mould 2004:211–13). Like the blowgun, this story is common to other Southeastern tribes. Similar fillers have included Choctaw or other princesses who are introduced and asked to say a few words and an emcee has done impressions of Elvis or Louis Armstrong.

A few of the hour-long entertainment slots have been assigned in recent years to a virtuosic hoop dancer: Derek Davis, who, although half Choctaw, was raised among the Hopi and is proficient in Southwestern Indian traditions. Also, within just one hour each year, Harold Comby emcees intertribal dancing. He presents exponents of the various powwow dance styles and efficiently conveys the overall feel of powwows by explaining the dance categories, plus offering a typical raffle, a giveaway, a story, and a joke. Last, during the first hour of evening entertainment (the main cultural offering during which is Social Dance), I have heard a young woman sing "The Star-Spangled Banner" in Choctaw and "Amazing Grace," sung partly in Choctaw and partly in English.

In sum, at the Choctaw Fair—the main public venue for Social Dance, the most specifically Choctaw form of cultural entertainment—many small but real bridges extend outward from the neighborhood and tribal levels of identity toward the regional level, the more broadly intertribal level, and the American rural spheres. The mixed parentage of two uncommon Social Dances adds to that linkage. The term House Dance formerly referred to night-long events in homes, where dances featured steps echoing those of Anglo square dances, accompanied by fiddlers (plus guitar or straws drumming the fiddle's strings) playing Anglo tunes such as "Sally Gooden." Those long nights of dancing are gone, but the individual dances were conflated into the one House Dance when this tradition passed under the umbrella of Social Dances. Also, in recent years, the Mystic Wind Choctaw Social Dancers have ended some of their sets with a Choctaw Two-Step, accompanied by a powwow drum (Southern Pine) and featuring a text including the phrases "I'm from Mississippi, you're from Oklahoma" and "Choctaw Saturday Night." As in the House Dance, Anglo-derived steps appear, now in follow-the-leader format, similar to Two-Step dances performed at intertribal powwows. But I believe that the most significant recent change in the world of Mississippi Choctaw Social Dance is the leap in popularity of the lively War Dances and especially Stealing Partners. These dances are indeed traditional, but emphasizing them statistically tilts the Social Dance experience from traditional ritual toward excitement, just as does the continued growth in popularity of the men's and women's Fancy Dances in the powwow world.

The Veteran's Day Powwow: Intertribal Culture with Tribal Accents

The main Mississippi Choctaw powwow today is their Veteran's Day Powwow, first arranged in 1995 by Harold Comby, who still organizes and emcees the event. The Choctaw also usually host a powwow for Mother's Day, plus occasional powwows, such as one in 2009 promoting education and one in 2010 encouraging tribal members to cooperate with the census. The Veteran's Day Powwow is small in national perspective, with two to five or six drums, probably fewer than one hundred dancers, no more than two dozen vendors, and an audience that seldom exceeds two hundred (mostly local Choctaw) at any given moment. But the physical layout of the event—the dance circle, surrounded by a convivial audience, in turn surrounded by food and craft vendors—and the series of dances and small ceremonies follow national norms.

Why do the Choctaw re-create what originally was a Plains intertribal event? First, inter-tribalism is not new here. Indian populations were more loosely woven long ago than in the current, restrictive U.S. government's definition of Indian tribes, and the Choctaw probably participated for centuries in a "pattern of reciprocal ceremonial ground visiting" with neighboring Woodlands populations (Levine, personal communication, 2013); some dances are still shared between Woodlands tribes. Second, many of today's Choctaw have lived among other Indian groups—as has Harold Comby—and wish to keep nourishing the "Indian" middle layer of identity. Third, the very high per capita rate of Native American enlistment in the armed forces is in part a pilgrimage to outer layers of identity, to both the Indian past (and the old warrior societies) and Southern rural layers; supporting the entire web of identity bolsters the coherence of personal and group psychology. Veteran's Day and the concept of the powwow are a good fit.

Just as the Choctaw Fair looked outward from the core of identity by peppering daily entertainment centered on Social Dance with regional and national elements, this broadly Indian powwow looks inward; it is tribe-specific in many small ways. During each Grand Entry each year, Comby names many of the veterans bearing flags—in most cases local Choctaw—and cites their past armed forces affiliations. He usually notes at some point that Choctaw soldiers served as code-talkers in World War I (antedating the more famous parallel work done by Navajo soldiers during World War II). He also mentions that three of his brothers served in the Marine Corps (he instead worked for years as a Bureau of Indian Affairs policeman in Native communities elsewhere in the United States and is now a captain in the Choctaw police force). He applies a local color to other regular powwow elements by naming other local individuals. In 2008, there was a blanket song for Lyndon Alex, a Choctaw who had "been dancing for thirty-seven years" (attendees honor such a dance's dedicatee by dropping dollars on a blanket). The prayer during the opening sequence of dances in 2009 was by Peggy Thompson, speaking in Choctaw. And a birthday song celebrating several named tribal members, done many years, has some of the words of the classic "Happy Birthday" song implanted into a Forty-Nine song performed by the local drum, Southern Pine.

Powwows of any size throughout North America feature several contrasting styles of drums (a "drum" is both the playing/singing ensemble and the large, horizontally suspended drum that all of the men play simultaneously). At least one drum will be "Northern" (with a relatively high singers' tessitura and tense timbre, in the style of Plains Indians) and at least one will be "Southern" (a style based in Oklahoma, with the men singing in somewhat more relaxed timbres in a lower tessitura, and often with some women and girls standing in an arc behind the players on one side of the drum, doubling the melody at the octave). Of the half-dozen Mississippi Choctaw drums, the most-heard Northern drum is Grey Wolf, and the most-heard Southern drum is the Southern Pine Singers, organized by Dan Isaac, whose large family also constitutes the core of the Mystic Wind Choctaw Social Dancers.

Tara Browner, when refining the categories of Northern and Southern drum styles, noted that "pow-wow musicians have a tendency to sing in styles not native to their geographic setting, [but] often adopt the pow-wow singing style closest in sound (that is, range and vocal production) to their own tribal repertoires." For instance, the high- and tense-singing Navajo prefer Northern drums, and the low- and relaxed-singing Pueblo favor Southern drums (Browner 2009:131). Among the Mississippi Choctaw, a majority of drums do opt for Southern style, which features vocal production closer in sound to the singing that accompanies their Social Dances. Further, Dan Isaac and the other main vocalists in Southern Pine sing with a level of tension that is low within the range delimited by the various Southern substyles; their sound is nearly identical to that of the chanters for Choctaw Social Dances.[6]

The powwow emcee calls for a Flag Song among the handful of songs immediately following the Grand Entry that initiates each long dance session of a powwow. Flag songs are tribe-specific and often include words, whereas most powwow and Social Dance songs feature vocables. When Comby assigns that song to Southern Pine, they do a specific Choctaw Flag Song bearing a text that Comby says was written in 1974 by Wagoner Amos (now deceased). "Dan Isaac added the big drum to the words," he continues, meaning that Isaac composed the music (Comby, emcee narration, 2012 Veteran's Day Powwow). It's relatively slow for a powwow song, indeed about the tempo of many Social Dance songs (MM=ca. 70). It's not shaped like typical Plains powwow songs, which start high, follow a terraced descent contour, leap up nearly as high, and flow downward again in asymmetrical repetition form (cf. Levine and Nettl 2011), with that sequence constituting each of several "push-ups" making up a performance. Instead, Isaac chose simplified melodic arcs that repeat quite literally and omitted the drummed honor beats, the placement of which helps differentiate Northern and Southern powwow singing style. To my ear, the form and general impression of this song places it squarely between Southern powwow drum conventions and the overall effect of Choctaw Social Dance songs.

Finally, just as the Social Dance–dominated Choctaw Fair had room for a fifty-minute demonstration of intertribal music and dance, the 2012 Veteran's Day Powwow, about half as long as the fair, included a twenty-minute demonstration of Social Dance, with the Elderly Social Dancers performing Stealing Partners, a Four-Step War Dance, their signature House Dance, and departing in a Walk Dance.

Country Music and National Native American Acts at the Choctaw Fair

Everyone in Neshoba County shares the same choices when they turn on their car or truck radios. Choctaw, young and old, favor core country music—many cite George Strait as a favorite performer—and, to a lesser degree, country's timbral cousin, classic rock. David Samuels noted that the "process that links Country Music to Native American ideologies of culture and history is the sense of connection to land and place" (2009:153), that is, it reflects the rural layer of their collective identity. The main occasion when these Indians can directly influence which pop music acts they hear is the Choctaw Fair. Most years, hired evening entertainment fits the same profile: affordable mainstream country music acts, plus a few nationally known Indian singers in the style of classic rock (in 2012, the Lumbee rhythm and blues singer Jana Mashonee, whose performances include Indian textual or visual references, and The Plateros, a Navajo family playing accessible blues).

Conclusions

The overall picture of identity displayed through music and dance among the Mississippi Choctaw is unsurprising in its broad outlines. Indeed, one subtopic—how powwows have been made tribe-specific in Native American cultures—has already attracted scholarly attention (Nettl 1989:41–42; Goertzen 2001; Jackson 2003). What I find most significant about how the Mississippi Choctaw shape music and dance to limn identity is a matter of symmetry. In the cases of both inherited tribal Social Dance and borrowed powwow culture, Mississippi Choctaw began with strong, well-developed, and internally varied cultural/aesthetic complexes, then treated them in a common way. In both cases, there has been a measured push toward vivid and fun dances. In addition to that shared impulse, rather than emphasizing the contrasting qualities of Social Dance and powwow dancing (and their musics), event arrangers and participants have carefully layered on similarly sized matrices of connections between these aesthetic complexes. Even the Mississippi Choctaw treatment of pop music exhibits parallel cultural-bridge building on a broader scale. In each genre of music and dance they favor, the Choctaw respect the essential nature of the cultural and aesthetic materials. They emphasize the middle ground of a practice, and don't insist on surrounding that practice with fortified borders; identity is treated in a confident, positive, and, above all, inclusive manner. Mississippi Choctaw identity is not about contrasts or stark choices, but rather about community.

Notes

1. The Choctaw Indian Princess is selected each year during the Choctaw Indian Fair. Whereas she may choose to attend several powwows during her reign, she is not

a "powwow princess" per se. She wears Choctaw Social Dance garb on all official occasions, including powwows.

2. Lewis and Hand sometimes disagreed about how the songs and dances should go, presaging today's low-key tension between cultivating a standard form for each dance and song versus cultivating localized versions.

3. Harold Comby, the most important figure in maintaining powwow culture on the reservation in recent decades, and his domestic partner, Peggy Thompson, were in the high school choirs Hand took on tour in the early 1970s. Thompson described their visits to the Smithsonian to demonstrate Choctaw Social Dance and its music, and also the ensemble's visits to powwows in several states (interviews, Hattiesburg, MS, April 2011).

4. Levine describes a different classification of dances in Oklahoma, one around which dance sets are structured (1993:402).

5. The dances were performed in 2008 in the number of repetitions indicated: Walk Dance, nearly all groups, twice each; Stealing Partners, 16; Snake Dance, 15; Fast War Dance, 8; Four-Step War Dance, 8; Corn Dance, 7; Friendship Dance, 7; Drunk Dance, 6; War Dance, 6; Raccoon Dance, 5; Mosquito Dance, 5; Duck Dance, 4; House Dance, 4; Jump Dance, 4; Quail Dance, 3; Wedding Dance, 3; *Kabocca Boli* (Ballgame Dance), 2; Tick Dance, 2; Turtle Dance, 1; and Choctaw Two-Step, 1. For excerpted examples of Choctaw Social Dances done on the tribal dance grounds in Mississippi, see the YouTube video "Voices of the Mississippi Band of Choctaw Indians" (www.youtube.com/watch?v=UmRxPK_-EYQ). The lady in the black baseball cap is Thallis Lewis. Several of the samples in this compilation feature Jump Dances. There's a fragment of a Snake Dance at 2'26". Near the middle of the video, when the fiddler R. J. Willis appears briefly, there's a short bit of the House Dance (at 6'23"). The video ends with the Walk Dance, as does any set of these dances. For audio examples see Choctaw Museum 2004.

6. Their collective timbre is closest to that of Browner's category of "Southern Prairie," although their approach to form better suits her category of "Southern Plains," since they often modulate up by a whole step at some point in their performance (Browner 2009:137).

References

Boykin, Deborah. 2002. "Choctaw Indians in the 21st Century." *Mississippi History Now: An Online Publication of the Mississippi Historical Society* (mshistory.k12.ms.us/articles/10/choctaw-indians-in-the-21st-century).

Browner, Tara. 2009. "An Acoustic Geography of Intertribal Pow-Wow Songs." In *Music of the First Nations: Tradition and Innovation in Native North America*, edited by Tara Browner, 131–40. Urbana: University of Illinois Press.

Choctaw Museum. 2004. *Choctaw Dance Songs*. Choctaw, MS: Choctaw Museum. Cassette tape.

Goertzen, Chris. 2001. "Powwows and Identity on the Piedmont and Coastal Plains of North Carolina." *Ethnomusicology* 45(1): 58–88.

Howard, James H., and Victoria Lindsay Levine. 1990. *Choctaw Music and Dance*. Norman: University of Oklahoma Press.

Jackson, Jason Baird. 2003. "The Opposite of Powwow: Ignoring and Incorporating the Intertribal War Dance in the Oklahoma Stomp Dance Community." *Plains Anthropologist* 48(187): 237–53.

Levine, Victoria Lindsay. 1990. "Choctaw Indian Musical Cultures in the Twentieth Century." Ph.D. dissertation, University of Illinois at Urbana-Champaign.

———. 1993. "Musical Revitalization among the Choctaw." *American Music* 11(4): 391–411.

———. 1997. "Music, Myth and Medicine in the Choctaw Indian Ballgame." In *Enchanting Powers: Music in the World's Religions*, edited by Lawrence E. Sullivan, 189–218. Cambridge, MA: Harvard University Center for the Study of World Religions.

Levine, Victoria Lindsay, and Bruno Nettl. 2011. "Strophic Form and Asymmetrical Repetition in Four American Indian Songs." *In Analytical and Cross-Cultural Studies in World Music*, edited by Michael Tenzer and John Roeder, 288–315. New York: Oxford University Press.

Mississippi Band of Choctaw Indians. 1972. *Mississippi Band of Choctaw Indians: An Era of Change*. Philadelphia, MS: Mississippi Band of Choctaw Indians.

Mould, Tom. 2004. *Choctaw Tales*. Jackson: University Press of Mississippi.

Nettl, Bruno. 1989. *Blackfoot Musical Thought: Comparative Perspectives*. Kent, OH: Kent State University Press.

Samuels, David. 2009. "Singing Indian Country: Country Music and Ethnic Boundary Crossing." In *Music of the First Nations: Tradition and Innovation in Native North America*, edited by Tara Browner, 141–59. Urbana: University of Illinois Press.

CHAPTER FOUR

St. Peter and the *Santarinas*

Celebrating Traditions over Time in Malacca, Malaysia

Margaret Sarkissian

I have conducted fieldwork in Malacca's Portuguese Settlement since 1990 and have been lucky enough to revisit the village almost every year since then. This has provided an extended ethnographic experience in a single, contained field site and allowed me to observe the ways in which change has occurred over time. My fascination with this topic was most likely influenced by my teacher, Bruno Nettl. Aged twenty-two, I arrived at the University of Illinois soon after *The Study of Ethnomusicology* first appeared (Nettl 1983); it was the textbook for my initial graduate school experience. One of my first jobs as Nettl's research assistant was to read the proofs of *The Western Impact on World Music: Change, Adaptation, and Survival* (Nettl 1985). Like a newborn duckling imprinting wildly, my scholarly brain was shaped by these formative intellectual experiences, and in 1990, I waddled off to Malaysia for my dissertation research. I had no idea then that this would become a lifetime commitment.

Without premeditation, I have been doing what Kay Shelemay calls "medium-term longitudinal or multi-temporal studies" (Shelemay 2013). It is from this perspective that I focus here on two of the community's most important celebrations: Festa San Pedro (the feast of St. Peter) and Christmas. While these are not their only celebrations, they neatly bisect the year, draw the largest number of tourists, and provide the main annual opportunities for those who live or work outstation to return. I am also intrigued by the comparative possibilities, given that my personal connection with the two traditions differs: I have attended and participated in Festa San Pedro regularly since 1990; in contrast, I have witnessed Christmas there only twice, in 1990 and 2005. Thus, while I have observed the incremental process of change over time in the case of Festa San Pedro, I have two discrete snapshots of Christmas fifteen years apart.

The ways in which these celebrations have changed illuminate important tensions and continuities within the community. Both display characteristics typical of festivals: "They occur at calendrically regulated intervals and are public in nature, participatory in ethos, complex in structure, and multiple in voice, scene, and purpose" (Stoeltje 1992:261). Over time, however, Festa San Pedro has been transformed from a saint's feast day into a scripted folkloric event, simultaneously a valued and visible part of the national calendar and a public demonstration of local Portuguese identity (Sarkissian 1999). The figure of St. Peter is central, but is represented more as genial ancestor/Ur-fisherman than major Catholic icon. Christmas, in contrast, is a potentially riskier enterprise, because it celebrates a core Christian religious event amid a majority Muslim nation. In 1990, Christmas was a low-key community-centered celebration. By 2005, a new, oddly unscripted version had emerged and become a flexible marker of contemporary Portuguese Settlement identity. Characterized by excess, Christmas present is now embodied in dozens of boys and girls who run around the Settlement dressed as Santas and Santarinas.[1]

Festa San Pedro

St. Peter is the patron saint of fishermen and by extension of the Portuguese Settlement, historically, at least, a fishing village. His feast day (June 29) was traditionally a special day for the fishermen. It was simultaneously a holiday and a holy day, providing the fishermen a day's respite from the sea and an opportunity for their small wooden fishing boats to be cleaned, repaired, and—most importantly—blessed by the priest for the upcoming year. The day always ended with a party, with musicians playing the local social dance, *branyo*, and singers improvising verses to songs in Kristang (local creole Portuguese) such as "Jinkly Nona."[2] Today, Festa San Pedro no longer belongs to the fishermen; it is a signature event on the national calendar, promoted in domestic tourist literature and international guidebooks alike.

The modern Festa San Pedro lasts anywhere from three to ten days depending on the enthusiasm of the organizing committee and the level of sponsorship from state government and local businesses. As merits a public display of this magnitude, the modern festival includes multiple activities that occur in a structured order (Turner and McArthur 1990:84–85). Certain events have become mandatory: a formal opening ceremony, the boat-decorating competition, Mass followed by a procession and blessing of the boats, plentiful local food and drink, cultural shows, and a closing *branyo* dance. The opening ceremony—not necessarily on the first day—provides an opportunity for the *Regedor* (Settlement headman), local politicians, and an invited state or national dignitary to make political capital. The other events constitute an annual public expression of the community's Portuguese face. The boat decorations make reference to Portugal's glorious seafaring past; the Mass, procession, and blessing of the boats link the community to Portuguese fishing villages worldwide; the cultural shows display local (perhaps at times imagined) versions of Portuguese music and dance for visitors; and the *branyo*, always dedicated to "the fishermen," links the Settlement musically to other parts of the Asian Portuguese diaspora (see Sarkissian 1995–1996; Jackson 2006). In short, the modern Festa San Pedro includes all the elements necessary to express group identity and articulate the heritage of the community (Stoeltje 1992:261).

This public face of the festival covers internal tensions that swirl beneath the surface. For example, the boat-decorating competition has gradually become more of a draw for tourists than a meaningful activity for residents. No longer is the Settlement abuzz as it was in the cool early morning of St. Peter's Day 1990, with dozens of fishermen busily decorating their newly repainted wooden boats, transforming each into a unique Portuguese galleon-shaped work of art, complete with painted sails, rigging made from fresh-cut green sugar cane, and even children dressed as angels or mermaids (figure 4.1). Each year there are fewer full- and part-time fishermen, partly due to massive land reclamation projects that have destroyed the fragile aquatic ecosystem. Of those who remain, fewer choose to decorate their boats. Annual arguments with the organizing committee, usually over money, have sucked the fun out of the day, resulting in a dwindling pool of participants who compete for prize money that does not cover the cost of the decorations. I now watch the same half dozen hard-core residents competitively decorate their boats, displayed not along the old sea wall as in the past, but in the middle of a large parking lot built on newly reclaimed land. Yet even in this concrete expanse, there are signs that remind anyone who cares to notice that the day is not simply about public display. A few older fishermen who refuse to participate in the competition still clean their fiberglass boats (which no longer need annual repainting), put up simple bunting, and keep their boats in line to be blessed by the priest (figure 4.2).

Mass continues to be celebrated by the community, but has been the source of ongoing tension between parish priests and the organizing

Figure 4.1. Decorated boats on display on July 29, 1996. Notice the mud flats and sea in the background. ***Photo by Margaret Sarkissian***

committee for years. For obvious reasons, the priest has to come to the Settlement to bless the boats. From the committee's perspective, they need a priest to officiate, but it does not really matter *which* priest. Having Mass in situ is convenient for community members, but the essential thing is to have a priest lead the boat-blessing procession because this is what tourists come to see. If the local parish priest is unwilling or unable to come, the organizers simply call around until they find another Catholic priest, active or retired, who is willing to say Mass and bless the boats at the required time and date. This perceived lack of respect has been irritating to local priests over time, some of whom have even expressed reluctance at being co-opted into the public spectacle. From their perspective, they have become Pied Pipers, leading processions of residents and tourists to the seafront (nowadays, the parking lot). In effect, the priest has become a costumed actor playing the part of a priest; he blesses boats, some of which no longer sail.

The procession further blurs the line between the religious and the quaintly folkloric. It begins with half a dozen altar boys, in long white robes swinging censers or carrying crosses on long poles, leading the way out of Mass and toward the boats. They are followed by a dozen or so *Irmang de Greza* (Kristang: "Brothers of the Church"),[3] wearing distinctive uniforms—

Figure 4.2. Gregory de Roche, one of the few active older fishermen, putting finishing touches to his boat, July 29, 2006. The painted cross, displaying the colors of Portugal's soccer team, is a reference to the ongoing 2006 World Cup. *Photo by Margaret Sarkissian*

black pants, crisp white shirts, and short red capes—as they walk two abreast. The last four *Irmang* carry a statue of St. Peter on a palanquin decorated with flowers. Next comes the priest (or priests, on grander occasions), who pauses in front of each boat to make the sign of the cross and sprinkle Holy Water as he recites his blessing. The long, unruly tail of the procession is a colorful snaking line of congregants intermingled with tourists. The former carry lighted white candles; the latter carry backpacks and cameras. On the surface, it looks like a time-honored part of the community's Iberian Catholic heritage. But all is not what it seems: St. Peter only joined the procession in 1994, a last-minute idea derived from other para-liturgical processions (Good Friday, Easter Saturday, and the Feast of the Assumption) at which statues are carried. Although the *Irmang* regularly attended Mass and joined the procession "out of respect to St. Peter," it was not one of their official duties, according to senior *Irmang* Michael Lazaroo (interview, 19 August 1994, Malacca, Malaysia). Like the priest, the *Irmang*, St. Peter, and the decorated boats all add color to, and become part of, the public spectacle, enhancing the folk-like elements and obscuring the deeper religious foundation. And yet, although the procession is filled with outsiders for whom religious experience is clearly secondary (few, for example, attend Mass), many older Settlement residents still follow the priest, reciting their prayers as they carry their lighted candles.

As for the evening entertainment, there is always some social drama unfolding. In the case of the Portuguese cultural shows, there are annual arguments over which groups will perform and how much they will be paid. In the early 1990s there were as many as five Portuguese cultural groups competing for or sharing nights among them. Even though only two—Rancho Folclorico San Pedro and Tropa de Malaca—survived through the mid-2000s, there were still disagreements between organizing committees and group leaders. At the very least, personality conflicts between group leaders and organizing committee members complicated the situation.

Sometimes, the drama illuminates deeper conflicts within the community. For example, in 1996, a dispute between the Settlement leadership and a newly formed "Fishermen's Action Committee" over the state government's ongoing land reclamation project almost disrupted performances.[4] But somehow, the show always went on—until 2006, the first year that there were no cultural shows at Festa San Pedro. This time the organizing committee had not only renewed its annual battle with Joe Lazaroo (leader of Rancho Folclorico San Pedro), but had also managed to irritate the usually placid Noel Felix (leader of Tropa de Malaca). Felix's public reason for not performing was the recent death of his brother, but that did not stop him from performing on the last night for the fishermen's *branyo*. Privately, he was angry that the organizers were paying a local Indian hip-hop group more than they had offered Tropa de Malaca.

The fishermen's *branyo* has suffered similarly. What used to be a social dance primarily for community members (though stray tourists were always welcome) has become another evening performance that draws large numbers of outsiders and alienates older residents. A significant number of the outsiders are local youths, some of whom come in gangs to drink and cause fights. The part-time Settlement bands that used to play for the *branyo* are increasingly displaced by professional Kuala Lumpur–based bands, which even if they do perform *branyo*, rarely do so to the liking of older residents. In 2006, the schism between the public Festa San Pedro and the community dance grew so wide that there were actually two simultaneous performances on the final evening. On the amplified main stage, a Kuala Lumpur–based band[5] and other invited entertainers (including emcees from a popular radio station, who were broadcasting live) performed to an audience of tourists and local (non-Settlement) revelers. At the same time, in a dark section of newly reclaimed land well behind the main stage (though hardly out of earshot of the enormous speakers), on a makeshift stage, local musicians—including Noel Felix—performed *branyo* and "golden oldies" "free, for the fishermen." Practically the entire Settlement community was there, drinking beer and having their own private dance party.

In between the requisite public events are events for community members. Although these vary from year to year, they usually include game stalls and a variety of traditional competitions—children's games, women's and men's sports, coconut peeling or smashing, duck catching, and prawn fishing (using the traditional *langgiang* butterfly net). Most are held during the hot afternoons, when few tourists are around, though fishing competitions depend on tides. There are also staged events for community members in the early evenings, the most popular being beauty pageants (for girls, occasionally for young women) and modern dance competitions. The latter demonstrate clearly the extent to which Settlement children are embedded in global popular culture. Teams of four to six children, ranging from about six years old to mid-teens (usually same sex, rarely co-ed), perform dance routines they have choreographed to the latest pop hits. Whether it is small boys perfectly imitating the latest hip-hop sensation or pre-teen girls in skimpy costumes copying the latest tween idol, the modern dancing skill and talent of the children is clear. Many of these children will join the Settlement cultural troupes and perform Portuguese folk dances in their turn. The old-fashioned "Talent Time" competition was even infused with new life in 2005, when the organizing committee ran its first "Settlement Idol" competition, complete with community voting. While non-Settlement spectators are welcome at any of these staged events, the audience consists mostly of Settlement residents, cheering on their children and grandchildren.

As the government-approved public face of the Portuguese Settlement, secular and cultural elements of the Festa San Pedro are promoted and religious aspects downplayed. On the one hand, decorated boats, cultural shows, games, competitions, stage shows, and non-stop music blaring from the public address system all contribute to the festive atmosphere. On the other, Mass is barely noticed by visitors and even the procession seems more folkloric than religious. Since 1990 I have watched Festa San Pedro grow into a major annual commercial opportunity: each year the two main beer companies, Carlsberg and Tiger, compete for prominence. Games stalls, once run by residents, have been gradually replaced by market stalls run by outsiders and, in 2006, even by the local Starbucks franchise; even the temporary food stalls, once open to any Settlement family to make a bit of money, are now dominated by outsiders. Despite this commercialization, there are moments of resistance, small ways in which residents reclaim their space and contest the public version of Festa San Pedro.

Christmas

Christmas, in contrast, was never considered a tourist event that belonged to the Settlement. In 1990 it was very much a self-contained community celebration, a religious holy day infused with the smell of fresh paint and the excitement of getting new clothes. In the days leading up to Christmas, Settlement residents busily repainted the outsides of their wooden houses and spruced up their front yards. On Christmas Eve everyone went to Midnight Mass at St. Peter's Church in town, wearing dressy new clothes bought especially for the occasion. After Mass residents returned to the Settlement and extended families got together for late-night suppers, one of the rare occasions at which whole families ate together. Christmas morning was eerily quiet, as residents slept off the late night, but from about eleven o'clock in the morning, there was a steady stream of visitors for "Open House."[6] Homes were open to family and friends; children scurried from house to house to offer season's greetings to their relatives and godparents; and friends of other races and religions (often colleagues from work) stopped by for twenty or thirty minutes to share some food and drink. Households prepared large pots of Curry Devil (spicy chicken curry, a Settlement specialty), mutton curry, and other favorite dishes. Crates of beer and bottles of whiskey were on offer to those who drank. By mid-afternoon, many Settlement boys who had sneaked drinks from their relatives were fast asleep under shady trees.

By 2005 Christmas had become a chaotic mega-event. Sometime between 1990 and 2005, residents discovered Christmas lights. The entire Settlement was lit up like fairyland (figure 4.3). Though there was no official competition or prize money, most of the 120 households expended tremendous effort and money to outdo each other with Christmas kitsch. Practically the only dark houses were those in mourning for a recently deceased family member. Not advertised in any way, the Settlement display was packed every evening with literally thousands of sightseers who came to see the lights. Although the promenaders included foreign tourists, they were mostly local: Chinese families with small children eager to be photographed next to Santa Claus or a giant inflatable snowman, Indian boys in gangs carrying motorcycle helmets on their arms, and Malay couples, the women easily visible in their *tudung* (headscarves).

In 2005 the Portuguese Settlement Youth Group hijacked Christmas. They hung strings of white fairy lights along the road leading into the Settlement; built a ninety-foot-tall Christmas tree out of green fairy lights in the

Figure 4.3. No. 12 Jalan D'Albuquerque illuminated for Christmas, December 2005. ***Photo by Margaret Sarkissian***

main open area; took over the outdoor stage and set up a nativity scene on one side, with life-sized statues carved from Styrofoam blocks and painted by members of the "Art and Decoration Subcommittee"; and organized ten days of activities, raffles, and stage events leading up to Christmas and through New Year's Eve. This time, however, the events were intended for Settlement residents. Two competitions in particular—"Supermodels 2005" (a drag contest for boys) and "Miss Santarina 2005" (a beauty pageant/talent show for girls dressed in *santarina* outfits)—drew large crowds of residents (figure 4.4). However, the Christmas lights and DJ music that went on into the wee hours every morning drew even bigger crowds of young Malaccans of all races. In fact, the crowds on Christmas Eve and New Year's Eve were larger than any I have seen at Festa San Pedro.

The crowd density made it impossible to leave the Settlement for Midnight Mass on Christmas Eve, so the parish priest of St. Peter's scheduled an open-air Mass at eight o'clock at night on the Settlement stage. By then, the open area was densely packed with residents and outsiders, including a sprinkling of young Western tourists. It was surreal: in the middle of fairyland, with large brightly colored Styrofoam nativity figures peering over his

Figure 4.4. Winners and participants of Miss Santarina, December 2005. ***Photo by Margaret Sarkissian***

shoulder, Father Moses (the Malaysian-Chinese parish priest) tried to bring his Christmas message to the multitude, many of whom were too busy to listen, talking, setting off firecrackers, or buying flashing Santa hats at one of the market stalls that had sprung up around the periphery. Following the Mass, Malacca's (Malay) chief minister was scheduled to appear, Father Christmas-like, to give presents to the poor children of the community. Lacking reindeer and a sleigh, however, his arrival was delayed by a couple of hours because he couldn't get into the Settlement for the sheer volume of foot traffic along the single entrance road.

On Christmas morning, the Settlement was awash in empty beer cans, silly string, and firecracker shells. Two elderly Indians wearing Public Works Department uniforms leaned on their brooms as they surveyed the colorful mess with resignation. As the day progressed, there was little of the usual Open House activity. Instead of staying home to await a succession of brief visits from non-Settlement friends, families visited each other. Few households had prepared the traditional food for guests; instead they informally offered their own relatives beer and cake, while children aggressively solicited *ang pows* (Chinese red envelopes containing money) from their adult relatives. In lieu of Open House, many families invited friends and colleagues to scheduled evening parties between Christmas and New Year. Rather than a steady stream of guests dropping in briefly throughout the day, chairs were set out in front yards and guests were expected to arrive around the appointed time, stay longer, and socialize with each other as well as with the host family.

In contrast to Festa San Pedro, there were no live bands, no Portuguese cultural dances, and not even a single *branyo*. Instead, competing gangs of children roamed the Settlement before dawn each morning, singing carols in several keys simultaneously as they incensed houses, collecting money to buy breakfast. After night fell, younger children ran around in Santa suits and scary latex Santa masks. Music, which was constant and ear-splitting, came from a DJ's console via an enormous outdoor speaker system that almost reached the roof of the stage. From mid-morning until two or three o'clock in the morning in the days leading up to Christmas, the Settlement was subjected to a continuous diet of Christmas songs. We all dreamed of white Christmases in the tropical heat while anticipating Santa Claus coming to town. Between Christmas and New Year, however, the Youth Group drove everyone to distraction with a different soundscape: hip-hop music played at extreme volumes. Their New Year's Eve Countdown turned into a public rave that went on until four o'clock in the morning, with no one in the village able to hear themselves talk, think, or sleep for the reverberations of the giant speakers.

In 1990 Christmas had been a private, community-centered celebration of a central Catholic holy day. Friends of other races and religions visited on Christmas Day to pay respects and share food, but otherwise there was little outside presence; it was a time to take a few days off work, eat, drink, and perhaps gamble a little among family. By 2005, Christmas in the Settlement was part Disney theme park and part non-stop rock concert. Thousands of outsiders came to see the lights, listen to the music, or simply to eat, drink, and be merry. Practically the only visible sign of anything religious was the Styrofoam nativity tableau, with its Magi, shepherds, and angels watching silently from one corner of the stage.

Conclusions

On the surface, these celebrations demonstrate, to me at least, competing faces of the Portuguese Settlement. One face (the Festa San Pedro) presents a self-consciously constructed Portuguese identity. "Traditions" are repeated because they are expected—by the government and the tourist industry—and because they create national visibility and generate revenue. They have meaning to the participants, to be sure, but this meaning is often submerged beneath the internal conflicts that arise each year, most of which are related to where the money goes. There are prominent signs of this public face everywhere—large plastic neon-lit advertisements with pictures of decorated boats, cultural group dancers, and the two main singers, Joe Lazaroo and Noel Felix, framed by beer company logos. Such images dominate the visual landscape year round, while their voices provide a temporary soundtrack: each day from mid-morning until the evening events begin, recordings of Lazaroo and Felix singing "Portuguese songs" are played over the public address system.

Yet there are significant moments of resistance to this public, folkloricized version of the Settlement. The fishermen who choose not to decorate their boats elaborately remind us of the day's deeper meaning: a ritual in which boats are blessed for the coming year. Though many boats no longer sail, the act of blessing them is still important to their owners. The residents who carry their candles in the procession remind us that the ritual is, for some at least, still a religious experience. They recite their prayers and sing their hymns, as they have always done, unperturbed by the tourists and their cameras. And as the absent cultural troupes and alternative *branyo* of 2006 remind us, Festa San Pedro does not always privilege the demonstration of "Portuguese identity" (or national multicultural diversity, for that matter) to outsiders above the celebration of Portuguese Settlement community. The fishermen's holy day/holiday has not been completely erased by the scheduled festival on the national tourism calendar.

The other face (Christmas) presents a different identity, one that is fluid and emergent. The youth of the Settlement have grown up in the middle of a tourist site, putting on costumes to dance on stage for the tourists; now they are starting to organize activities themselves. They have no direct connection with Portugal; rather, they live in a truly global world. They wear American street clothes, listen to the latest hip-hop artists, support Manchester United or other English Premier League teams (but always root for Portugal or Brazil during the World Cup), interact with each other on Facebook, and have relatives in Australia, Germany, and the United States. Yet a sense of community is truly important to many of them. Donny de Costa, president of the Youth Group in 2005, described plans to form a band to play for Sunday Masses and for youth praise and worship, language classes to promote the speaking of Kristang, and their own cultural dance group (interview, 16 January 2006, Malacca, Malaysia).

In 1990, residents of the Portuguese Settlement, like other Christians nationwide, celebrated core religious holy days quietly. By 2005, a secularized version of Christmas, devoid of religious symbols, was embraced throughout Malaysia except in the most fundamental Islamic strongholds. Santa Clauses, reindeers, snowmen, and elves adorned shopping malls across the nation—at least until they were supplanted by the Chinese New Year decorations that followed closely on the heels of Christmas. This Malaysian version of Christmas was embraced by the younger generation of Settlement residents, with the exception of the onstage Styrofoam nativity scene, the single visible reminder of the reason for Christmas. Artistic talents, used by previous generations to decorate boats, were now illuminating the Settlement quite literally. There was a new sense of fun and freedom, unhampered by official competition for token prizes. And yet, underneath all this, these young people—most of whom I have known all their lives—are preoccupied by the same issues as their parents: religion, language, heritage, culture, and education. Donny and his friends think about providing role models, keeping kids off drugs and in school, and creating a sense of community. It's a tall order, but if they fail, the Portuguese Settlement will lose much of its special identity, especially when Joe Lazaroo hangs up his guitar and Noel Felix no longer sings *branyo*. From my perspective, this is a positive sign, a small green shoot after a long tropical winter.

I continue to observe Festa San Pedro in person, and each year my understanding of the social structure of the community deepens. In some years, like 2007, the fiftieth anniversary of the nation's independence, the Festa

San Pedro is grand; in others, like 2013, it is minimal or "boring" in the words of residents. I continue to observe Christmas from a distance, now sharing photographs on Facebook and WhatsApp posted by Settlement friends. Newly rebuilt cement houses have rendered the Christmas-tide smell of freshly painted woodwork anachronistic, but the decorations have become ever more elaborate and advertising companies have joined the bandwagon, providing lavish illuminations for strategically placed homes in order to advertise their products. Instead of living in a tourist site visited by the world as they were even in 1990, Portuguese Settlement residents now engage in global culture, traveling more widely, both virtually and literally. The wonderful thing about studying change over time is that one never runs out of new material.

Notes

1. Of unclear origin, "santarina" appeared in Malaysian and Singaporean English in the mid-2000s to describe a young woman dressed in a Santa costume. The costume, which ranges from cute for small girls to sexy for teens, is a red dress (or miniskirt) with white fur-like trimmings and a red elf's hat with white edging and pom-pom; fur-trimmed boots are optional. See also a blog post by a Malaysian called Naith KK (2009).

2. For a description of Festa San Pedro in the old days and its subsequent transformation, see Sarkissian 1999:327–39.

3. The *Irmang de Greza* is a male para-religious confraternity founded in 1553 by the Dominican Fr. Gaspar da Cruz. There are frequent tensions between the *Irmang* and the official church hierarchy.

4. This social drama is described and analyzed in detail in Sarkissian 2000:150–58.

5. Family connections between a band member and an organizing committee member did not help.

6. "Open House" or *rumah terbuka* is a Malaysian practice surrounding the major festivals of each race and religion: *Hari Raya Aidilfitri* (Malay/Muslim), *Chap Goh Mei* (Chinese/Buddhist), *Deepavali* (Indian/Hindu), and Christmas (Eurasian/Christian). On a community's appropriate special day, homes are opened and relatives, friends (often of other races or religions), and even strangers are invited to share the celebrations.

References

"Christmas and a Little History." 2009. Posted on Naith's Myst blog, 6 December. Retrieved from naith.kuiki.net/blog/2009/12/christmas-and-a-little-history.html (accessed 5 September 2013).

Jackson, K. David. 2006. "*Sinhelle Nona/Jinggli Nona*: A Traveling Portuguese Burgher Music." Paper presented at the conference Portuguese World Music: Luso-African Forms and Their Diaspora, Yale University, 25 March.

Nettl, Bruno. 1983. *The Study of Ethnomusicology: Thirty-One Issues and Concepts*. Urbana: University of Illinois Press.

———. 1985. *The Western Impact on World Music: Change, Adaptation, and Survival*. New York: Schirmer Books.

Sarkissian, Margaret. 1995–1996. "'Sinhalese Girl' Meets 'Aunty Annie': Competing Expressions of Ethnic Identity in the Portuguese Settlement, Melaka, Malaysia." *Asian Music* 27(1): 37–62.

———. 1999. "Patron Saints, Decorated Boats, and the Sugar Cane Story: Holidays and Holy Days in the Construction of a Malaysian Community." In *Structuralism's Transformations: Order and Revisions in Indonesian and Malaysian Societies*, edited by Susan Russell and Lorraine Aragon, 323–56. Tempe: Arizona State University, Center for Southeast Asian Studies.

———. 2000. *D'Albuquerque's Children: Performing Tradition in Malaysia's Portuguese Settlement*. Chicago: University of Chicago Press.

Shelemay, Kay Kaufman. 2013. "When Ethnography Meets History: Longitudinal Research in Ethnomusicology." Paper presented at the 42nd World Conference of the International Council for Traditional Music, Shanghai, China, 11–17 July.

Stoeltje, Beverly J. 1992. "Festival." In *Folklore, Cultural Performances, and Popular Entertainments*, edited by Richard Bauman, 261–71. New York: Oxford University Press.

Turner, Rory, and Phillip H. McArthur. 1990. "Cultural Performances: Public Display, Events, and Festival." In *The Emergence of Folklore in Everyday Life: A Fieldguide and Sourcebook*, edited by George H. Shoemaker, 83–93. Bloomington, IN: Trickster Press.

CHAPTER FIVE

~

Performing Translation in Jewish India

Kirtan of the Bene Israel

Anna Schultz

Several years ago I was interviewing a performer of *naradiya kirtan*—a Marathi-language Hindu performance medium that combines song, storytelling, and religious discourse—as part of my dissertation research on music, religion, and nationalism in India. Our conversation was cut short when his brother called to announce an exciting new discovery: a Jewish Marathi kirtan organization called the *Kirtanottejak Mandal* had been founded in Mumbai in 1880, three years before the first Hindu *kirtan* organization. I later learned that kirtan was arguably the most important Marathi Jewish performance medium of the next forty years and that it was revived in Israel in the 1990s as a prime exemplar of Bene Israel (Marathi Jewish) identity. I was as intrigued to learn of Jewish kirtan as I was that lifelong proponents of naradiya kirtan had never heard of it. Why would Jews adopt a performance form that had been firmly attached to Hindu temple worship for seven hundred years? Did the *Kirtanottejak Mandal* signify a lost history of Hindu-Jewish cultural exchange?

In this chapter I reflect on dialogues of the past, when Hindu *kirtankars* *did* know of Jewish kirtan and Indian Jewish scholars were inspired by Hindu performers, and attempt to address how and why a Hindu temple genre was translated for Jewish purposes. My preliminary findings suggest that the adaptation of Hindu devotional traditions helped Bene Israel people navigate the difficult task of connecting with global Judaism while negotiating a voice as a tiny minority within the Indian nationalist movement. It was no easy task to generate a sense of Jewish authenticity through Hindu song, but the socio-political climate of the late nineteenth century made it a project worth pursuing. When Bene Israel leaders first adopted Hindu kirtan in the late nineteenth century, they translated languages, religious practices, and musical styles to negotiate an Indian Jewish voice vis-à-vis Hindus, Christian missionaries, Indian Christians and Muslims, and global Jewry. They were careful about which songs they performed, what words they chose, which stories they told, and what ceremonial clothes they wore, but many aspects of Maharashtrian Hinduism remained untranslated in Jewish kirtan without censure.

The Bene Israel *Kirtanottejak Mandal* (Kirtan Inspiration Society) shaped a new performance style and provided a modern institutional structure to support a minority religious community's entry into an incipient sphere of religious nationalism. As argued by Partha Chatterjee in *The Nation and its Fragments* (1993), anti-colonial nationalists in India turned toward the "inside" sphere of religion and spirituality when frustrated by attempts for political autonomy in the "outside" realm. This inside space was constructed implicitly and explicitly as Hindu, and was both embraced and resisted by the religious minorities who were excluded from its majoritarian imaginary (Chatterjee 1993:5–13). Kirtan provided a means for Bene Israel people to ally their identities with a Marathi Hindu past that was becoming a resource in the creation of national identity, and it helped them to carve a particularly Jewish space within the nation.[1] My initial research suggests that the sonic aspects of kirtan were particularly powerful in generating affective attachment to Jewish texts because of their resonance with Marathi modes of Hindu devotion that were familiar to Bene Israel people, and also because of the power of music to encourage participation and activate memory.

This chapter also addresses the regendering of kirtan during its revival in late twentieth-century Bombay and Israel. From the 1880s through the 1920s, Bene Israel men published dozens of Marathi Jewish kirtans, plays, songbooks, and ritual instruction books, but Marathi performing arts publishing waned in the 1920s as interest in Zionism increased. When attention shifted toward learning Hebrew, Bene Israel men left a lacuna in Marathi Jewish musical song and literature. Women filled that space by maintaining kirtan in the oral tradition. In the 1960s, as Indian Jewish people became increasingly dissatisfied with their marginal status in India and Israel, Bene Israel women proudly performed kirtan to convince people that being Indian made them no less Jewish and that being Jewish made them no less Indian.

Translation theory provides a nuanced way to understand how literature and culture are transformed through adaptation (Mandair 2009; Niranjana 1992; Clifford 1997). Because Bene Israel kirtan has translated men's music into women's music, Hindu music into Jewish music, and Indian Jewish music into Indo-Israeli music, it is particularly ripe for study through a translational lens. Translation theories have been used in post-colonial literary theory to help explain how power is maintained and resisted through the imperfect glosses of translation between European languages and languages of colonized people (Niranjana 1992). Literary theorists Tejaswini Niranjana and Homi Bhabha are among those who have applied the concept of translation to cultural production more generally, arguing that people are translators not just of written texts, but also of practices and ideas (Bhabha 1994; Niranjana 1992). The cultural translations introduced in this chapter were articulated in a colonial context, but the play of power between Indian Jews and British colonizers was refracted by the presence of the Hindu majority. Bene Israel people not only translated Marathi Hindu practice into Jewish practice; they also conversely translated Jewish texts into a South Asian idiom. It was this second element that proved most messy for Bene Israel people claiming Jewish identity at the dawn of Israeli nationhood and in the face of Indian emigration to Israel.

Christians, Kerala Jews, and the Bene Israel Revival

Bene Israel community memory says that they arrived in the Konkan region of what is now the state of Maharashtra via shipwreck about two thousand years ago, but undisputed written documentation of the Bene Israel exists only as far back as the eighteenth century, first with a 1738 letter by the Danish Christian missionary J. A. Sartorius (Israel 1984:10–11, 54; Katz 2000:91–93; Numark 2012). Thirty years later, in 1768, a letter from Yechezkel Rahabi of Cochin to his Dutch business partner acknowledges the presence of the Bene Israel and describes their limited religious observances: reciting the Sabbath-evening prayer, "Shema," and resting on the Sabbath (cf. Katz 2000:91). Rahabi's letter also marks the beginning of Bene Israel religious revival. His son David (1721–1791) was the first of many teachers to travel from Kerala in South India to Maharashtra (Israel 1984:12; Isenberg 1988:44–45). David Rahabi taught the Bene Israel to recite important Jewish prayers, and he appointed three young men known as *kazis* to serve as ritual specialists. With this training firmly in place, the first synagogue in Marathi-speaking areas was built in Bombay in 1796, with services led by Cochini *hazzanim*, or cantors (Fischel 1968:2–3; Israel 1984:56, 63; Katz 2000:96–97).

Following the Bene Israel revival fueled by Jews from Cochin in the eighteenth century, Marathi Jews began to crave firsthand experience with Jewish *texts*. Paradoxically, it was Christian missionaries who helped them to realize that ambition in the nineteenth century. When the British ban on missionary activity in India was lifted in 1813, Christian missionaries taught Hebrew and the Bible to the Bene Israel with the hope of converting them to Christianity. That plan backfired: instead of inspiring them to become Christians, knowledge of Hebrew intensified their commitment to Judaism and set in motion a vibrant Marathi Jewish publishing scene that flourished throughout the nineteenth century.

The first translation of the Old Testament into widely intelligible Marathi was published in 1832, with new editions emerging throughout the nineteenth century (American Marathi Mission 1882:76–77; Katz 2000:95; Fischel 1968:3). Earlier New Testament translations in Marathi had been distributed among multiple communities, but the first printing of the Old Testament was distributed primarily among Jews, producing such a great demand that a second printing was issued in 1833 (American Marathi Mission 1882:76–91). At around the same time that books of the Bible were being published by the American Marathi Mission, they were also publishing works of Hebrew grammar intended for the Bene Israel (Numark 2012:28–29). Quickly mastering Hebrew, Bene Israel authors published a flurry of Marathi translations of Hebrew prayers and ceremonies, and by the 1880s, were producing huge numbers of versified Bible stories, some of which were in indigenous poetic, theatrical, and song forms, including kirtan.

Marathi Kirtan as Jewish Performance

The thrilling but contentious beginnings of Bene Israel kirtan have been well documented in Marathi Jewish publications. In a 1918 article on kirtan in his *Prasangik Vichar* (Occasional Thoughts) series, Samuel Mazgaokar recounted how he and his friends David Haeem Divekar and Benjamin Shimshon Ashtamkar, along with three other Bene Israel men, were inspired to found the Kirtanottejak Mandal. On the last day of an annual Hindu festival in 1880, the six friends decided to attend a kirtan by a Hindu kirtankar named Raosaheb Shankar Panduranga Pandit (Mazgaokar 1918:4–5). They were captivated by what Mazgaokar called the "trance-inducing" effect of the performance. As they giddily reflected on Raosaheb's kirtan on the way home, they made a commitment to introduce kirtan to the Bene Israel community (Gadkar 1996:61; Mazgaokar 1918:5).

What might this group of friends have heard on that fateful occasion? As mentioned above, Marathi kirtan is a devotional performance medium that combines singing, storytelling, and didactic religious discourse. Though Mazgaokar does not give many details, the form of Bene Israel kirtans based on Hindu kirtans suggest that he and his friends probably heard naradiya kirtan, a style of Marathi kirtan performed almost entirely by Brahmin men in the nineteenth century. Panduranga Pandit would have been standing in a Hindu temple, facing his audience and flanked by his accompanists. During the 1880s, naradiya kirtankars played small, flat cymbals known as *jhanj* and were accompanied by players of *pakhawaj* (a double-headed drum) and a plucked string drone. In the first part of his performance, Panduranga Pandit would have expounded on some devotional theme for about an hour, then there would have been a break, and in the second half, he would have told a story in speech and song to illustrate that theme. He probably sang and recited verses in a wide range of Marathi genres, including *arya*, *saki*, *dindi*, *ovi*, *shloka*, and *abhanga*, and chose a few points in the kirtan to improvise melodies in the manner of Hindustani rāga music. A kirtankar must be a captivating orator and singer with deep knowledge of scripture and vernacular literature, and Mazgaokar's account suggests that Panduranga Pandit was a master of these many dimensions of kirtan.

Very soon after hearing Panduranga Pandit's kirtan, Mazgaokar and his friends formed the Kirtanottejak Mandal, a group that composed and performed kirtans based on Bible stories (Roland 2000:33; Mazgaokar 1918:5–7). Mazgaokar's origin story affirms dialogue between Bene Israel people and their Hindu neighbors, but the Mandal was concerned that some people might object to the adaptation of a Hindu temple medium. He wrote:

> After the kirtan was finished, the *arti* was over, and we had received the pearls of wisdom, we brothers all voiced the same sentiment: "This could lead to great progress in teaching the scriptures to our people." In response, Davidbaba said, "Truly, this idea is excellent, but it is not clear to me how we will lay the first stone ["pound in the first post"]! This type of performance does not exist in our caste, and because there are several simple religious brothers who would not like it and who would raise oppositions, there's a big chance that they'll harass and pursue us if we adopt it! If we dare to try to perform a kirtan, I am afraid that it is very likely that *gondhal* [mayhem] will ensue; before beginning this work we should take great care!" (Mazgaokar 1918:5–6, translation by the author)

As a result of these concerns, they met to decide on a list of seven rules for kirtan performance so that they would not be accused of what Benjamin Shimshon Ashtamkar called "pick[ing] up the Hindu type completely" (Gadkar 1996:61; Mazgaokar 1918:6).

1. Davidbaba or Benjamin Master should do the job of *haridas*.[2]
2. Kirtan should be performed according to the plans established by the chairman.

3. The haridas should not expect "*bidagi*"—gifts.
4. *Prasad* (sacralized food offerings) should not be distributed.
5. Don't touch the feet of the haridas.[3] Those who want to may kiss his hand.
6. Don't chant "*Pundalika Varda Hari Vitthala.*"[4]
7. A collection plate will be passed at the kirtan to support it, and through that the entire expenses of the kirtan will be fulfilled.[5]

Additionally, in an article on Bene Israel kirtan, Rachel Gadkar noted that Mazgaokar also mentioned that the kirtankar should wear a long silk gown, a turban, and a garland around the neck and hands, but no *tilak* on the forehead (Gadkar 1996:61). The silk gown, or kaftan, is more commonly associated with Muslims in India, but was adopted by the Bene Israel (Fischel 1968:2). (See figure 5.1.)

What strikes me about the Kirtanottejak Mandal's list is its brevity and the fact that, except for the proscription against chanting "Pundalika Varda Hari Vitthala," all of the other items have visual or physical, rather than sonic, impact. According to the Mandal, then, almost any song genre was fair game. Following these seven guidelines, Benjamin Shimshon Ashtamkar performed the first Bene Israel kirtan, *Sadhu Abraham Charitra* (The Deeds of Abraham the Ascetic) in 1880 under the auspices of the Harikirtanottejak Mandal, and the text of his kirtan was published in 1882 (Mazgaokar 1918:6–7; Ashtamkar and Talkar 1882). The openness to Hindu songs was borne out in practice—Hindu and Jewish kirtans from that era used the same genres, including several that are associated with Maharashtrian Hindu worship and the poet-saint tradition.

In addition to the self-conscious alterations to Hindu kirtan made by the Kirtanottejak Mandal, a few other differences can be gleaned from nineteenth-century Bene Israel kirtan publications. Most obviously, Hindu kirtankars performed stories of Marathi saints and deities from the epics and puranas, while Bene Israel kirtankars sang and narrated Bible stories. Another difference is that the work of narration and singing in Bene Israel kirtan was split between the kirtankar and a group of singers, while Hindu naradiya kirtankars performed the entire kirtan as a solo (Mazgaokar 1918:6; Samuel 1998:9–11). The Harikirtanottejak Mandal decided that Benjamin Master or David Baba, senior members of their group, would serve as kirtankars and that the remaining four friends would sing the songs (Mazgaokar 1918:6). Finally, and perhaps most important, the context changed. Kirtan was transferred not from temple to synagogue but from temple to school, home, or hall, where it was performed for naming ceremonies, weddings,

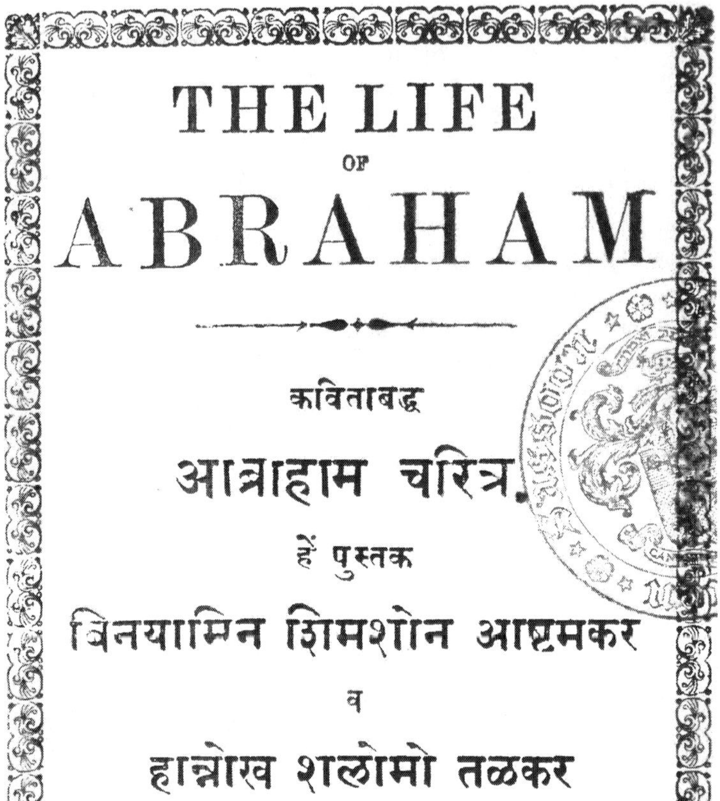

THE LIFE
OF
ABRAHAM

कविताबद्ध

आब्राहाम चरित्र.

हें पुस्तक

बिनयाम्मिन शिमशोन आष्टमकर

व

हान्नोख शलोमो तळकर

यांनीं तयार केलें

तें

एथील "कीर्त्तनोत्तेजक" मंडळीनें

आंग्लो-वर्नाक्युलर छापखान्यांत छापवून प्रसिद्ध केलें.

प्रती १०००

५६४३

१८८२

किम्मत ४ आणे.

Figure 5.1. Bene Israel kirtankar, Benjamin Shimshon Ashtamkar

and housewarming parties (Gadkar 1996:62–63). In other words, Bene Israel kirtan did not become liturgical, as it had been for Hindus.

Despite the Mandal's safeguards against the seepage of Hindu ideas, Jewish kirtankars faced significant obstruction by orthodox segments of Bene Israel society, who even attacked members of the Kirtanottejak Mandal after one kirtan performance. In a "Short Report from the Secretary of the Kirtanottejak Mandal," Mazgaokar wrote that he and his friends had suffered "psychological conflicts" with other community members during their first five years, and "we shudder when we remember the difficulties we had to face directly or indirectly when we undertook this endeavor" (Mazgaokar 1889:9). Shaken but not defeated, Mandal members sought Bible verses to support kirtan performance, and found what they wanted in the 150th Psalm (Gadkar 1996:62). The Marathi terms in brackets below are from an 1886 translation of this Psalm by the Bombay Auxiliary Bible Society.

1. Hallelujah. Praise God in His sanctuary; praise Him in the firmament of His power.
2. Praise Him for His mighty acts; praise Him according to His abundant greatness.
3. Praise Him with the blast of the horn [Hebrew: *shofar*, Marathi: *karana*]; praise Him with the psaltery [Hebrew: *kinnor*, Marathi: *sitar*] and harp [Hebrew: *nevel*, Marathi: *vina*].
4. Praise Him with the timbrel [Hebrew: *tof*, Marathi: *daf*] and dance; praise Him with stringed instruments [Marathi: *yantravadye*] and the pipe [Hebrew: *ugav*, Marathi: *tantravadye*].
5. Praise Him with the loud-sounding cymbals [Hebrew: *bethsilthey*, Marathi: *manjutal jhanja*]; praise Him with the clanging cymbals [Hebrew: *bethsiltheytheru*, Marathi: *uncatal jhanj*].
6. Let everything that hath breath praise the LORD. Hallelujah.[6]

In the Marathi translation, the psaltery and harp are translated as "sitar" and "vina," cymbals are translated as "jhanj," and timbrel as "daf." Because jhanj, vina, and daf were associated with Marathi Hindu devotional music, readers of this verse may have pictured something not unlike kirtan. Instruments aside, the Kirtanottejak Mandal argued that this important Psalm enjoined devotees to perform kirtan, arguing that kirtan is at its heart the praise of God in collective song with instrumental accompaniment (Gadkar 1996:62). The Christian missionaries who translated the Bible into Marathi with the assistance of Hindu pandits had unwittingly provided community leaders with justification to perform Hindu song in Jewish worship

(American Marathi Mission 1882:78). This biblical defense, as well as kirtan's enthusiastic reception, put the initial criticisms to rest after just a few years, and Bene Israel kirtankars trained by the Mandal performed throughout Marathi-speaking India (Gadkar 1996:62–63).

Popular accounts and author introductions to kirtan texts suggest that nineteenth- and early twentieth-century Bene Israel kirtankars drew considerable crowds through their ability to elicit fevered responses from listeners. Printed texts were eagerly sought out by people wanting to follow along during the performance or relive it afterward (Ashtamkar 1888; Ashtamkar and Talkar 1882:6; Israel 1984:70–71). Between 1882, when *Abraham Charitra* was published, and 1960, when the last kirtan was published, approximately forty-two kirtans found their way into print, with activity concentrated between 1882 and 1918, a thirty-six-year span during which thirty-five Bene Israel kirtans were published (figure 5.2). According to Ashtamkar, he and the other members of the Mandali could not meet the incredible demand for new kirtan publications and performances because kirtan was not their primary occupation (Ashtamkar 1888).

I find a couple of hints that Bene Israel kirtankars were sonically and textually negotiating a minority religious identity in more subtle ways than the Kirtanottejak Mandal's seven rules might lead us to believe. The first hint comes from the politics of song choice and genre naming. During the heyday of Bene Israel kirtan between the 1880s and 1910s, some kirtankars chose Marathi poetic meters set to traditional tunes (saki, arya, dindi, abhanga, etc.) while others used the catch-all category of *pad*. This is not unlike naradiya kirtan texts of the same era, though Bene Israel kirtankars incorporated more popular songs under the heading of "pad" than did their Hindu counterparts of the same era. In the 1920s, when Brahmin naradiya kirtankar Vasudeo Kolhatkar began setting his kirtan poems to popular songs and tunes composed by his brother-in-law, he met with resistance from the fairly conservative naradiya kirtan community. Even in the second decade of the twenty-first century, very few naradiya kirtankars use more than two or three popular songs per kirtan.

By way of contrast, Bene Israel kirtankars had been singing popular songs in their kirtans since the 1880s. In the introduction to his *Kavitabaddha Moshe Charitra* (Versified History of Moses) of 1884, David Haeem Divekar wrote, "Seeing that people are inclined more toward songs sung in a popular style rather than sakis, aryas, etc., we made this collection; these poems were lovingly made to increase the devotion, religious knowledge, and brotherhood of our young people" (Divekar 1884:3). It includes twenty-eight pads, many of which are popular songs of the day; a number of thumris; ghazals;

Figure 5.2. Binyamin Shimshon Ashtamkar. *Abraham Caritra* (The Life of Abraham). Kirtanottejak Mandal, 1882

a hori (North Indian Holi song); and a garba (Gujarati women's folk song), plus a small smattering of traditional Marathi genres like abhanga, saki, dindi, and ovi (Divekar 1884). While popular songs may have been seen as a threat to the six-hundred-year-old devotional tradition of Hindu kirtan, Bene Israel kirtan was undeniably new and its links to that ancient tradition were anyway held with some suspicion in Indian Jewish society. Moving beyond the traditional repertory may actually have assuaged the fears of more orthodox listeners.

Marathi naradiya kirtan and its Bene Israel cousin are inherently eclectic, which makes the range of repertory choices I have described not only possible but even expected. Given kirtan's flexibility, it is striking that Bene Israel kirtankars incorporated song genres so firmly attached to Maharashtrian Hindu devotional practice. Most Bene Israel kirtans of the nineteenth century included at least one or two abhangas, abhanga being the meter in which Marathi Hindu poet-saints composed, and ended with an arti (the song sung at the conclusion of Hindu worship). In short, the emphasis on popular pads notwithstanding, Bene Israel kirtankars found it unnecessary to translate song genres indexing Hindu worship into others that were more firmly attached to Judaism.

In a similar vein, many Marathi Hindu terms, figures, and images were incorporated into Bene Israel kirtans without Jewish/Hebrew glosses. This contrasts starkly with the journalistic writings of the Bene Israel from the same era, which are peppered with Hebrew words like *bima*, *Torah*, *Tanakh*, *yom*, *kashrut*, and so on. A few examples from a kirtan by N. S. Satamkar on Rabbi Akiba (Akiva), illustrate the prevalence of untranslated Hindu concepts in Jewish kirtan. Rabbi Akiva (ca. 40–137 CE), a founder of rabbinical Judaism, was hacked into pieces on the Roman king Hadrian's orders while reciting *Prabhu-nama* (Lord's name) as he achieved *moksha* (release from the cycle of death and rebirth), images that resonate with bhakti notions of *namjap* and *namkirtan* (repeating God's names) and with more general Hindu philosophies of reincarnation (Satamkar 1950:10). Other less Hindu-laden but nonetheless potentially confusing concepts include *gun* (virtue), *bhakti* (devotion, usually used in relation to Hindu devotional sects), and *mukti* (a synonym for moksha). Figures from Hindu scriptures, such as Yama (God of Death) and Kaama (God of love), also find their way into the Rabbi Akiva story, and Akiva's wife, Rachel, falls at the "lotus feet" (*pad kamala*) of her husband, an image that is familiar to those of us who work with Hindu bhakti sources (Satamkar 1950:6).

Kirtan Goes to Israel

The Harikirtanottejak Mandal disbanded in around 1900 and other groups supported kirtan in its place, including the Jewish Union Singing Club, the Jewish Amateurs Singing Club, the Kirtan Mandal of Pune, the Satamkar Music School, and the Bene Israel Youth Convention (Isenberg 1988:263). Indian and Israeli independence interrupted this process in the mid-twentieth century and kirtan went through a period of dormancy. There was little Bene Israel interest in an Israeli state until the 1920s and 1930s, when the first Indian Zionist organization was founded and the Jewish Agency began sending Zionist representatives to India. After Indian independence in 1947 and the founding of the State of Israel in 1948, masses of Bene Israel people migrated to Israel. Because of emigration, the Bene Israel population in India dropped from twenty thousand to sixteen thousand between 1948 and 1961 (Weil 2001).

Bene Israel people, who say they never experienced anti-Semitism in India, faced serious discrimination in the Israel of the 1950s and 1960s. For many, it was serious enough that they sought repatriation in India (Weil 2001). The height of prejudice against the Bene Israel was a 1962 ruling by the Chief Rabbi of Israel, who decreed that weddings between Bene Israel and other Jews could be performed only after the genealogy of the Bene Israel partner was investigated for non-Jewish descent. Before and after this ruling, many rabbis refused to officiate Bene Israel weddings because they claimed that the Bene Israel were not truly Jewish (Roland 1995:1). Following two years of steady Bene Israel protest, the Israel Rabbinate finally declared the Bene Israel "full Jews in every respect" (Weil 2001). This gesture of acceptance led to a dramatic increase in Indo-Israeli migration after 1963, and by 2001, there were sixty thousand Bene Israel in Israel and only five thousand in India (Weil 2001).

The State of Israel was founded on a principle of rapid assimilation, and immigrants became absorbed in learning modern spoken Hebrew. Children of Bene Israel immigrants were rarely taught Marathi, and there was a serious decline in Marathi Jewish arts and publishing. Throughout the 1950s, 1960s, and 1970s, though, women continued singing Marathi songs in their homes, and by the 1980s, they used these songs as a resource in the creation of a new Bene Israel identity that was proudly Marathi. A Bene Israel educator named Flora Samuel led this charge through her revival of kirtan in the 1990s. Before migrating to Israel from Bombay in 1964, Samuel had been the headmistress of Sir Eli Kadourie School in Mumbai and she continued teaching after emigration. She taught kirtan to a women's organization in the town of Lod, published kirtan texts, performed kirtan, and wrote articles on Jewish kirtan (Samuel 1996, 1998; Roland 2000; Weil 1999).

With Hannah "Annie" Rohekar and Ivy Jhirad, Flora Samuel performed kirtans on Joseph, Moses, Hannah and her seven sons, and Ruth. The three women received kirtan texts and learned melodies from a Lod resident whose father-in-law had been a kirtankar in India. Annie composed the remaining melodies and her husband accompanied the group on *bulbul tarang* (banjo).[7] In these performances, one woman provided the discourse and a small chorus of women sang the songs (Samuel 1998). Although Samuel wrote the kirtan narrations, Ivy and Annie told me that she appointed a different woman as narrator/kirtankar for each performance. It was a successful enterprise—the group was invited all over Israel to perform, and Samuel even performed kirtan at an exhibit on the Bene Israel at the Jewish Museum in New York.

Through her *re*-translations of kirtan, Samuel contributed to emergent articulations of Indo-Israeli minority identity. In the second decade of the twenty-first century, Bene Israel people are well versed in Jewish scriptures so there is no urgent need to teach Bible stories, but Samuel found a new use for kirtan: to teach *Marathi* Jewish cultural heritage to younger generations and to non-Indians in Israel. There are very few second-generation Bene Israel in Israel who speak Marathi—even Samuel's own children do not speak Marathi—and many of the forty thousand Indian Israelis are still marginalized in today's Israel. While late nineteenth-century kirtan was created in a context of anxiety about Bene Israel religious identity, its revival in the late twentieth century was again related to a crisis of identity, but this time of ethnic identity following a period of mass migration. Through kirtan, Samuel communicated to younger Indian Jews and to non-Indian Israelis that Bene Israel heritage is rich, complex, and hybrid, and that its hybridity makes it no less Jewish.

While some critics have regarded Bene Israel syncretism as evidence of the inauthenticity of Bene Israel Jewishness, I hope to help counter those claims through a careful historicization of Bene Israel kirtan, one emphasizing the modernity of Bene Israel engagement with kirtan and their strategic and selective translations of Hindu performance. Kirtan may seem an unlikely beacon of Indian Jewish identity—early opponents certainly thought so—but I hope to have shown that its intermedial nature presented a rich set of resources for Bene Israel cultural translators articulating identities in dialogue with other Jews and other Indians. The translation from Hindu kirtan to Bene Israel kirtan is uneven—not all aspects of its text and performance are translated in the same way or to the same extent. The Hindu indexicality of artis and abhangas dies hard, but when combined with Jewish texts, performed by people in Jewish dress at Jewish events, these songs are transformed into Jewish devotional music inscribed with cultural memories of intercommunal exchange.

Notes

1. I am grateful to Philip V. Bohlman for formulating the idea for a joint paper we presented at the 2010 annual conference of the Midwest Chapter of the Society for Ethnomusicology in Chicago.
2. A synonym for kirtankar, literally, "servant of Vishnu."
3. At the end of Hindu naradiya kirtans, listeners touch the kirtankar's feet and give him an offering of money or uncooked rice.
4. Pundalika was a great devotee of Lord Vitthala, a form of Krishna associated with the varkari devotional sect. Hari is a name of Vishnu. This phrase is commonly chanted at Hindu kirtans and means, "Vishnu Vitthala, who blessed Pundalika."
5. At Hindu kirtans, offerings are made directly to the kirtankar or are placed on the *arti* (ritual fire) plate at the end of the kirtan.
6. This translation is from the Jewish Publishing Society's Hebrew Bible in English (1917): www.mechon-mamre.org/e/et/et0.htm. A transliteration of the Hebrew was found at www.hebrewsongs.com/psalm150.htm and descriptions of Hebrew instrument names are from Rubin and Baron (2006:36–41).
7. Interviews with Annie Rohekar, Ivy Jhirad, and Iris Goldstein (daughter of Flora Samuel), August 2012.

References

American Marathi Mission. 1882. *Memorial Papers of the American Marathi Mission, 1813–1881*. Bombay: Education Society's Press.

Ashtamkar, Benjamin Samson. 1888. *Suddh Vasana Kivha Noahca Bhakti Bhav* [Pure Longing or Noah's Devotion]. Mumbai: Nirnayasagar.

Ashtamkar, Benjamin Samson, and Hannokh Shlomo Talkar. 1882. *Abraham Charitra, The Life of Abraham in Marathi Verses*. Mumbai: Kirtanottejakmandali.

Bhabha, Homi. 1994. "How Newness Enters the World: Postmodern Space, Postcolonial Times and the Trials of Cultural Translation." In *The Location of Culture*, by Homi Bhabha. New York: Routledge.

Bombay Auxiliary Bible Society. 1886. *The Holy Bible in the Marathi Language*. Bombay: Nirnayasagar Press.

Chatterjee, Partha. 1993. *The Nation and Its Fragments: Colonial and Postcolonial Histories*. Princeton, NJ: Princeton University Press.

Clifford, James. 1997. *Routes: Travel and Translation in the Late Twentieth Century*. Cambridge, MA: Harvard University Press.

Divekar, David Haeem. 1884. *Kavitabaddha Moshe Charitra* [Versified History of Moses]. Mumbai: Anglo-Jewish and Vernacular Press.

Fischel, Walter. 1968. *Hagadat Bene Yisra'el = The Haggadah of the Bene Israel of India.* New York: Orphan Hospital Ward of Israel.

Gadkar, Rachel. 1996. "Amhi Bharatvasi Bene Israel" [We are the Bene Israel of India]. *Shaili* 32 (September): 60–64.

———. 2001. *Bharatvasi Beneisraeli* [Indian Bene Israelis]. Mumbai: Granthali.

Isenberg, Shirley Berry. 1988. *India's Bene Israel: A Comprehensive Inquiry and Sourcebook.* Berkeley, CA: J. L. Magnes Museum.

Israel, Benjamin. 1984. *The Bene Israel of India: Some Studies.* Bombay: Orient Longman.

Katz, Nathan. 2000. *Who Are the Jews of India?* Berkeley: University of California Press.

Mandair, Arvind. 2009. *Religion and the Specter of the West: Sikhism, India, Postcoloniality and the Politics of Translation.* New York: Columbia University Press.

Mazgaokar, Samuel Siloman. 1889. "Kirtanottejak Mandalicya Citnisaca Sanksipta Report" [Short Report from the Secretary of the Kirtanottejak Mandal]. Introduction to Benyamin Shimshon Ashtamkar, *Shmuelakhyan* [Story of Samuel]. Bombay: Kirtanottejak Mandal.

———. 1918. *Prasangik Vichar* [Occasional Thoughts], no. 10. Bombay: Kirtanottejak Mandal.

Niranjana, Tejaswini. 1992. *Siting Translation: History, Post-Structuralism, and the Colonial Context.* Berkeley: University of California Press.

Numark, Mitch. 2012. "Hebrew School in Nineteenth-Century Bombay: Protestant Missionaries, Cochin Jews, and the Hebraization of India's Bene Israel Community." *Modern Asian Studies* 46(6).

Roland, Joan. 1995. *The Jewish Communities of India: Identity in a Colonial Era.* New Brunswick, NJ: Transaction Publishers.

———. 2000. "Religious Observances of the Bene Israel: Persistence and Refashioning of Tradition." *Journal of Indo-Judaic Studies* 3 (June): 22–47.

Rubin, Emmanuel, and John H. Baron. 2006. *Music in Jewish History and Culture.* Detroit Monographs in Musicology 47. Detroit: Harmonie Park Press.

Samuel, Flora (Manik Ashtamkar). 1996. *Sanskrutisangam* (Marathi). Mumbai: n.p.

———. 1998. "The Kirtan." *Pe'amim* 71: 121–28. In Hebrew with songs in Marathi. (English translation of the Hebrew by the author).

Satamkar, N. S. 1950. *Rabbi Akiba.* Mumbai: Satamkar Sangit Vidyalaya.

Weil, Shalva. 1999. "Flora Samuel—In Memoriam." *Journal of Indo-Judaic Studies* 1, 2 (April).

———. 2001. "Bene Israel of Mumbai, India." Tel Aviv: Beit Hatfutsot. www.bh.org.il/database-article.aspx?48701 (accessed 29 September 2013).

———. 2007. "On Origins, the Arts, and Transformed Identities: Foci of Research into the Bene Israel." In *Indo-Judaic Studies in the Twenty-First Century: A View from the Margin*, edited by Nathan Katz, 147–57. New York: Palgrave Macmillan.

PART II

INTELLECTUAL HISTORY OF ETHNOMUSICOLOGY

CHAPTER SIX

~

Guerra-Peixe, Cold War Politics, and Ethnomusicology in Brazil, 1950–1952

Samuel Araújo

The Brazilian composer Guerra-Peixe (1914–1993) felt stranded in what he termed a "crisis of aesthetic orientation" following the international repercussions of his serial music, after a 1946 BBC broadcast of his *Symphony No. 1* and further premieres in England, Switzerland, and Canada. Reflecting on this period (Guerra-Peixe 1971), he attributed it to the shock between the rationalist brand of universalism of the Second Viennese School with which his music was in dialogue at the time, and the resulting communicatory impasses regarding its public reception. By then he had already read the Brazilian modernist poet and musicologist Mario de Andrade's ideas on systematic folklore studies as the basis of an art simultaneously national and universal (1928). Later, he would also be impacted by the ideals expressed in the Prague Manifesto, which resulted from the Second International Congress of Composers and Music Critics in 1948 (cf. Carroll 2009). The manifesto promoted national folklore as the basis for overcoming perceived contradictions between "bourgeois" avant-garde music and a revolutionary proletarian art, the central aesthetic position prescribed to composers affiliated with, or close to, Communist parties the world over in the early years of the Cold War.[1]

In December 1949, Guerra-Peixe left Rio de Janeiro and took a radio job in the northeastern town of Recife, the capital of Pernambuco state, where he worked until June 1952. In Recife, he studied musical practices in oral traditions in an effort to overcome the communicatory dilemmas mentioned above. Determined to create conditions for more effective public reception of his "concert hall music" (the term he preferred to either "art music" or "erudite music"), he conducted research on musical practices in oral traditions, using largely self-taught methods. While in the field he became acquainted with articles by authors such as Richard Waterman, Mieczyslaw Kolinski, and Melville Herskovits,[2] which appeared in Spanish in the *Revista de Estudios Musicales* (Review of Musical Studies). He also corresponded with both the German-Uruguayan musicologist Curt Lange (1903–1997), a former student of Erich von Hornbostel and Curt Sachs, who edited the *Revista*, as well as the Brazilian music scholar Mozart de Araújo (1904–1988).

Beginning in 1950, Guerra-Peixe wrote several articles on both oral and written musical traditions. These appeared in daily newspapers in Recife, Salvador, São Paulo, and Rio de Janeiro, and some were original in approach and subject matter (cf. Guerra-Peixe 2007). In 1953, he moved to São Paulo, where his major monograph, *Maracatus do Recife*, appeared in 1954. This was the pioneer publication in Brazilian music based on ethnographic fieldwork and intensive participant observation. Therefore, in 1954, when the International Folk Music Council (IFMC; forerunner of the International Council for Traditional Music) held its seventh annual conference in São Paulo in conjunction with an International Folklore Congress, Guerra-Peixe was invited to serve as director of the music and dance festival associated with the conference. However, he did not present a paper at the conference, perhaps because of his lifelong intellectual modesty as a self-taught music scholar with no academic credentials.

The main theme of the São Paulo congress was to elaborate a definition of folklore that could accommodate the idiosyncrasies of New World folk music while distinguishing it from commercialized popular music. According to Maud Karpeles (1955), this theme was suggested by the Brazilian national representative, Renato Almeida, at the annual conference in 1952. Several major scholars presented papers on this theme in São Paulo, including Karpeles and Almeida, all of whom highlighted the difficulties of establishing a definition of folklore that might apply universally, from relatively recent New World postcolonial traditions to ancient forms established and documented in Asia and elsewhere, including the European cultural traditions for which the term *folklore* was coined.[3]

In light of ideological and aesthetic debates in the early Cold War context (1945–1950s), this chapter examines Guerra-Peixe's distinctive and still largely ignored contribution, both to the field of traditional music studies and to the debate on the concept of folklore. It highlights in particular his relatively sustainable position in defining "folk" knowledge not as a foundation of conservative life ways, but as a dynamic and necessary countercommentary to uncritical submission of social life to scientific reasoning.[4] This chapter argues that Guerra-Peixe's interrelated work in studies of both traditional music and musical composition clarifies the contours of a cultural praxis that processes reality in multiple, complementary, and contradictory levels. Using examples from his compositions as well as his ethnographic research, I attempt to demonstrate how a largely self-taught scholar achieved a singular position in the early history of ethnomusicology in Brazil.

Guerra-Peixe, Tradition, and Modernity

Born into a family of Portuguese Roma origins, Guerra-Peixe began playing the mandolin and guitar with his father, a blacksmith and guitarist, at family gatherings. He became noticed for his talent as a violinist at the age of eight in his native town, Petrópolis, and moved to the city of Rio de Janeiro when he was fourteen years old. He earned a scholarship to study with a local teacher, and a few years later, he started formal composition classes. He adopted serialism by 1945, after studying with Hans Joachim Koellreutter, a German flute player, composer, and influential teacher, who had been a student of René Leibowitz and had migrated to Brazil shortly before the end of World War II.

In his compositions, Guerra-Peixe applied serial structuring principles in increasingly unorthodox ways until 1949, when he faced the dilemma that concerned many composers of his generation, namely, how to align his creative output to an aesthetic simultaneously contemporary in sophistication yet engaged in the social struggles of the time.[5] As indicated above, his search for politically aimed communicability had two main sources. First, he admired Mario de Andrade's proposals of a modern music informed by folklore studies. Secondly, in the 1940s, and particularly with the Cold War divide of the intellectual milieu and amid a politically charged radicalization of the aesthetic debate in Brazil, he found himself very close to the call for a revolutionary proletarian art prescribed in the 1948 Prague Manifesto. The convoluted intellectual climate in Rio de Janeiro, however, made extremely difficult going beyond general aesthetic ideals toward their materialization in musical action.

Exemplifying such dilemmas, his 1947 *Peça p'ra dois minutos* (Piece for Two Minutes) for solo piano attempted to break with tonal hierarchies central to atonal serialism, but in an experimental manner (Guerra-Peixe 1971). He employed a series of ten pitches, broken down into two cells of six and four pitches each, plus the bracketed C, which he conceived as independent from those two cells. He set the series in 4/4 meter, but with breaks in 3/4, which he thought would infuse the melodic lines with elusive tonal centers present in certain urban popular music (figure 6.1a and 6.1b).

Figure 6.1a. ***Peça p'ra dois minutos*** **original series + 1 independent pitch (Source: Guerra-Peixe 1971)**

When Guerra-Peixe's music was first heard abroad through the BBC radio broadcast, the aesthetic and ideological opposition between supporters of *l'art-pour-l'art* and those of socialist realism had reached its peak, dividing international intellectuals in many parts of the world. In Brazil and elsewhere, such polarization resulted in the publication of manifestos and accusatory exchanges around aesthetic and political affiliations during the 1940s and 1950s. It is important to note this moment in history, when political motivations either conjoined or distanced social classes through their symbolic production. Such a situation seems out of place in the early twenty-first century, when class struggles are no longer at the core of social causes. Yet during the Cold War, thinking about the place of "pre-modern" traditions in art, literature, and scholarship stimulated heated debates on the formation of a proletarian, revolutionary culture. Guerra-Peixe's crisis of aesthetic orientation thus resonated with the dilemmas of a specific trend in twentieth-century art, which aimed at forging a radically new proletarian culture, derived from tradition while simultaneously breaking with traditional patterns of elaboration. For Guerra-Peixe, the crisis had to do mainly with a stagnation of the rhythmic component in contemporary art music, a component that had received little, if any, attention from the Second Viennese School.[6] In light of his fieldwork during the early 1950s, this lack of attention to rhythm would have contrasted drastically with the complex and detailed rhythmic processes of elaboration and transformation he had studied and notated among Afro-Brazilian musicians in Recife.

In a letter he wrote to Mozart de Araújo in 1950, Guerra-Peixe suggested that *maracatu* players thought of time in structural ways comparable in sophistication to the ways in which serialist and dodecaphonic composers thought of pitch organization:

> As I had observed in June, the Zabumbas [*alfaia* bass drums] do not perfectly coordinate their drum strokes [*pancadas*]. Some always fall behind in the first note [*sic*] of each rhythmic pattern. It does work like this, I think, because the guys are ready for Carnival and I've also had confirmation from several people.

Figure 6.1b. *Peça p'ra dois minutos* **piano score, measures 1–12**

> Môzar [*sic*], for you to have an Idea of the *apparent disconnection* [underlined in the original] of maracatu drumming you might imagine a music which might be called: Rhythmic Dodecaphony!!!! It looks like each one keeps the rhythm as he pleases, as long as it makes noise. Now I understand why composers who have been here did not write down the Zabumba rhythms. They cannot really write them down, so difficult they are. . . . I send you some of these rhythms collected in the rehearsal I've been to. Capiba [a fellow composer and former student] agreed with what I notated, while the maracatu went on. I've done all the calculations possible to verify whether there was any displacement of the beats or of their parts, even taking the eighth-note as the minimal unit. However, every sum I've done only took me to the conclusion that they really are different rhythms. (letter to Mozart de Araújo, 6 February 1950, Acervo Sala Mozart Araújo, Centro Cultural Banco do Brasil, Rio de Janeiro)

This letter, written after a few months of residence in Recife, raises an issue Guerra-Peixe seemingly found too difficult to deal with, that is, the lack of synchronicity among the drum strokes. He did not go back to systematize the drum strokes in either his writings or his musical compositions, and this issue was only addressed much later in African American music studies (Keil and Feld 1994; Keil 1995) and maracatu studies (Barbosa 2005).

Guerra-Peixe later wrote to Curt Lange, asking whether a few scholars whose work he had read were "musicians too or were just smart sociologists who had produced a better work," since he found that their work on Afro-Bahian drumming (Herskovits and Waterman 1949) and West African rhythm (Kolinski 1949) valuable, although it did not address the structuring principles of the music. The letter ultimately exposes one of Guerra-Peixe's more original insights: "I have tried to reproduce as faithfully as possible the rhythms I have notated here. But there are certain drum strokes which produce certain tonalities I have not found a way of writing" (letter to Curt Lange, 2 October 1950, Curt Lange Archive, Federal University of Minas Gerais).[7]

Inspired by his research findings, Guerra-Peixe's work developed in two new directions in 1954. First, he composed concert music using stylized musical processes found in oral traditions. Second, he published his first major monograph, *Maracatus do Recife* (1954), on the music, dance cortèges, and social context of the Afro-Brazilian maracatus tradition.[8] The transcription in figure 6.2 illustrates his tentative analytical responses to what he heard as tonalities. The melodic sense of drum tones he inferred could not be conceptualized by drummers simply as durational values, as Africanist scholars believed before Arthur M. Jones's groundbreaking studies (1952, 1954, 1959). They were conceptualized as melodies in counterpoint and tonalities

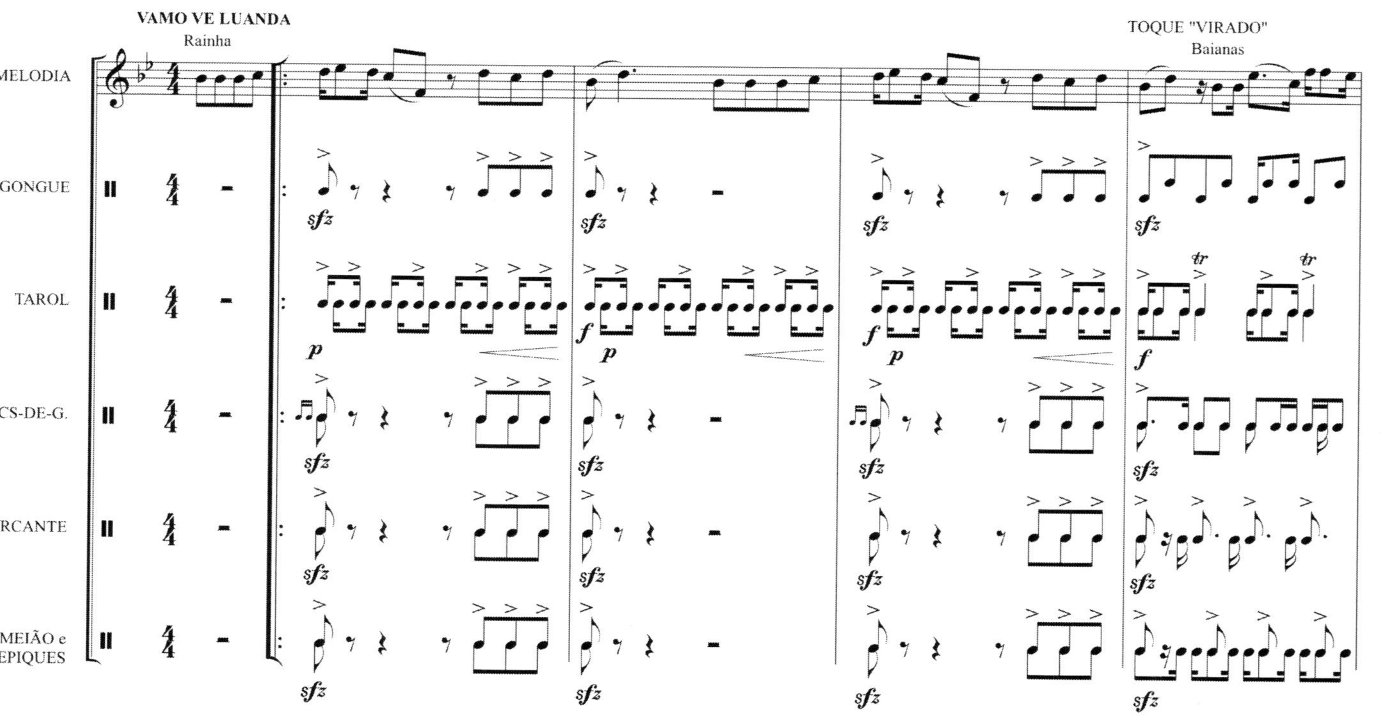

Figure 6.2. Transcription of *maracatu* drumming (Guerra-Peixe 1954:82)

Figure 6.2. (continued)

tempered according to listening conventions different from those of European temperament, which remained intact even in serialism. Guerra-Peixe used modified notation, such as upward or downward stems, to indicate pitch and timbre variation of alternating hands in the drum or bell (*gonguê*) parts. He also differentiated higher and lower pitches and indicated expressive accents on certain sounds.

Guerra-Peixe's concern with temporal matters is reflected not only in his detailed analytical transcriptions of *maracatu* drumming and singing, but also in the stylization procedures he adopted and refined in his concert music. An excerpt from "*Violeiros*" (Guitar Players), *Suite No. 2, Nordestina* (Northeastern), illustrates a prototypical melo-rhythmic structure heard in *gemedeira* (moaning), a subgenre of the *cantoria* (singing dispute), an improvised practice of sung poetry involving two singers in a song duel in strophic form (figure 6.3). The last three measures resemble a "folk" (modal) pitch sequence in gemedeira style, in which the A♯ alternates with A natural. However, their break with the isochronous 4/4 design, first with a duple and then a triple meter, introduces a disturbing element from the cantoria initiates' perspective.[9] This difference is further enhanced by the dissonant harmony, introducing additional ambiguity to the modal sound.

The pitch material might signal an alternative to both strict tonalism and serialism, perhaps indicating a desire to communicate more immediately with the northeastern working-class audiences still immersed in modalism, but Guerra-Peixe also consciously invested in prosodic characteristics of cantoria to escape from strict obedience to meters standardized in European concert music since the eighteenth century.[10] In his view, the conscious and continuous re-elaboration of folk materials, by combining them in ways not found in the original sources, resonated with Mario de Andrade's (1928) concepts of contemporary art rooted in the traditional. These included adherence to the folk models with minor modifications based on academic principles; stylization embedded in direct knowledge, analysis, and "conscious" manipulation of folk models; and free composition in which folk models and the composer's own creativity produce an organic, or "unconscious," synthesis.

Defining Folk and Traditional Music: Guerra-Peixe and the 1954 IFMC Conference

Despite his growing reputation, Guerra-Peixe did not deliver a paper at the 1954 IFMC World Conference, limiting his participation to service as director of the musical program. Karpeles, the IFMC secretary general, suggests that the conference's major theme was a concession to Latin American

Figure 6.3. "Violeiros" (measures 9–14, right hand), from Suite No. 2, *Nordestina* for piano by Guerra-Peixe

scholars, and particularly to the Brazilian local organizers who wished to expand the Council's earlier definition of folk music (Karpeles 1955). The Latin American scholars were concerned mainly with European-derived criteria, such as longevity, anonymity, and oral transmission, in defining "folk" music, criteria that excluded nearly all New World, non-hegemonic musical expressions from being defined as folk music. Mario de Andrade had written, "A new concept of folklore is indispensable to the peoples of recently imported civilization and culture, such as the ones of our America. But this new concept has to be 'scientific,' because if the European concept leads to the ridiculous and socially inefficient lessening of whatever among us is folkloric fact, giving up on it has led to an equally absurd *confusionism*, making certain authors take as folkloric any singer's romance and any urban authored piece" (Andrade 1949:298).

Andrade's concern regarding socially compromised aesthetic values that did not communicate with those of the working class had no direct ties to socialist realism; rather, it derived from a different, if contemporary, aesthetic debate, however convergent on the surface (Travassos 1997). Meanwhile, Guerra-Peixe's fellow composer Claudio Santoro, who was affiliated with the Communist Party of Brazil and who was also at odds with his previous attachment to serial music, spoke of the relationships between "pre-modern" and "modern" art models in more openly political overtones aligned with the theses approved in the 1948 Prague Congress:

> Before the rise of socialism, the artist gave the impression of being ahead, giving impulse to the development of society, because the people, not being in power, represented in fact the vanguard. But today, in socialist countries, the people being in power, the revolutionary class is ahead; the artist who marches side by side with the proletariat must be in line with progress and not with the last tendencies of the bourgeoisie. (Santoro 1948:232)

> If atonal art is by no means in touch with the musical language used by our people, which is in essence either tonal or modal, it has to be put aside, so that it does not mislead the proper characteristics of our musical language. (Santoro 1950:n.p.)

The intellectuals engaged in this debate could thus refer to quite distinct and even antagonistic ideological camps, but the concern for communicating with the audience led some of them, such as Andrade and Santoro, to converge in the defense of serious artistic consideration of non-hegemonic musical creations as part of their respective aesthetic and political projects.

Guerra-Peixe expressed his own stance concerning this issue through the music festival he organized in connection with the IFMC conference. The 1955 issue of the IFMC journal presents a review of the festival program by Douglas Kennedy (1955), a member of the IFMC Executive Board. He highlighted the features of a number of the folk groups brought from distinct parts of Brazil and suggested their apparent similarities to European sources. The festival program is included in the review. An *escola de samba* (samba school) from Rio de Janeiro made an especially good impression on Kennedy. Samba fit well with what Latin American and Brazilian scholars wanted to discuss—the particularities of folk knowledge in the New World, which went beyond European definitions. The Brazilian scholar Renato Almeida had already proposed samba as an example of urban folklore in his writings prior to the conference, and Kennedy unknowingly endorsed this proposition with some enthusiasm in his review.

Even if Guerra-Peixe's choice of repertory for the festival program had been accidental, he made clear his stances on the conference's theme in a later article that bore more than one association with the Cold War, beginning with its curious title, "The Sputnik and Folklore." His title alluded to the oral narratives that spread about the successful launch of the Soviet satellite. The article appeared in a 1957 Brazilian Communist Party daily newspaper. The article was meant to highlight the ways in which technology and profound social transformations, aimed at eliminating illiteracy and socializing the benefits of technological progress, did not preclude the emergence of new forms of human wisdom referencing tradition and used as a counternarrative to the sometimes arrogant and predatory hegemony of rationalism. In other words, oral tradition can provide a necessary source of alternative critical views on human affairs. Guerra Peixe explained:

> In Old Europe there is a generalized opinion that the essential characteristics of a "folkloric fact" lay on two principles: tradition and anonymity. It is worth saying that to the European only the persistence over the years or centuries and the ignorance about who invented a theme attribute validity to given material. Taking as source the Charter of Brazilian Folklore, the "folkloric fact" is constituted not only of what exists for centuries, God knows by whom, but also by what the people create on the spur of the moment, under the impulse of events, and since whatever is invented is collectively accepted—or, as I prefer to say, collective "use." Scientific conquests sometimes induce the people to create new songs or modify older ones. Printed music, the piano, the phonograph, and the radio form a launching pool in such cases. (Guerra-Peixe 2007:185)

Conclusions

According to recent work by historians from countries situated on both sides of the Cold War, its motivations and dynamics cannot be accounted for without deep consideration of the geopolitical particularities of World War II itself. This context of external and internal politics, international alliances and ruptures had as its substratum a profound mistrust in the foundations of capitalism as a way to prevent widespread world conflict and poverty (see Leffler 1999). If this situation has gone through dramatic changes particularly after the downfall of the Soviet regime in 1991, its somber spectrum, so to speak, seems more alive than ever after the 2008 stock market crash and the derived world crisis. Events such as the People's Summit, an event parallel to the Rio+20 United Nations conference on the climate, was co-organized by world NGOs that defend dialogic and collective global solutions against the arrogance and predation fostered by capitalist logics in the post-Soviet Union era, by no means discontinuous with the ones that astonished Europe and the rest of the world since the 1930s, resulting in the Cold War. In its final document (People's Summit 2012) one can also read a defense of traditional lifeways no longer for the sake of museum-like preservation but in terms of a vivid argument articulated by communities for the strategic importance of their alternative worldviews, in a manner analogous to the role of "folk knowledge" in Guerra-Peixe's definition.

The relatively original and insightful contributions of Guerra-Peixe to both the study of traditional music in the 1950s and the beginnings of ethnomusicology in Brazil have been presented here under the light of Cold War politics as well as of aesthetic and scholarly debates, highlighting simultaneously the role played by both national and international contexts in his personal dilemmas and adopted paths in both music scholarship and musical composition. Worth noticing in this concise picture was Guerra-Peixe's relative synchronicity, in spite of his non-academic training, with artistic and scholarly insights on compositional and research issues, as well as with their eventual interrelationships, occupying contemporary Western European and North American discussions, among which was the one on the concept of folklore in general and folk music in particular, to which the IFMC was so intensely associated.

If in the 1950s one of the effects of the polarization between the two major world power blocs, socialist and capitalist, was turning a number of Brazilian scholars and composers such as Guerra-Peixe closer to the musical and expressive creations of nonhegemonic groups in the national arena, the motivations and conceptual concerns of present generations interested in studying similar expressive forms today seem to show an increasing interest in the larger struggles for autonomy these populations continue waging in order to resist and overcome the pressures of capital accumulation, commodification of human relations, and increasing social exclusion. Signs of such rising nonconformism can be read for instance in the criticism of reifying discourses on structural aspects of music and social life in academic texts or in the increasing space in scholarly forums and publications devoted to larger political and conceptual matters of today, including a reappraisal of the position and role of traditional music in the contemporary world. One consequence of this may be, and in my view has been, growing demands to well-established institutions such as academic programs and societies to rethink their goals and intensify their initiatives against the threats to alternative modes of musical and social coexistence, joining even more actively than before the emerging collective voices articulating resistance and alternatives to one-sided authoritarian and predatory logics the world over.

Acknowledgments

This chapter reexamines materials analyzed in the course of a project funded by the National Center for Scientific and Technological Development (1997–2001). The main results of the project appear in Guerra-Peixe 2007. I read an earlier version of the chapter at the Symposium on Traditional Music in Contemporary Society, organized by Xiao Mei and colleagues at the Shanghai Conservatory of Music (June 2012). I thank the members of the Shanghai Conservatory of Music and the Local Arrangements Committee for the generous funding that supported my participation in the symposium.

Notes

1. Carroll (2003) provides a detailed account of the Prague Congress.

2. There is a growing literature on early dialogues between Brazilian music scholars and comparative musicologists and ethnomusicologists from the 1920s through the 1960s, for example, Zamith 1992, Travassos 1997, Aragão 2006, Araújo 2007, Lima Barros 2009, Drach 2011, and Machado de Barros 2013.

3. The conference's inconclusiveness led to a public debate on the event's "failure" between at least two eminent Brazilian folklore scholars, Joaquim Ribeiro and Edison Carneiro.

4. Guerra-Peixe's definitions resonated with those formulated by scholars from the socialist countries of Eastern Europe (I thank my colleague, Naila Ceribasić, for pointing that out to me), despite the lack of evidence concerning his awareness of any related literature.

5. See Carroll's discussion of debates among French composers (2009).

6. This impression was widespread among European composers who were inspired by Webern's ideas about expanding serial structuring to parameters other than pitch, such as Pierre Boulez and Karel Goeyvaerts, whose *Nummer 2* (1951) has been regarded as the first piece of integral serialism. An interest in Asian timbres and rhythmic structuring models inspired Boulez's composition of another icon of integral serialism, *Le Marteau Sans Maître* (1953–1954) (see de Tugny 1998; Araújo 2007).

7. On this innovative topic, the convergent and apparently simultaneous research insights of Guerra-Peixe and Arthur M. Jones are remarkable, despite the Brazilian composer's considerable distance from the academic milieu. His contemporary, Jones, was an acknowledged Africanist music scholar who wrote in 1952 of the organization of African drumming as "total patterns of sounds," aggregating sound and duration in time (Blacking 1958).

8. During his intensive fieldwork in Pernambuco (1950–1952), Guerra-Peixe only transcribed real-time performances, since he did not have access to sound recording equipment.

9. In the gemedeira syllabic style, as well as in other poetic subgenres of cantoria, each line of the verse contains seven or eight syllables. Therefore, the changing meters in the three concluding measures disrupt the insider's expectations.

10. Guerra-Peixe seems to have been unaware of the related research and compositional techniques simultaneously being developed by Bartók during the 1950s.

References

Andrade, Mário. 1928. *Ensaio sobre música brasileira*. São Paulo: Chiaratto.

———. 1949. "Folclore." In *Manual bibliográfico de estudos brasileiros* [Brazilian Bibliographical Handbook], edited by Rubens Borba Moraes and William Berrien, 421–70. São Paulo: Instituto Progresso Editorial.

Aragão, Pedro de Moura. 2006. "Luiz Heitor Corrêa de Azevedo e os estudos de folclore no Brasil: Uma análise de sua trajetória na Escola Nacional de Música (1932–1947)" [Luiz Heitor Correa de Azevedo and Folklore Studies in Brazil: An Analysis of His Trajectory at the National School of Music (1932–1947)]. M.M. Thesis (Ethnomusicology), Universidade Federal do Rio de Janeiro.

Araújo, Samuel, ed. 2007. "Introdução." In *Estudos de Folclore e Música Popular Urbana*, by César Guerra-Peixe, 13–32. Belo Horizonte: Editora da UFMG.

Barbosa, Virginia. 2005. "A continuidade das mudanças musicais construindo reconhecimento: A experiência do Maracatu Nação Estrela Brilhante (Recife)" [The Continuity of Musical Change Generating Acknowledgement: The Maracatu Nação Estrela Brilhante Experience]. M.M. Thesis (Ethnomusicology), Universidade Federal do Rio de Janeiro.

Blacking, John. 1958. "Review of *African Rhythm* by A. M. Jones." *Ethnomusicology* 2(3): 127–29.

Carroll, Mark. 2003. *Music and Ideology in Cold War Europe*. Cambridge: Cambridge University Press.

———. 2009. "All Together Now: The Prague Manifesto (1948) and the *Association Française des Musiciens Progressistes*." In *French History and Civilisation: Papers from the George Rude Seminar*, Vol. 2, edited by Vesna Drapac and Andre Lambelet. Available at: www.h-france.net/rude/rudepapers.html (accessed 19 January 2014).

De Tugny, Rosângela Pereira, ed. 1998. *Pierre Boulez, André Shaeffner: Correspondance*. Paris: Fayard.

Drach, Henrique. 2011. "A rabeca de José Gerôncio: Luiz Heitor Corrêa de Azevedo, música, folclore e academia na primeira metade do século XX" [José Gerôncio's Fiddle: Luiz Heitor Corrêa de Azevedo, Music, Folklore, and the Academy in the First Half of the Twentieth Century]. Ph.D. Dissertation (History), Universidade Federal Fluminense.

Guerra-Peixe, César. 1954. *Maracatus do Recife*. São Paulo: Ricordi.

———. 1957. "Sputnik e Folclore." *Notícias de Hoje*, São Paulo, 24 November.

———. 1971. "*Catálogo de obras* [Work Catalog]." Unpublished Ms., Rio de Janeiro.

———. 2007. *Estudos de Folclore e Música Popular Urbana* [Studies on Folklore and Urban Popular Music], edited by Samuel Araújo. Belo Horizonte: Editora da UFMG.

Herskovits, Melville J., and Richard Waterman. 1949. *Revista de Estudios Musicales* 1 (December): 65–127.

Jones, Arthur M. 1954. *African Rhythm*. London: International African Institute.

———. 1959. *Studies in African Music*, 2 vols. London: Oxford University Press.

Jones, Arthur M., and L. Kombe. 1952. *The Icila Dance, Old Style: A Study in African Music and Dance of the Lala Tribe of Northern Rhodesia*. Roodepoort, South Africa: Longmans, Green and Co. for the African Music Society.

Karpeles, Maud. 1955. "Definition of Folk Music." *Journal of the International Folk Music Council* 7: 6–7.

Keil, Charles. 1995. "The Theory of Participatory Discrepancies: A Progress Report." *Ethnomusicology* 39(19): 1–19.

Keil, Charles, and Steven Feld. 1994. *Music Grooves*. Chicago: University of Chicago Press.

Kennedy, Douglas. 1955. "Festival Performance of Dance at São Paulo." *Journal of the International Folk Music Council* 7: 4–5.

Kolinski, Mieczyslaw. 1949. "*La Música del oeste africano: música europea y extraeuropea*." *Revista de estudios musicales* 1 (December): 191–215.

Leffler, Melvyn P. 1999. "The Cold War: What Do 'We Now Know'?" *American Historical Review* 104(2): 501–24.

Lima Barros, Felipe Santos de. 2009. "Construindo um acervo etnográfico-musical: Um estudo etnográfico sobre o arquivo de Luiz Heitor Correa de Azevedo, seu método de campo e documentação produzida durante suas viagens a Goiás (1942), Ceará (1943) e Minas Gerais (1944)" [The Making of a Musico-Ethnographic Archive: An Ethnographic Study on the Archives of Luiz Heitor Correa de Azevedo,

His Field Methods and the Documentation Produced During His Trips to Goiás (1942), Ceará (1943), and Minas Gerais (1944)]. M.M. Thesis (Ethnomusicology), Universidade Federal do Rio de Janeiro.

Machado de Barros, Frederico. 2013. "César Guerra-Peixe: A modernidade em busca de uma tradição" [César Guerra-Peixe: Modernity in Search of a Tradition]. Ph.D. Dissertation (Sociology), Universidade de São Paulo.

Peoples' Summit. 2012. *Peoples' Summit—Final Declaration.* cupuladospovos.org.br/wp-content/uploads/2012/07/FinalDeclaration-ENG.pdf (accessed 15 January 2014).

Santoro, Cláudio. 1948. "Problema da música contemporânea brasileira em face das Resoluções e Apelo do Congresso de Praga" [Problems in Contemporary Brazilian Music in the Face of the Resolutions and Appeal of the Prague Congress]. *Fundamentos* 2(2): 232–40.

———. 1950. *O progresso em música.* Brasília Arquivo Cláudio Santoro.

Travassos, Elizabeth. 1997. *Os Mandarins Milagrosos: Arte e etnografia em Mário de Andrade e Béla Bartók* [The Miraculous Mandarins: Art and Ethnography in Mário de Andrade and Béla Bartók]. Rio de Janeiro: Funarte/Jorge Zahar Editor.

Zamith, Rosa Maria Barbosa. 1992. "A Escola de Música da UFRJ e o estudo e pesquisa do folclore musical: Problemas e perspectivas" [The UFRJ School of Music and the Study and Research of Folk Music: Problems and Perspectives]." In *Anais do Simpósio Nacional de Ensino e Pesquisa de Folclore*, 135–45. São José dos Campos: Fundação Cultural Cassiano Ricardo.

CHAPTER SEVEN

~

Bohemian Traces in the World of Ethnomusicology

Zuzana Jurková

This chapter presents the story of Czech ethnomusicology as I have understood it from archival sources, books, and my own experience.[1] My narrative oscillates between the historical approach and personal recollections, a method partially inspired by Bruno Nettl's latest books (2002, 2010, 2013) and those of several younger Czech historians, my colleagues (such as Horský 2009, 2013). In the words of Paul Veyne, I cut the story "out of the tissue of history" (1978:36), certainly subjectively, but perhaps not unjustifiably. And those who are not otherwise interested in situations in the Czech Lands may read it as an illustration of at least two general features. The first is diachronic continuity: even in very unfavorable times, it is possible to follow the transfer of the baton of an interest in music (often music of "those Others") and its cultural connection. The second is interlocking—a sort of pas de deux—of that interest with social conditions.

Amateur Proto-Ethnomusicologists

The first figure in our story is Ludvík Kuba (1863–1956).[2] This high school teacher was later famous not only for his musical-ethnographic activities, but also as a painter. Had he been American, English, French, or German, he surely would have been included by Mervyn McLean among the "pioneers in ethnomusicology" (2006). Driven by ideas of Slavic solidarity, still alive in the patriotically oriented part of Czech society of the second half of the nineteenth century, Kuba collected folk songs of the Slavs and published some of them in various arrangements in his ten-part, seventeen-volume work, *Slavs in Their Songs* (1884–1927).[3] His Balkan collection is the most famous; for example, his 1883 transcriptions of more than twelve hundred songs hitherto unknown substantially enriched the collections of the Sarajevo museum. Moreover, Kuba did not limit himself to dry transcriptions; he also documented his travels in ethnographically rich texts, which he also published.[4]

It was precisely Ludvík Kuba who wrote an enthusiastic foreword to the book *Living Song* (1949) by the one-generation-younger biologist Vladimír Úlehla (1888–1947), whom he knew for many years. *Living Song* is an extremely thorough musical ethnography of the South Moravian town of Strážnice, a center of wine production and cimbalom bands. However, the book is especially remarkable because of the view Úlehla takes: as a world-famous biologist-ecologist,[5] he used ecological argumentation to clarify the dynamics of musical phenomena.[6] Apart from this, he developed—primarily again with the needs of biology—a method of documentary filming, which he also applied to collecting Moravian folklore. Thus, in his *Disappearing World* (1932) he captured the *verbunk*, a Moravian dance, in sound film. This dance was the first phenomenon from the Czech Lands to be included in 2005 on the UNESCO list of intangible cultural heritage, partly thanks to its documented continuity of performance.

The third member of this group of pre-war amateur proto-ethnomusicologists was the famous writer and journalist Karel Čapek (1890–1938). The enormously popular and influential writer[7] had many hobbies, among which, at the end of the 1920s, was collecting recordings of "Other" musics—European folk music and especially non-European music—what two decades later Jaap Kunst designated as the subject of ethnomusicology. In Čapek's collection are not only recordings available in Europe, such as Hornbostel's album *Musik des Orients*, but also recordings Čapek ordered from overseas catalogues.[8] Čapek rarely refers to them in his novels, but he popularized them both in newspapers and on the radio.[9]

I am convinced that the activities of these three famous, visible amateurs both characterized the music research during the First Republic and also shaped it.

Professional Ethnomusicologists

The professional trend in pre-war Czech ethnomusicology may be traced mainly through the Prague University. Over the past 150 years, the fate of this institution—the oldest university north of the Alps and east of Paris, as the witticism goes[10]—faithfully reflects the social situation in the Czech

Lands. As a result of the growing tension between the Czechs and Germans, the famous Charles University split in 1882 into two separate institutions, the Czech-language Charles-Ferdinand University and the German-language Charles-Ferdinand University. The German branch, known from 1918 as the Deutsche Universität Prag, became the alma mater of Czech German-speaking students, and "a significant number of Jewish students were represented in it. . . . They constantly made up about one third of the student body" (Hlaváček and Radovanovič 2013:14). The situation on the teaching force was probably similar.[11] A certain tension—considered, however, by many as stimulating, even beneficial—among the Czech and German segments of Prague life, not only in the university, continued after the establishment of the independent Czechoslovakia in 1918. Furthermore, at the German university of the 1930s, the tension grew stronger between National-Socialist-oriented professors and the liberal wing loyal to the Czechoslovak state, among whom were primarily Jewish professors. The situation was similar in the 1920s and 1930s, when Czechoslovakia granted asylum to people from the east and west,[12] and emigrants from surrounding lands found refuge at the German university in the first half of the 1930s. By contrast, at the end of this same decade, all teachers of Jewish origin were dismissed, and on September 1, 1939, the German university was subordinated directly to German jurisdiction.[13] During the war, the university became a tool of the German National Socialists. Therefore, right after the war it was closed by presidential decree retroactively from November 17, 1939. Thus began the gradual process of expunging Czech cultural memory, a process that also suited the following totalitarian regime in Czechoslovakia, of which I myself have been a product. Only after the revolution in 1989 did the gap—which absorbed not only the German university but also a large part of Czech-German-Jewish culture, for which the term *Bohemian* is so fitting—begin to be filled.[14]

During my studies in musicology at the beginning of the 1980s, I myself perhaps fleetingly heard of August Wilhelm Ambros (1816–1876), who in 1869 became the first Professor Ordinarius—the highest rank at a German university—in the field of musicology in Prague. I knew the name Guido Adler (1855–1941), whose publication in 1885 marks the birth of a systematic approach to the study of music, as well as the concept of comparative musicology. However, I learned only from his quotation in the lobby of Vienna University that he had formulated his thoughts in Prague. I am quite sure that at that time I had not heard of Adler's pupil, Paul Nettl (1889–1972),[15] whom Bruno Nettl characterizes as a "pioneer of intercultural studies, studies that typify ethnomusicology" (Nettl 1994:227). Of course, I did not learn of Paul Nettl's 1923 book about Jewish musicians in small-town Bohemian life.[16] I knew the name Alois Hába (1893–1973), whom Paul Nettl interviewed right before he emigrated, but only as a composer of micro-interval music. I had not the slightest idea about his involvement in the field of non-European musical cultures. Quite surely I had not heard of Nettl's pupil Walter Kaufmann (1907–1984), who, as it will be apparent later, posthumously accompanied me on a part of my trip of discovery, not only of Bohemian ethnomusicology.

In 1983, shortly before the end of my studies, I made the acquaintance of Václav Kubica. At that time he was working as an ethnomusicologist in the Náprstek Museum of non-European cultures, which received, among others, a collection of phonograph records from Karel Čapek in 1981.[17] Until that time I knew the term "ethnomusicologist" as a synonym for music folklorist; in socialist Czechoslovakia, with its closed borders, no subject of research other than local folk music was conceivable.[18]

Václav Kubica (1926–1992), however, was a different case. He studied music at the conservatory and musicology at Charles University. He later spent many years in the Middle East.[19] From there he brought back an extensive library, hundreds of phonograph records, and dozens of musical instruments.[20] In the lands where he stayed, Kubica studied local classical and folk music, and he published the results of his field collections in a book titled *Nordafrika* (Collaer and Elsner 1983), a volume in the only ethnomusicological series available in Czechoslovakia—the German *Musikgeschichte in Bildern.* Eager for any kind of information, I acquired another volume in this series, *Altindien* (1981). The amount of material in this book, and its systematic presentation, impressed me so much that I remembered the author's name: Walter Kaufmann. A few years later, this man became my virtual gatekeeper to the past and to the future.

Once again I came across Kaufmann's name in the Academy of Sciences, in a quotation by one of the Theresienstadt composers, Karel Reiner (1910–1979), who had been a pupil of Alois Hába. Reiner wrote that "it seems that today nobody knows about the Carlsbad Walter Kaufmann, the gifted composer and conductor."[21] I could not imagine that the brilliant author of *Altindien* could have something in common with Carlsbad. Nevertheless, I started to trace him in my Ph.D. dissertation about Czech ethnomusicological traditions. I discovered the book *Music East and West: Essays in Honor of Walter Kaufmann* (Noblitt 1981). Kaufmann's biography only begins in 1934, when he became the director of European Music at the All-India Radio in Bombay. But in this same volume was an article by Bruno Nettl containing a passage about how his father's student, Walter Kaufmann, "expertly taught" him as a four-year-old "how to squirt water through his hands in order to drench the walls of the bathroom," but what was most important to me was that this took place *in Nettl's apartment in Prague* (Nettl 1981:111).

Walter Kaufmann thus turned my attention to that interwar line in ethnomusicological research (and at least to a notion of the existence of "Bohemian" culture), and also to its continuation. I learned that Hába was not only the composer of the opera *Mother* (1929), which used micro-intervals (and at the time of my studies was still considered to be avant-garde), but that he was interested in micro-intervals in a broader context. Reports have been preserved of how he played recordings of non-European, mainly Middle Eastern music for his pupils at the conservatory and how he researched their intervals with his Turkish students (Vysloužil 1996). Hába devoted several publications in Czech- and German-language periodicals to this topic (Hába 1934, 1956). In 1932, he participated in the famous Congress of Arabic Music in Cairo (Nettl 2002:28; Vysloužil 1996:84–85), for which he wrote "Memorandum," dedicated to questions of the Egyptian music education system (Vysloužil 1974).

The Committee for Non-European Music

One of Hába's students was Miloslav Kabeláč (1908–1979), who was "one of the most outstanding Czech composers of the 20th century. Soon he created an original style. . . . His economical expression consists mainly of conscious work with intervals which shows the application of original non-octave modes to musical structure, but also of investigation of the possibilities of so-called interval augmentation and diminution. . . . His interest in non-European musical cultures also became apparent" (cs.wikipedia.org/wiki/Miloslav_Kabel%C3%A1%C48D, accessed 24 November 2013). And indeed, Kabeláč was an informal leader of the so-called Committee for Non-European Music,[22] which began in 1962 in affiliation with the Oriental Institute of the Czechoslovak Academy of Sciences (activity of the Committee for Non-European Music was forbidden in 1972). The Committee was remarkable for several reasons, including, for example, because it broke through the traditional ignorance of music of Czech Oriental Studies. Its interdisciplinarity was also unusual; it gathered together musicologists (Herzog, Stanislav), scholars in Oriental studies (Merhautová, Dvorská), musicians (Kabeláč, Kubica), and others such as the geodesist Mácha, who collaborated with Lomax. The Committee sponsored lectures, discussion evenings, and biennial conferences, the papers of which were published in limited printings by *Reports of the Czechoslovak Society of Oriental Studies*.

One of the members of the Committee was my old friend Xenie Dvorská (1932–1991), who majored in Sinology in Prague and graduated from the Beijing Conservatory of Music, where she studied the *pipa*. Her basic interest was the aesthetics of Chinese theater; nevertheless, after entering the Czechoslovak Academy of Sciences, one of two institutions of Oriental studies in socialist Czechoslovakia, her job was to translate a political newspaper.[23] Fulfillment of her real expertise came after the revolution of 1989, when she prepared a distinguished album, *Traditional Music of China*, published in 1991, the year of her death. Other members of the Committee included, for example, Josef Stanislav (1897–1971), a professor of musicology and music folklore studies at the Music Academy and the author of a comprehensive monograph about the biologist and music ethnographer Vladimir Úlehla (1963), as well as Václav Kubica, who was later my mentor from the Náprstek Museum.

Walter Kaufmann, apart from the fact that he drew my attention to the interwar Prague University scene, also to a certain extent steered my professional future. His bequest, which in the mid-1990s remained unprocessed, was left to the Music Library of Indiana University in Bloomington, where Alan P. Merriam had earlier taught. Indiana University was, at that time, the seat of the Society for Ethnomusicology and was where Paul Nettl worked during the last quarter century of his life. Supported by a recommendation from Bruno Nettl, I was granted a Fulbright scholarship to work on Kaufmann's bequest,[24] and I lived it up for half a year in that ethnomusicological metropolis. I returned home equipped with basic literature, an idea of ethnomusicology as a multi-paradigmatic discipline, and the daring to collaborate across borders.

Minorities

In 1999, at a conference of the International Council on Traditional Music in Hiroshima, I participated in founding the Study Group on Music and Minorities. In the photograph of that founding meeting are Svanibor Pettan (Slovenia), Ursula Hemetek (Austria), Anka Giurchescu (Denmark), and I. At that time, we were all engaged in studying the music of Roma. I began to study this topic shortly before my stay in the United States. Apart from various evident, practical reasons, I strongly felt that "Other" people lived close to me about whom I knew very little, which was definitely to my detriment. Looking back, perhaps I was puzzled by the fact that I didn't know a large area of my own culture at all—that interwar Jewish-German one.

I researched the music of the Roma both by myself in the Czech Republic and also with colleagues from neighboring areas, approximately covering the territory of the former Austria-Hungary.[25] To a certain extent, this was stimulated by the existence and helpfulness of the Vienna Phonogramm-Archiv,[26] which was so important in the early years of ethnomusicology.

A broader view of minorities was (and is) provided to me by the Music and Minorities Study Group. In 2008, its fifth conference took place in Prague; some of my Charles University students participated in its organization.[27] A few of them are also involved in research on music and minorities. For her baccalaureate thesis, Veronika Seidlová prepared an edition of recordings of *The Forgotten Voice of the Prague Jerusalem Synagogue: Cantor Mose Blum* (2008). Zita Skořepová Honzlová wrote her thesis on musical self-presentations of immigrant communities of today's Prague. She published an article summarizing the main information in the ethnomusicological volume of the journal *Urban People* (2012), an issue centered primarily on papers from the international round table organized by our faculty in the summer of 2011 titled "Theory and Methods in Urban Ethnomusicology."[28] One of my doctoral students who researches music and minorities is Martha Stellmacher of Hannover, who focuses on musical practices in Prague synagogues in the interwar period. One of the first items in her project's bibliography is, understandably, *Alte jüdische Spielleute und Musiker* by Paul Nettl.

Conclusions

It would be possible to continue telling this story,[29] to focus on various details,[30] or to expand various episodes.[31] But I have tried to emphasize a certain line. One of its characteristics is continuity—passing on an interest in the music of "Others," most often in its cultural context—from teacher to student or colleague, a continuity that persisted, even in the unfavorable periods of totalitarian regimes. To use Úlehla's ecological metaphor, this interest is like a plant, the roots of which grew out of the multinational environment in Austria-Hungary, but which grew and spread in the interwar period. Sprouts are then traceable after the war and became institutionalized only in the 1960s, those years our history calls the Prague Spring, and again only after the revolution of 1989.

The development of that metaphoric plant in time reveals, apart from continuity, another basic feature: conditions of growth. When for the first time after the Velvet Revolution, Bruno Nettl took part in a conference in the Czech Lands (1992) and presented his father, Paul, as a pioneer of intercultural studies, he linked his father's approach with the character of the environment of interwar Czechoslovakia: "I think that a major reason for his approach was his origin and life in Bohemia and Czechoslovakia, and his strong feeling of belonging to the Czech Lands, with their significant German and Jewish minorities, and especially with the intercultural character of the historic city of Prague," and later spoke about "the democratic and culturally tolerant character of the Czechoslovak Republic of the '20s and '30s" and "cultural equilibrium" (Nettl 1994:224).

It is almost impossible to overestimate the importance of the democratic and culturally tolerant environment creating *a cultural equilibrium*. Like interwar Czechoslovakia, today's Czech Republic is, in the fields of politics and everyday life, far from a perfect democracy; nevertheless, it has again become a state where people seek asylum rather than from which they leave. And again it is acquiring an intercultural character that is stimulating for our ethnomusicological study. Focusing on our minorities we, perhaps unconsciously, remind ourselves that any one of us could be considered, in the words of Bruno Nettl, "a member of a group with undesirable qualities of some sort or other" (Nettl 2009:13). Moreover, when looking back, we are aware of the time continuity—in the words of Jan Assmann, the time dimension of connective structure—creating a "shared space of experience" that "contributes to the development of confidence and orientation" (Assmann 2001:20). Or, like Bruno Nettl, one can call it *belonging*: belonging to our nearest world and the world of ethnomusicology.

Notes

1. I use the term "Bohemian" as a synonym for the German *böhmisch*, which refers to the Czech Lands in opposition to "Czech" (German *tschechisch*), which refers to the Czech language. I use the word "ethnomusicology" in the broad sense of the study of music while taking culture into account.

2. For further information on Kuba, see Stanislav 1963.

3. The primary source for Kuba's research was his own field collections, which he complemented with songs from already published collections. Of about 4,000 songs collected, *Slavs in their Songs* includes 1,510.

4. The most famous of these is his *Quest of Slavic Song* (1953).

5. Among other organizations, he belonged to the American Society of Plant Physiology and the American Ecological Society.

6. For example, Úlehla stated, "So that we may speak with biologists, every song has its microclimate. . . . It is closely connected with its environment" (1949:12).

7. The contemporary intellectual elite—including Tomas Garrigue Masaryk, the first president of Czechoslovakia—met in discussion groups in Čapek's home in Prague's Vinohrady district. Čapek also published an extensive, three-volume book of dialogues with Masaryk, *Conversations with TGM* (1928–1935).

8. Approximately five hundred phonograph records are in Čapek's collection.

9. Čapek's four-part radio program, "Trip Around the World on Phonograph Records," was broadcast by Czechoslovak Radio between August 1 and October 10, 1933.

10. Charles University was founded in 1348.

11. This is suggested by the fact that during the "Aryanization process" at the beginning of 1939, 34 percent of the teaching force had to leave (Hlaváček and Radovanovič 2013:20).

12. These included the Mann brothers, Arnold Schoenberg, and members of the Prague Linguistic Circle.

13. At this time the German University became known as the Deutsche Karls-Universität Prag.

14. For further information, see Nettl 2002 and 2013. In November 2011, the Philosophical Faculty of Charles University mounted an exhibition titled "The Crowded-Out Elite: Forgotten Scholars of the German University in Prague," which was dedicated to "important and, at the same time, neglected personalities" (Hlaváček and Radovanovič 2013:9). Hlaváček and Radovanovič based a publication by the same name on the exhibit. Among the eighteen personalities, Paul Nettl is mentioned.

15. Bruno Nettl explains the relationship as follows: "My father considered himself a disciple of Adler, having served for a time as his assistant" (Nettl 2002:19).

16. For more details concerning Paul Nettl, see Nettl 2013:127–98 and Reittererová 2002.

17. Čapek's heir, Karel Scheinpflug, donated the collection to the museum. After years of procrastination, it was digitized with the support of the Czech commission of UNESCO and some of the recordings were published along with accompanying texts on CD-Roms (Jurková 1999b, 2001). Because of Čapek's continuing popularity, the entire printing immediately sold out.

18. For further information, see Elschek 1991.

19. Kubica was in Morocco from 1957 to 1959, in Iraq from 1960 to 1962 and from 1964 to 1968, and in Algeria from 1973 to 1975. He lived abroad mainly because his wife, Bozena Kubicová, had engagements as a professional clarinetist. For further information, see Jurková 1996.

20. After Václav Kubic's death, the Institute for Musicology of the Academy of Sciences of the Czech Republic purchased his phonograph record collection.

21. Reiner made the comment in an unpublished biography (110), quoted in Schindler and Jurková 1996:233.

22. Sometimes also known as the Section of Music Sciences of the Czechoslovak Society of Oriental Studies.

23. For a selected bibliography of work by Xenie Dvorská, see Jurková 1996:161.

24. The electronic catalog of the bequest may be accessed at library.music.indiana.edu/collections/kaufmann/kaufmann.html (accessed 25 November 2013). See also Schindler and Jurková 1996; Jurková 1999a.

25. See Jurková, Lechleitner, Muszkalska, Seidlová, and Fennesz-Juhasz 2007.

26. The second half of the 1990s saw the rise of an extensive collection of field recordings of Romani musics in the Phonogramm Archiv; the most important contributors, apart from Mozes Heinschink, were two Czech scholars, Milena Hübschmannová and Eva Davidová. See also Jurková and Davidová 2001.

27. For the publication of selected papers, including Nettl 2009, see Jurková and Bidgood 2009.

28. Available online at lidemesta.cz/index.php?id=28&issue=842 (2013).

29. For example, about the preparation for the conference of the European Seminar in Ethnomusicology in September 2014 with the topic "Crossing Bridges," inspired by Prague's topography and history.

30. Such as the enthusiastically welcome cycle of lectures Bruno Nettl presented at the Faculty of Humanities of Charles University, 2010.

31. Here could be mentioned the activities and publications of the Ethnological Institute of the Academy of Sciences, where, for example, musical transcriptions by Ludvík Kuba are deposited, along with other collections of folk songs. Only in 1996 did it become possible to publish a collection of "Bohemian," that is, German and Czech dances from the Czech territory (Tyllner 1996). Besides traditional methodological and thematic foci on rural folk music, the ethnochoreologist Daniela Stavělová (2008a, b) often studies various folk-dance phenomena from an anthropological perspective.

References

Assmann, Jan. 2001. *Kultura a paměť*. Prague: Prostor. (Originally *Das kulturelle Gedächtnis: Schrift, Erinnerung und politische Identität in frühen Hochkulturen*, Munich 1992).

Collaer, Paul, and Jürgen Elsner. 1983. *Nordafrika*. Leipzig: VEB Deutscher Verlag für Musik.

Dvorská, Xenie, ed. 1991. *Tradiční hudba Číny*. Prague: Supraphon.

Elschek, Oskár. 1991. "Ideas, Principles, Motivations, and Results in Eastern European Folk-Music Research." In *Comparative Musicology and Anthropology of Music*, edited by Bruno Nettl and Philip V. Bohlman, 91–112. Chicago: University of Chicago Press.

Hába, Alois. 1934. "*Tschechoslowakisch-türkische Zusammenarbeit in Prag* [Czechoslovak-Turkish Collaboration in Prague]." *Der Auftakt* 14: 131.

———. 1956. "Čtvrttóny v libanonské hudbě" [Quarter-Tones in Lebanese Music]. *Hudební rozhledy* 9: 940.

Hlaváček, Petr, and Radovanovič, Dušan. 2013. *Vytěsněná elita. Zapomínaní učenci z německé univerzity v Praze*. Prague: Philosophical Faculty, Charles University in Prague.

Horský, Jan. 2009. *Dějepisectví mezi vědou a vyprávěním* [Historiography between Science and Narration]. Prague: Argo.

———. 2013. "Teorie a narace." In *Narace a (živá) realita*, edited by Jan Horský and Juraj Šuch, 9–27. Prague: Togga.

Jurková, Zuzana. 1996. *Česká etnomiuzikologie: O českém poznávání cizích hudebních kultur* [Czech Musicology: About the Czech Study of Foreign Musical Culture]. Ph.D. dissertation, Palacký University, Olomouc.

———. 1999a. "Nad pozůstalostí Waltera Kaufmanna." *Hudební věda* 1: 32–48.

———, ed. 1999b. *Mimoevropská hudba v původních nahrávkách ze sbírky Karla Čapka/ Non-European Music in Original Recordings from Karel Čapek Collection*. 5 CD-Roms. Prague: Náprstek Museum.

———, ed. 2001. *Evropská hudba v původních nahrávkách ze sbírky Karla Čapka/European Music in Original Recordings from Karel Čapek Collection*. Prague: Náprstek Museum.

Jurková, Zuzana, and Lee Bidgood, eds. 2009. *Voices of the Weak: Music and Minorities*. Prague: Slovo 21.

Jurková, Zuzana, and Eva Davidová. 2001. *Vlachicka Djila* (in cooperation with the Vienna Phonogramm-Archiv of the Austrian Academy of Sciences). Prague: Academia.

Jurková, Zuzana, Gerda Lechleitner, Božena Muszkalska, Veronika Seidlová, and Christiane Fennesz-Juhasz. 2007. "Uncovering Layers of Memory: A Diachronic Approach to the Music of Central European Jews and Roma." In *Minority: Construct or Reality?* edited by Zuzana Jurková, Blanka Soukupová, Hedvika Novotná, and Peter Salner, 100–156. Bratislava: ZingPrint.

Kaufmann, Walter. 1981. *Altindien*. Leipzig: VEB Deutscher Verlag für Musik.

Kuba, Ludvík. 1884–1927. *Slovanstvo ve svých zpěvech*. 10 parts, 17 volumes. Prague: Hudební matice Umělecké besedy.

McLean, Mervyn. 2006. *Pioneers in Ethnomusicology*. Coral Springs, FL: Llumina Press.

Nettl, Bruno. 1981. "Comments on the Persian Radif." In *Music East and West: Essays in Honor of Walter Kaufmann*, edited by Thomas Noblitt, 111–22. New York: Pendragon Press.

———. 1994. "Paul Nettl and the Musicological Study of Culture Contact." In *Colloquium Ethnonationale Wechselbeziehungen in der mitteleuropäischen Musik mit besonderer Berücktischtigung der Situation in den böhmischen Ländern*, 223–28. Brno.

———. 2002. *Encounters in Ethnomusicology: A Memoir*. Warren, MI: Harmonie Park Press.

———. 2009. "Minorities in the Study of Ethnomusicology: A Meditation on Experience in Three Cultures." In *Voices of the Weak*, edited by Zuzana Jurková and Lee Bidgood, 12– 23. Prague: Slovo21.

———. 2010. *Nettl's Elephant: On the History of Ethnomusicology*. Urbana: University of Illinois Press.

———. 2013. *Becoming an Ethnomusicologist: A Miscellany of Influences*. Lanham, MD: Scarecrow Press.

Nettl, Paul. 1923. *Alte jüdische Spielleute und Musiker*. Prague: Verlag Dr. Josef Flesch.

Noblitt, Thomas, ed. 1981. *Music East and West: Essays in Honor of Walter Kaufmann.* New York: Pendragon Press.

Reittererová, Vlasta. 2002. "Die jüdische Musik im Werk von Paul Nettl." In *Kontexte: Musica Iudaica*, edited by Vlasta Reittererová and Hubert Reitterer, 77–109. Prague: Charles University, Philosophical Faculty.

Schindler, Agata, and Zuzana Jurková. 1996. "Kdo byl Walter Kaufmann?" *Hudební věda* 3: 233–44.

Seidlová, Veronika. 2008. *Zapomenutý hlas pražské Jeruzalémské synagogy*. Prague: Jewish Museum.

Skořepová Honzlová, Zita. 2012. "Acculturation Strategies in Musical Self-Presentations of Immigrants in the Czech Republic." *Urban People* 2: 369–84.

Stanislav, Josef. 1963. *Ludvík Kuba: Zakladatel slovanské hudební folkloristiky*. Prague: Panton.

Stavělová, Daniela, ed. 2008a. *Červená růžičko, proč se nerozvíjíš: Doudlebská masopustní koleda: Tanec, identita, status a integrace: Multimediální studie*. Prague: EÚ AV ČR.

———, ed. 2008b. *Prostředí tance: Hranice identity a jejich překračování*. Prague: EÚ AV ČR.

Tyllner, Lubonír, ed. 1996. *Tomáš Antonín Kunz: Böhmische Nationalgesänge und Tänze-České národní zpěvy a tance*. Prague: EÚ AV ČR.

Úlehla, Vladimír. 1932. *Mizející svět* [Disappearing World]. A documentary film, Czechoslovakia.

———. 1949. *Živá píseň* [Living Song]. Prague: Fr. Borový. Reprint Strážnice: ÚNLK 2008.

Veyne, Paul. 1978. *Comment on écrit l'histoire, suivi de "Foucault révolutionne l'histoire."* Paris: Édition du Seuil.

Vysloužil, Jiří. 1974. *Alois Hába*. Prague: Panton.

———. 1996. "*Alois Hába und die Musik des Orients*." In *Gedanken an Alois Hába*, edited by Horst Hesse and Wolfgang Thies, 82–87. Salzburg: Verlag Müller-Speiser.

CHAPTER EIGHT

Music Scholarship and Politics in Munich, 1918–1945

William Kinderman

The period from the collapse of the Central Powers in 1918 to World War II was a turbulent era of decline for humanistic scholarship in Munich, the city recognized by the National Socialists as the "capital" of their movement. Long before Hitler's seizure of control in 1933, anti-Semitic agitation had an impact on Munich cultural life, damaging the careers of Jewish musicians in that city such as the conductor Bruno Walter and the critic and scholar Alfred Einstein. So strong was the National Socialist network in Munich by early 1933 that the Nobel Prize–winning author and defender of democracy Thomas Mann was forced into exile in response to his lecture held at the Ludwig Maximilian University on "The Suffering and Greatness of Richard Wagner," a lecture that treated Wagner with much insight and sympathy.[1] In contrast, the career of Wagner scholar Alfred Lorenz during the 1920s and 1930s was promoted precisely because of his National Socialist orientation. In this context, the career of Kurt Huber also assumes importance and merits examination. Huber's work focused on *vergleichende Musikwissenschaft* (comparative musicology) or ethnomusicology, an orientation he pursued in sharp contrast to his university colleague, Lorenz. By 1942, Huber joined the "White Rose" resistance group centered at the Ludwig Maximilian University; shortly thereafter, he served as a main author of the final brochure or *Flugblatt* before the group's members were arrested and executed. Huber's sad fate and the stark contrast with Lorenz displays to what extreme the discipline of music scholarship became twisted by ideology in Hitler's "New Germany."

This chapter compares the highly divergent paths of three music scholars whose activities brought them to Munich and to the Ludwig Maximilian University during the years following World War I: Alfred Lorenz, Alfred Einstein, and Kurt Huber. Whereas Lorenz's writings received much praise at the time, their serious flaws and limitations have become increasingly evident. Einstein was forced to emigrate from Germany on account of his status as a Jew, but he succeeded in continuing his distinguished career in the United States, and his scholarly contributions have had enduring impact. Of these three figures, it was Kurt Huber whose professional goals were most severely curtailed, and whose contributions to music scholarship remain least familiar.

Alfred Lorenz (1868–1939)

Rich documentary material related to Alfred Lorenz is held in the archive of the Ludwig Maximilliam University in Munich.[2] These files are unusually informative, since Lorenz came to his position at the university late in his career and he repeatedly petitioned the administration to upgrade or extend his status as professor. He received his doctorate in 1922 for a study of Wagner's *Der Ring des Nibelungen*, which formed the basis for the first of his four analytical books on Wagner. Lorenz finished his second dissertation, or *Habilitationsschrift*, in 1926 and thereafter taught at the Institute for Musicology until he fell ill in 1938. He died in 1939 around the time World War II began.

Lorenz was born in 1868 in Vienna, where his father, the historian Ottokar Lorenz, held a professorship at the University of Vienna. In 1898, Alfred Lorenz became second *Kapellmeister*, and in 1904 first *Kapellmeister* in the service of Duke Alfred von Sachsen-Coburg-Gotha. The core of his conducting repertory consisted of Wagner's works as well as operas and symphonic poems of Richard Strauss. Until 1920, Lorenz remained music director of the theater in Coburg-Gotha.

At various times Lorenz offered differing explanations for the end of his work as a conductor in Coburg at the age of fifty-two. In one document he describes the situation as follows: "Whereas after the revolution the theater passed into other hands and circumstances ensued that were intolerable for me, I terminated my role and again took up my music-theoretical studies." At a later point Lorenz depicted these events differently: "Shortly after the shift to the red system in 1920 I lost my permanent position as Music Director of the Coburg-Gotha Theater on account of my convictions."[3] According to this second explanation, the reason for his early retirement lay beyond his control, with the "red system" (*im roten System*). Only after Hitler's rise to power in 1933 did Lorenz send a letter to the Prussian Cultural Ministry—a letter that now is found in the documents of the *Reichskanzlei*—that contains a *third* explanation of these events, whereby Lorenz depicts himself as a victim. He writes here that after his outstanding and long-standing contributions to musical life in Gotha and Coburg, he had been removed "in order to make room for a Jew." Lorenz's claim is not convincing, since his successor, Ewald Lindemann, was professionally active at various German opera houses during the Third Reich, and therefore must have produced documentation of his Aryan status. In any event, Lorenz was successful with his strategy and remained active teaching at the Institute for Musicology for fifteen years, from 1923 until 1938.

Lorenz took pride in his political activity and convictions. He emphasized during the 1930s that before the beginning of World War I, he had been a member of the "German Union" (*Deutschbund*), an association that "already at that time strove for *racial purity*."[4] The files at the university archive document his ideological convictions in detail. On a form dated 9 August 1935, Lorenz claims to have been a member of the Deutschbund, a "thoroughly anti-Semitic association." Shortly before, on 4 July 1935, Lorenz wrote the following to the rector of the Ludwig Maximilian University: "Confirmation for my partaking in the young spirit of the university and for my political beliefs is provided through the date of my joining the Nazi party: Nov[ember] 1931, as well as through the fact, that I for instance already in 1933 held a lecture course on 'Race and Music.' Heil Hitler!"[5]

Lorenz mentioned as well that his son joined the march to the *Feldherrnhalle* during the Hitler *Putsch* in 1923. According to the records, he was the sole professor at the university who belonged to the Nazi Party before Hitler came to power. Especially detailed is Lorenz's report to the dean of the Philosophical Faculty from the beginning of 1939. He describes here how he resumed his musicological studies in Munich beginning in 1920 and, at the same time, became a "passionate follower" (*glühender Anhänger*) of Hitler:

> Returning to the musicological studies I pursued in my youth, I came to Munich, where I immediately visited the early Hitler gatherings and became his passionate follower. It was the same with my family, which followed me a year later, after we had successfully found an apartment. Our connection to the party was established according to the National Socialist doctrine, whereby the future belongs to the youth, and hence my son became at once with my encouragement a member and made the march to the Feldherrnhalle. Once my situation was somewhat stabilized (during the time of inflation we barely

> got by) we the parents became party members in 1931 and received on 1 December [19]31 our party books. . . .
>
> In 1934 a series of radio broadcasts about Richard Wagner were held, in which I gave an extended lecture from Breslau, "On the Structure of Wagnerian Music drama." I was asked to give a similar lecture on the 29th October 1934 by the Nazi Cultural Commission of Coburg. All of my other lectures (Würzburg, Vienna, Zurich, Basel, Berne, Stuttgart, Heidelberg, Mannheim, Karlsruhe, Leipzig, Cologne, Berlin, Zwickau, and Munich, courses for foreigners, etc.) were devoted fully to the dissemination of the National Socialist cultural perspective.[6]

Lorenz stresses here how his lecturing activities promoted National Socialist ideology. His publications were by no means limited to formal analysis. He wrote in 1933 in the journal *Deutsches Wesen* about "Richard Wagner's 'Parsifal' and National Socialism," and articles from his last years carry titles such as "Musicology and Racial Research," "Musicology and the Jewish Question," "Musicology and Inherited Biology," as well as "Music Greets the Führer!"

His main contribution to analysis of Wagner's works consists of his series of four volumes, *Das Geheimnis der Form bei Richard Wagner* (The Secret of Form in Richard Wagner), in which he claims to reveal the "secret of form" in Wagner's later works. The last of these books, devoted to the opera *Parsifal*, appeared by the summer of 1933, perfect timing for the "New Germany" and for the Bayreuth Wagner Festival, where Hitler's visit that year aroused much attention. Granting Wagner the power of political prophecy, Lorenz announces in his preface (with spaced-out words for emphasis) that "Wagner conveyed his prophetic thoughts about leadership of the Führer and regeneration in his work and bequeathed thereby an *exalted mission*." Elsewhere in his *Parsifal* book, and in a separate essay on "The Religion of Parsifal" (*Die Religion des Parsifal*), which appeared in February 1933 in the journal *Die Musik*, Lorenz wrote about the "new *Parsifal* religion." His argument focuses on Parsifal's raised Holy Spear at the end of the drama and, as he writes, the "marvelous rise" of the musical motif that he dubbed as the "word of redemption" (*Erlösungswort*), which forms the culmination of the drama. Lorenz draws a conclusion equating this gesture with the implementation of the National Socialist agenda:

> *Wir sollen den Verfall überwinden und als rassisch hochgezüchtetes Volk zum Siege schreiten*, will Wagner. [*We should overcome decay and as a racially high bred people advance to victory*, Wagner wishes.]
> (Lorenz 1933a, 153)[7]

Lorenz's words "Wagner wishes" are highly questionable; he even adds a footnote at this point to Wagner's essay "Religion und Kunst" (Religion and Art), to a passage that does not support his racial interpretation. Lorenz hardly acknowledges the theme of compassion (*Mitleid*) that is embedded in Wagner's drama through the prophecy of the Grail, "Knowing through compassion, the pure fool" (*durch Mitleid wissend, der reine Thor*), anticipating Parsifal's role. Lorenz also does not recognize that Parsifal, differently from Amfortas, does not use the Holy Spear aggressively as a weapon, but as an instrument for healing. On the contrary, the Nazi ideologist Alfred Rosenberg, who was sentenced to death at Nuremberg for crimes against humanity, had a different view of *Parsifal*, finding it incompatible with National Socialist ideology, since in his opinion it represented "a church-influenced enfeeblement in favor of the value of renunciation" (Rosenberg 1930:434). For his part, Lorenz was determined to counter this impression, writing in the preface to his *Parsifal* book that "the character of *Parsifal* has generally been understood to be too gentle" (for detailed discussion of Lorenz and the reception history of Wagner's work, see Kinderman 2013).

Kurt Huber (1893–1943)

Let us return to the context of the Institute of Musicology at the Ludwig Maximilian University during the 1930s. Which colleagues apart from Lorenz offered courses at this time? Each Wednesday morning at ten o'clock during the winter semester of 1934, students at the institute could choose between attending "Musik und Rasse" (Music and Race) with Lorenz or "Einführung in die psychologische Volksliedkunde" (Introduction to the Psychological Study of Folk Song) with Kurt Huber, who lectured enthusiastically about the artistic value of the music of various peoples, and who also led ensemble performances of world music at the university.[8]

Huber was born in 1893 in Chur, Switzerland. After moving to Munich in 1912, he studied musicology, psychology, and philosophy at the Ludwig Maximilian University. His plan to concentrate his activity there in musicology was unsuccessful, but his 1919 dissertation on "The Expression of Elemental Motives" remained centered on music (Huber 1919). Beginning in 1926, he taught courses at the Institute for Musicology on folk song, although his main appointment was in the Philosophical Faculty. In 1942, Huber came into contact with the "White Rose" (*Weiße Rose*) resistance group. Early in 1943, he acted as main author of the final brochure critiquing the Hitler regime, the pamphlet that led to a fatal outcome for all concerned when members of the group were apprehended while distributing copies at the atrium of the main university building, adjacent to the Institute of Musicology. Like other members of the Weiße Rose, Huber was sentenced to death; he was decapitated on 13 July 1943.[9]

Huber's viewpoint diverged very sharply from that of Lorenz. As Pamela Potter has observed, Lorenz was fundamentally concerned to assert the musical superiority of the German race (see Potter 1998 and Potter 2000). From his standpoint, the psychology of music and above all the detailed study of "exotic music" were superfluous. He considered the music of "inferior" races as an unworthy pursuit, believing that engagement with such music involved the false assumption of an equality of races. Lorenz presents this argument in his essay "Musikwissenschaft im Aufbau" (Building Musicology; 1939). He fervently encouraged younger scholars to absorb racial ideology into their work, stressing anti-Semitic convictions in accordance with National Socialist doctrine. In this political context, Lorenz stood for narrowly "systematic" as opposed to "comparative" musicology, which was Huber's field of research.

As Bruno Nettl has pointed out, *vergleichende Musikwissenschaft* was a burgeoning field during the 1930s. In 1933, the short-lived *Zeitschrift für vergleichende Musikwissenschaft* began to be published under the editorship of the Jewish scholar Robert Lachmann, and included other Jewish contributors; this publication anticipated the development of the field of ethnomusicology in the United States, with the founding of the Society for Ethnomusicology roughly twenty years later (Nettl 2013:50–51). Kurt Huber's career can be regarded in this larger context of ideological conflict, intolerance, and persecution. A popular teacher whose philosophical and ethical perspective was indebted to Gottfried Leibniz, Huber properly stressed experience as the indispensable basis for an "aesthetic from below" (*Ästhetik von unten*), maintaining that "we must build up our entire aesthetics from experience [*wir müssen unsere ganze Ästhetik wieder aufbauen auf dem Erleben*]" (Haase 1957:814). Sadly, many of Huber's studies failed to reach publication during his lifetime, although some studies by Huber were published posthumously (cf. Huber 1959).

Even after the death of Lorenz in 1939, Huber's work situation at the university cannot have been easy, in part because of the appointment in 1937 of Hans Alfred Grunsky, son of the Wagner scholar Karl Grunsky. The younger Grunsky was made professor of philosophy and psychology that year through the direct intervention of Adolf Hitler, an unprecedented act in the history of the institution.[10] Grunsky was unqualified for the position, not having written a *Habilitationsschrift* (the German second doctorate). His dissertation from 1923 was an attack on the "Jewish claims" of Albert Einstein's theory of relativity (Grunsky 1923). Like Hitler, Grunsky was inspired around this time by having met Houston Stewart Chamberlain at Bayreuth.[11] Hans Grunsky had scant background in philosophy but wrote glowing reviews of Alfred Lorenz's work on Wagner. Once installed at the university in Munich, Grunsky showed himself to be a quarrelsome fanatic. That he was made professor through Hitler's decree suggests a link to Winifred Wagner, since the elder Grunsky had long been active in the Bayreuth circle.

In his detailed study of Lorenz, Stephen McClatchie comments that "the remarkable uniformity of critical opinion about Lorenz's work during his lifetime may be attributed to the then prevailing philosophical and aesthetic climate" (McClatchie 1998:178). It was not, however, simply the "philosophical and aesthetic climate," but rather the brutal politics of the Third Reich that account for the overwhelmingly positive response to Lorenz's writings at that time. Lorenz had already embraced National Socialist ideology earlier, but from 1933 during the Hitler dictatorship, his work was practically immune from critique in Germany.

Alfred Einstein (1880–1952)

Thomas Mann was not the only critical admirer of Wagner's art forced to leave Germany after Hitler took power. Another was Munich's finest musicologist, Alfred Einstein, who later wrote about Wagner that his "creative power was equal to his intellectual abilities, or, better, [and he] used his phenomenal intellectual faculties in the defense of his very personal art work, in order to secure the cohesion of so doubtful and artificial a building as the Wagnerian *Gesamtkunstwerk*" (Einstein 1941:284). With Mann, Einstein, and others in exile, German discourse about Wagner became dominated by racist ideologues whose analytical methods tended to be severely reductionist.

Anti-Semitism exerted an impact on Einstein's career well before 1933, since Adolf Sandberger, the influential senior professor of musicology at the Ludwig Maximilian University, declined to offer Einstein the possibility of the *Habilitation* necessary for an academic position, whereas he supported Lorenz. Sandberger was openly nationalistic and anti-Semitic and had long been interested in Wagner; he had contributed an essay on "Richard Wagner in Würzburg: *Die Hochzeit, Die Feen*" as early as 1888 to the *Neue Zeitschrift für Musik*. This essay displays his prejudice, in that, for example, he conspicuously ignores the decisive role of the Venetian dramatist Carlo Gozzi in supplying Wagner the model for the text of his first opera (Sandberger 1888). In response to limited professional opportunities as well as Hitler's ascent to power, Einstein left Germany in 1933 and took up residence in the United States a few years later, teaching at Smith College in Massachusetts from 1939 until 1950. In 1944, Einstein took American citizenship.

Like Thomas Mann, Einstein never again resided in Germany, but the cultural legacy of European music remained at the center of his productive creative life. Impressive contributions on the Italian madrigal, Gluck, Mozart, and Schubert characterized his scholarship of the 1930s and 1940s, with his revision of the Köchel catalog of Mozart's works (1937) representing a landmark achievement. During the first years that Einstein taught at Smith College, Thomas Mann had taken up residence on the other side of the country, in Pacific Palisades, California. Mann, in his last major novel, *Doktor Faustus*—which he sometimes regarded as a "late work" parallel to Wagner's final drama, *Parsifal*—charted the crisis and collapse of Germany through his Faustian figure Adrian Leverkühn. The writer locates his narrator, the humanist Sererus Zeitblom, near Munich, Mann's home until he was driven into exile. Within the narrative structure of *Doktor Faustus*, Zeitblom begins writing this biography of his artistic friend Leverkühn on 27 May 1943, and he completes the last chapter of the tome in April 1945, while witnessing the downfall of a Germany "surrounded by demons, with a hand over one eye and the other staring down into horrors, from despair to despair."

In his scholarship, Alfred Einstein remained more detached in his writings about the disaster that befell his birthplace, the "capital" of the National Socialist movement. A passage in his book *Greatness in Music* (1941) nevertheless addresses the provinciality, bias, and hypocrisy that mars the work of National Socialist writers like Lorenz:

> We cannot . . . subscribe to the theory and practice of the race fanatics—people who, while they do not altogether deny to the French or British some knowledge of, and general approach to, Beethoven, nevertheless deny to them the profounder understanding of the "German" master. These people have driven Mendelssohn from the German concert hall as a "Near-Easterner," and would eliminate Heinrich Heine from the history of German literature—while they do not shy at appropriating Shakespeare to themselves. How singular! Beethoven entrusted the first performance of his *Kreutzer Sonata* to a mulatto; and Carl Maria von Weber, next to Wagner the most "German" of all masters, made not the slightest objection to having a Mr. Braham, alias Abraham, sing the part of Hüron in the world première of *Oberon*. The interpretation of Beethoven's last quartets which made the deepest and strongest impression upon me was that of the Frenchman Capet and his colleagues, and the greatest performer of Bach's Partitas and Beethoven's sonatas is the Catalan cellist, Pablo Casals. (Einstein 1941:24–25)

Just two years earlier, shortly after his arrival in America, Einstein had helped his fellow immigrant and Mozart scholar Paul Nettl and his family to reach America, assisting them in purchasing their boat tickets in U.S. currency, thereby enabling their passage to safety (Nettl 2013:166–67). Einstein's generosity was important not only for Paul and Gertrud Nettl, but for their young son, Bruno Nettl, then just nine years old, who was to become that outstanding scholar whom we so proudly honor in the present volume.

Notes

1. For detailed discussion of Thomas Mann's lecture and his situation at Munich in 1933, see especially Vaget 2005:87–143. For an English translation of Mann's essay, see among other sources Mann 1957.

2. The documents cited below are held in the University Archive of the Ludwig Maximillian University of Munich in the Freimann district of the city. I thank the archivist Claudius Stein for facilitating my access to these sources. All translations are my own.

3. The first of these explanations is contained in a "Lebenslauf" (curriculum vitae) in the file for Lorenz; the second is found in his letter to the university administration labeled O-XIV-501.

4. On the form cited (labeled "S.AKT 862/3" in the Lorenz file in the university archive), Lorenz underlines "Rassenreinheit" (racial purity) for emphasis.

5. Lorenz file in the archive of the Ludwig Maximillian University, numbered E-II-2316.

6. Lorenz file, O-XIV-501.

7. Lorenz footnotes at this point his essay on "Die Religion des Parsifal" (1933b:341–48).

8. The information about these courses stems from the doctoral dissertation by Andreas Elsner (1982:534).

9. For information on Huber's role in the White Rose group, see among other sources, Steffahn 1992:101–3 and *Weiße Rose* (2005), a publication of the Denkstätte Weiße Rose (Memorial Room to the White Rose) at the Ludwig Maximilian University in Munich (www.weisse-rose-stiftung.de).

10. The University Archive at Munich holds a copy of the communication from Hitler from 26 May 1937 naming Grunsky a professor, an appointment made effective 1 April 1937, as other documents confirm.

11. The source of this information is Grunsky's own personal statement (Lebensabriss) on file in the University Archive of the Ludwig Maximilian University. Houston Stewart Chamberlain was the author of *Die Grundlagen des neunzehnten Jahrhunderts* (The Foundations of the Nineteenth Century), a book that contributed to the formation of National Socialist ideology. He married Wagner's daughter Eva

in 1908, and became a central figure in the circle that had formed around the aging Cosima Wagner at Bayreuth.

References

Chamberlain, Houston Stewart. 1899. *Die Grundlagen des neunzehnten Jahrhunderts*. Munich: F. Bruckmann.

Einstein, Alfred. 1941. *Greatness in Music*. Translated by César Saerchinger. New York: Oxford University Press.

Elsner, Andreas. 1982. "Zur Geschichte des musikwissenschaftlichen Lehrstuhls an der Universität München." Ph.D. dissertation, Ludwig-Maximilians-Universität, Munich.

Grunsky, Hans Alfred. 1923. "Das Problem der Gleichzeitigkeit in der Relativitätstheorie." Ph.D. dissertation, Ludwig-Maximilians-Universität, Munich.

Haase, Hans. 1957. "Huber, Kurt." In *Die Musik in Geschichte und Gegenwart*, edited by Friedrich Blume, Vol. 6: 814. Cassel: Bärenreiter.

Huber, Kurt. 1919. "Der Ausdruck mus. Elementarmotive: Eine experimentalpsychologische Untersuchung." Ph.D. dissertation, Ludwig Maximillian University Munich.

———. 1959. *Volkslied und Volkstanz: Aufsätze zur Volksliedkunde des bajuwarischen Raumes*, edited by Clara Huber and Otto Alexander von Müller. Weilheim in Oberbayern: Buch-Kunstverlag Ettal.

Kinderman, William. 2013. *Wagner's "Parsifal."* New York: Oxford University Press.

Lorenz, Alfred. 1933a. *Der musikalische Aufbau von Richard Wagners "Parsifal."* Berlin: Max Hesses Verlag.

———. 1933b. "Die Religion des Parsifal." *Die Musik* 25: 341–48.

———. 1939. "Musikwissenschaft im Aufbau." *Zeitschrift für Musikwissenschaft*.

Mann, Thomas. 1957. *Essays by Thomas Mann*. Translated by H. T. Lowe-Porter. New York: Vintage.

McClatchie, Stephen. 1998. *Analyzing Wagner's Operas: Alfred Lorenz and German Nationalist Ideology*. Rochester, NY: University of Rochester Press.

Nettl, Bruno. 2013. *Becoming an Ethnomusicologist: A Miscellany of Influences*. Lanham, MD: Scarecrow Press.

Potter, Pamela M. 1998. *Most German of the Arts: Musicology and Society from the Weimar Republic to the End of Hitler's Reich*. New Haven, CT: Yale University Press.

———. 2000. *Die deutscheste der Künste: Musikwissenschaft und Gesellschaft von der Weimarer Republik bis zum Ende des Dritten Reiches*. Stuttgart: Klett-Cotta.

Rosenberg, Alfred. 1930. *Der Mythus des 20. Jahrhunderts*. Munich: Hoheneichen Verlag.

Sandberger, Adolf. 1888. "Richard Wagner in Würzburg: *Die Hochzeit, Die Feen*." *Neue Zeitschrift für Musik*. Reprinted in *Richard Wagner: Die Feen*, edited by Michael von Soden and Andreas Loesch, 176–97. Frankfurt am Main: Insel Verlag, 1983.

Steffahn, Harald. 1992. *Die Weiße Rose mit Selbstzeugnissen und Bilddokumenten*. Reinbek bei Hamburg: Rowohlt.

Vaget, Hans. 2005. *"Im Schatten Wagners"—Thomas Mann über Richard Wagner: Texte und Zeugnisse 1895–1955*. Frankfurt am Main: Fischer.

Weiße Rose. 2005. *Die Weiße Rose*. Munich: Weiße Rose Foundation.

CHAPTER NINE

Harry Partch and Jacques Barzun

A Historical-Musical Duet on the Subject "Western Civ"

Harry Liebersohn

"Shantih shantih shantih" ends T. S. Eliot's poem *The Waste Land* (1922).[1] In his footnote to this line the poet comments: "Repeated as here, a formal ending to an Upanishad. 'The Peace which passeth understanding' is our equivalent to this word." Eliot's turn to ancient India is more than just a testimony to the monumental learning of his undergraduate years at Harvard, where according to Stephen Spender, he spent two years studying Sanskrit and Indian philosophy (Spender 1975:20). The signal poem of its age also reminds us of the anxious cosmopolitanism of a significant number of intellectuals after World War I. Eliot's poem famously envisions a Europe in spiritual ruins, its present-day inner impoverishment alternating with memories of its former splendors. The turn to the Upanishads suggests a kind of desperate gesture of reaching beyond Europe for deliverance. One could hardly imagine a poem from before 1914 ending this way, or if it did, having the resonance with contemporaries of Eliot's work; but the poem quickly and lastingly took its place in the landscape of the postwar era. Because Eliot retreated later in the 1920s into an arch Christianity, the final line is not often noted. But it captured a widespread curiosity of Western artists and intellectuals about whether non-European cultures could soothe their sense of crisis (Eliot 1971:50, 55).[2]

You didn't have to go abroad after 1918 to hear that Western Civ (to invoke the later courses of the same name) had reached its limits and that, to recover your creative élan, you had better look somewhere else. The music and writings of Harry Partch (1901–1974) contain a homegrown American version of the same impulse. Partch spent time in New York and visited Europe, but he was nonetheless a fierce critic of European high culture and, in contrast to American-born Eliot, made repeated declarations of independence from it. After spending years as a hobo during the Great Depression, Partch captured the rhythms of the rails across the United States; he lovingly and satirically made the punch of its rhetoric and the inflections of its down-home folk the subject of his bardic declamations and dramas. While California became the nearest thing to home, he spent his childhood in the Southwest and did some of his best writing and composing in the Midwest, including the completion of his book-length manifesto, *Genesis of a Music* (1949), at the University of Wisconsin, Madison, and the composing and staging of the drama *The Bewitched* (1957) at the University of Illinois at Urbana-Champaign.[3] Always suspicious of the snobbery of East Coast Americans, Europeans, and (worst of all) East Coast Americans who shone with the prestige of time spent in Europe, he wrote in 1959: "I believe thoroughly in an integrated arts center in the middle of the prairie, in decentralization, and in self-sufficiency in the realm of ideas."[4] With these words Partch put his finger on some of the reasons for the creativity of ethnomusicology as well as his own art at Midwestern public universities, which is nowhere more richly in evidence than in the scholarship of Bruno Nettl.

Harry Partch and Twentieth-Century Music

In one of those oddities of intellectual history that are more revealing than the conventional affinities, Partch attracted the support and admiration of Jacques Barzun (1907–2012). A greater contrast between biographies could hardly be imagined. Partch resented East Coast and European elites, whereas Barzun was the embodiment of those elites on both sides of the Atlantic; Partch was always an institutional outsider, never able to snag a regular musical or academic job for very long, whereas Barzun was the consummate insider, a longtime member of the Columbia University history department; Partch always worried about money, and during the Depression went hungry while hoboing, whereas Barzun had a knack for writing best-sellers; Partch struggled for public recognition, whereas Barzun garnered honors all the way up to the National Humanities Medal, awarded by President Obama in 2010. Partch's and Barzun's correspondence from 1952 to 1968 confronts wayward genius with breezy virtuosity (on Barzun see Murray 2011).

How can we explain their mutual admiration? The answer has to do with the cultural crisis of the 1920s. They shared the widespread belief that European civilization after World War I was a wasteland, but were largely skeptical toward both conservatives such as Eliot and the avant-garde. Even though their own programs for cultural renewal were different, they were capacious enough cosmopolitans to appreciate one another's creations. Their exchange is an exemplary dialogue between a historian and a composer-critic; to reconstruct it today is to uphold the value of conversation between scholarship and art.

Partch drew on many sources for his defiantly original compositions, and several of them cross, without exactly settling into, the course of comparative musicology in the late nineteenth and twentieth centuries. The resources for Partch's turn to extra-European music emerged naturally enough from his early biography—were prepared for him, in fact, before he was born. His parents went to southeast China at the end of 1888 as Presbyterian missionaries and stayed, with a two-year break, until 1900. They experienced a crisis of faith, in part because they learned to admire Chinese culture as they got to know it in Zhejiang and later Shandong provinces, places of ancient beauty, wisdom, and commerce (on Partch's parents see Gilmore 1998:14–15). While the immediate cause of their return to the United States was the Boxer Rebellion and attendant dangers to Westerners, especially missionaries, Partch's father had already lost his religious faith. Harry Partch was born shortly after the family's return to the United States, where his father found employment working for the U.S. Immigration Service. They settled in small-town Arizona, where Partch grew up in a rough and colorful frontier atmosphere that colors his later music about life on the road. Partch later recalled the Chinese books in the house, his father's conversations in Mandarin with Chinese guests, and the Chinese songs that his mother sang to him, which he remembered into his twenties. Later, the Chinese influence continued, stiffening his critical distance toward Western classical music. His resistance grew as he explored the cultural milieus of southern and northern California, for he hated the stuffy Angelinos who attended the concerts of the newly founded Los Angeles Symphony. Instead, his taste ran to the Cantonese opera performances that he attended in San Francisco, where he enjoyed the music and the immigrant audience, objecting only to the noise from the peanut shells that were cracked and strewn on the floor.[5]

Partch's early exposure to Chinese music and culture led him to an imagined cultural home outside of Europe that provided him with the material for his first mature work, *Seventeen Li Po Lyrics* (composed 1930–1933) (Gilmore 1998:76–77). Li Bai (Li Po) (701–762 CE) was a poet from the Tang dynasty who first enjoyed imperial favor and later was exiled: He was a wanderer, a dreamer, who celebrated the pleasures of alcohol, women, and the freedom of life on the road—not a bad historical counterpart to Partch himself (though

Partch turned to men, not women, for erotic company), who could never stay put in one place for very long and who also turned to drink for pleasure and consolation. Partch could read an intelligent summary of Li Po's life in the introduction to a 1922 translation of his poetry. There was a mystical side to Li Po that would also have appealed to Partch, always in search of a deeper, precivilized stratum of human subjectivity, which, along with rough times, he experienced on the road. The availability of Li Po's poetry was in itself a sign of the times: several translations of the interwar period introduced Chinese poetry to American readers, and Ezra Pound loosely retranslated it to demonstrate the fit between its imagery and the demands of modern poetry. Partch, more honest than Pound, did not claim to "translate" Chinese music to accompany the poetry; rather, he used the translations of poems of Li Po as a subject to animate the bardic, cantillating sound of heightened speech.[6]

Other influences, too, streamed into Partch's music in the interwar years and beyond. As a boy he had met Yaqui Indians in Arizona—and sympathized with them and not the police who harassed them; later he transcribed samples of their music from ethnographic recordings made by Charles F. Lummis and deposited with the Southwest Museum in Los Angeles. He approached a Los Angeles rabbi in the hope of hearing a recitation in Jewish cantorial style, in preparation for his setting of Psalm 137 (again, about a wandering artist) (Gilmore 1998:19, 86, 93; Partch 1974:ix). A more profound influence was W. B. Yeats, who shared the dream of an incantatory art that would merge words with a music remote from anything modern.

The intellectual revelation that set the course of Partch's composing came from a book he discovered in the Sacramento Public Library in 1923, Hermann Helmholtz's *On the Sensations of Tone*, in the 1885 translation by Alexander J. Ellis. Without knowing it, Partch had stumbled on one of the urtexts of comparative musicology, a work whose mathematical analysis of tone or pitch was for Partch a demystification of the tempered diatonic scale and a recipe for departures from it. Helmholtz's book was the first work to show Partch how to peer beneath the lettered system of labeling notes and to understand the Western scale instead as a mathematical system derived from the overtones of the tonic (Partch 1974:vii; Gilmore 1998:49–50). With broad learning as well as mathematical precision and acoustic experimentation, Helmholtz showed that the well-tempered scale was an invention of recent centuries, that other tonal systems had been alternatives even within the West, and that the Greeks and other peoples had used different scales. He discarded the idea that there was a superior naturalness to the well-tempered scale and in fact complained that he disliked some of the artificial displacements of pitch that it required in order to make the notes acoustically equidistant. Ellis powerfully reinforced this message. His own essay "On the Musical Scales of Various Nations" (1885) inventoried the musical scales of Greece, the Arab world, India, Japan, China, Indonesia, Persia, and other places, replacing a hierarchical and ignorant view of musical scales with a cosmopolitan smorgasbord of many different possibilities. Ellis summarized the results of his own work in an appendix to Helmholtz that reported on what he had learned from performances of actual instruments. Yet the implications were not restricted to historical examples. As Helmholtz and Ellis made clear, if the pitches of the notes on the Western scale were arbitrarily assigned, one could also hear pitches "between" or other than these notes—that is, microtones. Non-Western musics made use of those notes. Beyond this, it took just a small step to conclude that the individual artist could plunge into the sea of microtones for himself and pull out new, strange, brilliant, and different notes (see Helmholtz 1954; Ellis 1885). Partch set about finding those notes and making them part of his own musical scales; he wanted to fashion them into patterns that better approximated, but also heightened, the passions of the human voice. And so he did. For the rest of his life he experimented with microtones. And since the tyrannical rationality of Western instruments excluded them, he built his own instruments and constructed his own scales, ever experimenting with different numbers of tones and different instruments to sound them.

Jacques Barzun and Harry Partch

For Partch, spending his early years in the Southwest and California, World War I was a distant if formative event; the decay of European culture and its suffocating effects on music and the arts were the circumstances for his fierce loyalty to American vernacular experience and search for extra-European means to express it. For Barzun, the impact of the war was more direct. His first seven years were spent in Paris, where his parents, apparently comfortable from inherited wealth, cultivated a circle of avant-garde friends, including the poet Guillaume Apollinaire. Then came the war, a collective trauma for Western European society, with the deaths and deprivation that touched virtually every family. At the war's end, his parents decided that he should continue his education in the United States and moved with him to New Rochelle, New Jersey, in 1920. Barzun seems to have made the transition smoothly and picked up English and a love of baseball even while retaining his native French; he thrived at Columbia University with the seeming effortlessness—behind which lay hard work and formidable powers of concentration—that marked all his later life into his nineties. From his parents he took the best of French humanism, as derived from his lifetime favorite author, Montaigne: nothing human was foreign to him; everything merited his critical examination (summarized from Murray 2011:3–60).

For the most part during his undergraduate years, Barzun stuck to courses in Western civilization; but when he heard that Franz Boas was going to teach his graduate course in linguistics for the last time, he pushed his way in and apparently was well received by Boas (Murray 2011:38–39). This exposure to Boasian anthropology turned into an invaluable resource, for when he went on to graduate studies in history at Columbia, the historian Carlton J. H. Hayes insisted that he write his dissertation on the subject of race, which Barzun did, surveying the development before 1789 of the idea of the French nobility as a Germanic race apart from the plebeian Gauls. Barzun went on to write a monograph on the ideology of race published in 1937, in urgent response to the ideologies of race that had brimmed over from kooky and scientific babble into a devastating form of political madness. Barzun's study was a superb historical complement to Boas's critical writings on the subject; he cited Boas's *Mind of Primitive Man* as a plausible starting point for the discipline of anthropology and cited Boas and his students in order to dismiss the belief that physical appearance defined a racial difference (Barzun 1932; Barzun 1965:34, 216–17). While Barzun himself did not write about extra-European cultures, he was unusually free of the racial prejudices that pervaded twentieth-century Europe and America.

Barzun became a cultural historian and a cultural critic. As a cultural historian he took as his chief domain the Western European culture of the nineteenth century. As a cultural critic he was the champion of the first hopeful cultural moment of the post–French Revolutionary era, Romanticism. Across the arts it responded to the democratic and economic revolutions of the eighteenth century with humanity, breadth, and an absorption of eighteenth-century neo-classicism into a greater range of human experience. Barzun specialized in the cultural history of music, championing the reputation of Berlioz. In the course of his defense of the composer, he also attacked the idea of pure music and the mathematical game playing and devotion to rules which underlay it, in favor of a musical art that was grounded in the feeling and cultural moment of real human beings (from Barzun's writings on Berlioz see above all Barzun 1950, especially volume 1:171–98 and volume 2:360–70). He furthered the defense of Romanticism through an attack on its enemies in his *Darwin, Marx, Wagner: Critique of a Heritage* (Barzun 1958 [1941]). Published in 1941, the book turned back to the mid-nineteenth century as the source of the pathologies that had overwhelmed Europe in his own time. His chronological point of departure was 1859, the year Marx published the preliminary version of *Capital*, Darwin published *The Origin of Species*, and Wagner completed *Tristan and Isolde*. Despite the coincidence of dates, the conjuncture was an odd one: Darwin and Marx, yes—but how did Wagner fit in with them? Barzun argued that Wagner, like Darwin and Marx, was a materialist for whom the all-enveloping love of Tristan and Isolde was nothing more than biological attraction. Like Darwin and Marx, he put forth a body of work that reduced the individual to insignificance in the service of self-interest. Gone was an appreciation for, a cultivation of, individual personality. The book concluded not with a plea for a return to early Romanticism—Barzun was too sophisticated a thinker to suggest such a nostalgic program—but with a yank away from the materialism and collectivism that in his view characterized the realist movement in the arts and sciences of the mid-nineteenth century and a return to the liberal spirit, if not the substance, of Romanticism (Barzun 1958[1941]).

There was romantic individualism aplenty in the music of Partch and in the letters that he sent Barzun from 1952 to 1968. Partch railed through the years against musical establishments, starting with "the music business and its once-removed hirelings in publications offices and musical schools," who, he wrote to Barzun in 1952, stood for "anti-music." In the same letter he went on to state his disgust with the music executives who were enthralled by European music stars.[7] Three years later, Partch compared his obscurity to the public recognition for other musicians and pointed out one of the ways his artistic integrity, his attention to "disturbing, or confusing, or ineffable experience" made him an irritant.[8] Two years thereafter it was the musicologists who set off his rage: "For some quite mysterious reason many key people insist on consulting musicologists before coming to any conclusion regarding new music. I say mysterious because the incompetence of musicologists in this area seems to me beyond argument. It is implicit in the idea of present-day musical scholarship, as a profession, that great music, great ideas, living music as a vital ingredient of our culture, are of the past, and more particularly a European past."[9]

Barzun's reaction to these outbursts was patient, practical, and encouraging. He was frank with Partch, asking him to tone down his anger at the world. But he did more than rein him in; he also became a patron. Writing to the editor of the *American Record Guide* to ask whether Partch's latest recorded work, *Oedipus*, would be reviewed, he stated:

> To those who know only that Mr. Partch is an American composer living in California and whose works are scored for instruments of his own devising, based on the 43-tone scale, the announcement of a new score by him will

> perhaps be classed as "experimentation" and thereby disposed of. To those, on the contrary, who have followed his career with their ears open, he seems with each new work to deserve a greater place among contemporary artists. He is a born musical dramatist and in all his productions, particularly when he himself takes part as a singer, one hears the unmistakable note of power.[10]

In 1959, Barzun intervened in a more public way: Partch was negotiating (ultimately unsuccessfully) for a fellowship from the Rockefeller Foundation to study theater and music in Japan for a year. To further the application, Barzun solicited an honorific post from the Columbia University music department (which did come through), telling Partch when he promised this assistance: "I have heard from them nothing but admiration of your genius and courage. For my part, I have long been convinced that you were making the most original and powerful contribution to dramatic music on this continent. If my poor words should be deemed helpful, you may quote me at any time anywhere."[11] Six years later Barzun was still writing to let Partch know how much he relished the new composition *Petaluma* and how delighted he was that Partch was enjoying a stint as composer in residence at the University of California, San Diego.[12] Barzun's civility and encouragement were unflagging.

Nor was it just in letter and conversation that he campaigned for Partch. Subsequent praise in print makes it clear that Barzun preferred Partch to virtually all the other composers of his time. Indeed he agreed with Partch's own radical view that the Western musical system of the past three hundred years had exhausted itself, with tiresome variations all that remained to accomplish within it:

> It is evident that by 1911 (the date of his [Schoenberg's, H.L.] *Harmonielehre*), the European system of major-minor harmony and tonal enharmony had yielded all it could possibly give. It had been exhausted in a few centuries by an extraordinary number of composers and their patrons. After Richard Strauss any further exploiting of it could only fall into meaningless repetition, clever allusiveness, or deliberate pastiche. . . . And what had happened to music was also happening to the other arts. Five hundred years of creation and logical evolution were everywhere coming to an end; an era of civilization was reaching its close—political, social, and cultural. (Barzun 1982:58)

Enter Partch as one of the few to escape the iron cage: "I happen to think that only in music have truly new directions been found, and that these are two and only two: electronic music and the 43-tone works and instruments of Harry Partch" (Barzun 1982; Weber 1958:181). Barzun added that, "knowingly or not, the Beatles partake of Partch, who antedates them by twenty years"—a statement verging either on the prophetic or the tongue-in-cheek, either one a possibility for Barzun, whose writings combined American flamboyance with Gallic wit (Barzun 1982).

What was it that made Barzun so unfailingly dedicated to Partch? *The Bewitched*, which figures in their correspondence, gives a good demonstration of the attractiveness. The "argument" Partch wrote in his notes to the recording was just the kind of thing to appeal to Barzun, deliciously witty but fundamentally serious. "We are all bewitched," wrote Partch, "and mostly by accident: the accident of form, color, and sex; of prejudices conditioned from the cradle on up, of the particular ruts we have found ourselves in or have dug for ourselves because of our individual needs." The voice-drama offers scenes of "unwitching," emancipation by a chorus he called the lost or displaced musicians. As part of his witch's brew, Partch transports his listeners to musical realms beyond the West—and does so with a sardonic humor that Barzun could have appreciated. For example, scene one is called "Three Undergrads Become Transfigured in a Hong Kong Music Hall." The displaced musicians' job is "to divest the undergrads of the confirmed xenophobia that once blanketed them so lovingly in their cradles." Barzun never made a journey to the East; but he had always battled the conformity of the West, and his genuinely open mind easily followed Partch's lead.[13]

Conclusions

Despite their different personalities and careers, Partch and Barzun forged a firm alliance in one of the twentieth century's culture wars. Both of them battled against the supremacy of *form* in high modernism, offered up as a higher artistic revelation in abstract expressionism in the visual arts and symbolism in literature as well as twelve-tone music, and stood instead for art as a recognizable extension of human *experience*. This position led both of them to excesses. It led Barzun to argue that because Berlioz was a compassionate, generous, broad-minded human being, and his music breathed those qualities, it was superior to the music of the vicious Richard Wagner: there was to be no separation of art and character, no worship of *l'art pour l'art*, self-contained, an immaculate conception having nothing to do with the sins of its creator. It led Partch to insist that music without words was meaningless, that the greats of Western music since Bach had gone down a lifeless path, that the return to a sane and profound music required the confluence of word, gesture, and tone. And yet: the historian and composer have a legacy. The liberality of Barzun's many-sided oeuvre continues to shake us out of our dogmatic slumbers. Partch's music at its best has real magic, and perhaps we are readier than earlier generations for its incantations, its percussive energy, and its turn to the extra-European world's resources of human experience and artistic expression. In their different ways, they are exemplars of a hard-fought personal freedom in an age of cultural conformity.

Barzun yielded more and more to pessimism in his extreme old age. His last book, *From Dawn to Decadence* (2000), deepened his youthful doubts about the West's cultural creativity into a firm conviction of decline. Is it not one of history's ironies that Partch, the misfit, the outsider, was, in the end, the optimist? Perhaps if Barzun had spent less time on Morningside Heights and had joined Partch for a stretch on the road, he would have seen a clearer way into the future. Perhaps if he had taught at a Midwestern university such as the University of Illinois, he would have found like-minded students of music and discovered more affinities with the non-West, building on his early brush with Boas . . . but this is mere speculation. Instead of tinkering with might-have-beens, we may take away from their encounter a more certain conclusion: by crossing academic and artistic borders, we, like Partch and Barzun, may return to our home disciplines with creativity renewed.

Notes

1. Full disclosure statement: The author of this essay has frequently taught "Western Civ" at the University of Illinois at Urbana-Champaign, since 1990. He believes that this can be done in the cosmopolitan spirit of Jacques Barzun and Harry Partch.

2. On Eliot's undergraduate studies see Spender 1975:20. Michael Adas makes the case for World War I as the turning point from European imperial self-confidence to self-doubt (see Adas 2004).

3. *The Bewitched* was first performed at the University of Illinois on 26 March 1957 (see Gilmore 1998:248–59). Gilmore's biography is a model synthesis of musical and historical studies. It reconstructs Partch's life in sympathetic detail but writes with critical detachment, setting Partch's music and writings in numerous cultural contexts from Los Angeles to Dublin. See also Kassel 2013, a valuable summary with an up-to-date bibliography. Partch speaks in his own autobiographical voice in Partch 1991.

4. Harry Partch to Jacques Barzun, 17 May 1959, Harry Partch Estate Archive, 1918–1991, Record Series 12/05/045, Folder 23, Sousa Archives and Center for American Music, University of Illinois at Urbana-Champaign. Hereinafter cited as UIUC Partch Estate Archive.

5. For Partch's own account of the Chinese influences, see Partch 1974:viii–ix. For a fuller account of these and his rebellion against the concert format as he experienced it in Los Angeles, see Gilmore 1998:38–39, 52–53, 77.

6. See Pound 1915 and Obata 1935. Shigeyoshi Obata's introduction is highly critical of the non-Mandarin reader Pound's self-proclaimed "translations."

7. Harry Partch to Jacques Barzun, 17 December 1952, UIUC Partch Estate Archive.

8. Partch to Barzun, 4 April 1956, UIUC Partch Estate Archive.

9. Partch to Barzun, 27 February 1958, UIUC Partch Estate Archive.

10. A copy of this letter of 20 September 1954 was enclosed in a note from Barzun to Partch, 15 October 1954, UIUC Partch Estate Archive.

11. Barzun to Partch, 25 May 1959; see also Partch to Barzun, 28 December 1961, Barzun to Partch, 23 May 1962, Barzun to Partch, 11 June 1962, Partch to Barzun, 15 May 1962, Partch to Barzun, 2 June 1962, and Partch to Barzun, 14 June 1962, UIUC Partch Estate Archive.

12. Barzun to Partch, 12 January 1968, UIUC Partch Estate Archive.

13. In another comic touch, the scene includes a parody of Chinese music as imagined by the undergrads. Harry Partch, *The Bewitched*, the Harry Partch Collection volume 4, accompanying booklet by the composer, Composers Recordings, 754 (1997).

References

Adas, Michael. 2004. "Contested Hegemony: The Great War and the Afro-Asian Assault on the Civilizing Mission Ideology." *Journal of World History* 15(1): 31–63.

Barzun, Jacques. 1932. *The French Race: Theories of Its Origins and Their Social and Political Implications Prior to the Revolution*. New York: Columbia University Press.

———. 1950. *Berlioz and the Romantic Century*, two volumes. Boston: Little, Brown.

———. 1958[1941]. *Darwin, Marx, Wagner: Critique of a Heritage*, second edition, revised. New York: Doubleday.

———. 1965[1937]. *Race: A Study in Superstition*, revised edition. New York: Harper and Row.

———. 1982. "Harry Partch and the Moderns." In *Critical Questions: On Music and Letters, Culture and Biography, 1940–1980*, edited by Bea Friedland, 58–62. Chicago: University of Chicago Press.

———. 2000. *From Dawn to Decadence: 500 Years of Western Cultural Life, 1500 to the Present*. New York: HarperCollins.

Eliot, T. S. 1971. *The Complete Poems and Plays, 1909–1950*. New York: Harcourt, Brace and World.

Ellis, Alexander John. 1885. "On the Musical Scales of Various Nations." *Journal of the Society of Arts* 33(1688): 485–527.

Gilmore, Bob. 1998. *Harry Partch: A Biography*. New Haven, CT: Yale University Press.

Helmholtz, Hermann L. F. 1954[1877]. *On the Sensations of Tone as a Physiological Basis for the Theory of Music*. Translated by Alexander J. Ellis with a new introduction by Henry Margenau. New York: Dover.

Kassel, Richard. 2013. "Partch, Harry." *Grove Music Online*. Oxford University Press. www.oxfordmusiconline.com/subscriber/article/grove/music/20967 (accessed 2 July 2013).

Murray, Michael. 2011. *Jacques Barzun: Portrait of a Mind*. Savannah, GA: Beil.

Obata, Shigeyoshi. 1935[1922]. *The Works of Li-Po, the Chinese Poet*. Translated and with an introduction by Obata. Kanda, Japan: Hokuseido Press.

Partch, Harry. 1974[1949]. *Genesis of a Music: An Account of a Creative Work, Its Roots and Its Fulfillments*, second edition. New York: Da Capo.

———. 1991. *Bitter Music: Collected Journals, Essays, Introductions, and Librettos*. Edited and with an introduction by Thomas McGeary. Urbana: University of Illinois Press.

Pound, Ezra. 1915. *Cathay: Translations by Ezra Pound, for the Most Part from the Chinese of Rihaku, from the Notes of the Late Ernest Fenollosa, and the Decipherings of the Professors Mori and Ariga*. London: Elkin Mathews.

Spender, Stephen. 1975. *T. S. Eliot*. New York: Penguin.

Weber, Max. 1958. *The Protestant Ethic and the Spirit of Capitalism*. Translated by Talcott Parsons with a foreword by R. H. Tawney. New York: Scribner's.

CHAPTER TEN

The Times They Are a-Changin'

Daniel M. Neuman

For those of us around at the time, it is hard to believe that a half-century has passed since Bob Dylan announced a new social and cultural era,[1] a time-post that also coincides with the establishment of ethnomusicology as an academic institution in the United States.[2] In this chapter I step back a little before considering how we might move forward toward what looks like yet another new era for ethnomusicology.

Four hundred years ago, in April 1613, Paul Canning, traveling overland from the port of Surat, finally reached Agra, the court of the Mughal emperor, Jahangir.[3] Canning was accompanied by two musicians; one played the virginals, the other the cornet. The virginals made no impression on the court, but "Trully's cornet, on the other hand, created an immense sensation; Jahangir himself attempted to blow the novel instrument" (Foster 1921:189–90). Three-hundred and ninety years later, Abigail Wood wrote that in 2003 she typed the word "music" into Google and came up with about 112 million hits. Two years later, the number had grown to 389 million (see Wood 2008). I did the same just eight years later and came up with more than seven billion hits. Similarly, cell phone use in India increased from 45 million in 2002 to 925 million in 2012 (Doron and Jeffrey 2013:6). These unprecedented changes happened in a space of just a decade. This chapter is not a report on the well-known growth of web or cell-phone use. In 2013 I referred to a 2008 publication, Wood's chapter in *The New (Ethno)Musicologies*, and called it recent. Not so long ago, referring to a book published five years earlier as "recent" would have been unremarkable. Wood's chapter, however, is severely dated. It's not her fault. In 2015 it is superseded not only by new facts, but by a world that seems to create them more quickly then we can digest them. Two large problems index a new era: the time problem and the space problem. The time problem is that ethnography instantly becomes history and the ethnographic present disappears before you can declare it. The space problem is that modernity has now turned into globality.

Why did I begin in 1613? To remind the reader that the engagement with other people's music—ethnomusicology's trademark identity—is an old story. The story was not only a one-way direction from West to East. There had been lots of musical mingling for centuries, for example, between the Ottoman, Persian, and Indian empires. Three hundred years later, the decisive technological turn meant that musicians no longer had to be transported; their sounds alone became portable through recordings. If three or four hundred years seem like a long time, think about the impact of just the past ten years. My question now is, where do we go from here?

In 1926: Living at the Edge of Time

> The present appears to be a moment of great sophistication when it comes to affirming that some certainties and assumptions "no longer work"—and of even greater reluctance when it comes to filling the gaps that the vanished certainties and assumptions have left. . . . We also lack strong alternatives to options that no longer seem viable. To make matters worse, the author feels that a great deal of pressure is being brought to bear on his generation to come up with something new, something not exclusively skeptical; but he thinks he is not particularly good at programmatic writing—i.e., at the genre of writing that, undoubtedly is required here. (Gumbrecht 1997:xii–xiii)

Hans Ulrich Gumbrecht's *In 1926* is not meant to be read sequentially as the reader is advised in the opening "User's Manual." Its chapters include interconnected essays, including among many others, ones on boxing, airplanes, trains, gramophones, jazz, elevators, and bars, all in 1926. On bars, for example, Gumbrecht is writing about Babe Ruth's frequenting them and prohibition. Bars also appear in another chapter titled "Gomina," which is the hair application made out of rubber to create the shiny, slicked-down look of the roaring twenties. Starting with a famous tango singer in Argentina—who re-emerges importantly in the gramophone chapter—gomina is the hirsute expression of the slinky, tight-fitting clothes of the era, soon to be rejected by Adolf Hitler during the rise of fascism. Gumbrecht attempts here to project another way of "doing" history, in an age when ordinary history seems to have lost its moorings.[4] Gumbrecht intends to illustrate what I call "post-everything exhaustion."[5] His remarks can help us think through our discipline that was born with the gramophone and needs now, I aver, to adapt to a radically new information environment.

The great turn[6] to critical and cultural studies starting in the 1970s included questioning the very foundations of our disciplines and the manner in which we conducted research. This was a moment of profound reflexivity and fundamental rethinking. What I want to suggest here is a reassembling of ethnomusicology as a field, a reset of the *praxis*. I approach this by considering two conceptual dimensions: the scale of times we *personally* encounter, and the scale of things we now engage.

Time Dimensions

Whereas the observations in Abigail Wood's article became dated after just five years, we might consider another scale of time, the genealogical. Reading Bruno Nettl's *Becoming an Ethnomusicologist*, I learned that Bruno's father had been an associate of the Czech-Austrian musicologist Guido Adler, who famously defined the modern understanding of musicology in 1885 (Nettl 2013:178–79). In 2015, our genealogical connection to the beginnings of musicology extends back only three generations. Our complete history of what we have been doing and what we are as ethnomusicologists and musicologists can be fitted into two or three lifetimes, all connected to living memories of today. After looking at the recent scales of five years and a bit more than a century, I should like to refocus our view on a third and last scale, a middle range of roughly the past three decades.

In 1987, Philip Bohlman invited me to chair a conference session titled "Music and Its Canons," which produced Bergeron and Bohlman's *Disciplining Music* (1992). Instructive for me is to read two very different reviews of the book, one by Leon Botstein, who found the whole idea of the book somewhat suspect but lists a number of articles he found useful, and the other by Robert Walser, who celebrates the intent of the volume but finds a number of articles not sufficiently with the program. It will be no surprise to learn that the articles Botstein favors are precisely those Walser finds wanting. About the Schenkerian essay Botstein writes: "Their contribution is particularly welcome because it represents an exercise in how one might innovate methodologically from within, so to speak" (Botstein 1994:343). Walser on the same essay writes they "contribute the least self-reflexive essay in the book. . . . They proceed without even the slightest trace of that interest in examining premisses [*sic*] that distinguishes the volume and the other contributors" (Walser 1993:571). If one knows Botstein and Walser, these differences are far from unexpected. Their autobiographies write their own subjectivities. Isn't that the fundamental rediscovery of the critical turn?[7] I am making no judgment about either viewpoint; rather, I want to consider the difference in their views as a *topic*, a way to think about the critical exercise. This middle-range perspective leads me to reiterate that we are suffering thirty years later from a form of post-everything fatigue. I write this recognizing the signal contributions to musicology by renowned scholars such as Gary Tomlinson, Susan McClary, and Lawrence Kramer, who introduce new ways of thinking about their subject, their discipline's subjectivities, and their own subjectivity. We might consider Richard Taruskin, for example, and his discussion of Beethoven's Ninth in "Resisting the Ninth" (Taruskin 1989). He despairs about what we can no longer recover, but nevertheless concludes: "We are still in the valley of the Ninth. And that gives hope."[8]

The critical juncture at which we find ourselves suggests that we need to rethink how we shall engage an era in which we have moved from not enough information to too much information. One possible first step is to take the critical gesture and think of it as a topic to be examined, not a resource to be used. The new criticism of the past few decades has itself become normalized, and we have to think about how we move on from here.[9]

Iconoclashes

In a recent introduction to a catalog of an exhibition called "Iconoclashes," Bruno Latour lays out his program, "which aims at turning iconoclasm—and more generally the critical gesture—into a topic rather than a resource."[10] Iconoclasm, the tearing down of icons, of which canonic classical music and its precursors in medieval and Renaissance musics are our exemplars, is the subject of much critical study. Latour wants to change the entire discourse and put together the brokenness of the pieces. He is not trying to reassemble an original, but taking the pieces themselves as the topic and reassembling them into new forms, iconoclashes. Elsewhere, Latour writes: "While we spent years trying to detect the real prejudices hidden behind the appearance of objective statements, do we now have to reveal the real objective and incontrovertible facts hidden behind the *illusion* of prejudices?" (Latour 2004:227). Latour, like Gumbrecht, is reacting to what he believes to have been the critical shortcomings of the past several decades. Indeed, Latour admits to his own complicity in this enterprise, and he is appealing to a wholesale rethinking of what we are doing as critics. But what was the real reason for his change of heart?

Latour's concern is not musicology, but ecology. He is reacting to the argument that anti-environmentalists make in denying a human cause for global warming: because there is as yet no scientific certainty, global warming can confidently be ignored. Previously, Latour had himself argued against the lack of scientific certainty, hoping to "emancipate the public from prematurely naturalized objectified facts." This same argument, the absence of scientific certainty, was being used to fool the public. All of *our* thinking, however, is located in a place, and I now shift to our place, the academy in which ethnomusicology mostly resides.

Musicologies

Inspired by Bruno Nettl, let us consider the location of ethnomusicology in the setting of the university today. Ethnomusicology became a critical "topic" for historical musicology, even though ethnomusicology was not intended as such a critique. Indeed, Nettl writes, "I sometimes think that if the holocaust had not driven so many European musicologists into the paradise of North America, music scholarship in America might have ended up being principally ethnomusicological" (Nettl 2002:39). It did, however, have the effect of entering musicological discourse explicitly in 1995 with a special issue of the *Journal of the American Musicological Society* (see especially the introduction by Qureshi). Musicology's resistance, nonetheless, was highlighted two years later by Kofi Agawu.[11] American ethnomusicology was a development of the post–World War II American engagement with the world, the enabling technologies of cheap transportation to far climes, and the political position that the United States had assumed. This new ecological context created opportunities for field research that benefited both anthropology and ethnomusicology.

Ethnomusicology emerged as a distinct institutional practice in the 1960s and is almost always located in the humanities, mostly in music schools and departments. This was a first for the humanities—linguistics being a possible exception—where research gets mostly conducted not in archives and libraries, but in the field, with the voices of live people, not the writings of dead ones, as the primary source. The critical argument in ethnomusicology was—and in a sense still is—how to claim the mantle of musicology for only one music, and that of a particular type, when there are thousands in existence.[12] I have always thought this a somewhat weak argument. Indians, for example, have their own musicology. Had traditional musicology in the West acted more like history, engaging world history or area histories, it might have had a more legitimate claim to its moniker from an ethnomusicological perspective. Musicology did not have a corpus of texts from around the world and thought of its music score-based study not as an anomaly but as normal.[13]

Actually studying other people's music in the field was a postwar luxury that only rich countries could afford. The practice of engaging other people's music in many parts of the world itself has a long history. This was not ethnomusicology as we understand it, but it was a practice, as Anthony Seeger demonstrated, prevalent in small societies such as the Suyá, as well as in large empires (Seeger 1987). What changed with ethnomusicology was the formal scholarly study of other peoples' music in the field. Lest we think that musicology and ethnomusicology are increasingly blurred genres, as Roger Savage recently (Savage 2009) and Regula Qureshi previously suggested (Qureshi 1995), their major differences being text and field, I want to highlight one other major difference still between them: archives. Musicologists work in archives and ethnomusicologists create them. At their extremes their materialities differ most fundamentally as well. Lest the reader think this distinction too glib, we might think about the number of musicologists who founded archives, and think about the number of ethnomusicologists today whose studies rely on them. Ethnomusicologists have founded archives, though they rarely work in them.[14] Among those who founded archives are Bruno Nettl, Mantle Hood, Robert Garfias, and Nazir Jairazbhoy. In 1982, Nazir Jairazbhoy founded the Archive and Research Centre for Ethnomusicology in India in order to repatriate field recordings to India. Repatriation was also a facet of the critical turn to reflexivity. Jairazbhoy exemplified and exhibited the responsibility of his own situational contingency as a scholar.

Contingencies Considered

Sometimes this recognition has turned into an inventory of sins and sinning. In ethnomusicology such inventories include hegemonic neo-colonialists in a postcolonial world extending neo-liberal capitalism via globalization through a post-Fordist modality. Granting such hyperbole, there is the palpable sense that if one does not adopt this dystopian view of the world—populated principally by exploiters, victims, and resistance—one is a culpable actor in it.

For more than four decades I have worked in India—that classic locus of postcolonial and subaltern thinking—but the experience of my own research has been very different. I'll provide two brief examples. My initial work was with a group of hereditary Muslim musicians in India. They were very poor, and many had little or no education outside of music. As Muslims they were also a minority community. Many were identified with a caste, which was widely disparaged. Today, however, the grandson of my primary consultant performs around the world. He is on television regularly and gets invited to perform in Europe. He performs Hindustani classical music, but his fame comes from a band he organized and leads, now signed with EMI. He teaches at an institution called the Global Music School in Delhi. His is not a unique case. Indeed, all younger musicians from this caste that I engaged in my most recent fieldwork (2010–2011) are vastly better off than were their parents and grandparents. If they are victims of the new world order of music production, distribution, and exploitation, one could not tell it from how they live or express how they think.

My second example comes from the rustic hinterlands of desert Rajasthan, the Manganiar musicians, who were the lowest of the low in the village hierarchy. Many of them have successfully entered a global network of American, French, and Indian supporters, who tour different groups on a regular basis. A Google search for "Musicians of Rajasthan" produces 1.3 million results. Most of these musicians were born in villages in which there was no electricity and no running water twenty years back. Scarcity of a very extreme kind was the central feature of rural Rajasthan for centuries. This has all changed dramatically during exactly the same decades the great critical turn was taking place. This is neither an argument to whitewash the terrible sufferings of the last century nor a call to ignore the complicity of American and European power in the expansion of global capitalism's influence. Still, one could rarely point to ethnomusicologists as the bad people here, and the preoccupation with a Foucauldian perspective in which dominance, exploitation, and resistance become not only the central moral subject, but the central subject itself, leads sometimes to a righteousness and dogmatism closely analogous to the Christian missionaries of earlier centuries. For all the self-questioning that has taken place in our disciplines, the critique itself is something that also needs to be interrogated. This is why Bruno Latour's project is ideologically something very much worth considering.

Our Future Turn

The future augurs one major difference in particular: It will be characterized by large-scale, project-oriented research as an increasingly important component of doing ethnomusicology. This will revolve around the fact of big data, what I earlier referred to as "too much data."

Collaborative Research

Though our research has tended to be isolated and slow moving, the success of the life sciences in promoting collaborative research should inspire ethnomusicology. Some of it is already happening. My own *Ethnographic Atlas of Rajasthan Musicians* (Neuman, Chaudhuri, and Kothari 2006) was the result of collaborative research not only with co-authors, but with a number of musicians who went out to collect much of the actual data on more than two thousand individuals in regional survey work. It may be true that this work has had virtually no impact in ethnomusicology, but for the musician communities in the *Atlas*—those I earlier described as occupying a very low status—it has been a source of great pride.

Another example is the "Audio Cultures of India" project, organized and directed by Philip Bohlman, Kaley Mason, James Nye, and Laura Ring at the Neubauer Collegium of the University of Chicago.[15] This considered how existing researchers in South Asian studies, ethnomusicology, and other disciplines, including computer science, could be directed toward thinking about how scientific and technological approaches might produce an aural history of modern India.

Collaborative research generously funded by the European Union is considerable. I might point toward two projects of many: (1) collecting all the *khayal* compositions that are now extant in India and publishing them as a two volume work (Magriel and Perron 2013), and (2) collecting, copying, and eventually studying all manuscripts relevant to the history of music in India. This brings me to the next anticipated big change in ethnomusicology.

Historical Work

When I first started my own research on Indian musicians in 1967, it was through examining the Indian decennial censuses starting in 1881 through 1931. Today, this kind of research would be considered historical, but at the time, with very little information otherwise available, I saw my research in the censuses then as *ethnographic*, not *historical*. In the twenty-first century, we have access to much more historical data. This actually *contradicts* my earlier assertion that ethnomusicologists create archives but do not work in them. Ethnomusicologists may still not use audio archives much,[16] but new manuscript sources are emerging in significant ways. One personal example about historical research follows here.

While I was working on the manuscript for my first book in the 1970s (Neuman 1980), I came across a reference to Wajid Ali Shah, the last ruler of Oudh, headquartered in Lucknow, and famous himself as a composer of *thumri* and a dancer of *kathak*. I found only one secondary source about how the British viewed Wajid Ali Shah; he was controlled by "fiddlers and poetasters," as it was put, and spending all his time in their company along with his courtesan dancers. It was this rationale—poor governance—that the British gave for removing him from power in 1856. This removal was an important basis for the great uprising—what the British called the Sepoy Mutiny—of 1857. Wajid Ali Shah was exiled to Calcutta with his retinue of musicians and dancers, and this laid the basis for Calcutta's centrality in the musical culture of early twentieth-century Hindustani music. The secondary source I had used, Michael Edwardes's *The Orchid House* (1960), relied on a diary that had been published as a two-volume work by W. H. Sleeman in 1858. I could not find a copy of this work, fascinated though I was with the possible significance of *sarangi* players—the instrument I learned to play in India—in the war of 1857 and the removal of the last Mughal ruler.

By the time Allyn Miner published her magisterial work in the 1990s on the sitar and sarod, she had been able to get a copy of the work and was able to provide much more detail on individual musicians, because Sleeman actually named them. One of them, Gholam Ruza, was famous as the inventor of the fast compositional form on sitar known as *rezakhani gat* (Miner 1993:112). Today, these volumes are even downloadable. Katherine Butler Schofield has been leading the team of researchers I mentioned above, collecting all available manuscripts pertinent to Hindustani music history. Schofield's team has so far collected more than two hundred treatises written on music and dance that were previously unknown (Schofield 2013). In the 1970s, I could never imagine we would ever be able to recover this kind of detail.

Conclusion

Now that we have access to musical information on a scale unimagined before the mid-1990s, we can begin to rethink the questions we are able to ask. Ethnomusicologists are faced with orders of magnitude and a vastly changed landscape in which data are located. Such big data, both diachronic and synchronic, not only invite us, but require us to rethink what constitutes the arenas of our research activities; it also requires us to rethink how we get such collaborative research funded. What is fundamentally changed from just ten years ago is the sheer scale of what we are now engaging in the musical universe. Many of the new tools needed have yet to be invented, for example, algorithms to mine and analyze large quantities of sound data.[17]

Where does all this lead us? I began this chapter suggesting that we have a time problem and a space problem. In a sense, both time and space have shrunk dramatically. Although an ethnographic present may now have a half-life too short to be useful, our access to historical materials is greatly enhanced and can usefully extend time backward. The collapse of space through globality greatly enhances our access to the diversity of musical experiences, even as this diversity, like the universe, continuously expands. If studying other people's music is what we actually mostly did, how can we think of a future in which the otherness of others' music becomes both more heterogeneous as well as less so? This is all very tough terrain and suggests the need for new *original* theorizing on the part of ethnomusicologists. I for one am optimistic about that future. Ethnomusicology is already well-primed to engage this complex new world, with its own encompassing perspective and basic humanity.

Notes

1. This is a revised version of a talk given at the celebration of the sixtieth anniversary of musicology at the University of Illinois, 25 October 2013.

2. Programs at the University of California, Los Angeles, the University of Illinois at Urbana-Champaign, Wesleyan University, and the University of Washington all began around this time.

3. Jahangir's father was the great Akbar, and his son was Shah Jahan, builder of the Taj Mahal.

4. Again, literary criticism seems prescient in this regard (cf. White 2008; Elias 2008; Poster 2008; Gumbrecht 2008).

5. For a useful, albeit different perspective on music issues in the academy, see Narmour 2011.

6. "Turns" are a favorite trope and include ethical, global, historic, interpretive, and political turns.

7. I say rediscovery because the problem of subjectivity has itself a long and distinguished genealogy.

8. For an exceptionally illuminating overview of these stances, see Susan McClary's very positive review of Richard Taruskin's six-volume *The Oxford History of Western Music* (McClary 2006). She also takes him to task about what he had left out, for example, "It's a dirty job factoring in popular music, but somebody's got to do it. Because like it or not, it's history" (McClary 2006:414).

9. For a trenchant critique in another area, that of Indian history generally, see Eaton 2000.

10. www.bruno-latour.fr/node/64. The introduction is available at the same site as a PDF file.

11. See Agawu 1997. A recent and useful overview including ethnomusicology's own turn to the study of Western music is Nooshin 2011.

12. Bruno Nettl reminds me that he always insisted that the term "musicology" should include both historical and ethnomusicology, and that "musicology" alone

ought not to be used as a synonym for historical musicology. For purposes of my discussion, however, I am sometimes conflating the term musicology with historical musicology. Still, it appears in my readings that traditional musicologists seem to prefer the expression music anthropology to ethnomusicology, suggesting ownership of the rubric "musicology" remains much contested.

13. Susan McClary draws attention to the limitations of a wholly "literate" approach in musicology (McClary 2006:413).

14. Of course, ethnomusicologists occasionally use them, but most studies do not rely on the mainly audio archives that ethnomusicologists have founded.

15. Held at the University of Chicago on 16 September 2013.

16. Philip Yampolsky stresses the importance of commercial recordings (cf. Yampolsky 2013 and in his contribution to the present volume).

17. See, for example, research.microsoft.com/apps/pubs/?id=198396 and autrimncpa.wordpress.com/ for Indian examples.

References

Agawu, Kofi. 1997. "Analyzing Music under the New Musicological Regime." *Journal of Musicology* 15(3): 297–307.

Bergeron, Katherine, and Philip V. Bohlman, eds. 1992. *Disciplining Music: Musicology and Its Canons*. Chicago: University of Chicago Press.

Botstein, Leon. 1994. "Review of *Disciplining Music: Musicology and Its Canons*." *Journal of the American Musicological Society* 47(2): 340–47.

Doron, Assa, and Robin Jeffrey. 2013. *The Great Indian Phone Book*. Cambridge, MA: Harvard University Press.

Eaton, Richard M. 2000. "(Re)Imag(in)Ing Otherness: A Postmortem for the Postmodern in India." *Journal of World History* 11(1): 57–78.

Edwardes, Michael. 1960. *The Orchid House*. London: Cassell.

Elias, Amy J. 2008. "Interactive Cosmopolitanism and Collaborative Technologies: New Foundations for Global Literary History." *New Literary History* 39(3): 705–25.

Foster, Willam, ed. 1921. *Early Travels in India 1583–1619*. Edited by Nicholas Withington. London: Oxford University Press.

Gumbrecht, Hans Ulrich. 1997. *In 1926: Living at the Edge of Time*. Cambridge, MA: Harvard University Press.

———. 2008. "Shall We Continue to Write Histories of Literature?" *New Literary History* 39(3): 519–32.

Lal, Vinay. 2001. "Subaltern Studies and Its Critics: Debates over Indian History." *History and Theory* 40(1): 135–48.

Latour, Bruno. 2004. "Why Has Critique Run out of Steam? From Matters of Fact to Matters of Concern." *Critical Inquiry* 30(2): 225–48.

Latour, Bruno, and Catherine Porter. 2013. *An Inquiry into Modes of Existence: An Anthropology of the Moderns*. Cambridge, MA: Harvard University Press.

Magriel, Nicolas, and Lalita du Perron. 2013. *The Songs of Khayal*, two volumes. New Delhi: Manohar.

McClary, Susan. 2006. "The World According to Taruskin." *Music and Letters* 87(3): 408–15.

Miner, Allyn. 1993. *Sitar and Sarod in the 18th and 19th Centuries*. Wilhelmshaven: Noetzel.

Narmour, Eugene. 2011. "Our Varying Histories and Future Potential: Models and Maps in Science, the Humanities, and in Music Theory." *Music Perception* 29(1): 1–21.

Nettl, Bruno. 2002. *Encounters in Ethnomusicology: A Memoir*. Warren, MI: Harmonie Park Press.

———. 2013. *Becoming an Ethnomusicologist: A Miscellany of Influences*. Lanham, MD: Scarecrow Press.

Neuman, Daniel M. 1980. *The Life of Music in North India: The Organization of an Artistic Tradition*. Detroit, MI: Wayne State University Press.

Neuman, Daniel M., and Shubha Chaudhuri, with Komal Kothari. 2006. *Bards, Ballads and Boundaries: An Ethnographic Atlas of Music Traditions in West Rajasthan*. Kolkata: Seagull.

Nooshin, Laudan. 2011. "Introduction to the Special Issue: The Ethnomusicology of Western Art Music." *Ethnomusicology Forum* 20(3): 285–300.

Poster, Mark. 2008. "Global Media and Culture." *New Literary History* 39(3): 685–703.

Qureshi, Regula Burckhardt. 1995. "Music Anthropologies and Music Histories: A Preface and an Agenda." *Journal of the American Musicological Society* 48(3): 331–42.

Savage, Roger W. H. 2009. "Crossing the Disciplinary Divide: Hermeneutics, Ethnomusicology and Musicology." *College Music Symposium* 49/50: 402–8.

Schofield, Katherine Butler. 2013. "Chief Musicians to the Mughal Emperors: The Delhi Kalāwant Birāderī, 17th to 19th Centuries." Unpublished manuscript.

Seeger, Anthony. 1987. *Why Suyá Sing: A Musical Anthropology of an Amazonian People*. Cambridge: Cambridge University Press.

Sleeman, W. H. 1858. *A Journey through the Kingdom of Oudh in 1849–1850*, two volumes. London: Richard Bentley.

Stobart, Henry, ed. 2008. *The New (Ethno)Musicologies*. Lanham, MD: Scarecrow Press.

Taruskin, Richard. 1989. "Resisting the Ninth." *19th-Century Music* 12(3): 241–56.

———. 2005. *The Oxford History of Western Music*, six volumes. New York: Oxford University Press.

Walser, Robert. 1993. Review of *Disciplining Music: Musicology and Its Canons*. *Music and Letters* 74(4): 569–72.

White, Hayden. 2008. "Commentary: 'With No Particular Place to Go': Literary History in the Age of the Global Picture." *New Literary History* 39(3): 727–45.

Wood, Abigail. 2008. "E-Fieldwork: A Paradigm for the Twenty-First Century?" In *The New (Ethno)Musicologies*, edited by Henry Stobart, 170–87. Lanham, MD: Scarecrow Press.

Yampolsky, Philip. 2013. "Three Genres of Indonesian Popular Music: Their Trajectories in the Colonial Era and After." *Asian Music* 44(2): 24–80.

CHAPTER ELEVEN

Comparative Musicologists in the Field

Reflections on the Cairo Congress of Arab Music, 1932

A. J. Racy

The history of ethnomusicology is the history of fieldwork.

—Bruno Nettl, *The Study of Ethnomusicology*

In recent decades, ethnomusicologists have taken special interest in the topic of fieldwork. They frequently discuss the relation between field research and the researcher's own theoretical perspective and, as Bruno Nettl has noted, the social and intellectual backgrounds of the researchers themselves (1983:29–40). Obviously, scholarly orientations, and by extension field inquiries, have changed significantly. In this study, I revisit the field research carried out by the European comparative musicologists in Egypt in connection with the 1932 Cairo Congress of Arab Music. Envisioning these scholars' work in the field closely—"in practice" or "on the ground"—I attempt to gain a closer look at the connections between musical worldviews and field applications. I also hope to shed light on these scholars' research methods, which, though they may have differed significantly from other research orientations, have in some ways left a lasting imprint on ethnomusicology.[1]

The Cairo Encounter

The 1932 Congress of Arab Music, held between 14 March and 3 April at Cairo's Eastern Music Academy (Ma'had al-Mūsīqá al-Sharqī),[2] was a landmark in the history of Arab and Egyptian music. It was particularly remarkable because of its international and interdisciplinary orientation, for it hosted dozens of distinguished Europeans and Middle Easterners, including music historians, composers, theorists, educators, and instrument makers, as well as musicians (figure 11.1). Among the prominent figures at the Congress were the German composer Paul Hindemith, the Czech composer Alois Hába (known for employing microtonality), and the music historian and specialist in medieval Arab music Henry George Farmer. Participants from neighboring countries included the notable Turkish music theorist and composer Rauf Yektah Bey (1871–1935), the Turkish composer and performer on the *tanbur* (long-necked lute) and the cello Mes'ut Camil (Mas'ūd Jamīl) Bey (1902–1963), and the well-known Syrian composer and music savant Shaykh 'Alī al-Darwīsh (1884–1952). Also present were several performing ensembles that included singers and instrumentalists, most prominently from Iraq and North Africa, as well as from Egypt itself.

In this chapter I focus on the distinguished group of European comparative musicologists associated with the Berlin School, primarily Erich M. von Hornbostel (1877–1935), Curt Sachs (1881–1959), and Robert Lachmann

Figure 11.1. Participants at the 1932 Cairo Congress (Kitāb Mu'tamar al-Mūsīqá al-'Arabiyyah 1933, 40 verso)

(1892–1939), and other notable guests, especially Béla Bartók (1881–1945). Several Berlin scholars already had educational and research connections with the German-educated Egyptian music scholar and historian Dr. Maḥmūd al-Ḥifnī (1896–1973).[3] In collaboration with the French musicologist and expert on Arab music Baron Rodolphe d'Erlanger (1872–1932), who incidentally was unable to attend the Congress, al-Ḥifnī played an important role in organizing the Congress event. The Congress centered on committee work. Depending on his or her specialty, each participant was assigned to one of seven specialized committees, usually containing both local and international members.

The Congress event was well documented. In 1933 the general Congress Committee published *Kitāb Mu'tamar al-Mūsīqá al-'Arabiyyah* (KMM'A), or the Book of the Congress of Arab Music, in Arabic, with a 1934 rendition in French (see *Recueil des Travaux* 1934). An all-encompassing volume, KMM'A incorporated committee proceedings, including their deliberations and recommendations.[4] It also contained a copious collection of photographic illustrations of musical instruments, musicians, musical ensembles, and schoolchildren's music groups, and, quite importantly, a substantial inventory of sound recordings made by the Recording Committee and subsequently issued on 78-rpm discs by the British company Gramophone on its His Master's Voice label. Dominated by the comparative musicologists, this particular committee consisted of fourteen members working under Robert Lachmann, among them Bartók, Chottin, and Hornbostel. At the Congress, the Committee was able to record musicians from different countries, including Morocco, Algeria, Tunisia, Iraq, and Turkey, as well as Egypt.

The Egyptian Setting

Invited guests who arrived at Cairo in March 1932 may have encountered a country that seemed both very old and very new. Egypt may have impressed them for its pyramids, the eternal Nile, the pharaonic antiquities, the old palaces and mosques, and the country's ethnic and religious diversity. At the time, however, Egypt had already been touched by decades of European influence, at least since the Napoleonic occupation of Egypt (1798–1805). Apart from the British protectorate over Egypt (1882–1922), moreover, the country had enjoyed a significant measure of political autonomy. Under the originally non-Egyptian Khedival dynasty, which ruled Egypt beginning with Muḥammad 'Alī (r. 1805–1848) and continued through the middle of the twentieth century, the country made significant contact with the West. Many rulers were known for their efforts to westernize Egypt by emulating

European educational, military, and artistic models. The importation of Western culture reached its height under the cosmopolitan Khedive Ismāʼīl (r. 1863–1879), who, aside from sponsoring local Egyptian musicians, built the Cairo Opera House and commissioned Verdi's *Aida* for the inauguration of the Suez Canal (constructed 1859–1869).[5]

By World War I, Cairo had witnessed a flourishing theatrical movement with local acting troupes that sometimes presented Arabic adaptations of European classical dramas. Similarly popular were musical plays, or operettas, for example, those by the modernist Egyptian composer Shaykh Sayyid Darwīsh (1892–1923). Moreover, commercial sound recording had become well established in Cairo since the early years of the twentieth century (Racy 1976:23–48). Soon thereafter, Egypt developed an influential film industry, which released its first sound film in 1932.

In 1932, many Egyptians were concerned about their nation's own historical past and its present position in the modern world. A scenario of progress inspired the official agenda of the 1932 Congress, whose prestigious sponsor was none other than the country's highest-ranking figure, the youngest son of Khedive Ismāʼīl, Aḥmad Fuʼād Pasha (1868–1936), or King Fuʼād himself. Fuʼād was European-educated and was impressed by the West. Acquiring the title of king in 1922, he is known for his interest in military and educational affairs, for serving as rector (1908–1913) of Cairo University, and for inaugurating the Eastern Music Academy in 1929 (figure 11.2).

Local Musical Outlooks

The Congress's official mission was expressed in general yet clearly ambitious terms. In his introduction to KMMʼA, al-Ḥifnī wrote about the king "taking upon his shoulders elevating Arab music to the high level that it shall be worthy of, and eventually, making the music widely known and promising to promote its evolution" (KMMʼA 1933:19).[6] Al-Ḥifnī detailed how the idea of a congress came about during one of Cairo's auspicious events:

> When his Majesty obliged to officially inaugurate the [Eastern Music] Academy on 26 December in 1929, he expressed his noble desire to plan a congress for Arab music to take place in Egypt, and in which Western researchers who are connected with music would meet together in order to discuss all that is needed to help civilize it [Egyptian music], teach it, and set it on fixed and recognized scientific principles. Since then, the preparatory work for this congress began under the sponsorship of his Majesty and through his gracious guidance.

Figure 11.2. The Eastern Music Academy, where the Congress convened (Kitāb Mu'tamar al-Mūsīqá al-'Arabiyyah 1933, 48 verso)

> Then, in the Spring of 1930 the Academy, with the approval of the Ministry of Public Education, brought in his Honor Professor Dr. Curt Sachs, who teaches music at the University of Berlin to give his opinion on related technical issues. In a report that he submitted, he endorsed the idea of holding the congress and gave his input on this matter. (KMM'A 1933:19)

In essence, the articulation of the congress plan, which carried distinct evolutionist overtones, emphasized: (a) the need to develop or promote the evolution (*taṭwīr*)[7] of local music, and (b) to seek Western expertise, in other words the advice of foreign (*ajānib*) specialists.[8] This plan meant emulating Europe's patterns of historical and cultural "progress," through "reviving and systematizing Arab music so that it will rise upon a proper artistic foundation, as did Western music earlier" (KMM'A 1933:23). The salient view was that the Arab world had witnessed a golden era at the height of medieval Islamic civilization, but later had undergone drastic decline. It was not until the recent Khedival epoch that Egypt had begun to experience a national and cultural renaissance. Such reawakening, however, had to be nourished through innovation and modernization, as well as through the reassessment of local cultural expression and cultivating a new local music that was "scientific" and "advanced." The underlying assumption was that "catching up" with the West could be officially expedited and systematically induced through official decrees and government programs.

The Comparativist Worldview

The scholarly outlooks of the comparative musicologists were compatible with those of many Western social scientists of the time (Nettl 1984:39). While accepting the broader implications of cultural evolution, the comparativists explained the world's variety of musical traditions as diverse evolutionary processes that were old, gradual, and discrete. Revolution, thus, could not simply be induced, or even tampered with, using short-term and expedient policies. As Robert Lachmann explained at the Congress, such endeavors would be artificial and arbitrary and would work against the natural flow of history (KMM'A 1933:439). Because of different evolutionary histories, world communities had developed their own racial, cultural, and musical traits (Hornbostel 1933:17).

Unlike the binary East vs. West worldview held by many Near Easterners, especially in Egypt, the comparative musicologists took account of the entire world's rich cultural and musical diversity. They were particularly interested in musical profiles that were "pure," "authentic," and "old," criteria that, at least implicitly, contrasted with more recent urban musics of the West. The notions of folk culture and, by extension, folk music seemed to embrace a particular significance. As Bartók stressed, folk music was not only old and pure, but also vigorous and spontaneous (cf. Bartók 1976a, 1976b). It was largely connected with people's livelihood and survival. Presumably, it was least affected by urban music, considered by Bartók and others as being largely impure and of recent origins. Folk music was communally shared and maintained. The glorification of individual composers was a Western trait that was incompatible with the orally transmitted music of peasants and tribal groups (see Nettl 1984:39). This view was clearly expressed at the Congress by Lachmann, who stressed that "in our concern for the future of Eastern music, we are not interested merely in the artistic level of professionals and the benefit of the listeners, but also in the people's musical feelings, whose manifestations frequently emanate spontaneously throughout daily life" (KMM'A 1933:440). Ultimately, the comparativists advocated the preservation of the world's old and pure musical traditions, which were in increasing danger of being uprooted or diluted by urban and modern Western styles. With this in mind Robert Lachmann expressed an urgent desire to preserve the "timelessness" of the Eastern world's oral musics (Bohlman and Davis 2007:116).

The Field Mission

Representing their own discipline, *vergleichende Musikwissenschaft*, the Western Recording Committee members viewed themselves as comparative musical scientists who sought direct contact with the music. Their domain of activity emphasized recording in the field using the phonograph as their paramount tool of research. As music historians at the Congress discussed early manuscripts, educators explored modern teaching methods, music theorists proposed a universal "Arab scale" with fixed intervals, and instrument makers displayed their equal-tempered quarter-tone pianos; it is no wonder that the comparativists were so enthusiastic about going to the field.[9] For them, the field recording project, designed to be continued by the Egyptians themselves, aimed at preserving the local musical heritage and making it available as an indigenous source of inspiration for present and future Egyptian musicians, composers, and educators. Besides being archived and made accessible for scholars and scientists, the recorded material would also be played at Egyptian schools and listened to through local radio broadcasts.

The Recording Project

In the field, recording took place with technical assistance from the British Gramophone company through its local Egyptian music director, a musician and also a member of the Recording Committee, Manṣūr 'Awaḍ (1880–1954). Recording may have taken place at Cairo locations designated by the company's recording staff. The recording project, however, extended beyond Cairo. With local logistic support, Robert Lachmann took an entire month (7 April to 6 May) to visit and record music in various Egyptian rural areas. His recording tour included visits to villages of the Delta, the Luxor area and the outer oases, the Fayyūm region, and Bedouin groups in the Sinai. After the Congress, he provided a report documenting his findings (see KMM'A 1933:129–32).

The Recording Committee followed a number of guidelines. In principle, the recorded material had to be pure, locally representative, and devoid of foreign, especially Western, influences. For field documentation, certain procedures were implemented: ending the discs with a note A on a pitch pipe to synchronize the disc speed with the original pitch of the performance; ending the disc by sounding the open strings, for example, on such instruments as the *santur*; announcing the names of the pieces at the beginning of the disc; and in some cases ending with a single-measure demonstration of the metric mode used in the recorded performance.[10]

The emphasis on authentic, and presumably old, musical expressions was a guiding principle. Besides the fifty-two listed discs of urban Egyptian secular music, the recorded Egyptian repertory included three records of *baladī*, or folk-oriented music, by the singer Muḥammad al-'Arabī and his ensemble; two records of *'awālim*, professional female singers, who traditionally performed folk songs at weddings; five records of folk dance music; three records of music by Bedouin nomads from the Fayyūm area; two discs of *zār* music, used for spirit-possession healing rituals; eight records of Sufi music by the Mawlawiyyah (Mevlevi) order; five records featuring *dhkir*, or Sufi ritual music, by the Laythī order (both Sufi groups reportedly no longer exist in Egypt); and nine records of Coptic church music. Within the entire collection of Egyptian recordings, this portion (thirty-seven discs) was relatively sizable, as well as geographically and stylistically varied. The Committee's strong interest in recording ritual-related music was reflected in a commentary by Johannes Wolf, a member of the German group at the Congress: "But the greatest attention and interest was certainly paid to the folk musicians: folk singers and sorceresses who, through hypnosis and music brought young girls to dance until they collapsed unconscious, also Negroes with work songs, dancing dervishes, *fallāḥīn* [peasants] with their primitive songs, and many others" (Wolf 1932:122).

Meanwhile, regardless of genre, the Committee sought to record what seemed unique and historically interesting. In post-Congress commentaries, Curt Sachs explained that at the Congress, Moroccan Andalusian music was particularly interesting because "more than information about Eastern music is what we can gain in knowledge about Western music of the Middle Ages" (Sachs 1933:18). Hornbostel stated that the Iraqi troupe, which presented a locally established repertory known generically as *maqām 'Irāqī* (Iraqi maqām), was "probably the best representative of the various delegations from the Arab nations" (Hornbostel 1933:17). By the same token, however, Bartók expressed disdain toward the urban ensemble from Syria, thus commenting sarcastically that "when stale waltz and gallop imitations were served up by a Syrian city Orchestra (the first violin's compositions, in a marvelous notation), we were anything but pleased; in fact, we unanimously voiced our displeasure" (Bartók 1976c:38). Similarly, Hornbostel lamented the hegemony of the Western violin in Arab music because this instrument brought in with it such things as the European vibrato and sentimentality, adding that: "especially painful is this manner of playing music, to the very expressive 'Planets Dance' of the Whirling Dervishes. What comes out is a laughable travesty—the Syrian new music composers evoke visions of splashing about in the waves of Danube" (1933:17). In light of such purist attitudes, we may speculate why the Syrian ensemble was not recorded save for one disc of *taqāsīm*, or instrumental improvisation, on the *qānūn* (plucked zither). We may similarly conjecture why the Congress's Egyptian urban recordings seemed to eliminate the violin and to restrict the performances to two or three traditional instruments, usually the *qānūn*, the *'ūd*, and the *riqq*, in addition to a singer and a few vocal accompanists.[11]

Lack of interest in celebrities was also clear. The Congress seemed little concerned with the professional musical milieu of Cairo. Although the singer Umm Kulthūm was invited to give an evening concert at the Congress, those who were recorded were chosen primarily for their knowledge of the traditional repertories. For example, on the twenty-three discs of Eastern Arab *muwashshaḥāt* (singular *muwashshaḥ*, a traditional vocal genre), the singer was Shaykh Darwīsh al-Ḥarīrī, a well-recognized authority on this musical genre. Similarly, Dāwud Ḥusnī, who sang on many Congress discs, was a highly respected traditional composer. Muḥammad Najīb, Muḥammad al-Baḥr, and 'Azīz 'Uthmān knew the musical heritage firsthand. 'Uthmān rendered a number of *adāwr* (singular *dawr*, a traditional Egyptian vocal genre that gradually phased out after the 1930s) composed by renowned late nineteenth-century composers, such as his father Muḥammad 'Uthmān (1855–1900) and 'Abduh al-Ḥāmūlī (1843–1901). Al-Baḥr sang theatrical and nationalistic popular songs by his father, Sayyid Darwīsh.

The Congress performances by these Egyptian artists can be contrasted with others that had been available on commercial recordings; they provided good representations of the sonorities, intricate group interactions, and complex heterophonic effects typical of Cairo's musical mainstream. The mainstream repertory, furthermore, was directly linked to the feeling of *ṭarab*, the ecstatic state that indigenous music evoked and that was often mediated through the recordings of the inspired artists (see Racy 2003). By comparison, the Congress recordings of Egyptian urban music seem austere and static. They tend to present the music not as a process generated through spontaneous creativity and individual display of talent, but rather in terms of self-contained musical documents, or "works." These Egyptian records have left little room for improvisation. Although improvisatory segments would have been included on other Congress recordings, essentially we find no separate urban Egyptian recordings of *taqāsīm*.

Meanwhile, the comparativists' aversion to musical westernization and their lack of interest in novel creations by individual celebrities may explain the somewhat "traditionalized" Congress renditions of Sayyid Darwīsh's urban popular songs. Darwīsh's commercial recordings occasionally incorporated polyphony and used such instruments as the piano, violin, and Western flute. The Congress recordings of his works, however, used minimal, basically monophonic instrumental accompaniment on a few traditional instruments in renditions that may have seemed sterile or musically subdued to the record audiences of the 1920s and 1930s. This and other comparable treatments may have constituted a compromise of sorts, namely between the Egyptian Committee members, who viewed Darwīsh's music as being basic to Egypt's futuristic vision, and the Western comparativists, who sought to exclude musical manifestations that to them may have seemed inauthentic or foreign.

Conclusions

By reflecting upon the comparative musicologists' contributions to the 1932 Cairo Congress of Arab Music, this chapter provides fresh insights into both the research legacy of these European scholars and the modalities of field research in general. To begin with, the discussion has illustrated the complexities of fieldwork as an experience. At the Congress, the scholars seemed to acquire roles that extended beyond conventional fieldwork. They were viewed and treated as educators, world-music experts, foreign consultants, field scholars, and musical visionaries. Their multilayered profile as such may have both complicated their research mission and aroused their enthusiasm and anticipation, given their systemic and reform-minded outlooks. Today, such multitasking finds parallels in our own research as ethnomusicologists. We often find that our fieldwork is not limited to work in the field; rather, it becomes entangled with such domains as public relations and social obligations, and even with local political and nationalist agendas. In reality, the concept of "field" may transcend the narrowly defined concept of physical or sonic space, or the mere implementation of conventional research tools.[12]

My research also calls attention to the delicate power relations implicit in field research, in particular, with the comparativists' own positioning as foreign guests vis-à-vis the Egyptians' role as hosts. For their part, the guests may have assumed a sense of privilege as Europeans, as well as experts and educators in their own right. At the same time, they may have felt a genuine sense of indebtedness to those who had welcomed them in their own country. In turn, the locals may have claimed certain prerogatives as hosts. A significant number of local participants may have already possessed added social and political capital, as Egyptian administrators, government officials, music educators, and locally well-connected individuals.[13] Their prestige, furthermore, may have been boosted symbolically through the use of Cairo's impressive Eastern Music Academy as the Congress venue. They would have looked, nevertheless, at their distinguished invitees with certain deference. Such an intricate relation between the two differently positioned groups is encountered in our own experiences as modern ethnomusicologists, especially when we interact with our foreign, or "native," field sponsors. In such contexts, we negotiate our own research space in light of both our and their, real or perceived, prerogatives and obligations.

More specifically, this chapter shows how such negotiations shape field research itself. In this case, the recording project was entrusted to a relatively sizable committee. Thus, the work in the field, including the process of decision making, may have been complicated, especially given the striking differences between the musical and cultural outlooks. At least on the surface, the comparativists' position was firmly held and methodically implemented. The work conducted, especially through the input of the committee's chair, Robert Lachmann, clearly reflected these scholars' musical perspectives. In retrospect, these scholars seemed to maintain strong loyalties to their own disciplinary paradigm, especially in comparison to other scholars who in later years upheld the tenets of cultural relativism. Ironically, perhaps, the comparativists' forthright subjectivity reminds us of our present acknowledgment of the researcher's own individuality, and of the biases typifying scholarly disciplines in general.

A closer look at the work of the Recording Committee reveals a certain measure of cross-cultural or cross-musicological negotiation. The recorded material attests to notable compromises between the foreign comparativists and their local colleagues. Local input may have played a key role in the decision to record a significant collection of urban performances, for example, of traditional dawr compositions and of modern Darwīsh songs. Such gestures of compromise may have foreshadowed our own dialectical interactions with our local field collaborators, as interpreters and research partners.

To close, the comparative musicologists, though their individual backgrounds and interests varied, seemed to espouse a study approach that was theoretically coherent, as well as practically motivated. From our present perspective, their own convictions may appear rigid and single-minded, and their broader mission may seem extremely idealistic, romantic, and utopian. In many respects, their research agendas are different from ours (see Fargion 2009). Arguably, their fundamental rationale for preservation has become less of a focus in our own field research. Similarly, their ambitious reformist projections, which, as time has shown, appear to have left little impact on Egypt's contemporary musical scene (Racy 1991:87–90), may have become less central to our ethnomusicological investigations. On a certain human and practical level, however, I use this chapter to show that the field-related encounters, dilemmas, and strategies of 1932 are by no means foreign to our present experiences as field workers and musical analysts. In particular, the Recording Committee's discs must be recognized for their potential musical and scholarly significance. Despite their overall idiosyncratic traits and the minimal ethnographic documentation, they capture the impressive artistry of traditional Arab world ensembles and the performance legacies of little-known Egyptian folk singers, healers, and mystics. They also memorialize musical practices that may have significantly changed or no longer exist today. Last but not least, the field recordings constitute a rare sonic representation of a significant stage in the development of ethnomusicology as a discipline.

Notes

1. This study draws upon my previous related research (Racy 1991, 1992). I am thankful to Tony Hampton, Dr. Barbara Racy, and others who have contributed in various ways to the preparation of the original manuscript of this work.

2. In Arabic usage, the term "*Sharqī*," like the term "Oriental," literally, "Eastern," is applied specifically to the Near or Middle East.

3. In his probing book on the Congress, Victor Saḥḥāb wrote that al-Ḥifnī received his higher education in Berlin, where he earned a doctorate in musicology in 1930 with a dissertation on the medieval music theorist Ibn Sīna. In Berlin al-Ḥifnī studied with distinguished scholars, including Hornbostel, Lachmann, Wolf, and Sachs. Robert Lachmann and he also translated a treatise by the medieval theorist al-Kindī into German. In Egypt, al-Ḥifnī played an active role in promoting music education (Saḥḥāb 1997:60, 226).

4. For specific information on the individual Congress committees and their work, see Racy 1991.

5. At the inauguration, Verdi's *Rigoletto* was presented, since *Aida* was not ready for the event. For more information on this event and on Cairo's music in the late nineteenth and early twentieth centuries, see Racy 1983.

6. In this chapter, all translations from the Arabic language are by the author.

7. The concept of *taṭwīr* was a central theme in the local Congress-related rhetoric and to a large extent has continued to dominate the Egyptian modernist discourse. Whereas the term *taṭawwur* is equivalent to the intransitive English verb "to evolve," the favored Egyptian usage has been the transitive verb *taṭwīr*, which translates as "to make something evolve."

8. In Arabic usage, *ajānib* (sing., *ajnabī*) literally means "foreigners," but strongly implies that they would be European, or Westerners.

9. Such enthusiasm was expressed by Bartók as follows: "Since we dealt with the kinds of Arabic music still living, rather than with abstract or theoretical questions concerning it, a consequence of our activity was a much closer contact with Arabic life than had our colleagues in the other sections. No wonder they envied us a little!" (Bartók 1976c:33).

10. My observations on the recorded material are based on listening to copies of Congress discs found during 1971 and 1972 in Cairo collections, as well as to recent selective releases of Congress recordings mostly by Europe-based institutions.

11. Similarly, the Musical Instruments Committee under Curt Sachs advised against the use of the cello and the double bass in Arab music, given their domineering sound and their repertory's tendency to evoke extreme emotional indulgence, excessive sentimentality, and "shedding of tears."

12. For recent discussions on field-related human interactions, see Titon 2008:25–41. For the expanded nature of the "field" as a site of investigation, see Cooley, Meizel, and Syed 2008:90–107.

13. Apparently, the prominence of high-ranking Egyptians at the Congress, including Congress planners such as al-Ḥifnī, evoked strong criticism from many well-known Egyptian musicians, who felt ignored or excluded. For more on Congress politics, see Saḥḥāb 1997:41–45.

References

Bartók, Béla. 1976a. "What is Folk Music?" In *Béla Bartók Essays*, edited by Benjamin Suchoff, 5–8. New York: St. Martin's Press.

———. 1976b. "Comparative Music Folklore." In *Béla Bartók Essays*, edited by Benjamin Suchoff, 155–63. New York: St. Martin's Press.

———. 1976c. "At the Congress for Arab Music—Cairo, 1932." In *Béla Bartók Essays*, edited by Benjamin Suchoff, 38–39. New York: St. Martin's Press.

Bohlman, Philip V., and Ruth F. Davis. 2007. "*Mizrakh*, Jewish Music and the Journey to the East." In *Music and Orientalism in the British Empire, 1780s–1940s: Portrayal of the East*, edited by Martin Clayton and Bennett Zon, 95–125. Aldershot: Ashgate.

Cooley, Timothy J., Katherine Meizel, and Nasir Syed. 2008. "Virtual Fieldwork: Three Case Studies." In *Shadows in the Field: New Perspectives for Fieldwork in Ethnomusicology*, second edition, revised, edited by Gregory Barz and Timothy J. Cooley, 90–107. New York: Oxford University Press.

Fargion, Janet Topp. 2009. "'For My Own Research Purposes?': Examining Ethnomusicology Field Methods for a Sustainable Music." *World of Music* 51(1): 75–93.

Hornbostel, Erich M. von. 1933. "Zum Kongress für arabische Musik-Kairo 1932." *Zeitschrift für vergleichende Musikwissenschaft* 1: 16–17.

Kitāb Mu'tamar al-Mūsīqá al-'Arabiyyah (KMM'A). 1933. Cairo: al-Maṭba'ah al Amīriyyah bil-Qāhirah.

Nettl, Bruno. 1983. *The Study of Ethnomusicology: Twenty-Nine Issues and Concepts*. Urbana: University of Illinois Press.

———. 1984. "Western Musical Values and the Character of Ethnomusicology." *World of Music* 24(1): 29–40.

Racy, A. J. 1976. "Record Industry and Egyptian Traditional Music: 1904–1932." *Ethnomusicology* 2(1): 23–48.

———. 1983. "Music in Nineteenth-Century Egypt: An Historical Sketch." *Selected Reports in Ethnomusicology* 4: 157–79.

———. 1991. "Historical Worldviews of Early Ethnomusicologists: An East-West Encounter in Cairo, 1932." In *Ethnomusicology and Modern Music History*, edited by Stephen Blum, Philip V. Bohlman, and Daniel M. Neuman, 68–91. Urbana: University of Illinois Press.

———. 1992. "Musicologues Comparatistes Europeens et Musique Egyptienne au Congrès du Caire." In *Musique Arabe: Le Congrès du Caire de 1932*, 109–22. Cairo: CEDEJ.

———. 2003. *Making Music in the Arab World: The Culture and Artistry of Ṭarab*. Cambridge: Cambridge University Press.

Recueil des Travaux du Congrès de Musique Arabe. 1934. Cairo: Imprimerie Nationale Boulac.

Sachs, Curt. 1933. "Zum Kongress für Arabische Musik–Kairo 1932: Die Marokkaner." *Zeitschrift für vergleichende Musikwissenschaft* 1: 17–18.

Saḥḥāb, Victor. 1997. *Mu'tamar al-Mūsīqá al-'Arabiyyah al-Awwal, al-Qāhirah 1932*. Beirut: Al-Sharikah al-'ālamiyyah li al-kitāb.

Titon, Jeff Todd. 2008. "Knowing Fieldwork." In *Shadows in the Field: New Perspectives for Fieldwork in Ethnomusicology*, second edition, revised, edited by Gregory Barz and Timothy J. Cooley, 25–41. New York: Oxford University Press.

Wolf, Johannes. 1932. "Die Tagung über arabische Musikreform in Kairo." *Deutsche Tonkünstler-Zeitung* 30(1): 121–22.

CHAPTER TWELVE

Ethnomusicological Marginalia

On Reading Charles Seeger Reading The Anthropology of Music

Anthony Seeger

"Well, that's a question I've never been asked, and I'm not even sure I know the true answer," responded Bruno Nettl in an e-mail replying to a query from me on 18 June 2013 (Nettl 2013b).[1] That encouraged me to write this essay, because in eighty-five active years he had probably been asked about—or written about—almost everything else. The question I had posed to him was how he keeps track of the ideas in all the books he reads and uses in his extensively documented discussions of the history of ethnomusicology. This appears to be a research technique ethnomusicologists have not much reflected upon, even in the shadows of our field.[2] For those of us learning the field, teaching, or advising before online library catalogs and Google Scholar, the handiest source of bibliography on any given topic in ethnomusicology was often to be found at the back of Bruno Nettl's books. We had them on our shelves, and they were extensive and helpful. I had asked him whether he put checkmarks next to key points, underlined text, or put pieces of paper between the pages. Did he take notes, or did he just tuck things away in his mind for later recall? He replied: "I guess I have done a little of all the things you mention, but I haven't been the least bit systematic. Early in my life I did have an exceptionally good memory and felt I could remember everything without taking notes. And later I began to place bits of paper as bookmarks, or write some notes in separate notebooks and rarely (but sometimes) underlined or marked passages. Most typically, I guess, I'd do what is the least efficient: try to remember what of interest I read in a book or article, and later look through it and try to find the citation I like" (Nettl 2013b).

One of the striking features of *Nettl's Elephant: On the History of Ethnomusicology* is his personal and autobiographical insertions in the historical essays (Nettl 2010). Arguing that he was born into musicology and has grown old with the discipline of ethnomusicology (see also Nettl 2013a), he was a contemporary of the founding of both the Society for Ethnomusicology and the early years of the International Folk Music Council (now called the International Council for Traditional Music). In celebration of his eighty-fifth birthday, I write here about how one of his colleagues, Charles Seeger (1886–1979)—whose involvement in musicology predated Nettl's by about forty years—read books. Like Bruno Nettl, I am part of this story, because I discuss the books I inherited from Charles Seeger in 1979. I discuss how Seeger marked an important book in the history of ethnomusicology and figuratively look over his shoulder as he reads Alan Merriam's *The Anthropology of Music* (1964) by examining the markings he penciled in the margins.

I was teaching anthropology and ethnomusicology in Brazil when my grandfather Charles died in early 1979. Thus I missed the family celebration of his life, held that spring in Bridgewater, Connecticut, and documented in now-faded color photographs of his seven children and many of his grandchildren. When I visited the United States in 1980, however, I discovered I had inherited the books Charles had taken with him to his retirement in Bridgewater, his morning coat, and a Stetson hat. The hat was too big and the suit was too thin and long, but the books were very interesting indeed.

There were fewer books than I expected. I suspect Charles had thinned down his library when he left Los Angeles and moved to his sister's house in Bridgewater in 1971. His papers were deposited at the Library of Congress and some publications went to the UCLA Library. He kept some classics in ethnomusicology written by friends and colleagues, among them Gilbert Chase's *American Music* (1966), Mantle Hood's *The Ethnomusicologist* (1971), Jaap Kunst's *Ethno-Musicology* (1950, 1955, 1959), Alan Lomax's *Folk Song Style and Culture* (1968), Alan Merriam's *The Anthropology of Music* (1964), and Bruno Nettl's *Music in Primitive Culture* (1956). Some of these contained dedications; most did not. Charles had written his own name on the inside of Bruno Nettl's *Music in Primitive Culture* and may have purchased the book himself. I also received a full set of the journal *Ethnomusicology*, including the first mimeographed newsletters, which I added to my own set that began in the early 1970s. The other main subject matter of the books I received was philosophy, with both primary and secondary sources. When Charles left the University of California, Los Angeles, he was revising his essays for *Studies in Musicology 1935–1975* (1977), several of which required access to those volumes on philosophy. Bridgewater, in the far western part of Connecticut, did not have convenient research libraries nearby.

Marginalia

Anyone who has borrowed a library book knows that readers interact with books in many ways. Some mark interesting passages with small checkmarks, while others underline whole paragraphs, and still others make extensive comments wherever there is some white space. H. J. Jackson has written a very helpful introduction to the subject, filled with examples of the different ways readers have interacted with texts over the past three hundred years. Charles's markings conform to the general pattern she describes, with his name and a date on the flyleaf, interest lines and short comments in the margins next to specific passages, longer comments at the foot of the page, and more general discussions at the end of a chapter (Jackson 2001:36). Compared with some of her examples, Charles was a neat reader and parsimonious in his markings, except when reading published versions of his own articles, where he sometimes corrected typos and changed wording in the margins of his offprints. He always marked with a hard pencil and his marks are often quite faint and at times barely legible.[3] There were no slips of paper between the pages of his book, and I do not know if he kept separate reading notes. Like Bruno Nettl, he rarely underlined sections of text. Charles would usually simply mark an interesting paragraph or sentence in his books with a light vertical pencil mark. This is the most common mark in the books I surveyed. Occasionally, he would write a comment in the margin, like "WOW" and "to hell with attitude" (figure 12.1), and sometimes he would write longer comments at the bottom of the page or in white space at the end of a chapter.

Most of the books I inherited from Charles had neither dedications nor markings. Of the books I surveyed, Merriam's *The Anthropology of Music* (1964) had the most marginalia, with thirty marks of interest, three question marks, four "Xs" (indicating disagreement), and twenty-three comments in the margins. The number of marks indicates something about Charles's interest in the subject matter. In this case, however, they go beyond that and reveal something of his thinking on a number of ethnomusicological issues.

Reading Alan Merriam over Charles Seeger's Shoulder

It is hard to tell exactly when Charles read *The Anthropology of Music*. He wrote the year 1965 underneath his name on the upper right center of a

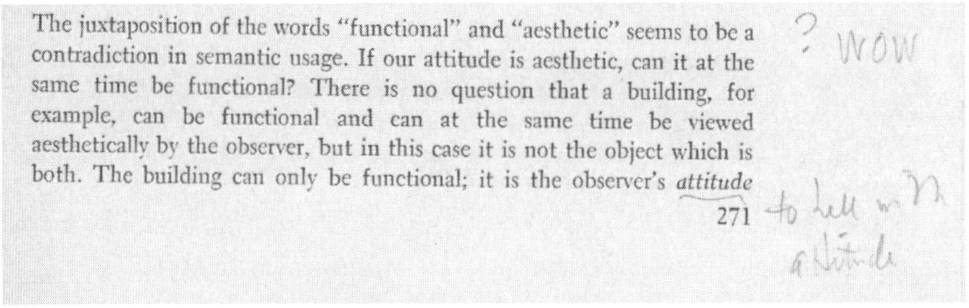

The juxtaposition of the words "functional" and "aesthetic" seems to be a contradiction in semantic usage. If our attitude is aesthetic, can it at the same time be functional? There is no question that a building, for example, can be functional and can at the same time be viewed aesthetically by the observer, but in this case it is not the object which is both. The building can only be functional; it is the observer's *attitude*

271

Figure 12.1. "WOW" and "To hell with attitude" from *The Anthropology of Music*, p. 271

brown page just inside the cover, but he may have read it somewhat later, perhaps before Merriam visited UCLA to give a series of lectures in May 1968.[4] From the comments about bimusicality I think Charles read the book during the years he was at UCLA (before 1971). This was not Charles's first close reading of and reaction to Merriam's work. He presented a response to Merriam's position paper at the 1962 meeting of the Society for Ethnomusicology, two years before the publication of *The Anthropology of Music*. Both the paper and Charles's response to it were published in the tenth-anniversary issue of *Ethnomusicology* (Merriam 1963; Seeger 1963).[5] Seeger and Merriam also both participated in a symposium at the University of Washington called "Symposium of the Current State of Research in Ethnomusicology" in March 1963 (the proceedings and discussions from this symposium are now available online; Garfias 2013a and 2013b). The proceedings reveal that Charles had certainly been exposed to Merriam's ideas before 1964.[6]

Charles's marks in *The Anthropology of Music* indicate that his attention was focused especially on part I, chapters 1 and 2 (Merriam 1964:3–16 and 17–36) and part III, chapters 11, 13, and 15 (209–28, 259–76, and 303–19). The bulk of his margin comments are in chapter 13. Here, I discuss only his reactions to chapters 2 (17–36) and 13 (259–76) because they receive the most comment. I indicate markings on the pages to these chapters in boldface in table 12.1.

Charles's marks in chapter 2 largely focus on a single subject, the importance of an ethnomusicologist's being able to create (perform or compose) in the tradition she or he is studying and the significance of musical knowledge as distinct from speech knowledge. Charles's criticisms of Merriam's presentation largely stem from his own writing about the linguo-centric predicament. Merriam draws a very hard and clear distinction between performance and analysis in this chapter and cites the philosopher Howard Gomes Cassidy

Table 12.1. Page numbers of marks in Charles Seeger's copy of Alan Merriam's *The Anthropology of Music*

Handwritten name and date on flyleaf	
Simple interest marks	viii; 8; 9; 10; 11; 13; **27**; **31**; **32**; 90; 210; 211; 212; 217; 220; 221; 223; 224; 225; 226; 227; **259**; **260**; **275**; 298; 303; 304; 305; 307; 308
Question marks	14; 226; 307
Xs	**19**; **20**; **23** (erased); 298
Comments on text in margins	**19**; **23** (two comments erased); **24**; **25**; **26**; **32**; **259**; **261** (extensive comments); **262**; **263**; **264**; **265**; **266**; **268**; **269**; **270**; **271**; **272**; **273**; **274**; **276**—a long, multipoint comment here.

(1962), who uses Bertrand Russell's concept of knowledge. Charles disputes Cassidy's statement that "the conveyance of knowledge is not the primary concern of the nonlinguistic arts" (p. 19, lines 7–8) with the margin comment: "He thinks the only knowledge is speech knowledge." Charles put one of his rare "X" marks next to another of Merriam's quotations from Cassidy: "But the artist is not, in the same sense as the scientist, *primarily* concerned with developing and communicating knowledge through the work of art. If he conveys knowledge, it comes as a bonus" (Cassidy 1962:14, cited in Merriam 1964:19). This is something Charles rejected out of hand. He rejects Merriam's restatement of the claim with another "X" on page 20 opposite lines 17–19, where Merriam writes: "The conclusion is almost inescapable that what the ethnomusicologist does is not the subjective, qualitative, discursive, esthetic, and so forth, but rather the objective, quantitative, and theoretical, wherever this is possible. There is a valid distinction to be drawn between the process of creating art and the artistic outlook, as opposed to the study of such processes" (Merriam 1964:17–19). Charles's final margin comment on the subject comes on page 25, where he has underlined eight words of the following sentence and written an emphatic "He *should* be!" in the margin next to these words: "The ethnomusicologist is *not the creator of the music he studies*, nor is his basic aim to participate aesthetically in that music (though he may seek to do so through re-creation) [underlined by Charles]." Charles is clearly opposing Merriam's position to his own, based on his philosophical position regarding speech knowledge and music knowledge, and the approach to music taken in the Institute for Ethnomusicology, in which students were encouraged to learn to perform non-Western musical traditions as part of their training, research, and analysis.

The disagreement over the importance of music knowledge, and of being able to create in the musical tradition one is writing about, was not a trivial point. It formed the basis of the different approaches to ethnomusicology at Indiana University and at UCLA. It was based on different philosophical positions regarding knowledge and different educational principles. It had a strong impact on shaping the curricula. Even if Bruno Nettl could later argue that the differences between the two schools of thought were more ideological than evident in the actual practice of their students, this chapter marked one of the defining differences in the approaches to ethnomusicology between Alan Merriam's position and that at the UCLA Institute of Ethnomusicology, where Charles Seeger was working.

Charles Seeger was a creator of the music he wrote about, or at least some of it. He wrote about European art music, ballad singing, and a variety of traditional musical styles in the United States. He was a composer and composition teacher, had studied conducting, and composed in a variety of musical idioms, ranging from dissonant counterpoint to his jazzy "Lenin, Who's That Guy?" (published under his pseudonym Carl Sands), to a round about Rockefeller begging for dimes, to performances of American traditional songs. Three of his performances appear on a compilation of political songs (Seeger 1996), and Alexia Smith Seeger is in possession of others. Members of his second family, the children of his marriage with Ruth Crawford, recalled evenings when the family would sit in the living room of their home in Chevy Chase, Maryland, and play American traditional music. They also recalled their mother playing the piano and her painstaking efforts at transcribing Library of Congress acetate recordings. Charles's familiarity with Euro-American musical traditions and performance lies at the heart of the criticisms he levels at the contrasts between music of "the West" and musical traditions in Africa that Merriam draws in chapter 11, "Aesthetics and the Interrelationship of the Arts." Charles put all these criticisms into a list of six points in the white space after the final paragraph of the chapter on page 276. Merriam has just finished writing that the nature of the interrelationship of the arts and ideas of aesthetics are questions "of enormous interest and concern to the ethnomusicologist who, almost by definition a comparative scholar, is in a superb position to contribute to our further understanding of them" (Merriam 1964:276). Under this Charles writes:

> But:
> 1) He's got to know the music of his own culture better than APM [Alan P. Merriam] does;
> 2) He must talk the language of the people he is investigating, WELL;

3) He must be able to *make the music* he is *making speech about* [underlined in original];
4) He must be fully aware of the extent he is talking about talking and talking about music;
5) He must cite more first-hand data from a more varied collection of cultures;
6) He must STOP dichotomizing in terms of either-or-ness [see figure 12.2].

Each of these final points is anticipated by a lively interaction with the text in the margins of the chapter. Regarding points 1 and 6, Charles repeatedly challenges Merriam's statements about European music in the margins. Merriam, based on his research among the Basongye in Africa and the Flathead Indians in the United States, contrasts their music with "European music" as strict oppositions. On line 5 of the chapter's opening paragraph on page 259, where Merriam writes "In Western art . . ." Charles inserts the word "fine" before the word art, to modify a generalization he believed to be too general. On page 261, in response to Merriam's statement that "In Western culture . . . we tend to stand away from our own 'art' music and look at it as an object by and of itself, examining it critically not only for its form but for what it expresses," Charles writes: "You can do this with a poem, a picture, a statue, a building, a dance—anything. . . . We *think* we do (better, pretend)." Right under that at the bottom of the page he adds: "Does an Appalachian folk-singer *necessarily* do this? Do rural jazz-men? Shape-note hymn singers?" Charles suggests that what Merriam refers to as "Western" musical traditions are not all alike on these issues. Similarly, on page 262 (lines 31–34), where Merriam writes that the Basongye conceptual system does not allow them to abstract music from its cultural context, Charles writes in the margin: "Neither can patrons of the Boston Symphony Orchestra."

There are no marginal comments related to point 2, but Merriam's extensive use of his research among the Basongye and Flathead and the complexity of the concept of value is such that Charles (in my view entirely appropriately) thinks that anyone investigating this subject needs to know the native language of the people she or he works with very well.

Point 3, about the importance of making the music one talks about, was the subject of many of his marginal comments on chapter 2 (see above). It is also central to Charles's idea that music knowledge and speech knowledge are fundamentally different. This observation comes less from the subject matter of this chapter than from chapter 2, but the position is strongly stated, with underlining, on page 276.

Regarding point 4, Charles criticizes Merriam for not clearly indicating when he is talking about "words" and when he is talking about "music." On

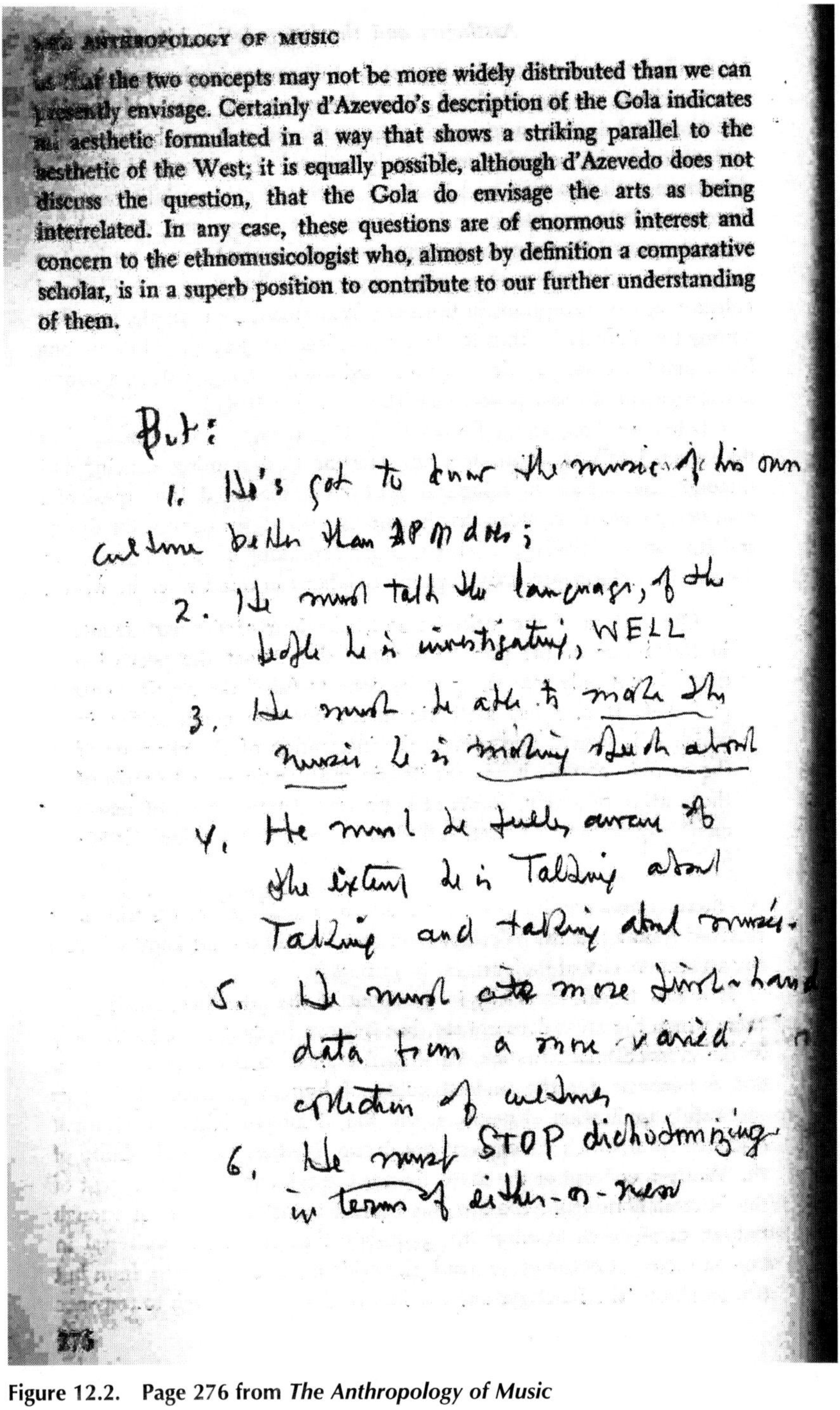

THE ANTHROPOLOGY OF MUSIC

us that the two concepts may not be more widely distributed than we can presently envisage. Certainly d'Azevedo's description of the Gola indicates an aesthetic formulated in a way that shows a striking parallel to the aesthetic of the West; it is equally possible, although d'Azevedo does not discuss the question, that the Gola do envisage the arts as being interrelated. In any case, these questions are of enormous interest and concern to the ethnomusicologist who, almost by definition a comparative scholar, is in a superb position to contribute to our further understanding of them.

But:

1. He's got to know the music of his own culture better than APM does;
2. He must talk the language, of the people he is investigating, WELL
3. He must be able to make the music he is making such about
4. He must be fully aware of the extent he is talking about talking and talking about music.
5. He must get more first-hand data from a more 'varied' collection of cultures
6. He must STOP dichotomizing in terms of either-or-ness

276

Figure 12.2. Page 276 from *The Anthropology of Music*

page 261, Merriam proposes to investigate whether the European aesthetic and abstract approach to music is applied by other societies, using the Basongye and Flathead as his cases. He argues that six factors are relevant to the contrast. Charles's marginal comments indicate that he thinks five of the six factors (1–5) are about speech, not about music. Later, on page 262 where Merriam states that neither the Basongye nor Flathead analyze music objectively, divorced from themselves and context, Charles writes: "I don't do this either when I *make* music. I do it when I talk about it." He wonders about the Basongye on page 266: "Do they do any abstracting?"

Later in the chapter (p. 271), Merriam begins to question the concept of aesthetics he has been applying, and that Charles has been rebutting in his margin comments. Merriam cites Roy Seiber's proposal that there is an "unvoiced aesthetic" applied to African visual art because they have no need to analyze and dissect their art. The assumptions that lie behind the art constitute the unvoiced aesthetic (Merriam 1964:271). Charles places an interest line next to this paragraph and writes, "Better!" In the next paragraph, where Merriam writes, "Unless we are willing to alter our understanding of the meaning of the word aesthetic, it seems that a new term must be coined" (lines 21–22), Charles writes: "We'd better if we want to talk sense." He also places an interest line and the word "Better!" next to the citation of David McAllester further down the page, in which he proposes a "functional aesthetic." Merriam, however, goes on to say that the words "functional" and "aesthetic" seem to be a contradiction in semantic usage (lines 35–37), next to which Charles places a question mark and the word "WOW." Where Merriam writes, "The building can only be functional; it is the observer's *attitude* which is aesthetic," Charles finally appears to lose patience. He writes at the bottom of 271, "To hell with attitude."[7] Opposite lines 8–16 on the next page, he writes, "Yes, if aesthetic means attitude (Where did APM [Alan P. Merriam] get this notion?)." After that remark, Charles's comments are few until the final list.

Regarding point 5, Merriam bases most of his discussion of non-Western aesthetics on his own field research among the Basongye and the Flathead. From my perspective, this choice was justifiable insofar as the subject of aesthetics had not yet been widely investigated outside of European art music. Merriam noted, however, that other researchers had worked in groups that appear to have an aesthetic perspective on their arts. Charles is correct to argue that if one is going to make universal statements about the West and the Rest, these should be based on more than just a few societies. This reflects an enduring problem in ethnomusicology, and one that we have not really settled today: how does one compare musical and conceptual systems across cultures? The largest and most systematic attempt to do so, Alan Lomax's cantometrics (Lomax 1968),[8] was not entirely successful and has not served as a model for much subsequent research. Citing more firsthand data from a more varied collection of cultures remains a challenge in our field.

Alan Merriam, in his attempt to establish an anthropology of music, was surely guilty of an almost Manichaean tendency to oppose concepts, methods, and approaches to music radically. This was partly his way of establishing a clearly defined field of the anthropology of music and ethnomusicology, but it was also open to criticism, which Charles made throughout the text in areas where he thought it was too extreme (see point 6). Interestingly, Charles never really criticized the absoluteness of his own dichotomy of "music knowledge" and "speech knowledge," although Steven Feld did this rather elegantly some years later (Feld 1984; see also Greer 1998). When, however, Charles created his elaborate diagrams—most fully presented in the fold-out table in his *Studies in Musicology* (Seeger 1977)—he also used dualisms. He expresses them, nonetheless, as continua and urges readers to move from one pole to the other, not to become too fixed on any one position. This approach to dualism is very different from Merriam's in *The Anthropology of Music*, especially in chapter 11.

Conclusions

I think it worth examining *The Anthropology of Music* using Charles Seeger's marginalia because I believe it to be one of the most important books in the short history of ethnomusicology. It certainly profoundly influenced my own work. Charles Seeger rarely wrote detailed critiques of his colleagues' work of the kind he wrote in this book. His markings reveal a thoughtful and critical reader whose own ideas were well formulated and yet being refined as he revised his own essays (e.g., Seeger 1977) and worked on one of the manuscripts in the posthumous *Studies in Musicology II 1929–1979* (Seeger and Pescatello 1994), certain features of which are prefigured in his markings. Here, we have two of the major conceptualizers of our field at the time facing off against one another—but on the pages of Charles's copy of Merriam's book, rather than in a conference room at a professional meeting, a book review, or over a dinner in Westwood, Bridgewater, or Bloomington.

H. J. Jackson argues strongly for the importance of marginalia of the type I have discussed in this chapter. She suggests that the practice of writing them is fairly extensive, if woefully overlooked, and that studying them can lead to exciting insights. Marginalia, used as an English word by Samuel Taylor Coleridge (a prolific marker of books including those loaned to him to mark up and then return to their owners) in 1819 (Jackson 2001:7), have a long history. Studies of marginalia are fairly well developed in literary studies, biography, and history, but as far as I am aware they have never been considered in the histories of ethnomusicology—even though many of us mark up our books. In the e-book and social-media era, the way readers interact with texts is changing in interesting ways (Wagstaff 2012:8). Marginalia are now increasingly becoming parts of a wider conversation among readers of certain texts, rather than private thoughts that only many years later may be uncovered and reflected upon.

Ethnomusicologists in the future may be parsing our underlining and comments in an effort to figure out what we were thinking when we read each other's books.[9] It is interesting to consider that marking up our books may not simply be part of the process of doing research, but one more product (like our field notes and recordings) of research that others may use long after the research is over (or, in the case of social media, as we are doing it).

As he himself notes in the remarks that open this chapter, Bruno Nettl has rarely written extensive notes in his books, so it will be left to future generations to puzzle over any markings to be found in them (he comments elsewhere in his e-mail [Nettl 2013b] that his handwriting is sometimes illegible even to himself). We, however, do know a great deal about what he has read and what he thinks about it from thousands of pages of writing. Thanks, Bruno! We don't need to hover over your shoulder because you have passed your ideas on to us already in elegant and often very witty prose, complemented by extensive and very useful bibliographies that so many of us have mined, often marked up, and used in our own work.

Notes

1. I am grateful to Charles Seeger for leaving me his professional books, to Bonnie Wade for help reading Charles Seeger's handwriting, to Bruno Nettl for permission to publish the contents of his e-mail, and to Robert Garfias and the editors of this volume for their very helpful suggestions as I was writing.

2. We do have some reflections on field notes, notably by Gregory Barz in the collection *Shadows in the Field*, to whose title I allude (Barz 2007), but nothing on methods of reading and remembering the content of books and articles.

3. I am grateful to Bonnie Wade for her assistance in deciphering Charles Seeger's marginalia. As one of his students and collaborators, she was more familiar with his handwriting than I.

4. In his memoirs, recorded at UCLA, Charles called Merriam's visit to UCLA one of the "big events" of the year. He describes how the students took Merriam out to dinner and recalls the following: "Well, of course, the students were absolutely

delighted, and I understand they pitched into Merriam pretty hard, but I'm sure it made no impression whatever. It rolled off his back like water off a duck's. Alan's a good man, but he definitely looks at music from the out-side [*sic*] and can't conceive that looking at it from the inside can see anything" (Seeger 1972:426).

5. Other respondents to Merriam's presentation included John H. Mueller (a sociologist at Indiana University) and Bruno Nettl, published in the same issue of *Ethnomusicology*.

6. I recommend Robert Garfias's reflections on the symposium for an impression of the field at that time (Garfias 2013a).

7. Both Bonnie Wade and I think Charles has written "hell" but we also agree that this was unlike his normal language. I suggest that his unusual use of the word "hell" indicates how deeply Charles was involved in this section and explains why he took the time to write out the six points at the end of the chapter, a few pages later.

8. Alan Lomax's *Folk Song Style and Culture* was second in the use of marginalia in Charles Seeger's books that I examined, providing evidence that Charles read it carefully as well.

9. For those still reading and writing on paper, Jackson recommends writing your name and the date of purchase in the front, and then identifying as yours the marginalia you produce as you read it (separating the different times you go back to the text). She also recommends that scholars who examine marginalia put the word in the titles of their works—hence my title for this chapter.

References

Barz, Gregory. 2007. "Confronting the Field(note) in and out of the Field: Music, Voices, Texts and Experiences in Dialogue." In *Shadows in the Field: New Perspectives for Fieldwork in Ethnomusicology*, revised second edition, edited by Gregory Barz and Timothy Cooley, 206–13. New York: Oxford University Press.

Cassidy, Harold Gomes. 1962. *The Sciences and the Arts: A New Alliance*. New York: Harper.

Chase, Gilbert. 1966. *America's Music from the Pilgrims to the Present*, revised second edition. New York: McGraw-Hill.

Feld, Steven. 1984. "Speech, Music, and Speech about Music." *Ethnomusicology* 16(1): 1–18.

Garfias, Robert. 2013a. "Reflections on the 1963 Symposium." aris.ss.uci.edu/rgarfias/1963/ (accessed 26 June 2014).

———. 2013b. "Symposium of the Current State of Research in Ethnomusicology." aris.ss.uci.edu/rgarfias/1963/ (text); eee.uci.edu/programs/rgarfias/photos/symposium-1963/index.html (photographs) (accessed 26 June 2014).

Greer, Taylor Aitkin. 1998. *A Question of Balance: Charles Seeger's Philosophy of Music*. Berkeley: University of California Press.

Hood, Mantle. 1971. *The Ethnomusicologist*. New York: McGraw-Hill.

Jackson, H. J. 2001. *Marginalia: Readers Writing in Books*. New Haven, CT: Yale University Press.

Kunst, Jaap. 1950. *Musicologica (A Study of the Nature of Ethno-musicology, Its Problems, Methods and Representative Personalities)*. Amsterdam: Uitgave van bet Indisch Institut.

———. 1955. *Ethno-Musicology: A Study of Its Nature, Its Problems, Methods and Representative Personalities to Which Is Added a Bibliography*, second enlarged edition. The Hague: Nijhoff.

———. 1959. *Ethno-Musicology: A Study of Its Nature, Its Problems, Methods and Representative Personalities to Which Is Added a Bibliography*, third enlarged edition. The Hague: Nijhoff.

Lomax, Alan. 1968. *Folk Song Style and Culture*. Washington, DC: American Association for the Advancement of Science.

Merriam, Alan P. 1964. "The Purposes of Ethnomusicology: An Anthropological View." *Ethnomusicology* 7(3): 206–13.

———. 1964. *The Anthropology of Music*. Evanston, IL: Northwestern University Press.

Nettl, Bruno. 1956. *Music in Primitive Culture*. Cambridge, MA: Harvard University Press.

———. 2010. *Nettl's Elephant: On the History of Ethnomusicology*. Urbana: University of Illinois Press.

———. 2013a. *Becoming an Ethnomusicologist: A Miscellany of Influences*. Lanham, MD: Scarecrow Press.

———. 2013b. Personal Communication. (E-mail to Anthony Seeger of 18 June 2013; permission to publish excerpts on 19 June 2013).

Seeger, Charles L. 1963. "On the Tasks of Musicology (Comments on Merriam, 'Purposes of Ethnomusicology')." *Ethnomusicology* 7(3): 214–15.

———. 1972. "Reminiscences of an American Musicologist." Charles Seeger Interviewed by Adelaide G. Tusler and Ann M. Briegleb. Completed under the auspices of the Oral History Program, University of California, Los Angeles. Regents of the University of California: archive.org/stream/reminiscencesofa00seeg#page/n9/mode/2up (accessed 14 June 2014).

———. 1977. *Studies in Musicology, 1935–1975*. Berkeley: University of California Press.

———. 1996. "London's Bridge Is Falling Down," "Risselty Rosselty," and "Hands." In *Songs for Political Action* [sound recording, 10 CDs]. Hamburg: Bear Family Records, BCD 15 720 JL CD I tracks 3, 4, 6.

Seeger. Charles L., and Ann Pescatello. 1994. *Studies in Musicology II: 1929–1979*. Berkeley: University of California Press.

Wagstaff, Kiri L. 2012. "The Evolution of Marginalia." www.wkiri.com/slis/wagstaff-libr200-marginalia-1col.pdf (accessed 7 August 2013).

PART III

ANALYTICAL STUDIES

CHAPTER THIRTEEN

The Persian *Radif* in Relation to the Tajik-Uzbek *Šašmaqom*

Stephen Blum

In conversations with Bruno Nettl, the distinguished Persian musician Nur 'Ali Borumand (1905–1977) emphasized his belief that the Persian *radif* "is really something extraordinary and fine, something quite unique . . . that we have created in Iran" (Nettl 1984:184).[1] Accepting Borumand's view, which "informs and governs" Nettl's book on the radif (1992 [1987]:xii), we may nonetheless compare the radif, viewed as a substantial collection of resources for the singing of Persian poetry, with other repertories composed of named musical units that are used in various ways.[2] Notable among these are the Azeri *muğam*, the Iraqi *maqām*, the Tajik-Uzbek (or "Bukharan") *šašmaqom*, the Khwarezm *altıyorım maqom*, the Tashkent-Ferghana *čahormaqom*, and the Uyghur *on iki muqam*. While each is unique, extraordinary, and fine, the seven repertories bear traces of intricate processes of cultural exchange and exhibit numerous affinities in both structure and content. One such affinity is hierarchical organization of the named units: the primary groupings; their "branches" (often with further subdivisions); the named units themselves; and distinctive phases within certain units.[3] The number of primary groupings is made explicit in the names of the last four of these repertories: *šaš*—"six" (Persian), *altıyorım*—"six and a half" (Turkic), *čahor*—"four" (Tajik Persian), and *on iki*—"twelve" (Turkic). Likewise, the Persian radif is commonly said to comprise *haft dastgāh*—"seven systems"—or *davāzdah dastgāh*—"twelve systems"—as explained below.

The radif's closest cousin is the Azeri muğam, now used for the singing of poetry in Azerbaijani Turkish. If we think of the radif and the muğam as gradually diverging branches of what was once a common system (cf. During 1988:16, 181–91; Djani-Zade 2008), that system would presumably have enabled a bilingual performance practice, and indeed we know of bilingual singers like Mirzā Sattār, born around 1820 in Ardebil (Shushinski 1979:29–40; During 1988:182). In the case of the Iraqi maqām, singers reportedly believed at one time that no less than thirty-three of fifty-three Iraqi *maqāmāt* would accommodate sung poetry in Persian and Baghdadi Turkish as well as in literary Arabic (Hassan 2009). From Baghdad to Samarqand and Dushambe, the loss of this multilingualism is one of several respects in which musical life suffered as state institutions promulgated doctrines (borrowed from Europe) of "one nation, one language, one race" (on Iran, see Manafzadeh 2009:149–227).

At present, the Tajik-Uzbek *šašmaqom* is the great system that enables singers to use the same rhythmic and melodic resources for verses in Persian and in Turkic languages—the Chaghatay Turkish of Navā'i and Bābur, the Baghdadi Turkish of Füzuli, and modern Uzbek. The first published notations that do full justice to this vital attribute of the *šašmaqom* (in Jung 2010) are those of Ari Babakhanov (b. 1934), whose grandfather, Levi Babakhan (1873–1926), was active at the court of the last Emir of Bukhara until the emirate was abolished in 1920.[4] This essay considers a few of the Persian radif's affinities with the šašmaqom.

In both the radif and the šašmaqom, the proper names attached to individual units, and to sequences of those units, designate bundles of features with varying degrees of relevance to performers and listeners, depending on their experience and their interests (cf. Blum 2009).[5] Among the distinctive features of each unit (*guše*, also *tekke*—"piece") in the radif are its relative length, the units it may follow or precede in a sequence of gušes, the frequency with which it is included in performances, and the degree of rhythmic and melodic variation allowable in performance (including its suitability for singing verses in more than one poetic meter). The name serves as a convenient label for the full configuration of distinctive features and for the knowledge a performer or a listener has come to associate with that guše. In teaching the radif, musicians may note that a particular guše refers to some other genre of performance. As he demonstrated the guše *Azarbāyjāni* in the *dastgāh* of *Māhur* on a recording made by Hormoz Farhat, Borumand sang a verse from one of the religious dramas called *ta'ziye* to a tune from that guše (Borumand 2005: disc 2, track 2, 1:49–2:34).

The late Harold Powers made valuable contributions to the comparative study of West and Central Asian musical systems by investigating what he termed *nominal equivalences* among *modal entities* (a term that covers what are here called sequences or groupings of units as well as the individual units). Having first explored that topic with reference to the rāgas of Karnatak and Hindustani music (Powers 1970), Powers was able to contrast the functions of the proper names of rāgas with those of the names given to modal entities in West and Central Asia, where names have long conveyed information about the ordering of units in extended sequences (Powers 1989:51–53). Powers's studies of proper names formed part of a much-needed critique of the concept *mode*, as extended by twentieth-century scholars to embrace a wide range of musical resources that musicians have understood and employed in quite different ways.

Nominal equivalences between units of the radif and the *šašmaqom* are more difficult to interpret than those between units of the radif and the Azerbaijani muğam (which are well treated in During 1988). Although the radif and the *šašmaqom* share several proper names along with terms for genres and functions, these do not always carry the same implications, as the two repertories result from different approaches to organizing a comprehensive collection of musical resources. Despite their differences, both approaches convey information bearing on the sequencing of units in performance, and both address the need to arrange units in an order that can be taught and remembered.

The six primary divisions of the *šašmaqom* are understood to follow one another in a fixed order, which at this level has no bearing on performance: *Buzruk*, *Rost*, *Navo*, *Segoh*, *Dugoh*, and *Iroq*. Each primary division begins with a series of instrumental pieces (*muškilot* or "shapings") in a conventional ordering of genres (*tasnif*, *tarji*, *gardun*, *muxammas*, *saqil*) and is followed by a longer series of vocal genres, which normally includes a few secondary groupings (*šo'ab*, sing. *šo'ba*, or "branch") with their own proper names, likewise following a relatively fixed sequence of genres. For example, each maqom except for *Iroq* has a secondary grouping, the *Muğulča* of that maqom, composed of the genres *muğulča* itself, sometimes *čapandoz*, then *talqin*, *qašqarča*, *soqinoma*, and *ufar*. Hence most names of pieces follow one of two formulas: *genre X of name Y* (e.g., *saraxbori Buzruk*) or *genre X of name Y of name Z* (e.g., *soqinomai Muğulčai Buzruk*). In both formulas, *name Y* often designates a melody type that takes on rhythmic features of each genre in turn (cf. Levin 1984:117), including both its rhythmic cycle (*usul*) and the poetic meter or meters that are most appropriate. Terms for specific structural functions such as *darxat* or *daromad*, *miyonxat* or *miyonparda*, *namud*, *furovard*, *avj*, and *suporiš* can be applied to the successive phases of each piece (*šo'ba*), as shown in Ari Babakhanov's notations (Jung 2010).[6] At some point in its history, the šašmaqom became above all a repertory of pieces, each of which follows the norms and bears the name of a genre (such as *saraxbor*, *talqin*, *nasr*, and *ufar* in the main part of each maqom, before the secondary groupings). Only rarely do performances of one maqom include all or even most of the possible pieces, though musicians normally adhere to the appropriate ordering of whichever genres they have chosen to perform on a given occasion (see Rapport 2014 for discussion of the current practice of Bukharian Jewish musicians in New York City).

Unlike the *šašmaqom*, a *radif* is transmitted in a redaction meant for the voice or for specific instruments. At present there is no universally accepted ordering of the seven principal *dastgāh*-s ("systems"), which differ significantly among themselves in the arrangement of gušes. Two of the seven, *Šur* and *Homāyun*, are said to have "derivatives" (*mota'alleqāt*) or "branches" (*šo'ab*, sing. *šo'ba*) called āvāz or, in the usage of some musicians and scholars, dastgāh. That usage is justified by the fact that these "branches" are performed independently and can be regarded as primary units within a system of twelve dastgāhs, rather than just seven.

Recognizable sequences of gušes within a dastgāh or āvāz may be comparable in length to a secondary grouping in the *šašmaqom*, but only a few sequences carry their own proper names (for instance, the *Rāk* group, discussed below, or the multiple parts of *Hesār* in *čahārgāh*). Rather, each guše has either a proper or a generic name, so that a chain of names can mark successive phases of a coherent musical process (though many sets of names can be arranged in more than one order). Certain generic names of gušes are comparable, even identical, to those for phases of individual pieces in the *šašmaqom* (e.g., *darāmad* and *owj*). Most gušes have been assigned proper names like *Rāk* and *Azarbāyjāni*. In current practice certain units of the radif function as models that provide a basis for improvisation, whereas other units are understood as pieces to be reproduced in a relatively fixed form, like those of the šašmaqom.

The nominal equivalence between the second, third, and fifth principal divisions of the šašmaqom and three principal dastgāhs of the radif—*Rost/Rāst Panjgāh*, *Navo/Navā*, and *Segoh/Segāh*—is not an index of identical content. Most shared names are applied at different levels. *Čahārgāh* is a primary dastgāh in the radif, whereas *čahorgoh* is the first secondary grouping (or "suite") of *Dugoh* in the *šašmaqom*. In the radif, *Dogāh* is one guše within one branch (āvāz) of *Šur*, and in various radifs *'Erāq* is the name of a guše in a different branch of *Šur* as well as in no less than three dastgāhs: Māhur, *Navā*, and *Rāst Panjgāh*.[7] Eight names of secondary divisions in the *šašmaqom* are shared with gušes of the radif: *Uzzal/'Ozzāl*, *Rok/Rāk*, *Uššok/'Oššāq*, *Navrozi Sabo/Nowruz-e Sabā*, *Panjgoh/Panjgāh*, *Hoseyni*, *Navrozi Xoro/Nowruz-i Xārā*, and *Muhayyar/Mohayyer*. In the radif, *Rāk* differs from the other seven names in designating a group of gušes, potentially similar in overall duration to the secondary grouping called *Rok* in maqom *Buzruk*. In this case, moreover, the nominal equivalence points to similarities in melodic contour.[8]

In the Razhabii-Karomatov edition of the *šašmaqom*, *Rok* is composed of pieces in the familiar sequence of five genres mentioned above: *Rok* itself, followed by the *talqinča*, *qašqarča*, *soqinoma*, and *ufor* of *Rok*. The sequence in Beliaev's edition is almost the same, with a *mustazod* rather than a *talqinča*.[9] The proper names given to gušes of the *Rāk* group in vocal and instrumental radifs include *Rāk*, *naghme-ye Rāk*, *safir-e Rāk*, *Rāk-e hendi*, *Rāk-e 'Abdollāh*, and *Rāk-e Keshmir*; the instrumental radifs of Mirzā 'Abdollāh and his brother Hoseyn Qoli also allow for the genre *čahār mezrāb* and the rhythmic pattern *kerešme* in *Rāk* (During 2006:178 and Pirniyākān 2001:134, respectively). There is no standard order of the *Rāk* gušes, and the names do not consistently designate the same melodies. *Rāk-e hend* may be the first of these names documented in treatises, as it is one of the thirty-three *maqāmāt* listed in the *Wajdiyya* of the essayist Mollā Toghrā Mashhadi, who died before 1667 in Kashmir after spending most of his career in India (Massoudieh 1996:174). In Persia, by the eighteenth or early nineteenth century, *Rāk* was one unit within the dastgāh of *Rāst*, as evidenced by the *Risāla dar bayān-e čahār dastgāh-e a'zam* (Purjavādy 2001:91).[10]

Just as *Rok* is the final šo'be of maqom *Buzruk*, in current practice the *Rāk* sequence comes toward the end of the dastgāh *Māhur* and, in some radifs, toward the end of *Rāst Panjgāh*. The name is spelled with a final consonant equivalent to g rather than *k* in the *Bohur al-alhān* ("Meters of Melodies"), an important text published in 1914, which lists *Rāg-e hendi*, *nağme-ye Rāg*, and *Rāg-e 'Abdollāh* among the gušes of both *Māhur* and *Rāst Panjgāh*. *Rāk-e hendi* is one of the seventeen units of *Rāst*, the first of the six dastgāhs described in an Azerbaijani text, the *Vozuh al-arqām dar 'elm-e musiqi* or "Explanation of Calculation in the Science of Music," which was published in 1913 though compiled in 1884 (Navvāb 1913:23). *Rāk*, *Rāk-e hendi*, and *Rāk-e khorāsāni* were included in the versions of *Rāst* performed in the muğam circles of three Azerbaijani cities: Baku, Shushā, and Shamākhā (Zohrābov 1999[1991]:143–44). The great muğamist Bahram Mansurov (1911–1985) included *Rāk-e Kešmir* and *Rāk-e 'Abdollāh* among the seventeen gušes of the dastgāh *Māhur hendi* (During 1988:77), and his version of the dastgāh *Rāst* includes *Rāk-e khorāsāni* (During 1988:70).[11]

Figure 13.1 compares the contours of the initial phrase of *Rāk-e Kešmir* as sung by Mahmud Karimi (1927–1984) with the initial phrase of *mustazodi Rok* in Ari Babakhanov's notation of *Buzruk*. In his studies of nominally

Figure 13.1. **(a) Initial phrase of *Rāk*-e *Kešmir* in the *dastgāh* of** *Māhur* **as sung by Mahmud Karimi (Massoudieh 1978:142 and Mas'udiye 1997:114) (b) Initial phrase of *mustazodi Rok* in Ari Babakhanov's notation of *maqom Buzruk* (Jung 2010:71)**

equivalent Karnatak and Hindustani rāgas, Powers (1970:16) found that "melodic characteristics—emphasis, contour, and the like—seem to be more persistent than scale-type," and that is also the case in this instance. The two initial phrases are comparable in length to the characteristic *tahrīr* that identifies each Iraqi *maqām* (Hassan 1987:145–46). They belong to the *Rāk* group only in some radifs, not in all, and other melodies in the group also have analogues in the *šašmaqom*. For example, the contour of *safir-e Rāk* in the vocal radif of Karimi (but not in that of his master, 'Abdollāh Davāmi, as notated in Pāyvar 1999[1996]:144) resembles that shared by *qašqarčai Rok* and *soqinomai Rok* in Beliaev's and Razhabii's editions of *Buzruk* (Massoudieh 1978:140 and Mas'udiye 1997:137 for Karimi's radif; Beliaev 1950–1967:i, 250, 252 and Razhabii and Karomatov 1966–1975:i, 168, 170 for Buzruk).

A comparison of *soqinomai Rok* in *Buzruk* with the guše-s called sāqi-nāme, *košte-morde*, and *sufi-nāme* in the radif may shed light on the different implications of names in the *šašmaqom* and the radif.[12] The three guše-s, which may be sung or played toward the end of a performance in the dastgāh of *Māhur*, require verses in the *motaqāreb* poetic meter, sung to a distinctive rhythmic pattern over a cycle of eight slow beats that can be understood as an alternation of downbeat and upbeat, thesis and arsis (see figure 13.2). This combination of a poetic meter, an eight-beat cycle, and a rhythmic pattern constitutes a rhythmic template (cf. Blum 2006:41–44), heard in many, though not all, of the *soqinoma* pieces in the *šašmaqom* as well as in the three gušes of Māhur.[13] We can regard the components of this rhythmic template as sequences of events defined in three ways: a cycle of beats, each distinguished by its ordinal number and as thesis or arsis; a fixed number of syllables in each half-line of verse, also distinguished by ordinal numbers and marked as either short, long, or long-plus-short; and a series of interonset intervals[14] that is retained or varied as a rhythmic framework to which the successive half-lines are sung. In the *šašmaqom*, the rhythmic template for each genre has a fourth component, the rhythmic cycle (*usul*).

A rhythmic template enables variation in certain respects, while at the same time specifying the moments when some, or even all, of the sequences must coincide. Levin (1984:143) suggested that, for performers of the *šašmaqom*, "there must be a type of metric 'common denominator' encompassing *usul* and verse meter that assures metro-rhythmic accommodation between them," and I mean for the term "rhythmic template" to cover the accommodation or coordination of whatever features are pertinent in a given unit. In Ari Babakhanov's notation of the *šašmaqom* (Jung 2010), thirteen of the twenty-two *soqinoma* movements have verses in the *motaqāreb* meter,

Figure 13.2. Rhythmic template of all sāqi-nāme pieces in the Persian radif and of certain soqinoma-s in the *šašmaqom*

and most of those thirteen set the Persian or Uzbek verses to the rhythmic pattern shown in figure 13.2.[15]

To summarize the different implications of *sāqi-nāme* in the radif and *soqi-noma* in the *šašmaqom*: in the radif, the term prescribes all three components of the rhythmic template, whereas in the *šašmaqom*, the term designates a piece performed after a *qašqarča* and before an *ufar*, and it allows for more than one poetic meter and more than one rhythmic pattern (but only one *usul*). In the radif, relatively few gušes restrict the singer to verses in a single poetic meter. The great singer Mohammad Rezā Shajariān (b. 1941) has argued that, with those few exceptions, "any poem may be sung to any gushe" (Sims and Koushkani 2012:191). This is a departure from the doctrine laid out in the treatise mentioned above, *Bohur al-alhān dar 'elm-e musiqi va nesbat-e ān bā 'aruz* ("Meters of Melodies in Musical Science and Their Relation to the System of Poetic Meter") (Forsat al-Dowla 1966[1914]), and evidently taught by Davāmi and his student Karimi.

Be this as it may, both the šašmaqom and the radif require performers who have learned to coordinate verse, rhythm, and melody. That requirement is obscured by continued use of the unfortunate terms "unmetered melodies" and "unrhythmic melodies," products of ideologies that fail to treat music and poetry as constituents of one art of performance. There are better alternatives, such as Daryush Talā'i's term "flexible [*en'etāf pazir*] melodies" (Talā'i 1993:16 and 2002:867), which is compatible both with the doctrine of the *Bohur al-alhān* and with Shajariān's practice.

Notes

1. A version of this paper was read on 4 November 2011 at a symposium on "Music as Intangible Cultural Heritage: Bukharan Shashmaqam, the Classical Music of Central Asia," convened by Angelika Jung and Tiago de Oliveira Pinto at the University of Weimar-Jena.

2. At least for much of the twentieth century, vocal radifs were distinguished from instrumental, though students of instruments have been expected to learn how to provide instrumental responses (*javāb-e āvāz*) to singers, an obligation that requires sensitivity to the poetic meters associated with units (*guše*-s) of the radif.

3. Overviews of the terminology by which various levels of these hierarchies have been distinguished at different times can be obtained by perusing Shiloah 1979 and 2003 for Arabic treatises, Massoudieh 1996 for Persian, and Jung 1989:137–66 for those most pertinent to Central Asian practices. Some terms have moved among levels: for example, one of the most common terms for "branch," *šo'ba* (pl. *šo'ab*), is now applied to individual pieces in the šašmaqom.

4. The Razhabii-Karomatov edition of the šašmaqom (1966–1975) provided supplementary Persian verses from an early nineteenth-century manuscript (see Levin 1984:40).

5. For the names of units in the radif, I have adopted conventions that are commonly used for the Persian of Iran. For names of units in the šašmaqom, I have generally followed Ari Babakhanov's spellings (in Jung 2010), which are closer to current usage for Tajik Persian and Uzbek: hence, *Rāst* in the radif, *Rost* in the šašmaqom.

6. Theodore Levin's annotations to his translation of the introduction to Razhabii and Karomatov 1966–1975 provide concise definitions of many technical terms associated with the šašmaqom (Karomatov and Radjabov 1981:114–17).

7. In the *Bohur al-alhān* and in Hoseyn Qoli's radif for tār and setār, *'Erāq* is assigned to all three dastgāhs (Forsat al-Dowla 1966 [1914]:34, 36; Pirniyākān 2001:136, 248, 274). In the vocal radifs of Davāmi and Karimi, it belongs only to *Māhur* and *Navā* (as well as to the āvāz of *Afshāri* in Davāmi's radif). *'Erāq* commonly includes or is followed by *Mohayyer*, and in the *šašmaqom* the first subdivision of maqom *'Erāq* is likewise *Mohayyer*.

8. Similarities in melodic contour are also evident in the units called *Mohayyer*.

9. In Babakhanov's notation, this subdivision is called *mustazodi Rok*, and the piece of that name is followed by a *talqin*, two *tarana*-s, and an *ufar*.

10. The unique source of the treatise, which is not listed in Massoudieh 1996, is ms. 3536.12 in the Malek National Library, Tehran, 323b–327b. It has been edited by Purjavādy (2001).

11. *Rāk* is the penultimate guše in a recorded performance of *Rāst* by the Muğam Ensemble Jabbar Karyagdy, Pan Records PAN 2017CD, p1993. The curriculum for *tār* adopted in 1925 at the Faculty for Folk Musical Instruments in Baku included *Rāk-e khorāsāni* in the *dastgāh* of Rāst and *Rāk-e hendi/'abdollāhi* in the *dastgāh* of *Rohāb* (Abdulgassimov 1990:104).

12. For an excellent description of the *sāqi-nāma* as a poetic genre, see Losensky 2009.

13. The dastgāh repertory of the Azerbaijani muğam, in the tradition of the Mansurov family, includes a "Persian sāqi-nāma" in the dastgāh of *Šur* and an "Arab sāqi-nāma" in the dastgāh of *Homāyun* (During 1988:46–47, 99; Mansurov 1995).

14. An interonset interval (IOI) is the duration defined by two successive attacks.

15. Monājāt Yultchieva sings an Uzbek ğazal by Munis (*uzoriŋda nure ayondur ayon* "Your face radiant with light") in the *soqinoma* from the *Bayot* branch of *maqom Navo* on OCORA C 560060, p1994.

References

Abdulgassimov, Vagif. 1990. *Azerbaijanian tar*. Baku: Ishyg.

Beliaev, Viktor M. 1950–1967. *Shashmaqom: Tartibdihandagon: Boboqul Faizulloev, Shohnazar Sohibov va Fazliddin Shahobov*. 5 vols. Moscow: Nashrieti Davlatii Muzikali.

Blum, Stephen. 2006. "Navā'i, a Musical Genre of Northeastern Iran." In *Analytical Studies in World Music*, edited by Michael Tenzer, 41–57. New York: Oxford University Press.

———. 2009. "Şah Xəta'i as Name and Genre." In *Proceedings of International Musicological Symposium "Space of Muğam," 18–20 March, 2009, Baku*, 92–97. Baku: Şərq-Qərb.

Borumand, Nur 'Ali. 2005. *Descriptive Analysis of the Dastgāh of Māhur by Ostād Nurali Borumand*. Recordings and interview by Hormoz Farhat. Tehran: Mahur Institute of Culture and Art. Four compact discs with notes by Hooman Asadi, Mahur M.CD-176.

Djani-Zade, Tamila. 2008. "The Concept of *Radif* in Iranian and Azerbaijanian *Dastgāh*." In *Intercultural Comparison of Maqām and Related Phenomena. Proceedings of the Fifth Meeting of the ICTM Study Group "maqām," Samarkand, 26–30 August 2001*, ed. Jürgen Elsner and Gisa Jähnichen, 41–66. Berlin: Trafo Verlag.

During, Jean. 1988. *La musique traditionnelle de l'Azerbayjan et la science des muqams*. Collection d' études musicologiques/Sammlung musikwissenschaftlicher Abhandlungen, 80. Baden-Baden: Koerner.

———. 2006. *The* Radif *of Mirzā 'Abdollāh, a Canonic Repertoire of Persian Music: Notation and Presentation*. Tehran: Mahoor Institute of Culture and Art.

Forsat al-Dowla Shirāzi, Nasir. 1966[1914]. *Bohur al-alhān dar 'elm-e musiqi va nesbat-e ān bā 'aruz*. Tehran: Foroughi. Facsimile of book published in Bombay, 1914.

Hassan, Schéhérazade Qassim. 1987. "Le makām irakien: structures et *réalisations*." In *L'improvisation dans les musiques de tradition orale*, edited by Bernard Lortat-Jacob, 143–49. Paris: SELAF.

———. 2009. "The Iraqi Maqam: Elements of Continuity and Change." Paper presented at conference on Musical Traditions in the Middle East, University of Leiden.

Jung, Angelika. 1989. *Quellen der traditionellen Kunstmusik der Usbeken und Tadshiken Mittelasiens: Untersuchung zur Entstehung und Entwicklung des šašmaqām*. Beiträge zur Ethnomusikologie, 23. Hamburg: Karl Dieter Wagner.

———. 2010. *Der Shashmaqam aus Buchara, überliefert von den alten Meistern, notiert von Ari Babakhanov*. Berlin: Schiler. Two accompanying compact discs.

Karomatov, Faizulla M., and Ishaq Radjabov. 1981. "Introduction to the *Šašmaqom*, Translated and Annotated by Theodore Levin." *Asian Music* 13(1): 97–118.

Levin, Theodore C. 1984. "The Music and Tradition of the Bukharan Shashmaqam in Soviet Uzbekistan." Ph.D. Dissertation, Princeton University.

Losensky, Paul. 2009. "Sāqi-nāma." *Encyclopaedia Iranica*, online edition: iranica.com.

Manafzadeh, Alireza. 2009. *La construction identitaire en Iran*. Comprendre le Moyen Orient. Paris: L'Harmattan.

Mänsurov, Eldar. 1995. *Muğam düşüncälärım*. Baku: n.p.

Massoudieh, Mohammad Taghi, ed. 1978. *Radif vocal de la musique traditionnelle de l'Iran*. Tehran: Ministry of Culture and Arts.

———. 1996. *Manuscrits persans concernant la musique*. Répertoire International des Sources Musicales, B, xii. Munich: Henle.

Mas'udiye, Mohammad Taghi, ed. 1997. *Radif-e āvāzi-e musiqi-e sonnati-e Irān be ravāyat-e Mahmud Karimi*, second edition. Tehran: Mahur Institute of Culture and Art.

Navvāb Mir Mohsen ebn Hāji Seyyed Ahmad Qarabāghi. 1913. *Vozuh al-arqām dar 'elm-e musiqi*. Baku: n.p. (In Azeri, written 1884.)

Nettl, Bruno. 1984. "In Honor of Our Principal Teachers." *Ethnomusicology* 28(2): 173–85.

———. 1992[1987]. *The Radif of Persian Music: Studies of Structure and Context*. Champaign, IL: Elephant and Cat.

Pāyvar, Farāmarz, ed. 1999[1996]. *Radif-e āvāzi va tasnif-hā-e qadimi, be ravāyat-e Ostād 'Abdollāh Davāmi*, second edition. Tehran: Māhur.

Pirniyākān, Daryoosh. 2001. *Musiqi-ye dastgāhi-ye Irān: radif-e Mirzā Hoseynqoli be ravāyat-e'Ali Akbar Shahnāzi*. Tehran: Māhur.

Powers, Harold S. 1970. "An Historical and Comparative Approach to the Classification of Ragas (with an Appendix on Ancient Indian Tunings)." *Selected Reports in Ethnomusicology* 1(3): 1–78. Los Angeles: Department of Ethnomusicology, University of California.

———. 1989. "'International Segah' and its Nominal Equivalents in Central Asia and Kashmir." In *Maqām—rāga—Zeilenmelodik: Konzeptionen und Prinzipien der Musikproduktion. Materialien der 1. Arbeitstagung der Study Group 'maqām' beim International Council for Traditional Music vom 28. Juni bis 2. Juli 1988 in Berlin*, edited by Jürgen Elsner, 40–85. Berlin: Nationalkomitee DDR des International Council for Traditional Music in Verbindung mit dem Sekretariat Internationale Nichtstaaliche Musikorganisationen.

Purjavādy, Amir Hosein, ed. 2001. "Risāla dar bayān-e chahār dastgāh-e 'azam." *Fasl-nāme Māhur* 3(12): 81–92.

Rapport, Evan. 2014. *Greeted with Smiles: Bukharian Jewish Music and Musicians in New York*. New York: Oxford University Press.

Razhabii, Iunus, and Faizulla M. Karomatov. 1966–1975. *Shashmaqom*. 6 vols. Toshkent: "Toshkent."

Shiloah, Amnon. 1979. *The Theory of Music in Arabic Writings (c. 900–1900): Descriptive Catalogue of Manuscripts in Libraries of Europe and the U.S.A.* Répertoire International des Sources Musicales, B, x. Munich: G. Henle.

———. 2003. *The Theory of Music in Arabic Writings (c. 900-1900): Descriptive Catalogue of Manuscripts in Libraries of Egypt, Israel, Morocco, Russia, Tunisia, Uzbekistan, and supplement to B X*. Répertoire International des Sources Musicales, B, x-A. Munich: G. Henle.

Shushinski, Firidun. 1979. *Narodnye pesni i muzykanty Azerbaidzhana*. Moscow: Sovetskii Kompozitor.

Sims, Rob, and Air Koushkani. 2012. *The Art of Avaz and Mohammad Reza Shajarian: Foundations and Contexts*. Lanham, MD: Lexington Books.

Talā'i, Daryush. 1993. *A New Approach to the Theory of Persian Art Music/negāreshi now be te'uri-ye musiqi-ye irāni*. Tehran: Māhur. (Text in English and Persian.)

———. 2002. "A New Approach to the Theory of Persian Art Music: The *Radif* and the Modal System." In *The Garland Encyclopedia of World Music*, Volume VI: *The Middle East*, edited by Virginia Danielson, Scott Marcus, and Dwight Reynolds, 865–74. New York: Routledge.

Yultchieva, Monājāt. 1994. *Maqām d'Asie Centrale, 1: Ouzbékistan-Ferghāna*. Paris: OCORA. Compact disc, C 560060, with booklet of notes by Jean During.

Zohrābov, Rāmez. 1999[1991]. *Muqām: Musiqi-e maqāmi-e Azerbāijān*. Translated by 'Alā'addin Hoseyni. Tehran: Sorush.

CHAPTER FOURTEEN

~

The *Saz Semaisi* in *Evcara* by Dilhayat Kalfa and the Turkish Makam after the Ottoman Golden Age

Robert Garfias

I embarked on the study of the Turkish *makam* after meeting the excellent Turkish musician Necdet Yaşar. I was intrigued by his performance, especially his profound understanding of the Turkish makam system. I did not think it possible, however, that I could come to grasp the elements of this system in the complete manner that Bruno Nettl had done with the Persian *radif* (Nettl 1987). After working on elements of the Turkish makam in Romanian urban Rom music (Garfias 1981), I was at last lured into pursuing it further. I spent about two years at different times studying in Turkey, a period during which I discovered some fascinating gems. The *saz semaisi* in *makam evcara* by Dilhayat Kalfa is one of these.

Turkish classical music, called *Türk Sanat Musikisi* in Turkish, grew out of the music of the court of the Ottoman Empire and from the *Mevlevi Hane*, the mystic Sufi houses that developed and sustained a music tradition parallel to, but distinct from, that of the court. The repertory of several thousand compositions regularly practiced and performed by many musicians in Turkey today is regarded much like the radif in Iran. It is a vast, complex tradition that is not so much defined by any single work, but by the cohesiveness and integrity of the entire body.

The key to the structure of Turkish classical music is the system of makam, which is similar to but distinct from the Persian system of *dastgah* and *gushe*. Each composition in the Turkish repertory is created in one makam or another, and certain compositions are regarded as good examples of a particular makam. Yet some compositions are highly regarded for their form or integrity, even while they may not best exemplify the character of a given makam. Thus while all compositions in the Ottoman tradition are in a makam, some may not be considered good examples of the makam but are nevertheless regarded as very good compositions. An analysis of the saz semaisi in evcara by Dilhayat Kalfa illustrates this point.

For many Turkish musicians, a makam is defined by all of its extant compositions. It is not possible to know exactly how many compositions exist in the Turkish classical music repertory, but there are at least ten thousand pieces. Many are recent compositions dating from the twentieth century, but more than half originated in the days of the Ottoman Sultanate. A commonly played makam such as *hicaz* comprises hundreds of examples, offering a great range of compositions that serve to define it. Others, such as evcara, comprise fewer than two hundred compositions, and thus are defined by a narrower range of examples. Most compositions in evcara date from the twentieth century. Yet several of the existing compositions in evcara are quite old, and a good number are by some of the most eminent and respected composers of the tradition, such as Sultan Selim III and Dede Efendi.

Many Turkish musicians cite the saz semaisi by Dilhayat Kalfa (1710–1780) to exemplify the complex makam evcara. Her composition is the earliest extant example in this makam and it is likely that she created it. Soon after, composers such as Sultan Selim III (1761–1808) and Dede Efendi (1778–1846) also created compositions in evcara that are thought to exemplify it better. This suggests that the conception of evcara changed soon after Dilhayat's time. Some sources suggest that Sultan Selim III created evcara, but this seems unlikely. The connection between Dilhayat and Sultan Selim III was close; some twenty years overlapped between the time of his birth and her death. Since he was a prince in the court, Sultan Selim III may have been allowed access to the women's quarters, and this would open the possibility that Dilhayat might have been one of his teachers, although there is no proof of this.

Within the world of Turkish classical music today, there is a clear distinction between the old court *fasıl*, a suite of some five or six compositions, and the late-nineteenth and twentieth-century fasıl, made up of several *şarkı* (a song type) framed by instrumental pieces. The old court fasıl began with an instrumental prelude, the *peşrev*, followed by a few songs in classic forms (one or two *beste*, one *ağir semai*, and one *yürük semai*), and ended with an instrumental composition, the saz semaisi. Hundreds of works had been created in this form before composers adopted the newer style of fasıl. Much of the oldest part of the repertory has been transmitted orally; what is available for study is the music as it is performed today, which is based on notated versions from the late eighteenth century.

The Ottoman Court Ensemble

Changes in the instrumental ensemble used to play court music have been gradual but continuous until the present day. Certain instruments came into and went out of fashion; as the musical styles changed, new interpretations and performance styles made the use of some instruments unfavorable. Such must have been the case with the angular harp, *çeng*, and the pan pipes, *mıskal*. Both have disappeared completely in Turkish music, except for recent historical reconstructions. Various lutes, bowed and plucked, have fallen out of use and were replaced by other instruments. The dominant instruments during much of the late eighteenth and early nineteenth century, the period discussed here, were the end-blown flute (*ney*) and the long-necked lute (*tanbur*). Other instruments have become standard, including the lute (*ud*) and the plucked trapezoidal zither (*qanun*). Until the early twentieth century, a bowed spike fiddle (*rebab*) was in common use, but it has been replaced by a Turkish folk instrument (*kemançe*). For compositions most associated with the Ottoman Court, the small timpani (*kudüm*) are the sole percussion instruments. Ensembles play in heterophony. Each instrument sounds the main melody, adding its characteristic embellishments; thus one hears the main melody played simultaneously on several different instruments with slight individual inflections.

All Turkish music from the Ottoman period features fixed rhythmic patterns called *usul*. Hundreds of usul patterns exist and are used regularly, and there are often several different usul in the same meter. The kudüm steadily marks out the simple usul pattern without variation. But in the Ottoman music tradition as it is played today, the kudüm plays a set of variant usul patterns called *velvele*. These are somewhat more complex patterns based on the usul of the composition (figure 14.1).

There may have been much more improvisation of individual parts formerly than is permitted today. In the case of the kudüm part, one can well imagine that some improvisation on the usul probably took place. In the early twenty-first century, however, in the performance of the old-style fasıl, kudüm players stay close to the usul as notated.

The Makam System

The makam system used during this epoch of the Ottoman Sultanate developed in a manner different from its Persian roots. Rather than following the path that led to the contemporary Persian system, a complex of small and large melodic fragments (gushe) grouped into larger melodic units (dastgah),

Figure 14.1. Basic *usul* and *kudüm velvele* for *aksak semai* and *yürük semai*

Ottoman practice evolved a system in which two or more makams were combined into a single new makam. Before 1700, Ottoman music had a system of makam and *terkib*; terkib were more fragmentary than the main makam. The terkib developed and began to be treated as makam; some were further combined into new makams. By the late seventeenth century, the makam system as a whole resembled the system as we understand it today (Feldman 1996:253).

The definition of a makam during the Ottoman Empire appears to have been based on the body of compositions in each makam. In 1922, the Turkish musicologist Rauf Yekta Bey (1871–1935) published an important work titled "La musique turque." Yekta's work stands out as the first substantial publication on Turkish music in a Western language, but it appears to represent his own unique interpretation of makam. Yekta traces the roots of the Turkish system back to ancient Greek models and provides precise mathematical calculations of interval structure. He emphasizes the pentachord and tetrachord components of each makam. This concept of makam is not in itself antithetical to the view that each makam is an integrated entity, and others gradually adopted the clarity and logic of Yekta's theory, most notably Hüseyin Sadettin Arel (1880–1955). It quickly became the established theory of makam and eventually was adopted by performing musicians.

The theory of makam as defined by Yekta, Arel, and others does not account for gradual changes that have occurred in each makam over time; in addition, the theoretical rules are not always faithfully observed in performance. Some makams, such as *sevkefza* (which is attributed to Sultan Selim

III), would be described as going through five separate makams or fragments of them before reaching the final cadence point. The sequence through the sub-makam is flexible and fluid. The range of surviving compositions in sevkefza from the time of Sultan Selim III shows considerable variety in the balance and duration of the component makams.

Many makam from this period have an implied pattern of balance among the various component makam that dictates the length of time spent on each. The amount of time spent on each component makam is determined by the fixed, notated composition. However, there is a balance of emphasis and a pattern of steps to be followed in the order and presentation of the component makam. Certain makam, such as *nuhüft* and *büzürk*, which were once popular in the court, rely so heavily on one of the component makam that the main makam itself appears to be merely another component. Only at the end does the composition resolve on the main makam. One can imagine that in an entire set of six or seven compositions in a fasıl suite, the listener would feel some suspense without knowing from the start what the final makam would be. Given the frequency with which this kind of makam occurs in Ottoman compositions, it may well have been a source of listening pleasure in the court. This deliberate play with time is in keeping with the calm, elegance, gravity, and solemnity of the Ottoman court.

Makam Evcara

Arel, and those who followed him, classed the makam evcara as a *şed makam* (transposed makam). However, in its structure it behaves like what is called a combined makam (*mürekkeb* or *bileşik makam*). This is the view of most contemporary Turkish musicians and theorists. Evcara is less complex than many other makam dating from the Ottoman period. In practice, combined makam are made up of two or more component makam. The concluding makam is the most important or main makam. The Turkish musician Necati Çelik explains that "the most important note in the makam is the last one you hear" (personal communication, July 1994). Compositions in evcara are regularly performed in Turkey today. One that is heard with some regularity is the saz semaisi composed by Dilhayat Kalfa, a woman living in the harem of the Sultan who was regarded as an important teacher and composer. Her rank as a *Kalfa* indicates her status as a leader or teacher, someone with responsibility, status, and skill. Of the hundreds of compositions she is said to have composed, only a few survive in notation. As was the common practice of Turkish composers in the late eighteenth century, Dilhayat composed a set of two instrumental pieces as part of the larger court fasıl. She composed two pieces in evcara, a peşrev (prelude) and a saz semaisi (the closing piece). Whereas some Turkish sources attribute the creation of makam evcara to Sultan Selim III, these two compositions by Dilhayat suggest otherwise. Dilhayat was fifty-one years senior to Selim; he would have been nineteen years old at the time of her death. Later historians may have thought it more fitting to attribute the creation of evcara to the Sultan rather than to a woman (Feldman 1996:71).

According to current theory, the scale and component makam structure of evcara appears in figure 14.2.[1] In the Turkish system, each pitch has its own name; therefore, the octave duplications of a pitch each have different names. In theory, the Turkish tonal system contains twenty-two pitches to the octave, but in practice, certain makams require more than twenty-two pitches, because there are different species of whole tones and semitones. In other words, the interval structure in Turkish classical music is quite different from what is suggested by staff notation. The pitches and interval structure of evcara as represented in staff notation, with their acoustical measurements in commas and cents, appears in Figure 14.3.

Evcara is thought to consist of a main component, makam hicaz on the pitch *irak* (low F♯). Specifically, this is the *zirgule* variant of makam hicaz on irak. This portion of evcara can be considered the main component of the makam. Two other makams are additional components of evcara and they usually appear in fragmentary form. It is worth noting that Yekta shows three additional components of evcara rather than two. A well-known performer of Turkish classical music, Münir Beken, composed a *seyir* in evcara (figure 14.4) that corresponds closely with Yekta's interpretation of this makam. A

Figure 14.2. The scale and component *makam* structure of *evcara*

Figure 14.3. ***Evcara*** **and component** ***makam*** **in staff notation with acoustical measurements in commas and cents**

Figure 14.4. ***Evcara seyir*** **as performed by Münir Beken.** ***Courtesy of Münir Beken***

seyir is an abstracted melodic essence of a makam used for practice, but not in performance. Although one could look for the classic subcomponents here as well, Beken and Signell suggest that it is more effective to perceive makam in terms of broad tonal movement and strategic points of emphasis and rest (2006:211). In this light, we see evcara as beginning around *evic* (high F♯), moving eventually to rest on *nim hicaz* (C♯), and finally moving down to irak (low F♯). Yekta provides a short *semai*[2] of his own creation as an example of the melodic tendencies of evcara (1922:3008), which can also serve as an example of the seyir of evcara (figure 14.5).

These two seyir indicate that evcara hovers around the evic (high F♯). In fact, the name evcara (*evic-ara*) means "around evic" or "on evic." In this upper nucleus, the makam ascends from evic as far as *muhayyer* (high A), barely touches on *tiz segah* (high B),[3] and sometimes uses *şehnaz* (high G♯). It usually leaps up to *gerdaniye* (high G) and then moves stepwise back down to evic (high F♯), sometimes touching on tiz segah (high B) and gerdaniye (high G) in passing. Descending further, evcara temporarily hovers around nim hicaz (C♯) before gradually lowering to irak (low F♯). In Beken's seyir for evcara, the first eight measures center on evic (high F♯), the middle section (five measures) centers on nim hicaz (C♯), and the last four measures rest on irak (low F♯). Both Beken's seyir and Yekta's semai emphasize evic (high F♯),

Figure 14.5. Yekta's *evcara semai*

with less emphasis on nim hicaz (C♯) and even less on the final irak (low F♯), although irak has an inherent emphasis because it is the last note to be heard.

In terms of form, Dilhayat's saz semaisi follows the standard pattern for all saz semaisi (figure 14.6). It is divided into four phrase types called *hane*, each of which differs from the others. In performance, each hane is followed by a phrase called the *teslim*, which acts as a kind of refrain; the same teslim repeats after each different hane. All of the hane feature the same usul except the fourth hane, which is always in a contrasting meter (usually a triple meter). In general, saz semaisi use shorter usul patterns than preşrev. In this

Figure 14.6. Melodic movement in Dilhayat's *saz semaisi*

case, the usul for all but the fourth hane is *aksak semai* (figure 14.1). In modern Turkish notation, the shorter usul are written in measures. Aksak semai is a measure with ten beats, represented by the time signature 10/8. The teslim features four cycles of aksak semai that can be repeated once each time the teslim is played. The different hanes use varying numbers of usul cycles. The first hane contains nine aksak semai cycles, the second has ten aksak semai cycles, and the third consists of eight cycles. The fourth hane, which is in yürük semai (6/8; figure 14.1), uses thirty-two cycles. Even though the last meter contains only six beats (as opposed to ten), the fourth hane is considerably longer than the other three in this composition.

The earliest examples of saz semaisi feature the same general form outlined in figure 14.6. Perhaps the desire to expand the notated instrumental portion of the fasıl led to the origin of this instrumental genre. It is interesting to note that the saz semaisi form seems to reflect or to derive from the last two vocal compositions in the fasıl, that is, the ağir semai in ten beats and the yürük semai in six beats. Thus the saz semaisi nicely concludes the old court fasıl by reprising the rhythmic patterns of the last two songs in the suite.

A Melodic Analysis of Dilhayat's Saz Semaisi in Evcara

A detailed melodic analysis of Dilhayat's saz semaisi in evcara demonstrates some of the ways in which her interpretation of this makam differs from that of later performers and theorists (figure 14.7). The first hane begins on evic (high F♯) and descends not to irak (low F♯), but only to nim hicaz (C♯), creating the feeling of resting temporarily on nim hicaz. Measures 4 and 5 return to evic (high F♯). In measures 6 through 9, the melody descends to irak (low F♯). There is an interesting use of melodic sequence, a short melodic pattern repeated at different steps, throughout this composition. In addition, the last two measure of the first hane, measures 8 and 9, are later repeated in the last two measures of both the teslim and second hane, connecting these three sections. Its phrase is reinforced at the end of the composition, which closes with the teslim.

The teslim section of the composition contains eight ten-beat measures. These eight measures may be repeated. In Ottoman practice, it may have been either the composer's intention or the tradition of the era to repeat

Figure 14.7. Weighted scale for Dilhayat's *saz semaisi* in *evcara*

the teslim once after each iteration of the hane. Current practice, however, leaves this to the discretion of the performer or performers, and thus in many cases the teslim is heard only once after each hane. Dilhayat's teslim centers on the lower range of evcara, on nim hicaz (C♯) or irak (low F♯), beginning around nim hicaz. The repetitions of the teslim after each hane emphasize the final note on irak (low F♯).

The second hane contains ten measures of ten beats each. In many compositions, the second hane centers on a different tonal region than the first hane. In this piece, the second hane begins in the lower register on irak (low F♯) and maintains an overall ascending melodic pattern, in contrast to the remainder of the composition. Measure 8 introduces a variation not found elsewhere, and the melodic content suggests the *makam buselik* on the pitch irak (low F♯), rather than evcara. This one measure seems so uncharacteristic that it may have been a copyist's error, yet it does add spice to the phrase. The end of the second hane echoes the last phrase of the first hane and the teslim. The teslim is reprised after the second hane.

The third hane consists of eight ten-beat cycles. Like the first hane, it begins on evic (high F♯) but continues in the high range as though returning to the register that was gradually attained in the second hane. The third hane ascends to and emphasizes şehnaz (high G♯) and muhayyer (high A). The last two measures descend to a cadence that resembles the final phrases in the first two hane as well as the teslim. The openings of measures 4, 5, and 6 employ a stepwise descent that creates a feeling of melodic sequence before the modified repeat of the now established cadence pattern. The teslim is reprised following the third hane.

The fourth hane contains thirty-two six-beat cycles. This hane uses the most typical usul found in this part of all saz semaisi, the six-beat yürük semai (figure 14.1). Usually the fourth hane also represents the most radical change in melodic material. In Dilhayat's saz semaisi, the fourth hane begins on irak (low F♯) and introduces a four-measure melodic pattern with regular sets of triplets. The melody remains largely in makam hicaz on irak (low F♯), the dominant lower component in evcara. The fourth hane also has a unique internal structure. This, together with the meter change, suggests that the fourth hane is treated almost as a separate short composition at the end of the saz semaisi. The opening four-measure phrase repeats almost exactly in measures 5 to 8, except for each of the last measures; measure 4 leads to the repetition of the figure, whereas measure 8 transitions to the new melodic material in measure 9. The four-measure phrase beginning in measure 9 uses the same rhythmic motif as that of the first two phrases, with two clear differences. Measure 9 begins high and moves to şehnaz (high G♯), suggesting the first phrase of the first hane. Measure 10 breaks the pattern by repeating the rhythm of measures 1, 5, and 9, rather than the rhythm of measures 2 and 6. Measures 11 and 12 repeat measures 7 and 8. These three four-measure phrases contain yet another three-part melodic sequence. This time, Dilhayat uses three phrases that are internal variants of each other, strongly linked by repeated rhythmic and melodic figures.

The second part of the fourth hane begins at measure 13 with very different melodic material, which repeats through the four measures until returning in measures 17 through 19 to the melodic material of measures 1 through 12. This creates an eight-measure pattern of two contrasting four-measure phrases. This pattern repeats again in measures 20 through 28. The cadence points of each repetition (measures 19 and 28) occur on segah (low B) and then connect to the pitch of the subsequent phrase, evic (high F♯) in the first case and segah (low B) in the second. After this repeated eight-measure phrase is a new four-measure phrase using the material made familiar in the first measure of the fourth hane. Absent the triplet or sixteenth-note figures of the previous material, this signals a slowing down in preparation for the inevitable repetition of the teslim. In measures 17 and 25, after introducing the pitch şehnaz (high G♯), the same measure also introduces gerdaniye (high G), for the only time in the entire composition. This melodic activity hints at *makam segah* on the pitch evic (high F♯), which is a characteristic of compositions in evcara in the period following Dilhayat. The phrase then returns to the more established use of şehnaz (high G♯). The first three measures of this second part of the fourth hane are repeated, and then the melody descends to irak (low F♯). Interestingly, the last two measures of the fourth hane repeat the same material found in the last two measures of the first and second hane, as well as the last two measures of the teslim. These two measures thus prepare the teslim each time it occurs, and through repetitions of the teslim, they pave the way for the final cadence of the piece as a whole. The sole exception to this pattern occurs at the end of the third hane, which concludes in the mid-upper range of the melody and leads directly to the teslim. At this point in the fourth hane, the figure serves to switch back to the aksak semai meter, slowing the pace for the final reprise of the teslim, where the composition ends. The weighted scale for the entire saz semaisi (figure 14.8), together with the emphasis created by numerous repetitions of the teslim, demonstrates that the main tones of Dilhayat's composition differ markedly from those of later compositions in evcara. In particular, the dominance of segah (low B) and neva (D) differ markedly from the current standard practice.

Aksak Semai | Evcara Saz Semaisi | Dilhayat Kalfa

1st Hane

5

10 Teslim

14 2nd Hane

19

24 Teslim

27 3rd Hane

31

35 Teslim

39 4th Hane

46

Figure 14.8a. Dilhayat Kalfa's *saz semaisi* in *evcara*

Figure 14.8b. Dilhayat Kalfa's *saz semaisi* in *evcara* (*continued*)

To summarize, in terms of a broader seyir without specific reference to particular sub-component makams, Dilhayat's saz semaisi reveals the following pattern: the first hane opens on evic (high F♯) and rises only to şehnaz (high G♯) before descending to nim hicaz (C♯) in the first two measures. Measures 3 through 6 are much the same, but begin on *neva* (D), move up to evic (high F♯), descend to nim hicaz (C♯), and rest on *segah* (low B). Measures 7 through 9 descend from segah (low B) to irak (low F♯). The teslim seems to be based entirely on irak (low F♯), and because it is repeated so often during the composition, the teslim strongly defines the composition in the listener's memory. It begins on neva (D), then the second measure begins on segah (low B), and the last two measures begin on irak (low F♯), ascend to nim hicaz (C♯), and return to end on irak. The second hane begins on ırak (low F♯), ascends through *rast* (low G), segah (low B), and neva (D) to reach evic (high F♯). From there, it ascends as high as gerdaniye (high G), remains around high evic (high F♯), and finally descends until it reaches ırak (low F♯). The teslim recurs. The third hane begins on evic (high F♯) and remains largely in the high register hovering on şhenaz (high G♯) and gerdaniye (high G natural) before descending to end on nim hicaz (C♯). The third hane stands out because it remains in the higher register, and because until now, the first hane, the teslim, the second hane, and the second teslim have all ended on irak (low F♯); the third hane alone ends on nim hicaz (C♯). The third teslim follows, and once again ends on irak (low F♯). The fourth hane is distinct in both meter and melodic material. In the first four measures it moves from irak (low F♯) up to neva (D) and back to irak. The repeat of this melodic material ends by ascending to evic (high F♯). The next eight measures remain around evic, ascending to şhenaz (high G♯), and once touching on gerdaniye (high G natural).

Conclusions

As an example of makam evcara, Dilhayat Kalfa's saz semaisi differs from the interpretations of early twentieth-century Turkish theorists, which were based on compositions by Sultan Selim III, Dede Effendi, and later composers. It also deviates from the seyirs in evcara by Münir Beken and Yekta, which are also based on later compositions. The clearest distinction lies in the relatively infrequent appearance of the pitch gerdaniye (high G natural) and instead the regular use of şehnaz (high G♯). Rast (low G natural) is fundamental to the lower region and the cadential pattern of evcara; thus the use of şehnaz in the upper register is a strong characteristic of Dilhayat's evcara. Gerdaniye (high G natural) appears only once in her saz semaisi, and not at all in her paired peşrev, which tells us that to Dilhayat, gerdaniye did not have the melodic significance that was attached to it by later composers. The other important difference between Dilhayat's evcara and those that came later lies in the emphasis on neva (D) and segah (low B), which are further underlined by their repeated appearance in the teslim. Had other compositions in this older form of evcara survived, we might have been able to distinguish between an old version and a new version, as Turkish musicians have done for *makam siphir*. Yet the fact that so many Turkish musicians cite and perform Dilhayat's saz semaisi as an example of evcara, even while admitting that it may not be the most characteristic manifestation of this makam, reflects their appreciation for the composition itself. We can only regret that so few of Dilhayat Kalfa's compositions have survived. As it stands, the high value placed on this saz semaisi by contemporary Turkish musicians is a testament to this earliest iteration of evcara. The character of evcara changed soon after Dilhayat's time, and this makam, as it is understood by most Turkish musicians, derives from later versions. However, the integrity of the formal pattern and flow manifested in the saz semaisi by Dilhayat Kalfa demonstrates that this earlier rendition of evcara was, in its time, complete and well-expressed in her composition.

Notes

1. Although this pitch structure for evcara is in general use in the early twenty-first century, it is interesting that Ekrem Karadeniz, in his encyclopedic *Türk Musikisinin Nazariye ve Esaslar*, describes evcara (*evicara*) as a basic makam and places it on

the pitch *geveşt* (low F♯), eight commas above Huseyni Asiran or low E, rather than irak (low F♯), five commas above Huseyni Asiran) (Karadeniz n.d.:84). No other authority interprets evcara this way, and Turkish musicians use evcara on irak.

2. A semai in this context is the same as a semaisi, but the word semaisi is only used when preceded by the complete term, as in saz semaisi.

3. All of the examples in this chapter use the pitch segah (low B) or its upper variant, tiz segah. In modern Turkish notation, this pitch is indicated with the reversed flat accidental and the pitch is always 204 cents lower than nim hicaz (C♯) and 90 cents above kürdi (low A♯).

References

Arel, Huseyin Sadettin. 1991. *Türk mûsıkîsi nazariyatı dersleri*. Ankara: Kültür Bakanlığı.

Beken, Münir Nurettin, and Karl Signell. 2006. "The Problematic Nature of Defining a Turkish Makam." In *Maqam Traditions of Turkic Peoples*, edited by Jürgen Elsner, Gisa Jähnichen, Thomas Ogger, and Ildar Kharissov, 204–15. Berlin: Trafo Verlag.

Feldman, Walter. 1996. *Music of the Ottoman Court*. Berlin: VWB.

Garfias, Robert. 1981. "Survivals of Turkish Charateristics in Romanian Musica Lautareasca." *Yearbook for Traditional Music* 13: 97–107.

Karadeniz, M. Ekrem. N.d. *Türk Musikinin Nazariye ve Esaslari*. Ankara: Turkiye I° ankas.

Nettl, Bruno. 1987. *The Radif of Persian Music: Studies of Structure and Cultural Context*. Champaign, IL: Elephant and Cat.

Yekta Bey, Rauf. 1922. "La musique turque." In *Encyclopedie de la musique et dictionnaire du conservatoire, premiere partie*, edited by Albert Lavignac and Lionel de la Laurencie, 2945–3064. Paris: Librerie Delagrave.

CHAPTER FIFTEEN

~

When You Do This, I'll Hear You

Gros Ventre Songs and Supernatural Power

Orin Hatton

I was fortunate to meet Bruno Nettl in 1970, while I was still in high school. At his office in the Hill Annex on the University of Illinois campus, I remember asking if he would teach me Grass Dance songs. He was very polite of course, and gently pointed me in another direction. He gave me reprints of his articles on Blackfeet music (1967, 1968), and I studied those reprints for many years. His discussion of tune families, characteristics of style such as scale and rhythm, and specific form outlines and closing formulae have long held a fascination for me. In trying to learn more about Grass Dance songs, I found that songs and singing among Native Americans of the northwestern Plains represent a particular "way of speaking" (Hymes 1989:445–51), and their communicative function varies by genre and context. For example, Gros Ventre songs obtained during spirit visitations provide a means by which individuals may summon spirit helpers to elicit assistance in moments of need. These songs raise questions about their sources of agency and how they are acquired, and perhaps most importantly, when they are sung, who is listening? This chapter, based on a study of two dozen Gros Ventre songs, helps to answer these questions.

The songs used in this study were recorded in August 1940 by John M. Cooper, a Jesuit priest, at the Fort Belknap Reservation in Montana. His principal consultant was a seventy-year-old elder named The Boy, whose father had been a noted pipe keeper, doctor, and leader. The Boy had direct knowledge of historic Gros Ventre culture, and a number of the songs he sang for Cooper had been obtained by Gros Ventre men and women from spirit and ancestral helpers during the eighteenth and nineteenth centuries—giving his recordings both great authority and considerable time depth. Cooper recorded songs obtained from supernatural entities, what I call spirit helpers, that occur in a variety of genres within the overall Gros Ventre repertory, including the Chief Medicine Pipe rituals; the Sacred Lodges; personal songs used for doctoring or painting a shield or lodge cover; Victory songs received from ghost helpers (ancestral beings); and an old Victory Song, dating from perhaps the 1790s, when a new text was set to an existing melody to mark the return of a young man and his supernaturally directed war expedition (cf. Cooper 1957; Fort Belknap Indian Community 1982:129–38). Taken together, these songs suggest that for the Gros Ventres, song and singing occupy a central place in a continuum of speech behavior, and demonstrate how songs obtained during spirit visitations create a nexus of meaning, symbol, analogy, and incitation (cf. Wagner 1986; Hatton 1989, 1990).

Power and Agency in Gros Ventre Songs

The Gros Ventre people of north-central Montana, who call themselves *A'aninin* or White Clay People, were among the earliest inhabitants of the northwestern Plains. For the Gros Ventres, the physical landscape is inhabited by a variety of spirit beings, each possessing different powers and knowledge. Certain spirits were known to inhabit certain places. In published narratives of vision quests and spirit visitations—those encounters between a spirit helper and a human being—there is an ever-present community of spirit beings within hearing distance. Spirit beings coordinate which among them will provide what gifts to a particular person who is fasting for power (see Cooper 1957; Horse Capture 1980). For example, the spirit being residing in a butte on which a Gros Ventre man named Bull Lodge sought a vision told him, "It has been foretold that you would be here," and added, "Now it was told to me by the one who attended your last experience, that I was to provide you with instruction concerning gifts that have already been given to you" (Horse Capture 1980:38–39).

The concept of spirit helpers is tied to concepts of power and agency (Giddens 1979:55). Spirit helpers come to the aid of humans when they have been summoned, and before that can happen, the spirit being and the human will have established a relationship in which the spirit felt compelled to help the human. The gift of a song plays an instrumental role in engaging that process, inciting the relationship that has been established between the human and the spirit helper. The human accesses that relationship in the manner taught at the time the spirit helper took pity on the human and bestowed a gift of power. Before describing the ritual of fasting for power, the so-called vision quest young men used to elicit the help of a spirit being, it is necessary to explain certain Gros Ventre concepts of power and agency.

Gros Ventre concepts of power and agency may be explained in relation to a sacred narrative that is widespread among Native peoples of the northwestern Plains. This is not a creation story per se; rather, it involves the restoration or reordering of the earth following a deluge. In the Gros Ventre narrative, the first order of the earth was destroyed by a fire, and the second order was destroyed by a flood (Kroeber 1907:59–61; Cooper 1957). After the flood, a human known as Earthmaker or possibly *Ni:hehat* (The Trickster) restored earth to the water's surface and repopulated the land, thus initiating the current or third order of the earth. It is important to note here that the Gros Ventres believe there will be a fourth world or order in the future (Cooper 1957:18; Kroeber 1907:61). Earthmaker was apparently a Flat Pipe Keeper, for after the flood, he was alone with the Flat Pipe bundle and a crow; he thought, prayed, cried, and sang. He animated certain ducks and a turtle, animals known for their mastery of the water environment and preserved in the Flat Pipe bundle, by singing and commanding them to dive into the water and bring up mud from the bottom. Earthmaker used the mud to restore earth to the water's surface. The Gros Ventres believe that birds and animals "continued to sing as they had done at the earthmaking," and "did not . . . let their singing degenerate" (Cooper 1957:80).

Central to this narrative is the idea that Earthmaker used his innate talents and abilities—his power of mastery—to reorder the earth's surface and restore animal, plant, and human life. Earthmaker used the speech resources of thinking, praying, crying, and singing to gain the pity of the Supreme Being. The first utterance after the flood was Earthmaker's singing, and the words of his song mean "My holiness (or my power) respond to me (pity me)" (Cooper 1957:79). Although the Earthmaker had supernatural powers at his disposal, he relied first upon his own mastery and the power of thinking, praying, crying, and singing to restore the earth and its inhabitants (Hatton 1990:7–16). The salient point is that the Gros Ventres distinguish between the power of one's own talents and abilities (mastery) and the use of supernatural power (Cooper 1957:79–80). The opposition of two competing flows of agency, using speech behavior and mastery on the one hand, or using speech behavior and supernatural power on the other, in which each *contains* the other, is a concept that may be unique to the Gros Ventres among northwestern Plains groups. The idea of containment is evident in that an individual Gros Ventre used the instrumental nature of thinking, praying, crying, and singing to obtain the pity of the Supreme Being, just as the Earthmaker had done in reordering the earth. Similarly, these are the speech behaviors used to obtain the assistance of supernatural entities (Cooper 1957:280–82).

Gros Ventre children were taught to avoid the use of supernatural power because it was known to shorten a person's life. Cooper notes that "in general, the Gros Ventres distinguished between three chief methods of fulfilling their desires and wants: natural ability, prayer and power. A person was supposed to make best use of his native physical and mental endowments to acquire skills, to use his wits, to develop his capacities and personality." When an individual's natural or acquired abilities "threatened to fall short of enabling him to fulfill his wishes and needs," the Gros Ventre turned to prayer, "primarily although by no means exclusively to the Supreme Being." In this system, the least desirable choice was to "resort to [supernatural] power" (Cooper 1957:264).[1]

I approach Gros Ventre songs that were obtained through encounters with spirit beings as a particular way of speaking (after Hymes 1989:441–51). Key to this approach is the context in which the songs access or provide agency, the frame in which singing is instrumental behavior. Elsewhere I have noted that "as performance, singing is communication between humans and supernatural entities about a problematic subject: the acquisition and use of alternative resources of power" (Hatton 1989:40). According to the Gros Ventres, each of the eight Sacred Lodges was obtained from supernatural entities (cf. Cooper 1957). Songs and singing, as a way of speaking, are part of a body of speech genres among the Gros Ventres that include "wish (or wish-thought), prayer . . . vows, oaths . . . omens," narratives of dreams or visions, and the narration of war exploits (Cooper 1957:365). Thus, crying and singing occupy the same continuum of instrumental speech behavior.

Fasting for Power

Just as Earthmaker elicited the pity of the Supreme Being through thinking, praying, crying, and singing, Gros Ventre individuals summon spirit helpers in times of need. People acquired the personal song necessary to establish a relationship with a spirit helper through dreams, visions, or spirit visitations, typically through a process commonly known as the vision quest, or "fasting for power." The practice of fasting for power has been a widespread cultural practice among Plains peoples; individual narratives describing the vision quest and spirit visitations appear in many sources (see Irwin 1994). Prior to the twentieth century, such encounters were important sources for obtaining new ceremonies or ritual practices, as well as ritual paraphernalia; songs were typically a part of such gifts to humans.[2]

The ritual that Gros Ventre men practiced when seeking supernatural power for success in war, acquiring wealth, or doctoring centered on sleeping, fasting, crying, and praying on top of a hill, butte, or mountain for as many as seven days (Cooper 1957:275). The speech genre of crying is instrumental in establishing a relationship with a potential spirit helper. The spirit community hears the human crying, and the spirits decide among them who might help the quester. It is worth noting that the majority of those who sought a vision were unsuccessful (Cooper 1957:273–74). Although women did not undertake vision quests, they might be offered supernatural power without asking (Cooper 1957:292). A woman named Singer Sleeping Bear, remarked that "when they lost a loved one, [women] would go up into the mountains and cry themselves to sleep, and that is when a lot of them would get power" (Cooper 1957:293). Some women made sacrifices of personal objects, such as a blanket, and prayed that a spirit might have pity on them, and thus received an offer of power (Cooper 1957:266–67).

The young man undertaking a quest for power traveled some distance away from his band's encampment and climbed atop a hill, butte, or mountain (Cooper 1957:275). There he built a shelter of rocks, typically about two feet high and in the shape of a U, for a windbreak (Horse Capture 1980:47). This was known as a "call-for-power lodge" (Cooper 1957:281). The practice is evident today, and according to Dormaar and Reeves, "several of the areas with old vision quest sites [in southern Alberta and northern Montana] are being used again for spiritual activities" (1993:167; see also Fowler 1987).[3]

Fasting for power involved careful preparation. Young men bathed and perfumed themselves before setting out for a mountaintop, so that the spirit being who lived there would not send them away because of their body odor (Cooper 1957:277). Questers unbraided their hair and took with them a pipe with tobacco, moccasins, a breechcloth, and a blanket (Cooper 1957:278–79). An elder might accompany the quester to help him get settled and take his horse back to camp. In addition to helping build the call-for-power lodge, the elder might also help the quester make sacrifices of skin or a finger joint (Cooper 1957:277–78; Horse Capture 1980:35, 38). Questers fasted, prayed, and cried for the duration of their time on the mountain, thinking about the gift of power they sought. A spirit who was moved by the quester's crying took pity and generally wanted to help in some way, but did not necessarily possess the gift being sought. The spirit might offer certain gifts and it was up to the faster to decide whether to accept them.

The spirit helper might visit the faster at any time of the day or night in the course of a fast for power. Often, the spirit approached the faster with the appearance of a human, but the faster knew it was a spirit by the way it approached him. For example, during their fasting experiences, the renowned Gros Ventre leaders Bull Lodge (Horse Capture 1980:38) and Running Fisher (Curtis 1909:120) recount that a small boy approached them in their dreams and led them down the butte (i.e., lodge) to its door. On entering the lodge, the faster observed that it was a tipi, and there was typically an old man and woman sitting at the back of the lodge. At the point when the owner of the butte (the lodge keeper or spirit being) had taken pity on the faster and was about to offer some type of power, the lodge keeper said, "I give you my body" (Cooper 1957:266). Similarly, in writing about Blackfeet spirit visitations, Clark Wissler explained that "the being manifest in the vision announces that he will give his body to the recipient and cause a small object to pass into the body of the recipient, which passes out again at death" (1912:105). The metaphor "I give you my body" thus signals the establishment of a relationship between the lodge keeper and the quester.

Another metaphor in vision quest narratives was explained by the Gros Ventre elder Fred Gone: "Occasionally a certain phrase is heard in the story: 'When you do this, I'll hear.' This means that the supernatural giver of some article will hear and recognize its special sound, whether it be a whistle, a song, a drum, or even a certain way of shouting. If the sound is made in a true way, exactly as it was told to be used, the giver will be present to insure success" (Horse Capture 1980:24–25). Phrases such as "When you do this, I'll hear," elaborate the relationship between the prescribed sound that summons a spirit helper, and the agency residing in the power obtained from the spirit helper. The power does not reside in the amulet, shield, or other object given to a quester, nor in the song itself; it is the presence of the spirit helper that ensures the effectiveness of a gift of power. To use the power, it is not necessary for the recipient to go through the entire process of eliciting pity from the spirit helper. The song or other sound activates and mobilizes the recipient's relationship with a particular spirit helper. What the song does in this process is to formalize the relationship between the human and the spirit being in a repeatable and recognizable way.

Two other important figures emerge from vision quest narratives. First, the butte or mountain where the faster sleeps and prays is called the "lodge," which belongs to the spirit being or "lodge keeper." Similarly, the social structure of the spirit being's lodge is modeled on the household of the Pipe Keepers of the Chief Medicine Pipes: the Keeper, the Co-Keeper (Keeper's wife), and the Pipe Child (Hatton 1990:42–43). During the fasting experience, the lodge keeper's son, analogous to the Pipe Child, summons the faster and leads him inside the lodge to meet his father, the lodge keeper; the lodge keeper's child may also instruct the faster on important protocols that must be observed once he is inside the lodge.

Native American myths and narratives such as Earthmaker's story often contain a rhetorical structure, which may have three corresponding parts: an onset, an ongoing, and an outcome (cf. Hymes 1981:321). However, in Gros Ventre narratives, the action itself may unfold in four or more scenes during the section identified as the "ongoing." Many Gros Ventre stories open with an appeal to tradition, phrases that point to a particular time or place in the past. Examples of this include "There was a camp circle" (Kroeber 1907:76) or "The Gros Ventre were camped where the Bear River . . . and the Knee River . . . come together" (Fort Belknap Indian Community 1982:1). Similarly, a Blackfeet example begins, "In the time when the Indians had no horses, and travelled on foot and with dog-travois" (Wissler and Duvall 1995:138). Narratives often end with a short closing phrase, such as a Gros Ventre example, "He speaks well. Let it be done that way" (Cooper 1957:155), or these Blackfeet examples: "That is what I know about it" (Uhlenbeck 1912:58); "And that is all" (Uhlenbeck 1912:195). These phrases mark closure at the end of a narrative and correlate with phrase endings in strophic song structures.

Form, Texts, and Meaning in Songs Obtained from Spirit Helpers

The Gros Ventre songs used in this study conform to the typical Plains style, including strophic forms with asymmetrical repetition, a characteristic terrace-shaped melodic contour, and a final flattening of the phrases at the end of each section within the form (Nettl 1954, 1968; Levine and Nettl 2011). My transcriptions of Gros Ventre songs focus on notating musical phrases, much like the line and verse notation of First Nations narratives used by Dell and Virginia Hymes as well as Anthony Woodbury (cf. Sherzer and Woodbury 1987). Line and verse notation enables us to discern underlying structures in the typical Plains form, including introductory phrases, internal melodic phrases, and characteristic phrase endings. To highlight my identification of lines or phrases, I use bar lines to separate individual phrases and remove all but the first clef sign. In this regard I follow the method used by Hymes to identify measured verse, more so than the pause phrasing used by Tedlock (1983). These distinctions can be made in a systematic, repeatable way from one song to the next, giving rise to a rhetorical structure that I have termed announcement, thought, and closure (Hatton 1990:55–60). The use of this model permits a comparison of the similar parts within each song, such as the B and C sections of the song in figure 15.1, and enables us to identify the closing formulae within individual A, B, or C phrases.

The song notated in figure 15.1, "Ghost Helper Summoning Song," is an example of a Gros Ventre song with the strophic form; the transcription illustrates one rendition or strophe of the song.[4] The descending melodic contour of Gros Ventre songs is one characteristic of an underlying rhetorical structure (see Woodbury 1987:178–81). Beginning on a high pitch (with a corresponding schwa sound in the text), the announcement phrase of the melody correlates with the speech behavior of crying, raising or "pushing up" the song to the attention of the Supreme Being or a spirit helper. At the same time, this melodic gesture references tradition—pointing to the figures of thought, wish, prayer, and tobacco smoke used in rituals—in the same way that Earthmaker sought pity from the Supreme Being in the process of reordering the earth. This is the way the Gros Ventres traditionally approached the Supreme Being and other spirit beings. The announcement phrase in figure 15.1 is marked A. Following the announcement, the next melodic

Figure 15.1. "Ghost Helper Summoning Song"

motive contains the thought, which is the narrative that informs a song. The thought phrase in figure 15.1 is marked B. The closure phrase in figure 15.1 is marked C. Closure in Plains songs is often prepared by the rhythmic figure of an eighth note followed by two sixteenth notes, usually within the context of an interval of a perfect fourth or a minor third, which prepares the final flattening of the phrase. In figure 15.1, the B and C sections each contain this cadence; for example, the figure marking closure in the B section starts on a G, followed by an F and E, ending on the F.

Some Gros Ventre songs modify this form, as shown in the "Lodge Painting Song" (figure 15.2).[5] Here there is only one long phrase marked A, which is repeated. The repeat of the A phrase, marked A2, is preceded by a short motive that Nettl referred to as "a short bridge between the repetitions of the main body of the song" (1968:12), which I call a launching phrase. In figure 15.2, the bridge or launching phrase repeats some melodic material from section A, but in other songs, it is often sung on one pitch.[6]

The texts of the two dozen Gros Ventre songs used in this study consist primarily of vocables, such as "hey" or "yey." Figures 15.1 and 15.2 present the texts in an informal phonetic transcription, together with a more precise transcription of the text using the International Phonetic Alphabet. Although vocables may not carry specific lexical content, their appearance in repeatable sequences that align with melodic and rhythmic phrases must be considered for their deictic function, especially when marking closure within a phrase or preparing the final flattening at the end of a section. They point to meanings or symbols outside the specific structure of the text (cf. Hanks 2000). It is worth noting that a song text includes three parts: the sung vocables and words, the "reported text" or what the singer states are the words of a song, and the narrative that explains the acquisition of the song during a spirit visitation. In some cases, there are words, or constructions of the words, that the singer may be unable to translate. Some song "words" appear to be proxies for the actual, meaningful text. Whether this is a strategy to prevent others from appropriating a person's song, especially in the case of a doctoring song, is unclear.

One of Cooper's primary consultants, The Boy, made every effort to "perform" all of the songs he recorded, as if singing during a ritual or ceremony.[7] For instance, he recorded three sets of three songs for the Flat Pipe ritual, singing three renditions of each song. This points to the significance of the pattern number three associated with the Flat Pipe ritual and cosmology. In addition, The Boy's songs are highly consistent from one rendition to the next, suggesting that the sequence of intervals comprising a melodic phrase was primary, and variability arose in the duration of certain long note val-

Figure 15.2. "Lodge Painting Song"

ues, especially the closing formulae at phrase endings. Thus, the systematic appearance of semitones in three songs associated with the Flat Pipe ritual is most likely intentional, rather than an artifact of vocal fatigue or variable memory.

Conclusions

I have demonstrated that Gros Ventre songs and singing belong to a range of speech genres that include thought, crying, and prayer, which are central to Earthmaker's narrative about the reordering of the world, as well as to individual vision quests for supernatural power. What we often think of as a characteristic of Plains performance practice—the repetition of a strophic song three or four times—takes on new meaning when framed by the question, who is listening? Each rendition of the song has a deictic function in that it points to a particular ordering of the earth and the spirit beings that lived during that period. For example, the pattern number associated with the Gros Ventre Flat Pipe ritual is three, aligning each rendition of a song with one of the first three orders of the world. That the songs used in other ritual contexts lacking the same antiquity are repeated four times may point to a fourth order of the world to come, or to a parallel tradition of alignment with the four cardinal directions. A Gros Ventre person who obtained the help of a spirit being with a resource of power from a past or future order of the world would have received a precious gift indeed. For the Gros Ventres, singing constitutes a system of meta-communication about a problematic subject—the use of competing resources of power and agency, each contained within the other in a dialectic relationship. Singing provides a nexus of meaning, symbol, analogy, incitation, and communication (after Wagner 1986:34–80). This perspective of approaching song and singing as a way of speaking adds a level of complexity to our understanding and appreciation of northwestern Plains singing.

Acknowledgments

I will always be grateful to Bruno Nettl for introducing me to the study of First Nations music, and for his patient advice and counsel over the past forty-five years. I am grateful to Vicki Levine for her comments on earlier drafts of this chapter. I must also thank Connor Rice for his careful notation of the song transcriptions using the line and verse notation. I also want to thank Mark Thiel, archivist at the Marquette University Library, for his help in locating old manuscripts concerning Gros Ventre language and culture. I have benefited in ways I may not be aware of from discussions of Gros Ventre history and culture with Harold "Jiggs" Main, James Main Jr., and the late Regina Flannery; I am of course responsible for ways in which I may have used their ideas. Copies of the recordings used in this study are archived at the Catholic University of America (Washington, D.C.), Indiana University, and the Fort Belknap Indian Community (Harlem, Montana).

Notes

1. During the historic period, many Gros Ventre men received gifts or objects of power, such as a strip of otter fur, from a relative or through purchase (see Curtis 1909).

2. Although all of the known Gros Ventre Sacred Lodges were obtained during spirit visitations, none was the result of an intentional vision quest (Cooper 1957).

3. The majority of known vision quest sites are in remote areas, either on private property or federal or tribal land.

4. A Gros Ventre woman named Woman, or Bear Old Woman, received this song from her late husband, and she used it both to summon him and for doctoring (Cooper 1957:259).

5. This song may have been given to Bull Lodge at the time he received the gift of a lodge during his first fasting experience (Horse Capture 1980:35–36).

6. I borrowed the concept of a launching phrase from the field of discourse analysis. A similar type of figure is the "launching beat" that prepares the hard beat pattern in Grass Dance songs that I naively termed the "Hot Five" drumming pattern, in which *one accented beat* is followed four drumbeats later by *four accented beats*, each of which alternates with an unaccented beat (Hatton 1974).

7. For more on the subject of "performance," see Bauman (1984) and Hatton (1990).

References

Bauman, Richard. 1984. *Verbal Art as Performance*. Prospect Heights, IL: Waveland Press.

Cooper, John M. 1957. *The Gros Ventres of Montana: Part II, Religion and Ritual*. Edited by Regina Flannery. Washington, DC: Catholic University of America Press.

Curtis, Edward S. 1909. *The North American Indian, Volume 5*. Cambridge, MA: The University Press.

Dormaar, J. F., and Brian O. K. Reeves. 1993. "Vision Quest Sites in Southern Alberta and Northern Montana." In *Kunaitupii: Coming Together on Native Sacred Sites*, edited by Brian O. K. Reeves and Margaret Kennedy, 162–78. Calgary: Archaeological Society of Alberta.

Fort Belknap Indian Community. 1982. *War Stories of the White Clay People*. Harlem, MT: Gros Ventre and Assiniboine Indian Tribes.

Fowler, Loretta. 1987. *Shared Symbols, Contested Meanings: Gros Ventre Culture and History, 1778–1984*. Ithaca, NY: Cornell University Press.

Giddens, Anthony. 1979. *Central Problems in Social Theory: Action, Structure and Contradiction in Social Analysis*. Berkeley: University of California Press.

Hanks, William F. 2000. *Intertexts: Writings on Language, Utterance, and Context*. Oxford: Rowman and Littlefield.

Hatton, Orin T. 1974. "Performance Practices of Northern Plains Pow-wow Singing Groups." *Yearbook for Inter-American Musical Research* 10: 123–37.

———. 1989. "Gender and Musical Style in Gros Ventre War Expedition Songs." In *Women in North American Indian Music: Six Essays*, edited by Richard Keeling, 39–54. Special Series Number 6. Bloomington, IN: Society for Ethnomusicology.

———. 1990. *Power and Performance in Gros Ventre War Expedition Songs*. Canadian Ethnology Service, Mercury Series Paper No. 114. Ottawa: Canadian Museum of Civilization.

Horse Capture, George. 1980. *The Seven Visions of Bull Lodge, by Garter Snake and Fred Gone*. Ann Arbor: Bear Claw Press.

Hymes, Dell. 1981. *"In Vain I Tried to Tell You": Essays in Native American Ethnopoetics*. Philadelphia: University of Pennsylvania Press.

———. 1989. "Ways of Speaking." In *Explorations in the Ethnography of Speaking*, second edition, edited by Richard Bauman and Joel Sherzer, 433–51. Cambridge: Cambridge University Press.

Irwin, Lee. 1994. *The Dream Seekers, Native American Visionary Traditions of the Great Plains*. Norman: University of Oklahoma Press.

Kroeber, Alfred L. 1907. *Gros Ventre Myths and Tales*. Anthropological Papers of the American Museum of Natural History, Volume 1, Part 3, 59–64. New York: American Museum of Natural History.

Levine, Victoria Lindsay, and Bruno Nettl. 2011. "Strophic Form and Asymmetrical Repetition in Four American Indian Songs." In *Analytical and Cross-Cultural Studies in World Music*, edited by Michael Tenzer and John Roeder, 288–315. New York: Oxford University Press.

Nettl, Bruno. 1954. *North American Indian Musical Styles*. Philadelphia: American Folklore Society.

———. 1967. "Studies in Blackfoot Indian Musical Culture." Parts 1, 2. *Ethnomusicology* 11: 141–60, 292–309.

———. 1968. "Studies in Blackfoot Indian Musical Culture." Parts 3, 4. *Ethnomusicology* 12: 11–48, 192–207. (Part 4 written with Stephen Blum.)

Sherzer, Joel, and Anthony C. Woodbury. 1987. *Native American Discourse: Poetics and Rhetoric*. Cambridge: Cambridge University Press.

Tedlock, Dennis. 1983. *The Spoken Word and the Work of Interpretation*. Philadelphia: University of Pennsylvania Press.

Uhlenbeck, C. C. 1912. *A New Series of Blackfoot Texts, from the Southern Piegan Blackfoot Reservation, Teton County, Montana*. Amsterdam: Johannes Muller.

Wagner, Roy. 1986. *Symbols That Stand for Themselves*. Chicago: University of Chicago Press.

Wissler, Clark. 1912. *Ceremonial Bundles of the Blackfoot Indians*. Anthropological Papers of the American Museum of Natural History, Volume 7, Part 2. New York: American Museum of Natural History.

Wissler, Clark, and D. C. Duvall. 1995[1909]. *Mythology of the Blackfoot Indians*. Lincoln: University of Nebraska Press.

Woodbury, Anthony C. 1987. "Rhetorical Structure in a Central Alaskan Yupik Eskimo Traditional Narrative." In *Native American Discourse: Poetics and Rhetoric*, edited by Joel Sherzer and Anthony C. Woodbury, 176–239. Cambridge: Cambridge University Press.

CHAPTER SIXTEEN

Permutation as a Basic Concept of Rāga Elaboration in North Indian Music

Lars-Christian Koch

Few areas of ethnomusicological research are as critical to Bruno Nettl's international influence as the study of improvisation. Improvisation has provided a connective tissue for Nettl's comparative studies, and it is that connective tissue that makes his publications on such diverse topics as the relation of oral to written tradition in European folk music and the classical musics of Asia, especially in Iran and South India, foundations for European ethnomusicology. Indeed, it is in large measure because his studies of improvisation cross historical and geographical borders that European ethnomusicologists have considered Bruno Nettl one of their own. The real point is, nonetheless, that Nettl has long called for an ethnomusicology that transcends the historical divisions into national schools and regional repertories. It is not just that call, moreover, that is important for his European colleagues; his analytical studies of the Persian *radif* and Karnatak improvisation remain inspiring models for a new era of comparative study for twenty-first-century ethnomusicology. With my contribution to the study of improvisation in the Hindustani *rāga*, I embrace the new comparative methods that Bruno Nettl has inspired, and I join him as an international colleague in a shared ethnomusicology of the twenty-first century.

This chapter also provides me with an opportunity to reflect on the influence of teachers on the ethnomusicologist as scholar and performer. In a volume filled with essays by many of Bruno Nettl's students, whose visions of music in the world have been shaped profoundly by their teacher, I offer my contribution as a chronicle to the influence of my teacher in Hindustani music, Trina Purohit-Roy, who passed away as I was writing the chapter. My understanding of rāga owes much to her, and this chapter represents one small measure of my homage to her and the lessons and lives we acquire from our teachers in ethnomusicology. These are the lessons that so many in the field of ethnomusicology have learned from Bruno Nettl (cf. Nettl 1984).

When the ethnomusicologist begins to consider North Indian rāga music, two matters of melodic form arise immediately: scale models and improvisation. Most publications further strengthen the presence of these issues, for they include clarification of the ascent and descent of rāgas. It is entirely correct to approach rāga in this way, but it explains only a small part of what rāga really is. In the present chapter, I use selected examples to illustrate rāga in ways that go far beyond the usual scale models. My concern is far more with rāga as patterns of melodic movement and structure in both pedagogy and practice, particularly in the ways they provide the primary foundations for improvisation.[1] Throughout the chapter I emphasize the ways in which permutation plays a central role in the process of rāga improvisation. Permutation also provides a basis for teaching in this genre. With case studies of selected rāgas, I illustrate how the ability to improvise is taught in a traditional way and how this art is applied in performance.[2] The chapter also includes a short comparative statement concerning similar aspects of jazz improvisation, which opens further perspectives on improvisation more globally.

Rāga

The Indian subcontinent is home to a rich musical life with a considerable number of different music cultures. If we talk about Indian music today, we most often mean a set of practices that is usually connected to the phenomenon of rāga music,[3] a term characterizing a central part of Indian music cultures.[4] According to Matanga (800–900 CE), the author of the *Bṛhad-deśī*, "peculiar melody (*dhvani*) which is defined through tones (*svara*) and their combination (*varna*) and which colors the minds of human beings is called a rāga by the sages" (Zimmerman 1984:240). Trina Purohit-Roy defines a rāga as "a fixed combination of successive tones following certain rules, which follows an inner sentiment" (Purohit-Roy 1967:286). The term rāga in the cultural setting we know today was first mentioned in Nārada's *Saṅgīta-makaranda* (1978). He classifies the rāgas according to the time of performance (morning, midday, evening, night), the number of pitches (five, six, or seven), gender (male, female, or neuter), family structure (eight male rāgas, with three "wives" each and several sons), and the degree of ornamentation.

The word rāga derives from the Sanskrit root *rañj*, "to be colored, to redden," in a broader sense also "to be affected, delighted." It is the quality that arouses feeling and delight, and refers in a nontechnical sense, for example, to the "passion" of a song, but should not be misunderstood as an equivalent to the term *rasa* (see Koch 1995). From the time of the theorist Matanga onward (ca. tenth century CE), it was used to denote a melody type that delights the listener. The sense of rapture is kindled by the particular pitches and melodic movement that distinguish the rāga or rāgas from all other melody types. A kind of melodic individuality is created in this process.

The creation of musical individuality also extended to extra-musical aspects, such as supernatural powers and association with certain divinities, specific human characters, the moods of the seasons, and times of day. These aspects have endured through the ages and are still important in South Asian culture today. After the theoretical formulation of the basic elements of Indian music by the end of the first millennium, not a single music-theory treatise would contain concepts or ideas significant enough to change Indian music culture.

The musical practices of the surrounding culture of the courts were of primary importance, but the old writings, the *śāstras*, lost none of their importance. The transmission of musical knowledge, which took place in closely knit family circles, underwent considerable change along with modernization. The phenomenon of the *gharāna* (house or school) came into being and remained influential through the twentieth century (cf. Neuman 1990). In response to rapidly changing social relations, gharānas developed at the beginning of the nineteenth century. The gharāna became the basis for the emergence of sociomusical identity; it became increasingly significant for the listener and the expansion of difference among gharānas, which formed distinctive patterns of reception history. At the same time, the ruler at whose court a gharāna formed increasingly identified with it. It was customary for students in a gharāna to live in the house of their teachers and to take part in the household. The term gharāna itself, meaning "house" or "household," grew from a social situation, though it actually referred to stylistic distinctiveness in music, and accordingly, gharāna became widely influential in the social organization of Hindustani music (Neuman 1990).

At the beginning of the twentieth century, Vishnu Narayan Bhatkhande (1860–1936) came to play a particularly distinctive role in transforming the sociocultural contexts of Indian music. V. N. Bhatkhande was born into a Brahmin family of Mumbai and received his education in the law, while also studying Indian vocal and instrumental music at an early age. After several years of practicing law, he turned to the study of music, thereafter dedicating his entire life to music. In numerous libraries he researched writings on Indian music theory, while at the same time seeking to establish ties with the major Indian musicians of the day. He worked intensively with these musicians, writing out the details of their teaching methods. Both the manuscripts and the teaching methods were to become the basis for his numerous publications (cf. Bhatkhande 1957, 1963–1968). Between 1900 and 1907, he transcribed hundreds of compositions in many different styles, developing for these a form of notation that would become the standard for Hindustani music (see also Bakhle 2005).

In 1916, he organized the first All India Music Conference in the city of Baroda, at which the learned representatives from different gharānas gathered to speak about music. Bhatkhande himself presented a paper, which he later published with the title *A Short Historical Survey of the Music of Upper India*, in which he sought to provide an introduction to music theory from musical writings of the sixteenth and seventeenth centuries. This became the basis of later theoretical work (Bhatkhande 1974). The second conference took place in Delhi in 1917, and it was here that leading musicians were enjoined to unify their distinctive interpretations of different rāgas.

The results of the discussions at the conference entered Bhatkhande's theoretical works, which he published between 1920 and 1937; they remain among the standard works of North Indian music (Bhatkhande 1963–1968). More than one thousand compositions appear in the volumes, interpreted by the musicians Bhatkhande interviewed and classified by him. Soon thereafter, he published a second standard work, *Saṅgītaśāstra*, which includes four volumes of more than two thousand pages, describing and analyzing 150 North Indian rāgas (Bhatkhande 1957). Bhatkhande's intensive theoretical work opens many different points of departure. First, he considered the situation of court music in his own age to be desolate and almost entirely without theoretical reflection. He attributed this to the growing distance from the early musical manuscripts, which were primarily written in Sanskrit:

> Our music changed its form slowly due to various reasons but even now it retains enough facts which can help us to connect it with the music mentioned in the ancient *granthas*. It is understandable that as music changed inevitably due to different circumstances, the writer of the subsequent ages also had to add new facts and figures according to the available material. This is not a surprising fact. With the progress of centuries when the writers could no longer master Sanskrit for writing they started writing in the language in vogue as a natural rule. When the *Deshi* language also became illegible, music fell into

> the hands of the illiterates and even now it remains in that state. The practical musicians of today have cultured and polished their voice in a whimsical manner and have taken the taste of the public astray with their vocal power. This distorted taste has found its grip strong in holding the society. (Nayar 1989:129–30)

Second, during Bhatkhande's life, it was the practical side of music that was dominant. Musicians were expected to "copy" from their teachers; the oral explanations given by learned musicians provided the standards for teaching, and their opinions were transmitted through oral explanations. Only about ten gharānas determined the larger context of the music scene of the time. Bhatkhande, however, turned teaching methods on their head by arguing that rāgas should be learned through notation and its theoretical implications. At the very least, the classification and standardization of rāgas were considerably expanded, which was precisely the goal at the 1916 All India Music Conference, at which each musician was asked to perform his own rendition of a given rāga so that a majority opinion from those in attendance could determine the standard version.

Bhatkhande's larger goal was to make Indian music accessible to a broader interest group, so that music would remain vital for the future. At his music conferences—eventually there would be a total of five, the first one at Baroda in 1916—he took a twenty-one-point manifesto as his point of departure, from which I extract the following critical points (the numbering follows Nayar 1989:160):

1. Indian music needs to be firmly established on an international plane.
2. It is necessary to develop an effective program of pedagogy that makes rāga and tāla easier to transmit.
3. The differences between North and South Indian music should be narrowed as much as possible through the use of a common notation.
4. The masterpieces of earlier eras should be protected.
5. A national music academy should be established, so that musicians can be trained explicitly, while at the same time a common introduction to music from music schools should make music accessible to all segments of society.

These points were broadly embraced and introduced in many areas. Still, Bhatkhande's music theoretical work received considerable criticism. Despite the inexactitude of certain theories, such as the division of rāgas into the ten ṭhāṭas (roughly, larger scale families) or the often questionable connection of single rāgas to times of the day, Bhatkhande's work remains of considerable importance and influence on teaching until the present (see Nayar 1989). Accordingly, the following rules about rāga interpretation remain relevant:

1. Every rāga is based on a defined scale in an ascending and a descending order. This scale is established from a fixed, constantly sounding fundamental tone. In this way all tonal intervals can be assigned a precise tonal classification.
2. Every rāga has as tonal material at least five pitches in its ascending and descending scales, whereby the fundamental root has to sound continuously. The fifth or fourth can be omitted but not simultaneously. Instead of the fourth, the augmented fourth could be part of the tonal material. In a linear progression, tones and their alterations are not allowed to follow each other successively; for example, in Western terms, a major third is not allowed to follow directly after a minor third.
3. In every rāga the musician has to follow specific rules in playing certain notes, including subtle rules in the sense of the melodic or ornamental shaping of the rāga. In this way, every rāga acquires its characteristic melody-structure.
4. Every rāga has two main tones (*vādi* and *saṃvādi*), which are of central significance in the upper and lower tetrachord, for vādi and saṃvādi are either in the upper or lower tetrachord with an interval of a fifth or a fourth. Most melodic movements either start or end with these tones. If the vādi is located in the upper tetrachord, it is a morning rāga; in the lower tetrachord, it is an evening rāga. All other tones belonging to the rāga-structure are called *anuvādi*, but there are also tones that could destroy the mood of a rāga or, to be more precise, could even kill the musical personality of a rāga; such tones are called *vivādi.*
5. Every rāga contains a small combination of tones (*pakaḍa*) that immediately identify the rāga.
6. On the basis of its musical structure, every rāga has a fixed performance time in the cycle of a day or a season.
7. The mood of a rāga and its musical structure determine the preference for certain interpretational styles.
8. Rāga is a content-oriented term, not a form-oriented one.

There are exceptions to all of these rules, something acknowledged by most musicians and even Bhatkhande himself. However, it does remain the most important theory on rāga in North India today, dominating the music-education system. Nevertheless, in contemporary theory based on the works of Bhatkhande, eight main characteristics of a rāga are of importance:

1. ārohī (ascending scale)
2. avarohī (descending scale)
3. vādi (central tone)
4. saṃvādi (corresponding central tone)
5. pakaḍa (typical short melodic combination)
6. ṭhāṭa (basic scale in which the raga is classified)
7. *jāti* (classification category according to the number of tones in a ṭhāṭa)
8. *kāla* (performance time)

The fact that many rāgas have changed in structure over the centuries while retaining earlier temporal associations suggests that structural and non-structural aspects are not directly interdependent; rather, each rāga evokes aesthetic and extra-musical associations in the knowledgeable listener's mind by its correct rendition according to the current concept of its structure. Despite all the extra-musical concepts connected with rāga, over hundreds of years its connection to religious meaning has always remained vital. Even with the emergence of new and different styles (e.g., *khyāl* or *thumrī*) and theoretical classifications at the courts, religious or supernatural association always remains present. What is even more astonishing is its persistence, whether performed by Hindu or Muslim musicians. There has always been a deep respect for the personality of the rāga.

Equally important for the distinctive character of Indian music is tāla, the concept of rhythmic-metric arrangement based on a system in which the rhythmic and metric elements of the music are measured in "cycles" (see Clayton 2000; for a criticism of cyclical metaphor, see Clayton 2013). The main purpose of a tāla is to order the measurement of time so that it is repeated in patterns across the entire flow of music. Within this framework it becomes possible to improvise.

Rāga and Patterns of Melodic Movement

Melodic arcs form around the movement of a rāga according to the ways basic rhythmic models are conceived; in instrumental music, these are often realized through specific patterns. These patterns are not like the measures that divide Western musical time; rather, they are determined through cyclic repetition. The fundamental elements of variation, often referred to as improvisation, lie in interpretation. Indian music assumes complex forms in the domain of movement, making it difficult to grasp from a Western music theoretical standpoint. Instead, there are principles of mathematical calculation that dominate variation. There is great value in examining these closely, not least because they have served as the basis for North Indian rāga music for centuries and offer an entirely different way of understanding the music itself.

A rāga is basically a melodic movement pattern. When we recognize this principle, it becomes obvious that in teaching and practice, different models and patterns of melodic movement have come to serve as the main principle for learning Indian rāga music. Every student of Indian music faces three specific practices of learning early on: *palta*, *mūrchanā*, and *khaṇḍa meru*.[5] Palta means "pattern"; it provides patterns for arranging musical tones in a successive manner.

We witness this use of notation to form the arches of melodic movement in table 16.1 and figure 16.1.[6]

Palta exercises keep the student of Indian music busy for the early years of study, and it is hardly surprising that every Indian musician develops a rich repertory of paltas. Additionally, musicians regularly practice mūrchanā. Not to be confused with the same term in ancient Indian music, a mūrchanā today is a pattern that arises within a given ṭhāṭa—one of the ten basic scales of North Indian music—within an octave and using linear patterns of melodic movement.

The most important category concerning patterns of movement is the concept of khaṇḍa meru, or *mirkhand*. Its literal meaning is close to "cross-section of steps," which is obvious in the following diagram (table 16.2) from the *Saṅgītaratnākara*, an extremely important thirteenth-century treatise on music, attributed to Sārṅgadēva.

Table 16.1. Palta patterns for an abstract rāga.

S
SRS
SRGRS
SRGMGRS
SRGMPMGRS
SRGMPDPMGRS
SRGMPDNDPMGRS
SRGMPDNSNDPMGRS

Figure 16.1. Palta patterns for an abstract rāga

The permutation calculator in table 16.2 allows the musician to count the possible combinations with a fixed set of notes (for a detailed explanation, see Roychaudhuri 1981). Whereas the permutational calculus of the tetratonic series shows how the possible permutations within a set of notes are arranged, it also establishes a single note as an ending note in each

Table 16.2. Khaṇḍa meru in *Saṅgītaratnākara*

Sa	Re	Ga	Ma	Pa	Dha	Ni
1	0	0	0	0	0	0
	1	2	6	24	120	720
		4	12	48	240	1440
			18	72	360	2160
				96	480	2880
					600	3600
						4320

Table 16.3. The permutational calculus of the tetratonic series

	Series with Ma as fourth		*Series with Re as fourth*		*Series with Ga as fourth*		*Series with Sa as fourth*
1	Sa Re Ga Ma	7	Sa Ga Ma Re	13	Sa Re Ma Ga	19	Re Ga Ma Sa
2	Re Sa Ga Ma	8	Ga Sa Ma Re	14	Re Sa Ma Ga	20	Ga Re Ma Sa
3	Sa Ga Re Ma	9	Sa Ma Ga Re	15	Sa Ma Re Ga	21	Re Ma Ga Sa
4	Ga Sa Re Ma	10	Ma Sa Ga Re	16	Ma Sa Re Ga	22	Ma Re Ga Sa
5	Re Ga Sa Ma	11	Ga Ma Sa Re	17	Re Ma Sa Ga	23	Ga Ma Re Sa
6	Ga Re Sa Ma	12	Ma Ga Sa Re	18	Ma Re Sa Ga	24	Ma Ga Re Sa

column (table 16.3). This process is explained in table 16.4, also taken from the *Saṅgītaratnākara.*

The important music scholar and musician Bimalakanta Roychaudhuri revived the concept of khaṇḍa meru (though it was never really forgotten) in his 1993 book on the aesthetics of North Indian classical music.

In practice, the most important aspect of the concepts of palta, mūrchanā, and khaṇḍa meru is to transfer them to a particular rāga. Here is just a short example from the afternoon rāga, *Bhīmpalāsī*, with an ascending structure of S $\underline{\text{G}}$ M P $\underline{\text{N}}$ S and a descending structure of S $\underline{\text{N}}$ D P M $\underline{\text{G}}$ R S, manifested in its typical melodic pattern, $\underline{\text{N}}$ S M, M $\underline{\text{G}}$ P M, $\underline{\text{G}}$ M $\underline{\text{G}}$ R S ($\underline{\text{G}}$ and $\underline{\text{N}}$ identify the flat third and seventh). The first simple palta from figure 16.1 would sound in this rāga, as shown in table 16.5 and figure 16.2.

Obviously it becomes more complicated if this is applied to the permutations for khaṇḍa meru, but at the same time, it provides a wide field of material for creative improvisation.

The question now arises, just how does one really perceive rāga music? Do musicians and other listeners primarily hear distinctions between pitch level, or are the patterns of movement predominant in any given tonal material? What happens in cases when particular rāgas do not conform to the usual

Table 16.4. Explanation of permutations from the *Saṅgītaratnākara*

Sequence of the Note Series	*Note Series*	*Notes Transposed*
1st series	Sa Re Ga Ma	
2nd series	Re Sa Ga Ma	Sa for Re
3rd series	Sa Ga Re Ma	Re for Ga
4th series	Ga Sa Re Ma	Sa for Ga
5th series	Re Ga Sa Ma	Ga for Re
6th series	Ga Re Sa Ma	Re for Ga
7th series	Sa Re Ga Ma	Ga for Ma

Table 16.5. Palta patterns in *rāga Bhīmpalāsī*

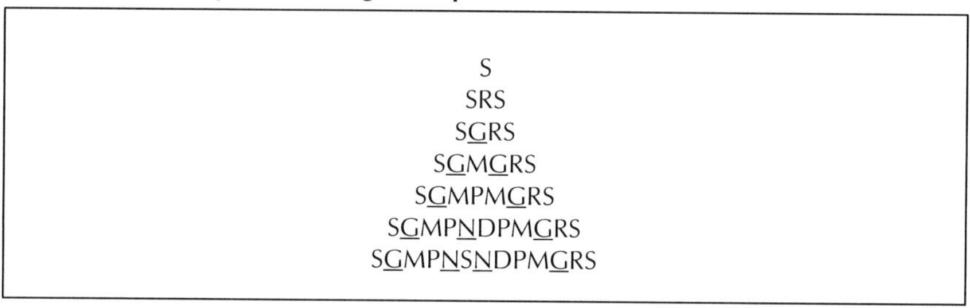
S
SRS
SG̲RS
SG̲MG̲RS
SG̲MPMG̲RS
SG̲MPN̲DPMG̲RS
SG̲MPN̲SN̲DPMG̲RS

patterns, for example, when some aspect thereof is absent? Individual tones are seldom regarded as isolated phenomena; rather, they are understood in relation to other tones, which specify the ways in which a rāga acquires its specific characteristics and identity. It is important to understand that small changes in pitch have the greatest impact on the sonic entity and personality of a rāga. These may be retained in the rāga's skeletal structure, but when the ways in which individual tones move are altered, a rāga loses its identity. It is in this regard that the complex of palta, mūrchanā, and khaṇḍa meru provides the most important basis for establishing the rāga in both its essence and its musical presentation. One builds upon this basis in order to awaken the rāga to life in all of its aspects. The requirement is, nonetheless, that an artist uses palta, mūrchanā, and khaṇḍa meru as creatively as possible in order to display her or his musical personality.

During my own early studies, I was perplexed as to why certain recordings or concerts were not positively received by other musicians, even though the "right tones" had actually been played. The response to my confusion was usually something like "The rāga isn't there." When I then replied, "But

Figure 16.2. *Palta* patterns in *rāga Bhīmpalāsī*

the ascent and descent of the scale was correct," I received the answer, "But that does not make the rāga what it is." Further clarification then followed, in which musicians pointed out discrepancies that might have seemed of little importance, but in the end proved to be critical. When examined more closely, all these discrepancies arose because the rāga's melodic patterns were not present. Individual tones were not really perceived as such; rather, they acquired meaning only when in movement with other tones. The skeleton of the scale was only an abstract representation consisting of individual tones. We witness here distinctions between South Asian and European concepts of pitch, scale, and melody, but even more importantly, we recognize the critical importance of understanding meaning and identity through performance, especially through improvisation. In order to clarify that importance, I briefly turn to improvisation comparatively, as has Bruno Nettl throughout his career (see especially Nettl and Russell 1998).

Chords and Arpeggios—Structure in Jazz Improvisation

Jazz, with its musical heritage from Africa, incorporating blues mixed with Western harmony and instrumentation, is perhaps the genre most often associated directly with concepts of improvisation. Its own history, with transitional moments, has been similar to that of Indian music, for example, during the important turning point in the 1920s and 1930s in New Orleans. With a strong influence of ex-military marching band instruments—mostly wind instruments—a unique style of playing variations over chord progressions was established, a mixture of *arpeggios* (chords played in a horizontal way using the root, third, fifth, and seventh) and corresponding *scales*, during performance with solos on the chord changes. We might speculate that it is much easier to play arpeggios on these marching-band instruments—saxophones, trumpets, and clarinets—than it is to play scales. Thus in standard jazz styles, such as bebop, a solo could be understood as arpeggio lines joined together by a few scale and chromatic notes. These arpeggios directly resemble the chords. For a minor seventh chord, a minor seventh arpeggio is played; for a dominant seventh chord, a dominant seventh arpeggio fits most closely; and for a major seventh chord, obviously, the jazz musician plays a major seventh arpeggio, keeping in mind that the typical II-V-I harmonic model provides the basic structure.

If we compare this approach to jazz improvisation, using II-V-I chord progressions and the corresponding arpeggios as a pattern-based improvisational tool, to improvisation in Indian music, we find that the major difference is the pure melodic permutation in Indian music connected to cyclical perceptions of rhythm and bodily movement, which in turn are connected to the conceptualized movement pattern in playing (*bol* patterns) as well as melodic construction. In jazz, the main aspect is how harmonic progressions generate sound and aesthetic qualities within a melodic concept based on chord arpeggios, which are by extension transformed into linear concepts. Improvisation in both music cultures depends, ultimately, on the transformation of melody into the periodicity of repeating structures.

Conclusions

The concept of saṅgīta, with its embrace of vocal and instrumental music as well as dance, established in the thirteenth-century *Saṅgītaratnākara*, reflects an expansion of cultural practice. The qualitative, aesthetic implication of the phenomenon rāga and the cyclical orientation of fundamental rhythmic parameters play an important role in this expansion. *Nāda* (sound) is a constitutive element of saṅgīta through ways it denotes a resonating body, which by extension manifests itself in the human body, which in turn is distinguished by the ways in which it moves. In this way, sound connects to concepts of dance and, in turn, connects dance to saṅgīta. Consequently, the complex domain of movement is transferred to all aspects of music. In India, musical thought has been gathered in many written forms and under different historical concepts and perspectives. Throughout the centuries, all these writings have been examined in order to understand their connections, which form a unified Indian music theory only in their approaches.

At the end of the nineteenth century, Vishnu Narayan Bhatkhande sought to establish just such a unified Indian music theory, and he was successful in doing so in several central areas. Many of his theories about rāga music, particularly those bound up with standardization, have not entered those central areas. Still, the musical "calculation-concept," khaṇḍa meru, with its identification of structures of melodic movement, remains one of the first successful approaches that reveals rāga in all its depth, and it does so by opening an understanding of the vast range of variation and improvisation. These concepts still lived in the older generation of Indian musicians, but they were known and practiced largely by family members and students. Though they have not found their way entirely into ethnomusicology, the connection between theoretical understanding and the continuing role of the teacher as a source of musical knowledge and practice has the potential to open the channels of transmission between the past and the present, so that we learn ever more from our principal teachers.

Notes

1. Throughout this chapter I use improvisation in the sense that Indian musicians themselves do when they say, "We are improvising."

2. Parts of this article have appeared in Koch 2011.

3. Just as it is in the West, the most commercially important music in India today is popular music, which is significantly influenced by film music and is disseminated through many of the same media. Popular music overlaps with rāga music in only limited ways.

4. The terms "art music" and "classical music" derive from the European tradition, but are used to allow comparison between Indian and European music.

5. For the following exercises and composition, I draw upon the teaching of Dr. Trina Purohit-Roy, with whom I studied over the course of many years.

6. The use of letters to represent pitches in Indian music is very common, and, accordingly, I apply it to the discussion of improvisation in this chapter, for example, in presenting paltas. This type of notation, moreover, makes it easier to recognize movement patterns and melodic structures.

References

Bakhle, Janaki. 2005. *Two Men and Music: Nationalism in the Making of an Indian Classical Tradition*. New York: Oxford University Press.

Bhatkhande, Vishnu Narayan. 1957. *Bhātakhaṇḍe-saṅgītaśāstra/mūla lekhaka Vishnunārāyaṇa Bhātakhaṇḍe Vishṇu* Śarmā. 4 volumes. Hātharasa: Saṅgīta-Kāryalaya.

———. 1963–1968. *Hindustānī saṅgīta-paddhati kramika pustaka-mālikā: Hindī anuvāda/ mūla granthakāra Vishṇunārāyaṇa Bhātakhaṇḍe; sampādaka Lakshmīnārāyaṇa Garga.* 6 volumes. Hātharasa: Saṅgīta Kāryalaya.

———. 1974. *A Short Historical Survey of the Music of Upper India*. Baroda: Indian Musicological Society.

Clayton, Martin. 2000. *Time in Indian Music: Rhythm, Metre, and Form in North Indian Rāg Performance*. Oxford: Oxford University Press.

———. 2013. "The Time of Music and the Time of History." In *The Cambridge History of World Music*, edited by Philip V. Bohlman, 767–85. Cambridge: Cambridge University Press.

Koch, Lars-Christian. 1995. *Zur Bedeutung der Rasa-Lehre für die zeitgenössische nordindische Kunstmusik: Mit einem Vergleich mit der Affektenlehre des 17. und 18. Jahrhunderts*. Bonn: Holos Verlag.

———. 2011. "Rāga und Khaṇḍa Meru: Einige Gedanken zur Bedeutung von Musiktheorie, Klassifikationen und Standardisierungen im Umfeld der Raga-Musik Nordindiens." ANKLAENGE 2010-*Wiener Jahrbuch für Musikwissenschaft*: 133–65.

Nārada. 1978. *Saṅgīta-makarandaḥ*. Hātharasa: Saṅgīta Kāryālaya.

Nayar, Sobhana. 1989. *Bhatkhande's Contribution to Music: A Historical Perspective*. Bombay: Popular Prakashan.

Nettl, Bruno. 1984. "In Honor of Our Principal Teachers." *Ethnomusicology* 28(2): 173–85.

Nettl, Bruno, and Melinda Russell, eds. 1998. *In the Course of Performance: Studies in the World of Improvisation*. Chicago: University of Chicago Press.

Neuman, Daniel M. 1990. *The Life of Music in North India: The Organization of an Artistic Tradition*. Chicago: University of Chicago Press.

Purohit-Roy, Trina. 1967. "Zur Improvisation indischer Ragas." In *Colloquium Amicorum-Joseph Schmidt-Görg zum 70. Geburtstag*, edited by Sigfried Kross and Hans Schmidt, 283–95. Bonn: Beethovenhaus.

Roychaudhuri, Bimalakanta. 1981. *Rāga vyākaraṇa* (Grammar of Music). Nayī Dillī: Bhāratīya Jñānapīha Prakāśana.

———. 1993. *Aesthetics of North Indian Classical Music*. Calcutta: Imdakhani School of Sitar.

Sanyal, Ritwik, and Richard Widdess. 2004. *Dhrupad: Tradition and Performance in Indian Music*. Aldershot: Ashgate.

Zimmerman, Heinz. 1984. "Der indische Kulturbereich." In *Neues Handbuch der Musikwissenschaft, Volume 8: Aussereuropäische Musik*, edited by Hans Oesch, 197–301. Regensburg: Laaber-Verlag.

CHAPTER SEVENTEEN

~

Aspects of Sound Recording and Sound Analysis

Albrecht Schneider

The Basic Problem: Music as "Volatile Sound"

The present chapter is a continuation of my previous studies devoted to sound analysis of ethnic music with regard to perception, tone systems, scale types, and sonic phenomena of various kinds (cf. Schneider 1997, 2000, 2001, 2013). In this chapter, I focus on aspects of computer-based melography. According to some Renaissance writings on the arts, sculpture and painting are regarded as superior to music since they create tangible objects that persist through time, whereas music is volatile when it sounds. Leonardo da Vinci, in his *Trattato di Pittura*, remarks that a work of music, when performed, is complete only when the last note has been played and heard, but at that very moment the music disappears (cf. Schneider 1984:222). Of course, one could notate music, and even multiply notation in print. Notation (including tablature), however, is a symbolic representation of music and not actual music realized and perceived as sound.

Attempts at recording sound, in particular human speech and singing, date back well into the nineteenth century (cf. Beyer 1999; Kittler 1999; Schneider 2009). Edison's "perfected phonograph" of 1888 was perhaps the first device suited for recording music with sufficient "fidelity." It is well known that the phonograph (as well as offspring such as the "Viennese Archive Phonograph") was soon used for recordings in the field and thus provided a basis for the documentation and study of traditional music from many ethnic groups and cultures. Sound archives established in Vienna in 1899 (Hajek 1928), in Berlin in 1900 (cf. Berlin and Simon 2000), and elsewhere, soon housed thousands of recordings of non-Western musics as well as folk music, spoken language, and regional dialects. In retrospect, the foundation of such sound archives may be viewed as a primarily ethnographic enterprise. Though documentation of music in particular from "primitive" cultures endangered by modern civilization was an important goal from the very beginning, sound recordings at Berlin and Vienna served likewise as source material for scientific investigation and comparative study (e.g., Abraham and Hornbostel 1902/1903; Stumpf 1911, 2012; cf. Lach 1924:17). Also, phonographic recordings (accompanied by film, as encouraged by Abraham and Hornbostel 1904) were regarded as an objective method necessary to control transcription by scholars who may have been inclined to perceive non-Western music along learned schemata of melody, harmony, meter, and rhythm.

In the course of the twentieth century, recording music on various media, filming musicians, and filming music and dance in specific sociocultural contexts have become techniques of documentation for which specific guidelines have been proposed (e.g., Simon 1994). Music performed in sociocultural settings was, and is, also of interest for media and entertainment industries (as is obvious from the huge number of sound and film recordings available on- and offline).

Sound Recording and Sound Analysis of Ethnic Music

Though the desire to store sound in a nonvolatile format seems to have included personal motivations (e.g., preserving the voice of a beloved relative or friend), most early attempts at sound recording had a scientific background. One has to remember that in acoustics, the study of the sound wave had begun before 1800, and soon it was found that the shape of a given sound wave and the number of cycles a periodic sound completes per time unit were enough to assess its pitch, loudness, and timbre. The development of mechanical sound recorders was therefore pursued decades before Charles Cros, Thomas Edison, and Emil Berliner came up with inventions that allowed a more or less faithful *reproduction* of prerecorded sound waves as audible sound. Leaving aside all commercial aspects sound recording and reproduction gained even before 1900 (and massively since), it is of interest to see that in Germany and other European countries, phonographic recordings of speech and singing were made with Edison's machines from the 1880s for the analysis of pitch, timbre, and other constituents of sound (Schneider 2013).

Carl Stumpf had done research on the perception of pitch and timbre (Stumpf 1883, 1890) before he came to Berlin in 1893. As a professor of psychology, he added systematic and comparative musicology as fields suited to investigate psychological issues. Stumpf had also expressed interest in non-Western music before his Berlin appointment; evidently, Benjamin Ives Gilman's transcriptions of the Passamaquoddy songs Jesse Walter Fewkes had recorded in 1890 led Stumpf (1892) to a critical evaluation of the prospects and also problems of phonographic recordings. He argued that while the phonograph for the first time allowed an objective registration of music and the possibility to reproduce music recorded in the field for scientific investigation, transcription of recorded music, even if done with great precision and detail (in regard to pitch and the duration of tone), might not necessarily capture musically meaningful phrases, or reflect the intentions of singers or musicians. Hence, Stumpf recommended that close observation of musical performances in the field should accompany phonographic recording. In most of the ethnomusicological fieldwork carried out during the past century, observation of behavior in regard to music, even participation of researchers in the music-making events of ethnic groups, along with sound recording and film or video documentation, has become general practice.

For decades, the transcription of non-Western music and also of European folk music recorded in the field (plus some laboratory recordings) into staff notation was considered a fundamental task of ethnomusicology. Our system of notation had to be adapted in certain ways to cover pitch and time structures not known (or rarely observed) in Western music. The aims of transcription as a basis for music analyses, or as part thereof, as well as methods employed are quite diverse (for an overview, see Nettl 2005:74–91). In relevant publications, one can find anything from "melody skeletons" to detailed transcriptions up to Béla Bartók's meticulous efforts to provide a "microscopic" representation of music. Bartók aimed at capturing even tiny deviations in pitch and time (relative to scale steps, tempo, and meter), small embellishments, rubati, and so forth. Bartók's approach (cf. Bartók and Somfai 1981) is of particular interest because, in most of his transcriptions of Hungarian folk songs of the 1930s and in other works, he rendered transcriptions that are close to a *quasi-continuous* symbolic representation of musical streams. To be sure, the musical stream a singer or instrumentalist (e.g., a flute or saxophone player) produces is also quasi-continuous in regard to the flow of sound over time. In this respect, Bartók's transcriptions indeed seek to preserve the modulation inherent in the sound signal that is aptly transferred to musical notation. In a way, one could call his approach of microscopic transcription a "Bartók transform" (quasi-continuous musical sound to chains of densely packed musical symbols). Though one criterion relevant for technical signal transformations (inverse transformation leads to restoring the original signal) would not be met, Bartók succeeded in preserving most of the musically relevant information contained in a recording when transcribing sound to staff notation.

Transcribing music in such detail as Bartók's, of course, is a very arduous and time-consuming task. Also, even a very detailed transcription remains the result of the ears and mind of a single scholar, and may not always be accepted as an "objective" representation of musical sound. The quest for "automated" transcription and "melography" that has been followed since appropriate technology (electric sound recording, amplifiers, and filters) became available, stems from objectives that, from recorded musical sound, a representation in a graphic format should be derived in which (1) the pitch and the duration of tones is given in standard physical units (frequency [Hz], milliseconds or seconds) to ensure reliability and control of measurement. If possible, (2) the graphic representation should be similar to musical notation, for example, by using semilogarithmic graphs with log for pitch and lin for time (see figure 17.1). Furthermore, (3) the changes of pitch over time should be indicated in a quantitative manner on a (lin or log) scale so that deviations from predefined scale positions or intonation variants can be measured and expressed as numerical data suited to statistical or similar processing.

Pitch, in this respect, typically stands for the fundamental frequency f_1 (Hz) of a complex harmonic sound (cf. Schneider 1997, 2000, 2001). Since the repetition frequency f_0 of a complex waveshape with a period T(ms) equals that of the fundamental ($f_1 = f_0$), one could derive pitch also by measuring the period length (ms) and then calculate the corresponding frequency as its inverse ($f = 1/T$). Though such measurement had been done on a mechanical basis as soon as phonographic recording was possible, this was cumbersome and prone to error. Progress was made when registration of sound waves on film became available, and "phonophotography" became a tool also in the study of intonation in African American folk song (Metfessel 1928). One has to remember that, in an interdisciplinary perspective, such investigations were of interest to both comparative and systematic musicology. The method of phonophotography was advocated by the well-known psychologist of music Carl Seashore for the documentation of "primitive" music, as well as for the precise study of intonation in singing or playing (Seashore 1928:10). As is obvious from the title of Metfessel's book (1928) as well as from its content, phonophotography not only allowed precise measurement of pitches, but also provided a new notation, including subtle pitch changes, for which conventional staff notation could not account as effectively.

Along with developments in electronics, subsequent decades saw the advent of so-called pitch meters, of Seeger's melograph (Seeger 1951, 1958), and of similar devices designed and built in Norway (Dahlback 1958) and Israel (Cohen and Katz 1960). A more refined melograph was designed and built by the Slovak physicist and musicologist Miroslav Filip (Filip 1969). It has been used in folk-music research, for example, in the analysis of flute music (Elschek 1979). In the analog era, melographs were either based on low-pass or band-pass filters with which the fundamental (f_1) of a voice or instrument was filtered out from the spectrum of a monophonic sound source, or were using zero-crossing detectors to determine the period length (ms) of a complex waveshape from which the corresponding frequency (f_0) is derived as pitch. Both f_1 and f_0 can be plotted continuously over time so that exact readings of pitch and duration of tones are available.

With digital signal processing, an alternative approach to pitch and time analysis based on auto-correlation (ac) or cross-correlation (cc) analysis has proved useful. Auto-correlation determines periodicities in signals (e.g., in recordings of brain waves for which the methodology was developed, among other applications, by the mathematician Norbert Wiener; cf. Wiener 1961). Soon, ac and cc analyses were used widely in musical acoustics. Leaving technical details aside (cf. Schneider 2000, 2013; Klapuri and Davy 2006), we can say that an instantaneous frequency $f_i(t)$ corresponds to each period of a (quasi-)periodic signal $x(t)$. If we assume that for signals produced by aerophones, as well as the human voice and tones from plucked and bowed chordophones, the period length for a given tone fluctuates within narrow limits in a small time interval (say, 20 ms), f_0 derived from integration over an interval relevant to perception can be taken to represent the pitch of a tone (since we can perceive pitches from f_0).

As with analog melography, typically monophonic sounds are subjected to analysis to determine the pitch contours of a single voice or instrument. If sound sources are polyphonic—containing several voices or instruments that sing or play simultaneously—analysis is more difficult and can result in ambiguous readings (see articles in Klapuri and Davy 2006). Digital melography (ac or cc method) of single sound sources is very precise and suited to investigate such phenomena as intonation (including glissandi, melismata, and small vibrati). As an illustration, part of the melographic analysis of a recording made by Poul Rovsing Olsen of a woman from Lebanon, Dunya Yunis, rendering a song titled or referring to "Abu Zeluf"[1] is analyzed here for two reasons: (1) the recording is fairly well known and is found in many archives so that the analysis can be checked easily; and (2) the singing of

Dunya Yunis contains melismata and other embellishments that are of interest for understanding issues of intonation.

"Abu Zeluf" is segmented by the singer into phrases, roughly determined as "breath periods." Analysis of the first long phrase (the first twenty seconds of the recording) has been published elsewhere (Schneider 2013) and may be consulted as reference material. I concentrate, therefore, on phrase 4, which starts at about forty-three seconds and ends at one minute, five seconds on the recording.[2] A first glance at the melogram of this segment (figure 17.1) reveals that there is upward melodic motion (comprising, as in phrase 1, the notes C4, D4, and E4 at ca. 264, 295, and 330 Hz, respectively) toward a stable E4 that lasts for almost three seconds before a melisma sets in for another three and a half seconds. The E4 is the central tone and most stable pitch in several of the phrases. After the melisma, which sweeps at a modulation frequency of 3–5 Hz between the E4 at ca. 330 Hz and a pitch close to F♯4 (peaking at ca. 363 Hz, meaning the interval E4–F♯4 is about 165 cents wide), again the pitch level of E4 appears (at 51–52 seconds in the recording). Then, a sudden jump from E4 to a pitch level peaking clearly above F♯4 takes place (333 à 388 Hz ~ 265 cents), which is followed by another

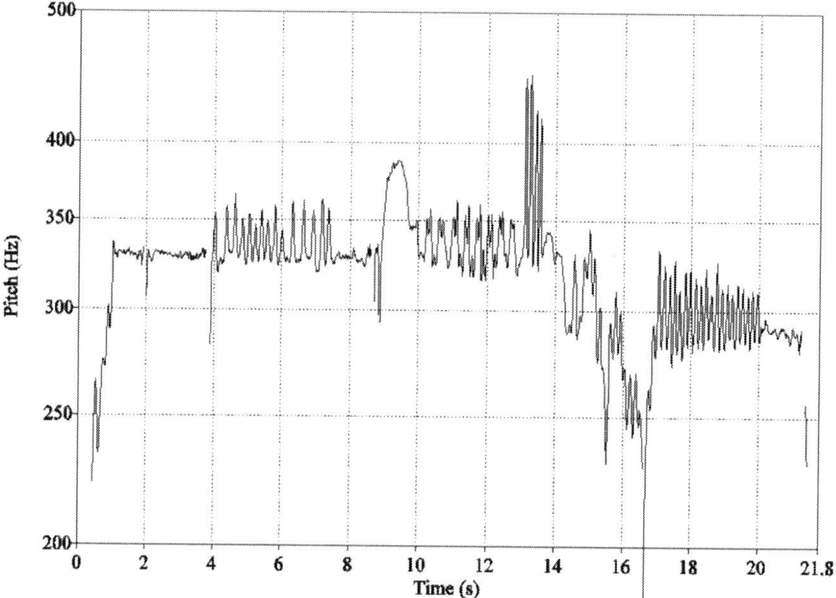

Figure 17.1. ***"Abu Zeluf,"*** **melogram of phrase 4 (duration ca. 22 seconds)**

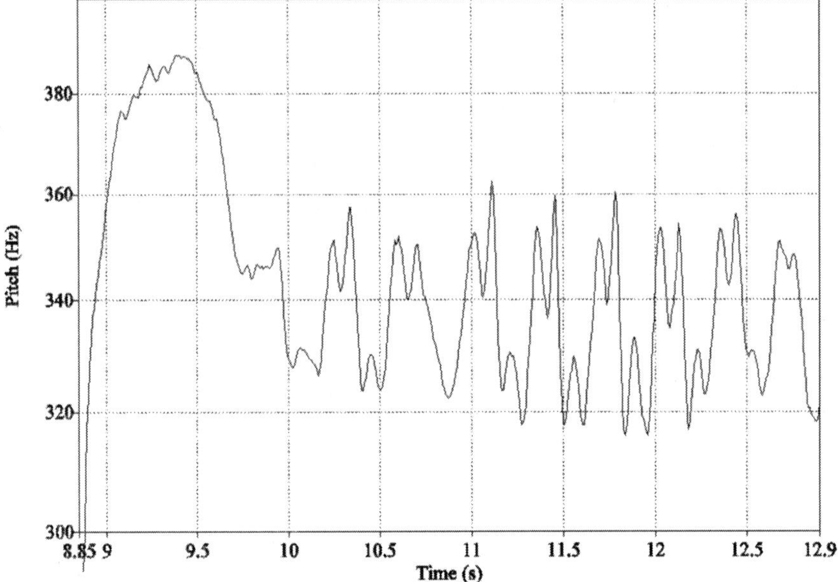

Figure 17.2. *"Abu Zeluf,"* segment of phrase 4, pitch jump and complex modulation

melisma (figure 17.2). As a fine-grained analysis of this section reveals, this melisma is not of the usual (more or less sinusoidal) type, yet it shows a fairly complex modulation in which smaller frequency shifts are superimposed on larger up-and-down sweeps.

The singer then adds a swift melisma that gives four nearly periodic pitch shifts from the level of E4 (ca. 330 Hz) to ca. 450 and 420 Hz, respectively, in only 0.5 seconds (13 seconds–13.5 seconds in figure 17.3). After briefly passing through the central note/pitch of E4, Yunis produces a fast micromelodic figure that, within a span of about three seconds, includes pitches from ca. 340 down to ca. 220 Hz and back to ca. 280 Hz. The corresponding musical notes very roughly would be F4, E4, D4, . . . ,[3] A3, D4; however, there are no steady pitches while there are inflections to every note/pitch produced by the singer. The micromelodic figure is followed by another melisma that yields an almost sinusoidal modulation lasting for three seconds, and with pitch shifts ranging from ca. 280 to 330 Hz (peak to peak; ca. 285 cents). The pitch shifts become smaller at the end of the melisma that leads to the final long note sung on a vowel at ca. 291 Hz (D4) before the phrase ends (w'a – a – u – f 'a).

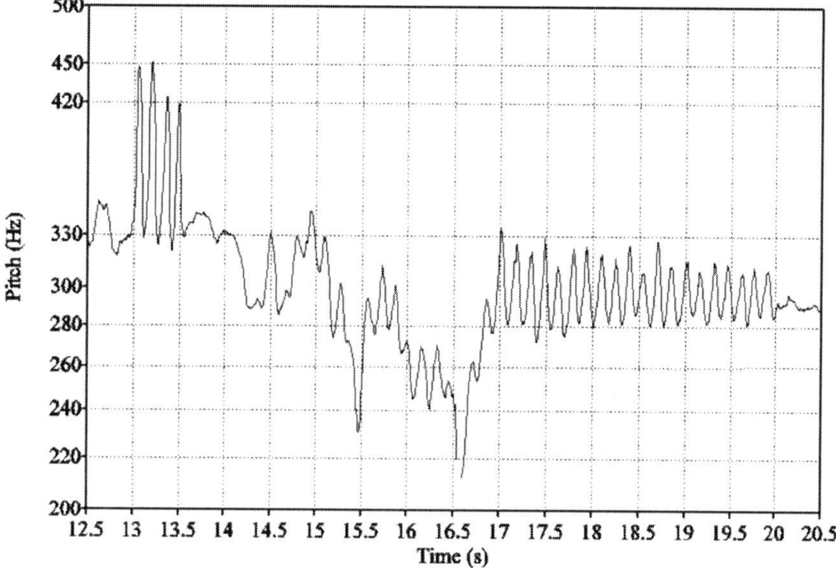

Figure 17.3. *"Abu Zeluf,"* phrase 4, final section, micromelodic shifts, melismata

Though transcription of the phrase from "Abu Zeluf" subjected to melographic analysis into conventional notation might be feasible, it would necessitate special signs to mark deviations from standard pitch notation and still would fail to indicate precisely the size of particular deviations. The temporal and pitch microstructure of melismata and other modulations, moreover, can hardly be shown in conventional notation (the use of zigzag lines is common practice in transcriptions of ethnic music to denote pitch shifts such as glissandi and melismata, yet lacks precision).

A special problem for transcription and analysis arises from polyphonic music like the vocal polyphony found in various parts of Georgia. Three-part polyphony is very common in Georgian traditions, and also four-part vocal polyphony was and still is practiced (for an overview, see Chkhikvadze 1969, 2010[1960]). Though detailed transcriptions of Georgian polyphony have been published (e.g., Nadel 1933), movement of individual voices, and interval structure as well as intonation, deserves further investigation. In recent years, there have been many attempts to develop software capable of transcribing polyphonic music (see Klapuri and Davy 2006). Most of the codes can handle several voices; however, the level of correctness is hardly perfect—depending on conditions; good codes are said to reach a level of about 70 percent correct pitch and time information—since (a) several sources such as human voices singing together have common partials when singing harmonic intervals such as fifths and major thirds. This makes automated separation of voices by use of spectral information difficult (partials have to be assigned to particular voices by some decision criteria). Additionally, (b) onset-time differences for tones from two or more voices can be small, thus onset will not help much as clues for voice separation. Furthermore, (c) algorithmic tracking of pitch contours can be confused if voices often cross each other, as in certain types of polyphony.

To avoid difficulties, it makes sense to record polyphonic music on (analog or digital) multitrack machines, on which one track per voice or instrument can be used at a time. This allows separate analysis per voice yet requires nearly complete acoustical separation of sources. This cannot always be achieved in recording a live performance. To illustrate, I present one brief example here.

In May 2001, our institute participated in a festival of Georgian music in Hamburg and, as part of that event, held a workshop on Georgian polyphony at which an ensemble from Tbilisi, the Anchiskhati Choir, consisting of nine male singers and instrumentalists (two folklorists, four composers, a conductor, a pianist, a mathematician, and a theologian), performed both folk and church music in front of an invited audience. This choir, though specializing in medieval church music, was proficient also in folk music styles of eastern and western Georgia, and performs songs and styles from various ethnic groups and regions. I recorded the concert on DAT and a selection of songs also on analog 8-track (Otari 80-8, ½-inch tape at 38 cm/s), so that nine voices were assigned to eight separate tracks. For the recording, I used a mixing desk (sixteen mic inputs, eight subgroups) and professional condenser mics (Neumann, AKG, Sennheiser), all set to a cardioid pattern. Since the singers said they could perform best standing close to each other in a semi-circle, the microphones had to be placed accordingly, with the result that complete separation of the voices could not be achieved, and some leakage of sound from each singer into neighboring mics and recording channels occurred. We could have avoided this mishap by using contact microphones; however, these were not at hand when the recording was made. Leakage of this sort is consequential for melographic analysis based on ac method since, for two or more voices forming harmonic intervals (i.e., fundamental frequencies are in a ratio of 2:3, 3:4, 3:4:5, etc.), auto-correlation may calculate their common denominator (musically speaking, the "root" of a given harmonic interval or chord). Typically, this is f_0—equal to the first partial of a harmonic series, f_1—that will be plotted as pitch in an ac-based melogram, even if f_1 does not exist in the sound spectrum. The period length relevant for f_0 calculation remains identical when there is a missing or weak f_1.

To analyze some of the songs with ac-based melography, I prepared digital copies (24 and 16 bit/48 kHz sampling), and from each track created a mono sound file normalized to -1 dBFS. Accordingly, eight melograms per segment of a given song were produced, plus a number of melograms showing several or all voices simultaneously.

One melogram presented here is from the song "Elesa," a work song from Guria (western Georgia) traditionally sung by men working in the woods. The word *elesa* serves as a signal to coordinate the work, namely to pull a heavy tree or other load. "Elesa" is basically in three-part polyphony, whereby the uppermost voice produces a kind of *Pendelmelodik* (a sequence of wide intervals sung upward and downward). Two and occasionally three voices in the middle and bass register form a complex polyphonic texture including many chord-like sonorities. Each of the chords lasts from about 750 to about 850 milliseconds, so that the pulse one can infer rather than feel (no foot tapping or other bodily expression was observed) from the flow of the chords is at about 72 beats per minute.

The song in its first phrase (duration about sixteen seconds) starts with but two voices, which have their f_1 at 175 and 257 Hz, respectively (F3 and C4). The first chord-like sonority that follows comprises four voices, of which three (with fundamentals at about 192, 285, and 683 Hz corresponding roughly to the notes G3, C♯4, and F5) can be identified unambiguously by spectral components. This requires that spectral analysis with manual assignment of partials to notes must complement melography.[4]

Since the nine voices performing "Elesa" were recorded on eight tracks, one melogram per track could be calculated; for readability, segments of ten to twenty seconds per track were chosen. It is possible to write several melograms into one graph so that the intervallic and temporal relation of voices can be studied in detail. Figure 17.4 shows pitch trajectories for two voices from the opening phrase of "Elesa." Because of the leakage problem described above, all pitches were controlled by means of spectral analysis (using both the DAT stereo recording and the 8-track recording of "Elesa"). The analysis of the upper voice proved to be fairly accurate, whereas for the lower voice some dubious readings were found (one such spot is indicated by the circle in figure 17.4). However, it is obvious from figure 17.4 that the phrase ends on B♭3 (ca. 230 Hz) and F4 (ca. 341 Hz) for the two voices displayed. The "open" fifth can also be easily identified by ear.

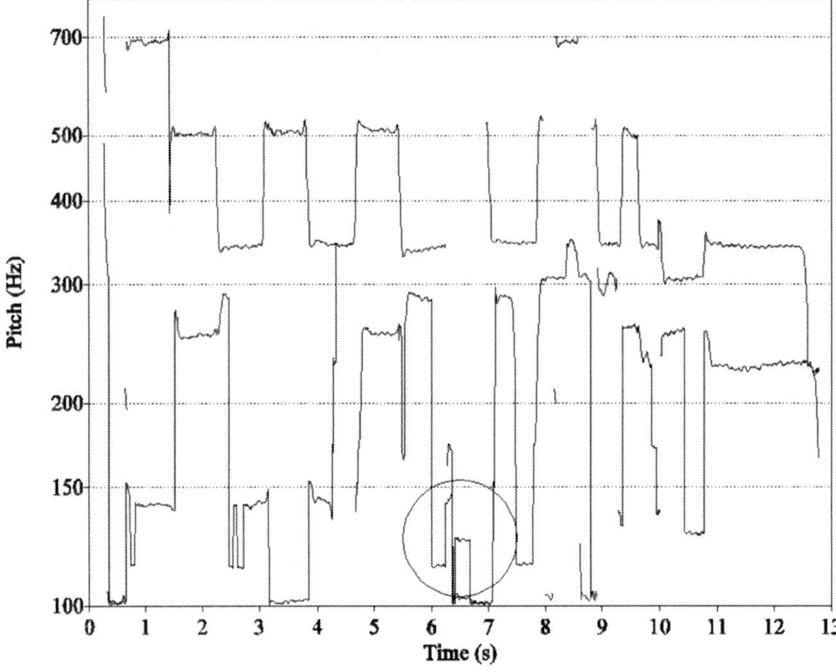

Figure 17.4. Segment of "*Elesa*" (first phrase), melograms of two voices

In regard to vertical sonorities resulting from polyphony as in "Elesa," spectrum analysis can help to reveal the intervallic structure of vertical sonorities in polyphony such as that in "Elesa." For example, the main spectral data (0–1 kHz) for sonorities number 3 and 4 are the following:

Table 17.1. Spectrum analysis of the Georgian song "Elesa"

Sonority No. 3		*Sonority No. 4*	
Main Frequencies (Hz)	*Note (approx.)*	*Main Frequencies (Hz)*	*Note (approx.)*
184.37	F#3	210.21	G#3
207.94	G#3	228.88	A#3
302.57	D#4	344–347	F4
368.1		406	G#4
403.53	G4/G#4	455.47	A4/A#4
515.5	C5	473.97	
607.58	D#5	571.5	D5
806.77	G#5	686.54	F5

Among the spectral data, including SPL for each component not listed here, those referring to fundamental frequencies f_1 of individual voices must be distinguished from those representing higher partials. This is not always easy, and especially so for the dense spectra produced by nine singers who show some variability in intonation. Sonorities 3 and 4 can be viewed as representing two major chords that constitute a harmonic shift by a whole tone (to simplify things, one could label the shift A♭ à B♭ instead of G♯ à A♯). Somewhat surprising is the lowest component in both chords, suggesting either a seventh or a very flat intonation of one of the nine singers.

Conclusions

Melographic analysis based on analog or digital signal processing is a useful tool for understanding the musical and sonic details of recorded sound. With ethnic music, one can investigate in particular the fine structure of melodic contours as well as intonation of single notes with high time and frequency resolution. Readings are reliable as long as monophonic sound is analyzed. With polyphonic music, analysis is much more complicated, since voices or instruments interact so that separation of sources can be difficult, and questionable results from processing of sound data can occur. Therefore, one should try different models and parameter settings to optimize results. It is probably more adequate to speak of computer-assisted than of automated transcription, since the process in fact needs to be monitored in many ways, and one still needs ears to analyze music and to check the outcome of whatever model is employed in computer-assisted transcription.

Notes

1. The recording was made in Beirut on 4 February 1972. It was originally published on the LP *Music in the World of Islam 1*, and has been (mis)used later as an example of "world music" (cf. Feld and Kierkegaard 2010) and even in a popular-music production, "Santiago" by the Swiss group, Yello, in 1987. The meaning of the expression "Abu Zeluf" is not quite clear (literally, "the one [guy] with sideburns"); see forum.wordreference.com/showthread.php?t=1250869&langid=3.
2. Melographic analyses use Praat software (Boersma and Weenink 2011).
3. The ellipses mean that after D4 and before A3, there are some very swift pitch shifts that do not lead to a clear pitch or note level.
4. Spectrum analysis was performed with tools available on the Audacity platform and with Spectro 3.1 (Cook and Scavone ca. 1993). Parameter settings were identical (FFT: 16384 pts, Hanning, frequency-at-peak).

References

Abraham, Otto, and Erich von Hornbostel. 1902/1903. "Tonsystem und Musik der Japaner." *Sammelbände der internationalen Musikgesellschaft* 4: 302–60.

———. 1904. "Über die Bedeutung des Phonographen für vergleichende Musikwissenschaft." *Zeitschrift für Ethnologie* 36: 222–31.

Bartók, Béla, and László Somfai, eds. 1981. *Hungarian Folk Music: Gramophone Records with Béla Bartók's Transcriptions*. Budapest: Hungaroton.

Berlin, Gabriele, and Artur Simon, eds. 2000. *Music Archiving in the World: Papers Presented at the Conference on the Occasion of the 100th Anniversary of the Berlin Phonogramm-Archiv*. Berlin: VWB—Verlag für Wissenschaft und Bildung.

Beyer, Robert T. 1999. *Sounds of Our Time: Two Hundred Years of Acoustics*. New York: Springer.

Boersma, Paul, and David Weenink. 2011. *Praat: Doing Phonetics by Computer* (Software version 5.2.17). Amsterdam: University of Amsterdam, Institute of Phonetics.

Chkhikvadze, Grigol. 2010[1960]. "Main Types of Georgian Folk Polyphony." In *Echoes from Georgia: Seventeen Arguments on Georgian Polyphony*, edited by R. Curcumia and Joseph Jordania, 97–110. Hauppauge, NY: Nova Science Publishers.

———. 1969. "La culture musicale populaire Géorgienne." *Bedi Kartlisa: Études géorgiennes et caucasiennes* 26: 18–66.

Cohen, Dalia, and Ruth Katz. 1960. "Explorations in the Music of the Samaritans: An Illustration of the Utility of Graphic Notation." *Ethnomusicology* 4: 67–73.

Cook, Perry, and Gary Scavone. 1993. *Spectro: A Spectrum Analysis Program*. Stanford, CA: CCRMA (version 3.1).

Dahlback, Karl. 1958. *New Methods in Vocal Folk Music Research*. Oslo: Oslo University Press.

Edison, Thomas A. 1888. "The Perfected Phonograph." *North American Review* 126(262): 527–36.

Elschek, Oskár. 1979. "Melographische Interpretationscharakteristika von Flötenmusik." *Studia instrumentorum musicae popularis*, volume 6, 43–58. Stockholm: Musik Museet.

Feld, Steven, and Annemette Kierkegaard. 2010. "Entangled Complicities in the Prehistory of 'World Music': Poul Rovsing Olsen and Jean Jenkins Encounter Brian Eno and David Byrne in the Bush of Ghosts." *Popular Musicology Online*. www.popular-musicology-online.com/issues/04/feld.html (accessed 30 August 2012).

Filip, Miroslav. 1969. "Envelope Periodicity Detection." *Journal of the Acoustical Society of America* 45: 719–32.

Graf, Walter. 1980. *Vergleichende Musikwissenschaft*. Edited by Franz Födermayr. Vienna: Stiglmayr.

Hajek, Leo. 1928. *Das Phonogrammarchiv der Akademie der Wissenschaften in Wien von seiner Gründung bis zur Neueinrichtung im Jahre 1927*. Vienna: Hölder-Pichler-Tempsky.

Kittler, Friedrich. 1999. *Gramophone, Film, Typewriter*. Stanford, CA: Stanford University Press.

Klapuri, Anssi, and Manuel Davy, eds. 2006. *Signal Processing Methods for Music Transcriptions*. New York: Springer.

Lach, Robert. 1924. *Die vergleichende Musikwissenschaft, ihre Methoden und Probleme*. Vienna: Hölder-Pichler-Tempsky.

Metfessel, Milton. 1928. *Phonophotography in Folk Music: American Negro Songs in New Notation*. Chapel Hill: University of North Carolina Press.

Music in the World of Islam, Volume I: The Human Voice. 1976. London: Tangent Records TGS 131.

Nadel, Siegfried. 1933. *Georgische Gesänge*. Leipzig: Harrassowitz.

Nettl, Bruno. 2005. *The Study of Ethnomusicology: Thirty-One Issues and Concepts*, second edition. Urbana: University of Illinois Press.

Schneider, Albrecht. 1984. *Analogie und Rekonstruktion*, Volume 1. Bonn: Verlag für Systematische Musikwissenschaft.

———. 1997. *Skala–Tonhöhe–Klang: Akustische, tonometrische und psychoakustische Untersuchungen auf vergleichender Grundlage*. Bonn: Verlag für Systematische Musikwissenschaft.

———. 2000. "Inharmonic Sounds: Implications as to 'Pitch,' 'Timbre' and 'Consonance.'" *Journal of New Music Research* 29: 275–301.

———. 2001. "Sound, Pitch, and Scale: From 'Tone Measurements' to Sonological Analysis in Ethnomusicology." *Ethnomusicology* 45(3): 489–519.

———. 2009. "Konservierung von Musik durch Erfindung der technischen Schallaufzeichnung." In *Handbuch Musik und Medien*, edited by Holger Schramm, 31–46. Constance: UVK Verlagsgesellschaft.

———. 2013. "Change and Continuity in Sound Analysis: A Review of Concepts in Regard to Musical Acoustics, Music Perception, and Transcription." In *Sound–Perception–Performance*, edited by Rolf Bader, 71–111. New York: Springer.

Seashore, Carl. 1928. *The Present Status of Research in the Psychology of Music at the University of Iowa*. Iowa City: University of Iowa Press.

Seeger, Charles. 1951. "An Instantaneous Music Notator." *Journal of the International Folk Music Council* 3: 103–6.

———. 1958. "Prescriptive and Descriptive Music-Writing." *Musical Quarterly* 44: 184–95.

Simon, Artur. 1994. "Die methodischen Implikationen der aufnahmetechnischen Medien in der Ethnomusikologie." In *Vergleichend-Systematische Musikwissenschaft*, edited by Elisabeth T. Hielscher and Theophil Antonicek, 93–118. Tutzing: Schneider.

Stumpf, Carl. 1883 and 1890. *Tonpsychologie*, two volumes. Leipzig: Barth.

———. 1892. "Phonographierte Indianermelodien." *Vierteljahrsschrift für Musikwissenschaft* 8: 127–44. Reprinted *Sammelbände für Vergleichende Musikwissenschaft* 1: 113–26 (1922).

———. 1911. *Anfänge der Musik*. Leipzig: Barth.

———. 2012. *The Origins of Music*. Translated and edited by David Trippett. Oxford: Oxford University Press.

Wiener, Norbert. 1961. *Cybernetics: or Control and Communication in the Animal and in the Machine*, second edition. Cambridge: MIT Press.

PART IV

HISTORICAL STUDIES

CHAPTER EIGHTEEN

In Search of Music's Intimate Moments

Philip V. Bohlman

What message does the tin sign with "Theresienstadt Water" on it tell us? And what of the meanings in the miniature hurdy-gurdy?[1]

—W. G. Sebald, *Austerlitz* (2001)

And courage has become so very weary, and longing so great

The rise of ethnomusicology's modern intellectual history has frequently followed the course of grand narratives that recognize the singular and distinctive contributions of the field to the sweeping historical, political, and cultural changes of modernity. Paradigm shifts and disciplinary revolutions follow upon technological innovation, the implementation of new theory, and the radical rethinking of music in its many ontologies. The ethnomusicological concern for agency and mobility generates activism and the engagement with the movements of immigrants and refugees. Many, if not most, ethnomusicologists enter the field with a belief that the possibility of bringing real change accompanies a moral imperative at the core of the field's grand narratives.

In this chapter I follow a different journey through and with the grand narratives of ethnomusicology's history, pausing and reflecting on what I call here music's intimate moments, in which musical experience and meaning are intensely personal, and change may assume the course of the few rather than the many. In so doing, I also reflect on Bruno Nettl's concern for the intimacy of the ethnomusicological experience, demonstrated by the ways he has consistently engaged with learning from his own teachers and students, and he has insisted on the ways in which influences, often profoundly intimate, shape the course of intellectual history (cf. Nettl 2013).

In recent years, intimacy in several theoretical formulations has shaped ethnomusicological thought in important ways. Michael Herzfeld's work on cultural intimacy (1997) has shaped the ways in which histories of nationalism have coalesced around the enactment of shared pasts, making the political personal. Popular music, as Martin Stokes has eloquently argued in the case of modern Turkey, may evoke the nation in forms that broad segments of society share at the moments they make music their own (Stokes 2010; see also Dueck 2007). In the historical *longue durée*, music is notable for the ways in which it collapses the dissonance of differences. Music's intimate moments, thus, often arise in the places where they seem incongruous and unexpected. At moments of cataclysm and violence, music may be the catalyst for deeper understanding, at once transcendent and redemptive. It may be music that makes intimacy possible where it would otherwise be absent. Music may literally fill the void separating human experiences.

In the course of this chapter, I turn to musical experiences not customarily studied for their intimacy, those I have found in the many years I have devoted to studying musicians whose lives were swept up in the Holocaust. The narrative path of the chapter follows the ways I have traveled "in search of" affective eschatological moments of music that took place at the end of life and that marked the end of history. I structure the chapter around the many paths necessary for a journey in search of intimacy where it was most fragile and endangered, paths emerging from my scholarship but shaped no less from my activities as a performer of melodramas with my pianist wife, Christine Wilkie Bohlman, and music from the concentration camps with my cabaret troupe, the New Budapest Orpheum Society.

The music and texts that fill the chapter, punctuating its journey as moments that at once arrest our attention and enjoin us to continue in search of further intimate moments, are themselves from musical and literary work produced in or about the concentration camp at Terezín/Theresienstadt. This work is remarkable not only for its abundance and extraordinary quality, but also for its evocation of intimacy, indeed, its testament to the possibility of shared journey. The composition with which I concern myself most deeply is Viktor Ullmann's *Die Weise von Liebe und Tod des Cornets Christoph Rilke* (hereinafter, *Cornet*), a melodrama for speaker and piano (eventually intended for orchestra), which Ullmann left in sketches at the time of his deportation to and murder in Auschwitz. I approach *Cornet* from different perspectives in the chapter, using fragments of texts as section headings, reflecting analytically on both Ullmann's music and the poetry by Rainer Maria Rilke. Intimate moments multiply through the intertextuality of *Cornet*, particularly the passage symbolized by its journey.

It is journey, moreover, that connects all the texts I weave into the chapter. It is journey at time of war that draws Christoph Rilke into war; the title of the great novel from Terezín, *Eine Reise* (The Journey) by H. G. Adler, makes journey explicit; W. G. Sebald's *Austerlitz*, the source of the epigraph above, unfolds as journey in counterpoint to and from Terezín; the music sounds the journey of time and history, in search of the resolution that it will always forestall, save for the few moments of intimacy it bequeaths to those who experience it.

Finally, and most intimately, I search for these moments because of their meaning for Bruno Nettl, for many of them shaped the everyday of the concentration camp at Terezín, to which three of his grandparents were deported. In particular, I embark on the allegorical journeys in the final compositions of the Czech-Jewish composer Viktor Ullmann (1898–1944), not only *Cornet* but other works I have brought to the stage and recorded with my own ensemble (see New Budapest Orpheum Society 2002, 2009, and 2014). Bruno Nettl's parents and Viktor Ullmann shared many of the same musical circles in Prague prior to and in the early years of the Holocaust. Bruno Nettl has himself written, not extensively but with intimacy, about the meaning of Ullmann's piano sonatas for his mother, the pianist Gertrud Nettl: "Hearing Ullmann's music, I can see him in my mind's eye, looking upset, making angular motions with his arms, walking into our apartment and out again" (Nettl 2013:12). It was not by chance that my own search for the music of the Holocaust, especially in Terezín, began when Bruno Nettl introduced me to Alice Herz Sommer (1903–2014), Gertrud Nettl's friend and pianist colleague, whose influence and inspiration would shape not only my Ph.D. dissertation in the early 1980s, but the course of my own life as an ethnomusicologist (for recordings of performances in the intimacy of her own Jerusalem home, see Herz-Sommer n.d.; see also Bohlman 1991).

This sense of intimacy is, as the chapters that honor Bruno Nettl throughout this volume make clear, a guiding force in the many moments that constitute the intellectual history of ethnomusicology that has so powerfully engaged him throughout his career. In the course of my own chapter, I, too, move between and among music's intimate moments to ethnomusicology's history, reminding us that our common search for the latter may well begin with our personal concern with the former.

As if there were only *one* mother

thus the searched search and thus search
searched thus be searched thus
be searched thus search
searched thus
search
—H. G. Adler, "Auf der Suche" (In Search)

Rainer Maria Rilke's *Die Weise von Liebe und Tod des Cornets Christoph Rilke* (Rilke 1912) was one of the most beloved literary works of early twentieth-century Central Europe, and it is hardly surprising that its literary and historical meaning would become even more intense in Terezín. Written in 1899, the prose-poem passed through several versions before appearing in print in 1912 as the first volume of the most influential German-language literary series of the twentieth century, "Insel-Bücherei." Terezín survivors speak of physical copies of the volume in the camp. They speak also of many residents capable of reciting passages from *Cornet* from memory. Moving between written and oral tradition, the poem expanded to create an aesthetic space that drew many into it. In that space, the Terezín residents encountered a world whose dimensions were familiar, albeit a world they could only approach from the distance of history. Just as the flag-bearer (Cornet) in the Rilke poem traveled to the edges of the Habsburg world, so too had the Terezín residents themselves come to occupy that world once again: Theresienstadt, the "city of Maria Theresa," an eighteenth-century Habsburg garrison city at the edge of empire repurposed as a concentration camp.

Viktor Ullmann's setting of Rilke's *Cornet* is, according to the composer's sketches, a monodrama for narrator and piano. Even the genre of monodrama, adapted from the Czech tradition of melodrama, intensified the intimacy of the composition, for it drew together the abundant references to the Czech Lands and history. Ullmann, like Rilke, was Czech, as were many of those who might witness *Cornet* in Terezín. The sketches survived because they were retrieved by H. G. Adler, who would preserve many of Ullmann's musical and literary works before donating them to the archives of the Paul Sacher Stiftung in Basel, where I studied them in preparation for this chapter and my own performances. The fragments, written with pens, pencils, and crayons of several colors on staves prepared in Terezín, stunningly cohere to the eschatological aesthetics that *Cornet* tragically embodies. The prose-poem's narrative itself is told from a number of different perspectives and in a number of different voices: Rilke's narrator, the flag-bearer himself, his lover, the civil servant preparing the final report of Christoph Rilke's death. Textually, Rainer Maria Rilke employs different genres as well—traditional narration, fragments from letters, dream sequences, and battle chronicles. Compositionally, Viktor Ullmann reaches in many directions, borrowing tunes and shaping them, sometimes grotesquely, sometimes with exquisite beauty, to portray the Central European past and the horrors of war that had so often consumed it—and were, again in 1944, consuming it.

Let yourself love me: I am the flag-bearer

Cornet is a narrative of the ultimate destruction and final tragedy of war, the end of time, and accordingly it is one of the most allegorical of all Ullmann compositions. The story begins in the decades after the Thirty Years War (1618–1648), when troops were mustered from the culturally diverse lands of Habsburg Central Europe to defend its eastern borders against the Ottoman armies. Fired by patriotism and military adventure, Christoph Rilke goes off to war for the imperial army, coming of age in war. For Ullmann, the allegory would be deeply personal, as if the monodrama he created might also stage the final moments of Terezín itself. The intimate and the eschatological—*Liebe und Tod*—would become one. In Rilke's text and Ullmann's score, questions abound, about Terezín and about the Holocaust. Destruction in war, the eschatological end of love, can ultimately not be restrained. In the closing scene—at the moment when the intimacy of love yields to the transcendence of death—Rainer Maria Rilke gazes into the future, while Viktor Ullmann musters themes and motifs that return to a past that never existed, where all that Ullmann, or anyone seeing *Cornet*, will witness is an old woman, weeping at the loss of all who had shared the world with her.

As he worked on the sketches for *Cornet*, time and the end of time increasingly formed a performative counterpoint for Viktor Ullmann. The sketches reveal the extent to which the compositional work began with great deliberation in the summer of 1944, probably July, only to accelerate and intensify until the compositional process itself formed a temporal stretto, a race against time. Working from beginning to end and laying out one scene after the other and following the course of Rilke's prose-poem, Ullmann clearly makes decisions that enable him to reach the final scenes with as much dispatch as possible. As the texture of leitmotifs becomes denser, so do the techniques with which Ullmann calls them forth, allowing the early scenes to push the later scenes forward. Early in the manuscript, he fits the text to themes and leitmotifs carefully, but by the second part, he begins writing them on the page, with a crayon rather than pen and pencil, proximate to the musical passage individual phrases might accompany. The several early scenes he rescored for orchestra waited for the final stages, when time itself would prove insufficient. The sketches come to their end in the late summer of 1944, or at the very beginning of the autumn. The dedication to Ullmann's sister Elly for her birthday on 27 September 1944 is the clearest indication of the moment of conclusion toward which he was working. Several weeks after his sister's birthday, Viktor Ullmann was deported to Auschwitz, where he was murdered upon his arrival, generally believed to be 16 October 1944.

During the years he spent in Terezín, Viktor Ullmann forged a compositional process that remarkably wove intimate moments from the everyday of the concentration camp into the scores he was composing. He did this figuratively and metaphorically, but he also did so in the most literal sense possible, in *Cornet* as well as other compositions in Terezín, some of which received performances. The typed final libretto by Peter Kien (1919–1944) for the 1943 opera *Der Kaiser von Atlantis* (The Emperor of Atlantis), for example, appears on the reverse side—in the libretto, thus, the recto side—of completed camp registration forms, literal representations of the life and death of real people.

Are you the night?

Ullmann's compositional procedures mirror the very allegory of journey and the *Liebestod* (love-death) of Rilke's poetry, for Ullmann reveals and records his acute awareness of the end of time powerfully shaping the decisions made while composing a moment of musical intimacy. That awareness led him to choose sonorities to represent time, but beyond such aesthetic decisions, the awareness was coupled with decisions he made about inscribing time with modernist musical techniques. Ullmann's choice to spell chords in certain ways actually provided him vocabulary for marking music's intimacy and then affording it with transcendent meaning. As the composition moves forward, following the flag-bearer's journey and mirroring its complex intertextuality, Ullmann consistently juxtaposes two areas of harmonic texture, the first consonant, the second dissonant in its reliance on quartal and quintal extensions of consonance, but actually marked in the score by the addition of accidentals that seemingly spurn diatonic and chromatic tradition.

By using mirroring techniques, in which different spellings of the same notes and intervals occupy the same space, realizing its sameness as different, Ullmann opens the musical portal for allegories of intimacy. One of the most intense of these moments is found in the third scene of part 2, in which the flag-bearer finds repose in the days before the battle that will lead to his

Table 18.1. Chord progressions as the flag-bearer flees from reality to dream

C♯m (added 6th) — gmin7/F — B♭ mM7—	D♭ 7/A♭ — F♯9 — C2 —	D♭7	
m.10	m.11	m.12	m.13

death. At the beginning of the scene the flag-bearer believes he is dreaming, but when he seeks to waken himself from the dream, he finds he is already awake, yet "confused by reality." Harmonically, Ullmann represents the confusion of reality in hymn-like fashion, using triadic structures that, however, follow the confused path of spellings that invert sharps and flats, dissolving into a dissonance in which the flag-bearer encounters his lover (table 18.1).

Metaphors, musical and poetic, surround the flag-bearer, enclosing him as the night and as a woman approaches him, closing the space of intimacy. The layers of spoken text Ullmann writes in his score do not fit the space, or rather they spill over its edges (figure 18.1), multiplying the growing dissonance in the piano, resolving it by forestalling the answer to the allegorical question of love and death: "Are you the night?"

Figure 18.1. The intimate space of love and death (Teil 2, Bild III)

> And the celebration is far away. And the light lies. And the night draws closely about him and is cool. And he asks a woman who approaches him: "Are you the night?"

How they sing their laughter

> *Everything that sounds in nature is music.* It contains all music's elements in it and requires only a hand that draws them out, an ear that hears, and a common feeling that is sensitive to it. . . . The sensation of music is not generated from the outside, but rather is within us, within us. (Herder 1998[1800]:812–13; italics in the original)

The aesthetic concern with music's intimate moments enters Western musical thought most fully at the confluence of the Enlightenment and the growing awareness of world music. The moment of this confluence, stretching from the late decades of the eighteenth century through the opening decades of the nineteenth century and enunciated through Johann Gottfried Herder's coinage of the concept *Volkslied* (folk song), was accompanied by an inward movement, thereby reconfiguring the universal as the personal. A new aesthetic language came into being to express the movement of music between the outside and the inside: *Empfindung*, *Empfindsamkeit*, *Sentimentales*, *Sinnlichkeit*, *Erhabenes*—feeling, sensibility, sentimentality, sentience, sublime. These were active qualities, and they accompanied the growing consciousness of musical meaning in a vastly greater world beyond the self (cf. the tension between "naïve" and "sentimental" in Schiller 2002). Herder (1744–1803), and the generations that succeeded him, also gave temporal meaning to the musical moment of intimacy, locating it in the history of aesthetic engagement between self and other that would be foundational for modern ethnomusicology: "Every moment is *temporary* for this art [music], and so it must be, for it is precisely the ways in which it is *shorter* and *longer*, *stronger* and *weaker*, *more* and *less*, that produces its *meaning*, its *impression*. In its *arrival* and *departure*, in its *becoming* and *being*, there lies the conquering strength of the sound and its perception" (Herder 1998[1800]:819, italics in the original).

The temporal and the spatial converge to yield music's intimate moment, the properties of which, according to Herder, underwent a process of fusion (*Verschmelzen*), a metaphor that would expand to become theoretically central for comparative musicology by the turn of the twentieth century (cf. Stumpf 2012[1911]). Critical to perceiving the moment of intimacy in an expanding intellectual history was the transitoriness of its immanence. Lying within, it was reached from without. Its dimensions were realized through arrival and departure, being and becoming. Music's moment of intimacy was realized by the body and on the body. Herder, above, and nineteenth-century German Romantics most commonly used *Augenblick* (the glance or blink of an eye) for "moment." The intimacy of the moment notwithstanding, it was only through journey that it was reachable. Already in the late Enlightenment, Herder recognized that the sentient being entered upon journey to experience folk song. The decade he devoted most intensively to folk song, the 1770s, followed immediately on the heels of a transformative sea journey in 1769 (see Herder 1997).

It is these metaphors that we encounter again as we search for music's intimate moment in Terezín. Christoph Rilke embarks upon his journey, pausing again and again at moments of intimacy. H. G. Adler's prose and poetry lead us on journeys, into and through and beyond the moment. Leo Strauss's Terezín cabaret players look beyond the stage in order to perform a moment made meaningful because it is shared. Together, such musical moments in Terezín lived in the intimacy through which they cohered.

The hour rushes toward the dreams of the night

If so very gently
my heart longs
to take a journey
back home.

To hear the music
playing in my own home,
just as it was sung
by Oscar Straus.

Just one last time to visit,
before it's all gone,
just one last time to see Vienna,
just once in May.

—Leo Strauss, "Aus der Familie der Sträusse," closing stanzas (1944)

Leo Strauss's "Aus der Familie der Sträusse" (From the Family of the Strausses) was one of the best-known potpourris for Terezín cabaret stage (in Migdal 1986:67–70; for a recording by Philip Bohlman and Ilya Levinson, see New Budapest Orpheum Society 2014, tr. 10). Leo Strauss (also Straus,

1897–1944) came from a long lineage of cabaret players, and it was his father, Oscar Straus (1870–1954), who had been one of the leading composers of music for the cabaret and the operetta stage, sharing the former with Arnold Schoenberg when both performed cabaret at the Überbrettl in fin-de-siècle Berlin. Leo Strauss's "From the Family of the Strausses" was autobiographical no less than allegorical.

In Terezín, moments of intimacy broke the silence between ending and beginning, sounding what, in drawing upon Mikhail Bakhtin's concept of the carnivalesque (see Bakhtin 1984), I call the cabaretesque. In the theological temporality of the Holocaust, eschatology may mark the end of things—the end of life or humankind in apocalyptic thought, or simply "just one last time to see Vienna"—but it is also in a rerouting through the cabaretesque that emptiness and silence open as spaces toward new beginning. It is in the cabaretesque that the journey of intimacy is sounded anew. The traveler enters into sounded silence, seeking meaning beyond the end of things. The ability to sound silence in order to open its meanings is one of music's richest attributes. Sounded silence defies the assertion that there is no meaning beyond the end. Music transforms silence from emptiness to fullness. It becomes the command to listen and to hear: listening into silence affords action and agency; hearing the silence opens it toward the intimacy of the cabaretesque.

On the cabaret stage many whose voices might otherwise be silenced find them again. It was the possibility of reclaiming silence for the marginalized that led to the spread of cabaret in the Jewish communities of the modern era, above all as they were forced from rural to urban settlement. The cabarets of the twentieth century sounded the telos moving toward the end of history. There were new voices and new songs to take up the cause of denying finality. By the beginning of the twentieth century, Jewish cabaret had achieved a remarkable degree of urban density across Europe, but also in North and South America. The silence of modernity was sounded with a fullness that might seem to forestall the eschatological telos of the Holocaust.

That moment came, approaching with deafening silence. And yet, the cabaretesque did not fall silent. As the rise of fascism turned into political reality and then, beyond, unleashed genocide, the cabaretesque rose as well in resistance. Jewish political song increased, profoundly shaping the new recording and film technologies. The first sound films—*The Jazz Singer* (1927) and *Der blaue Engel* (The Blue Angel; 1930)—were even filmed largely in cabaretesque settings.

By the late 1930s, nonetheless, the setting for the cabaretesque in Jewish Central Europe had shifted to places that were for many unexpected, if not unimaginable: the concentration camps. Both the ghettos and the concentration camps had cabaret stages. In several notable cases, cabaret could be said to thrive, leaving documentation of the resistance against falling silent. This was the case in Terezín, which at various times could claim nine cabaret stages, seven with performances in German, two with performances in Czech (cf. Migdal 1986; Peschal 2008). Great cabaret performers appeared on the Terezín cabaret stages—Kurt Gerron (1897–1944), who had played the *conférencier* in *Der Blaue Engel*, and Coco Schumann (b. 1924), who would become one of the great jazz musicians in postwar Berlin (Schumann 1997). Cabaret lineages stretching from Budapest to Vienna to Berlin intersected in Terezín, making it possible to establish new troupes, such as the Strauß-Ensemble. Musicians found a new métier for composition and performance, a moment made intimate by a long history of the cabaretesque.

The cabaretesque is the art of the small stage, the *Kleinkunstbühne*, where the intimacy between performers and audiences is most intense. Accordingly, it shaped moments that many, indeed most, musical activities at Terezín shared. The orchestra for Viktor Ullmann's *Kaiser von Atlantis* (1943) combined the instrumental sound of a jazz ensemble—guitar, saxophone, banjo—with that of commedia dell'arte. The experience that would have been shared by those on and off the stage of Ullmann's *Cornet* combined the Czech tradition of the melodrama with the cabaretesque, allowing them to search, once again, for the intimate.

And from the ruins of time they blossom

Peacefully, peacefully rock your little green-braided cap.
My little white birch, which offers a song in prayer.
Each little leaf quietly makes a wish,
Dear little birch, be sweet and pray also for me.

"Berjoskele" (The Little Birch) is the first of three Yiddish songs (*Březulinka*, op. 53; Julia Bentley sings all three on New Budapest Orpheum Society 2009, tracks 18, 19, and 20) that Viktor Ullmann composed in 1944, also around the time of his work on *Cornet*. Again, we witness allegory; again Ullmann leads us on the musical journey from far away (*fun vayt'n*, in the Yiddish at the beginning of verse 2) to a moment of music's intimacy, the prayer of the birch tree, borne by lullaby. Unlike *Cornet*, the text to the little birch was not originally familiar to Ullmann. He did not know Yiddish, nor had he employed it when using material from other folk-music traditions for his compositions. Many things may have drawn him to a Yiddish lullaby, but it was surely the physical copy of Menakhem Kipnis's collection of Yiddish

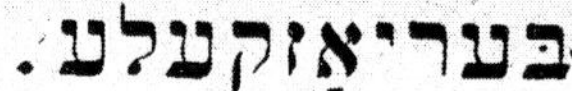

I.

רואיג, רואיג שאָקעלט איר געלאָקטעס גרינעס קעמעל
מיין ווייסינקע בעריאָזקעלע און דאַווענט אָן א שיעור;
יעדעס, יעדעס בלעטעלע איר'ס שעפּטשעט שטיל א תּפילה
זיי שוין, קליין בעריאָזקעלע, מתפלל אויף פאר מיר.

II.

איך בין דאָאַן עלענטער געקומען פון דער ווייטען,
פרעמד איז מיר דער גאָט פון דאַן' און פרעמד
איז מיר זיין שפּראַך;
נישט ער וועט מיין טרויער זען און נישט פאַרשטיין
מיין תּפילה,
כאָטש איך וועל מתפלל זיין, מתפלל זיין א סך.

63

Figure 18.2. "Berjoskele" (The Little Birch), Menakhem Kipnis, *Folkslieder Konzert-Repertoir*, Warsaw: Di Welt, n.d.

folk songs that he used when deciding not to alter the melody and to use the same key signature. The journey realized by the song—not just that of the unnamed narrator in the Yiddish text, but all those who had traveled to and through and beyond Terezín—was coming to its close. The song offered as prayer realizes a moment of intimacy, perhaps even as redemption.

Journey translated musically into song, however, reaches its end only by reckoning with the pain of living. Can that pain be fully reconciled through song? Such is the question that Viktor Ullmann, also as poet, puts to music. Is the fullness of stretto, of music and poetry intertwined in the common act of performing, ultimately a witness to the moment in which intimacy remains unfulfilled? From that question issues Ullmann's own voice as a poet, singing of the immortality that joins, tragically, only with mortality. Still in search of redemption, this chapter closes with Viktor Ullmann's own realization of the transcendence between mortality and immortality, his poem "The Deepest Pain Cannot Become Music," in which he sings of the frailty of music's intimate moment.

The deepest pain cannot become music,
no word alters that pain,
it does not assume its shape from the rock of the earth—
it remains in muffled silence.
Thus, I bear silent sadness about the saddening silence
that I missed,
and it is silent, that it only hums
what I dreamed.
The deepest pain cannot go back
into the farthest time,
it strikes the wounds, that now deadly burn:
It has passed!

—Viktor Ullmann, "Der tiefste Schmerz kann zu Musik nicht werden"

Note

1. All translations are those of the author.

References

Adler, H. G. 1980. *Stimme und Zuruf: Gedichte*. Hamburg: Knaus.

———. 2008[1962]. *The Journey: A Novel*. Translated by Peter Filkins. New York: Random House.

Bakhtin, Mikhail. 1984. *Rabelais and His World*. Translated by Hélène Iswolsky. Bloomington: Indiana University Press.

Bohlman, Philip V. 1991. "Of *Yekkes* and Chamber Music in Israel: Ethnomusicological Meaning in Western Art Music." In *Ethnomusicology and Modern Music History*, edited by Stephen Blum, Philip V. Bohlman, and Daniel M. Neuman, 254–67. Urbana: University of Illinois Press.

Dueck, Byron. 2007. "Public and Intimate Sociability in First Nations and Métis Fiddling." *Ethnomusicology* 51(2): 30–63.

Herder, Johann Gottfried. 1997. *Journal meiner Reise im Jahr 1769*. In *Johann Gottfried Herder Werke*, volume 9/2: *Journal meiner Reise iim Jahr 1769, Pädagogische Schriften*, edited by Rainer Wisbert and Klaus Pradel, 9–126. Frankfurt am Main: Deutscher Klassiker Verlag.

———. 1998 [1800]. *Kalligone*. In *Johann Gottfried Herder Werke*, volume 8: *Schriften zu Literatur und Philosophie 1792–1800*, edited by Hans Dietrich Irmscher, 641–964. Frankfurt am Main: Deutscher Klassiker Verlag.

Herz-Sommer, Alice. N.d. *Alice Herz-Sommer spielt Bach, Beethoven, Schubert, Chopin, Smetana, Debussy*. AHS Records.

Herzfeld, Michael. 1997. *Cultural Intimacy: Social Poetics in the Nation-State*. New York: Routledge.

Kipnis, Menakhem. N.d. *Folkslider: Konzert-Repertoire*. Warsaw: Di Welt.

Migdal, Ulrike, ed. 1986. *Und die Musik spielt dazu: Chansons und Satiren aus dem KZ Theresienstadt*. Munich: Piper.

Nettl, Bruno. 2013. *Becoming an Ethnomusicologist: A Miscellany of Influences*. Lanham, MD: Scarecrow Press.

New Budapest Orpheum Society. 2002. *Dancing on the Edge of a Volcano: Jewish Cabaret, Popular, and Political Songs, 1900–1945*. Cedille Records CDR 90000 065.

———. 2009. *Jewish Cabaret in Exile*. Cedille Records CDR 90000 110.

———. 2014. *As Dreams Fall Apart: The Golden Age of Jewish Stage and Film Music, 1925–1955*. Chicago: Cedille Records.

Peschal, Lisa, ed. 2008. *Divadelní texty z terezínského ghetta 1941–1945* [Theater Texts from the Theresienstadt Ghetto, 1941–1945]. Prague: Akropolis.

Rilke, Rainer Maria. 1912. *Die Weise von Liebe und Tod des Cornets Christoph Rilke*. Leipzig: Insel-Verlag. (Insel-Bücherei, 1).

Schiller, Friedrich. 2002. *Über naïve und sentimentalische Dichtung*. Stuttgart: Reclam.

Schumann, Coco. 1997. *Der Ghetto-Swinger: Eine Jazzlegende erzählt*. Munich: Deutscher Taschenbuch Verlag.

Sebald, W. G. 2001. *Austerlitz*. Translated by Anthea Bell. New York: Random House.

Stokes, Martin. 2010. *The Republic of Love: Cultural Intimacy in Turkish Popular Music*. Chicago: University of Chicago Press.

Stumpf, Carl. 2012[1911]. *The Origins of Music*. Translated and edited by David Trippett. Oxford: Oxford University Press.

Ullmann, Viktor. 1993. *Der Kaiser von Atlantis, oder die Tod-Verweigerung*, Op. 49. Libretto by Peter Kien. Mainz: Schott.

———. 1995. *Die Weise von Liebe und Tod des Cornets Christoph Rilke*. Mainz: Schott.

CHAPTER NINETEEN

~

Oral History, Musical Biography, and Historical Ethnomusicology

Martha Ellen Davis

Guido Adler's seminal publication of 1885 defined musicology as comprising systematic and historical dimensions (Nettl 1958:173; C. Seeger 1977:1–15). The historical dimension became the domain of musicology, whereas the systematic dimension, with its synchronic perspective, was subsumed by ethnomusicology. The lack of emphasis on history within ethnomusicology may be attributable to its division from historical musicology (Shelemay 1980:233), the influence of folklore's collection and anthropology's ethnography as their respective goals (Kirshenblatt-Gimblett 1989:128), and the static nature of British social anthropology's structural functionalism. The result is a notable "dearth of historical perspective in ethnomusicology from the 1950s to the late 1980s" (Stone 2008:181). Since the late 1970s, this has been changing (Ruskin and Rice 2012:301). For example, as Bruno Nettl's second doctoral student in anthropology, I particularly recall his presentation of Native American musical areas not as an ossified taxonomy, but as the result of dynamic historical processes. This chapter traces the intersections among oral history, musical biography, and historical ethnomusicology that have emerged since the 1970s. I echo Timothy Rice's call for a "remodeling" of ethnomusicology (1987) and argue for the reinstatement of the historical dimension in ethnomusicology, such that largely nonliterate musical traditions, creations, and practices are documented and examined in historical as well as social context.

Oral Tradition, Oral History, and Ethnomusicology

The relationship between historical perspectives and ethnomusicology entails *oral tradition* and *oral history* (cf. Vansina 1985; Ritchie 1995). Oral tradition is usually collective and inherited. The culture bearers of oral traditions remember and transmit the history or knowledge of their community, group, or family. In contrast, oral history generally refers to personally lived or eyewitness accounts of individuals. In ethnomusicology, for example, the praise song as funeral dirge (cf. Nketia 1955) can be seen as an oral tradition, as it is an interpretive biographical account of someone else, the deceased, which may be somewhat distorted in that person's favor. Ballads that narrate legends, such as the French "La Chanson de Roland," also represent oral traditions. However, other ballads describe current or historic events that the composer personally witnessed or experienced, such as many Mexican *corridos*, a modern version of the Spanish ballad. Corridos were an important means of describing and interpreting events of the Mexican Revolution of 1910 among the illiterate peasantry fighting for land and freedom, as evidenced, for example, in a documentary film with testimonies of centenarians who lived through the Mexican Revolution (cf. Taboada Tabone and Perrig 2001). The corrido, therefore, exemplifies oral history as performed in song.

Oral history is a growing subfield within the field of history on a worldwide basis. In the United States, the study of oral history in the university context was established as the Oral History Research Office at Columbia University in 1948 by Allan Nevins. It was followed in 1953 with the Oral History Archives at the University of California, Berkeley, and, in 1958, was introduced at the University of California, Los Angeles. In Europe during that period, oral history was less institutionalized, but was carried out by individual scholars. The Oral History Association of the United States was founded in 1966, and the International Oral History Association in 1987 in Oxford, England. The Oral History Association offers the following definition: "Oral history is a field of study and a method of gathering, preserving, and interpreting the voices and memories of people, communities, and participants in past events. Oral history is both the oldest type of historical inquiry, predating the written word, and one of the most modern, initiated with tape recorders in the 1940s and now using 21st-century digital technologies" (www.oralhistory.org/about/do-oral-history/, after Ritchie 2003 [1995]). As the oldest type of historical inquiry, early examples of oral history include the collection of sayings of the people by Chinese court historians during the Zhou dynasty (ca. 1046–256 BCE). Several centuries later, the Greek historian Thucydides (ca. 471–396 BCE) interviewed participants in the Peloponnesian War, using the method of multiple sources for corroboration (Ritchie 2003[1995]:19–20, citing Thucydides 1972; cited in Davis 2006:642).

Studies in oral history may be focused on a specific topic, in which the researcher elicits historical knowledge or lived experience from one or more people regarding a subject such as the Mexican Revolution. I myself conducted such a study in oral history on the Cuban and Dominican music and dance genre, the *son*, in the city of Santo Domingo (Davis 2007). Or an oral history may focus on an individual *life history*, in which consultants narrate their personal experiences to provide insight into their lives and times. Benjamin Botkin, the director of the United States Federal Writer's Project in the 1930s, explained that life history makes possible connections between the histories of individuals, groups, and communities (Botkin 1946). With regard to the use of oral history in music, Kirshenblatt-Gimblett states in reference to the study of the blues singer Lead Belly (Lomax and Lomax 1936) that life history offers "not only a way to structure ethnographic interviews, but also a heuristic device for integrating fragmentary material gathered in studies of 'culture at a distance' and a literary genre for capturing the vividness of the speaker" (1989:128).

Music Biography in Ethnomusicology

The focus on an individual composer or performer is the norm in historical musicology, jazz, or popular music studies, and "the biographies of composers lie like steppingstones across the ocean of European music history" (Wilcken 2013:2). But historically, biography has not been featured in ethnomusicology or folklore (Kirshenblatt-Gimblett 1989:136), though it has long been part of American cultural anthropology (cf. Langness 1965). Bruno Nettl observes that "the literature of ethnomusicology overstresses the homogeneity of the world's music" (1984:179), despite the fact that the researcher's conclusions are usually compiled from in-depth interaction with key informants in a collaborative approach based on shared knowledge (A. Seeger 1987:19–21; Vander 1988:xiii). Yet the documentation of a musician's life history has many applications in ethnomusicology. Nettl calls the collection of a musician's life history the study of a musical idiolect, that is, the study of an individual's complete repertory, musical life, and experience in relation to his or her society as a whole (2010a:67, 68). The study of the individual can be expanded to include a family. In turn these microcosmic, individual portrayals can be combined to construct a larger, community-based view.

Jesse Ruskin and Timothy Rice comment that "ethnomusicologists treat individuals more often as members of communities than as autonomous actors" (2012:303). However, individual musicians can be critical in the history of musical cultures and their social contexts. For example, the Cuban religious, cultural, and musical complex known as *santería* (more correctly and respectfully known as Regla de Ocha) developed in the way it did due to the specific African individuals transported to Cuba in the nineteenth century. Nettl states that "I got quite a different sense of the place of music in life from an autobiographical account than from conventional ethnography." He goes on to say about his Blackfeet consultant that "if Calvin was representative of the homogeneous side of Blackfeet culture, he also had a unique story to tell" (Nettl 1984:178; see also Nettl 1968). Thus, in any ethnomusicological study, the focus on an individual can provide insight.

Whether the musician studied should be a well-known performer and master teacher or an ordinary member of the community is a matter of debate. I think the particular musical culture, research design, and circumstances determine each case. For example, an advisee who was studying the musical culture of the Kumeyaay (formerly known as Diegueño), several related Native American peoples living in San Diego County and northern Baja California, asked whether he should try to gain access to a well-known culture bearer, who was hounded by researchers. I suggested that he focus on a less well-known singer instead; he found this person to be more accessible, and therefore his research was more fruitful.

Rice suggests that ethnomusicologists should fully acknowledge the work of individual culture bearers in our research and respect their knowledge as intellectual property. This, too, appears to be a current trend in ethnomusicology. Rice terms this approach "subject-centered ethnomusicology" (2003:156–58). The subject-centered approach focuses not on the "data" (meaning "that which is given"), the collective society, or extrapolated conclusions. Rather, subject-centered ethnomusicology focuses on the culture bearer. In this approach, one's informants transcend the formal role of subjects and become consultants, and ultimately teachers, because that is precisely what they are (Nettl 2005:144; 2010b:xix). This was the message of Nettl's Charles Seeger Lecture, "In Honor of Our Principal Teachers," delivered to the Society for Ethnomusicology in 1983 (Nettl 1984). It was an acknowledgment of his teachers' fundamental role in his effort to understand their musical cultures and in his professional development.

The focus on our teachers as research collaborators is a methodology that yields better data, which is the basis of good science. Studying the musical behavior of our own species requires behaving like our own species; that is, good social science requires good social relations. It depends on not just the analytical dimension of our minds, but what could be termed emotional intelligence (akin to subjective and intuitive intelligence). Otherwise, "that which is given"—our data—may be flawed or misunderstood. The most successful qualitative studies of human behavior often depend on establishing bonds of friendship, which are developed over years of residence or revisits; the scholarly product is the result of a relationship based on trust and affection, as well as the researcher's deep, intuitive knowledge of a musical culture and practices.

A pioneering biographical study in ethnomusicology was the autobiography of Frank Mitchell, a Navajo Blessingway Singer, edited by Charlotte J. Frisbie and David McAllester (1978); Ruskin and Rice called this an "assisted autobiography" (2012:313). Other longitudinal studies that combine oral history and music biography include Judith Vander's research on Shoshone women's music (1988) and Carol Babiracki's work with a *nacni* (female professional singer and dancer) in Jharkhand, India (2008). Interestingly, both studies involved woman-to-woman bonds of friendship developed over many years and revisits, enhanced by extensive musical and dance participation.

Vander's study of five Native American women resulted in five "songprints," or total repertories, including passive repertories, and musical experiences of individuals, each one unique, in the contexts of their lives and communities. When superimposed, they formed a "cumulative songprint," which Vander calls an "archaeological slice" of Shoshone music making in the twentieth century (1988:287). She thus developed a musical taxonomy of Shoshone genres and their historical trajectories in which some have become archaic, some have been added, some have substituted for others in specific social functions, and there have been changes with regard to gender in musical roles and performance practices in music and dance. Nettl remarks that it is surprising that this approach has not been used more frequently (2005:182).

Babiracki's work with a nacni, whom she has known since 1993, involved her active participation in music and dance performances. Her consultant's husband also collaborated with Babiracki in translating song texts from Nagpuri to Hindi. Her study is remarkably ambitious and successful in connecting life history, performance, and scholarship. She states, "We acknowledge that we arrive at our interpretations in the course of field research through complex, intersubjective and dialogic processes, but few of us manage to carry that insight through to our writing or our conclusions," with the exception of Hagedorn (2001) and Kisliuk (1998) (Babiracki 2008:26). When I complimented her on accomplishing this, Babiracki said that she must return yet again for there have been more changes in her consultant's life. Science is slow and social science yet slower, for the best understanding of human phenomena requires a long and deep engagement, exemplified by the work of Frisbie, McAllester, Babiracki, and Vander.

A focus on specific musicians contextualizes and adds a diachronic perspective to the ethnomusicological dimensions of concept, behavior, sound (Merriam 1964), and, today, commodification (added by Rice). The subject-centered approach contributes "narrative coherence to . . . [today's] . . . complex and seemingly fragmented world" (Rice 2003:157) of global versus local dialectics. Within the social sciences, it "reflects a broader shift . . . toward theories of agency, practice, power, and historical change" (Ruskin and Rice 2012:318). This methodology also allows the reader to comprehend social and musical theory and phenomena in the tangible, applied context of human lives.

People find stories of other people engaging; it appears to be human nature, as social animals, to be interested in others' stories, as well as to think narratively and anecdotally. Scholars, as people, are equally fascinated by human narrative and human artistic expression, which facilitate intellectual and emotional comprehension of concept and experience. For this reason, the narrative approach is successful in contemporary American journalism and seems to be increasingly attractive for academic writing in the humanities and social sciences, as well. Narrative journalism engages the reader with an anecdotal lead to personalize a problem or incident. Then, throughout the story, the case study is referenced or perhaps expanded through other cases. This approach succeeds because

> the subjects of research, the researchers themselves, and the readers are all human, meaning that they have feelings and are interested in other people and their stories. The somewhat arid forms of conventional journalistic or academic writing which have evolved in the last 100 or 200 years leave out human sources or they are described with nothing more than a name or impersonal label. Little or nothing about their lives, circumstances, histories, or unique personal characteristics is included. Any traces of storytelling or indications of emotion are rigorously suppressed. Non-fiction narrative writing is about putting some of these human qualities and sensibilities back, making academic writing more memorable, more informative, and more interesting. (Guy Baehr, personal communication, 2013)

Similarly, in writing about the arts, such as music, people want to engage in the experience of art (cf. Dewey 1934), for the arts are an "affecting presence" (cf. Armstrong 1971), and readers want to be affected.

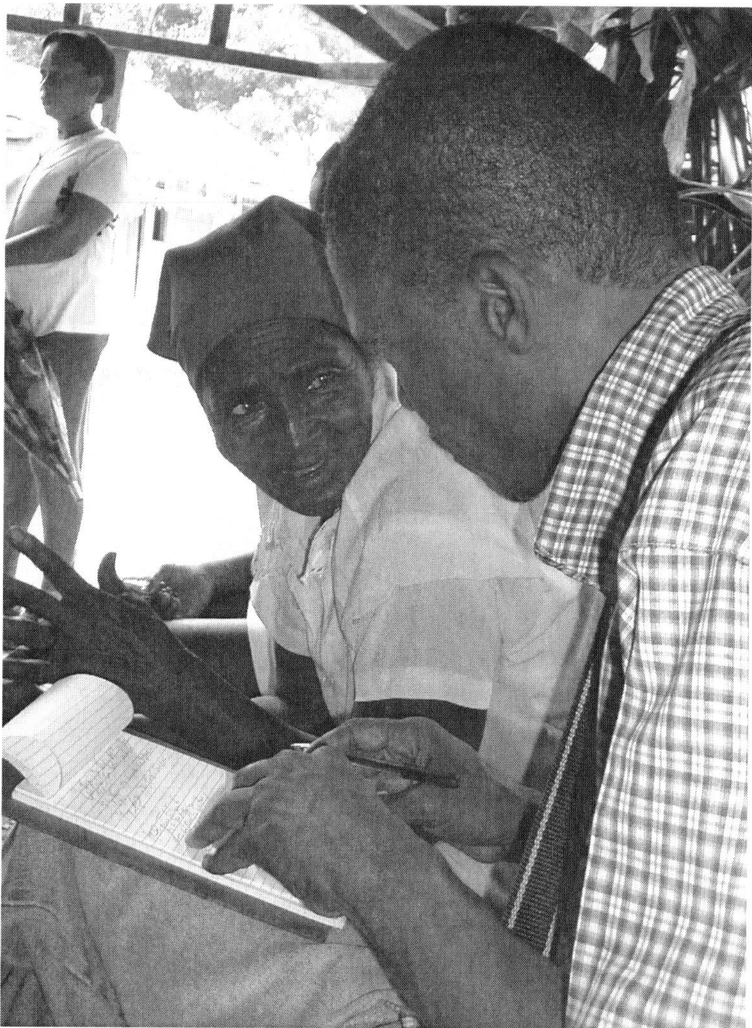

Figure 19.1. Aquiles Castro of the Oral History Program at the Dominican National Archive (Archivo General de la Nación) interviews the sister of the capitán (master musician) Sixto Miniel of the UNESCO-recognized Brotherhood of the Holy Spirit in Villa Mella, Dominican Republic, whose signature instruments, music, and dance are called the congos. He asks about the social organization during the annual vow-based family saint's festival in the rural area of Mata los Indios featuring congos and Salves at the family altar. *Photo by Martha Ellen Davis*

Historical Ethnomusicology

Ethnomusicologists are increasingly interested in a historical approach, including oral history and life history or biography. Edited collections focused on historical ethnomusicology began to appear in the 1990s (cf. Blum, Bohlman, and Neuman 1991). In addition, book-length biographical studies of individual performers, based on archival research and oral history, began to appear in the same decade. For example, Virginia Danielson published an outstanding study of Umm Kulthūm, the most popular Egyptian singer of the twentieth century (1997). Although Danielson never met Umm Kulthūm, she contextualized her life in music both socially and historically through documentary evidence and interviews with people who had been close to the singer. Another important biographical study from the 1990s focuses on the fiddler Émile Benoit of French Newfoundland, Canada (Quigley 1995).

At the book display during the annual meetings of the Society for Ethnomusicology in 2013, the proliferation of music biographies was clear. In addition to a second biography of Umm Kulthūm, there was the well-known work by María Teresa Vélez on the Afro-Cuban musician and folk-religious practitioner Felipe García Villamil (2000), Michael E. Veal's work on an African musician in the United States (2000), Sean Williams and Lillis Ó Laoire's biography of the Irish singer Joe Heaney (2011), and a work by David F. García on the commercially successful Latino musician Arsenio Rodríguez (2006). It was interesting to find two assisted autobiographies in which the consultant figures as the co-author: a work on the Cuban *batá* drummer Carlos Aldama, co-authored by Umi Vaughan and Aldama (2012), and, in the role of principal author, an autobiography of Frankie Manning, the "ambassador of Lindy Hop," co-authored with Cynthia R. Millman (2007). At the same conference, conversations with colleagues about their current research topics yielded a surprising number of ongoing studies on an oral history of single musicians of traditional and popular musics. These include Lois Wilcken's biographical study of the late Haitian master drummer Frisner Augustin (Wilcken 2013) and Jocelyne Guilbault's study of the Trinidadian saxophonist and band leader Roy Cate (Guilbault 2014). Two landmark collections on historical ethnomusicology appeared in 2014 (Bohlman 2014; McCollum, Hebert, and Howard 2014).

Musical biography also lends itself to film documentation. Three good examples portray musicians separated from their homelands, two due to warfare and insecurity and the other, economic opportunity abroad. The former include the film *Amir: An Afghan Refugee Musician's Life in Peshawar, Pakistan*, directed by John Baily (1985), and *The Key from Spain: The Songs and Stories of Flory Jagoda*, directed by Ankica Petrović, about the life and repertory of a Sephardic Jewish singer of Sarajevo, now in the United States (2000). The third film is *Journey of a Badiu: The Story of a Cape Verdean-American Musician, Norberto Tavares*, directed by Susan Hurley-Glowa (2010), which documents the musician's life in the Boston area and then follows him on a trip back to Cape Verde.

Much of the present interest in historical ethnomusicology has been stimulated, nurtured, and supported by the Society for Ethnomusicology's Historical Ethnomusicology Special Interest Group, established in 2005. In 2014, when the group had some eighty-eight members, it became a Section, which is an acknowledgment of its vitality and the consistent record of activities it sponsors.

Other dimensions of historical ethnomusicology, which fall outside the purview of this brief chapter, include the following:

- The impact of the research experience and of informants-as-teachers upon the researchers themselves and the collegial relationship between researcher and subject.
- Biographies and autobiographies of ethnomusicologists.
- The topic of oral history and identity, including the role of music for remembrance, significant for war-torn or dispersed communities (cf. Shelemay 1998; Olsen 2008).
- The role of ethnomusicologists in documenting recorded sound, and the role of archives in safeguarding it, thus protecting the oral history and intellectual property of musicians of endangered traditions (cf. Petrović and Levin 1993), and in reconstructing lost or fragmented traditions or a contested past.
- The empowerment of musicians through receiving a voice and a venue in print, recording, or film. In the 1930s, Benjamin Botkin considered oral history "a way to empower the marginalized, to give voice to the silent, and democratize the making of history" in reference to his compilation of slave narratives (Kirshenblatt-Gimblett 1989:137). In other words, as Daniel Sheehy, director of Smithsonian Folkways Recordings, stated at the 2013 annual meetings of the Society for Ethnomusicology, "Ethnomusicology has to do with social justice."

Conclusions

This chapter supports the current interest of many colleagues in incorporating a historical dimension in ethnomusicology, thus adding to the study of largely nonliterate musical cultures the diachronic perspective formerly the domain of historical musicology. I advocate for the inclusion in musical ethnography of a temporal component, which would imply that such depictions of a musical culture represent but a slice in time. Finally, I suggest that the goal of our studies should be not only summary views and extrapolations, often based on data from a few key informants; rather, those informants should be duly acknowledged as teachers and collaborators in our academic studies of their traditions. I propose that oral history, music biography, and historical ethnomusicology are integral to our work. This approach is not only ethically correct, but may yield greater scholarly accuracy, while changing the lives of researchers and musicians for the better.

References

Adler, Guido. 1885. "Umfang, Methode und Ziel der Musikwissenschaft." *Vierteljahresschrift für Musikwissenschaft* 1: 5–20.

Armstrong, Robert Plant. 1971. *The Affecting Presence: An Essay in Humanistic Anthropology*. Urbana: University of Illinois Press.

Babiracki, Carol M. 2008. "Between Life History and Performance: Sundari Devi and the Art of Allusion." *Ethnomusicology* 52(1): 1–30.

Baehr, Guy. 2013. E-mail communication (16 December).

Baily, John. 1985. *Amir: An Afghan Refugee Musician's Life in Peshawar, Pakistan.* Documentary film. Watertown, MA: Documentary Educational Resources.

Blum, Stephen, Philip V. Bohlman, and Daniel M. Neuman, eds. 1991. *Ethnomusicology and Modern Music History*. Urbana: University of Illinois Press.

Bohlman, Philip V., ed. 2014. *The Cambridge History of World Music*. Cambridge: Cambridge University Press.

Botkin, Benjamin A. 1946. "Living Lore on the New York City Writers' Project." *New York Folklore Quarterly* 2(4): 252–63.

Danielson, Virginia. 1997. *The Voice of Egypt: Umm Kulthūm, Arabic Song and Egyptian Society in the Twentieth Century*. Chicago: University of Chicago Press.

Davis, Martha Ellen. 2006. "Historia oral: Recurso histórico y base de la dominicanidad." *Boletín del Archivo General de la Nación* 31(116): 637–70.

———. 2007. "La historia oral del son vivo de la capital dominicana." *Boletín del Archivo General de la Nación* 32(117): 175–97.

Dewey, John. 1934. *Art as Experience*. New York: Minton, Balch and Company.

García, David F. 2006. *Arsenio Rodríguez and the Transnational Flows of Latin Popular Music*. Philadelphia: Temple University Press.

Guilbault, Jocelyne. 2014. *Roy Cape: A Life on the Calypso and Soca Bandstand*. Durham, NC: Duke University Press.

Hagedorn, Katherine. 2001. *Divine Utterances: The Performance of Afro-Cuban Santería*. Washington, DC: Smithsonian Institution Press.

Hurley-Glowa, Susan. 2010. *Journey of a Badiu: The Story of a Cape Verdean-American Musician, Norberto Tavares*. Documentary film. Vancouver, BC: Villon Films.

Kirshenblatt-Gimblett, Barbara. 1989. "Authoring Lives." *Journal of Folklore Research* 26(2): 123–49.

Kisliuk, Michelle. 1998. *Seize the Dance!: BaAka Musical Life and the Ethnography of Performance*. New York: Oxford University Press.

Langness, Lewis L. 1965. *The Life History in Anthropological Science*. New York: Holt, Rinehart and Winston.

Lomax, John A., and Alan Lomax. 1936. *Negro Folk Songs as Sung by Lead Belly*. New York: Macmillan.

Manning, Frankie, and Cynthia R. Millman. 2007. *Frankie Manning: Ambassador of Lindy Hop*. Philadelphia: Temple University Press.

McCollum, Jonathan, David Hebert, and Keith Howard. 2014. *Theory and Method in Historical Ethnomusicology*. Lanham, MD: Rowman and Littlefield/Lexington Books.

Merriam, Alan. 1964. *The Anthropology of Music*. Evanston, IL: Northwestern University Press.

Mitchell, Frank. 1978. *Blessingway Singer: The Autobiography of Frank Mitchell, 1881–1967*. Edited by Charlotte J. Frisbie and David P. McAllester. Tucson: University of Arizona Press.

Nettl, Bruno. 1958. "Historical Aspects of Ethnomusicology." *American Anthropologist*, New Series 60(3): 518–32.

———. 1968. "Biography of a Blackfoot Indian Singer." *Musical Quarterly* 54(2): 199–207.

———. 1984. "In Honor of Our Principal Teachers." *Ethnomusicology* 28(2): 173–85.

———. 2005. *The Study of Ethnomusicology: Thirty-One Issues and Concepts*, second edition. Urbana: University of Illinois Press.

———. 2010a. "Contemplating Ethnomusicology Past and Present: Ten Abiding Questions." In *Concepts, Experiments, and Fieldwork: Studies in Systematic Musicology and Ethnomusicology*, edited by Rolf Bader, Christiane Neuhaus, and Ulrich Morgenstern, 64–76. Frankfurt am Main: Peter Lang.

———. 2010b. *Nettl's Elephant: On the History of Ethnomusicology*. Urbana: University of Illinois Press.

Nketia, J. H. Kwabena. 1955. *Funeral Dirges of the Akan People*. Exeter: Achimota.

Olsen, Dale A. 2008. *Popular Music of Vietnam: The Politics of Remembering, the Economics of Forgetting*. New York: Routledge.

Petrović, Ankica. 2000. *The Key from Spain: The Songs and Stories of Flory Jagoda*. Watertown, MA: DER.

Petrović, Ankica, and Theodore Levin. 1993. *Bosnia: Echoes from an Endangered World*. Documentary film. Washington, DC: Smithsonian Folkways Recordings.

Quigley, Colin. 1995. *Music from the Heart: Compositions of a Folk Fiddler*. Athens: University of Georgia Press.

Rice, Timothy. 1987. "Toward the Remodeling of Ethnomusicology." *Ethnomusicology* 31(3): 469–88.

———. 2003. "Time, Place, and Metaphor in Musical Experience and Ethnography." *Ethnomusicology* 47(2): 151–79.
Ritchie, Donald. 1995. *Doing Oral History*. New York: Twayne Publishers.
Ruskin, Jesse D., and Timothy Rice. 2012. "The Individual in Musical Ethnography." *Ethnomusicology* 56(2): 299–327.
Seeger, Anthony. 1987. *Why Suyá Sing: A Musical Anthropology of an Amazonian People*. Cambridge: Cambridge University Press.
Seeger, Charles. 1977. *Studies in Musicology, 1935–1975*. Berkeley: University of California Press.
Shelemay, Kay Kaufman. 1980. "'Historical Ethnomusicology': Reconstructing Falasha Liturgical History." *Ethnomusicology* 24(2): 233–58.
———. 1998. *Let Jasmine Rain Down: Song and Remembrance among Syrian Jews*. Chicago: University of Chicago Press.
Stone, Ruth M. 2008. *Theory for Ethnomusicology*. Upper Saddle River, NJ: Pearson/Prentice Hall.
Taboada Tabone, Francesco, and Sarah Perrig. 2001. *Los últimos zapatistas: Héroes olvidados*. Documentary film. México: Universidad de Morelos.
Vander, Judith. 1988. *Songprints: The Musical Experience of Five Shoshone Women*. Urbana: University of Illinois Press.
Vansina, Jan. 1985. *Oral Tradition as History*. Madison: University of Wisconsin Press.
Vaughan, Umi, and Carlos Aldama. 2012. *Carlos Aldama's Life in Batá: Cuba, Diaspora, and the Drum*. Bloomington: Indiana University Press.
Veal, Michael E. 2000. *Fela: The Life and Times of an African Musical Icon*. Philadelphia: Temple University Press.
Vélez, María Teresa. 2000. *Drumming for the Gods: The Life and Times of Felipe García Villamil, Santero, Palero, and Abakuá*. Philadelphia: Temple University Press.
Wilcken, Lois. 2013. "Biography, an Emergent Genre in Ethnomusicology." Paper read at the 58th Annual Meetings of the Society for Ethnomusicology.
Williams, Sean, and Lillis Ó Laoire. 2011. *Bright Star of the West: Joe Heaney, Irish Songman*. New York: Oxford University Press.

CHAPTER TWENTY

The Doubleness of Sound in Canada's Indian Residential Schools

Beverley Diamond

Bruno Nettl is one of the pioneers in the study of Native American music and encouraged many, including me, to further that study. His work has borne enormous fruit, not only through his own scholarship and that of his students, but through the unprecedented number of young scholars—many of them of First Nations, Inuit, or Métis descent—now engaged in the ethnomusicology of Native America. When Nettl began his research in the 1950s, many Native Americans chose to be silent about the traumatic experiences they had and were having in government boarding schools throughout North America. This chapter, then, also honors the courage of the many survivors who have broken that silence. It emerged from an interdisciplinary project on the uses of expressive culture in the work of the Truth and Reconciliation Commission (TRC) on Indian Residential Schools in Canada (Robinson and Martin forthcoming). Sound was a double-edged sword in the Indian Residential Schools (IRS) that operated in Canada from the late nineteenth century until the 1990s. It functioned as a mechanism of assimilation and control, but also as a form of student resistance and resilience. Yet sonic culture within the Canadian-based schools has rarely been studied, although passing references abound in residential school histories. By assembling shards of evidence about music and other sonic expression in the schools, I reflect on the expediency[1] of sonic expression in the schools and describe some recent responses by contemporary musicians to the residential school tragedy.

Indian Residential Schools in Canada

Like the boarding schools to which Indian children were sent in the United States, the residential school system in Canada was designed to assimilate First Nations, Inuit, and Métis children by removing them from their families, denying traditional lifeways, and forbidding the use of their own languages. Whereas missionary-run schools were established as early as the seventeenth century, an official policy of religious-based, government-funded industrial and residential schools was adopted in 1847 and the government played an active role beginning in the 1870s. The last government-run school closed in 1996. Couched in euphemistic metaphors of "civilizing" and "Christianizing" Indian children, the system was bent on destroying First Nations, Inuit, and Métis cultures, which constitutes genocide by the terms of the UN Convention on the Prevention and Punishment of the Crime of Genocide (1948). It was a form of "slow violence" (Nixon 2011), or destructive actions that occur over a long period with devastating social and environmental effects that only become evident generations later.

The histories of former IRS students constitute a "counter-narrative to those of Canada's celebratory past," one that contests the nation's repeated image as a "peacemaker" (Regan 2010). Such stories "call upon us to rethink our ideas about what constitutes violence and to recognize the more subtle forms of violence embedded in Indigenous-settler relations" (2010:37).

A potential turning point was the 2008 apology for the residential school system offered by Prime Minister Stephen Harper, the implementation of a settlement agreement[2] for survivors, and the establishment of the TRC. As many have observed,[3] however, the Harper government described the abuses as a "sad chapter" implying closure, ignoring continued inequities in the provision of housing, education, and health services. Signs of government insincerity include subsequent decisions such as the termination of the Aboriginal Healing Foundation, which provided assistance to survivors; funding cuts to other Aboriginal organizations; failure to meet with Aboriginal leaders such as Chief Theresa Spence (of Attiwapiskat, Ontario), who undertook a hunger strike on behalf of her people; or the lack of response to the demands of the Idle No More movement that began in the winter of 2012.

Problematizing Narratives of Victimization and Agency

Assumptions underpinning responses to narratives of trauma are often problematic. If settlers read victimization and respond with pity to the testimony of survivors, they reify settler privilege rather than unsettle it.[4] Even the hopefulness of the concept of reconciliation may obscure assumptions of social hierarchies, ignoring the fundamental need to respect incomprehensibility and difference—to recognize the independent co-existence of indigenous and settler sovereignty—rather than seek some sort of cultural merger.

Aboriginal scholars and elders recognize these problems. An Anishnabe survivor identified as Henri (Pikogan, Quebec) asserted that "the version that everyone knows makes us out to be victims. This is dangerous. I don't want to be a victim. I can be someone who went through a terrible experience but I refuse to be a victim" (First Nations of Quebec and Labrador 2010:39). A Mi'kmaw survivor, Isabelle Knockwood, similarly refused a victim position when she ended her testimony before the TRC by saying, "My happiness is my revenge."[5] Stereotypes of Aboriginal people as "passive victims in the era of settlement" (Brownlie and Kelm 1994:544) are antiquated in academia, but the role of witnessing at the TRC may reanimate traces of this stereotype, as one hears hundreds of hours of stories of physical, psychological, and sexual abuse. Listening *for* victimhood, however, may be a form of settler condescension that obscures clear thinking about collaborative action for social change.

Rather, like Aboriginal writers who emphasize resistance in both historical and contemporary work,[6] I am drawn to small expressive acts of agency and resistance by children in the schools, acts that sometimes provided personal solace or reconnected to pleasant memories, sometimes parodied what they were taught, or subverted the schools' restrictions, particularly bans on their own languages. But this position, too, may have unhelpful implications. A debate among Canadian historians in the 1990s problematized an emphasis on Native agency as "colonialist alibi." With reference to studies that emphasized agency, Brownlie and Kelm observe that some "uses of Native resilience and strength may soften, and at times deny, the impact of colonialism, and thus, implicitly . . . absolve its perpetrators" (1994:545). They suggest that scholars who "minimize the extent of the very real and observable damage inflicted on Aboriginal societies" can assert the right of settler governments and religious institutions to intervene and may overdraw the "altruistic intent of the colonizers" (1994:545). Some scholars whose work was criticized defended their evidence and raised the very tension between narratives of victimization and agency addressed here. Kelm responded with a personal narrative about the "sigh of relief" she sensed among fellow graduate students when they read historical accounts of agency in the wake of the Oka stand-off in 1990. She asks, "How were we, in our own writing, to examine power relations under colonialism in a way that did not underestimate Aboriginal agency, yet would not produce that 'sigh of relief' which said that maybe colonialism never happened at all?" (1994:640).

As a settler, I find it hard to write about the testimony I have had the difficult privilege of hearing. How can I acknowledge the suffering without implying victimhood, without trading on the pain of others and subsuming their autonomous voices? I've chosen to search the historical record for the multiple functions—oppressive, assimilative, or resistant—that music served within the schools themselves. Agency is prominent here, but includes the agency of several different players: the Canadian government, church authorities, teachers and IRS administrators, and the children themselves. My hope is that a more balanced picture emerges, one that struggles toward the rejection of alibis of any sort.

The individual experiences of survivors appear in a large number of print and video sources,[7] and are theirs to tell. However, having attended four of the seven national events of the TRC, I play a role as a witness. I am outraged by the stories of sexual abuse, but also cognizant of the fact that other types of abuse have been dismissed at times in the courts as less serious and less provable. The lasting physical effects of concussions from being struck repeatedly on the head, broken ear drums from cuffs on the ears, scars from burns, injuries from hard physical labor or corporal punishments, injuries from heavy equipment that did not function properly, jaw dislocation from wedges placed in the mouth for speaking one's language, and many others are unthinkable but true. Equally traumatic are the psychological effects of repeated attempted drowning, head shearing, removal of clothes or toys, isolation in dark cells, separation from one's brothers and sisters, shaming for bed-wetting or vomiting, and very few expressions of love or affection. I acknowledge that there were devoted and caring teachers as well as abusive ones, but the system tolerated and even encouraged abuse.

Children were forcibly taken from their homes at as young as four years of age. They often remained in the school until they were about sixteen. Statistics show that in some schools, fewer than half of the children survived. Inadequate health care, particularly intentional neglect of tuberculosis,[8] was partially responsible for the high death rates. Government officials selected certain schools as part of an experiment on the health impact of malnutrition.[9] At the best of times, the food given to the children was meager, but undernourishment was part of a scientific agenda in some places.

Music in the Schools

The violence at the heart of the Canadian IRS is clear, but the uses of sound and music in the schools complicate the human encounter, both reinforcing the slow violence but also, in some instances, ameliorating the students' negative experiences. The children's sonic experiences at school differed dramatically from those at home. Survivors describe the oppressive bells that regulated their lives from the moment they awakened until the moment they slept. This regimentation that distressed the children was a source of pride for school officials (cf. Shingwauk Archives, Dora Cliff fonds, 2010-024-001-004-010). Individual stories itemize as many as eighteen bells or buzzers daily, signaling scheduled activities but symbolizing "obedience, conformity, dependence, subservience, uniformity, docility, surrender" (Johnston 1988:43). Survivors also describe the silence and silencing that brought terror to their hearts: teachers and clergy who silently walked the aisles of the school with a sharp stick that might be used at any moment. The prohibition on speaking their Aboriginal languages drove some to be silent for several years, since they knew no other language. Knockwood explained, "For a long while, about three years, I kept so quiet I wouldn't be noticed" (2001[1992]:56).

Music was a tool of control and assimilation. Although policy concerning what music should be taught was rarely articulated in government or church documents, Knockwood located a set of "Instructions to teachers printed on Residential School Registers," which directs teachers to "insist on English during even the supervised play," to teach calisthenics "frequently accompanied by singing," and to teach "simple songs and hymns. The themes of the former to be interesting and patriotic. The tunes bright and cheerful." These instructions reflect the low opinion of the children's potential that pervaded the racist system: "Instruction is to be direct, the voice and blackboard the principal agents. The unnecessary use of textbooks is to be avoided. Do not classify students in advance of their ability" (2001:49–50).

Most schools used songbooks, generally with nursery rhymes or Christmas carols. Some teachers wrote out songs and may have composed teaching material themselves. Hymnbooks and liturgical music prevailed. A Cree student at the Shingwauk IRS in the late 1950s explained, "The only time I felt peace was in the church, sitting there listening to the hymns especially. . . . I heard the choir singing and somehow my soul got lifted."[10] Students with good singing voices were sometimes selected for participation in the choir, and this was regarded by many as a positive experience.[11] The Sto:lo elder Flora Wallace enjoyed learning harmony for hymns, although she maintained traditional repertories during and after her school days. When her family formed the musical ensemble Tzo'kam in the 1990s, they used harmony because it gave her pleasure (interview, Russell Wallace, 8 September 2004). The singer-songwriter Florent Vollant (Innu) explained, "At residential school I learned and I heard religious chants. . . . I found

Gregorian chants were fascinating—I really liked them" (Audet 2012:410). These individuals enjoyed diverse repertories and had an appetite for learning any kind of music they encountered. By contrast, some children who sang at home were not given the chance to participate in ensembles. Some individuals were taken under the wing of teachers who knew how to play the piano or violin. These special arrangements were important for skill acquisition, but even more because they were rare instances of being recognized as individuals. One girl who received piano lessons from a teacher at the Shingwauk school in Sault Ste. Marie, Ontario, explained the lessons were important because "you felt validated, in a way, that you were a person."[12]

Most information available about music in the schools was written for school newsletters, often by students under the close supervision of teachers and administrators. These articles presented the schools in a positive light, as if they were the equivalent of other schools across the country.[13] The newsletters describe formal and informal music making, pageants and theatrical productions, play, and handicrafts. Most often, the performances described were church-related special events, however, and not part of the curriculum. By the late 1960s, some schools had richer and more diverse music programs. The Muscowequan school had both a band instructor and a "music and upgrading" teacher by 1969. The girls' programs included concerts and dances: "Friday or Saturday nights we have concerts or dances in the playroom. Our program consists of songs, dances—modern, square, jigs, Scottish [*sic*] and pow-wow; baton twirling, guitar playing and imitations such as our hippies. These are enjoyable ways to spend evenings and everyone does something. When a concert isn't planned we have a dance—old time or modern. . . . When there is no organized activity the girls bead, read books . . . listen to records or provide their own entertainment with a make-up band—spoons, guitars, tin cans and our own western singers" (Muscowequan School newsletter, Easter 1969; Grey Nuns fonds; accessed at Shingwauk Archives). There is less information about music for the boys, whose recreation seemed more committed to sports or band practice.

Mr. P. Koett, the Shingwauk music teacher in the late 1960s, reported that twelve students were learning the guitar, they had learned to recognize instruments by listening to records, they could read music, and they were making progress on "the Bell recorders" (newsletter for the Catholic Indian Missionary Record, 1969, Grey Nuns fonds, Shingwauk Archives 2012-21-001). Somewhat rarer were popular music ensembles. When they existed, there was often a teacher who wanted to play a particular style and may have formed a student band to facilitate his own musical ambitions. One example was The Eagles of the Muscowequan IRS, a group of five students under the direction of Father Plamondon (newsletter for the Catholic Indian Missionary Record, 1969, Grey Nuns fonds, Shingwauk Archives 2012-21-001).

Documents offer some indications about musical instruments in the school, but survivors rarely mention them, except for band instruments in certain regions. In British Columbia, a tradition of brass band music flourished in Aboriginal communities independently of the schools; both English-style brass bands and American-style marching bands had taken root there in settler and Aboriginal communities at least as early as the 1870s (Stride 2012). Non-Indigenous scholars and civic leaders point to these institutions as evidence of high achievement within the residential schools, usually failing to note the irony of their establishment around the time when traditional ceremonial practices were being criminalized. Survivors, including the TRC commissioner Chief Wilton Littlechild, mention the bands as a source of pleasure, in contrast to the oppression of the schools in other respects.

In both Canadian and U.S. Indian boarding schools, bands were public symbols that marked the schools as successful (cf. Troutman 2009:123). There were, however, marked differences between, for example, the British Columbian bands and their U.S. counterparts. In British Columbia, prior to the IRS period, instruments and repertory often came from the British brass band tradition and its French relative, the fanfare band, rather than the military-style concert or marching bands of the United States. Furthermore, the functions of British Columbian bands included imperial events (e.g., Dominion Day and visits by royalty or civic authorities) and community functions such as weddings, fishery worker strikes, and welcome home celebrations for seasonal cannery workers. Community bands mirrored those in the schools and indigenized the practices of band performance. The structures of band leadership replicated the traditional hierarchies relating to clan roles and functions (Neylan and Meyer 2006). One First Nations band leader, Job Nelson, conducted bands in New Metlakatla (Alaska), Port Simpson, and Aiyansh and was also a composer. His march, "Aiyansh," was performed at one of the most famous band competitions of the early twentieth century, the Dominion Exhibition in New Westminster in 1905, and was later published (and ironically renamed) as the "Imperial Native March."

Expressive Culture as Resistance

Control of the children was paramount for the school authorities, but there were rare opportunities for challenging the system. A common form of sonic resistance was language. Larger schools had extensive grounds with places out of earshot of the school staff. A student at the Shingwauk school in the

1950s explained, "We couldn't speak our language in front of a staff member. But again, because of the expanse of Shingwauk and the bush and everything else, it was pretty hard for them to enforce it."[14] There was a downside to the inability to enforce regulations, however, in that many children were accused unfairly of speaking their language and punished accordingly. A Mi'kmaq student who attended Shubenacadie IRS in Nova Scotia wrote that, whereas speaking one's language was forbidden, "that didn't keep me from thinking in my language" (First Nations of Quebec 2010:23).

Some children used traditional sonic means to connect with their families and ancestors in the spirit world. They listened for birds, which in some traditions are the voices of ancestors. One Mi'kmaq survivor commented that she had not heard an eagle during her time at the Shubenacadie RI (Nova Scotia), but after the school burned down, seventeen eagle feathers were found near the ruins, the exact number of children who died in the school (tribute to Sarah Barnard, Halifax national event, 26–29 October 2011). The Rev. Henry Morrow, a teacher at Shingwauk (Sault Ste. Marie, Ontario) from 1947 to 1952, related that a Cree student from Saskatchewan broke a window to whistle down the Northern Lights, where the ancestors reside in many First Nations traditions, attempting, according to Morrow, to test whether traditional medicine was stronger than that of the clergy.[15]

Both listening and performance were vehicles for personalizing the meaning of song. Children developed keen capacities for double meanings, some of which were only thought since they dared not express them. A young woman at Shingwauk in the late 1930s and early 1940s relates a story about a Cole Porter hit of the 1930s: "I remember when that song first came out. I think it was Roy Rogers made that song 'Don't Fence Me In.' I never forgot that song. We used to go around and around in circles, singing that song. We made sure the matrons heard us, eh? We used to reach a certain spot and just shout it, 'Don't fence me in!' I never forgot that song. None of us have. We thought it was a very good song" (Shingwuak Archive, Wilshire 2010-047-001-010).

Opportunities for parody were limited, but there are traces of creative revisions of music taught in the schools. Elizabeth Graham printed a hymn parody on the cover of her book at the residential school in Brantford, Ontario, with reference to the food served there, sung to the tune of the hymn "There Is a Green Hill Far Away" composed by William Horsely in the mid-nineteenth century. Graham's words became "There is a boarding school far far away/ Where we get mush 'n' milk three times a day" (Graham 1997:back cover). Littlechild performed what he described as a "residential school song" at the talent show[16] of the Inuvik national event. "I'm going to teach you a residential school song but it only works between 2:15 and 2:30," he quipped referencing the regimentation of activities at the schools. He carefully taught the Cree words the children adapted to a simple tune. He then translated the playful text: "Tomorrow I'm going home [repeated]. If you love me, kiss me right away." Knockwood describes how "children would use their knowledge of language to undermine the nun's authority." She illustrates this with a story about a classmate, Clara Julian, who "could reduce us all to helpless laughter in church when she would take a line from the Latin hymn for Benediction, '*Resurrecsit sicut dixit*' [He said he would rise again]. But Clara would sing at the top of her voice, '*Resurrecsit kisiku piktit*,' which in Mi'kmaq means, 'When the old man got up, he farted.' The whole choir would start laughing and poor Sister Eleanor Marie thought we were laughing at Clara for mispronouncing Latin and she'd stop and patiently teach Clara the proper pronunciation. Clara would just stand there and grin" (2001:126). Residential school students also created songs or wrote poetry in private contexts to express loneliness, sadness, and fear, such as "I Want to Go Home to Nain" by Beatrice Hope and Joan Dicker (n.d.). Such counter-narratives—"hidden transcripts" to use Scott's terminology (1990)—were probably used more widely as forms of resistance than these few examples suggest.

Music as Reflection and Critique

In the post-IRS era, music has served several purposes for individual survivors; only a few examples are referenced here. Singers have created songs to honor parents or grandparents who suffered in the schools. Russell Wallace and his sisters effected their own healing and paid tribute to their mother's courage and resilience in the first album they produced as Tzo'kam, on which they sang the "Gathering Song" she learned from her schoolmates. The Métis songwriter Fara Palmer traces an emotional journey in "Bring Back Yesterday" from the album *Pretty Brown* (1999). It begins with an explicit narrative about her mother's abuse in the schools, intensifies as it sonically depicts a storm, and ends with a calm choral response interlaced with an archival recording that brings the voices of the past into the present. Jani Lauzon's instrumental trio, "Stolen," honors her father and other survivors. It begins with somber minor chords and sustained notes played on a traditional block flute, but the feeling shifts when jazz inflections in the keyboard and plucked cello are introduced. The final section of the composition is dominated by the flute, the sound of which now has more traditional elements and eventually transforms into an eagle call.

Some musicians created songs as part of personal healing. Mike MacInnes, a Mohawk social worker in the Mi'kmaq community of Eskasoni, Nova

Scotia, worked with men in his "Tunes and Talk" healing circle to make *Journey of Healing* (2013), recording their songs professionally to build pride. Mishi Donovan (Métis) regards much of her music as part of personal healing. Some of her songs about residential school abuse, particularly "Almost Broken," address the perpetrators: "We've done nothing to your children/ We've not locked away the sun/ We've not given you food to eat that is strange upon your tongue./ We've not shaved your heads, or took away your spoken words./ We've not taken your dances and blamed you of devil's work" (2000). Many other examples exist.

Songs also address the fears that elders had about speaking publicly of their traumatic experiences. Susan Aglukark (Inuit) explained that she wrote "Circle of the Old" because of the "particularly heart-breaking realization of the deep, deep fear entrenched in our elders to speak out, just simply to speak out" (e-mail, 17 January 2013). The song switches to Inuktitut for one phrase, when she addresses the elders directly: "*Kappiasungilanga, Ilirasungilanga, Ilirasungilanga, Kappiasungilanga*" (May I not be afraid. May I not feel fear of disapproval) (2006). The language shift, break from stanzaic form, and change to chromatic harmony mark this line as different, arguably outside the pop genre world (Negus 1999) and its mainstream expectations.

Many contemporary singers refuse to see the residential school issue in isolation as they describe the inter-related social challenges that emerged from colonialism and the continuation of social inequities, among them youth suicide, missing and murdered Aboriginal women, racism, second-tier health and education, and poor housing. Their music articulates the slow violence of settler colonialism. Wabkinew's "Last Word" has a YouTube video in which participants, some wearing T-shirts with "Survivor" written boldly across their chest, carry R.I.P signs for those named in his rap, victims of many sorts of social violence. Cheryl Bear has written a residential school song but also addresses other tragic social issues such as the murdered and missing Aboriginal women. In varied genres and styles, many songs use Indigenous languages as well as English and incorporate traditional elements, insisting on a modernity that reflects the wholeness of Indigenous experience and asserts expressive sovereignty by playing on the varied sonic memories that bring the past into the present with a view to the future.

Notes

1. I use George Yúdice's concept (2003) while also suggesting that expediency is applicable much earlier than the late twentieth century, when we saw the emergence of the neoliberal regard for culture as a manageable resource.

2. See the website of the Truth and Reconciliation Commission of Canada (www.trc.ca) for the text of the Harper apology and explanation of the Settlement Agreement, which offers modest financial compensation to survivors but places the onus on them to apply with the appropriate documents verifying their attendance at one of the schools.

3. Cf. Martin 2009.

4. See Simon 2013:131–35.

5. TRC testimony, Halifax, 26 October 2011, livestream.com/trc_cvr (accessed 24 June 2014).

6. Cf. LaRocque 2010:164–65.

7. In addition to documents in print (2012) and on the website of the Truth and Reconciliation Commission (www.trc.ca), there are numerous publications, among them Knockwood (2013); Haig-Brown (1993); Archibald (2008); Rogers, DeGagné, and Dewar (2012); and several volumes published online by the Aboriginal Healing Foundation (www.ahf.ca).

8. See www.cbc.ca, 18 February 2013 and 19 August 2013.

9. The *Globe and Mail* newspaper, for example, reported evidence of "a post-Second World War experiment in which food was deliberately withheld from some aboriginal students at six schools in four communities across the country" (www.globeandmail.ca, 13 December 2013). See also www.cbc.ca, 16 July 2013.

10. Interview in Shingwauk Archives 2010-047-001-016.

11. One narrative stated that enforced participation in the chapel choir was used as punishment for talking during a service, but this is the only negative comment uncovered thus far (Shingwauk Archives Collection 2010-047-001-008).

12. Shingwauk Archives, 2010-047-001-038.

13. Cf. YouTube, *Canadian Residential School Propaganda Video 1955* (video.search.yahoo.com/video/play;_yit+A2KLqlVLC7BTBmgAnGT7w8QF;_ylu=X3oDMTByZWc0dGJtBHNIYwNzcgRzbGsDdmlkBHZOaWQDBGdwb3MCMQ-?p=Indian=residential=propoganda=video&vid=323423d60b137dcc01e33498462a543b&l=2%3A38&turl=http%3A%2F%2Fwww.youtube.com%2Fc%3Ds_V4d7sXoqU&tit=Canadian=Residential+School+Propaganda+Video+1955&c=0&sigr=11afo4gb0&sigt=11hnesa1a&age=0&fr=chr-greentree_ff&tt=b).

14. Shingwauk Archives collection 2010-047-001-008.

15. Harry Morrow fonds, Shingwauk Archives 2010-047-001-027. Undated interview.

16. National TRC events have social gatherings for survivors, many of whom are seeing their fellow students for the first time since they left school. Talent shows are held on one evening.

References

Archibald, Jo-ann. 2008. *Indigenous Storywork: Educating the Heart, Mind, Body and Spirit.* Vancouver: University of British Columbia Press.

Audet, Veronique, with Florent Vollant. 2012. "Aboriginal Popular Music in Quebec: Influences, Issues, and Rewards." In *Aboriginal Music in Contemporary Canada: Echoes and Exchanges*, edited by Anna Hoefnagels and Beverley Diamond, 408–18. Montreal: McGill-Queen's University Press.

Brownlie, Robert, and Mary-Ellen Kelm. 1994. "Desperately Seeking Absolution: Native Agency as Colonialist Alibi." *Canadian Historical Review* 75(4): 543–56.

Cole, Douglas, J. R. Miller, and Mary-Ellen Kelm. 1994. "Responses and a Reply." *Canadian Historical Review* 75(4): 628–40.

First Nations of Quebec and Labrador Health and Social Services Commission. 2010. *Collection of Life Stories of the Survivors of the Quebec Indian Residential Schools*. Wendake: Les Copies de la Capitale Inc.

Graham, Elizabeth. 1997. *The Mush Hole: Life at Two Indian Residential Schools*. Waterloo: Heffle Publishing.

Haig-Brown, Celia. 1993. *Resistance and Renewal*, sixth edition. Vancouver: Arsenal Pulp Press.

Johnston, Basil. 1988. *Indian School Days*. Norman, OK: University of Oklahoma Press.

Knockwood, Isabelle, with Gillian Thomas. 2013[1992]. *Out of the Depths*, new extended edition. Black Point, NS: Fernwood Publishing.

La Roque, Emma. 2010. *When the Other Is Me: Native Resistance Discourse 1850–1990*. Winnipeg: University of Manitoba Press.

Martin, Keavy. 2009. "Truth, Reconciliation, and Amnesia: Porcupines and China Dolls and the Canadian Conscience." *English Studies in Canada* 35(1): 47–65.

Negus, Keith. 1999. *Music Genres and Corporate Cultures*. London: Routledge.

Neylan, Susan, with Melissa Meyer. 2006. "'Here Comes the Band!' Cultural Collaboration, Connective Traditions, and Aboriginal Brass Bands on British Columbia's North Coast, 1875–1964." *BC Studies* 152 (Winter 2006–2007): 35–66.

Nixon, Rob. 2011. *Slow Violence and the Environmentalism of the Poor*. Cambridge, MA: Harvard University Press.

Regan, Paulette. 2010. *Unsettling the Settler Within: Indian Residential Schools, Truth Telling, and Reconciliation in Canada*. Vancouver: University of British Columbia Press.

Robinson, Dylan, and Keavy Martin, eds. Forthcoming. *Taking Aesthetic Action*. Waterloo: Wilfrid Laurier University Press.

Rogers, Shelagh, Mike DeGagné, and Jonathan Dewar, eds. 2012. *Speaking My Truth: Reflections on Reconciliation and Residential School*. Ottawa: Aboriginal Healing Foundation.

Scott, James C. 1990. *Domination and the Arts of Resistance: Hidden Transcripts*. New Haven, CT: Yale University Press.

Shingwauk Archives. Algoma University, Sault Ste Marie, ON.

Simon, Roger. 2013. "Towards a Hopeful Practice of Worrying: The Problematics of Listening and the Educative Responsibilities of Canada's Truth and Reconciliation Commission." In *Reconciling Canada: Critical Perspectives on the Culture of*

Redress, edited by Jennifer Henderson and Pauline Wakeham, 129–42. Toronto: University of Toronto Press.

Stride, Brian. 2012. "First Nations Brass Bands." In *History of Brass Bands in British Columbia*. Vancouver: Vancouver Association of Brass Bands (vabbs.org/hist_bb_bc.php, accessed 8 January 2014).

Troutman, John. 2009. *Indian Blues: American Indians and the Politics of Music*. Norman: University of Oklahoma Press.

Truth and Reconciliation Commission of Canada. 2012. *They Came for the Children: Canada, Aboriginal Peoples, and Residential Schools*. Interim Report of the TRC Commission on Indian Residential Schools. Winnipeg: Truth and Reconciliation Commission of Canada.

Truth and Reconciliation Commission of Canada. www.trc.ca (accessed 8 January 2014).

U.N. Convention on the Prevention and Punishment of the Crime of Genocide. 1948. legal.un.org/avl/ha/cppcg/cppcg.html.

Yúdice, George. 2003. *The Expediency of Culture: Uses of Culture in the Global Era*. Durham, NC: Duke University Press.

Discography

Aglukark, Susan. 2006. *Blood Red Earth*. Aglukark Entertainment under license to Arbor Records.

Donovan, Mishi. 2000. *Journey Home*. Arbor Records AR-11192.

Hope, Beatrice. N.d. *Panik Labradorimiuk/Daughter of Labrador*. Independent.

Lauzon, Jani. 2006. *Mixed Blessings*. Ra Records RR 0117.

MacInnes, Mike, producer. 2013. *Journey of Healing*. Eskasoni. Independent CD.

Palmer, Fara. 1999. *Pretty Brown*. New Hayden Music Corporation NHMC1717.

Tzo'kam. 2000. *Īt'em: 'To Sing.'* Red Planet Records RP1011-0103.

Wabkinew. 2009. *Live By the Drum*. Winnipeg: Indie Ends.

CHAPTER TWENTY-ONE

Passages on Music in the Accounts of Medieval Arab Travelers

Amnon Shiloah

The scholar wishing to explore the past of an oral musical tradition often clings to fragments of information that she or he finds from every available type of material. The authors of travel accounts report eyewitness events, though rarely are such writers musical experts. Such firsthand observations, nonetheless, often provide evidence rarely found in systematic or anecdotal writings on music. Travelers may refer to the place of music in a given culture; to the function of a given term; to the relations of sacred to secular music, of art to folk music, and of vocal to instrumental music; as well as to the degree of stability and change. One should be careful, of course, when using this kind of information, to avoid erroneous or fanciful interpretations from travelers, who otherwise might lack general knowledge about the culture they are describing. The use of historical evidence in ethnomusicology has always been a critical part of Bruno Nettl's research. His historical studies of the Middle East and South Asia, as well as European folk music and the musics of Native Americans, have contributed substantially to the common foundations of ethnomusicology itself, and it is hardly surprising that he has inspired the historical turn in our field. It is through our common interest in the historical sources for the music of North Africa and the Middle East, moreover, that Bruno Nettl and I have worked together, seeking a historiography based on ethnography in the present (cf. Nettl and Shiloah 1986).

In this chapter, I have selected two important Arab medieval sources that are the works of two famous Muslim medieval travelers. The first, by Ibn Jubayr (1145–1217), a native of Valencia in Muslim Spain, comes from a book recounting his pilgrimage to Mecca, beginning in 1183 and ending with his return to Granada in 1185. Ibn Jubayr's travel account is considered a valuable and reliable source for the history of the time. The second work considered in this chapter is by the Moroccan Ibn Battuta (1304–1368), whose family belonged to the Berber tribe of Luwata. Ibn Battuta was born in Tangier and journeyed farther perhaps than any other medieval traveler, covering seventy-five thousand miles through most Muslim countries of the time during some thirty years. For several years, he served as the great *qāḍī* (judge) of Delhi, and also as a qāḍī on the Maldive Islands. His travel accounts include some of the most interesting and important documents for the political and social history of the Muslim world during the second quarter of the fourteenth century. Ibn Battuta covered more area than did Marco Polo. Both Ibn Jubayr and Ibn Battuta were perceptive and keen observers, who offer global views of the cultures of their times. The music passages in both sources may be divided into three major categories: music in military contexts, music in ceremonies with entertainment, and music in ritual chanting.

Music in Military Contexts

Interestingly, most of the musical passages in both sources dealt with the musical domain known as *ṭablkhānah* (the drum house), practiced by military bands in Muslim lands. These bands were initially used in battle to inspire the soldiers as well as to overwhelm the enemy. They also were used as an emblem of royalty for ruling caliphs during peaceful times. In such cases the band brandished colorful banners and insignias to augment the pomp of royal processions and festivals. Such honors, initially reserved for the caliph alone, became symbols of rank and prestige for petty rulers and various classes of officers and court officials, who were entitled to have their own ceremonies. According to the historian Ibn Khaldûn (1332–1406), the *'ala* (literally, outfit) under the Fatimid rulers in Egypt (eleventh century) included five hundred banners, five hundred trumpets, and fifty *naqqārāt* (kettle drums). The Egyptian historian Ibn Taghribirdi (1409–1470) reports that fifty *kusāt* cylindrical drums and fifty naqqārāt players, all mounted on mules, participated in the grand procession as well as vast ensembles of *tubul* (drums), *sunuj* (cymbals), and *safāfīr* (whistles) (see Ibn Khaldûn 1958, volume 2:48–40).

The ṭablkhānah bands described by Ibn Jubayr and Ibn Battuta had an excessively large number of drums, from small kettle drums placed on the backs of camels or horses, to sizable drums used for signals. They were joined by *anfār* (trumpets), *buqāt* (horns), and *surnāyāt* (reedpipes). Among the major events for which these instruments were used in time of peace were daily performance at the gates to a ruler's compound; religious functions on Fridays and feast days; journeying, hunting, and public and private audiences and religious processions; pilgrimage to holy shrines; the *ḥajj* pilgrimage to Mecca; and folk festivals. On such occasions it was customary that rulers, chamberlains, and emirs had their own bands. It should be noted that the larger or smaller number of instruments depended on the choice imposed by the different rulers. Indeed, the size and content of the bands, their hierarchical placement, their partition into distinctive groups, and the order, time, and nature of performance were subject to strict regulations established in accordance with the event in which they were participating.

A band's performance often alternated with singing and dancing by a special performing group always labeled by Ibn Battuta as *ahl al-ṭarab*. The term *ṭarab* (emotion, delight, and entertainment) refers to a wide range of emotional reactions from subtle delight to great excitement. Over the course of history, the term became synonymous with music and its derivatives—*muṭrib* (male musician) and *muṭriba* (female musician)—designated artist-musicians endowed with the power to arouse emotion through their art (for a study of ṭarab in the contemporary Middle East, see Racy 2003). In this spirit, Ibn Battuta also used the expression "ahl al-ṭarab" to designate expert male and female singers, dancers, and instrumentalists playing art music, *ālāt al-ṭarab*. Travel references do not include the names and types of the instruments played by these musicians. We might attribute this to Ibn Battuta's lack of familiarity with those foreign instruments. Ibn Battuta also uses the term *nawba* to indicate the singing of the vocalists of ahl al-ṭarab alternatively with the players of the military band. This appellation needs clarification in order to verify its relation to the well-known compound suite form, the same name widely used in both Middle Eastern and Maghrebi styles of Arab classical music. Are we concerned here with the same forms? The immediate answer is no, for it does not fit the usual definition of the compound form in art music. One thing is certain, namely, that the instrumental part belongs to the realm of the ṭablkhānah, whose instruments are dedicated to martial music and are not those usually belonging to art music and performing compound suites.

Literally, the term "nawba" signifies, according to Edward William Lane, a "turn which comes to one; or which one takes, or during which, anything is, or is to be" (Lane 1863–1893). This explanation is somehow externally close to the playing and singing in the passages cited here, but not to the type and style of the musical pieces exchanged between martial instrumental music of the ṭablkhānah and the refined male singing of ahl al-ṭarab, or to the exact function and times of Muslim Islamic prayer. Henry George Farmer discusses the meaning of the nawba in connection with the ṭablkhānah and its context: Many observers, including Farmer, recognized that the *nawba* was a special piece of music, performed by the *naqqārah khanah* for royalty during the five hours of Muslim prayer, as well as for other prayer occasions by lesser dignitaries (cf. Farmer 1931). The nawba in this case probably refers to melodic vocal segments alternating with instrumental passages of martial character at particular hours of the day, as well as at official ceremonies. There is also an anonymous work reporting that the Sultan of Tabriz, Jalal al-Dīn Ḥusain, commissioned a musician to compose a nawba for each day of the month of Ramadan. This undertaking seems feasible if the nawba is similar to the one depicted in the passage above (Shiloah 2003:205–6).

Passages from the travel reports of Ibn Battuta provide good illustrations of the terms ahl al-ṭarab and nawba. For example, in the following passage, Ibn Battuta provides details of a military ceremony of the Sultan Abu Sa'id (736/1355), the king of al-'Iraq, in Baghdad. Journeying as part of the military encampments, Battuta gained entry into the sultan's *ma ḥalla* (a mobile camp of the Mongol khan), about which he writes:

> On setting out with the rising of the dawn, each of the emirs comes up with his troops, his drums and his standards and halts in a position that has been assigned to him. Then the king mounts, and the drums, trumpets and horns are sounded for the departure. Each emir salutes the king and returns to his place. The chamberlains and the marshals move forward ahead of the king and are followed by ahl al-ṭarab whose number is about a hundred musicians wearing handsome dresses. Ahead of ahl al-ṭarab are ten horsemen with drums carried on slings round their necks; five other horsemen carried five surnayat (reed-pipes), or "*ghaitas* in our countries." Then these drums and surnayat play a piece and stop. And then ten singers perform their nawba and stop; then one more time the instruments play and another ten singers perform their nawba and they continue so until ten nawbat are completed. When the hour of departure comes, the great drum is beaten. It is followed by the drum of the queen beating, the drums of all the ladies, the vizier drum, all of them the same and one beat. (Ibn Battuta 1958–1971, volume 1:342–43)

We find a similar nawba in Ibn Battuta's account of the journey of the Muslim governor along the Indus River. The two performing groups began to perform their nawbas from two different boats accompanying the ship of the governor. In the center of the governor's ship there was a wooden cabin, and on top of this there was a place prepared for the governor to sit. Accompanying the governor's ship were four vessels to the right and left. Two of these carried the emblems of the emir's sovereignty: the insignia, the drums (tubul), horns (*abwāq*), trumpets (anfār), and reed-pipes (surnāyāt, i.e., ghaitas). The other two carried the singers (ahl al-ṭarab). Concerning the nawba, Ibn Battuta writes:

> First the drums and horns play a nawba and the singers perform a nawba and keep this up alternately from early morning to the lunch hour. Then the singers of ahl al-ṭarab go on board the governor's ship and sing until he finishes eating. The journey continued thereafter as before until nightfall. The camp was then set up on the bank of the river, and the governor disembarked. At dawn the trumpets and drums sounded and the dawn prayer was said, then food was brought and when the meal was finished they resumed their journey. (Ibn Battuta 1958–1971, volume 3:600–601)

Music in Ceremonies with Entertainment

Ibn Battuta also provides accounts of music in palace ceremonies that included entertainment. For example, he described how the sultan held audience on feast days in the following passage:

> The palace was sumptuously adorned especially for the event. In the audience-hall a vast tent surrounded by pavilions and of artificial trees made of silk, the great throne in pure gold throughout, its legs are encrusted with jewels and many other numerous fantastic details help depicting the enchanted ambiance of the event. When the sultan mounts the throne those present come forward to salute him, in accordance of the established protocol. In this established order the ahl al-ṭarab are placed right behind the vizier with the secretaries, the chamberlains, and the chiefs comprising the following order: first come the daughters of the infidel Indian kings who have been taken as captives of war during that year who after they have sung and danced are given by the Sultan given to the emirs and to the distinguished foreigners, then after them the rest of the daughters of the infidels and these, after they have sung and danced, are given to his brothers and kinsmen and relatives by request. The next day after the hour of the afternoon prayer, the Sultan holds a session at the same manner to which are brought female singers after they have sung and danced to the emirs of white slaves. On the third day he celebrates the marriages of his relatives and makes gifts to them; on the fourth day he emancipates male slaves; on the fifth he emancipates female slaves; on the sixth he marries male slaves to female slaves and on the seventh he distributes alms. (Ibn Battuta 1958–1971, volume 3:666–67)

A noble wedding is surely full of colorful and grandiose events, which also include some references to music and dance. At the beginning of his report on the marriage of the Amir Saif al-Dīn to the Sultan's sister, Ibn Battuta mentions the arrival of an ensemble of male singers, female singers, and dancers, all of whom are the sultan's slaves. The grand ensemble was led by the *Emir al-muṭribīn* (the chief of the musicians), Shams al-dīn al Tibrizi. The description also contains a note referring to unnamed instruments linked to ahl al-ṭarab.

> Two nights before the wedding ceremony, a group of distinguished ladies went at night from the sultan's habitations to the Red palace and after having decorated a special mansion in it they summoned the bridegroom Amir Saif al-din and put him in the midst of them and made him sit on a cushion and dyed his hands and his feet with henna. Other women who attended the ceremony and stood before him intoned songs and danced and thereafter withdrew to the audience-hall where the ceremony of wedding was to take place. This singing and dancing were of a folk nature not connected with the artists of ahl al-tarab. In the audience-hall, filled with women after the female musicians had brought all kinds of instruments, the bride had been placed on a high pulpit. The bridegroom Amir Saif al-Din entered on horseback and proceeded until he reached the pulpit, where he dismounted, and made the gesture of homage on reaching its first step. The bride rose up, and standing until he mounted to the top, then he sat down below the step on which she had stood. Gold dinars were thrown over those of his friends who were present, and the women picked them up; then the female singers performed song while the playing of the drums, horns and trumpets and reed-pipes were sounding outside the gate. . . . It is the custom in India that no one should give presents to ahl al-ṭarab. (Ibn Battuta 1958–1971, volume 3:686–89)

Elsewhere, Ibn Battuta describes music and musicians in an Indian bazaar:

> In Dawlat Abad [India] there is a bazaar of male and female musicians called *tarab Abad*. This bazaar is spacious and a most beautiful one. It contains numerous shops, each of which has a door leading to the house of its proprietor. This shop is beautified with carpets, and in the center of it there is a sort of large cradle on which the female singer sits and reclines and it is swung by her attendants. In the centre of the bazaar there is a large carpeted and decorated pavilion in which emir al-mutribin [the chief musician] sits every Thursday after the afternoon prayer, with his servants and slaves in front of him. The female musicians come group after group, they sing and dance before him till the sunset prayer, and then they withdraw. In the same bazaar there are mosques for the prayer services where the imams also lead the presentation of the special spiritual hymns [*rawāih*] sung during the month of Ramadan. One of the infidel rulers in India used, on passing through this bazaar, to alight

at the female musicians' pavilion and these female musicians used to sing before him. One of the Muslim sultans used also to do the same. (Ibn Battuta 1958–1971, volume 3:624–25)

Ibn Battuta also traveled in East Asia, eventually reaching China, from which he began his slow return to his native country, the present-day Morocco. At the final stage of his travel to the east, the supreme commander in China, the great Amir Qurtay, offered Ibn Battuta hospitality in his house, where he stayed for three days. Ibn Battuta describes a reception given by Qurtay at which the leading figures in the city were present:

> The Amir sent his son with him to the canal, where he went on board a ship resembling a vessel of the fire department, and the Amir's son went on another along with ahl al-tarab and *ahl al-musiqa* vocalists and instrumentalists singers; this ensemble performed songs in Chinese, Arabic and Persian. The Amir's son was a great admirer of Persian music, therefore the ensemble sung a Persian song verse, which he commanded them to repeat it over and over again, until I learned it by heart. Its melody is indeed extraordinary.
>
> A large number of ships assembled on that canal. The people on them began a mimic battle and bombarded each other with oranges and lemon. In the evening we returned to the Amir's house and spent the night there, the ahl al-tarab came and sang kinds of remarkable and strange songs. (Ibn Battuta 1958–1971, volume 4:903

Music in Ritual Chanting

I now turn to witnesses dealing with religious song and the role played by the ṭablkhānah in the ceremonies included in the account of the ḥajj—the pilgrimage to Mecca—by Ibn Jubayr, who embarked on a ḥajj from Granada in March 1183. He remained in Mecca for about eight months and devoted more than two hundred pages in his travel account to this long sojourn. In part, Ibn Jubayr deals conspicuously with all the monuments and shrines found in the holy city of Mecca, indicating their unique religious and devotional functions. He also provides an eyewitness account of the variety of ceremonies held during the month of Ramadan (18 December 1183 to 16 January 1184).

Ibn Jubayr gives special attention to the sacred well, *Zamzam*, located at the perimeter of the sacred complex of Mecca. The muezzin, writes Ibn Jubayr, is the chief of all the muezzins of the noble complex. He is the first to recite, while all the other muezzins imitate him and follow in his footsteps

(Ibn Jubayr 1907:91). He is charged with the duty of announcing the daybreak meal (*sahur*) during the fast of Ramadan. He does it from a minaret close to the Emir's house. Also at the zamzam are two younger brothers, who answer him and call the faithful to prayer in their turn (Ibn Jubayr 1907:147). The *khatib* (preacher) is led by the zamzam muezzin to the pulpit, where he is girded with a sword. A group of muezzins places itself in front of the preacher and call the *adhān* in one voice before the khatib delivers his address (Ibn Jubayr 1907:91–92). On the second day of Ramadan, reports Ibn Jubayr, the Emir of Mecca left the city to meet the Emir Sayf al-Islam, the brother of Saladin, who was on his way from Egypt to Mecca (Ibn Jubayr 1907:147). When the latter reached the holy places, the kettle drums, drums, and trumpets announced his arrival as a mark of respect for the prince and an affirmation of his standing. Ibn Jubayr described the effect of the kettle drums, drums, and trumpets, stating that they "smote the ears and all parts of the noble Haram shook from it" (Ibn Jubayr 1907:150).

Collective recitation of the Qur'an will be my last example drawn from Ibn Jubayr's travel account: "The readers whose number is more than twenty, began to recite the Koran. Two of them spoke [chanted] a verse of the Koran in a moving and impassioned rhythm and when they were done, another group of the same number recited another verse. So they went on, alternately reciting verses" (Ibn Jubayr 1907:230). In the same context there is another example of collective Qur'an recitation: "The Koran readers, who were arranged in a line before him [the preacher] in chairs, soon began to recite in order, filling one with longing and emotion as they wished, and the eye speedily dropped tears. When they had ended, and we have counted them as doing nine verses from different chapters [of the Qur'an], he began a discourse that was brilliant and superb, and set throughout with the opening words of the verses" (Ibn Jubayr 1907:231). Such recitation is very close to spiritual vocal artistry.

When at the end of the month of Ramadan, there was proof of the sighting of the new moon, the Emir ordered the beating of kettle drums and drums and the sounding of trumpets as a sign indicating that it was the night of the festival. The camel riders raced with the horsemen, revealing marvels of all kinds in their skillful contest.

During his visit to the Iraqi city of al-Wāsiṭ on the main channel of the Tigris, Ibn Battuta offers impressions of the considerable familiarity of its inhabitants with the Qur'an and its correct recitation. He observes that most residents of al-Wāsiṭ could recite the Qur'an from memory and excelled in chanting it according to the science of the *tajwīd* (embellishment and rules of recitation). Tajwīd is a remarkable system regulating cantillation with respect to phonetics, correct diction, and rendition of the sacred text. Ibn Battuta adds that "all those in the Iraqi countries who wish to learn this art come to them. There are also many students from abroad, who are housed in a large and magnificent college, which contained some three hundred rooms. The sheikh Taqi al-dīn al-Wāsiti, who built the college, also gave each student a set of clothing every year and supplied money for living expenses" (Ibn Battuta 1958–1971, volume 1:272).

Ibn Battuta described an extravagant mystical ritual he observed in Iraq. The grave of the celebrated founder of the Rifā'i Sufi brotherhood was located about a day's journey from the city of al-Wāsit. Ibn Battuta made the trip to visit this brotherhood, whose vast monastery was located nearby. In summary, he writes that after afternoon prayers the drums and tambourines were beaten and the *faqirs* (members of the brotherhood) began to dance. Thereafter, they offered up the sunset prayer and brought in the evening meal, consisting of rice-bread, fish, milk, and dates. When all had eaten and prayed the first prayers of the night, they began to perform the *dhikr* (literally, remembrance), which refers to the quranic injunction "To remember God as often as possible." Shaikh Ahmad was sitting on his grandfather's prayer rug, and then they began the *samā*, both the dhikr ritual and the careful listening to sacred cantillation. Having already prepared loads of firewood, they went into the midst of its flames while dancing. Some of them rolled in the fire, and others put coals in their mouths and chewed them until finally they were extinguished. This ritual was undertaken with persistence, with the Aḥmadiya brotherhood known as specialists. There are some of them who take an enormous serpent, grabbing its head before severing it (cf. Lane 1842:273).

The Ithnā 'Asharya (The Twelvers) is a major sect of Shi'a Islam, which believes in the succession of twelve imams from the death of Muhammad, beginning with 'Ali, the fourth caliph. The last imam of the twelve successors, who disappeared in 878, is thought to be alive and in hiding, ready to return at the last judgment. Ibn Battuta provides the following description of a performance by members of this sect, which he witnessed in the Iraqi city of al-Hillah on the Euphrates.

> The inhabitants of this city are all Shi'ites but are divided into two factions which are always in fighting between them. There is a mosque they call "the Master of the Age." Every evening before sunset, a hundred of the townsmen, following their custom, go with arms and drawn swords to the governor of the city and receive from him a saddled and bridled horse or mule. With this they go in procession, with beating drums and blowing trumpets and horns. They

> halt at the door and call out: "In the name of God! O Master of the Age, in the name of God come forth. Corruption is abroad and injustice is rife! This is the hour for thy advent; that by thee God may discover the true from the false." They continue to call out thus, sounding their drums and horns and trumpets, until the hour of sunset prayer, for they hold that Muhammad al-'Askari, entered this mosque and disappeared from sight in it, and that he will emerge from it for he, in their view is the expected Imam. (Ibn Battuta 1958–1971, volume 2:324–25)

In the foreword to his translation of Ibn Battuta's travel book, Hamilton A. R. Gibb wrote that after his visit to Bulgaria, Ibn Battuta had an unexpected opportunity to visit Constantinople in the retinue of the khan's third wife, a Greek princess who was returning from a visit to her parents (Ibn Battuta 1958–1971, volume 1:xii). Ibn Battuta's account of this important Christian site displays admiration for what he saw and heard with the assistance of an official guide provided by the khan. Ibn Battuta called this guide "the Greek" and was led by him to the most important churches and impressive monasteries. The guide reported to Ibn Battuta that "the number of monks and priests in one principal church runs into thousands. Other special Convents containing more than a thousand virgins consecrated to religious devotions" (Ibn Battuta 1958–1971). The hospitality of his Christian hosts also contained warmth and objectivity, which the Muslim qāḍī describes with great sympathy, especially in a Christian holy city conquered by the Ottoman armies 150 years later. It is significant that Ibn Battuta devoted a special section to the numerous "monasteries." The term appears as a title in Arabic transliteration, with an explanation of how this word should be pronounced and how it relates to the Islamic *zawiya*, a hospice attached to the establishment of a religious order. Describing a church within one of the monasteries he visited with his host, Ibn Battuta writes:

> The church contained about five hundred virgins wearing cilices, and with their heads shaved and covered with felt bonnets. They were of exceeding beauty and show the traces of their austerities. A boy was sitting on a pulpit chanting the gospel to them in the most beautiful voice that I have ever heard; round him were eight other boys on pulpits accompanied by their priest, and when this boy chanted another boy chanted [probably antiphonally or simultaneously]. The Greek said to me, "These girls are kings' daughters who have given themselves to the service of this church, and the boys who are reading also [are kings' sons]." (Ibn Battuta 1958–1971, volume 2:510–11)

In another monastery Ibn Battuta reports a similar sequence of events with the presence of about five hundred virgins and boys chanting as in the former monastery, but the Greek guide reported that these "are daughters of viziers and emirs, who engage in devotional exercises in this church. With this one more encounter with other religions in peaceful mind it is good to come to an end of my selection of passages on music" (Ibn Battuta 1958–1971). And so, too, do I reach the end of my accounts on music by medieval Arab travelers, contributing this chapter to the growing body of literature that fills the history of ethnomusicology, on whose journeys so many of us have been privileged to accompany Bruno Nettl.

References

Farmer, Henry George. 1931. *Studies in Oriental Musical Instruments*. London: H. Reeves.

Ibn-Battuta, Muhammad Ibn-'Abdallah. 1958–1971. *The Travels of Ibn Battuta: A.D. 1325–1354*. 4 volumes. Edited by C. Defrémery and B. R. Sanguinetti and translated by Hamilton A. R. Gibb. Cambridge: Cambridge University Press.

Ibn Jubayr. 1907. *The Travels of Ibn Jubair*. Translated by R. J. C. Broadhurst. Leyden: Brill.

Ibn Khaldûn. 1958. *The Muqadimmah: An Introduction to History*. 3 volumes. Translated by Franz Rosenthal. New York: Pantheon.

Lane, Edward William. 1842. *An Account of the Manners and Customs of the Modern Egyptians*. London: C. K. Knight and Co.

———. 1863–1893. *An Arabic-English Lexicon: Derived from the Best and Most Copious Eastern Sources*. 2 volumes. Edinburgh: Williams and Norgate.

Nettl, Bruno, and Amnon Shiloah. 1986. "Persian Classical Music in Israel: A Preliminary Report." *Asian Music* 17(2): 69–87.

Racy, A. J. 2003. *Making Music in the Arab World: The Culture and Artistry of Ṭarab*. Cambridge: Cambridge University Press.

Shiloah, Amnon. 2003. *The Theory of Music in Arabic Writings (c. 900–1900)*, Volume 2. Munich: G. Henle.

CHAPTER TWENTY-TWO

~

Reconstructing Abbey Road

History and Mnemohistory in Memories of Working with the Beatles

Gordon Thompson

Few performers have had their work as fully documented and closely scrutinized as have the Beatles.[1] Numerous interviews with members of the network of individuals associated with the band have explored the gamut of the personal and professional lives of the "Fab Four." The Beatles themselves, moreover, have been actively involved in retelling and mediating their story, assisted by numerous biographers and technologists, not to mention lawyers. This saturated coverage extends to those who assisted them in the creation of their recording catalog, particularly the engineers who captured the sound. All of this material serves the information appetites of one of the most dedicated and extensive fan bases in the world. As we approach the fiftieth anniversary of the start of the band's rise to fame, the Beatles remain a mainstream topic in the popular press and imagination.

For an ethnomusicologist researching this music culture, fieldwork poses significant problems, in part because interviews function as both social and commercial commodities. The remaining members of the band—Paul McCartney and Ringo Starr—participate in interviews largely as part of marketing campaigns, and consequently limit their availability to publications that will further that end. Other participants in the creation of this musical catalog, however, appear to have been less calculating in their availability. Their accessibility and obvious pleasure in sharing memories help to establish alternative versions of the otherwise closely controlled story line.

A string of challenges, nevertheless, resides with any of these interviews. At the root of the problem, the stories originate decades in the past, such that their retelling can present psychological challenges for storytellers. Consequently, different versions of the same events often emerge, sometimes contributing to densely textured portrayals, but sometimes also leading to conflicting assertions. All involved understand the fragility of memory and often turn to documentation to anchor the direction of personal claims, but consensus can still be difficult.

A Gentlemen's Disagreement

In 2005, the balance engineer who had worked with the Beatles on the albums *Revolver*, *Sgt. Pepper's Lonely Hearts Club Band*, parts of *Abbey Road*, and other releases began putting the finishing touches on his memoir. In anticipation of the release of Geoff Emerick's *Here, There, and Everywhere: My Life Recording the Beatles* (2006), his publisher circulated copies of the manuscript to a select group of individuals for verification. Ken Scott read both an early edited version and a prepublication proof of the book and sent corrections and comments to the editor. Scott had replaced Emerick at the mixing desk for parts of *Magical Mystery Tour* and for most of *The Beatles* (the so-called White Album) and had worked on Beatles sessions since 1964, sometimes alongside Emerick as the tape operator. After reading the drafts, however, he questioned Emerick's assertions about dates and technology, including the engineer's claims of being the first to apply techniques that had clearly already become standard practice. An ultimately public set of Internet exchanges between the two recording professionals ensued, with one declaring that the perceived inaccuracies reflected differences of opinion and the other claiming sloppiness on the part of his former colleague (cf. Emerick 2006; Scott 2006a, 2006b). Poignantly, Scott chastised Emerick by saying: "As part of that history, Geoff did AMAZING work recording them, but if one can't remember or take the time to double check the facts, DON'T WRITE A BOOK" (Scott 2006a).

In the context of the remarkable documentation of Beatles sessions, these two veterans proposed competing narratives, each asserting his own authentic memories of recording the twentieth century's most influential rock band. As Scott began work on his own book, he doubled his efforts to confirm his memories. His *Abbey Road to Ziggy Stardust* discusses working with the Beatles and others, including David Bowie, Lou Reed, and George Harrison. Notably, Scott began fact-checking his recollections by contacting others who had worked with him at EMI, Trident, and other studios. Scott admits, "I have come to learn . . . how strangely the memory works" (Scott and Owsinski 2007:2).

The very notion of fact-checking assumes that the accuracy of memories and the consistency of documentation can be challenged. In my interviews with musicians, songwriters, music directors, balance engineers, and producers active in the London music and recording industries of the 1950s and 1960s, the ability to recall events has always been an issue. Cross-referencing interviews with release information and press reports often helps to verify accounts, but even here both memories and documentation can deceive. In addition to routine hyperbole, press agents often altered birthdates to make performers appear younger than they were and also invented other information about them.

For professionals such as Emerick and Scott, music and recording were daily events, sometimes tedious, sometimes exciting, but almost always with elements of predictability and repetitiveness. "Just another day at the office" is how Scott describes some of his work at EMI's Abbey Road facilities (Ken Scott, interview, 3 October 2013). The very predictability that frees us from having to ponder every action we take, however, also potentially impedes our ability to remember.

Memory

Memory is very much a part of how we know we exist. As a psychological, biological, and social process, memory involves registering experience, storing references to stimuli in a retrievable form, and reconstructing that information when circumstances demand. Every time we recall an event, we reimagine that experience from clusters of neurological connections established through the very patterns by which we have learned to access them. Intriguing recent research (Doeller, Caswell, and Burgess 2010) into the role of "grid cells" in the hippocampus and the entorhinal cortex that "remember" place and on which we build memory finds confirmation in the monuments we erect and our veneration of locations. In short, the origins of memory lie in some of the most primal portions of the brain, where a grid of cells literally serves as a topographical map of our environment over which we lay other important information. Thus, in our ability to recall the past, location plays a fundamental role.

Equally important, reconstructing memories is routinely a collaborative act so that we collectively agree on who people are and were, what they did, and where we encountered them. Any discussion of the idea of collective memory should start with Maurice Halbwachs (1877–1945), who first articulated the concept in *Les cadres sociaux de la mémoire* (1925). He asserted that we construct memory in the context of society and that we build our memories through our interactions with others in ways that are both "public and shareable" (Halbwachs 1980[1950]:12). He explored these ideas further in *La mémoire collective chez les musiciens* (1939) and more completely in the posthumous *La mémoire collective* (1980[1950]). Notably, he argued against the notion that our minds record all of our experiences and that all we need are the right tools to recall them. Recent research has borne out his predictions (cf. Coman, Brown, Koppel, and Hurst 2009; Cowan 2000).

Halbwachs understood memory as dependent on different kinds of recall: "autobiographical memory" (which grows from personal experience), "historical memory" (personal knowledge supported by documentation), and, even more discretely, "history" (documentation of events to which we have no "organic" connection). These elements combine in "collective memory" to articulate how we actively shape our identities, both personally and communally (Olick 2007:7).

Historically, governments, businesses, and individuals routinely have manipulated the fluidity of memory, such that Jan Assmann's (1997) construct of mnemohistory includes a combination of "memory culture" and the "past as remembered" (Holtorf 1999). By "memory culture," Assmann intends "the way a society ensures cultural continuity by preserving, with the help of cultural mnemonics, its collective knowledge from one generation to the next" (1997). By the "past as remembered," he suggests that some memories "reassure the members of a society of their collective identity and [supply] them with an awareness of their unity and singularity in time and space" (Assmann 1997).

Individuals, in other words, might promote accounts of the past that they see as truthful, but ultimately cultures decide how they wish to remember history. Assmann (1997:9), referring to archaeology, sees memory as an active process of meaning-making through time and "the ongoing work of reconstructive imagination," for which he proposes a "theory of cultural transmission that helps us understand history" (Olick 2007:8). For individuals, the loss of memory, combined with a quest for authenticity, is manifest in our concern for the accuracy of history. If our identity derives in significant part from who we were, then our very conscious existence depends on our ability to remember, especially as the Internet allows multiple, often unchallenged assertions about the past and predictions for the future. Our individuality, moreover, relates to the communities to which we imagine we belong and with whom we share common interpretations of history. Perhaps most important, we tell stories as a way to know who we are and to serve as the vehicles for the construction of memory.

Popular Music Studies and Memory

Jan Assmann suggests that some collective memory comes from distinct contexts, while we concretize others through "ritual, architecture, and texts" (quoted in Strachan 2008:6). The not-unique challenge of popular-music history often lies in the ways individuals and organizations have attempted to manipulate that history. In an industry where fiction commonly passes as reality, the subjects we interview sometimes consciously attempt to shape how we tell their stories. Consistent with the human condition, they also subconsciously remember in ways that support their particular narrative, even when confronted with evidence to the contrary. In many cases, managers, agents, and promoters have created stories around performers as a way to optimize audience interest. Similarly, when asked to narrate stories about ourselves, we all predictably shape the plots to support outcomes we believe to be true, but that others might question. Popular-music marketing takes this notion much further, occasionally positioning intentionally theatrical identities as a way to attract audiences, identities that performers themselves sometimes embrace as reality.

Not all accounts of popular music, however, are quite so intentionally deceptive. Increasingly, individual narratives have sought to correct the informational excesses of the intervening decades by sharing memories that serve as valuable sources of information about popular music making. Robert Strachan (2008), referring to Assmann's research, has commented on the role that biographies in popular music play in shaping the collective memory of audiences and, notably, how publishers and other institutions shape the stories that fans actively embrace. Balancing autobiographical memory (personal recollections) with historical memory (e.g., recording release dates) often has the effect of individuals realigning their stories to match the facts. Thus, the exchange mentioned earlier in this chapter between Ken Scott and Geoff Emerick—in which the former questions the latter about the accuracy of his memories—occupies familiar territory.

Kay Kaufman Shelemay (2006:21) observes another factor that affects these memoirs as the storytellers seek the assistance of informed others in the construction of their narrations. She describes a trilateral structure of the "narrator" (the individual whose story forms the core of the exchange), the "mentor" (someone who helps the narrator tell the story), and the "monitor" (the ethnographer who shapes the telling of the memory).

In the commercial contexts of popular music, that model commonly takes on an exaggerated form: press agents serve as mentors who actively rewrite the story, while journalists function as interested monitors. The goal of each party is readership, rather than accuracy per se. Importantly, these actors function in unofficial collusions, each benefiting from the contributions and exaggerations of the other. What they create serves as a kind of transient mnemohistory, not a factually accurate depiction of the creation of music and recordings, but clearly a communally mediated representation. As in Assmann's approach, they help to build communal memory with both an imagined present and past.

With memoirs, the role of co-writers in the creation of biographies can range from benign to significant. Emerick chose as his co-author Howard Massey, an engineer who writes about production techniques. In the minds of many familiar with this era in Beatles history, the choice of Massey clearly shaped how Emerick's work with the Beatles would be presented and, some would argue, how his memory lapses would be filled. Ken Scott, commenting on the role played by his co-author, Bobby Owsinski, asserts that his collaborator only served to organize his ideas: "Bobby had very little to do with the process of remembering. I gave him the information which he then put into some semblance of order and then I put it into my own words" (Ken Scott, interview, 3 October 2013).

Owsinski, like Massey, is also a producer and engineer who writes about production; thus, he too would be familiar with the technology and methods of recording. Facilitators, however, leave their mark on anything that passes through their hands and Owsinski helped Scott with his verification process, contacting individuals to seek their recollections of events. Owsinski writes, "Whenever possible we attempted to cross-check the facts with other people who were there. . . . Frequently, we interviewed multiple people on the same topic, where all remembered an event differently. When that occurred we kept on interviewing, usually to find out that everyone was right" (Scott and Owsinski 2007:xvi). Notably, both Emerick and Scott turned to other author/engineers to help them interpret and present their stories, suggesting that they wanted someone familiar with the language and everyday reality of their craft to help them convey their version of history.

What would be different about how an ethnomusicologist might interpret their story? How do we approach forming productive questions for narrators such as Scott, who have not only been interviewed numerous times about work over the past fifty years, but who have also compiled official versions of their memories? What can we learn about their world that they have not already recounted numerous times? How would an ethnomusicologist, in Shelemay's terms, be a different kind of "mentor," and is it any different from the role of a "monitor"?

"While My Guitar Gently Weeps"

In preparing his book, Ken Scott knew that he would struggle to recall a particular day in Beatles history when Eric Clapton (at that point celebrated for his role in the band Cream) arrived to dub in the guitar solo for George Harrison's "While My Guitar Gently Weeps." Fans have consistently asked Scott about the session, and much to the engineer's chagrin, he has very few recollections of the event. His frustrations have even led to undergoing regression therapy in an attempt to recapture memory fragments of what happened on 6 September 1968.

The end of August 1968 had been particularly difficult in the studio, with drummer Ringo Starr walking out of the sessions after a verbal altercation with Paul McCartney and, around the same time, John Lennon's wife Cynthia publicly suing for divorce. Of more immediate importance for Scott, producer George Martin had gone on holiday, leaving the band in charge for around two weeks, with Scott serving as both engineer and objective ears.

The day before Clapton arrived to record, Ringo Starr had returned to the band and the studio, where he found his drums decked out in flowers. More importantly, Scott and accomplices had—against company protocol—moved one of EMI's first eight-track recorders (a 3M M23) from where it was being stored and, after installing it in studio two, were still dealing with the significant problems arising from its unfamiliar technology. George Harrison had discovered the recently purchased machine stored in a hallway outside the studio where they were recording and had insisted that they install it immediately.[2] The twenty-one-year-old Scott would have had much on his mind.

Part of an explanation of the memory gap might be found in the daily routine of recording and how potential disruptions might affect one's ability to remember. Working at EMI would have had predictable patterns: instruments and amplifiers would have been in place, and microphones would have been set up for recording. A nebula of factors on this occasion, however, presented unusual challenges, including (a) the absence of a producer, (b) the return of the drummer, (c) the potentially job-threatening appropriation of an eight-track recorder,[3] (d) the challenging installation of substantially new technology, and (e) the decision to hide Clapton's identity.

The five musicians on the studio floor and the engineers in the control room above confirm that numerous eyes were present, and yet different stories emerge about the details of that day. Memories of the 6 September 1968 session were already skewed less than two years later, when Clapton imagined that he had used his own guitar and amplifier, an arrangement that clearly did not happen (Stuckey 2010). At the very least, the studio microphones and levels would have been reset, with annotations documenting the precise setup.

Scott and Mnemohistory

Ken Scott has been a regular guest at conventions where he is routinely asked about his work. He diligently answers everyone, retelling his stories with verve and no small amount of charm. The predictability of these questions, however, has generated conditioned responses on his part. Scott admits: "I have become increasingly aware that these days I tend to answer the same every time. I have done SO many interviews . . . that I can't see how one could possibly answer the same questions without getting into that trap" (Ken Scott, interview, 4 November 2013).

I have interviewed Ken Scott in different contexts, the most low-key and predictable of which have been in front of groups of students where I gave him cues to talk about his most famous clients. The questions posed in these settings purposefully covered topics that would be new to the audience, but familiar to Scott; thus they were anticipated, and his answers were well formed and told compellingly. We have also had informal conversations where topics such as studio protocols and mutual acquaintances came up along with more mundane topics. Unsurprisingly, when we launched into a formal telephone interview specifically about his memories of recording at the EMI Recording Studios, his replies, rather than revealing anything new, veered back to his well-established responses. Even though "memory" was our prime topic (a subject in which Scott has been particularly interested), we returned repeatedly to answers he might well have given in any other forum.

Scott's conundrum parallels that of many other individuals involved with the Beatles. Most notoriously, Paul McCartney has been interviewed so often and his stories have been so remarkably consistent over the years that some interviewers have formed unofficial discussion groups to compare notes and form strategies. Even knowing where to begin asking a question for which McCartney would not veer into a stock answer is daunting. Indeed, the subject of "The Beatles" has been so heavily covered that the multitude of different interpretations of Beatles details could fill a small library.

Almost all of what we know about the Beatles has been reconstructed such that even the touchstones of the band's history are suspect. Moreover, the Beatles' recordings have been remastered such that the very sound of the core material is different from the original releases of the sixties. The Beatles themselves have participated in the creation of these variations, for example, when Paul McCartney instructed Ken Scott to create different endings for the mono and stereo recordings of "Helter Skelter." McCartney knew that fans would recognize the differences and would purchase both versions. More extremely, collectors seek out the different mixes, edits, and outtakes that have escaped EMI's vaults. Notably, even if we were to play the original recordings on period equipment, we still could not hear them the same way that we did when they were released. This reimagining of the past extends to the three-volume *Beatles Anthology*, recordings sometimes edited together to create the impression of immediacy and authenticity, but in actuality they serve as props for an elaborate representation of a corporate-approved story. Indeed, the story of the Beatles has grown exponentially since their unseemly demise in 1970 (see Tessler 2010).

Even the name of the location in which the recordings were made, moreover, has been reconstructed, with "Abbey Road Studios" (or simply "Abbey Road") replacing the formerly titled "EMI Recording Studios"—the name of the street and a Beatles album substituting for the more bureaucratic sign that once hung over the front door. And in narrow Mathew Street in their hometown of Liverpool, the place of their annunciation by soon-to-be manager Brian Epstein, the Cavern Club, has been rebuilt after being demolished by the city to create a parking garage.

As Ken Scott began to reconstruct his past, his methods unknowingly reflected the different aspects of Assmann's notions of mnemohistory. He worked within the realm of "memory culture," his memoir helping to shape "cultural continuity" with the intention of passing his experiences on to another generation by contributing to the "collective knowledge" of fans. To this end, Scott says, he wanted "to let people know more about what I experienced during my life in as accurate an account as possible" because "we are losing a lot of what made the music great back then" (Ken Scott, interview, 4 November 2013).

In this process, the recordings of the Beatles (reconstructed as they are) that Scott helped to record serve as the "cultural mnemonics" of this referencing process. Indeed, for the significantly large community of individuals interested in the Beatles, Scott also contributes to Assmann's notion of the "past as remembered," with the community seeking awareness of their group identity (e.g., the annual Beatles conventions on both sides of the Atlantic at which Scott has spoken). These audiences want reassurance that their experiences were real and important, and Scott's and other books support that goal. Indeed, a 2013 segment of CBS's *Sixty Minutes* intricately linked the assassination of John F. Kennedy with the arrival of the Beatles and the ensuing "Beatlemania" (Safer 2013).

In a reference intentionally echoing Kurosawa's film *Rashomon*, Scott notes that the individuals he consulted sometimes had different versions of events, but that each contributed a different perspective such that, not only does the story consist of multiple facets, it changes as the field of information changes around it. As he and I continue our "interview" virtually through e-mail, the subject of "memory" becomes more intense. Scott, as the "narrator," seldom questions his own recollections, even while referring to the memories of select individuals. Ironically, as we move even farther in time from those recording sessions and memories become even frailer, the mnemohistorical version of the events continues to evolve.

Notes

1. This chapter was first delivered as a paper at the annual meetings of the Society for Ethnomusicology (November 2013).

2. Unbeknownst to either the Beatles or the recording staff, EMI had offered use of the equipment to producer George Martin, who rejected it because "it wasn't up to the standard" of the equipment with which the band was already recording (Studer four-tracks), but also probably because its installation would have slowed down the creation of the album (Ken Scott, interview, 4 November 2013).

3. Scott and the tape operator who had moved and helped to install the 3M M23 were fired shortly after the completion of the album.

References

Assmann, Jan. 1997. *Moses the Egyptian: The Memory of Egypt in Western Monotheism*. Cambridge, MA: Harvard University Press.

Coman, Alin, Adam D. Brown, Jonathan Koppel, and William Hurst. 2009. "Collective Memory from a Psychological Perspective." *International Journal of Politics, Culture, and Society* 22: 125–41.

Cowan, Nelson. 2000. "The Magical Number 4 in Short-Term Memory: A Reconsideration of Mental Storage Capacity." *Behavioral and Brain Sciences* 24(1): 87–114; discussion 114–85.

Doeller, Christian F., Barry Caswell, and Neil Burgess. 2010. "Evidence for Grid Cells in a Human Memory Network." *Nature* 463(7281): 657–61.

Emerick, Geoff. 2006. Letter to *Daytrippin'* in response to Ken Scott's 3 March 2006 letter (8 March). daytrippin.com/letters.htm (accessed November 2013).

Emerick, Geoff, and Howard Massey. 2006. *Here, There, and Everywhere: My Life Recording the Music of the Beatles*. New York: Gotham Books.

Halbwachs, Maurice. 1925. *Les cadres sociaux de la mémoire*. Paris: Presses universitaires de France.

———. 1939. "La mémoire collective chez les musiciens." *Revue philosophique* (March–April): 136–65.

———. 1980[1950]. *La mémoire collective/The Collective* Memory. Translated by Francis J. Ditter Jr. and Vida Yazdi Ditter. New York: Harper and Row.

Holtorf, Cornelius J. 1999. *Monumental Past: An Hypermedia Exploration of Megaliths.* Toronto: CITD Press. tspace.library.utoronto.ca/citd/holtorf/ (accessed November 2013).

Olick, Jeffrey K. 2007. "Collective Memory." In *International Encyclopedia of the Social Sciences*, second edition, edited by William A. Darity, 7–8. New York: Macmillan Reference.

Safer, Morley. 2013. "Capturing History." *60 Minutes*. CBS television, 10 November. www.cbsnews.com/news/capturing-history/ (accessed November 2013).

Scott, Ken. 2006a. Letter to *Daytrippin'* (regarding the publication of Geoff Emerick's *Here, There, and Everywhere: My Life Recording the Beatles*) (3 March). Daytrippin.com/letters.htm (accessed November 2013).

———. 2006b. Letter to *Daytrippin'* (response to Geoff Emerick's 8 March letter) (12 March). Daytrippin.com/letters.htm (accessed November 2013).

Scott, Ken, and Bobby Owsinski. 2007. *Abbey Road to Ziggy Stardust: Off the Record with the Beatles, Bowie, Elton, and So Much More*. Los Angeles: Alfred Music Publishing.

Shelemay, Kay Kaufman. 2006. "Music, Memory, and History." *Ethnomusicology Forum* 15(1): 17–37.

Strachan, Robert. 2008. "'Where Do I Begin the Story': Collective Memory, Biographical Authority and the Rock Biography." *Popular Music History* 3(1): 65–80.

Stuckey, Fred. 2010. "GP Flashback: Eric Clapton, June 1970." *Guitar Player* (14 September). www.guitarplayer.com/article/GP-Flashback-Eric-Clapton-June-1970/1167 (accessed November 2013; originally published June 1970).

Tessler, Holly. 2010. "The Role and Significance of Storytelling in the Creation of the 'Post-Sixties' Beatles, 1970–1980." *Popular Music History* 5(2): 169–89.

CHAPTER TWENTY-THREE

~

Commercial 78s

A Rediscovered Resource for Ethnomusicology

Philip Yampolsky

Nothing is lost so irrevocably as the sound of a song.

—Frances Densmore (1945:639)

For almost forty years, Bruno Nettl has been sending out bulletins on the state of ethnomusicology and its current concerns and emphases (cf. Nettl 1975). In this spirit, and to contribute one more facet to his eyewitness history of the development of the field, I offer here a report on a trend that began slowly in the late 1970s but has gathered speed and amplitude in recent decades: the use of commercial recordings as sources for ethnomusicological study.

Resisting 78s

In a polemical article, Ronda Sewald argued that mid-twentieth-century ethnomusicology's mistrust of comparative musicology led influential scholars to deny the value of sound recordings in general (Sewald 2005). In particular, she refers to Alan Merriam's well-known criticism of "armchair analysis . . . by the laboratory technician of materials collected by others in the field" (Merriam 1964:39). The turn from "musical product" to "musical behavior," spearheaded by Merriam, further devalued the use of recordings and implicitly disparaged any musical analysis, even of one's own recordings.[1] Since that time, however, the emergence of magnetic tape recording as a field technology and LPs, CDs, and DVDs as publishing media has stimulated a profusion of published field recordings with scholarly annotation, sometimes supplemented by additional online materials, and the wave of interest in repatriation of archive recordings has brought new legitimacy and acclaim to archives for their public service. Even if some ethnomusicologists eschew archival recordings, other people—culture bearers eager to know the way things were done in the past, people longing to hear the voices of their parents and grandparents—seek them out.

While the regard for field recordings seems higher today than in the second half of the twentieth century, there is much less scholarly certainty about the value of commercial recordings, especially the cylinders and gramophone records (78s) produced for sale from the 1890s until World War II (and, in some markets, even into the 1960s)—even though, on the surface, this vast body of recorded material would seem perfect for ethnomusicologists. Rapidly expanding from its initial base in the United States and Western Europe, the recording industry sent "engineers" scurrying around the globe to record local music and build company catalogs. By 1906, the German firm Beka Record advertised "the largest and most comprehensive repertoire which has ever been compiled," itemizing it by language: "German, English, French, Italian, Portuguese, Russian, Austrian, Hungarian, Danish, Swiss, Dutch, Spanish, Chinese (Swatow, Guakau, Pekinese, Shansinese, Kiangnanese, Cantonese), Arabian, Turkish, Hindustanee (Urdu, Marathi, Gujarathi, Hindi, Tarsi, Tamil), Malayian." Burmese and Japanese were added in 1907. In 1913 another German firm, Lyrophon, advertised recordings in all of Beka's European languages, plus Belgian, Polish, Romanian, Bulgarian, Serbian, Greek, Swedish, Bohemian, Croatian, and Slovenian; and, outside of Europe, it listed (in addition to eight languages from Beka's list) Tatar, Creole, Tunisian, Moroccan, Bengali, Singhalese, Javanese, Sundanese, Siamese, and Annamese. And that is only two labels. Other companies recorded not only in Europe, Asia, North Africa, and the Middle East, but also in Central and South America, the Caribbean, Central Asia, and the Caucasus.[2]

The companies' motives were neither ethnographic nor documentarian: they were looking for music that would sell (and would synergistically stimulate the sales of gramophones and phonographs). Often they had no idea what that music would be, so they recorded whatever they could find, or whatever they thought might appeal to someone. They were interested, for the most part, in *local* markets—that is, they recorded Georgian choruses for consumers in the Caucasus and Peking opera for consumers in China and the Chinese diaspora, not for an exoticist market in Western Europe or the United States. Nevertheless, such records *were* of interest to the musically adventurous outside the local markets. The German music critic and composer Max Chop wrote reviews of some of the earliest Beka records from Asia in the *Phonographische Zeitschrift*, treating them as real music, not weird racket.[3] And over time the news of these localized musics filtered out. Colin McPhee traveled to Bali because he heard in New York the Balinese recordings Beka and Odeon had made in 1928 (Herbst 2012:95). Erich M. von Hornbostel—complaining that "records taken in the various countries of the Orient are not marketed in Europe and it is almost impossible to obtain anything but indiscriminate selections and that by the merest chance" (1934:1)—compiled a group of Odeon and Parlophone recordings from Japan, China, Java, Bali, Siam, India, Iran, Egypt, and Tunisia into a twelve-record set released in Germany in 1931 as *Musik des Orients* and later in England as *Music of the Orient* (1934).

Pekka Gronow has hazarded an estimate of five hundred thousand to one million unique commercial recordings (that is, "sides"—usually two per disc—or cylinders, not counting reissues, and disregarding production quantities per item) produced for all markets before World War II (Pekka Gronow, personal communication, 12 October 2013). Predating the era when every researcher could bring a tape recorder into the field and focusing often on popular music that most of them chose to ignore in favor of the traditional, the classical, and the "authentic," the records are, for many genres of prewar music, just about all we have.

If we have them. Surprisingly few archives collected 78s of any sort of music outside the Western mainstream.[4] The reason may in part go back to Merriam: his warnings against working with other people's recordings would apply all the more to working with commercial recordings made by company engineers. It must also lie partly in the fact that the mission of most archives was to house scholarly field recordings, and *their* mission was primarily to document endangered music. Both researchers and archives rejected the commercial genres, regarding them as debased, ephemeral, and destructive—as, in fact, the source of the danger.

This view was inaccurate even at the time. Much of the commercial recording in Asian, North African, and Middle Eastern markets was "classical," and in some others it was what could be called "traditional." Hornbostel's *Orient* collection, compiled entirely from commercial recordings, was devoted to "the principal musical products of all high Oriental Cultures" (1934:1). And today the issue is moot: ethnomusicology has dramatically shifted its focus and is now vitally interested in that ephemeral phenomenon popular music. But it's too late to recoup: the time for building collections of 78s has passed.

Fifty years ago, Pekka Gronow published an article urging scholars to pay more attention to commercial recordings (Gronow 1963). His discussion focused mainly on jazz records, but jazz and blues were actually areas where the study of 78s was already well established, while recognition of 78s as a resource for the study of music outside the Western mainstream (and also for the historical study of performance practice in European art music since the 1890s) came quite a bit later. Gronow followed, in the 1970s and 1980s, with pioneering articles on "ethnic records" in the Soviet Union, Scandinavia, the United States, and Asia. These were all essentially discographical or "paradiscographical" (indicating the range of material a discography would need to cover, or providing data on recording companies and their practices and procedures). They did not seem to elicit much reaction in ethnomusicology at the time.

Some ethnomusicologists did recognize early on the usefulness of commercial 78s, citing them as illustrative examples in their writings and using them for demonstration in their classes and lectures.[5] As far as I know, the first substantial studies exploring the content of 78s outside the mainstream did not appear until the late 1970s. Perhaps the first of these, and certainly one of the most thorough, was the 1977 dissertation by Bruno Nettl's student A. J. Racy on the impact of commercial recording on music in Egypt up to 1932; one chapter of this was devoted to changes in the *qaṣīdah* genre as revealed in the 78s.

Working with 78s: The Difficulties

The factor that greatly complicates the use of commercial 78s, and probably the one that has made them suspect as a source, is precisely that they are commercial. The companies produced what would sell, or what they thought would sell. Or, in the early period of the industry's exploration of the world, what they *hoped* would sell. The engineers of the Gramophone Company, Beka, Odeon, Pathé, and others, in their expeditions eastward, seem to have recorded almost anything, to see if it would fly. This was also the case in the mid-1920s in the United States, when recording scouts took chances on rural white and African American music in the South, against the assumptions of the home office. In later years, when the companies had refined their formulae, they became less daring and recorded only sure-fire genres.

In order to understand what *was* recorded, we have to understand what was *not*. Elijah Wald (2004) has convincingly shown that rural musicians in the South, both black and white, had repertories encompassing many kinds of popular music, but the record companies would not record them singing show tunes or Tin Pan Alley hits. Similarly, in Batavia (now Jakarta), the capital city of the Dutch East Indies, there was a lively jazz scene featuring mestizo Dutch-Indonesian musicians playing the dance tunes popular in Europe and the United States, but only one such disc by a Batavia jazz band was ever issued. Why would people buy local records when they could as easily buy recordings of Ellington or Goodman? In Turkey, labels carved out niches for themselves in recording *gazel*: HMV chose modernist performers, while Columbia recorded traditionalists, and thus a focus on one label's production skews one's understanding of the genre (O'Connell 2003:404–5). Again in the Dutch East Indies, record companies until the mid-1930s recorded only on Java and Bali, two out of the colony's six thousand inhabited islands; in the last years before the war they expanded to Sumatra. Moreover, they recorded primarily urban musicians, even though many of those performers had undoubtedly grown up in villages hearing village music. Thus, in a sense, *what was recorded was the political, social, and symbolic opposite of what was not recorded*, and this realization must inform our understanding not only of the "modern" tangos, rumbas, and *kroncong* (musically Western but sung in the colonial lingua franca), but also of the songs on Muslim themes and of the "traditional" genres in fully Indonesian idioms (Central Javanese and Balinese gamelan music; West Sumatran music for voice and *saluang* flute). In short, commercial recordings must be interpreted. It is crucial to know the full range of musical possibilities in a given locale, so as to know the context for what was recorded. And it is important also to know the full range of what actually was recorded. Myths and simplifications abound: kroncong is the music of nostalgia and sensual longing; *rebetika* is the music of dope fiends; blues is the music of black despair. But a look at the scope of these genres on records shows that there is more flirtation, social commentary, and conservative moralizing than nostalgia in kroncong; that "of the approximately 5,000 'rebetiko' recordings made during the 78 rpm era, only about 300 referred to drugs" (Klein 2012); and that many prewar records marketed as blues, or whose performers were marketed as blues singers, were dance tunes or "hokum" songs, and countless blues verses were devoted to double-entendre jokes and assertions of pride and confidence.

Working with 78s: The Payoff

Despite all the difficulties they pose, the 78s are a gold mine. They provide evidence of older styles, genres, and repertory that may have died out or been subsequently modified to suit more recent tastes (e.g., for smooth vocal quality, electric instruments, harmony, thematically unified lyrics). They present song texts from fifty to a hundred years ago and document vanished experiments.[6] While the time limitations of 78s mean that one cannot in most cases use them as evidence of the design or pace of a live performance, they have what Frances Densmore recognized was the unique capability to capture the timbre of voices and instruments, the technique of playing, the manner of singing, "the sound of a song" (1945).

Bruno Nettl observes that musical change has emerged since 1980 as a central topic in ethnomusicology (2005:284). He remarks, furthermore, that around 1990 popular music "came to occupy a central place in the development of ethnomusicological theory" (Nettl 2005:188). The 78s serve both of these now-central concerns: they enable ethnomusicologists to bring the whole first half of the twentieth century into the record of change, and much of what they document are genres of popular music. Moreover, they not only document change that occurred (and not only in popular music), they were a crucial *vehicle* of that change, teaching listeners new repertory and new techniques. Adrian McNeil, writing of *sarod* players in India, notes that since "the same performance could be heard over and over again, . . . the possibility was created for music to be recast as a text, which could be heard and studied repeatedly" (2004). Muddy Waters learned to play his first blues from a Leroy Carr record (Wald 2004:58). Roald Maliangkay quotes a scene from a memoir of Seoul in the 1930s: "The sound of a pop song poured from the music store's speakers. The lyrics had been attached to the huge shop window in large fonts. Students with lunchboxes under their arms were standing still learning the song. Some also wrote down the lyrics. . . . As they got more into a song, they would rock their bodies, tap the beat with one foot and make a rattling sound by shaking the small bowls inside their empty lunchbox" (2007:59).

The use of commercial recordings, including 78s, is now far more common in ethnomusicology than it was in the middle of the last century. What has brought about this change is the admission of popular music, along with the related fields of jazz and blues, into the discipline's field of study. The development and dissemination of popular music is so closely linked to recordings—their production, sale, promotion, and broadcasting—that the study of them is indispensable. Once popular music was admitted, its domain extended ever backward in time, encompassing not only current and recent popular musics but also their distant predecessors. Thus the study of popular music took on a historical dimension that had previously been questionable in ethnomusicology. And, finally, the historical perspective legitimized the study of *any* kind of mediated music, popular or not, in any period back to the introduction of recorded media.

Research on Commercial 78s

In the remaining pages I sketch some of the work that has been done since the 1970s on commercial 78s outside the Western mainstream. My overview is not comprehensive; it mentions only a few titles as illustrative of various lines of research.[7]

In the study of the pre–World War II commercial 78s, there are, I propose, four broad categories of work. One is discography, the nuts-and-bolts, recording-dates-and-matrix-numbers work without which research on 78s is severely limited. There are, of course, many types of discography: of genres, artists, labels, instruments, composers. The most comprehensive is the geographically defined, multi-label discography of an entire period, covering all genres or a large range of related genres (e.g., "traditional music"). Among the most impressive of this type are: Richard Spottswood's monumental discography of "ethnic recordings in the United States" (1990); Cristóbal Díaz Ayala's discographies of Cuban and Puerto Rican 78s (1994, 2009); Bill Dean-Myatt on Scotland (2013); Dionysis Maniatis on Greece (2006); the Academy of Korean Studies on Korea (Han'guk 1998); and Katarzyna Janczewska-Sołomko's seven volumes on Poland (2002, 2013). A variant form of these encyclopedic discographies tries to encompass all the records worldwide on a single multinational label—Alan Kelly's ongoing work on Gramophone Company catalogs and matrix series around the world is an example, as is the "Lindström Project," the discography of all recordings on the Lindström labels, now in progress under the auspices of the Gesellschaft für Historische Tonträger in Vienna.

A subcategory of discography includes works giving information about the *production* of the records: histories of record companies and labels, explanations of the workings of the industry, summaries of label activity around the world. A few outstanding examples: Michael Kinnear's encyclopedia of the record labels of India (2003); studies of the gramophone industry in Turkey (Ünlü 2004), Brazil (Franceschi 2002), and China (Steen 2006); Pekka Gronow's raft of articles, too numerous to cite; the many detailed articles published in the volumes of *The Lindström Project* (Gronow and Hofer 2009–); and Hugo Strötbaum's website, www.recordingpioneers.com, which identifies hundreds of recording engineers from the gramophone era and gives biographical and professional information about them and their recording itineraries. Discographies and recording-industry histories provide information crucial to the development initiated by Racy's 1977 dissertation: the careful examination of a body of commercial recordings in order to describe and analyze them and, when appropriate, trace changes perceptible in them—changes in a genre, performance style (of an artist or of the genre as a whole), and repertory. I can mention only some of these studies. They did not emerge immediately after Racy's dissertation but began to appear in force in the 1990s, with full-length books on *jùjú* (Waterman 1990), *isicathamiya* and other South African genres (Erlmann 1991, 1996), Umm Kulthūm (Danielson 1997), and Cuba (Moore 1997), and articles on *qawwali* (Qureshi 1999), *bangsawan* and popular music in Malaysia (Tan 1996/1997, 2013), sarod players (McNeil 2004), Korea (Maliangkay 2007), Bosnia-Herzegovina (Pennanen 2008), and kroncong (Yampolsky 2010). These studies devote attention to illuminating the character or tracing the development of a genre or musical sphere through relevant commercial recordings.

Another group of studies does not engage directly with the content of the 78s but instead looks at recording as a cultural phenomenon, highlighting such topics as the changing position of female performers, the implementation of various notions of modernity, and the growth and transformation of audiences (Farrell 1997, Jones 2001, Hughes 2002, Weidman 2006, Neuman 2009). All of these studies have the merit of bringing into the ethnomusicological purview a treasure trove of material. They are, necessarily, studies for specialists. There is also new work that is accessible to a broader, nonspecialist audience. This is the flood of reissues of 78s on compact discs (or, earlier, on LPs) that bring the recordings themselves back into circulation. For example, some sixty CDs of rebetika 78s have been published on British, French, German, and American labels, and roughly the same number again on Greek labels. There are at least sixty CDs of pre–World War II tango, mostly published in Latin America; at least thirty CDs of Irish 78s; another thirty of 78s from the Balkans. There are also recordings of flamenco, fado, mariachi, klezmer, Turkish, Chinese, Korean, Japanese, Maltese, Swedish fiddling, and on and on.

Some of these publications are audio monographs, substantially annotated and carefully structured in order to show the scope or historical development of a single genre or category, sampling its principal artists and substyles. A characteristic of the best of these is that the relevance of each track to the overall design is evident in the album notes. Excellent examples of the form are *Jùjú Roots* (Waterman) and *Mbube Roots* (Erlmann); the *Antología del tango rioplatense*; the book-and-CD packages on rebetika and Greek instrumental music (*Mortika* and *Greek Rhapsody*, respectively, both by Tony Klein); *Blowers from the Balkans* (Pennanen); *Song of the Crooked Dance* (Lauren Brody); and the East African collection *Something Is Wrong* (annotated by Peter Cooke).

Another type of narrowly focused reissue presents a delimited corpus: the Gramophone Company's 1903 visit to Japan (*1903 First Recordings*); a 1909 recording expedition to the Caucasus and Central Asia (*Before the Revolution*, edited by Will Prentice); the 1928 Balinese recordings by Odeon and Beka (*Bali 1928*, edited by Edward Herbst); or surveys of the recordings of a single featured artist or performing group.

Still others are broad-brush anthologies, presenting large categories or geographical areas. The broadest, such as the *Secret Museum of Mankind* series on Yazoo or Dust-to-Digital's *Victrola Favorites*, have no focus at all and are simply grab bags where the records' unfamiliarity or antiquity, or the compiler's personal taste, is the only rationale for their inclusion.[8] These random collections, with little or no annotation, are of scant scholarly value, although the selections may be of interest to listeners able to contextualize them. More useful, though still underannotated (probably at the insistence of the publishers), are anthologies with a broad but defined topic, such as Charles Howard's eight boxed sets of rebetika reissues on JSP Records (four CDs each) or JSP's other multiple-CD sets of music from Bulgaria (*Outsinging the Nightingale*, edited by Lauren Brody) and ethnic groups in the United States.

Since the usefulness of all reissues depends in large part on the depth of annotation that accompanies them, these broad-focus anthologies are of limited value to ethnomusicologists. They do, however, serve to immerse listeners in historical sound-worlds. While ethnomusicologists may wish for more systematic reissues and should themselves provide critical reviews to guide listeners through the welter of reissues from a given region, it is unequivocally a benefit to have returned to us the evanescent sounds that Frances Densmore feared would be so irrevocably lost.

Notes

1. Sewald points out that some partisans out-Merriamed Merriam, who devoted nearly half of *Ethnomusicology of the Flathead Indians* to transcription and analysis and included recordings by another researcher in the corpus he analyzed.

2. Beka advertisements in *The Talking Machine World*, 15 November 1906, and *Die Sprechmaschine*, 16 February 1907; Lyrophon advertisement in *Phonographische Zeitschrift*, 19 July 1913. By 1930 the only main areas of the world not yet mined by the recording companies were sub-Saharan Africa and Oceania (aside from Hawai'i).

3. Articles by Max Chop in *Phonographische Zeitschrift* 7(25) and 7(26), 1906; 9(3) and 9(4), 1908; 10(26), 1909.

4. Most collections today are in private hands. But public and private collections together probably hold only a small portion of what was published. For

Indonesia, Malaysia, and Singapore, for example, I estimate that no more than 30 percent of all the titles recorded before World War II are preserved in collections, public or private.

5. Robert Garfias tells an anecdote from Jaap Kunst's lecture tour to the United States in the early 1950s. At that time an undergraduate at San Francisco State University, Garfias went to all of Kunst's lectures in the Bay Area. At one point he managed to ask Kunst in private whether a certain Javanese modulation Kunst had described in theoretical terms was something listeners would actually notice. Kunst said yes, without elaborating, but in his next lecture he put on the turntable a 78 of the gamelan piece "Ladrang Babar Layar" (it would have been Beka B 15007-II), and as it played he walked up the aisle to where Garfias was sitting at the end of a row near the back. He timed it so he reached Garfias just at the dramatic gong on pitch 4, when the music does indeed seem to burst into new tonal territory. Looking Garfias straight in the eye, Kunst pointed down with his finger, as though striking an instrument, and said "Here!" (Robert Garfias, personal communication, 19 December 2013).

Although he made use of 78s, Kunst was generally disparaging of them: the record companies, he wrote in 1950, "have not rendered so much service to ethnomusicology as could be expected. . . . [They] usually pander completely to the—often regrettable—taste of the larger public and fight shy of the rare musical expression-forms which are important by virtue of their being ancient, but (possibly for that very reason) no longer generally current, let alone popular" (1950:34–35).

6. These include, for example, in Indonesia, the arrangements of Javanese gamelan music for an ensemble of Sundanese zithers (Columbia GJ 214-218), or pieces from the Sundanese *tembang* and *degung* repertories for what is essentially a kroncong orchestra (Tio Tek Hong 529-533).

7. Due to space limitations, I omit from the discussion the highly developed literature on English-language "non-mainstream" 78s in the United States: the essential genre discographies of Dixon, Godrich, and Rye (blues and gospel) and Tony Russell (country); the comprehensive label discographies of John Bolig (Victor) and Tim Brooks and Brian Rust (Columbia); and the historical studies of recording and recorded genres by Tim Brooks, Allan Sutton, Paul Oliver, Jeff Todd Titon, and many others.

8. The first volume of the *Secret Museum* series (Yazoo 7004) contains "ethnic music classics, 1925–1948" from Nigeria, Sardinia, Russia, Ceylon, Rajasthan, Cuba, Romania, Vietnam, Macedonia, Society Islands, Morocco, South Africa, Japan, India, the Basques, Sweden, Yiddish-speakers, Poland, Jamaica, Abyssinia, Andalusia, the Philippines, and Fiji.

References

Danielson, Virginia. 1997. *The Voice of Egypt: Umm Kulthūm, Arabic Song, and Egyptian Society in the Twentieth Century*. Chicago: University of Chicago Press.

Dean-Myatt, Bill. 2013. *A Scottish Vernacular Discography, 1888–1960*. Hailsham: City of London Phonograph & Gramophone Society Ltd. "Preview copy" posted on www.nls.uk/catalogues/scottish-discography.

Densmore, Frances. 1945. "The Importance of Recordings of Indian Songs." *American Anthropologist* 47 n.s. (4): 637–39.

Díaz Ayala, Cristóbal. 1994. *Cuba canta y baila: Discografía de la música cubana, 1898–1925*. San Juan, Puerto Rico: Fundación Musicalia.

———. 2009. *San Juan–New York: Discografía de la música puertorriqueña, 1900–1942*. Río Piedras, Puerto Rico: Publicaciones Gaviota.

Erlmann, Veit. 1991. *African Stars: Studies in Black South African Performance*. Chicago: University of Chicago Press.

———. 1996. *Nightsong: Performance, Power, and Practice in South Africa*. Chicago: University of Chicago Press.

Farrell, Gerry. 1997. *Indian Music and the West*. Oxford: Clarendon Press.

Franceschi, Humberto M. 2002. *A Casa Edison e seu tempo*. Rio de Janeiro: Petrobras/Sarapuí/Biscoito Fino.

Gronow, Pekka. 1963. "Phonograph Records as a Source for Musicological Research." *Ethnomusicology* 7(3): 225–28.

Gronow, Pekka, and Christiane Hofer, eds. 2009– . *The Lindström Project: Contributions to the History of the Record Industry*. 4 volumes. Vienna: Gesellschaft für Historische Tonträger.

Han'guk Chŏngsin Munhwa Yŏn'guwŏn P'yŏn [Academy of Korean Studies], ed. 1998. *Han'guk yusŏnggi ŭmban ch'ongmongnok* [A Comprehensive Discography of Korean Gramophone Records]. Seoul: Minsogwŏn.

Herbst, Edward. 2012. "Gamelan Gong Kebyar: Music from Belaluan, Pangkung, Busungbiu: Lindström in Bali 1928." In *The Lindström Project: Contributions to the History of the Record Industry, Volume 4*, edited by Pekka Gronow and Christiane Hofer, 93–122. Vienna: Gesellschaft für Historische Tonträger.

Hornbostel, Erich M. von. 1934. *Music of the Orient*. 12 78-rpm discs plus booklet. Hayes, Middlesex, England: Parlophone Company. (German edition 1931.)

Hughes, Stephen P. 2002. "The 'Music Boom' in Tamil South India: Gramophone, Radio and the Making of Mass Culture." *Historical Journal of Film, Radio and Television* 22(4): 445–73.

Janczewska-Sołomko, Katarzyna. 2002. *Dyskopedia Polonikówdo roku 1918*. 3 volumes. Warsaw: Biblioteka Narodowa.

———. 2013. *Dyskopedia Poloników 1919–1939*. 4 volumes. Warsaw: Biblioteka Narodowa.

Jones, Andrew F. 2001. *Yellow Music: Media Culture and Colonial Modernity in the Chinese Jazz Age*. Durham, NC: Duke University Press.

Kinnear, Michael. 2003. *The 78-r.p.m. Record Labels of India*. Heidelberg, Australia: author.

Klein, Tony. 2012. "Review of *Bed of Pain*." www.mustrad.org.uk/reviews/bed_pain.htm.

Kunst, Jaap. 1950. *Musicologica: A Study of the Nature of Ethno-Musicology, Its Problems, Methods and Representative Personalities*. Amsterdam: Indisch Instituut.

Maliangkay, Roald. 2007. "Their Masters' Voice: Korean Traditional Music Sps (Standard Play Records) under Japanese Colonial Rule." *World of Music* 49(3): 53–74.

Maniatis, Dionysis Dimitris. 2006. *I ek peráton diskografia grammofónou: 'Erga laïkón mas kallitechnón* [The complete gramophone discography: Works of our popular artists]. Athens: Mitropolis AE for Upourgeía Politismoú.

McNeil, Adrian. 2004. "Making Modernity Audible: *Sarodiyas* and the Early Recording Industry." *South Asia: Journal of South Asian Studies* 27 n.s. (3): 315–37.

Merriam, Alan P. 1964. *The Anthropology of Music*. Evanston, IL: Northwestern University Press.

———. 1967. *Ethnomusicology of the Flathead Indians*. Viking Fund Publications in Ethnomusicology, Number 44. Chicago: Aldine Publishing Company.

Moore, Robin D. 1997. *Nationalizing Blackness: Afrocubanismo and Artistic Revolution in Havana, 1920–1940*. Pittsburgh: University of Pittsburgh Press.

Nettl, Bruno. 1975. "The State of Research in Ethnomusicology, and Recent Developments." *Current Musicology* 20: 67–78.

———. 2005. *The Study of Ethnomusicology: Thirty-One Issues and Concepts*, second edition. Urbana: University of Illinois Press.

Neuman, Dard. 2009. "The Production of Aura in the Gramophone Age of the 'Live' Performance." *Asian Music* 40(2): 100–23.

O'Connell, John Morgan. 2003. "Song Cycle: The Life and Death of the Turkish Gazel: A Review Essay." *Ethnomusicology* 47(3): 399–414.

Pennanen, Risto Pekka. 2008. "Immortalised on Wax: Professional Folk Musicians and Their Gramophone Recordings Made in Sarajevo, 1907 and 1908." www.phonomuseum.at/includes/content/lindstroem/pennanen_immortalised.pdf.

Qureshi, Regula Burckhardt. 1999. "His Master's Voice? Exploring Qawwali and 'Gramophone Culture' in South Asia." *Popular Music* 18(1): 63–98.

Racy, Ali Jihad. 1977. "Musical Change and Commercial Recording in Egypt, 1904–1932." Ph.D. dissertation, University of Illinois at Urbana-Champaign.

Sewald, Ronda. 2005. "Sound Recordings and Ethnomusicology: Theoretical Barriers to the Use of Archival Collections." *ReSound: A Quarterly of the Archives of Traditional Music* 24(3/4): 1–10.

Spottswood, Richard K. 1990. *Ethnic Music on Records: A Discography of Ethnic Recordings Produced in the United States, 1893 to 1942*. 7 volumes. Urbana: University of Illinois Press.

Steen, Andreas. 2006. *Zwischen Unterhaltung und Revolution: Grammophone, Schallplatten und die Anfänge der Musikindustrie in Shanghai, 1878–1937*. Wiesbaden: Harrassowitz.

Tan Sooi Beng. 1996/1997. "The 78 rpm Record Industry in Malaya Prior to World War II." *Asian Music* 28(1): 1–41.

———. 2013. "Negotiating 'His Master's Voice': Gramophone Music and Cosmopolitan Modernity in British Malaya in the 1930s and early 1940s." *Bijdragen Tot de Taal-, Land- en Volkenkunde* 169(4): 457–94.

Ünlü, Cemal. 2004. *Git zaman gel zaman: Fonograf-gramofon-taş plak*. Istanbul: Pan Yayıncılık.

Wald, Elijah. 2004. *Escaping the Delta: Robert Johnson and the Invention of the Blues*. New York: HarperCollins Publishers.

Waterman, Christopher. 1990. *Jùjú: A Social History and Ethnography of an African Popular Music*. Chicago: University of Chicago Press.

Weidman, Amanda J. 2006. *Singing the Classical, Voicing the Modern: The Postcolonial Politics of Music in South India*. Durham, NC: Duke University Press.

Yampolsky, Philip. 2010. "*Kroncong* Revisited: New Evidence from Old Sources." *Archipel* 79: 7–56.

Reissue CDs

1903 Japanese First Recordings by Frederick Gaisberg. Toshiba-EMI TOCF 59051 [Tokyo]. 2000.

Antología del tango rioplatense, desde sus comienzos hasta 1920. 2 CDs. Instituto Nacional de Musicología Carlos Vega [Buenos Aires]. 2002.

Bali 1928, Volume 1: Gamelan Gong Kebyar. World Arbiter 2011. 2009.

Before the Revolution: A 1909 Recording Expedition in the Caucasus & Central Asia by the Gramophone Company. Topic TSCD 921. 2002.

Blowers from the Balkans: Classic Historic Recordings of Wind Instruments. Topic TSCD 928. 2005.

Cantors, Klezmorim, and Crooners, 1905–1953: Classic Yiddish 78s from the Mayrent Collection. 3 CDs and book. JSP 5201. 2009.

Greek Rhapsody: Instrumental Music from Greece, 1905–1956. 2 CDs and book. Dust-to-Digital 27. 2013.

Jùjú Roots, 1930s–1950s. Rounder CD 5017. 1993 [LP 1985].

Mbube Roots: Zulu Choral Music from South Africa, 1930s–1960s. Rounder CD 5025. 1988.

Mortika: Rare Vintage Recordings from a Greek Underworld. Arko CD 008 [Uppsala]. 2006.

Outsinging the Nightingale: Lost Treasures of Bulgarian Music. 4 CDs. JSP 77134. 2010.

Rembetika: Baglamas, Bouzoukis and Bravado. 4 CDs. JSP 7776. 2006. [The first of eight rembetika collections on JSP.]

Something Is Wrong: Vintage Recordings from East Africa. Honest Jon's HJRCD 50. 2010.

Songs of the Crooked Dance: Early Bulgarian Traditional Music 1927-42. Yazoo 7016. 1998.

PART V

ISSUES AND CONCEPTS

CHAPTER TWENTY-FOUR

~

One Hundred Years of Indian Folk Music

The Evolution of a Concept

Stefan Fiol

Bruno Nettl is the reason I became an ethnomusicologist. When I was six years old, my father, Steve, married Bruno's daughter Rebecca, and Bruno and Wanda quickly became my closest set of grandparents (my lineal sets were living in Paraguay and India at the time). Although I could barely pronounce the word "ethnomusicology," I saw Bruno traveling the globe and delivering lectures, and I decided that any field of study that combined my two great loves of travel and music would be worth pursuing. I am forever grateful to Bruno for opening this path for me and for patiently letting me find my own way, offering sage guidance whenever I needed it. By way of homage to Bruno, whose interests have long included folk music, the music of India, and historical and comparative topics, this article offers a broad diachronic survey of the folk concept in India over the past century, highlighting the shifts in the meaning and treatment of folk in musical and social discourse.

On one of his fieldwork expeditions just over a century ago, the English ethnologist Arthur H. Fox-Strangways, one of the pioneers of ethnomusicological fieldwork and ethnography, transcribed and recorded several songs performed by a group of "cheerful and honest" Garhwali migrants from Mussoorie who had arrived in Allahabad for training as rickshaw drivers (1914:51–72). When one of them indicated that he had performed a song in *Raga Behag*, Fox-Strangways was surprised: "That its singer knew so much about it as that, not to mention its carefully balanced sections (the same as in our National Anthem), removes it from the category of folk-song proper" (Fox-Strangways 1914:56). For Fox-Strangways, one may infer that the category folk song presupposes a *lack* of refinement and symmetry, and that the category of folk performer presupposes a lack of status and theoretical knowledge about the music.

The tendency to characterize folk music in negative terms, as an indication of low musical development, or as the antithesis of art music or popular music, has a long history in Indian music scholarship that continues to the present (see Paige 2009; Allen 1998). Ethnomusicologists, particularly those trained in North America, have developed a healthy skepticism of the term "folk" following a period of poststructural critique and reflexivity in the social sciences in the 1970s and 1980s (e.g., Keil 1978); nonetheless, most ethnomusicologists researching Indian music continue to use the term "folk" as a general label to identify musicians and musical styles, either because they demonstrate some combination of qualities normally identified with the term "folk" (Nettl 1976; Bohlman 1988) or simply because they are using local terminology.

Below I highlight three periods in which there has been a shift in the meaning and treatment of folk in musical and social discourse.[1] In the late nineteenth and early twentieth centuries, colonial administrators and academics studied folklore as a means of positioning rural India and hereditary, low-caste communities as primitive subjects within an evolutionary paradigm. In the mid-twentieth century, urban Indian elites positively resignified folk forms in the context of regionalist and nationalist goals, and in many cases appropriated these forms from rural, hereditary musicians with whom they had been associated previously. Finally, in the context of late twentieth- and early twenty-first-century neo-liberalism, the musical and social discourses of folk have become more diffused than ever, as hereditary musicians and urban cosmopolitans draw upon a range of decontextualized folk elements to serve various economic and political ends.

Collecting Folklore in Colonial India

The origins of the folk concept in India remain unclear. Scholars have been divided on the issue of whether the contemporary term *lok* (commonly understood to be synonymous with folk) carries precolonial meanings or whether it was essentially adapted to fit corresponding European concepts. The fact that there is considerable semantic overlap between the German *Volk*, the English *folk*, and the ancient Sanskrit *lok-a*—all of these terms can signify common people, local, provincial, or worldly, among other meanings—suggests at least the possibility of a shared Indo-European etymology, with the Sanskrit term likely predating the emergence of European cognates

(Chalmers 2002; Narayan 1993). Yet the emergence of the English word "folk" in India can be dated only to the late nineteenth century, when European social elites deployed the concepts of folk music and folk culture as part of a broader worldview rooted in cultural nationalism and colonial dominance. Frank Korom, for example, writes that the concept of folk was a "metaphorical invention" born out of the colonial encounter between British and Bengali social elites, and that each group subsequently channeled this concept into self-serving colonialist and nationalist ambitions, respectively (2006:39).

Only in the last decades of the nineteenth century, more than a century after J. G. Herder coined the term *Volkslied* in Germany, did the study of folk become a formalized discipline in South Asia. Three groups of people were largely responsible for the emergence of folklore studies: European women and missionaries, British military and administrative officers writing as "scientific scholars," and Indian social elites working in the colonial civil service. While individuals in each of these three groups obviously differed in terms of their relative access and prestige, there was interaction and a shared sense of purpose between them; moreover, all of them communicated almost exclusively in the English language and wrote for an educated readership (Naithani 2006:23).

The study of folklore in late colonial India consisted of collecting vast amounts of data and separating it into discrete genres such as superstitions, myths, rituals, songs, ballads, fables, proverbs, and stories. Scholars rarely described the sonic characteristics of the songs and ballads that they collected in any detail, but the texts were translated and scrutinized to reveal universally shared patterns of thought and behavior among primitive societies past and present. "It is not easy to distinguish between mythology and folklore," noted the educator and folklorist E. S. Oakley, "for both represent an early stage of consciousness when man's fancy worked with freedom and was employed to give an explanation of all things. We are apt to think too seriously of the so-called religious ideas of non-christian peoples. They are largely relics of man's early unrestrained fancy, consecrated, to some extent, in later times, by custom and priestly adoption; but, originally on the same level as our nursery tales. To the early intelligence of our remote ancestors everything was alive" (1990[1905]:174–75).

Although framed in terms of universal and monogenist evolutionary questions, late colonial writings often focused on issues of cultural particularism, specifically the need to demonstrate the otherness and fundamental difference of the folk in India. The expansion of British colonial dominance generated a desire for a specific kind of fractured and divided Oriental folk subject, one that would validate the racial and cultural unity and superiority of the colonial elite. The Aryan migration theory, a cornerstone for interpretations of race and caste in colonial India, also reveals the ambivalence between concepts of universalism and cultural particularism. The theory, which was controversial from the beginning, posited a series of migrations (or, according to some, one large-scale exodus) of proto-Indo-Aryans from Central Asia into northwest India and Europe (Bryant 2001).[2] First proposed by the illustrious Sir William Jones, various eighteenth- and nineteenth-century scholars offered iterations of the theory on the basis of linguistic, archaeological, and cultural observations. A key piece of evidence for the Aryan thesis was the supposedly similar form and content of folktales across Europe and India; for some Orientalists, such as Theodore Benfey, India was the *Urheimat*, or original home, of all folk narrative (Blackburn 2003:180).

If many early iterations of the Aryan migration theory supported a common origin for languages and cultural artifacts across Europe and South Asia, by the late nineteenth century, the theory was used to interpret phenotypic differences and to reify the imperial discourse of caste. Across South Asia, a "high" Indo-Aryan, Sanskritic, Brahmanic, and upper-caste cultural stratum was distinguished from a "low" Dravidian, lower-caste, folk cultural stratum (e.g., Gover 2002[1871]). In the central Himalayas, British administrators such as George Traill proposed that Brahman and Rajput residents had Aryan blood because of their fairer complexions and "higher culture" (1991[1828]). The aboriginal stratum of non-Aryan Doms, in contrast, demonstrated a "low culture," a darker appearance, and a condition of slavery (Traill 1991[1828]:25), but their anachronistic social customs were believed to preserve the secrets of ancient Indian civilization.

The coexistence of these universalist and particularist agendas in colonial folklore studies is consistent with Herder's conception of a national spirit (*Volksgeist*) (Nettl 2010:42). Volksgeist belonged to all peoples, in Herder's formulation, but it was the task of social elites to find and nurture the production of folklore in the "common man," among whom it was thought to emerge spontaneously and instinctually. The identification of the common man has always been an inherently unstable enterprise; it is easier to describe folklore than to identify "the folk." In India, the conception of the noble savage living in a state of balance with the natural environment emerged at the same time that urbanization, migration, deforestation, and military recruitment spread under British colonial rule. A sentiment of lost innocence pervades much late colonial writing, as British rule was thought to have spoiled much of the physical and moral terrain of the natives.

Late nineteenth- and early twentieth-century researchers in India held resolutely to the village as the ideal site of folklore studies, just as they maintained a concept of the rural peasant as the ideal, if vanishing, folk subject. Scholars rarely documented their methodologies or the names of individual consultants; in most cases, however, they collected songs, proverbs, ballads, and tales from low-caste, hereditary performers. Through the process of inscription, folklorists converted oral hereditary knowledge into literary knowledge. The study of folklore was a means of apprehending the "primitive" from a distance, thereby putting the observer on a higher stage of cultural evolution.

Codifying Folk for the New Nation

While a great deal has been written about the reform of classical music in the first half of the twentieth century (Allen 1998; Bakhle 2005; Weidman 2006), much less has been written about nationalist reconfigurations of folk music over the same period. Urban-educated Indians continued to seek out and discover folk culture among marginalized people (tribals, scheduled castes, remote hill populations) in an essentialized space (the village) and time (the unchanging past). Indian scholars may have inherited theoretical and methodological approaches from European scholars, but they also *responded* to colonization by asserting ownership over regional folklore as part of their national patrimony (Narayan 1993:187). In many parts of India, folklore collections became the primary means of accessing a pre-British historical record. Thus, scholars turned to folklore to counteract the ideas of rural depravity advanced by early folklore studies and to lay the groundwork for new national forms of music, poetry, and art. The study of folklore was a means by which "one's own 'contribution' [could be] demonstrated, and this often in reaction to feelings of inferiority in regions which were, in more than one sense, colonized" (Konrad quoted in Bendix 1997:184).

In his study of the Sauka, a community of trans-Himalayan traders living in the Chamoli district on the border of Garhwal and Tibet, the Kumaoni anthropologist Naresh Chandra wrote:

> There is now hardly any possibility of a diversity of opinions on the importance of *the preservation of folk-songs of our people, who have escaped the influences of the new hybrid culture* and have thus been able to preserve from its ravages the native beauty of their social customs and simple pastimes. . . . As these tribal people become aware of the more "advanced" cultures around them, they begin to be *obsessed by a consciousness of [their] backwardness and awkwardness.*

They are desirous to bring their native culture more in line with that of the outside world, and thus folk cultures and folk songs are pitched in a struggle for existence. (Chandra in Pangtey 2006[1949]:106, my emphasis)

This passage identifies folk culture as being in a perpetual state of decline; it needed to be protected from the "ravages . . . of the new hybrid culture." Yet Chandra's goal was not simply one of documenting the primitive state of the Sauka as a marginal folk community; crucially, the author framed the music of the Sauka as part of the threatened heritage of "our people," signaling a shift toward nationalist discourse. If the colonial elite's framing of folk marked alterity and marginality within the empire, the nationalist elite's framing of folk marked an experience of sameness, a collective heritage that could be claimed by each and every citizen. The goal of folklore studies was to reclaim the folk from the margins and to convert their cultural practices into a collective resource for the nation.

Some cultural policy makers argued against the use of folk music as a tool of cultural nationalism because of its supposedly provincial and backward qualities (see Blackburn 2003:16); usually classical music was advanced because of its purportedly pan-regional character. Yet folk music was valuable to mid-century cultural nationalists precisely because of its ability, in the words of the broadcasting and information minister B. V. Keskar, "to please and charm the mass of people" (1967:48). One of the core beliefs of cultural nationalists everywhere is that all subnational regions have a corresponding corpus of folk performance genres; it was only necessary to codify and develop these into vehicles of nationalist and regionalist sentiment.

Early in his first term as prime minister, Jawaharlal Nehru recognized the threat posed to the new nation by secessionist movements and calls for regional statehood across the subcontinent. Although all ethno-linguistic groups in the nation could not be granted their own regional state, Nehru recognized the importance of fostering artistic expression as a form of political representation. Nehru conceived of folk culture, in Srirupa Roy's words, "as a national and natural resource—available in abundance but requiring careful monitoring, management, and harvesting by the state" (Roy 2007:76). By encouraging folk performances among marginalized communities from around the subcontinent, the state could claim to offer a platform for regional diversity while subsuming antinationalist sentiment. Under Nehru's administration, central government initiatives like the Song and Drama Division, Sangeet Natak Akademi, the Gramophone Company of India, and All-India Radio (AIR) became central to codifying a national repertory of folk music. The postindependence period also saw a dramatic growth in the number of publishers, archives, museums, and academic departments specializing in regional folk studies.

The cultivation of folk music also flourished outside of official state sponsorship. Film music was a powerful means by which folk musical styles were codified and diffused across the nation. From the beginning of Hindi-language talkies in the 1930s, film sequences liberally employed rural imagery and musical characteristics from vernacular performance styles (Booth 1993). The reverse process of incorporating film music back into village-based performance traditions has at times resulted in the desire for larger ensembles and musical professionalism (Marcus 1993), and it has disseminated the idea of regional folk styles across the country.

From 1944 until the early 1950s, the Indian People's Theatre Association (IPTA) spearheaded one of the earliest efforts to use folk arts to create a national political movement. Linked to the political agenda of the Communist Party of India, IPTA artists selected vernacular forms and melodies from diverse regions in India—notably urban theatrical forms such as *jatra* in Bengal and *tamasha* and *powada* in Maharashtra—to create a nationwide artistic movement with the goal of unifying the working classes against fascism and imperialism (Bharucha 1998:32–45). Although the IPTA dissolved soon after its emergence, and did not achieve the political results for which many had hoped, it nonetheless became a platform for dozens of urban intellectuals to codify folk forms and to popularize them among a broader public. Many leading artists and intellectuals of postindependence India, including Habib Tanvir of Chattisgarh, Mohan Upreti of Kumaon, Bupen Hazarika of Assam, and Jhaverchand Mehgani of Gujarat, embraced folk arts first as a cornerstone of political activism and later as the legitimizing source of regional distinction within the nation. Rural, hereditary artists sometimes performed before urban audiences after attending workshops in which they were trained in cosmopolitan style and values; often, however, urban cosmopolitans usurped the title of folk artists and constructed their own hybridized, urban folkloric presentations. As the cultural critic Rustom Bharucha observed, "folk [became] a nomenclature for a wide range of supposedly non-urban performance traditions, that are primarily enjoyed by urban audiences" (1990:199).

These developments in the IPTA signal a broader shift in the identity of the folk performer over the mid-twentieth century, as performers from urban, middle-class, high-caste backgrounds were able to appropriate the repertory and imitate the styles of rural, low-caste, hereditary artists. This mirrors a similar demographic transformation in classical music that has been well documented by ethnomusicologists such as Daniel Neuman (1990).

Branding Folk in Neo-Liberal India

If academics and state institutions almost single-handedly cultivated an interest in folk arts in the mid-twentieth century, the discourse of folk has become widely diffused as a result of an expansion of the middle classes and the market-based economics of neo-liberal reform since the early 1990s. The spread of inexpensive recording and distribution technologies (Manuel 1993) as well as the "vast underbelly of live shows" (Tripathy 2012) have created burgeoning vernacular markets in the remotest corners of India. The title of folk artist and the musical signs of folkness are eagerly claimed by Indigenous performers, regional politicians, recording artists, and diasporic audiences for a variety of commercial and socio-political purposes. Folk music has become "one of the universally recognizable terms in which difference is represented" (Comaroff and Comaroff 2009:24). Although still mediated by nationalist sentiment and by entrenched notions of tradition, heritage, rurality, and backwardness, folk has become a commercial brand adopted by a wide range of individuals and institutions.

There is overwhelming evidence for the diffusion of folk brands across India.[3] Indian Idol introduced a folk category in 2008, requiring that all contestants sing folk songs from their respective regions. There has been an explosion of folk festivals across India, including *Virasat* (Dehradun), Blue Lotus Festival (Pushkar, Rajasthan), Rajasthan International Folk Festival (Jodhpur), Jaipur Literature Festival, and Kolkata International Folk Music Festival, among others. "The audience for Indian ethnic folk music is getting fashionable," notes one journalist, "with performers moving from their open air venues in jungles and villages to perform in closed spaces across cities" (Chatterjee 2011).

The fracturing of the Indian economic and political landscape has also contributed to the popularity of regional folk brands. Jharkhand, Chattisgarh, Uttarakhand, and most recently Telangana attained statehood after prolonged political movements, and more than a dozen movements for regional autonomy or statehood continue to simmer around the country. In each of these cases, music and dance have played an important role in mobilizing social identities on the basis of language, caste, tribe, and above all region (Fiol 2012). Many regional states have incentivized the development of vernacular entertainment industries by offering hefty subsidies and tax breaks to film and music production companies. As a result, new production centers have emerged across the country, offsetting the dominant position held by the urban hubs of Mumbai, Delhi, Kolkata, and Chennai.

Under these relatively new political and economic conditions, the stylistic parameters of what constitutes folk music are quite broad. A noticeable trend among performers marketing their music at regional, national, and international levels has been the isolation and juxtaposition of various folk elements within a cosmopolitan musical setting. In the Garhwali music industry with which I am most familiar, commercial recordings and stage shows rarely feature full-length performances of folk songs or dances; instead, they are liberally sprinkled with disparate folk elements (*lok pada*) that evoke a regional or rustic essence and are blended within a cosmopolitan musical setting (cf. Greene 2001). Folk elements might include the rhythmic patterns played on the *dholak* or *tabla* that are derived from the indigenous *dhol* and *damaun* repertory, the particular phrases or words from a regional dialect, the unique timbre of a *hurka* (hourglass-shaped pressure drum) or *binai* (Jew's harp), or the melodic formulae that evoke local performance genres. Some folk elements have little or no relationship to contemporary practice in Garhwal, such as the use of the bamboo flute (*bansuri*), which has become a sonic index of Himalayan folk music in recordings and stage performances, despite having almost entirely fallen out of use in the Garhwal mountains.

The use of folk elements has also become more common among urban cosmopolitan performers such as the Bangalore-based Raghu Dixit Project, who draw from a variety of vernacular musical and textual traditions in an attempt to broaden their appeal. Many urban performers likewise adopt Sufi influences in their music and lyrics, sometimes rearticulating qualities of *qawwali* or *sufiana kalam* in rock, popular, or classical settings (Manuel 2008). The Manipuri musicians Reuben Mashangva and Lou Majaw perform what they refer to as a folk-blues fusion, blending Tangkhul instruments and musical styles with stylistic elements of the North American singer-songwriter tradition, and citing Bob Dylan and Leonard Cohen as influences. In Mumbai's film music industry, according to the vocalist Shubha Mudgal, "There was a time when folk songs were part and parcel of Bollywood films, but now popular rustic tunes seem to have gone missing from movies even though composers are experimenting with different genres far more than they used to. Once in a while, a film song features a short opening section or a choral section in a folk singer's voice, but otherwise, folk music remains a musical reserve or bank, which music directors from the film industry poach on once in a while, taking the odd tune, song, phrase for unacknowledged use as their own compositions" (Mediaticks). In this way, folk elements have become floating signifiers in much contemporary music; they continue to index cultural authenticity for many, but they do so in increasingly general (and generic) ways that are removed from village-based musical practice.

Conclusions

In his study of race and musical performance in the United States, Karl Miller (2010) illuminates a transition from what he calls the "minstrelsy paradigm" of the late nineteenth and early twentieth centuries, when folk authenticity was performative (i.e., whites could employ and imitate black forms), to the "folklore paradigm" of the mid-twentieth century, when folk authenticity became part of an essentializing discourse through which racialized bodies were attached to distinct white and black performance styles and genres. A similar discursive shift occurred in the Indian context, but in reverse order (and with caste substituting for race). In early twentieth-century India, the colonial elite understood low-caste, rural, hereditary artisans to be the source of primitive folk culture. As the study of folklore grew into an important arm of cultural nationalism in the mid-twentieth century, however, high-caste and middle-class individuals began to appropriate folk forms and sometimes the title of folk artists—folk authenticity became performative rather than essentialized in particular types of bodies. By the late twentieth century, neo-liberal economic and political shifts had encouraged the widespread diffusion of folk signs across India and the diaspora, and anyone with adequate economic means could select decontextualized folk elements and reassemble them in an attempt to assert a distinctive cultural identity.

This historical survey has sketched the evolving discourse of folk in very broad strokes, and it is hoped that it will stimulate more detailed studies. The folk concept is now firmly entrenched in everyday and scholarly discourse, but there has been little attempt to uncover the discursive histories nested within the contemporary use of the term, nor to understand the impact of this discourse on contemporary Indian music and musicians. Beyond its use as a marketing brand, folk is a marker of style, conveying a sense of authenticity and rootedness in village-based traditions, even as the term commonly invokes elements that are decontextualized from village life. Folk also mediates status and professional identity, marking a performer's exclusion from, or inclusion in, various social groups. Until recently, for example, village-based hereditary musicians in the Garhwal Himalayas rarely identified themselves except by their personal or *jati* (occupational caste) names. If one asked to meet a *lok kalakar* (folk artist) in any village, one would likely be directed to the home of a high-status musician, often someone who has released an album in the vernacular music industry. More recently, however, some hereditary performers are reclaiming their identities as the "authentic" regional folk artists. The use of this title can be a point of pride and accomplishment for many musicians whose communities have long been relegated to the lowest position in society. Yet in claiming this identity, these musicians often revert to an earlier colonialist discourse linking folk music to low-caste, hereditary backgrounds, or an earlier nationalist discourse linking folk performance to sentiments of regional belonging and national sovereignty. The concepts of folk music and the folk artist will undoubtedly acquire new significance in the ensuing decades, but the older understandings of the term will continue to influence contemporary discourse.

Notes

1. Many of the examples in this essay are drawn from the first three chapters of my forthcoming book, *Producing Folk in the Indian Himalayas*.

2. Bryant notes that J. G. Herder was one of the most prominent supporters of the theory that "the central point of the largest quarter of the Globe, the primitive mountains of Asia, prepared the first abode of the human race" (2001:19).

3. Precursors to the recent craze for Indian folk music took place in the 1960s and 1970s, when a handful of Baul musicians from Bengal, and Langa and Manganiyar musicians from Rajasthan, recorded LPs and toured Europe and the United States (Capwell 1986).

References

Allen, Matthew Harp. 1998. "Tales Tunes Tell: Deepening the Dialogue between 'Classical' and 'Non-Classical' in the Music of India." *Yearbook for Traditional Music* 30: 22–52.

Bakhle, Janaki. 2005. *Two Men and Music*. New York: Oxford University Press.

Bendix, Regina. 1997. *In Search of Authenticity: The Formation of Folklore Studies*. Madison: University of Wisconsin Press.

Bharucha, Rustom. 1990. *Theatre and the World: Performance and the Politics of Culture*. Delhi: Manohar Publications.

———. 1998. *In the Name of the Secular: Contemporary Cultural Activism in India*. Calcutta: Oxford University Press.

Blackburn, Stuart H. 2003. *Print, Folklore, and Nationalism in Colonial South India*. Delhi: Permanent Black.

Bohlman, Philip V. 1988. *The Study of Folk Music in the Modern World*. Bloomington: Indiana University Press.

Booth, Gregory D. 1993. "Traditional Practice and Mass Mediated Music in India." *International Review of the Aesthetics and Sociology of Music* 24(2): 159–74.

Bryant, Edwin. 2001. *The Quest for the Origins of Vedic Culture: The Indo-Aryan Migration Debate*. New York: Oxford University Press.

Capwell, Charles. 1986. "The Changing Role of the Bauls in Modern Bengal." In *Explorations in Ethnomusicology: Essays in Honor of David P. McAllester*, edited by

Charlotte J. Frisbie, 47–58. Detroit Monographs in Musicology 9. Detroit: Information Coordinators.

Chalmers, Rhoderick. 2002. "Pandits and Pulp Fiction: Popular Publishing and the Birth of Nepali Print Capitalism in Banaras." *Studies in Nepali History and Society* 7(1): 35–97.

Chatterjee, Madhusree. 2011. "Ethnic Folk Music Finding Echoes in Capital." *Hindustan Times (New Delhi)*, 11 August. zeenews.india.com/entertainment/art-and-theatre/ethnic-folk-music-finding-echoes-in-capital_94094.html (accessed 2 January 2014).

Comaroff, John, and Jean Comaroff. 2009. *Ethnicity, Inc*. Chicago: University of Chicago Press.

Fiol, Stefan. 2012. "Articulating Regionalism through Popular Music: The Case of *Nauchami Narayana* in the Uttarakhand Himalayas." *Journal of Asian Studies* 71(2): 447–74.

Fox-Strangways, Arthur Henry. 1914. *The Music of Hindostan*. Oxford: Oxford University Press.

Gover, Charles E. 2002[1871]. *The Folk-Songs of Southern India*. New Delhi: Rupa Company.

Greene, Paul. 2001. "Authoring the Folk: The Crafting of a Rural Popular Music in South India." *Journal of Intercultural Studies* 22(2): 161–72.

Keil, Charles. 1978. "Who Needs 'the Folk'?" *Journal of the Folklore Institute* 15(3): 263–65.

Keskar, B. V. 1967. *Indian Music: Problems and Prospects*. Bombay: Popular Prakashan.

Korom, Frank J. 2006. *South Asian Folklore: A Handbook*. London: Greenwood Press.

Manuel, Peter. 1993. *Cassette Culture: Popular Music and Technology in North India*. Chicago: University of Chicago Press.

———. 2008. "North Indian Sufi Popular Music in the Age of Hindu and Muslim Fundamentalism." *Ethnomusicology* 52(3): 378–400.

Marcus, Scott L. 1993. "Recycling Indian Film-Songs: Popular Music as a Source of Melodies for North Indian Folk Musicians." *Asian Music* 24(1): 101–10.

Mediaticks. "Why Don't We Hear Folksongs in Bollywood Films These Days?" www.mediaticks.com/bollywood/bollywoodreviews.php?bollywood-type=Titbits&bollywood=Why-dont-we-hear-folk-songs-in-Bollywood-films-nowadays?&id=25618 (accessed 1 October 2013).

Miller, Karl Hagstrom. 2010. *Segregating Sound: Inventing Folk and Pop Music in the Age of Jim Crow*. Durham, NC: Duke University Press.

Naithani, Sadhana. 2006. *In Quest of Indian Folktales: Pandit Ram Gharib Chaube and William Crooke*. Bloomington: Indiana University Press.

Narayan, Kirin. 1993. "Banana Republics and V. I. Degrees: Rethinking Indian Folklore in a Postcolonial World." *Asian Folklore Studies* 52(1): 177–204.

Nettl, Bruno. 1976. *Folk Music in the United States: An Introduction*. Detroit: Wayne State University Press.

———. 2010. *Nettl's Elephant: On the History of Ethnomusicology*. Urbana: University of Illinois Press.

Neuman, Daniel M. 1990. *The Life of Music in North India: The Organization of an Artistic Tradition*. Chicago: University of Chicago Press.

Oakley, E. S. 1990[1905]. *Holy Himalaya*. Nainital: Gyanodaya Prakashan.

Paige, Aaron. 2009. "Acoustic Entanglements: Negotiating Folk Music in Naiyaṇṭi Melam Performance." *Indian Folklore Research Journal* 6(9): 45–66.

Pangtey, K. S. 2006[1949]. *Lonely Furrows of the Borderland*. Nainital: Pahar.

Roy, Srirupa. 2007. *Beyond Belief: India and the Politics of Postcolonial Nationalism*. Durham, NC: Duke University Press.

Traill, George William. 1991[1828]. "Statistical Sketch of Kamaon." *Himalaya: Past and Present*, Volume II, edited by M. P. Joshi, A. C. Fanger, and C. W. Brown, 1–97. Almora: Shree Almora Book Depot.

Tripathy, Ratnakar. 2012. "Music Mania in Small Town Bihar: Emergence of Vernacular Identities." *Economic and Political Weekly* 47(22): 58–66.

Weidman, Amanda. 2006. *Singing the Classical, Voicing the Modern: The Postcolonial Politics of Music in India*. Durham, NC: Duke University Press.

CHAPTER TWENTY-FIVE

~

Textual Relationships between O'odham Story and Song

J. Richard Haefer

Bruno Nettl, while a student in the 1940s, recalled that his teacher, George Herzog, "was often described as the leading . . . true professional in his field, then known . . . as comparative musicology" (2013:27). Herzog's studies focused on Native American music of the Southwestern United States, with brief excursions in the Plains, Great Basin, and other areas, topics, and regions of the world.[1] Herzog's influence appears in Nettl's descriptions of American Indian musical style areas and in many of his theoretical concepts. As Nettl's former student, I have found two of Herzog's publications have been especially significant to my research (Herzog 1936a and 1938). When Herzog retired from teaching, he held onto many of his field notes with the hope of continuing to write and publish, but unfortunately, his health did not permit him to fulfill that goal. The material from Herzog's manuscripts that is presented here is a step toward completing his goal, and this chapter, then, is a tribute to both Nettl and his teacher.

This chapter examines some of the relationships between O'odham story and song.[2] Whereas a number of studies exist of North American Indian song texts, only a few have examined their literary attributes within their traditional languages. The art of poetry in Akimel and Tohono O'odham songs (*ñe'ñei*) has been studied within various song cycles, but no studies to date have considered the relationships between song texts and pre-existing textual sources, including stories. Yet O'odham storytelling, with its interpolation of multiple songs, presents a unique opportunity to compare song texts to spoken prose and narrative speech. Contrary to the majority of O'odham songs, which tend to exist in song cycles without other literary references, the songs interpolated into stories have clear connections to the story's prose and narration. These songs therefore present an opportunity to compare song texts, spoken prose, and narration. Not only can they be examined for their literary connections to the story, they provide well-defined examples of O'odham song language, which is distinctly different from spoken Piman. For example, in creating song texts, the O'odham alter spoken language to fit musical meters. Metric organization differs in O'odham songs from phrase to phrase, and the first or second phrases are typically longer than the penultimate or final phrases. In addition, rhythmic vitality may be created in the text through syllabic reduplication, the insertion of new vowels or syllables, and the addition of suffix syllables. Vowel and consonant sounds may also be changed in song language.

Whereas O'odham songs are normally grouped in cycles of four, within stories, songs exist as individual items, in pairs, or even in groups of three. Their form is less predictable; most O'odham songs employ four phrases, whereas songs in stories may feature four or five phrases. These characteristics may be exemplified through an analysis of song texts in the O'odham creation story.

The O'odham Creation Story

The O'odham creation story is known as "O'o Sag Vavandag I Mot." Its literal translation means "to haul the rafter" or "the straightness of the spanner." Figuratively, it means that the speaker "brings it from memory" (Benedict and Bahr 2001:3). As a myth or sacred narrative, this is "a story about ancient times, that people retain, that they take on faith, and that is largely or entirely immune from proof or disproof" (Bahr, Paul, and Joseph 1997:26). The O'odham story and its songs present information to contemporary O'odham people in several respects. They portray the secular past (history), the sacred past (religion), the creative (imagination), and a shared reality (cultural knowledge from visions and associated values) (cf. Bahr, Paul, and Joseph 1997). Traditionally, the creation story is told over a four-night period at or near the winter solstice; tellers of the story may impart different versions of it, though the basic themes remain consistent.

Six versions of the creation story were recorded between 1901 and 1936 (table 25.1). Within these tellings, three main types of communication occur: prose, narration, and song (table 25.2). Each type of communication is thought to come from the ancients; the teller is only the vehicle for the story.[3] Prose is presented in common speech language, though it is believed

Table 25.1. Recorded tellings of the O'odham creation story

Teller	*Interpreter*	*Recorder*	*Language*	*Recorded*	*Published*
Thin Leather	Unknown	Frank Russell	Both	1901–1902	1908[1]
Thin Leather	Unknown	J.W. Floyd	Both	1908	1911
Unknown	Unknown	Elsie Parsons		1926	Ms.
Thomas Vanyiko	Paul Azul	George Herzog	Both	1927–1936	No Date[2]
Juan Smith	W. S. Allison	Julian Haydn	English	1933	1994[3]
William Blackwater and Thomas Vanyiko		Ruth Benedict	English	1927	2001[4]

1. Russell 1975.

2. A new edition by Bahr, Bahr, and Haefer is in progress. Herzog recorded the texts during a field trip to Sacaton, Arizona, in the summer of 1929. He recorded some of the songs during a brief stay with the Akimel O'odham in 1927. He reviewed the texts of the stories and songs, and collected additional songs, during two subsequent field trips in 1933 and 1936.

3. Bahr, Smith, Allison, and Hayden (1994).

4. Benedict and Bahr (2001).

to have originated among the ancients. Prose is considered to be the softest or weakest type of communication, and it is therefore the most variable part of the tellings. A somewhat harder type is what Benedict calls recitative, Bahr calls oration, and I call narration or dramatic oration. Narrations are verbatim quotes from the ancients, presented word for word, or phrase by phrase, in heightened speech. They are "more firmly retained and more

Table 25.2. Types of communication within tellings of the O'odham creation story

Prose
- Common speech language, but believed to have originated from the ancients
- The softest type of O'odham verbal communication

Narration (also called recitative, oration, or dramatic oration, depending upon the source)
- Heightened O'odham speech with verbatim quotes from the ancients
- A medium-hard type of O'odham verbal communication

Song (ñe'i/ñe'ñei)
- Melodic/rhythmic presentation of text in song language, which differs from common speech language
- The hardest type of O'odham verbal communication

Note: This typology derives from Benedict and Bahr (2001:xxxi).

strongly voiced than prose" (Benedict and Bahr 2001:xxxi) but are less strict, and are longer, than song texts (i.e., they are not in verse form). Therefore, they represent a medium-hard type of communication. Neither prose nor narrations are analyzed in this chapter, except for how they interrelate with song texts. Songs (ñe'i singular, ñe'ñei plural) occur in strictly metered melodic and rhythmic patterns and are interpolated at high moments of the telling.[4] They are, in essence, sung by the ancients, who are really doing the telling. Songs represent the hardest type of communication heard in O'odham language.

The Interpolation of Songs in the O'odham Creation Story[5]

The creation story begins with a character called *Jevut Ma:kai* (translated as Earth Magician, Earth Doctor, or Creator Being),[6] who lived in a "space" without light or solidity (Benedict and Bahr 2001:4f). He takes something solid from himself and causes it to grow into the earth where he dwells for a time. He then makes the sun, moon, and stars from water or his spit. Then he causes a few beings almost as powerful as he to exist: a man named *S-e'ehe*[7] (Elder Brother), who will be one of the most important characters in the large overall story; a Coyote man; a Buzzard man; and in some tellings, a woman named *Nasia*. Coyote and Buzzard are the basis for the two most important O'odham clans nowadays. After he created various animate and inanimate beings, Jevut Ma:kai gave songs to them, and they later transferred the songs to the O'odham through dreams. It is important to note that the O'odham believe that they themselves do not compose these songs. The O'odham use the word *neit* (to compose) only in relation to Jevut Ma:kai, who composed ñe'ñei. Therefore, this analysis examines how Jevut Ma:kai related song texts to his own story and how he evolved song language from his spoken language.

At the first high point of the telling (end of table 25.3), the narrator interpolates the first two songs. O'odham songs often occur in pairs as parts of song cycles and, in this telling, may occur either in pairs or singly. I present Songs 1 and 2 first in metrical song language and then in spoken Piman with a metaphrase English translation in parallel columns. The numbers at the top of each metrical phrase indicate individual pulses and do not appear in further examples. A slash indicates a sustained tone. Each line indicates an individual phrase of music and text. O'odham songs usually have four phrases; the earlier phrases are longer.

Table 25.3. The O'odham creation story

[Story begins] E**d**a'g scuhugam heg su:da'ki ve:na'ks.	At that time the darkness (was) mixed with the water.[1]
Voho i s-cuhugam. Pi an [h]u ha'icu o'otam an e**d**a.	It was truly dark. There were no people then.
Am ab a'i i s'e-juñim, ha'icu. Am si e-kavutka hek s-cuhugmam.	Then it wanted to happen, something. The darkness gathered itself.
Am si ku:p ialim, a p i vu:**s** a p amje**t** Jios i:bda'k. Amje**t** an ahava oimme**t** hek Jios i:bda'k. Cum p a'i oimme**t**.	It [darkness] was rolling over, and from it came forth God's heart.[2] After that God's heart was moving about. It was moving about everywhere.
Am e-a'i, am i vu:**s** mat al a'as ha'icu hab o o-ju:. Am na:to hek ku:daki. Hekaj am ahava e-tonoli'c [,] oime**t**.	Then it came (to him)[3] that he would do a little thing. He made a firebrand. Making light for himself with that, he moved about.
Am e-ai a p hahava e-ta:t[,] mat am [h] a'icu has o ju:[,] am na:to hek **s**egoi. Am ep ha-na:to hek s-cuck totoñ. (Kut) ap ha-dakto hek ab **s**egoi.	Afterward he felt, that he would do something, and he made the greasewood. He made also the black ants. He left them on the greasewood.
Kut ap ap oiyopo[,] hegam totoñ. K ap**s** we:s usapic[,] hegai **s**egoi. Kut am cum ñei g Jio**s**, pi ha'icu am has juñma cu'ik.	And they ran about on it, those ants. They just made it into tree-gum, that greasewood.[4] And when God saw it, it seemed that nothing could be done (with that).[5]
Am ahava ep ha-na:to heg hiopc. Ap ha-**s**ul ep ap heg **s**egoi. Kut ap oiopo[,] ap i jevu**t**c[,] hegam. K ve:s bit**s**[,] hegai **s**egoi. Hahava ha'icu has i juñma cu'ik.	Then he made the wood-lice. He dropped[6] them on the greasewood also. They ran about on it, were making it into earth, those. They covered it all with dirt, that greasewood.[7] Then it seemed that something could be done (with that).
Kut ab ve:s i bek[,] i hemapa. Ap i dagiovia. Am o:liat. Am cum dai[,] pi an [h]u dahiva. Pi ha'icuk a'i an [h]u dahivia. K ap**s** hi:[,] me:k.	And taking it all up, he gathered it. He kneaded it. He rounded it. He tried to set it down, it did not sit there. It did not sit on anything. It just went, away.
Kam i oi hek Jio**s**[,] hek am u ai[,] an bei[,] am ep cum dai[,] ep hi:. Kut am ep oi[,] m [h]u ai. Am ehe bei. Ep cum dai. Ep pi an [h]u dahiva.	And God followed it, he reached it, he took it, again he tried to make it sit, again it went. And again he followed it, reached it there. Again he took it. Again he tried to make it sit. Again it did not sit there.
Amahava ap si e-vancwa heg s-cuhugmam ha'apje**t**[,] ha'apje**t**[,] ha'apje**t**[,] ha'apje**t** heg Jio**s**. Anahava dai hek da:m[,] kut am i dahiva. Kut am i da'ak an da:m cudowa. Kam ciahañ.	Then God pulled[8] the darkness from there, there, there, there.[9] [W E N S] He set it [darkness] on top of that, and then it sat. He jumped and landed on it. He coaxed[10] it.

1. The following bracketed notes are from the edition in progress: ["Really fog or mist."]

2. ["It was his life, his spirit." God, whose name "*Jios*" is taken from the Spanish word "*Dios*," is mentioned just a few times in this telling. It is as if God, who lived in heaven on high, was the eternal and supreme power in the universe—as in this case where an act of God is the first remembered thing that ever happened—*ed.*]

3. [This is Herzog's parenthesis. Actually he didn't translate the phrase "am I vu:s," "then it came out." A better translation for the whole might be, "Then it came, it came out, that he would do . . ."—*ed.*]
4. ["They covered it all over with tree-gum, so that it seemed as if it was nothing but tree-gum."]
5. [Literally and word for word, "not something there some-way do-able is"—*ed.*]
6. [Or better, "threw," "tossed"—*ed.*]
7. [Literally and word for word, "And all-of-it they-excreted-on, that-one greasewood"—*ed.*]
8. ["With his power."]
9. [[The narrator points to West, East, South, and North. "There were no directions at that time, he just points them out when telling the story."]
10. [[The word can also be translated as "commanded"—*ed.*]

Song 1

1	2	3	4	5	6	7	8	9	10	11	12
"hi	hi me	lo	/	hi	he me	lo	/	hi	he me	lo	/.
he te	je	we na	ma	kai	je	we na	na	to.			
ta	ma na	ke ki	wa	ya a	/,						
hi me	co	hi me	co."								

None of the song text words (that is, spoken language and not song language words) actually appear in the opening prose telling. However, the central idea appears in the paragraph preceding the song. This will become clearer as we examine the second song in the pair.

Song 2

hi	hi me	lo	/	hi	hi me	lo	/	hi	hi me	lo	/.
he te	je	we na	ma	kai	je	we na	na	to	.		
ta	ma na	ke ki	wa	ya a	/,						
me le	co	me le	co.								

Table 25.4. Translation of Song 1

Himlo, himlo, himlo.	Spreading, spreading, spreading.
I:da Jevut Ma:kai jewut na:to.	This[1] Earth Magician made the earth.
Da:m ke:kiwa,	Standing on top of it,
Himc, himc.	Making it spread, making it spread.

1. [In the songs, "I" is at times expressed by "this." "It is Earth Magician that is talking here."]

Table 25.5. Translation of Song 2

Himlo, himlo, himlo.	Spreading, spreading, spreading.
I:da Jevut Ma:kai jewut na:to.	This Earth Magician made the earth.
Da:m ke:kiwa,	Standing on top of it,
Melc, melc.	Making it grow, making it grow.[1]

1. [This song is identical with the first one, except for the last word which literally means "make-it-run," as opposed to the last word of the first song which means "make-it-go." Herzog's translations of "grow" and "spread" are retained, but "run" and "go" are probably better as there are other Pima words for "grow" and "spread," and one thinks that if Earth Magician meant those ideas he would have used those words—ed.]

The previous spoken paragraph states, "Then pulled the darkness from there, there, there, there. He set it on top of that, and then it sat. He jumped and landed on it. He coaxed it." These two songs, then, paraphrase the spoken text, naming Jevut Ma:kai (Earth Magician) in the song and specifying the "coaxing" as "to spread" and "to grow." In other words, "He [Earth Magician] set it [darkness] on top of that [something he made], and then it [the something] sat [still]. He jumped and landed on it. He coaxed it." The songs paraphrase this as "he made it spread [and to] grow [into something, i.e., the earth]." The two song texts are virtually the same, as is often the case in paired songs, except for one word: *himc* changes to *melc*. In some other paired songs, two words are changed. These two songs elaborate on the prose in the creation story. Elaboration is one of the most frequent methods of relating songs to prose when they are interpolated into O'odham narratives. Other methods include paraphrase, amplification, use of direct quotes from the story, and explanation. Each is discussed in turn. Due to space limitations, I present only the spoken Piman version of the song texts, derived from the song language, along with the parallel English translation.

The relationships between song and prose in O'odham narratives are examined in table 25.6. For example, of the roughly sixty songs in Herzog's manuscript,[8] fifteen (25 percent) involve paraphrase. Paraphrase is defined as a restatement of a text passage using different words; it puts the source statement into perspective, while preserving the essential meaning of the prose. Song 6 exemplifies paraphrase while also clarifying how *Jios* (God) was known traditionally. Examples of amplification, elaboration, explanation, anticipation, and reiteration in other songs appear in the table.

Conclusions

Additional literary procedures such as parody, compilation, and summary occur in the songs interpolated into O'odham narrative as a means of transfer-

Table 25.6. Story, texts, and notes for six O'odham Songs

[Story] Hahava s-ap'e. Kut ab**s** gathu va:[,] am i ve:cik hek jevu**t**. Am da:m i vu:**s** hek **s**u:daki hek jewu**t**. Gat hu **s**u:dagic e**t** dahivua hek jeve**t**. Kut ama a'i gevckwua hek Jio**s** hek su:daki e-coikutkac.	Then it was good. And the earth just sank in there; it had become heavy. Water came out on the earth. There in the water sat the earth. And God pushed the water back in all directions with his staff.
Song 6	
A:ñi[,] si hai ju:kam[,][1]	I, wizard[,]
A:ñi[,] si hai ju:kam[,]	I, wizard[,]
A:ñi[,] si hai ju:kam[.]	I, wizard[.]
Su:daki[,]	The water[,]
a'ai himc.	In all directions[2] am moving [it].
The song paraphrases the last two lines of the story with an emphasis on the traditional O'odham "doer" as the one moving the water, as opposed to the prose statement of Jios (God).	
Of the sixty songs, twenty-four (40 percent) exemplify amplification, defined as embellishing the narrative by adding details to enhance understanding of the full story.	
Ma s-ap'e o. E**d**a heg jeve**t** pi am [h]u ap ka:c[,] a'ai e-vi**d**ut. Heg Jevu**t** Ma:kai am si va:m cu'i[g].	And it was good. Still this Earth did not lie well, it still swayed back and forth. Then Earth Magician did much more.
Song 22	
"Jevu**t** Ma:kai[,]	"Earth Magician[,]
Doa'ak na:to[.]	Made the mountains[.]
Vi:ki ku:kuk amai[,]	Tipped them with down [,]
Doa'ak na:to[.]"	He made the mountains."
In the song it is specified that what he "did much more" was to make the mountains, and furthermore that he made white clouds (down feathers signify white clouds).	
Songs 3 and 4 feature both direct quotes and elaboration, the latter filling in details of the story. The story text ends: *"Ndo matc hek do:do'ak"* (I will cause the mountains to bear a child).	
Song 4	
Doak ando ma**t**c.	I will cause the mountain to bear a child.
Doak ando ma**t**c,	I will cause the mountain to bear a child,
Heg Na:sia ab i vu:**s**.	And then Nasia[3] came forth.
After the singer quotes the story in the first two song lines (changing mountains to mountain), we learn that the child is none other than Nasia, an important female figure in O'odham mythology. In Song 3, whose Piman language text Herzog apparently neglected to notate, his English translation indicates that the child was Si'ehe (Elder Brother). In this song pair, number four states that two different beings are made. Interestingly, after Nasia is introduced in the song, the telling continues with the inclusion of her name:	

(*continued*)

Table 25.6 (*continued*)

Ab a'ai si e-gegavs da:m ka:cim jewut hek do:da'ak ve:m[,] ap i vu:sat hek Na:sia.	He pressed the sky and the mountains against each other, and made Nasia to come forth.

Here the teller says Nasia's name while explaining that she was brought forth by pressing the sky and mountains against each other, so the prose here amplifies the song text. The teller previously explained that Elder Brother was also created by pressing sky and mountains together, but Yellow Buzzard emerged from the shadow of Earth Magician's eyes. It is curious that Earth Magician caused three beings to be created (Yellow Buzzard, Elder Brother, and Nasia), since four is the typical O'odham sacred number, but only the latter two are emphasized in song. We are left to wonder whether the singer intentionally omitted Yellow Buzzard from the song, perhaps due to the nature of paired texting, or if the omission was unintentional.

Of the sixty songs, fifteen (25 percent) illustrate explanation, the process that describes facts to clarify the causes or consequences of the original statement. The story states:

Kut am ahawa vas heg su:daki[,] kut am kauvka[,] hab masma mo giw[,] kut ap hemackamc[,] ab vonamc[,] as k vonamc[,] abs o ce'evec vonamc[,] ap si ge'e ma: g s-toñ.	Then he poured out water, and it hardened, like ice, and he made it into a person, put a headdress on it [, just put a headdress on it], a headdress with long tips[4] he put on it,[5] gave it a very great heat.

Song 11

"Tas hemu i:yo na:to[.] Tas hemu i:yo na:to[,] Si'alik tagio vo vua[.] Gahu i dais[,] S-ap o metat[.]"	"Now making the sun here[.] Now making the sun here[,] Will drop in at the east [.] There it comes up[,] It will run well."

The song makes it clear that Earth Magician is making the sun, since he was the only being capable of doing so at that time. It also makes it clear that the headdress is the sun and that the sun rises in the East and will "run well" across the sky.

Clearly, paraphrase, amplification, and explanation are often intermixed within the song process. While 80 percent of the songs illustrate these three methods of relating the songs to the narrative, there is considerable overlap among them. Other methods of relating the songs to the narrative include anticipation and reiteration.

Of the sixty songs, seven (11 percent) exemplify anticipation, defined as foretelling the next subject of the story.

Hema da[ha g] ma:kai o'otam, am ki hugit-am ge doa'ak; hap ce:gik Hevel Ma'is. Am soak[,] am [h]a'icu si ma:ciok[;] am ep ñe'i[,] hegai ma:kai:	There was a magician person, he lived beside a mountain. His name was Wind Covered. He cried, since he knew [what was to come]; he also sang, that magician:

Song 31

Jevut me:mei[,] Jevut me:mei[,] Toak me:mei[.]	The earth will burn[,] The earth will burn[,] The mountains will burn.

(*continued*)

Table 25.6 (*continued*)

The story tells us that a magician person (Wind Covered) knew what was to come, but the teller does not say what that is. Song 31 explains that the earth will burn, and Song 32 informs us that [we] shall drown, leading to the need for a new race of people to cover the earth (the subject of the next portion of the story).

Reiteration is the process of repeating something already said in order to emphasize it. The example below clearly emphasizes through repetition the water swelling at the side of the boat due to a mass of driftwood.

Kut**s** **ed**a heg u'us vaku'ulu an s-mu'umvigim an **s**u:daki da:m. An ep ha-hugit-an heg **s**u:daki si e-kopotka.	The driftwood was piling up on the water. The water swelled at their side.
Song 39	
Ge'e **s**u:daki,	Big water,
Ge'e **s**u:daki,	Big water,
Ñ-[h]ukit-an mu'umvic vakulu'uk ge	Driftwood piles beside me big
Su:daki,	Water,
Ge'e **s**u:daki,	Big water,
Ñ-[h]ukit-an mu'umvic ko'okpotkat.	It swells up beside me.

1. [The phrase "si hai ju:k*am" must be* "sai ju:kam." The last word means "doer," and the first is an adverb little or never heard outside of telling about ancient times that means, more or less, "like a powerful medicine man." Thus, "like-a-medicine-man doer." "Wizard" is a fair translation—ed.]
2. [Better translation: "back-and-forth moving." And note, this song is attributed to God, not to Earth Magician. It is almost the last mention of God until much later in the mythology. God exists but the dramas of Pima ancientness involve other gods—ed.]
3. The complete story of Nasia occurs later within this telling of the creation narrative.
4. ["Long tips means long feathers; symbolically the rays of the sun."]
5. [Literally, "a tall headdress-[or hat]-he-put-on-it." Herzog didn't include the previous, bracketed, repetitional clause in his translation, but the Pima transcript has it—ed.]

ring and/or emphasizing the meaning of the original story. Some of the songs present mystical expressions. Many of the songs provide dynamic equivalents or formal equivalents (Nida and Taber 1969), which are often understood as sense-for-sense translation (translating the meanings of phrases or whole sentences) and word-for-word translation (translating the meanings of individual words in their more or less exact syntactic sequence). In other words, O'odham songs interpolated into narratives essentially translate the story, providing the same message (by morpheme, word, or phrase) encoded in the song language.

Space limitations prevent the discussion of additional rhetorical or literary devices, such as thematic patterning, motif, personification or anthropomorphism, alliteration, onomatopoeia, anecdote, verisimilitude, or even rhythm and rhyme in relation to interrelationships among prose, narration, and song texts. Parallelisms within the prose and songs also exist, especially in terms of color, character, and other paired expressions. Various other constructs, including ideas such as reimagining or canon-conscious revisions, also need to be examined. Certainly we are not dealing with revisionists rewriting the narratives, as all tellers agree that they are presenting the words of the ancients and are not telling their own story. Thus they represent a classic example of language ideology,[9] expressing the connections between what the speakers believe (that is, really the beliefs of the ancients) and the socio-cultural system of the O'odham. Ñe'ñei highlight, elaborate, and explain the prose narrative for the benefit of the listeners. A comparison with the songs in the other five tellings may reveal further relevant information.

Acknowledgments

I wish to thank the anthropologist Donald Bahr for giving me his edited version of Herzog's Piman creation story and suggesting that I analyze the songs, both textually and musically. Bahr and I have worked together since the mid-1970s; while this chapter reflects his imprint, I bear responsibility for the statements herein. I also wish to thank the Archive of Traditional Music, Indiana University, for providing Herzog's field notes for his work with the Pimas.

Notes

1. Cf. Herzog 1928, 1930, 1933, 1934, 1935, 1936a, 1936b, and 1938.
2. The Akimal O'odham (Pimas) and Tohono O'odham (formerly called Papagos) of Arizona speak dialects of the Piman language, which is phonologically part of the larger Uto-Aztecan language family. Piman language studies include Hale (1959), Saxton (1998), and Zepeda (1983), who is herself Tohono O'odham.
3. For the O'odham, the ancients are spiritual beings who have existed from the beginning of time, that is, prior to the Hohokam.
4. O'odham songs involve texts "whose melody and pitch, and some of whose articulated sounds, are [entirely] different from ordinary speech" (Bahr, Paul, and Joseph 1997:3).
5. In this analysis, I am using a version of Vanyiko's telling of the creation story to Herzog (see table 25.1), but comparisons can be made to the versions collected by Russell, Haydn, and Benedict. I am currently preparing a new edition of the story for publication in collaboration with Donald Bahr.
6. Juan Smith calls him *Jeoss* (God) from the Spanish *Dios* (Bahr, Smith, Allison, and Hayden 1994:45–46).
7. Bahr transliterates the word as *Siuhu* (Bahr, Smith, Allison, and Hayden 1994:11).
8. The number is approximate because Herzog did not separate some songs that may be pairs; he also does not appear to have collected all of the songs possible in the telling.

9. The concept of language ideology, outlined by Michael Silverstein, is a "set of beliefs about language articulated by users as a rationalization or justification of perceived language structure and use" (1979:193), quoted in Schieffelin, Woolard, and Kroskrity (1998:4).

References

Bahr, Donald, Juan Smith, William Smith Allison, and Julian Hayden. 1994. *The Short Swift Time of Gods on Earth: The Hohokam Chronicles*. Berkeley: University of California Press.

Bahr, Donald, Lloyd Paul, and Vincent Joseph. 1997. *Ants and Orioles: Showing the Art of Pima Poetry*. Salt Lake City: University of Utah Press.

Benedict, Ruth, and Donald Bahr. 2001. *O'odham Creation and Related Events*. Tucson: University of Arizona Press.

Hale, Kenneth L. 1959. *A Papago Grammar*. M.A. Thesis, Indiana University.

Herzog, George. 1928. "The Yuman Musical Style." *Journal of American Folklore* 41(160): 183–231.

———. 1930. "Musical Styles in North America." *Proceedings of the 23rd International Congress of Americanists, New York (1928)*, 455–58. New York: Random House.

———. 1933. "Maricopa Music." In *Yuman Tribes of the Gila River* by Leslie Spier, 271–79. Chicago: University of Chicago Press.

———. 1934. "Speech-Melody and Primitive Music." *Musical Quarterly* 20: 452–66.

———. 1935. "Plains Ghost Dance and Great Basin Music." *American Anthropologist* 7: 403–19.

———. 1936a. "A Comparison of Pueblo and Pima Musical Styles." *Journal of American Folklore* 49: 283–417.

———. 1936b. *Research in Primitive and Folk Music in the United States: A Survey*. American Council of Learned Societies, Bulletin 24.

———. 1938. "Music in the Thinking of the American Indian." *Peabody Bulletin* (May): 1–5.

Nettl, Bruno. 2013. *Becoming an Ethnomusicologist: A Miscellany of Influences*. Lanham, MD: Scarecrow Press.

Nida, Eugene A., and Charles R. Taber. 1969. *The Theory and Practice of Translation, With Special Reference to Bible Translating*. Leiden: Brill.

Parsons, Elsie Clews. 1926. "Notes on the Pima, 1926." *American Anthropologist* 30(3): 445–64.

Russell, Frank. 1975. *The Pima Indians*. Tucson: University of Arizona Press.

Saxton, Dean. 1998. *Papago/Pima–English Dictionary*. Tucson: University of Arizona Press.

Schieffelin, Bambi B., Kathryn Woolard, and Paul V. Kroskrity, eds. 1998. "Language Ideologies: Practice and Theory." *Oxford Studies in Anthropological Linguistics*. Oxford: Oxford University Press.

Zepeda, Ofelia. 1983. *A Papago Grammar*. Tucson: University of Arizona Press.

CHAPTER TWENTY-SIX

~

Finding and Recovering Musicality in a College Folk Music Class

Melinda Russell

In this chapter, I analyze student responses to an applied component in a college ethnomusicology course, finding that it provided a set of conditions favorable to the discovery or recovery of human musical potential. Students seized the opportunity to redefine themselves as musical people, leaning heavily for support on the ethos of the movement they were studying. In so doing, they illuminated the barriers to such musicality in their everyday experience.

For a decade or so, I have offered a class on the 1960s American folk revival. Students read scholarly work, examine primary sources, and study period audio and video recordings. Over the years, many students have replaced the course research paper with applied projects, ranging from writing protest songs to learning to play the harmonica. Struck by the productive connections students made between these personal endeavors and prominent themes in the course, I replaced a third of the lecture days with weekly applied sections. The class size is limited to twenty students, so that each of these Wednesday sections contains no more than ten students. In one section, students study beginning guitar with me, and in the other, students with at least one year of experience bring their own instruments (guitar, banjo, mandolin, fiddle, cello, and so forth) and work with Mark Kreitzer, an excellent local musician who leads them in learning to play together, improvise, and harmonize, and often they learn a bit of theory. On the last Wednesday, which is also the last class day, we organize a coffeehouse, and the two groups hear each other for the first time.

Whereas losing a third of the lecture and discussion time has necessitated some sacrifice of course content, there is no question that student benefit from the applied sections is enormous. Playing the music of the folk revival, and playing it with others, rewards them with a deeper knowledge of repertory, technique, and performance practice. Students notice similarities and departures in song form and harmony. They are able to think in some detail about individual performance styles. They hear and feel connections between songs in a way that was not prompted by listening exams, but rather by their own intellectual paths. Engaging the music as players helps them as scholars; their study of the period, in turn, informs their playing.

Reflecting on her satisfaction in breaking a longtime habit of dropping the guitar and thereafter recovering only to her previous level, RK[1] wrote about what else she derived from the class:

> I have been able to understand my positionality within the musical traditions I have been performing, and the styles in which this music was historically performed, practiced, sung and strummed. I have learned about the heritage of songs, which changes the way I understand them as being played "right" or "wrong."

KM wrote:

> I had barely heard of Phil Ochs before last week, but was pretty enamored with him by the end of class on Monday. On Wednesday, we split into groups to work on two of his songs, and it was great to get to engage his music even more intensely—not just listening to the music passively, but finding it on the guitar, tracing its movement. By the end, we had realized that the chords in the two songs . . . were identical—who would've known!

Students in the advanced section were able in the next class to contribute authoritatively to a discussion of Ochs's stylistic progression through later albums; normally, such discussion is only possible with music majors or a select few insiders.

These were the sorts of connections that motivated the addition of the applied component. What I expected somewhat less was just how moving it would be—for them and for me—for students to "do" the folk revival instead of just studying it. In particular, the discovery or recovery of a musical self, most visible in the beginning guitar section, was a shared central emotional event of the term. One young woman, LH, described her own transformation:

> The guitar section of the class has been really personally meaningful to me. For a long time, I thought of myself as someone who wasn't very good at music,

> either making it or recognizing/knowing about it. That started to change when I moved into Farm House my sophomore year. There were a lot of people living there who were really good at music (mostly singing and guitar) and they made music all the time, just as part of their daily lives, and always let other people join in. I loved it. That was when I started to get into folk music and also when I started to get more comfortable singing in public. Now, FINALLY learning folk guitar and practicing it at Farm, I feel like I've come full circle. . . . Now I'm the one singing downstairs. I feel so empowered! And beyond Farm House, learning guitar is helping me redefine myself as a more musical person.

Many students wrote powerfully about the coffeehouse, as had several the previous year. In the main, the groups shared their responses to hearing "the other group" play, noting the extreme difference between the two: Mark's experienced students, playing a variety of instruments, comfortably improvising and experimenting, and my beginning students, all on guitar, playing more rigidly and performing somewhat self-consciously. More than half of those who wrote about the coffeehouse had emotional reactions to it. LG, from the advanced group, wrote:

> On a personal level, the coffeehouse was very touching. I am generally a pretty quiet person, and, although I have performed music in front of a crowd before, I always preferred to stay out of the spotlight (either by playing drums or rhythm guitar; never did I dream of singing!). However, armed with the immensely accepting and open-minded ideology of the folk movement, I felt surprisingly comfortable singing along with my classmates. . . . Folk music was so inclusive, optimistic, and encouraging that it gave people the ability to at least feel free of judgment; it made people excited to try new things, express themselves, and ultimately break out of their self-conscious shell. By my diagnosis, I believe that America needs something today that could, like the folk revival did, inspire this attitude once again. I believe my generation would be the better for it.

Especially interesting were the romantic notions of inclusivity and acceptance often invoked in student writing. As they learned more about folk's manifestations, students could offer more sophisticated and nuanced discussion of inclusivity in the folk music revival. In their writing, however, they preferred uncomplicated versions of these ideas, evidently discovering there an important basis for and confirmation of the musical invitation they felt. Having read Peter Mercer-Taylor's (2007) article on Bill Staines, for example, LG was able to diagnose himself with a case of "secondary nostalgia" in the space shown by ellipses above, yet that did not dilute the power of the inclusivity and acceptance that dominate his understanding of the folk revival. We spent Mondays and Fridays problematizing aurality, authenticity, and participation, questioning much that had seemed clear the first day. For all the holes we collectively poked through folk's capacious umbrella, on Wednesdays we found it still offered shelter. Even students with significant musical experience found themselves in an altered musical reality, as was the case for a violist, MT:

> Finally, I actually wanted to reflect on the first song [we] played: "This Land Is Your Land." I initially thought it would be fun to play with the beginners, but having everyone there playing together as a group far surpassed my expectation of "fun." I have never been in a situation where every single person is participating in producing music in some way, because even in group music lessons there has always been an instructor there serving in a teacher/observer capacity. I did not realize this until about the middle of the song, and, as cheesy as this sounds, it was a very powerful moment for me. . . . I found myself really understanding the power of folk music at a level that I had never been able to before. It helped me believe in folk music as something with the power to change.

Similarly, another student wrote that the sense of power she felt in the moment was one that translated into politics for her: if her musical contribution could matter, maybe her political contribution could, too.

Emerging Themes

In considering student reactions to the course, I organize my thoughts according to four major themes that emerged from the experience: demusicalization, anxiety, safety, and recovery of the musical self. As much as possible, I use students' own descriptions of their experiences, drawing mainly on three assignments. First, students are required to turn in a progress report about halfway through the term. Most use these both to describe and to reflect on their progress in the applied section. Second, throughout the term, students write reading responses, sharing their reactions to class readings. The responses may also be about concerts or personal experiences. A number of students used a response (in most cases asking me in advance if they could save one for this purpose) to reflect on the coffeehouse at the end of the term.

Demusicalization

A third assignment on which I draw is received by students in the first week and completed in the following two. In this four-part assignment, I ask students to:

- list songs they believe they learned through oral/aural tradition, hence upsetting their notions of oral/aural tradition (concurrently, they read Bruno Nettl's 2005 chapter on "Traditions: Recorded, Printed, Oral, Written" and Charles Seeger's 1977 article, "The Folkness of the Nonfolk and the Nonfolkness of the Folk");
- collect the song list of another individual, removed by at least a generation;
- consider ways of organizing the resulting material;
- write, choosing their own focus, on what they learned or what strikes them.

Though rife with contradictions through which we struggle in class, the assignment produces reliably rich results and grounded contemplation of folk music, tradition, and the place of singing in American culture.

One strong conclusion reached by the students is that music making, or at least much informal and aurally transmitted music, is largely a thing of childhood, and thus their own pasts. They observe that religious and athletic affiliations account for many of the later additions to their lists. With few exceptions, those who are not invited or do not choose to specialize in music find that music making appears to be confined to particular life stages and contexts. This is especially true of playful group engagement.

Some students are conscious of having been what Christopher Small has called "demusicalized." Using the term "musicking"—engaging music, not just performing or practicing—Christopher Small asked himself, "If everyone *is* born capable of musicking, how is it that so many people in Western industrial societies believe themselves to be incapable of the simplest musical act?" (1998:210). He concludes that people "have been actively taught to be unmusical" (1998:210). He further references his experience with students, concluding that "there must be millions of people in Western industrial societies who have accepted the judgment passed upon them and classed themselves as unmusical and even as something called tone-deaf" (1998:210).

In its focus on simple, repetitive forms, inclusivity, and pedagogy, the folk revival provided a powerful rupture in the demusicalization trend. Pete Seeger personified this message. His 2014 death elicited fond remembrances, many of which center on his lifelong support of music making as a human capacity. Of the many iconic photos of Seeger, especially apt are the many in which he cups his hand around his ear, to encourage and to hear the singing of others. The iconic sound is his shouting, "Everybody, sing it!" as he did at the Obama inauguration, and lining out, yelling his lining-out louder than he sang the rest of it. His insistence on musicality as a way of being human was transformative for many, who often begin their stories as folk musicians with a Pete Seeger concert. This is true across a wide spectrum, from professionals such as Joan Baez (Hajdu 2001:8) to the ethnomusicologist Tom Turino. After pointing out that the "aesthetics of the 'folk revival' actually celebrated everyman voices and instrumental abilities; many of the songs were easy to learn and play," Turino turns immediately to Seeger, noting that "in a country where great importance is placed on specialization and professionalism . . . he, and others who followed, succeeded in opening up a variety of musical scenes that have enriched many people's lives—I count myself . . . among them" (Turino 2008:157).

My consultants from the Minneapolis folk scene of the 1960s have similar stories. Lyle Lofgren, who still plays with his band Uncle Willy and The Brandy Snifters, answered my question about how he started playing:

> **Melinda Russell**: So how did you pick up the instrument?
> **Lyle Lofgren**: Pete Seeger concert. 1957. I think John, Bud's brother, took me to a Pete Seeger concert . . . at the Unitarian Society. It struck a resonant chord because he got across the idea that anybody can do this. And I had grown up around fiddle music, Swedish fiddle music. But I didn't play; I was a pretty clumsy kid. And I'd taken some piano lessons, but like with Bud's guitar lessons, it didn't really take. So I never learned to read music. I can write music, but I can't read it. . . . And so I sent for a five-string banjo . . . and then . . . a cheap guitar. (Lyle Lofgren, interview, 10 December 2011)

It is particularly striking that Lyle's initial answer to my query about his becoming a musician is simply "Pete Seeger concert," and he has plenty of company. This connection, between Seeger's invitation and their own musicality, was one my own students made. As one beginning guitar student, LM, wrote in her progress report:

> Pete Seeger would often tell his audience, "Sing with me. Sing by yourself. Make your own music, pick up a guitar, or just sing a cappella. We don't need professional singers. We don't need stars. You can sing. Join me now." (Hajdu 2008:8). . . . This message, which was at the heart of the folk revival, comes alive as I, too, pick up the guitar and sing. A few weeks ago I had never intentionally played the guitar—all I had done was strum it and pluck notes on

> friends' guitars—and now I am playing "A Soalin'" and, what's more, it sounds similar to Peter, Paul and Mary!

In its inclusion of an applied component, especially one aimed at beginners, the folk music class moves beyond studying this moment of musical invitation to echo it, offering students the chance as adults to play together in a musical field whose name, folk, shouts its counterargument that music is for everyone.

Anxiety

When urging students to make music, I sometimes found that they had difficulty conceiving of themselves as musicians. They are exquisitely sensitive to the tendency, noted by Nettl, of societies to "distinguish, rank, or group musicians" (2005:366). In class and in their writing, many students disclosed anxiety about their status as musicians, seeking and giving assuagement. In the pre-registration period, I received several e-mails checking whether it was really okay (as clearly stated in the course description) to have no musical experience or to be unable to read music. Students wanted to confirm that expected barriers to beginning music study would not be in place. Were there really free instruments to borrow? After I met students, and especially after they completed the song-list assignment and shared stories about family music making, I learned that many had a story of being labeled unmusical or bad singers or tone-deaf. Parents, older siblings, and music teachers figure prominently in these stories. As the stories emerge, they are sometimes accompanied by visible pain and anger. More than once, attempting to offer help, I have unknowingly evoked a difficult memory or hurdle, and sometimes individual students, or all of us, have to stop playing to deal with the emotions.

Some students mask their anxiety while in class, but express it in writing. Here, EV shares her dismay at finding that we would be singing:

> And then there's singing. . . . I have to admit, I did not foresee that singing would be such a big part of the Wednesday lessons (shows how much I knew about folk music beforehand!). On the first day when we were asked to sing I just kinda thought to myself, "Oh, maybe I'll just opt out of this one." Then it became clearer that singing was a large part of the class and I got really nervous. I've never had any formal voice lessons and singing (along with dancing and similar ventures) are things I've always been fairly self-conscious about. But I *think* I'm becoming more comfortable with it. I appreciate that class is a really safe environment where everybody is asked to sing but no one is required to sing *well*. . . . I still wouldn't say I'm now totally brave enough to sing loud

> and proud but perhaps I am continually becoming more comfortable with the idea that it's ok to try something and still not be very good at it.

Two important patterns are evident in this response: confirming the "safety" of the class by spelling out what differentiates it from other settings—separating participation from perfection—and linking that difference to the revival itself.

Another student, AL, wrote of overcoming a sense of herself as unmusical:

> Thinking about my experience with respect to the folk revival, what stands out most to me is a sense of empowerment. This is the first time I have ever had any musical instruction, and I tend to perceive engaging with music as something intimidating and inaccessible, because I lack any acquaintance with either theoretical or applied terms or concepts. Nonetheless, I have been able to learn a few chords and play some songs. Simple as this is, it seems rather significant to me, because it has transformed something that seemed totally foreign and unapproachable into something that I can actually participate in.

SS, who was in the advanced section, noted that her minimal comfort as a singer made her a song leader in a context where so many students—students who had, after all, signed up for a folk music class and might have been presumed comfortable musicians—were too inhibited to sing:

> I'm not comfortable leading a song vocally myself, but the mere fact that I was willing to sing sometimes singled me out as the lead singer (or sole singer!) in the small group, which was challenging.

Many scholars have picked up Small's idea of demusicalization, but few have explored the attendant anxiety. An Internet search for "afraid to sing" or "why can't I sing" or "am I a bad singer" is simple proof of the depth of such feeling. Music therapists and educators, especially vocal instructors, confront musical anxiety in their work.[2] Jeanette Myers, a scholar and vocal instructor who teaches a class called "Singing for Those Who Have Been Asked Not To" writes poignantly of a ninety-two-year-old woman who has mourned her lost singing voice, silenced by very early criticism (2012). Myers's students, like mine, often report that criticism from teachers or parents foreclosed their musical exploration. They seek her help, she writes, in order to be able to sing in their own churches or to sing "Happy Birthday" to a grandchild.

Safety

While not every student in the class must overcome anxiety, it is prominent in the beginning guitar section. I occasionally take it on explicitly, especially in the first session. In a more general way I am conscious that the classroom must feel safe. Several elements help here. Students realize that, as Nettl noted (1995:84), folk music is not a central music department function but a peripheral one, and they further imagine it to be less governed by notions of talent than classical music. Since they sign up for a course, not an ensemble, students have a cover that allows them to pursue their own musicality within a setting that does not require them to declare themselves musicians, enter a music store, read music, or rent or own an instrument. The guitar itself is a sort of comfort object and a shield. Making one's way on the guitar, especially in the early stages, allows a lot of looking down. My own extremely modest guitar skills close the gulf between student and teacher.

It has been important to take great care in offering students encouragement, empathy, and success, and especially to maximize early success and reduce the potential for shame. On the first day, students play a rudimentary version of "Michael, Row the Boat Ashore," learning and then strumming its two chords. Though none of the students really like the song, all are delighted, and most surprised, to leave a single class playing a whole song. In each successive class, one or two new chords and a single new technique (e.g., thumb-brush) are added. Students enjoy (and sometimes note in their responses) the masking effect of playing in a group, where the musical fabric is dense enough that no error particularly stands out, and they also find comfort and progress in the breakout groups of three or four that I visit in rotation during class. In truth, I am pleased by their focus and progress and find it easy to compliment achievement and dismiss mistakes. I know from student responses that the advanced section has the same tenor, as BE wrote:

> What I've appreciated most about the applied lessons is that trying something that's just a little bit out of our comfort zones—even if we're not entirely successful—is rewarded. Rather than worrying about getting something exactly right the first time, I've been able to try and fail along the way and feel less self-conscious about it, which means I can focus more on how I'm playing with the people around me rather than on how self-aware I am.

Discovery and Recovery of the Musical Self and Community

Thomas Turino argues that "in fundamental ways, the mainstream 'folk revival' was a result of a mainstream need to make music without pressured comparison to the stars—to have music back for connecting with places, a past, and other people, with home, however it is conceived . . . *participatory* music and dance have special qualities and characteristics for creating solid feelings of community and identity. Sounding together articulates and realizes a special way of being together" (2008:157). I would add that folk reclaims music as a form of play. In its insistence on the use of strophic and verse-chorus structures, of simple and repetitive formats, of slow tempi and stepwise melodic motion, folk combines elements to offer a distinctly rewarding, safe, and confined musical space in which to be a learner, and to actually play with the materials. A first pass at a tune might involve simply strumming the basic chord on each bar. As her skill set grows, a player can experiment with adding melody, harmony, bass notes, picked lines, or countermelodies.

The coffeehouse at the end of the term was initially a concession to students who wanted to hear one another. It also presents tension, for as performance approaches, the class seems to diverge from the goals of comfort and low stakes. In the advanced group, most students had some previous experience with performances, and the coffeehouse setting was clearly informal in comparison with these. In the beginning section, the idea of any kind of performance, especially nine weeks after first holding an instrument, was daunting. We spent parts of the last four lessons planning subgroups, talking about ways to end songs, and ways to vary texture, for instance. Students who wrote responses to the coffeehouse found enjoyable and laudable aspects of both groups. Advanced students were impressed by the beginners' aplomb and progress, and the beginners were impressed with the advanced groups' technical prowess and ability to work within a less-defined form. All, like WT, commented on the accepting environment:

> It has been quite a long time since I performed on the guitar in front of any audience, and that was a fantastic feeling. Compared to almost any performance I have given, the coffeehouse gig had a sense of ease and community that let all our mistakes slide rather than dwelling on them. People just wanted to hear our own take on the songs; there was no thought of comparisons or failures. That acceptance was part of the folk tradition (outside of the realms of the critics, at least) and in finding that we were at least able to plug back into part of that past. It's what we love about that period in time, after all.

The coffeehouse performance of both groups offered evidence of playful engagement with music. In the advanced group, the comfort level was so great that improvising never really gave way to thinking about the performance as a product. In the beginning group, there was more self-conscious preparation for the performance, but this took the form of play, as when a subset sang "Goodnight Irene," introducing itself as "from Kentucky" (and thus taking on the anxiety of authenticity), then personalizing their verses with references to senior "comps" (theses) and post-graduation stress. That they sang these verses, each taking a vocal solo, deeply impressed their classmates. A transgender student who had been newly navigating the effect of hormone therapy on his voice inhabited it with confidence and humor. A second student, not fully comfortable singing, did something further on the speech end of the continuum. Of them, fellow student SS wrote:

> I was surprised and fascinated by the boldness with which each singer performed in their own unique style, whether it was semi-spoken, singing with high, ethereal vibrato, or simply singing with whatever vocal ability they had. W's constant smile throughout her solo, and her exceptionally wide grin at the end of the song epitomized the signs I saw from the other students of their enjoyment of the simple ability to make their own music and to share it with others. . . . This unashamed pleasure, with no hint of embarrassment and hardly any nerves, was inspiring for all in the room. When we saw how our peers were truly enjoying making music and sharing it with us, we were encouraged to add our own voices, our own expressions, and our own pleasure to the mix.

These students were not reviving "folk music," so much as they were reviving their own sense of being people, of being "folk." The coffeehouse was an affirmation and enactment of students' intent to take back music. Several wrote of the out-of-class implications of their playing experience. JS wrote:

> Playing and learning in front of the rest of the class has made me comfortable playing where others can hear me, and making mistakes where others can hear me. When I was afraid of the rest of the house hearing my playing, I would close the door each time I played, but as I've become more comfortable I leave the door open sometimes and people will often stop in and sing a few lines of whatever song I'm playing . . . people tend to gravitate towards music, even if it's pop songs shittily sung to simple chords by the guy who lives down the hall.

In a short ten weeks, we managed to form a community while studying a period. In it, we repeated and enacted a belief about musicality that bound us together. For all the complex forces pushing toward demusicalization, the antidote—Pete Seeger's antidote—is freely available and remarkably effective. In this case, dismantling commonplace barriers to novice music making and immersing ourselves in a period characterized by a redefinition of "musician" helped us establish an atmosphere conducive to everyone's participation. Though sensitive to society's tendency to mark off the role of musician as a particular territory, many people are equally awake to its exceptions and are quick to take up an invitation to make music, so long as the demand for excellence, and the risk of shame, are reasonably low.

Notes

1. All student comments are from written work in MUSC 247 at Carleton College (Spring 2013). My thanks, as always, to my wonderful students, and to the excellent Mark Kreitzer.

2. Cf. Chong (2010); Richards (1999).

References

Chong, Hyun Ju. 2010. "Do We All Enjoy Singing? A Content Analysis of Nonvocalists' Attitudes Towards Singing." *Arts in Psychotherapy* 37(1): 120–24.

Hajdu, David. 2001. *Positively 4th Street: The Lives and Times of Joan Baez, Bob Dylan, Mimi Baez Fariña, and Richard Fariña*. New York: Farrar, Straus and Giroux.

Mercer-Taylor, Peter. 2007. "Bill Staines's 'Bridges' and the Art of Meta-Folk." *Journal of the Society for American Music* 1(4): 423–52.

Myers, Jeanette S. 2012. "Teaching Adult Beginning Singing." *Journal of Singing* 69(1): 31–37.

Nettl, Bruno. 1995. *Heartland Excursions: Ethnomusicological Reflections on Schools of Music*. Urbana: University of Illinois Press.

———. 2005. *The Study of Ethnomusicology: Thirty-One Issues and Concepts*, second edition. Urbana: University of Illinois Press.

Richards, Carol. 1999. "Early Childhood Preservice Teachers' Confidence in Singing." *Journal of Music Teacher Education* 9(1): 6–17.

Seeger, Charles. 1977. "The Folkness of the Nonfolk and the Nonfolkness of the Folk." In *Studies in Musicology 1935–75*, 335–44. Berkeley: University of California Press.

Small, Christopher. 1998. *Musicking: The Meanings of Performing and Listening*. Middletown, CT: Wesleyan University Press.

Turino, Thomas. 2008. *Music as Social Life: The Politics of Participation*. Chicago: University of Chicago Press.

CHAPTER TWENTY-SEVEN

~

Transpacific Excursions

Multi-Sited Ethnomusicology, The Black Pacific, and Nettl's Comparative (Method)

Gabriel Solis

In 2002, I took up an assistant professorship at the University of Illinois as a newly minted Ph.D. I was soon greeted with the admonishment that I would be expected, as part of a tradition established by Bruno Nettl, to do research in a second area. Comparison, it was put to me, was an essential part of the ethnomusicological endeavor, and really only possible with deep knowledge of at least two musical traditions or culture areas. As readers of this volume will know, Nettl had done research with Native Americans and in Iran (and was deeply knowledgeable about the Western classical tradition and about Karnatak music for that matter); the rest of my senior colleagues in the department at that time had all followed in his footsteps, Charles Capwell in India and Indonesia, Thomas Turino in Peru and Zimbabwe, Donna Buchanan in Bulgaria and the wider Ottoman sphere.

I had done dissertation research on jazz, with a particular interest in the intersection of music, memory, and the politics of race in America. To the extent that I saw my work being geographically larger in scope than the United States, I was interested in diasporic connections—placing African American music in the Black Atlantic. Paul Gilroy's book by that name was fairly current at the time (Gilroy 1993), making the African diaspora—a subject that had been an important part of Afrocentric scholarship since at least the 1960s—visible and fashionable in cultural studies. Ingrid Monson had just edited the volume *The African Diaspora: A Musical Perspective* (Monson 2003), and Thomas Turino and James Lea's book on diasporas (Turino and Lea 2004) was about to be published, adding considerably to the literature on the topic. Moreover, I had trained with *capoeira* groups, and I had a considerable interest in Afro-Brazilian music more broadly.

With this range of research interests, it might have made sense for me to work in Brazil once I had finished my first book, but somehow I did not. By the time I got to that point, I had developed an abiding interest in Aboriginal and Torres Strait Islander music. With a semester's teaching leave in the fall of 2005, I pursued a project in Australia, studying ancestral performances in contemporary contexts as a way of understanding Indigenous modernity. I have been going to the Southwestern Pacific—Australia and Papua New Guinea—once or twice a year almost every year since then, slowly accumulating a level of knowledge and understanding necessary to write about music in the region. I initially imagined that the project would contribute to the large-scale comparative study of Anglo-settler colonialism worldwide. Since 2005, my research interests have shifted to some degree; I remain committed to understanding Indigenous modernity, but am no longer concerned only with the dynamic of ancestral traditions in contemporary spaces. I now see my work largely as a study of racialization—a system and practice that has fundamental and intertwined implications throughout global modernity. Most importantly, through this shift in focus I have pursued not so much an ethnographically comparative project (that is, a comparison of two instances of a type of social structure) as a historical one. Somewhat unexpectedly, I am now engaged in a study of connections—alliances and affiliations—that Indigenous artists and activists and their African diasporic counterparts have developed through music over slightly more than the last century.

The point of this expanding interest, and to me the reason to cast it as a comparative study, is that most of the individual stories that make up what I have started calling the "Black Pacific" have appeared in the scholarly record, but have never been described in terms of a single, overarching socio-musical process. I do not claim to have a unique archive in this project. Instead, by seeing all of these stories as historically continuous, I propose a new synthesis. I outline that synthesis in this chapter, offering at the same time an appreciation of the many ways Bruno Nettl's ideas—especially about comparison as a practice and "comparative method"—have informed my intellectual framework, and finally making a suggestion of what I think the stakes of this research are for ethnomusicology at large.

Nettl's Comparative (Method)

Bruno Nettl has written in a number of places about the role of comparative study in our field (2005, 2008, 2010, 2013). His refrain is that while it was probably just as well that we abandoned the name "comparative musicology" and its cognates in other European languages, we never really abandoned comparison as an intellectual practice: "We have not been able to get on without it" (Nettl 2010:89). Nettl's point about the change from "comparative" to "ethno-" musicology is clear: ultimately, he says, we don't engage in comparison more than other fields as such, and, moreover, in the period when the field was called "comparative musicology," its practitioners "didn't do all that much outright comparing" (Nettl 2010:74). Over time, he ventures, attitudes toward the prestige of comparison as a method or as a primary aim of the field have waxed and waned. We have engaged in lots of incidental comparison, but only occasionally based whole studies, much less the field itself, on systematic comparison.

What have we done in the way of comparison? Nettl sees comparative practices in a number of places, some of them more significant than others. First, comparison is a basic fact of human cognition: we come to understand things by comparison with other instances of more or less similar things. True, but perhaps not terribly significant to the discipline. Comparison covers an enormously wide range of studies (Nettl 2010:88). More relevant is the comparison that has implicitly or explicitly structured ethnomusicology's transcultural framework. Nettl has explored the ways in which the discipline moved from *Kulturkreis* (culture circle), based on an evolutionary framework, to culture areas, which offered more historical ways of casting this material, more or less concurrent with the shift from comparative musicology to ethnomusicology. Nettl's own work and that of his mentor, George Herzog, for instance, used the culture-area model to reconstruct the history of Native American demographic shifts.

This phase in the use of comparative study not only had a bearing on Indigenous history, but also played an important role in the study of music and diaspora. Richard Waterman's 1948 article on "'Hot' Rhythm in Negro Music," for instance, is a landmark in this tradition, because of its capacious, explicitly comparative argument. He offered a formal study of general features of rhythm in various diasporic black musics, looking for continuity and change. His article, and a host of others that came after it, demonstrated music's capacity to serve as evidence in ongoing anthropological debates, in this case over so-called African retentions in New World black culture. Melville Herskovits's emphasis on culture as a concrete collection of observable traits would ultimately lead later scholars to see his findings as limited, but his fundamental point, that the Middle Passage had not extinguished African memory and practice in the enslaved, proved persuasive (Mintz and Price 1976; Khan 2003:762). The idea that the New World could be seen as a culture area defined by the historical presence of African-descended people, words, sounds, tools, and ideas, and that comparative research was necessary to investigate this state of affairs, solidified over time with considerable input from ethnomusicology.

Comparative scholarship of this sort, drawing as it did on diffusionist, structural-functionalist, and structuralist paradigms in anthropology, did not require the people it studied to be aware of the historical relations it proposed, and might even have found such knowledge irrelevant. As a result such scholarship seems largely to have ignored the significant, explicit ways in which African diasporic communities maintained not only so-called African retentions or a deep-structural African cultural grammar, but purposefully developed social and political connections across the diaspora and with people on the African continent. It is ironic, given the significance of pan-Africanism in the twentieth century, that such connections were largely absent from analyses of diasporic culture until recently.

Comparative work, beyond the specific question of diaspora, was explicitly contested as part of what might be called a decolonizing moment in ethnomusicology in the 1980s. As American and European ethnomusicologists increasingly entered into dialogic relations with their interlocutors in field sites, and as scholars from outside the United States, United Kingdom, and continental Europe came to have a larger profile in the discipline, questions about the purpose and ideological underpinnings of comparison arose. Nettl describes this in *The Study of Ethnomusicology*, comparing the kinds of questions his students asked about comparison in the 1950s and the 1980s, as seen in his presentation of the range of Native American musical styles: "They took this exercise at face value, as it was clear to them that its purpose was simply to exhibit the variety, which struck them as important, and which could only be illustrated through comparison" (Nettl 2005:60). The later group "questioned the purposes of comparison, and wanted to know what valid conclusions one would draw from it. . . . They were suspicious of making comparisons of what they claimed were 'apples and oranges'" (Nettl 2005:61). Nettl concedes the critique that comparison undertaken with the goal of constructing evaluative hierarchies is grossly prejudicial and runs counter to the goals of ethnomusicology. He observes, nonetheless, that in "ethnomusicology, responsible comparative study has never been judgmental, and one wonders why this issue should have become such a bone of contention" (Nettl 2010:88). My sense is that generally, objections to comparative studies have been raised in relation to formalist comparison—comparisons of music, social structures, or both that objectify the cases being studied through trait lists and attempt to interpret those trait lists using statistical models, as with Alan Lomax's cantometrics.

My own work has led me to engage the cultural politics of comparison directly. This arises in two ways: first, as a concern that my work will suffer from a "similarity bias," that is, that my interest in connections between racialized peoples could lead to facile generalizations. Of course, the histories of race-based slavery and Jim Crow in the United States and of Indigenous genocide, displacement, and attempted deculturation in Australia are significantly different, as are the struggles against them—in the past and today. Second, as my interlocutors will readily note, such comparative work may serve no immediate value for the people whose music I study. Detailed, local anthropological studies of autochthonous cultural forms and ideas can be, and often are, used in the struggle for land rights, local language education, and so on, while the same is not clearly true for comparative studies of emphatically postcontact forms, ideas, and lives. I have, nevertheless, also found significant support for my research among interlocutors from the community. The history of connections I am teasing out is by no means a kind of complete ethnography of the people with whom I have worked, but it is a history that is known, at least in its outlines, and valued by many.

Bruno Nettl sees a return to questions requiring comparative approaches, if not a comparative "method," in recent ethnomusicology (Nettl 2008:71–73). He reminds us, in Alan Merriam's words, that we "must be cautious, that like things must be compared, that the comparisons must have some bearing upon a particular problem and be an integral part of the research design" (Merriam 1964:53, quoted in Nettl 2008:70). It seems, for the most part, that Nettl, like those he cites as interested in comparative studies, sees comparison as something best undertaken in essentially formalist projects, and with the idea of discrete musical entities (whether they be songs and song families, genres, or music cultures) serving as interpretive heuristics. Such a framework is indicative of much contemporary scholarship, but I believe it can be coupled with historicism and an orientation to music that sees genres and music cultures as essentially fluid and only thinly bounded.

The Black Pacific

My current research, as I noted, involves studying the connections—affinities, affiliations, and collaborations—between Indigenous artists and activists in the Southwestern Pacific and their counterparts in the African diaspora. These connections stretch back to at least the late nineteenth century and have historical continuity to the present. In line with the "intercultures" Mark Slobin describes in *Micromusics of the West*, the music and politics of transpacific blackness connect communities and cut across larger cultural formations (such as nations or ethnicities) without being defined by small-scale, shared descent lines and other features of a classic, anthropologically defined culture or society, or by what Slobin calls a "subculture" (Slobin 1993).

It is beyond the scope of this chapter to explore in detail the range of people, events, and musical works that constitute the history of the Black Pacific, but it is useful to give at least a cursory picture of the most important ones. In my view this history begins with the Fisk Jubilee Singers and with West Indian sailors and missionaries in the Tasman, Coral, and Arafura Sea fleets in the late nineteenth century, and continues through to the local interpretations of hip-hop today. Throughout this history the musical movement has been relatively unidirectional, with Indigenous musicians in Australia and Papua New Guinea adopting and adapting African diasporic genres, but relatively few diasporic musicians doing the same with Indigenous musics; the social and political relations that have developed in tandem with this musical process have, however, been more complex and less one-sided. African diasporic artists and activists have reached out to Indigenous people and have in a number of instances shown a keen interest in the politics of liberation in the region, especially in Australia.

It appears that this history starts with the Fisk Jubilee Singers' tour of the region in the 1880s and the return in 1890 of onetime Fisk member Orpheus McAdoo with the Virginia Jubilee Singers. It is plausible that further research, particularly in the Torres Strait region, might uncover earlier significant intersections, but it is unlikely that such connections would have involved African diasporic musicians of a profile similar to the Fisk and Virginia groups. The Fisk Jubilee singers were, as Sandra Graham and others have shown, an exceptionally prominent African American singing group in the second half of the nineteenth century (Erlmann 1988:333; Graham 2006). The singers' reception in Australia, in particular, was so positive that McAdoo, who had toured South Africa solo after his tours with the Fisk group, eventually returned to Australia, setting up a black theater company in Sydney in 1899 (Wright 1976:320).

The extent of their interactions with Indigenous people in Australia is hard to know at present. At least one instance of interaction, however, was documented and had important consequences for the longer history of musical blackness in the region. In his narrative of the Fisk singers' Australasian tour, Frederick J. Loudin devotes a considerable portion of the chapter on Australasia to the group's interactions with Aboriginal and Maori people, describing in particular an experience singing for Aboriginal residents of Maloga Mission (Marsh 2003:140–42). The Murray River people at Maloga, who later moved to Cummeragunja—a community that would continue to play an important role in the development of the Black Pacific over time—may or may not have wept "like children, tears of joy" at the Jubilee Singers' performance of spirituals, as Loudin writes, but there is evidence they were impressed by the music. Catherine Ellis recorded Sophie Briggs, a community leader at Cummeragunja, in January 1963, singing "Ngarra Burra Ferra," listed on the tape reel as "a hymn." The piece was inspired by the Jubilee Singers' favorite, "Turn Back Pharaoh's Army." The lyrics, in Yorta Yorta, draw on verses five and six of the published version of the song (Marsh 1883:132). The song begins with an invocation of Moses and continues to the critical point, the closing of the Red Sea, which drowns the Egyptian oppressors and saves the Jews. Similarly, the shape of the melody of "Ngarra Burra Ferra," particularly of the verse, is nearly identical to "Turn Back Pharaoh's Army."

Religious music and Christian missionaries were not the only African diasporic connections for Aboriginal and Torres Strait Islander musicians in the pre–World War II era. Black sailors from the West Indies, the United States, and the African continent were a significant presence in the Pacific fleets, and particularly in the pearling ships that worked the Coral Sea, the Arafura Sea, and the Torres Strait. There is good reason to think that the interchange between these sailors and Indigenous people was considerable. The most well-documented and thoroughly researched aspect of this part of the history of the Black Pacific is the spread of Marcus Garvey's philosophy in the region. John Maynard exhaustively documented the role of Garvey's UNIA (United Negro Improvement Association) in the development of early Aboriginal rights organizations in the early twentieth century, culminating in the establishment of a short-lived Australian chapter of the UNIA in 1920 (Maynard 2005:12–14, 16–19). I cannot say with any authority how extensive the relation between African diasporic music and Indigenous activists engaged with Garveyite ideas may have been. In Maynard's discussion of the boxer Jack Johnson's visit to Sydney for a world heavyweight championship bout in 1908, however, we find that commentators at the time focused on local black sailors' engagement in a quadrille, in which "some sable dancers were displaying bell bottom trousers with great effect" (Maynard 2005:6). Further archival research may bring more connections to light.

By the 1930s, there is substantial evidence of Indigenous music making in Australia that drew on African diasporic popular music, especially jazz, blues, and later rhythm and blues. Black American soldiers stationed in Australia during World War II were profoundly important vectors in transmitting musical styles and ideas about black pride and liberation. The impact of black soldiers in Australia on Indigenous communities has not been studied extensively, but it remains in the shared cultural memory among residents of the villages of the Northern Peninsula Area of Cape York, as I discovered in conversations with elders in Injinoo and New Mapoon. One man, Larry Woosup, reported that the visits were compelling because it was the first time they had seen Westerners who "looked like us" (Larry Woosup, personal communication, 4 October 2006). He described a kind of reciprocal meeting of the musical minds, in which they listened to the soldiers' recordings of the latest African American pop and learned the latest dances, and in exchange they sang and danced the local "shake-a-leg" dances for the soldiers. The years between the 1940s and 2006, when Woosup spoke with me, had worn it down to a somewhat vague story. Woosup did not have a clear sense of what songs the soldiers or the locals would have played and sung, not surprisingly, since this would have involved his father's and grandfather's generations.

Henry "Seaman" Dan, a Torres Strait Islander who worked in the pearling fleets in the 1940s, 1950s, and 1960s, similarly remembers the importance of African American soldiers in the transmission of this music to Australia. Dan grew up on Thursday Island, the administrative center of the Torres Strait Islands, and moved to the mainland with his mother during the World War II evacuation. He first learned to play the guitar and sing pop music in Cairns: "The American Negroes [soldiers] had a camp out at Redlynch. When they'd get their liberty they'd come into Cairns. They used to jive. An old fellow, Harry Hodges, used to play the button accordion. And another uncle, Fred Sailor's older brother, Ben Jacob, he'd play the mandolin. He was very good. They had good parties there. The [African] Americans they'd sing their blues and the jazz songs and they'd do jitterbug. . . . And that's how I got into jazz and blues. Just watching the American Negroes play" (Dan and Neuenfeldt 2013:30).

Marlene Cummings, a blues saxophonist and singer from Queensland, a DJ on Sydney's Koori Radio, and a onetime member of the Australian Panther Party, remembers her father playing in groups called the Opals and the Magpies (the second named after the striped bird for the band's black–white integration). The groups were progressive in their political orientation and drew on jazz as a style of music oriented toward liberation and integration in the 1950s (Marlene Cummings, personal communication, 12 March 2013). Cummings herself has continued in this vein, playing and recording blues as a political music, one that she believes can speak about issues of labor inequality, oppression, and police brutality in Australia as much as in the United States.

The 1970s were a period of intense growth in Indigenous movements in the Southwestern Pacific. Aboriginal and Torres Strait Islander activists consolidated political gains of the 1960s and demanded more with the Tent Embassy, erected on the grounds of the parliament house in Canberra in 1972, setting the tone for movement politics that continues today. Throughout the early 1970s, successful independence movements grew in intensity across Melanesia. Papua New Guinea (PNG) achieved independence through an act of Australia's parliament in 1975. The Solomon Islands followed shortly thereafter, in 1978, and Vanuatu achieved self-rule in 1980 after a somewhat more complicated process, due to its joint British–French colonial rule. Whereas each country has a distinct musical and political history, they have been significantly intertwined since at least the mid-twentieth century.

As Michael Webb has documented, the period immediately following independence in PNG was one of enormous productivity in popular music (Webb 1993:31). These recordings, which were made by artists across a spectrum of ages and from every region of the country, were largely in Tok Pisin, the national pidgin language, and drew heavily on foreign musical styles. Of particular relevance for my project is the enormous popularity of reggae, and especially of Bob Marley and the Wailers, in PNG. Webb describes, for example, the musico-political meaning of the song "Indonesia, Leave Our People Alone," by the artist Tony Subam. The song, which decries the Indonesian occupation of West Papua (then called Irian Jaya), connects the local struggle to the fight against apartheid in South Africa: "The adoption of the musical language of reggae seems deliberate in an album of songs decrying exploitation and foreign domination. . . . The diaspora of a portion of the original inhabitants of western New Guinea under the Indonesian government makes the use of the reggae idiom particularly pointed, drawing a comparison with the African diaspora in the Caribbean" (Webb 1993:64).

The 1980s and early 1990s formed an important turning point in Indigenous music history in Australia, as Aboriginal and Torres Strait Islander musicians developed a new genre that came to be known as Indigenous roots music. Starting with bands formed at the Center for Aboriginal Studies in Music (CASM) and shortly thereafter in dialogue with the Central Australian Aboriginal Media Association (CAAMA), Indigenous artists in Australia began developing a distinctive musical genre that fused the country and rock that were already popular in the Central Desert and Top End regions with reggae. This is perhaps the Indigenous music in the region most widely visible to non-Indigenous people, in large measure because of the success of the band Yothu Yindi and because of connections between the white Australian band, Midnight Oil, and the Aboriginal artist George Burarrwanga (known in life as George Rurrumbu) and the Warumpi Band. It is also the Indigenous music most widely present in the academic literature, with major studies by Aaron Corn (2009), as well as a number in edited volumes by Karl Neuenfeldt (1997) and Philip Heyward (1998), among others.

The Center for Aboriginal Studies in Music's role in instigating this growth in Indigenous popular music cannot be overstated. While artists from the far north have arguably had more prominence in Australia in the 1990s and 2000s, the earliest bands to be successful all had ties to CASM and were motivated not only by its music educational offerings, but also by its commitment to developing Indigenous internationalism. CASM's early leadership, especially Leila Rankine and Ben Yengi, were interested not only in developing pan-Aboriginal connections among the young people there, but also in developing musical and political connections outside Australia. The common wisdom regarding this period is that these bands were specifically interested in reggae, and that there was not a significant presence of African American musical influences. Such wisdom, however, is overly simplified. The extent of Indigenous interest in blues, soul, and funk in the 1980s and 1990s was more extensive than the canonical narrative suggests. In the second decade of the twenty-first century, Indigenous musicians in Australia and PNG maintain autochthonous forms, play reggae and roots music, have developed hip-hop scenes, and have distinguished themselves as R&B performers, locating themselves in relation to blackness in the transnational music industry.

Conclusions

To be sure, the project I have outlined here is distinct in its goals and methodologies from early comparative musicology and from the studies surveyed by Nettl in his recent publications on the topic. I make no claim to uncovering socio-musical prehistory through a study of the Black Pacific, nor to theorizing musical universals or the origins of music. While there are considerable formal coherences among the musics I am considering, moreover, comparison of musical elements occupies only a part of my project. Rather, I am engaged in a multi-sited, comparative project spanning two sides of the Pacific for the light it sheds on transnational social formations in modernity.

This project raises the question: what kinds of affiliations and alliances have the musicians and activists on two sides of the Pacific imagined themselves creating over the past century? The shared term "black" has served a useful purpose, allowing people on the ground to assert connections with some room for slippage, but it is worth probing the question further. Mark Slobin describes three kinds of intercultures, but none quite fits what I see here (Slobin 1993). Surely, this case includes elements of commodification and the spread of disembodied sounds in the industry, but it is more than that. Similarly, it includes elements of diaspora—without the Black Atlantic there would not be a Black Pacific. The history of connections I have sketched here is motivated by affinity, but it is deeper than Slobin's description of a "rather random bonding of individuals to musics," enabled by contemporary modes of mobility (Slobin 1993:68). Thomas Turino describes three "trans-state cultural formations"—immigrant communities, diasporas, and cosmopolitans—but again none quite fits the case of the Black Pacific. Immigration has played only a minuscule role in the connections I am studying, and while it may be similar to cosmopolitanism, or at least make use at times of cosmopolitan circuits, it is frankly the opposite of Turino's definition: a formation that "stresses individuality, placelessness, universalism, and a pan-historicism that results in ahistoricity" (Turino 2003:61). What I see in the Black Pacific is the intentional creation of a measure of cultural unity by people with historically convergent experiences, a process that has stressed commonality, emplacement, and historicity, but one that has also played with the limits of universalist discourse. For the moment I am calling this a postcolonial formation, inasmuch as the connections have been a socially, politically, and artistically creative process through which subjects of Anglo-settler colonial societies have used music to create livable spaces within modernity and to contest their subjugation within a fundamentally oppressive system.

References

Corn, Aaron. 2009. *Reflections and Voices: Exploring the Music of Yothu Yindi with Mandawuy Yunupingu*. Sydney: Sydney University Press.

Dan, Henry, and Karl Neuenfeldt. 2013. *Steady, Steady: The Life and Music of Seaman Dan*. Canberra: Aboriginal Studies Press.

Erlmann, Veit. 1988. "A Feeling of Prejudice: Orpheus McAdoo and the Virginia Jubilee Singers in South Africa, 1890–1898." *Journal of South African Studies* 14(3): 331–50.

Gilroy, Paul. 1993. *The Black Atlantic: Modernity and Double Consciousness*. Cambridge, MA: Harvard University Press.

Graham, Sandra. 2006. "On the Road to Freedom: The Contracts of the Fisk Jubilee Singers." *American Music* 24(1): 1–29.

Heyward, Philip, ed. 1998. *Sound Alliances: Indigenous Peoples, Cultural Politics, and Popular Music in the Pacific*. New York: Continuum.

Khan, Aisha. 2003. "Isms and Schisms: Interpreting Religion in the Americas." *Anthropological Quarterly* 76(4): 761–74.

Marsh, J. B. T. 1883. *The Story of the Jubilee Singers: With Their Songs*. New York: S. W. Green's and Son.

———. 2003. *The Jubilee Singers and Their Songs with Supplement Containing an Account of Their Six Years' Tour around the World, and with Many New Songs, by F. J. Loudin*. Minneola, NY: Dover.

Maynard, John. 2005. "In the Interests of Our People: The Influence of Garveyism on the Rise of Australian Aboriginal Political Action." *Aboriginal History* 29: 1–22.

Merriam, Alan P. 1964. *The Anthropology of Music*. Evanston, IL: Northwestern University Press.

Mintz, Sidney, and Richard Price. 1976. *The Birth of African-American Culture: An Anthropological Perspective*. Boston: Beacon Press.

Monson, Ingrid, ed. 2003. *The African Diaspora: A Musical Perspective*. New York: Taylor and Francis.

Nettl, Bruno. 2005. *The Study of Ethnomusicology: Thirty-One Issues and Concepts*. Urbana: University of Illinois Press.

———. 2008. "Comparative Study and Comparative Musicology: Comments on Disciplinary History." In *Systematic and Comparative Musicology: Concepts, Methods, Findings*, edited by Albrecht Schneider, 295–314. Berne: Peter Lang.

———. 2010. *Nettl's Elephant: On the History of Ethnomusicology*. Urbana: University of Illinois Press.

———. 2013. *Becoming an Ethnomusicologist: A Miscellany of Influences*. Lanham, MD: Scarecrow Press.

Neuenfeldt, Karl. 1997. *The Didjeridu: From Arnhem Land to Internet*. Sydney: J. Libbey/Perfect Beat Publications.

Slobin, Mark. 1993. *Subcultural Sounds: Micromusics of the West*. Hanover, NH: Wesleyan University Press.

Turino, Thomas. 2003. "Are We Global Yet? Globalist Discourse, Cultural Formations, and the Study of Zimbabwean Popular Music." *British Journal of Ethnomusicology* 12(2): 51–79.

Turino, Thomas, and James Lea, eds. 2004. *Identity and the Arts in Diaspora Communities*. Warren, MI: Harmonie Park Press.

Waterman, Richard. 1948. "'Hot' Rhythm in Negro Music." *Journal of the American Musicological Society* 1(1): 24–37.

Webb, Michael. 1993. Lokal Musik*: Lingua Franca Song and Identity in Papua New Guinea*. Port Moresby: Institute of Papua New Guinea Studies Press.

Wright, Josephine. 1976. "Orpheus Myron McAdoo: Singer, Impressario." *Black Perspective in Music* 4(3): 320–27.

CHAPTER TWENTY-EIGHT

~

The Emperor's New Clothes

Why Musicologies Do Not Always Wish to Know All They Could Know

Marcello Sorce Keller

> *Mankind have a great aversion to intellectual labour; but even supposing knowledge to be easily attainable, more people would be content to be ignorant than would take even a little trouble to acquire it.*
>
> —Samuel Johnson, Boswell's *The Life of Samuel Johnson*

Bruno Nettl and Me

Bruno Nettl has been something really important in my life. No one has ever influenced my relation to music as much as he has. I was always impressed by how, in his scholarship, the anthropological and the historical dimension activate each other, and offer countless possibilities for comparison. With Bruno Nettl not only can one better understand all kinds of fascinating sonic landscapes for what they are in themselves, but also, under his guidance, we can better comprehend the familiar music we grew up with—the literate tradition of the West (Nettl 1963, 2005). It is thanks to Bruno Nettl that I developed the inclination to look at things musical through the wide-angle lens (Nettl 1995, 2002). That is what I try to do in this chapter, and I am aware I may have overdone it a bit. Antonio Gramsci used to make fun of contributions that cast their net too wide, like this one, and used to file them under the dubious category of "Short remarks about the nature of the universe!" That is why I would like to remind the reader that all that follows is a bit tongue-in-cheek and to be taken as a divertissement.

One Question to Begin With

Is all knowledge in principle equally desirable? To be sure, not all is equally sought, or equally prestigious to possess. At times Christianity regarded knowledge as a sinful form of pride. Friedrich Schiller spoke of scientific inquiry as leading to what he called *Entzauberung der Welt* (a demystification of the world).[1] In contemporary Western culture we are definitely more knowledge-oriented. Research, however, is expensive, and the question of priorities necessarily comes up—the question, for instance, of whether immediately useful knowledge should come first. Fundamental as that question may be, an even more fundamental one needs to be asked: what to do with knowledge we already have. My feeling is that whatever knowledge we possess, once it is in our hands, we might as well try to keep it and make sure it remains available—which is not always done. Societies, cultures, human groups, and individuals do not always even wish to retain the knowledge they have. Eric Hoffer once wrote: "Far more crucial than what we know or do not know is what we do not want to know" (Hoffer 2006[1954]:38). That is why I titled this chapter "The Emperor's New Clothes." In Hans Christian Andersen's fairy tale bearing this title, no one wishes to realize that the emperor is wearing no clothes. Only a little boy at some point cannot refrain from observing out loud that he is clothed only in his underwear!

It does not only happen in fairy tales. Robert Proctor and Londa Schiebinger call "agnotology" the study of why we do not know, or no longer know, or do not even wish to know things well within our reach: the study of "ignorance making," if you like.[2] Part of our ignorance may be culturally produced and, to an extent, functional—which is a trivial observation from an anthropological standpoint. By carrying a culture, we develop one specific view of the world, which allows people to become more aware of some aspects of reality and, necessarily, less of others. Each culture makes some aspects of reality invisible or transparent.[3] Even when something is culturally noticeable, it may well be considered irrelevant and not even be given a name. In any case, precisely because Western culture is complex, made of layers, roads, corners, tunnels, detours, and dead ends, we have countless possibilities to bypass possible knowledge, or even forget or lose knowledge already acquired. A few such cases deserve to be mentioned.

Hopelessly Lost

Ötzi, the Stone Age mummy found in Southern Tirol in 1991, wore leather shoes that appeared rough and uncomfortable to wear. The Czech shoemaker

Petr Hlavacek, however, was curious enough to duplicate them and put them to the test. He described the experience: "The shoes are very comfortable. They protect feet from heat, cold, and hard terrain. . . . Despite their thin leather soles, the shoes hold very well, protect from humidity, and prevent blisters." Hlavacek's conclusion was that wearing such shoes is like walking barefoot, "only better."[4] There is little doubt that in the course of time knowledge can get lost or forgotten—not only in matters of shoemaking. Loss of knowledge is especially possible, as with Ötzi, when a tradition is not inherited, and so it comes to an end. For instance, the social use of sound as it was practiced by Ötzi and those with whom he lived is also something we do not know and are unlikely to ever know, though in principle such knowledge could have been transmitted. To be sure, there also was knowledge at the time, as at all times, of a different nature, unsuitable for handing down.

When people gain experience in dealing with specific situations, knowledge is acquired that is not easily transmissible when its owners pass away. Speaking of music, Charles Seeger called it "music-rationale," in contrast to the "speech-rationale of music" (Seeger 1976, 1977). Similarly, Anthony Giddens speaks of *practical consciousness* as opposed to *discursive consciousness* (Giddens 1984). My former professor of composition was a perfect example of *practical consciousness*. He could make fascinating music at the drop of a hat, but could never explain why one solution was more effective than another. He could only say: "It just sounds better so." Similarly, Michael Jackson developed unusual ideas and attitudes about the interaction of music, singing, dancing, choreography, and filmmaking, but he did not write books about that. He was no scholar, only a man of genius. A considerable amount of what he knew is now lost. What we cannot verbalize, what we can only express through action, can only to a limited extent be learned through imitation; much inevitably gets lost. Vere Gordon Childe, who considered knowledge a social process, went so far as to say that knowledge is not truly "knowledge" unless it can be communicated and transmitted (Gordon Childe 1956).[5]

I am no philosopher, and in no position to deal with complex issues of epistemology. That is why, in the following pages, I concentrate on communicable knowledge.

Of Laziness and Good Intentions

Mental laziness, my own included, often leads us astray. I do know that in the past music was experienced quite differently from the way it is experienced today. Still, I have a tendency—mental laziness—to look at the past through the eyes of the present. I was once observing a Greek amphora, on which musicians were painted playing instruments. It appeared to me rather bizarre that people surrounding them acted as if they were not listening. Of course, they were not; they were "hearing" the music rather than "listening" to it. The opening sentence of L. P. Hartley's novel *The Go-Between* (1958) puts it very well indeed: "The past is a foreign country: they do things differently there" (7). What the Greek amphora in all likelihood depicted was not "sound-centered" (like the modern concert of "classical" music), but rather "sound-complemented" or "sound-enhanced" (Sorce Keller 2010). We now take it for granted that music exists in order to be listened to, with full attention, maybe even holding our head in our hands to achieve maximum concentration. It is all too easy to forget how even in Western culture, where the anthropological singularity of "active listening" came about, "active music listening" is only an ideal type, to which we very seldom come close.[6] Our ingrained attitude to read the past in terms of the present is strong, and even an ethnomusicologist like myself can occasionally forget what he teaches in the classroom: music in most cultures, and even in some layers of our own, is not meant for pure aesthetic contemplation. Heinrich Besseler, therefore, made the significant distinction between *Umgangsmusik* and *Darbietungsmusik* (Besseler 1959).[7] Thomas Turino reminds us of the fundamental difference between music made to be "participatory" and that made to be "presentational" (Turino 2008). The danger is always there to make *Darbietung* or presentational music for the present out of *Umgang* or participatory music from the past. Madrigals were meant for communal singing, and surely not to be performed on stage in front of a public. Much keyboard music by Handel, Bach, Scarlatti, or Rameau was intended for personal entertainment.[8] Today, that keyboard music is experienced in a concert setting, and there is nothing inherently wrong with that—as long as we are aware it is a modern way of experiencing music. Framing an ancient music score in contemporary social practices is a creative act. The moment, however, we use ancient music as a frame to support the art experience we enjoy today, some forms of available knowledge are either bypassed or lost.

Paradoxically, even well-meaning forms of preserving and communicating knowledge may actually entail the loss of it. When we value pieces or traditions more deeply than they were in the past, by putting them on an altar and making them objects of veneration, we set them out of context. That can happen not only to artifacts, but also to scholarly work. It may have happened when, in the 1980s, several books by Carl Dahlhaus were translated into English. To be sure, the English-speaking readership was in no position to sense that Dahlhaus was not an isolated gem, but rather the product of a scholarly tradition that is very German. Most readers did not know that his writings were often tacitly directed to his East German antagonist Georg Knepler—who never was translated into English. Our appreciation of Dahlhaus leads us to take him out of context, and so to lose some of the knowledge his writings contain.[9]

Circumstances where we miss opportunities to learn something can occasionally be amusing. It is a rumor, circulating among Indonesia specialists, that whenever Jaap Kunst misunderstood something about the gamelan, his Javanese friends loved him too much to have the heart to tell him he was wrong. Usually, loss of knowledge is not amusing. It surely is not the case in Western culture, where an inhibition was developed against physically reacting to sound. In the West we developed the concept of "absolute music," music that only exists to be heard. The dance music we produced in the course of time tends to be made abstract, and so it becomes an occasion only for listening. We may "listen" to African music that, in Africa, could not be conceived without dancing. Deactivating the body is tantamount to deactivating a form of knowledge. When we listen to pieces by Joseph Lanner, Johann Strauss, or Paul Lincke, however, we retain some memory of what dancing the waltz is (or was). Today, nobody has the slightest notion of what it meant to dance a *chaconne*. We know from history that the *sarabande* and chaconne were perceived as erotic and arousing, and at the time of Bach, when the dance forms already were out of fashion, people probably retained an idea of their physical quality. I might ask how Bach's contemporaries reacted to the D-minor Chaconne. Did they still perceive erotic overtones? We do not know, and it is difficult even to imagine what area of scholarship, or concourse of disciplines, might bring back to us some of that lost knowledge.

The question of disciplinary boundaries is a major topic in itself. When areas of scholarly endeavor go their separate ways, there inevitably are advantages and disadvantages.[10] Disadvantages become tangible when separate disciplines no longer communicate with one another.[11] It happens in music studies where "musicologies" have proliferated: historical musicology, ethnomusicology, music theory, music education,[12] jazz studies, and popular music studies;[13] and there is, of course, the psychology of music as well.[14] We now also have biomusicology, zoomusicology, and ecomusicology. Our age could indeed be described as the "Era of Musicologies."

Never Mind Grieg

It is more than a century since sound recordings were invented. We can hear, if we so wish, Fritz Kreisler and his lush violin sound; the cellist Pablo Casals and all the notes he used to leave out in order to keep the pulse going; the many mistakes the pianist Alfred Cortot was able to collect in one single piece. One would imagine their recordings could be used to learn about performance practice in the late eighteenth and early nineteenth century. We have only limited ideas about how Bach used to perform or conduct his own music, but we can actually hear how Saint-Saëns, Grieg, Leoncavallo, Mahler, Paderewski, Debussy, Strauss, Reger, Hindemith, Busoni, and Elgar would perform their own. And yet, no contemporary performance of Grieg takes Mr. Grieg seriously as a pianist (because of his freedom of tempo, approximate durations, and so forth). The sound is there for us to hear, but musicians and scholars reject (what they feel) is the bad taste of Grieg, Rachmaninoff, and Debussy sitting at the piano. No one today who dared to play music as they used to play it themselves would ever get a piano degree in any reputable conservatory. Historical authenticity may be proclaimed, but only enforced when it does not clash with the aesthetics of our age. Once again, knowledge ignored.

Why Reject the Enjoyment of Music

Whenever I have the company of young people, I seldom miss the opportunity of asking them what kinds of music they listen to. The answer always is: "All kinds." As soon as I scan what they have in their iPod, I see that is not true. In what they think is "all kinds of music," about 99 percent of the musics of the world are missing: no Bach, Mozart, or Brahms; no Duke Ellington, Miles Davis, or Charlie Parker; no Philip Glass, John Williams, or Ennio Morricone; and no classical Indian music, *gagaku*, gamelan, or high-brow non-Western repertory. It is striking how often we all, not just young people, think ourselves musically open, though we usually only access the most easily available genres. It already is notable when people are open to classical, jazz, pop-rock, and world music.[15] Rarely do we take the pains of looking for music that is not easily available, and when we do, we immediately retreat as soon as we run across something we find distasteful. This is a crucial border that, in my view, deserves to be crossed. The point I would like to make is that, if we do not only look for pleasure in music, but also expect from it an opportunity to expand our knowledge, then the sole listening to the music we like and love brings us little in return.

The music genres we like and love connect us to familiar places, occasions, and rituals that make us feel comfortable. When we like the music, its social background is easily taken for granted, becoming unnoticeable, even transparent. When that happens, listening becomes, from the point of view of gaining knowledge, pretty much a waste of time. An exception occurs when, overcoming our bias, we look for the fundamental reasons why we find a given genre attractive. Then we unfailingly discover what we may not be consciously aware of: a sense of belonging to, or at least empathy for, the social environment where that music is practiced, which ultimately is ideological. Once such unconscious ideological choices are made, once we give in to the attraction for a genre that reassures us and supports our worldview, only at that point, within that genre, can we "aesthetically" appreciate single pieces, performances, or utterances that better than others exhibit the core values of the repertory at large. What I am suggesting is that the aesthetic experience only takes place within ideological frameworks that are accepted and understood by the community. Such empathy for the social environment to which we belong, or of which we may wish to be part, may be strong to the point that our taste is flaunted as a banner highlighting distinctions between ourselves and the others. That is why listening to or practicing the music others like helps us to come out of our shells and meet them where it certainly requires an effort to do so: meeting them in their symbolic world as it is represented through meaningful sound (Sorce Keller 2012:228–32).

My suggestion to consider the music genres we dislike should not be read puritanically, according to the motto: "You can do anything, unless it gives you pleasure!" Quite the contrary, I suggest that the music we instinctively like does us no good. We do not do ourselves a favor by giving up on one of the most effective instruments for understanding why and how other humans perceive and interpret reality differently from us. I can put it even more forcefully, by saying that we can only effectively prove we are neither racist nor xenophobic when we are ready, through the experience of meaningful sound, to enter the symbolic world of people who are culturally distant from us; and whose distance is revealed by sound practices that we do not like, we do not understand, or may even find irritating or antagonizing—after all, they were not meant for us.

That is why I fear that I, and all the people like me who will eventually be ending up in Hell, will be there endlessly force-fed with the music we most like, which entirely and unproblematically reflects our worldview. With that kind of punishment all possibilities of growth will be denied for eternity. We will be forced to be only the little thing we managed to be up until that point, with no hope to encounter any horrifyingly distasteful music that might lead us out of our niche, and help us understand some of the very many different ways to be human.

Screen Labels

It is inevitable for cultures to use what I call "screen labels." Cultures need to simplify reality, because reality is far too complex to be apprehended in its entirety. The trouble is when in the effort to simplify their worldview, cultures invent labels—I should better say terms and concepts—that postulate the existence of something that is not really out there. The terminology of Western music has quite a few such labels, and "classical music" is a good example. Actually, there is no such thing out there, but rather only a "classical formatting," where sonic products or processes that have little or nothing to do with one another are arbitrarily put into the same conceptual basket. All that Gesualdo's madrigals, Haydn's symphonies, Hugo Wolf's *Lieder*, and Stockhausen's *Klavierstücke* have in common is not much at all, except they all are (albeit in different ways) notated on paper and regarded today as "High Culture." They represent substantially different manners of socially using sound, realized following different recipes, and conceived for circumstances and expectations that could hardly be more diversified. When we put them into the same basket and call them classical music, in a single stroke we erase their original intention, and actually offend the specificity of the accomplishment they embody. It is in a way as if we put highways, city boulevards, classroom floors, or desk surfaces into the same conceptual category simply because on their surface—if we really wanted to—we could dance! But it would make no sense to speak of "danceable surfaces," because in doing so the distinctive characteristics of highways, boulevards, floors, and desk surfaces would become obscured. Something as repulsive as the basket where we collect what we like to call "classical music" is an idea worthy of Dr. Frankenstein.[16]

Of course, screen labels such as "classical," "folk," and "pop" are so established in common parlance that it would be impossible to do away with them. My plea is that we constantly be aware that they are not useful as tools for scholarship. Words that hide the complexity of reality do not favor the acquisition of knowledge. Language that labels and does not define is a dangerous tool. As Thomas Hobbes put it in his *Leviathan*: "A man that seeketh precise truth, had need to remember what every name he uses stands for; and to place it accordingly; or else he will find himselfe entangled in words, as a bird in lime-twiggs; the more he struggles, the more belimed" (Hobbes 1651:22).

Conclusions

At the outset of this chapter, I wrote that it is questionable whether useful knowledge should, in principle, be preferable to what appears to be useless.

By "useless," I am referring in particular to that kind of knowledge that gives us nothing more than the pleasure of satisfying curiosity. After all, mathematicians do not primarily work with mathematics just because what they do may at some point become useful but rather because it brings pleasure.[17] Pleasure and curiosity are important, and not only to mathematicians. I myself would like to know a lot of things that, in all likelihood, would be considered useless by most people. Permit me to offer a few examples. I grew up with Beethoven's music, and that is why I would love to know how Beethoven's laugh sounded. Could it communicate a sense of joy, human warmth, empathy, humor, and irony, like some of his music? Later in life, I listened to much Indian classical music, South Indian in particular, what Bruno Nettl once described during one of his seminars as the most beautiful music in the world. That is why, when I think of the great Thyāgarāja, I wish I could hear the tone and color of his voice when he sang, for instance, the *Jaga-dananda-karaka* melody. To be sure, like in such cases I mentioned, there is also such a thing as hopeless knowledge, unreachable knowledge. The painful awareness of that we could call, by using the title of the famous novel by André Malraux, "*la condition humaine*," the human condition. Painful as it is to accept that there is so much we will never know, in this chapter I tried to explain that it is even more regrettable if the knowledge we already have goes unnoticed and unheeded, and eventually gets lost altogether.

Notes

1. W. H. Auden put it somewhat differently: "This passion of our kind / For the process of finding out / Is a fact one can hardly doubt, / But I would rejoice in it more / If I knew more clearly what / We wanted the knowledge for, / Felt certain still the mind / Was free to know or not" (Auden 1966).

2. As Proctor and Schiebinger put it, "Our primary purpose here is to promote the study of ignorance, by developing tools for understanding how and why various forms of knowing have 'not come to be,' or disappeared, or have been delayed or long neglected, for better or worse, at various points in history" (2008:vii).

3. In Classical Greece, for instance, the economic dimension of life and politics was never the object of systematic investigation, hence, never consciously perceived. In our time, although cinema is the art form where one could more easily study the process of collective authorship than in any other, it is difficult for us to do so, because the idea is implanted in our aesthetic culture that "art" is the product of a single creative mind.

4. sciencev1.orf.at/news/137746.html.

5. For instance, if I am staying at a hotel in a foreign city, I may be able to retrace my steps from the train station without being able to tell a friend how to do the

same. That is because I collected impressions about the itinerary, like the smell of a coffee shop, a very ugly building, a windy street corner. All that makes up a bundle of knowledge not easy to communicate.

6. Theodor W. Adorno advocated "structural listening" and was disappointed to admit that most listening attitudes fall into inferior categories: the culture consumer, the emotional listener, the resented listener, and the pop music or regressive listener (Adorno 1962).

7. Questions about the many different ways music was used and regarded in past eras occupied his thoughts from his earliest years as a scholar, questions he explored up to the Romantic Era.

8. Nobody around 1800 would have conceived of presenting to a public Bach's *Well-Tempered Clavier* or Couperin's *Pièces de Clavecin*. By the time Brahms was asked by the publisher Novello to edit all four books of the latter, the idea of publicly performing "ancient" music was obviously already gaining ground.

9. Do we really wish to use all the knowledge we have about Beethoven? Although it is known that up until the time of Czerny, chords were usually arpeggiated, no pianist likes to do that today. How many pianists performing his sonatas have preliminarily studied the analyses and discussion of those pieces by Hugo Riemann, Rudolph Réti, Heinrich Schenker, or Charles Rosen?

10. It happened in North America when the Society for Music Theory was developed out of the American Musicological Society, in 1977, and became an independent association.

11. One is reminded here of C. P. Snow and his famous book *The Two Cultures* (Snow 1959).

12. Music educators often reproached me that ethnomusicologists have done remarkably little to make their knowledge useful for them to use in the classroom, and added that today, more than ever before, they need help in the classroom, where they have pupils coming from the most diverse cultures.

13. Jazz studies are not considered part of ethnomusicology by those who practice them, though many ethnomusicologists are indeed interested in jazz. As in the case of popular-music studies, we have here two substantially independent scholarly fields, often visited by ethnomusicologists.

14. What we call "music" (sound-centered, sound-complemented, sound-supported, social activities) is "nature" well before it becomes "culture." In other words, when we only investigate music "as culture," the "natural" layer of the process is overlooked. Although the natural sciences investigate music from their own angle, their findings are difficult to reconcile with those obtained by musicologies.

15. A musician's knowledge of music seldom goes beyond the genre she or he actually practices.

16. Hermann Hesse once expressed the same idea much more effectively: "One might imagine an orchard with hundreds of trees, with thousands of flowers, and with a hundred different sorts of fruit and vegetables. If this gardener knows no other botanical distinction than one between 'edible' and 'weeds,' he will only know to deal

with one-tenth of the vegetation in the orchard; he will weed out the most magical flowers, and cut down the most noble trees, hating everything he sees around him" (Hesse [2009]1927).

17. An excellent example of that was Évariste Galois (1811–1832), whose work laid the foundations for the theory of numbers and of function—totally useless at the time, a simple intellectual game—which much later became essential to develop a theoretical model of quark particles.

References

Adorno, Theodor W. 1962. *Einführung in die Soziologie der Musik: Zwölf theoretische Vorlesungen*. Frankfurt am Main: Suhrkamp.

Auden, W. H. 1966. "After Reading a Child's Guide to Modern Physics." In *About the House*. London: Faber.

Besseler, Heinrich. 1959. "Umgangsmusik und Darbietungsmusik im 16. Jahrhundert." *Archiv für Musikwissenschaft* 16: 21–43.

Giddens, Anthony. 1984. *The Constitution of Society*. Berkeley: University of California Press.

Gordon Childe, Vere. 1956. *Society and Knowledge*. London: George Allen & Unwin Ltd.

Hartley, Leslie Porter. 1958. *The Go-Between*. London: Penguin Books.

Hesse, Hermann. 2009[1927]. *Der Steppenwolf*. Frankfurt am Main: Suhrkamp.

Hobbes, Thomas. 1651. *Leviathan or the Matter, Forme and Power of a Commonwealth Ecclesiastical and Civil*. London: Andrew Crooke, at the Green Dragon in St. Pauls Church-yard.

Hoffer, Eric. 2006[1954]. *The Passionate State of Mind, and Other Aphorisms*. Titusville, NJ: Hopewell Publications.

Nettl, Bruno. 1963. "A Technique of Ethnomusicology Applied to Western Culture." *Ethnomusicology* 7(3): 221–24.

———. 1995. *Heartland Excursions: Ethnomusicological Reflections on Schools of Music*. Urbana: University of Illinois Press.

———. 2002. *Encounters in Ethnomusicology: A Memoir*. Warren, MI: Harmonie Park Press.

———. 2005. *The Study of Ethnomusicology: Thirty-One Issues and Concepts*, second edition. Urbana: University of Illinois Press.

Nettl, Bruno, and Philip V. Bohlman, eds. 1991. *Comparative Musicology and the Anthropology of Music: Essays on the History of Ethnomusicology*. Chicago: University of Chicago Press.

Proctor, Robert, and Londa Schiebinger, eds. 2008. *Agnotology: The Making and Unmaking of Ignorance*. Stanford, CA: Stanford University Press.

Riemann, Hugo. 1893. *Vereinfachte Harmonielehre oder die Lehre von den tonalen Funktionen der Harmonie*. London: Augener; New York: G. Schirmer.

Seeger, Charles. 1976. "Tractatus Esthetico-Semioticus: Model of the Systems of Human Communication." In *Current Thought in Musicology*, edited by J. W. Grubbs, 1–40. Austin: University of Texas Press.

———. 1977. "Speech Music and Speech about Music." In *Studies in Musicology 1935–1975*, 1–26. Berkeley: University of California Press.

Snow, Charles Percy. 1959. *The Two Cultures and the Scientific Revolution*. Cambridge: Cambridge University Press.

Sorce Keller, Marcello. 2010. "Was ist Musik? Einige Gründe dafür, warum wir die 'Musik' nicht mehr als 'Musik' bezeichnen sollten." *Schweizer Jahrbuch für Musikwissenschaft* 30: 11–26.

———. 2012. *What Makes Music European*. Lanham, MD: Scarecrow Press.

Turino, Thomas. 2008. *Music as Social Life: The Politics of Participation*. Chicago: University of Chicago Press.

Discography

Famous Composers Performing Their Own Works (Saint Saëns, Grieg, Leoncavallo, Mahler, Paderewski, Debussy, Strauss, Reger, Hindemith, Nikisch, Stevenhagen, Degreef, Lhevinne, D'Albert, Busoni, von Dohnanyi, Landowska, Petri, Schnabel, Backhaus, Fischer, Gieseking. CD, Zyx Classic 3001/2/3.

Welte-Mignon, Grieg, Mahler, Skrjabin, Debussy, Saint Saëns spielen eigene Werke. CD, Intercord INT 860.855.

CHAPTER TWENTY-NINE

~

On Theory and Models

How to Make Our Ideas Clear

Thomas Turino

Among his many theoretical contributions, Bruno Nettl created one of the major models for thinking about culture contact, musical syncretism, and musical change—central problems in ethnomusicology at the time—in a seminal 1978 article and in his 1985 book, *The Western Impact on World Music*. I will return to these publications and a recent interview I conducted with Nettl en route to my main purpose for this paper: to address the hows and whys of theoretical work in ethnomusicology and to consider what theory is, what conceptual models do, and why explicit model building is important for the progress of the discipline.

From Hornbostel's generation to mine, ethnomusicologists have been more interested in elaborating theories and coherent models than seems true among younger scholars today. In our conversation, Nettl concurred, remarking that it is curious that people aren't writing books like *The Study of Ethnomusicology* anymore. Maybe we *are* in a postmodern era in which grand theories and belief in the advancement of general knowledge have been discredited in the humanities. Or as Anthony Giddens would have it, maybe the acute reflexivity of science—that is, that any fact or theory can be overturned by the next discovery—in this high modernist period has led to profound uncertainty about what can be known and elaborated at a general level (Giddens 1990). Two current graduate students, Ian Middleton and Jud Wellington, suggested to me that like the incessant repetition and recombinations of sampled bits from the past in hip-hop, younger scholars' approach to theory has become a practice of bricolage, matching the fractured sense of contemporary selves and social realities. Ethnomusicologists have long used existing theory in a rather ad hoc way, fitting their data into preexisting conceptual boxes picked from here and there. I advocate for a more critical, creative, and holistic way of working with theory.

Over the years I have been confronted by students and colleagues who have stated that they "don't do theory," which strikes me as nonsensical if *theory* is defined simply as a generalization about some entity, phenomenon, or experience. Everyone acts every waking moment of every day on the basis of their theories about people and the world, which, in turn, are based on a whole series of premises that take the form of beliefs. It is important for people to move from what we could call *practical theory* and Gramsci would have called common sense (i.e., nonarticulated or reflected-upon bases of practice), to an explicit and continuous grappling with, and clear articulation of, our central concepts, premises, and general understandings.[1] Why is this important?

Like other social scientists and humanists, ethnomusicologists are engaged with extremely complex and messy human phenomena of which we, as social actors, are intimately a part. As scholars it is our job to make sense of the complexity—be it in regard to a specific ethnographic case or a general problem such as the dialectical relations between sonic-gestural performance, on the one hand, and broader patterns of social life, on the other. When the act of "making sense" involves explanations of the *whys* of the processes we study, this necessarily moves us from the realm of mere description to a more general understanding, that is, to Theory. In order to build better general knowledge about our subjects of study, it is necessary to create analytical concepts and models that are explicitly defined and articulated, that simplify the complexity, and that allow for a comparison of cases. This explicitness leads, most basically, to clearer thinking in the analyst and, thus, to better work. Concepts and models that have "hard edges," as Ming Kuo puts it (personal communication, October 2013),[2] allow for sharper understanding and communication among the community of scholars, which, in itself, is necessary for a furthering of knowledge. Finally, and most importantly, explicitness and clarity allow for the concepts and models to be tested against actualities, and to be accepted, built upon, modified, or rejected by the community; these processes are necessary to a progress of knowledge within a particular discipline, and I take such progress to be a foundational goal. A primary purpose in this paper is to suggest some guidelines for *how* we can become clearer conceptually, and to describe some examples of good theoretical models, a sort of "how-to" guide for younger scholars.

How to Make Our Ideas Clear

C. S. Peirce's ideas about different sign types offer a crucial foundation for creating clear analytical concepts and models. Peirce elaborated three different ways that signs are connected to what they stand for—their *objects*—to create different types of effects in specific perceivers. As one way, icons are signs that stand for something else through some type of resemblance between sign and object. As a second way, indices are signs that stand for their objects through co-occurrence, that is, individuals experience the sign and what it stands for together in their personal experience. Note that there may be mass indices, for example a TV show theme song that calls to mind the program for millions of viewers because they experienced the song and show together repeatedly. But indices are the most individualistic, context-based, and thus unpredictable signs because no two people have exactly the same background of experiences. Indices feel clear, in fact "real," to the perceiver but that clarity is illusory.

Peirce unfortunately chose the word *symbol* to refer to a third way that signs are connected to their objects beyond resemblance and co-ocurrence. Because in lay language *symbol* means the opposite of what it refers to within Peircean semiotics, I have renamed it P-symbol as a reminder that I mean something else and something quite specific (Turino 2014). P-symbols are signs that (1) are connected to what they stand for by linguistic definition; (2) in contexts where that definition is agreed upon by the relevant actors; and (3) they are general signs referring to general objects. That is, P-symbols have other P-symbols or general concepts as their referents (for example, cats in general as opposed to *my* cat). Because one of their fundamental characteristics is generality, P-symbols are the signs best suited for theoretical work. Because they are linguistically defined and the definitions agreed upon, P-symbols are the most explicit and predictable signs—the signs with the "hardest edges"—and are thus the best for clear thinking and specific communication. They are also most removed from the actuality of existents out in the world—they are generals about generals. In contrast, indices are the most individualistic and unpredictable signs and yet the most reality-laden and convincing because the sign-object relations are grounded in our own actual experiences. Understanding these differences between P-symbols and indices is crucial to the task of making our ideas clear.

We learn the meaning of most words indexically. Either we connect a word to some existent out in the world, as when a child says, "Mama, what's that?" or more often we learn the meaning of words indexically through their repeated co-occurrence with other words in linguistic contexts. Indexical words work well enough in general communication when people share common experiences with the language; and for such purposes explicit definition is not required. People commonly use terms like *music*, *identity*, *culture*, *symbol* without ever feeling the need to define them and, in fact, would be hard-pressed to do so. As with the judge asked to define pornography with a verdict hanging in the balance, we know the objects of indexical words when we see them. But we find it difficult to define such terms in the abstract, because indexical words are only tied to a conglomerate of concrete instances.

To transform a word into a P-symbol, these instances must be boiled down and synthesized to lay bare the essential features that unite their objects. This very process makes the concept (and our thinking) sharper and thus more useful for analysis. I submit that in order to make acute analytical distinctions, and to synthesize contrasting cases in terms of specific sets of features, one needs to go through the process of creating hard-edged concepts (P-symbols) out of the fuzzy indexical language we typically use. P-symbols are the most hermetically sealed signs and invite the least amount of creative interpretation, the least amount of "participation," on the part of the perceiver. This fact would make P-symbols less attractive for certain semiotic fields, for example, art and music, but it is this aspect of P-symbols that makes them the most useful for theoretical work.[3]

Let me suggest the following adequacy test for P-symbols that are created to be analytical tools. A good P-symbolic definition clearly delineates the conceptual/ontological *object* of the sign—especially from other related concepts/phenomena—in a manner such that the P-symbol will pertain in the widest variety of relevant instances—that is, will capture all instances without including non-instances—and will highlight the essential dynamics and/or features of the object(s) of the sign being defined. If the P-symbol does not designate something distinctive and essential about its object, it is of little use to us analytically. For example, if the words *society* and *culture* are used as synonyms, as they often are, then they provide no analytical purchase in relation to each other. If, however, one defines the *cultural realm* as "shared habits of thought and practice among two or more people" and one defines *society* as "the social relations, networks, and institutions to which individuals belong," then we can analyze how cultural processes affect the nature of social relations. In the very process of defining key analytical terms, we learn a lot about the concepts and the existents in the world to which they pertain. That is, this exercise is intellectually fruitful in and of itself and is extremely important for fostering clear thinking.

The career-long struggle to define my terms, however, has taught me an important lesson: not all indexical words can be domesticated as P-symbols, and there are various reasons for this. Some words are so thoroughly indexical—only sensible in relation to specific contexts—that they cannot be rendered as relatively context-free P-symbols and hence made analytically useful. The word *music* is like this. Typical attempts to define the word *music*, such as "humanly organized sound in time" fail the adequacy test for defining P-symbols. "Humanly organized sound in time" does not differentiate music from speech, poetry recitations, fire sirens, school bells, and wolf whistles. The reason for failure with signs such as *music* is that there are too many objects of radically different natures and discursive contexts to be grouped as a single concept. For some listeners, certain compositions by John Cage are not sufficiently iconic of sounds they indexically understand as music. Koranic chant and preaching are more iconically related but discursively distinct; in other words, practitioners of these forms adamantly deny their placement within the category music. As ethnomusicologists remind us repeatedly, many societies have no general word *music*, probably for the very reasons I have outlined—we might do well to follow their lead.

Failures to rework an indexical word as a clear P-symbol are often as intellectually and analytically rewarding as successes. Certain terms only function as indices in relation to a particular discourse. Failures at creating P-symbols out of such terms help lay bare the specific discourses to which such terms are tied, discourses that hinder analysis of the particular realities that they circumscribe and often distort. Thus, for example, if one works within the premises of Wilsonian nationalist discourse and defines *nation* as a preexisting cultural unit that has a right to its own state, then the concept *nation* cannot be used to analyze the processes of nation creation in places like Zimbabwe where a preexisting nation did not exist. A key rule for clear thinking is that signs such as *nation* or *folk* that depend on the premises of a particular discourse for their meaning and functions cannot be used to analyze the reality that that particular discourse propagates.

The terms we use and the discourses we buy into and perpetuate have real effects in the world. This is particularly true for media people, politicians, academic writers, and teachers, who, by repeating certain linguistic clusters again and again, create new indexical words and bring them to the level of naturalized common sense for the general public. What is at stake here is nothing less than a battle over worldviews that, in turn, influence people's practices in fundamental ways. The commonly heard and read phrase "we now live in a global world" should give us pause if, as once was the case, *globe* was a P-symbolic synonym for world and *global* referred to everyone everywhere. The phrase "we now live in a global world" only makes sense if *globe* is divorced from its P-symbolic meaning. Through think tanks, media blitzes, and newly funded academic units such as "Global Studies" since the 1990s, the term *global* has become an index for modernist-capitalist cosmopolitanism—the message here being "you're either on the bus or off the bus" to quote the Merry Pranksters. Discourses such as nationalism and globalism do fundamental political work by naturalizing particular worldviews, particularly those of cosmopolitan elites, thereby helping to erode the myriad alternative lifeways existing within a given state or in the world as a whole. As intellectuals and social theorists, it is worth deciding which political agendas we want to propagate or conversely help dismantle.

One guideline is to be on the lookout when there is a massive shift of a common P-symbol such as *global* to a new indexical usage. P-symbols typically inspire P-symbolic thought and critical assessment; indices typically ground our unassessed habits of thought, in other words, become common sense. The shift from P-symbolic to indexical language is very useful for corporations and politicians, often to our detriment, because indexical language dulls critical thinking. I developed my concept of cosmopolitanisms specifically and strategically as an alternative to globalist language for this very reason (Turino 2000, 2003).

On the Value of Conceptual Models in Ethnomusicology

For my generation of ethnomusicologists, there was a basic core of scholars, books, theories, and problems that one had to know. Nettl, Merriam, Hood, Blacking, and Lomax, among others, all wrote theoretical texts outlining what ethnomusicology was, was for, and, in certain cases, what ethnomusicologists ought to do. They gave my generation of scholars common platforms and language to think with and to think past. Theoretical advancement is possible, and in fact has occurred, in ethnomusicology—between Nettl's generation and the previous ones, and between Nettl's generation and mine. As the mothers and fathers of contemporary ethnomusicology, the members of Nettl's generation were concerned with devising conceptual models to make sense of the complexities of artistic and social life.

What is a conceptual model? It involves specifying relations between two or more P-symbolic concepts or categories to map onto existential phenomena in such a way as to clarify the fundamental nature, dynamics, and relations among the components of those phenomena. Richard Adams used the term "contentless models" and advocated their use; the idea here was that, as with the best P-symbolic concepts, the linked concepts of the model were open enough to make sense of the dynamics of a wide variety of cases. Adams's own model for *social power* provides a good example. Adams defined *power* as "that aspect of social relations that marks the relative equality of the actors or operating units; it is derived from the relative control by each actor or unit over elements of the environment of concern to the participants. It is therefore a social-psychological phenomenon, whereas control is a physical phenomenon" (1975:9–10). In this P-symbolic construction, power is circumscribed as social/psychological and it distinguishes *control of something significant to the other actors* as the active variable, or engine that drives the model. Note also that it does not assume a particular relation of dominance—this model can pertain to symmetrical as well as asymmetrical power relations. For example, this model can be used to explain a professor's power over students through the control of grades, or the prison system's power over inmates through the control of their bodies. If a student doesn't care about grades, or an inmate doesn't care about living, then the professor and the warden have no power over them. Compare this to Max Weber's definition. He writes, "We understand by 'power' the chance of a man or of a number of men to realize their own will in a communal action even against the resistance of others who are participating in the action" (1982:60). Weber's inclusion of "communal action" limits the model unnecessarily. The main thing Weber omits, however, is the key variable of the *control of something of concern to the other participants* in the interaction. By distinguishing the P-symbolic concepts of *control* and *power*, and relating them as active variables and results in his model, Adams pinpointed the very engine that drives social power relations of all types and instances.

One of the most lasting models in ethnomusicology comes from Alan Merriam: his elegant tripartite "sound-behavior-concepts" framework for studying music. The model suggests trialectic relations among the three concepts with sound influencing concepts that influence behavior that influences sound production that influences concepts ad infinitum through time. Merriam doesn't specify what the sounds, behaviors, and concepts are, any more than Adams specifies what types of things might be controlled to gain power; thus both models are, in Adams's terminology, "contentless" and can be applied universally if one accepts their P-symbolic constructions.

Taking on one of the central problems of his generation, variably framed then as "culture contact" or "the Western impact on world music," and tied directly to the problem of "musical change," Bruno Nettl proposed a major model in his 1978 article titled "Some Aspects of the History of World Music in the Twentieth Century: Questions, Problems, Concepts." In its explicitness and clarity, this article serves as an excellent example of model building. In the same year, Nettl published the book *Eight Urban Musical Cultures*, which championed and set the stage for the study of urban popular musics, by now a mainstay in ethnomusicological research. Both projects were linked conceptually and strategically in that both advocated the study of syncretic musical processes and musical change.

In our interview and as described in his 1985 book, *The Western Impact on World Music*, Nettl noted that in the 1970s the study of change, syncretism, and culture contact as processes was relatively new in ethnomusicology. He suggested that this new interest had to be understood as a reaction against earlier views of non-Western musics and cultures as static, isolated, homogeneous, and discrete. According to Nettl, this earlier view was a product of social evolutionist premises of earlier generations that Nettl and his cohort rightly felt needed to be superseded. In our conversation, Nettl noted further that coming from music theory, we also study and come to expect musics to be understandable systems, and he mentioned his teacher George Herzog as using the systems model for studying music. Nettl stated: "In George Herzog's time, change was something that was undesirable, and music resulting from culture contact was something that got in the way of his [Herzog's] way of operating. . . . Popular music was even more difficult to deal with; Herzog, and me in the beginning, found that it was so unstable that it didn't lend itself to being looked at as a system, making it something that we didn't want to get involved with" (Bruno Nettl, personal communication, 24 September 2013). This is a typical example of the way that the discourses and models we inherit and inculcate might limit the very things we will study. Nettl saw the inadequacies in the reach of his teacher's model for operating and so was able to make theoretical advances beyond it. Earlier I noted that failures to convert indexical words into P-symbols have often been as intellectually valuable as successes. In regard to our broader conceptual models, this is even more importantly true. In science it is not the places where the theory fits but rather instances where it doesn't that provide the Ah Ha! moments that drive new theory and insights. *This is precisely why a bricolage approach of picking theoretical bits piecemeal to fit our cases is unproductive*.

I asked Nettl why he created his 1978 model. He responded that models help us organize data, and he went on: "People were talking in very general terms about change. The idea of syncretism was there with Merriam. And I thought, you know, there are all these kinds of things that happen, there are all these kinds of motivations for change and so maybe I'll try to make a list" (Bruno Nettl, personal communication, 24 September 2013). His goal was to characterize and classify the types of relationships between societies for the comparison of different cases, and he set out a series of variables influencing the relationships including the relative complexity and technological development of the two societies in contact, political domination, relative size of populations, and, "of course, degree of compatibility of the cultures, providing or denying, for example, opportunities for syncretism," among other variables (1978:124–25). Nettl clearly and provocatively suggests his central premise upon which the whole model turns, his theory of musical energy, which, in turn, depends on understanding musical cultures as systems. He states that while societies vary in the amounts of energy expended in music making, his "basic assumption is that the amount of energy that a culture is willing to expend on music is a very basic and deep-rooted value and thus remains more or less constant over long periods, changing only slowly" (1978:129). The point is that if something new, musically, comes in, something else must be scaled back or go out.

Finally, the meat of the matter, Nettl provides eleven well-formed P-symbolic categories for the types of responses societies might have in relation to the coming of Western music. He ends his "list" with three large concepts. The first is syncretism, which presumably was involved at one or more levels of sound, behavior, and concept in a number of the foregoing categories. The final two responses were modernization and westernization. Having discussed the variables of compatibility and centrality, Nettl distinguishes these concepts as follows: "Syncretism results when the two musical systems in a state of confrontation have compatible central traits; westernization, when a non-Western music incorporates central, non-compatible Western traits; modernization, when it incorporates non-central but compatible Western traits" (1978:134).

Many of these ideas remain useful for thinking about any number of ethnographic instances in current research. His model is clear and logical. One might take issue with Nettl's fulcrum premises of musical energy and "musical culture as system," but he systematically lays out his central premises and concepts so that one can understand the relations among the model's components, and thus can use, refine, or reject the different components and so further one's own intellectual work.

Again writing against the evolutionist position and ethnocentrism, Nettl wrote, "The acceptance of individual creativity as characteristic of non-Western and especially folk and tribal music is somewhat newer; after all, the emphasis on their strong traditions, anonymous composition, and great age had long been juxtaposed to the constant innovation of Western music" (1985:18). Nettl paid close attention to the innovation and creativity of individual artists in different societies. In this way he laid the groundwork for the actor-centered approaches that are typical of my generation and the preceding one. But in the culture contact/ musical change literature of the 1970s and '80s, musics and cultures *were* typically treated as organic interacting systems; it is therefore striking how deeply the structuralism of Radcliffe-Brown and, indirectly, Saussure—the organic whole model of culture and the "music as language-system" metaphor—had penetrated the writing of the time. For Hornbostel's generation, evolutionism was not just a theoretical paradigm, it was a worldview; the same might be said of structuralism for ethnomusicologists in the 1970s and 1980s. Thus, in his famous article calling for a unified theory of musical change, John Blacking (1978) distinguished between changes "of the system," and "changes within the system." The problem that Blacking never solved, and with which Nettl struggled, was arriving at a clear conceptualization of musical or cultural systems.

When I arrived in Peru in the mid-1980s to conduct research on music in the rural Aymara district of Conima, Puno and among the migrants from that district in Lima, I was steeped in the culture contact/musical change literature. Another influence was Dick Schaedel's important work on the "Andeanization of Lima"—a city once the bastion of Euro-Peruvian society. Premised on the organic-whole concept of *culture*, Schaedel's notion was that Indigenous Andean culture was being transplanted in Lima whole hog. My project was to study musical change among the migrants in Lima against the backdrop of Conimeño culture in the highland district. From the start, this framing of my research caused problems, the main one being the systems or organic-whole concept of culture itself.

The Conimeño migrants in Lima were a special self-selecting group in two ways. First, many of the individuals who decided to migrate to Lima in their late teens and early twenties differed from many of those who stayed behind due to their ambition and desire for a different type of life; many were in some way discontent with Conima and were not particularly interested in Aymara lifeways. The Indigenous peasants who stayed in the rural district were by and large content and proud to be who and where they were. Second, the people I worked with in Lima also differed from other Conimeño migrants in the city in that they were members of three district-based regional associations, whereas the majority of Conimeño migrants did not join regional clubs or attempt to identify publicly as Conimeños in the capital. Right off I was unable to talk about Conimeños as a single cultural unit or Conimeño migrants as having a unified cultural core. What was going to be my cultural baseline against which to measure musical and cultural continuity and change?

The Conimeño regional club members created a whole series of new lifeways and musical practices that drew on models from Conima, Lima, other migrant groups, and cosmopolitan practices in unique combinations that fit their particular goals and circumstances, but that differed fairly radically from the ways people in the home district and Limeños operated (Turino 1993). Through the course of this research, my conception shifted from problems of cultural continuity and change to an emphasis on actor-centered creativity and the analysis of specific social conjunctures and strategies for living. This mode of thinking helped me deal with individual differences within the regional associations as well as the myriad variables and models for habit formation that influenced Conimeños in Lima.

Does the historical complexity of real life suggest that we should abandon model building and generalizing? My predictable answer is no. It was the Conimeño migrant case and others like it that led me to create a different series of models that helped me think about the complexity (e.g., Turino 2008). Equally important, however, were the well-formed models of the previous generation that I had internalized; these provided useful tools and insights as well as dilemmas that had to be overcome with different conceptualizations.

My hope for the next generation of ethnomusicologists is that they supersede mine, just as the leaders of Bruno's superseded the evolutionists, and members of my generation have theorized ourselves in various ways past the conceptual limits of structuralism and the organic-whole concept of culture. In order to move ahead, young scholars will need a deep understanding of their intellectual history; but theoretical pastiche, bricolage, and sampling are not useful responses to structuralism or to my generation's brand of "post-structuralism." What is needed is a continuation of the ongoing struggle to analyze the discourses, worldviews, and paradigms that we receive and inculcate. In order to do so, we must continue the process of creating better P-symbolic concepts out of the sea of indexical language. We must also comprehend received models as units of hierarchically related concepts and premises in order to discover where they work and where they fall short. As Kuo reminds us, it is the weak links in the models that generate the breakthrough moments of new thinking and insights, and thus disciplinary progress. Finally, young scholars need to build their own coherent conceptual models that make sense of and help simplify the messy complexities of social life and artistic practices as we now find them. Rather than working with inherited problems, concepts, and models from previous generations, I hope they inherit the *spirit* that led to that creative theoretical work in the first place, a spirit exemplified by Nettl's massive body of work. At the core of this spirit is the belief that a better *general* understanding of the subjects that we study is possible, but only if we make our ideas clear.

Acknowledgments

This paper was originally delivered as the 2013 Bruno and Wanda Nettl Distinguished Lecture in Ethnomusicology at the University of Illinois. I wish to thank my colleagues for the invitation to present this lecture. The second part of the title is taken from an article by C. S. Peirce.

Notes

1. Here I am defining "theory" in the most fundamental sense: simply as generality. As Gabriel Solis suggested to me, this conception of the term might be distinguished from contexts when the term is used to refer to "a Theory," a specific elaboration of premises, concepts, and processes to explain or predict something. I suggest that "theory as generality" undergirds specifically elaborated theories, and the two conceptions are linked through the process of moving from "practical theory" to "articulated theory."

2. Ming (Francis) Kuo is associate professor of environmental psychology at the University of Illinois at Urbana-Champaign. I am grateful to her for her careful reading and critiques of this paper.

3. The process of creating P-symbols is akin to what is also called making "operational definitions." When I make a P-symbol, I am not claiming a unique grasp of the truth about the sign-objects in question, only that I am specifying a sign to the best of my understanding *and for specific analytical purposes*, so that I can use the concept, communicate it to others, and perhaps continue to improve it over time.

References

Adams, Richard N. 1975. *Energy and Structure: A Theory of Social Power*. Austin: University of Texas Press.

Blacking, John. 1978. "Some Problems of Theory and Method in the Study of Musical Change." *Yearbook for Traditional Music* 9: 1–26.

Giddens, Anthony. 1990. *The Consequences of Modernity*. Stanford, CA: Stanford University Press.

Nettl, Bruno. 1978. "Some Aspects of the History of World Music in the Twentieth Century: Questions, Problems, and Concepts." *Ethnomusicology* 22(1): 123–36.

———. 1978. *Eight Urban Musical Cultures: Tradition and Change*. Urbana: University of Illinois Press.

———. 1983. *The Study of Ethnomusicology: Twenty-nine Issues and Concepts*. Urbana: University of Illinois Press.

———. 1985. *The Western Impact on World Music: Change, Adaptation, and Survival.* New York: Schirmer Books.

Turino, Thomas. 1993. *Moving Away from Silence: The Music of the Peruvian Altiplano and the Experience of Urban Migration*. Chicago: University of Chicago Press.
———. 2000. *Nationalists, Cosmopolitans, and Popular Music in Zimbabwe*. Chicago: University of Chicago Press.
———. 2003. "Are We Global Yet? Globalist Discourse, Cultural Formations and the Study of Zimbabwean Popular Music." *British Journal of Ethnomusicology* 12(2): 51–80.
———. 2008. *Music as Social Life: The Politics of Participation*. Chicago: University of Chicago Press.
———. 2014. "Peircean Thought as Core Theory for a Phenomenological Ethnomusicology." *Ethnomusicology* 58(2): 185–221.
Weber, Max. 1982. "The Distribution of Power: Class, Status, Party." In *Classes, Power, and Conflict: Classical and Contemporary Debates*, edited by Anthony Giddens and David Held, 60–76. Berkeley: University of California Press.

PART VI

~

CHANGE, ADAPTATION, AND SURVIVAL

CHAPTER THIRTY

~

Music, Modernity, and Islam in Indonesia

Charles Capwell

When I first met Bruno Nettl, he was already a legend in the field, so I was surprised he was only forty at the time and told him so. As his colleague over the next thirty years, I continued to observe his growing legend and to feel it a privilege to be able to talk with him nearly every day, often over coffee. Now, at eighty-five, he surprises me by being as productive as ever, and I would say he is a model for us all if he weren't, in fact, inimitable. Nettl has long been interested in musical modernity, and therefore in this chapter I consider from the viewpoint of literature on multiple modernities what it means to be Muslim, musical, modern, and Indonesian. Exploring how "modernity" takes a variety of forms in addition to the narrowly conceived one resulting from the European Enlightenment, I focus on an aspect of popular musical culture, "*musik yang bernafaskan Islam*" (music inspired by Islam), to demonstrate how a component of everyday culture can illuminate concepts about modernity and their actualization by the nation and its individual citizens.

The Study of Popular Culture and Islam in Indonesia

Scholarly interest in popular music was slow to develop, even in ethnomusicology. Regarding the popular music of Indonesia, for example, Jaap Kunst once said about *kroncong*, "I do not care much for this music myself. It strikes me as with a weak sensuality and lacking ethnic identity" (1994:293). But *pace* Kunst, recognizing the value of studying popular culture through musical media later endowed kroncong with a kind of canonic status in the ethnomusicology of Indonesia (Becker 1975; Heins 1975; Kornhauser 1978) and has broadened our perspective of Indonesia's cultural life.

The fact that early scholarly interest in Indonesian music focused largely on courtly repertories and, more recently, kroncong, is partly attributable to a Western perspective that saw in gamelan music an expressive medium replete with the aura of Hindu-Buddhist heritage and, in kroncong, the aura of a European folk heritage in the subaltern songs originating with a creole population in Batavia. Both perspectives reflected a willing blindness to Islam in the cultural history of Southeast Asia. Just as in colonial India, Indian music was often referred to as "Hindu Music"—as though Muslims had contributed nothing to it—in Indonesia, the prestige of Hindu-Buddhist culture left little room for attention to Islamic influence, as did the natural predilection for an interest in the history of European influences and their products, including kroncong.

During the colonial period, Islam was marginalized in the political field through the effort of the government's adviser on Islamic affairs, Christian Snouck-Hurgronje, who sought to limit its influence, paradoxically, to the cultural sphere. But his purpose was to circumscribe Islam's political influence, not to enhance its significance in cultural life. This situation continued until relatively recently, one reason being the conceptual tendency to exclude the Islamic world from the processes of modernity that is commonly described as a post-Enlightenment project. Dale Eickelman reminds us that in 1994, Ernest Gellner "reiterated the view that 'Muslim society' remained the exception to the pervasive trend toward a shared culture of nationalism with its ensuing fruit of modernity—commonly educated, mutually substitutable, atomized individuals with the potential for participating in a 'civil society'" (2000:119). Clifford Geertz (1960) acknowledged the importance of Islam in Java, but perhaps minimized the importance of Islam in general. In reaction, Mark Woodward (1989) attempted to uncover the way Islam cast its own legitimacy over many elements of indigenous and Hindu-Buddhist beliefs while rejecting others.

The marginalization of Islam in Indonesian culture has been exacerbated not only because it has been viewed as a nominal influence compared with other layers of culture, but also because the scriptural, legalistic, and other canonical elements of what might be called "scholarly" Islam traditionally held pride of place. Robert Hefner explains, "With several notable exceptions, the Orientalist commentaries that introduced Islamic civilization to a western readership in the late nineteenth and early twentieth centuries were concerned with high culture, not the everyday meaning of Islam for ordinary Muslims" (1997:9).

The historian William Frederick, rather than a musicologist, brought attention to the role of popular music in the everyday life of Indonesian Muslims in an article on Rhoma Irama. He found Rhoma's *dangdut* songs to be a "useful prism through which to view Indonesian society" in contrast to conventional data, "which tell us relatively little about . . . Islam in everyday life" (Frederick 1982:104).

Modernist and Traditionalist Attitudes in Islamic Indonesia

The dialectic between high culture and the culture of everyday life is transferable to the so-called modernist and traditionalist attitudes of Islam in Indonesia; these terms suggest that the one attitude is critical and inquiring, whereas the other is conventional and conformist. But what does it mean to be "modern" in this sense? A "modern" attitude toward music in this sense is revealed by Geertz, who encountered a style of music and dance called *gambus* that was popular among youths in Islamic schools (*pesantren*), but when he asked a Muslim modernist his opinion of it, the man scoffed that it was "like Africa in Indonesia," with all that was meant to imply about its primitiveness and backwardness (1960:156). Yet to a Westerner, this dismissal, based on religious scruple, might seem distinctly anti-modern, for it brings religion into the public sphere, when in the post-Weberian view of modernity, it should retreat to the individual and private. Geertz's adherent of Muhammdiyah, the modernist Islamic organization of Indonesia, saw no justification for such behavior in his version of Islam, which he wanted to free from accumulated perversions through the practice of *ijtihad*, critical reasoning. A tool of many Islamic reformists, ijtihad is particularly associated with the modernizing Egyptian Muhammad 'Abduh, of whom Alfian says, "The central thesis he was to construct about Islamic modernism was to reformulate the Islamic Faith to be in harmony with the beliefs of the early Muslims . . . and with the intellectual development of the modern thought" (1989:97).

The amalgam of a critical modernist stance with a puritanical reformism represents a conundrum in understanding the significance of modernity in the Indonesian context. Such conundrums have given rise to the concept of multiple or alternative modernities. The habit of viewing modernity as something for which Western Europe and America provided an inalterable template, with secularization at its core, is one reason that Islam has been marginalized in our understanding of Indonesia. Further, if the secular nation-state is seen as the corollary of modernity and is thought to require the removal of religion from the public sphere, then it is difficult to comprehend what is happening in Indonesia, where Islamic religiosity has been on the rise for decades. Shmuel Eisenstadt states that "the ideological and symbolic centrality of the nation-state, its position as the charismatic locus of the major components of the cultural program of modernity and collective identity, have [*sic*] been weakened; new political, social, and civilizational visions, new visions of collective identity, are being developed" (2000:16). Nilüfer Göle adds that "the presence of an Islamic idiom, of voices and practices in everyday life, in urban spaces, in public debate, and in the market-place, throws new challenges at classical premises of the modernist project—basically those of secularism and Western-boundedness" (2000:93).

But the picture of Islamic modernity is still more complicated than this, since the perspective of multiple modernities challenges what has been understood, paradoxically, as "modernist Islam." Göle explains that "the multiple-modernities project puts the emphasis on the inclusionary dynamic of modernity, on borrowing, blending, and cross-fertilization rather than on the logic of exclusionary divergence [like] binary oppositions (between traditionals and moderns)" (2000:91).

Musical Modernity in an Islamic Traditionalist Tract

A traditionalist tract on music from Indonesia sheds light on the notion of Islamic modernity. This work, *Laws on the Instrumental and Vocal Arts and on the Art of Dance in Islam* (*Hukum Seni Musik, Seni Suara, dan Seni Tari dalam Islam*), was written by H. M. Toha Yahya Omar (1964). He served as dean of the Faculty of Religious Principles (*usuluddin*) at the National Institute for Islamic Religion (IAIN), a traditionalist institution—that is, one under the influence of the largest Islamic organization, Nadhlatul Ulama—which trains religious scholars expected to be the arbiters of religious matters for the *ummat*. The tract addresses the *ḥadith* on the performing arts. It has several brief prefaces by Islamic notables that demonstrate how their authors viewed the place of music at that time. For example, Hazairin S. H., rector of the Islamic University of Jakarta, writes:

> Let us try to think—suppose we are still influenced by the old-fashioned views we still meet in this twentieth century among a group of people in the villages, those who forbid playing sports and dancing for women, those who forbid representing human beings, forbid sculpture and music, and only approve striking the frame drum and singing religious songs. Won't such a state as this become a major obstacle for the progress of our nation in the development of its culture?

> Let us hope, with this orderly and pure fatwa given by an expert, that all such obstacles to progress will be wiped out. (Toha 1964:xi)

A similar tone appears in the preface by then minister for religion K. H. Sjaifuddin Zuhri:

> We are living in a time of national development. . . . Developing a nation with its people and state by means of politics alone constitutes a worn out way of thinking whose efficacy has never been proven, even constitutes an old-fashioned way of thinking. . . .
>
> The ummat of Indonesia, as the most populous group in our country, has the largest responsibility in the charge of developing the nation and its people along with the state. And aside from the realm of politics and economy, that of art and culture constitutes a tool involved in determining the quality and character of our nation, whether in the present or the future.
>
> The field of arts and culture as a tool of national development has already been accepted by our age as an absolute path that has to be extended, and leaving this path would mean putting aside the path that will arrive at its destination. For this reason, within the Islamic populace itself, especially in the arenas where there are concentrated centers of the power of the ummat and the circle of the *ulamate*, let them seek to acquire determination in seeing and valuing the question of art and culture in all its forms. (Toha 1964:vii–ix)

Both men express the idea that music is tied to the need for development of the nation and is inextricably bound to the development of Islamic expressive culture. The traditional vocal *qasidah*, accompanied only by frame drums, is associated with the backwardness of village life, and such obstacles on the path to modernity must be bypassed with a new awareness of the value of a developing artistic culture.

In another prefatory note, Bustami A. Gani says that Toha's tract is useful "because in confronting our revolution which reaches every field, the field of culture is especially important and determines the battle lines for constructing a kind of national culture and eliminating those elements that are in opposition to our culture" (Toha 1964:xii). Conforming to Sukarno's call for ridding Indonesian performing arts of Western influences at a time when these were increasingly being felt in popular music around the world, this comment has enhanced meaning when its source is identified as the dean of Islamic Culture and Civilization (*adab*) at the National Institute for Islamic Religion. Music and dance are recognized as fields in which an individual identity can be constructed, on the one hand, among modern world states, and on the other, among modern world religions.

Finally, K. H. Idham Chalid, head of the Board of Curators of the National Institute for Islamic Religion, stated that in accordance with the determination made by the 1960 Provisional People's Deliberative Assembly (MPRS), several fields, including religion, the arts, and culture, should be thought about, set in motion, and settled according to the "rising demands" and "revolutionary demands" of the time. As music and dance had already been accepted into the category of the arts by the "International World," including the Arabic and Islamic world, and as students and youth are always attracted by musical entertainment, organizations such as the Muslim Cultural Association of Indonesia (Lembaga Seni Budayawan Indonesia) had been established in order to ensure that these arts were not monopolized by others (Toha 1964:xiv–xv).

These comments create a picture of an Islamic sensitivity that accepts the challenge of modernity, while resisting the equation of modernization with Westernization. Concordant with Sukarno's nationalist agenda, it nevertheless views the development of music and dance not as problems only of *Kultur*, but also of adab, that is, as questions pertaining to the spheres of both Islamic and Western behavior and belief. After citing various *aḥadith* that are pro and con the arts of music and dance, and arguing that "the condemnation of instrumental and vocal music and of dance is occasioned by other things and not by their own essence," Toha states his commitment to an idea of Islamic modernity: "We are now in an age of development, development in all fields, in which culture and the arts are included. . . . We the Muslim ummat of Indonesia certainly do not wish to live passively, to live as spectators of what is happening around us; rather we also want to engage in development, even to become pioneers and to develop in every field within the limits allowed by our religion. . . . We have to demonstrate that the religion of Islam can serve the development of 'rising demands' that are 'up to date' . . . and thus we soon will be able to maintain that the religion of Islam is truly suited to every time and place" (1964:56–58).

The concern displayed in this work reveals an attitude toward the place of music in Islam as a tool useful for engaging the project of modernity and preventing Islam from being marginalized. This should be underlined strongly, as musical culture is too often thought to be a decorative, but ultimately inconsequential, component of the way people contend with one another about appropriate ways of conducting their lives. Clearly, the writers quoted here considered music to be an essential component in the creation of national identity and pride, and in the demonstration that Islam is a religion adaptable to the needs of a modern society.

Ethnicity, Nationalism, and Transnationalism in Islamic Musical Modernity

One genre in particular embodies the concept of Islamic modernity in its very name: *qasidah moderen*. This name puts it into opposition with the genre known simply as qasidah, the type of religious song considered typical of backward village practices associated with proscriptions against dancing or musical instruments other than the frame drum. Traditional qasidah uses the Arabic language, but one of the hallmarks of qasidah moderen is the use of Indonesian, though "some singers apply an Arabic-sounding nasal voice quality . . . and vocal ornaments known from Arabic song are common. Some pronounce Arabic loan words in the lyrics, or even words of Austronesian origin, in a clearly Arabic manner" (Arps 1996:392). The Arabic language has a special place within Islam as the language of revelation; therefore songs with lyrics in Arabic carry an aura of the sacred, even to those who do not understand them. Ahmad Buchori Masruri stated that "because they don't know the meaning at all, the public usually listens to them and considers them as Islamic songs" (*Kompas* 1995:20). He mentioned a qasidah whose Arabic text began, "I say to you my love, don't leave me," to demonstrate that not all qasidah are religious, and like pop or Javanese songs, not all have an Islamic flavor. Because of his dissatisfaction with Arabic qasidah as a communicative medium, this former regional head of Nadhalatul Ulama became a pioneer in writing qasidah lyrics in the Indonesian language, including "Perdamaian," the evergreen hit of the qasidah moderen group Nasida Ria.

As adviser to and lyricist for Nasida Ria—an all-female band, like most qasidah groups—Masruri created texts for tunes provided by Astakona Hartono, owner of the Puspita recording label with studios in Semarang and Jakarta. Hartono claims outright to have developed the modern style of gambus and qasidah (Astakono Hartono, interview, Jakarta, 23 July 1993). As a marketing ploy by an Indo-Chinese Catholic business entrepreneur, this new genre, whether actually named by him or not, was promoted with the awareness that a market was developing for this kind of religiously tinged popular music in a newly emerging Islamic public sphere. In turn, the music nurtured that public sphere by bringing a new kind of religious behavior into it, though not without controversy as the language issue was contentious at first. The singer Rofiqoh Warto Wahab did not meet with unalloyed approbation when she, too, began to create Indonesian language qasā'id several decades ago; she needed the intercession with the ulamas of her respected grandfather so that "the teachings of Rasulullah could be more directly and quickly received by the public" (Dahana 1991:60).

Public electronic media have made Islamically oriented songs in Indonesian a commonplace in a way that Arabic songs were unlikely to become. But language remains a contentious issue within the modernizing ummat. The pop group Snada, which started at the University of Indonesia as a male a cappella ensemble in the 1990s, pride themselves on creating texts not only in Arabic and Indonesian but in English, too. Just as Rofiqoh used Indonesian in order to reach a wider Islamic public in her country, Snada wants to reach a youthful public with a global awareness, and to appropriate the transnational language and musical style of international pop, even covering some tunes. To their amusement, when they have performed their English songs at some mosques, they have found themselves without amplification when the religious authorities pulled the plug on them (Snada, interview, Jakarta, March 1996). Though willing to tolerate choral harmonies that smack to them of Christian hymn-singing practice, such authorities will not accept a religious message in English. Since Snada does not use instruments, I wondered whether, despite their appropriation of a Western pop vocal idiom, they were adhering to the traditional conservative Islamic ban on instruments. They replied that they had recently sung on the Indosiar television network accompanied by an instrumental group, so there was no objection to this practice; singing unaccompanied, however, allied their music with Islamic tradition. They remarked, nevertheless, that Indosiar had objected to their including songs in English in the broadcast for fear of criticism from the ulamate.

Another ensemble concerned with Islamic *dakwah* (Islamic predication), Ngek, originated at the University of Indonesia about the same time as Snada, but they based themselves firmly as an instrumentally accompanied group. The instruments and the musical sources relied on by Ngek, however, represent Indonesia rather than outside influences. They pointedly refer to the religious genre of vocal music known as *nasyid* as being of Middle Eastern and Malaysian provenance and particularly concerned with struggle and *jihad*. Instead, they are mining the ethnic musics in Indonesia, following the example set centuries ago by some of the Wali Songo, who used regional music and gamelan for dakwah. Imanjaya explained that the urban middle class "tends to push away things with an Arabic flavor as of inferior culture" (Imanjaya 1995:6). He describes nasyid as an example of extreme acculturation, or even colonization, which as an instance of the total acceptance of foreign culture is rather alien.

Ngek's approach to Islamic music opposes that of the qasidah moderen groups, but both aim to create a public sphere for Islamic expressive culture. Arps writes that "in the same way that the Arabic colouring of its melodic and vocal styles connotes Islam and not the Middle East, so does the mainly

Western instrumentation of qasidah modéren connote not America or Europe, but modernity" (1996:395). For the audience that enjoys qasidah moderen, the Arabic flavoring is a reference to the origin of the faith they publicly celebrate, and the instruments used reference their acceptance of a contemporary world. The first part of Arps's statement contradicts Imanjaya, for whom the "Arabic colouring" is an ethnic and geographic marker rather than a religious one, and his approach to modernity is that of the revivalist seeking nativist roots for the cultural expression of Islamic faith. The second part of Arps's statement clarifies the distinction between Westernization and modernity, and implicitly warns against confusing the two in qasidah moderen simply because Western artifacts are used. Similarly, we should not misunderstand Ngek's use of indigenous instruments, or Snada's preference for a cappella, as anti-modern moves, but rather the opposite.

Whereas some qasidah singers add Middle Eastern embellishments to melodies and pronounce even Indonesian with an Arabic inflection, Imanjaya views such sonic mannerisms as traces of a kind of internalized cultural imperialism that a modern awareness should eschew. But when Sam Bimbo sings his famous song "Tuhan," the tune is in the style of a pop ballad that appeals to the aesthetic sensibilities of his educated middle-class fans and has no suggestion of the Arabized qualities they might associate with "an inferior culture." Nevertheless, the visuals accompanying the song all refer to Middle Eastern venues with their splendidly gilded and tiled mosques, linking this Indonesian act of musical devotion to the international realm of *dar al-Islam*. Sam's video version of "Tuhan" brings a vision of transnational Islam into an Indonesian urban popular music style. As youngsters, Sam Bimbo and his brothers started out singing covers of Spanish songs to the accompaniment of acoustic guitars; when they ventured into qasidah, they brought to these songs, with their phrygian turns of phrase, what they consciously imagined as a flavor of high culture from Almoravid Spain and its diasporic Arabo-Islamic music, something quite different from the associations carried by the Arabisms of conventional qasidah. References to the Middle East can be references to Islam and not the region and its culture, for, in Sam's eyes, the term "*kebudayaan Arab*" (Arabic culture) is derogatory (Sam Bimbo, interview, Semarang, February 1996).

The Individual Musician as Agent and Creator of Modernity in Islam

The distinction between the Islamic world at large and the Arabic cultural realm is key to the conception of Islamic modernity in Indonesia's pop music with an Islamic bent, yet it can be confusing at times to separate them. A music video produced in 1999 by Tya Subiakto, the then twenty-year-old conductor of the TnT Orchestra, arranged the Egyptian song "Magadir," a favorite in Indonesia, for performance by an exceptionally large ensemble combining a Western orchestra with a gambus group featuring the *'ūd* (called gambus in Indonesia), violin, and *dombak*; in addition to the male vocal soloist, there was a large mixed chorus as well as a group of dancers, all dressed in "oriental" style. Subiakto conducted these forces with vigorous gestures, standing before a grand piano in a studio strewn with sand and punctuated with palm trees, among which the dancers cavorted and live camels occasionally promenaded. The Arabicism of this video could hardly have been criticized for suggesting that Islamic culture is "out of date"; its slick production techniques, sophisticated and complex musical arrangement, and competent execution all focused attention on the young *jilbab-* and *abaya-*wearing woman, who could hardly be conceived of as anything but modern. In fact, the use of Middle Eastern referents might be viewed as elements of a postmodern emptying of signs, a kind of meaning-deprived phantasmagoria, but this would impose an alien perspective that denies the experiences and convictions of the artists.

When I met her in 1999, Subiakto was making another music video urging the public to participate in the general election that year. Directed by her father—in whose TV advertising production firm she works—she again appeared as the jilbab-wearing conductor of a large ensemble, but this time she wore jeans and a shirt more appropriate to the video theme; thus her roles as Muslim musician and nationalist were prominent. The melding of political and Islamic engagement in the public sphere could hardly have been a better realization of the wishes expressed in the prefatory notes to Toha's 1964 booklet.

In 1997, when the New Order still controlled the engagement of Islam in politics through the Unity and Development Party (PPP), the *Economist* noted that "Islam as a focus for protest is growing, not just among the urban and rural poor, but among some students and intellectuals as well. For them, religion offers an alternative both to the stifling restrictions of the New Order and to the slavish aping of western models. It is quite a modern thing to be a practising Muslim" (1997:8). Two years later, with the New Order's restrictions lifted, Subiakto could join in a civil forum with a variety of other pop entertainers as a modern Muslim musician, not in protest, but in a mood of celebration and nationalistic exhortation for getting out the vote.

In 2002, as the recently divorced mother of a young child, Subiakto continued her career with single-minded determination. Her attitude to divorce is that of a modern woman with a clear sense of her individual needs, as she explained in an interview with *Kompas*: "'For nearly a year and a half my music career has been halted. Frankly, I feel constrained.' . . . Music for her is the breath of life. Since she was little she had the principle that music was her life's path. Even if someone should forbid her to be a musician, she would oppose him, not excepting her husband. 'Through music I can spread religion. Therefore, I can be separated from my husband, but not from my music,' she says" (2002). Recalling the motivation of the qasidah moderen singer Rofiqoh, Subiakto's commitment to musical dakwah expresses a striking attitude of self-individuation typically listed as one of the characteristics of modernity.

"Cultural Islam" as a Catalyst of Indonesian Modernity

Throughout the period of the New Order in Indonesia, Islam struggled to influence the social and political realms but was always viewed with suspicion by the military government, which sought to control it by circumscribing its sphere of activity in a government-sanctioned party. A later tactic was to co-opt Islamic restlessness by establishing the Association of Indonesian Muslim Intellectuals (ICMI) as a way of getting technocratic modernists to subscribe to government policy. In doing so, it tended to view cultural Islam as an arena devoid of political impact. But the result of this policy was to allow the evolution of a public sphere where it could become "quite a modern thing to be a practicing Muslim" (Hefner 1997:22–23).

Part and parcel of the Islamic revival has been the evolution of traditional Islamic music performances in a public arena, where the display of Islamic piety no longer represents a conservative rejection of modernity but an appropriation of it. If it is true that "there has been an unprecedented deepening of Islamic piety [in Indonesia] since the 1980s, a period during which political Islam has been far less influential than a civic-minded, cultural Islam" (Hefner 1997:30), then it is equally true that cultural Islam generated the rebirth of political Islam at the end of the New Order. Bruce Robbins explains that the media helped reinvent the concept of the public sphere "as an urban space of aesthetic self-presentation, sociability, theatricality, and pleasure" and "that participation in the making, exchanging, and mobilizing of political opinion—the defining characteristic of 'republican virtue'—has to some extent been reinvented or relocated as well, and that it is now discoverable to an unprecedented extent in the domain of culture" (1993:xix). Although the conception of the public sphere may pertain more to an arena of secularized discourse and social intercourse, it should also be seen as a place where ideas about such things as what it is to be Muslim and modern can be thought out through the arts, musical and otherwise.

At the 1999 annual meetings of the Society for Ethnomusicology, where I presented a paper on Islamic popular music in Indonesia, I was asked "Why is this music Islamic?" It was a reasonable question; the music I was discussing, after all, could not be considered liturgical in any way and could easily be seen as transgressive of Islamic legalistic proscriptions. I was unsatisfied with my response, which was along the lines of "Because it is designated as such by those who make and listen to it," having in mind the Indonesian phrase "musik yang bernafaskan Islam" (music inspired by Islam). Now, if I returned to this question, perhaps I could answer, "Because it is modern."

References

Alfian. 1989. *Muhammadiya: The Political Behavior of a Muslim Modernist Organization under Dutch Colonialism*. Yogyakarta: Gadjah Mada University Press.

Arps, Bernard. 1996. "To Propagate Morals through Popular Music: The Indonesian *Qasidah Moderen*." In *Qasida Poetry in Islamic Asia and Africa*, Volume I: *Classical Traditions and Modern Meanings*, edited by Stefan Sperl and Christopher Shackle. Studies in Arabic Literature: Supplements to the *Journal of Arabic Literature*, edited by J. E. Montgomery and R. M. A. Allen, 20(1): 389–409. Leiden: E. J. Brill.

Becker, Judith. 1975. "*Kroncong*, Indonesian Popular Music." *Asian Music* 7(1): 14–19.

Dahana, Radha Panca. 1991. "Sorotan: Pop and *Balada Dalam* Music." *Vista* 114: 60.

Economist. 1997. "Survey: Indonesia: The Mosque and the Palace." 6 July–1 August: 6-8.

Eickelman, Dale F. 2000. "Islam and the Languages of Modernity." *Daedalus* 129(1): 119–35.

Eisenstadt, Shmuel N. 2000. "Multiple Modernities." *Daedalus* 129(1): 1–29.

Frederick, William. 1982. "Rhoma Irama and the *Dangdut* Style: Aspects of Contemporary Indonesian Popular Culture." *Indonesia* 34: 103–30.

Geertz, Clifford. 1960. *The Religion of Java*. Glencoe, IL: Free Press.

Göle, Nilüfer. 2000. "Snapshots of Islamic Modernities." *Daedalus* 129(1): 91–117.

Hefner, Robert. 1997. "Islam in an Era of Nation-States: Politics and Religious Renewal in Muslim Southeast Asia." In *Islam in an Era of Nation-States: Politics and Religious Renewal in Muslim Southeast Asia*, edited by Robert W. Hefner and Patricia Hovatich, 3–40. Honolulu: University of Hawai'i Press.

Heins, Ernst. 1975. "*Kroncong* and Tanjidor—Two Cases of Urban Folk Music in Jakarta." *Asian Music* 7(1): 20–32.

Imanjaya, Ekky [Ekky al Maliki]. 1995. "*Nasyid: 'Penjajahan' Budaya?: (Persoalan Seputar Nasyid)*" [Cultural Colonizer?: (A Discussion about *Nasyid)*]. Unpublished paper for Dialog Islam dan Seni: Nasyid Sebagai Fenomena Budaya [Dialogue on

Islam and Art: Nasyid as a Cultural Phenomenon], 19 Desember 1995, Ruang 411 FSUI, Departemen Kerohanian Senat Mahasiswa FSUI [Fakultas Sastra Universitas Indonesia].

Kompas. 1995. "KH Ahmad Buchori Masruri: 'Qasidah' Yang Nikmat dan Memikat." March 17: 20.

———. 2002. "Tya Subiakto: Kado Ultah Menyakitkan." Gaya Hidup and Hiburan, 7 May. www.kompas.com/gayahidup/news/0205/07/003116.htm.

Kornhauser, Bronia. 1978. "In Defence of *Kroncong*." In *Studies in Indonesian Music*, edited by Margaret J. Kartomi, 104–83. Monash Papers on Southeast Asia, Number 7. Melbourne: Monash University.

Kunst, Jaap. 1994. *Indonesian Music and Dance: Traditional Music and Its Interaction with the West: A Compilation of Articles (1934–1952)*. Amsterdam: University of Amsterdam, Ethnomusicology Centre.

Robbins, Bruce, ed. 1993. *The Phantom Public Sphere*. Cultural Politics, Volume 5. Minneapolis: University of Minnesota Press.

Toha Yahya Omar, H. M. 1964. *Hukum Seni Musik Seni Suara Dan Seni Tari Dalam Islam*. Djakarta: Penerbit Widjaya.

Woodward, Mark R. 1989. *Islam in Java: Normative Piety and Mysticism in the Sultanate of Yogyakarta*. The Association for Asian Studies Monograph No. 45. Tucson: University of Arizona Press.

CHAPTER THIRTY-ONE

~

"Clubbing the Boots"

The Navajo Moccasin Game in Today's World

Charlotte J. Frisbie

In the late twentieth century, a public competition version of *Késhjéé'*, the Navajo Moccasin Game, became associated with New Year's Eve.[1] Evidence suggests that intentional sharing of knowledge about the game began in the 1970s in on-reservation schools and elsewhere, perhaps to ensure its future. As interest increased, more people wanted to play, and games moved from family hogans to larger spaces. At least by 1998, the game had become associated with New Year's Eve celebrations. Here, I describe the 2012 "4th Annual Moccasin Game Tournament" at the Navajo Nation Museum in Window Rock and share some mixed opinions Navajos verbalized about it. Having shared interests in Native American music and the history of ethnomusicology and service in the Society for Ethnomusicology for more than four decades, I have written this chapter to honor my esteemed colleague, Bruno Nettl. I begin with a synopsis of the game's origin and summaries of research on the game and its songs.

The Origins of *Késhjéé'* and Its History of Research

According to Navajo oral tradition and Blessingway creation narratives, after emerging into the present world, the Holy People gathered at Mt. Huerfano to consider several important questions. Among these was, should there be perpetual daylight or perpetual darkness? Big Giant, *Yé'iitsoh*, suggested playing a hidden ball/shoe game to decide the matter and challenged all animals and every other living being to attend. Everybody gathered at Big Snake's

House, a cave in Red Rock Canyon in the west, on the east side close to the Chuska Mountains. The game started at sunset, finishing at sunrise; participants divided into two teams with those preferring nighttime, such as bat, bear, lion, owl, fox, and bobcat, sitting in the north of the hogan, and those for daylight, such as jackrabbit, porcupine, antelope, locust, gopher, and bird people, sitting in the south. Four moccasins were buried in a row in front of each team. A blanket was held to conceal the action while each team had a chance to hide a yucca root ball in one of the shoes. The hiders sang a Moccasin Game Song while concealing the ball and continued singing while opponents "sent a person across to tap the moccasin" suspected of housing the ball. An elaborate scoring system was devised based on 102 yucca leaf counters. The original game had no winner, despite cheating and other antics during the night; thus, today we have both daytime and nighttime.

The earliest published account of Késhjéé', to my knowledge, is by Washington Matthews, an Army surgeon and field anthropologist stationed at Fort Wingate, New Mexico, in 1880–1884 and 1890–1894 (see Halpern and McGreevy 1997). While Matthews is better known for other publications, among his contributions is a paper on Navajo Gambling Songs. Matthews (1889) presents the Késhjéé', Shoe Game, within its oral narrative context, with documentation of purpose, rules, procedures, and twenty-one of its songs with Navajo and English texts and notes, but no musical transcriptions. Culin's (1907) description in his study of North American Indian games was based solely on Matthews's work. Others, such as the Franciscan Fathers (1910) and Kluckhohn (1944), added further information. Reichard's study of Navajo religion discusses the game and gives texts for several songs (gopher, chicken hawk, and owl) (1950:199–200, 287–88).

Musical transcriptions of Shoe Game Songs first appeared in the 1930s, based on George Herzog's collections at the Chicago World's Fair in 1933 (Herzog 1934). Willard Rhodes's work in the 1940s and early 1950s in cooperation with the Bureau of Indian Affairs led to ten long-playing vinyl discs. The eighth in the series, Library of Congress AFS L41, *Folk Music of the U.S. from the Archive of Folk Song, Navaho* (1954), included four Moccasin Game Songs. He described the songs (Red Rock wren, turkey, ears sticking up, and time to stop) as strong and rhythmically infectious, short, and sung with endless repetitions and with increasing tempo and volume during games. McAllester (1954:80–81) used some of the game's song texts to illustrate and expand Hill's (1943) discussion of Navajo humor. O'Bryan's (1956:63–70) study of Navajo origin myths included twenty-three (five unnumbered) Shoe Game texts in English she collected in 1928. Whereas Boulton recorded Moccasin Game Songs in both 1933 and 1940, these were not released until 1992 on Smithsonian Folkways 40403, *Navajo Songs Recorded by Laura Boulton in 1933 and 1940*. Reg Begay recorded three Shoe Game Songs in 1948; Canyon Records, founded in 1951 by Ray and Mary Boley, acquired these in 1955, released them as Canyon 186a, January 1956 (Stephen Butler, personal communication, 23 July 2013); and reissued them on Canyon ARP 6064, *Traditional Navajo Songs* (1969). McAllester transcribed the second of these Shoe Game Songs for inclusion in McAllester and Mitchell (1983:617), providing another transcription. Nettl (1956: ex. 53) had used one of Herzog's transcriptions in his text. The 1960s also brought the development of cassette tape technology (followed in 1982 by the compact disc) and the beginning of my fieldwork on aspects of Navajo music and culture, including Moccasin Game Songs. In 1966, Tony and Ida Isaacs founded Indian House, another recording company committed to Native American music.

These glimmers of interest among outsiders sparked no corresponding interest on the reservation. Until the 1970s, there was little mention of moccasin games outside of families; as RB explained, "Years ago, families used to host them at home with the hosts providing the main meal and all the materials needed to play the game. There were only two teams and you always bet with money, loose change or a dollar bill. If you bet on the winning team, you got double your money back. These were times of laughing, teaching about the game and the meaning of the songs, lots of teasing, and good fun" (RB, personal communication, 15 July 2013). Although some now claim these games had to go "underground" in this time period because they were illegal, neither fieldwork nor the Navajo Tribal Code (1962) support these statements.

In the 1970s, at least some educators on the Navajo reservation were growing concerned about cultural preservation. Stimulated by the 1975 Indian Self-Determination and Education Assistance Act (PL 93-638), Navajos and others increased their controls of Bureau of Indian Affairs schools, and with time, education became increasingly culturally relevant. Teachers began to discuss how to improve cultural content and sometimes suggestions appeared in the *Navajo Times*. Some districts started to host teacher training workshops on various aspects of Navajo culture. In music, Moccasin Game Songs began to appear in classroom materials developed with accompanying cassette tapes and appropriate warnings about restricting them to wintertime use. Examples include Diné Bi'ólta Association (1973) and Tsistł'ahnii Yázhí (1974). In 1975–1977, Charlotte Heth directed a two-year videotape project at the University of California, Los Angeles, *Interviews with American Indian Musicians*. Sam Yazzie Sr., one of the Navajo interviewees, sang shortened versions of two Shoe Game Songs on Tape III, Side A (Frisbie 1981). The recordings of the four Moccasin Game Songs on the 1990 New World Records album *Navajo Songs from Canyon de Chelly* were made in 1975. That same year, Indian House released a two-genre album, IH 1507, *Navajo Corn Grinding and Shoe Game Songs* (Frisbie 1977). In 1978, Lynn Huenemann, an educator at Navajo Community College (now Diné College, Tsaile), published a text-tape resource, *Songs and Dances of Native America.* The five pages (65–70) allotted to the Navajo Moccasin Game include the Navajo texts of five songs—bat, pheasant, bear, giant, and turkey—with diagram, scoring, paraphernalia, and one musical transcription (Bear Song).

The Resurgence of Navajo Moccasin Games

Whether public moccasin games started in the 1980s or early 1990s is unclear. By the 1980s, awareness of the game's importance as part of traditional culture had increased, and with time, there was what Navajo people call a resurgence or revival. How much of this was deliberately orchestrated by cultural brokers concerned about the potential disappearance of the game if its stories and songs were not made more accessible, I do not know, but I think it's a real possibility, as does SB, one of today's ceremonialists. Some claim the revival was stimulated by a broader interest in gambling as a way to improve the Navajo Nation's economy, but given minimal parallels between casinos[2] and public shoe games, I doubt it. In any case, by the early 1990s, it was not uncommon to hear and see announcements for shoe games planned at community centers, chapter houses, senior centers, or other political spaces affording more room than family hogans. Once the game started being played in public, the idea of associating it with New Year's Eve appeared. In 1998, the rehabilitation center in Gallup, Na'nizhoozhi Center, Inc. (NCI), began to sponsor a public shoe game on New Year's Eve as a way to spend the evening with family and friends having fun in a safe, sober environment. Perhaps this was the first New Year's Eve shoe game competition. NCI's games continued through 2012; their future is unclear (Bitsoi 2013), since on 4 November 2013, in an agreement to share costs between the tribe, Gallup, and the county, the tribe took over the operation, renamed it the Gallup Detox Center, and closed the rehabilitation program.

Both print and sound media continue to support the game's resurgence. New bilingual teaching materials assist teachers' efforts to include the game, when seasonally appropriate, in cultural awareness and enrichment activities (see Emery 1996; Mose 2004; Roessel 2004). Davidson James, a Blessingway singer, explained the game's narrative and how to play it in *Leading the Way*

(2004, 2006). Teachings about the game appear in Holiday and McPherson (2005:237–39) and McPherson, Dandy, and Burak (2012:217–23). The resurgence of interest in the Shoe Game is also reflected in recordings, an area more complicated than publications because of a proliferation of independent artists, record producers, and recording studios. Trying to keep up with releases is hopeless, even with regular assistance from Tony Isaacs (Indian House) and Bob Nuss and Chris Good (Drumbeat Indian Arts, formerly Canyon Records and Indian Arts). The major problem is "DIY (do-it-yourself) labels" (Scales 2012:7). As Nuss explained, this "individual production and marketing that consists of dropping some copies off at flea markets, this hit or miss marketing" makes it impossible, at least from a distance, to document what independent producers are doing (Bob Nuss, personal communication, 4 March 2013). In the Window Rock area between January and August 2013, Shoe Game compact discs were being sold at Cool Runnings, the Navajo Nation Arts and Crafts (and its branches), and flea markets. Nuss stated, "These independent guys . . . think they can get rich quick by making their own records and selling copies themselves. They put out one thing and then fold. They reject offers of help . . . to make one hundred copies for them and help them keep things in stock. None of them are trained to run a business and the whole thing folds up shortly. Recordings go out of print rapidly. And then too, there's the problem of bootlegging, although people tried to stop that happening to recordings, films, and other things" (Bob Nuss, personal communication, 4 March 2013).[3]

With ongoing print and sound support of the Shoe Game revival, it is no surprise that competitive New Year's Eve Shoe Game tournaments at museums, Indian centers, and elsewhere, in cities such as Tucson and Phoenix, receive media coverage (cf. *Navajo Times* 2013:C-5). Such a game was held at the Nation's fairgrounds (Fonesca 2007) in 2006, and the Nation's Museum began to host a New Year's Eve Shoe Game tournament in 2009, when the new director, Manny Wheeler, was hired.

The 2012 New Year's Eve Moccasin Game Tournament

The 2012 Moccasin Game Tournament was documented in the *Navajo Times* (Silversmith 2013). In June 2013, Char Kruger, education curator, and Robert Johnson, cultural specialist, both then museum employees, expanded my understanding of the event. From the many possible ways of running a tournament, the museum chose the gaming model known as "eight team single elimination, which allows both winners and losers to have play-offs. The new bracket system, double elimination and then single elimination, gave everybody a chance" (Char Kruger, personal communication, 18 June 2013). Participation was first come, first served; the museum limited the number of players on a team to eight, but each team decided its own size. Registration cost $100 per team. Names were drawn from a bowl to set up double eliminations, and four games were run to see who would play whom. All four games started at the same time. Eight teams registered, some having played in 2011. Local merchants provided support and prizes in exchange for radio, print, and online advertisements, as well as front-row tickets. Sponsors were needed in 2012 mainly to pay the radio station, KTNN, to come and do live broadcasting of the game from eight o'clock in the evening until one o'clock in the morning. A handout developed by Leroy Nelson, Avery Denny, and Robert Johnson (2010) and distributed that year by Denny "to enhance learning" (Avery Denny, personal communication 12 July 2013) was not used in 2012. New to the 2012, fourth annual event was a webcast, live-streamed video so people could watch online, and the use of an outside master of ceremonies to free Kruger from those responsibilities. The Nation's vice president, Rex Lee Jim, did the countdown to the New Year.

As always, the museum provided everything needed for the game, using its main lobby and two meeting rooms at the start, with the final game played in the main lobby after an intermission. Chairs were provided for each team, and food (hot mutton stew, fry bread, and coffee) was available. Among Johnson's pre-game responsibilities was going to surrounding areas to acquire, with appropriate prayers and offerings, the yucca materials and cedar stick needed for the game; fashioning the ball, counters, and tapping stick; and then after the game, appropriately returning these things to Mother Nature (Robert Johnson, personal communication, 18 June 2013). More than five hundred attended the tournament, and winners were as follows: first prize, five Makita chainsaws to the Winslow, Arizona, team named Slinkey Boots; second prize, five loads of firewood to the Badgers from Fort Defiance, Arizona; and third prize, ten bales of three-wire hay, to the Shoemakers from Jeddito, Arizona. Hourly door prizes, called sheepherder specials, were awarded, as was a grand door prize of another Makita chainsaw (see Kruger 2013). Museum administrators clearly saw the annual shoe game as an important way of contributing to cultural learning and teaching for the Navajo people, while "keeping the museum on the map." While this chapter was being written, the fourth annual game at the Museum was among other Navajo Shoe Games available via YouTube, Ustream, and other websites (see Ustream.tv and search Navajo Nation Museum 2012 Shoe Game). Media coverage in 2014 was more limited (see Quintero 2014:A-8; see also political cartoon on A-6). The first New Year's Eve shoe game sponsored by the

Tséhootsooí Medical Center in Fort Defiance, Arizona, was covered a week earlier (see Buffalo 2014:A-1, A-2).

Navajo Opinions about the Shoe Game Revival

Not everyone with whom I spoke was happy about the Shoe Game revival. Perhaps the greatest concern was the potential for angering the Holy People by having Moccasin Game tournaments and public competitions. The following comments, collected in 2013, illustrate a range of opinions; since speakers requested anonymity, identifications are not provided.

> You can't just come out and play the game the way they are now, in a tournament, a big competition. That's not traditional and it's going to cause us harm.

> Our weather is crazy now because some Navajos are mistreating sacred things, like the Moccasin Game. Of course, a lot of the people objecting to that are passed away now, and others just stay away from those tournaments, because that game is sacred.

> Now younger medicine men just do anything for money. They mix up their ceremonies and procedures from this and that. Look at what people have done to the Moccasin Game; they say those tournaments are educational entertainment, but that game is supposed to be sacred and respected. The whole world is suffering because of that.

> People only get involved because they might win something. They don't even understand what the game means.

> I totally object to the publicization [*sic*] and secularization of the game. I hear that now these games are even being put on as fund-raisers, where you pay to go in, and then again, if you want food, or want to play. Some even use the game to sponsor a benefit. This is wrong.

> The young are getting interested now but they're just playing it for the winnings, the money in the pot. The game is now being played for profit, so there's a lot of competition. The ceremonial part is out, and the application of treatment is out. Now it's a social event. This is wrong and it concerns me greatly.

> These songs are supposed to be very protected. None of my teachers ever said they could be used in public competitions.

> This does not respect the sacredness of the game; when we play the game for ourselves or during a Holyway ceremony, it is very sacred. The proper order of

songs is followed and some of us end with Blessingway songs and a corn pollen blessing to sanctify our practices and avoid overindulgence.

It's already clear that we've angered the Holy People by disrespecting the Shoe Game. They are retaliating by sending us the most severe, the worst drought we've ever had on the reservation, even worse than during the Great Depression.

But others with whom I spoke disagreed:

The game has always been about competition and winning the prize of day or night.

I'm not pro or con this. It's using cultural practices to try and remedy social disorder, to heal social discord. So the healing aspect is still there [at least in the NCI game]. I'm more concerned with cultural transference; these tournaments allow the old and young to share the game, techniques, stories, songs, and knowledge. This has made the game a positive social activity, and without these public tournaments, it probably would have become obsolete.

You can't say it's like casinos; nobody comes to do that kind of high stakes gambling at a shoe game. Nobody is ever going to strike it big shoe gaming; our pot may only be a couple of dollars. We shoe game to sing, laugh, connect with our kin. This is our Navajo way. This coming together has healing power.

The game is a deep-rez practice. I've never been to one where our Window Rock Navajo elite, cosmopolitan, Karrigan estates dwellers were playing or hosting.

The game has come out of the closet and isn't secret any more. It's good because that way, it won't go extinct. And it's a way of getting people to have fun with family and friends, to laugh and tease and joke around, and really to feel better about everything.

The game teaches a lot about thinking, concentrating, observing people, trusting and respecting your teammates, respecting all the natural processes, the universe and its rules and cycles. I heard that in my great-grandparents' time, people might bet with jewelry, bridles, blankets, saddles, and things like that. But nobody I know has ever seen wagers with anything but money. People bet as teams and individually; if you don't pay, you don't play; you can't go across to tap the shoes, club the cowboy boots. You can't share in the blessings acquired by the winners.

> You can't say this is wiping out the sacredness of the game or making it secular. The game has always involved the ideas of healing and gaining health and wealth.

Conclusions

Conversations in 2013 demonstrated that it is now much easier to discuss at least some things about the game, such as its timing, the total corpus of songs, their ordering during the game, possible regional differences, and the possibility of new compositions. The songs—which are short, unaccompanied, repetitive, often fast, bouncy, syncopated, and humorous *if* you know the oral narrative context—concern animals, birds, the game itself and its equipment, participants and their appearance, personalities, places, and so forth. Texts are either all vocables or a combination of vocables with words, and the former do occasionally include animal growls and bird cooings (see Frisbie 1980).

Whereas everybody recognizes the Moccasin Game as entertainment and a "good clean way of having fun," either at home with family and friends or now in public on New Year's Eve, there is another aspect to the game that Matthews did not consider, one not often mentioned in today's conversations. That is the game's ability to heal. While I was learning about the game and its components as part of Navajo culture, discussions always involved laughing, teasing, and joking as the songs were sung and the texts explained to me. It was always a joy to hear more of these songs and learn about where they fit in the narrative, and it was fun to see others around during recording sessions also enjoying them.

As more and more people now acknowledge, perhaps because there is more open discussion about social discord, abuse, gang violence, and mental health issues on the reservation, Moccasin Games are also times for healing. They allow families to gather, joke, laugh, share good times, and, by placing small wagers, participate in having fun and forgetting personal troubles. When they are over, people leave happier, less stressed, and less depressed. The fact that laughter is great medicine is hardly a twenty-first-century discovery. But there's another way in which the game heals, since under the right circumstances, a Shoe Game can be played during lulls in ceremonial activities during the night of wintertime curing ceremonies.

SB explained, "Shoe Games can be included if there's a Holyway ceremony going on, like Navajo Windway, Lightningway, Evilchasingway, Mountainway male or female branch, and it's wintertime. There have to be long interludes between ritual activities, and the game cannot be played during sandpainting or praying. [Other adjustments may include a difference in the ball that's hidden, and so forth.] The Ancient Night versus Day tug of war is central to the Holyway." But playing it during a curing ceremony is "at the discretion of the singer and the host. It depends on which day of the ceremony it is, how much work needs to be done that day. Usually you can work in a couple of games a night." Games have no set length, of course, but if the game is being played during an interlude in a curing ceremony, obviously it does not last all night. The patient or one-sung-over in the ceremony is expected to bet and automatically becomes part of the north team. "She or he is massaged when someone hits a wrong guess and has to pay ten yucca counters. All participating in Shoe Games conducted during a curing ceremony acquire both favor and good fortune of winning with long life" (SB, personal communications, June and July 2013).

Those who are not concerned about the appropriateness of the very public New Year's Eve competitive tournament Shoe Games say that even in these settings, the game has healing power:

> You participate to enjoy yourself; sure, you bet and hope to win prizes, material things, but just participating increases your good health, and chances for good fortune and wealth.

> Using the shoe game to say goodbye to the old year and welcome in the new one is an example of us calling on our traditions, using our cultural practices to address some of the social ills we are now experiencing as Navajos. That's a very positive development.

Given the resurgence of the Moccasin Game, perhaps the time is right to propose a serious study of it, along with its songs and all of its other components and layers of meaning. The Késhjéé' is anything but a simple "hide the ball" game. But recognizing that the game continues to be restricted to winter season nights, and that its songs are seen as sacred songs with a story, it's unclear whether a study by outsiders would even be approved by the Navajo Nation's Historic Preservation Office, which grants research permits. From my perspective, the right authors of such a study would be Navajo ceremonialists, those fully knowledgeable about the game and its multilayered meanings. I'd like to think that some of today's singers would be interested, have time, and see such labors as contributing to ongoing efforts at increasing cultural awareness and understanding, and transmitting important cultural knowledge to future generations of Navajos.

Acknowledgments

Many colleagues provided various kinds of invaluable assistance, without which writing this chapter would've been impossible. My deepest thanks to Navajo colleagues for willingness to discuss certain things even though summertime is totally inappropriate, as we all knew, for research on a game restricted to winter nights! Thanks and indebtedness are expressed to: Clarenda Begay, Richard Begay, Steven Begay, Martha Blue, Kristin Butler (Canyon Records' director of licenses), Avery Denny, Jim Faris, Blane Grein, Tony Isaacs (Indian House), Steve Jett, Robert Johnson, Klara Kelley, Char Kruger, Vicki Levine, Kathleen Manolescu, Judy McCulloh, Bob McPherson, Bob Nuss and Chris Good (Drumbeat Indian Arts, formerly Canyon Records), Augusta Sandoval, Will Tsosie, Eddie Weber (Cool Runnings), and six others who chose anonymity.

Notes

1. Steven Begay coined the expression "Clubbing the Boots," noting that now, cowboy boots are more commonly used than moccasins, and the game is usually called "the Shoe Game" (Steven Begay, personal communication, 29 July 2013).

2. The first Navajo casino, Fire Rock, opened in Church Rock, New Mexico, on 18 November 2008.

3. Despite other problems, reviewing available recordings in 2013 did reveal some surprises. For example, a Chieftain Tracks album by Gilbert Begaye Sr., *Traditional Navajo Shoe Songs* (now out of print), won a 2008 NAMMY Best Traditional Recording category award, and another Chieftain Tracks album, *Keshjee-Navajo Shoe Game Songs* by the Porcupine Singers (Patterson 2009), was nominated in the same category for 2009 and 2011 NAMMYs, though it did not win. The Porcupine Singers is a group with more women than men, unlike others recording Shoe Game songs. The album review also revealed some actual game sounds on Leo Nez's 2011 *Night vs. Day Navajo Shoegame Songs*, rattle accompaniment on Delphine Tsinajinnie's one song on *Mother's Word* (Canyon 6325), and drum on songs 2 through 4 (1954 AFS 41 album, Willard Rhodes series), despite statements that these songs are always unaccompanied.

References

Bitsoi, Alastair Lee. 2013. "*Késhjéé* a Wholesome Way to Ring in the Year." *Navajo Times*, 3 January: A-3.

Buffalo, Michael. 2014. "Kééshjéé Teaches Morals, Restores Spirituality." *Navajo Times*, 2 January: A-1, A-2.

Culin, Stewart. 1907. *Games of the North American Indians*. 24th Annual Report, Bureau of American Ethnology, 1902–1903: 3–846.

Diné Bi'ólta Association. 1973. *Winter Shoe Game Songs, DBA Winter Workshop '73*. Ganado: Diné Bi'ólta Association, Inc.

Emery, Nedra. 1996. *Day and Night: Jí dóó Tł'éé'*. Bilingual book on the story of the Moccasin Game. Flagstaff: Salina Bookshelf.

Fonesca, Felicia. 2007. "Traditional Navajo Game Teaches Lessons." *Albuquerque Journal*, 12 January.

Franciscan Fathers. 1910. *An Ethnologic Dictionary of the Navaho Language*. St. Michaels, AZ: Franciscan Fathers.

Frisbie, Charlotte J. 1977. "Review of Navajo Corn Grinding and Shoe Game Songs." 1 12" 33 and 1/3 rpm disc. Recording and commentary by Tony Isaacs. Indian House IH 1507. *Ethnomusicology* 21 (2):355–56.

———. 1980. "Vocables in Navajo Ceremonial Music." *Ethnomusicology* 24(3): 347–92.

———. 1981. "Review of Interviews with American Indian Musicians, videotapes by Charlotte Heth, 1978." *Ethnomusicology* 25(2): 365–81.

Halpern, Katherine Spencer, and Susan Brown McGreevy. 1997. *Washington Matthews: Studies in Navajo Culture, 1880–1894*. Albuquerque: University of New Mexico Press in cooperation with the Wheelwright Museum of the American Indian.

Herzog, George. 1934. "Speech Melody and Primitive Music." *Musical Quarterly* 20(4): 452–66.

Hill, Willard W. 1943. *Navajo Humor*. General Series in Anthropology 9. Menasha: George Banta Publishing Company.

Holiday, John, and Robert S. McPherson. 2005. *A Navajo Legacy: The Life and Teachings of John Holiday*. Norman: University of Oklahoma Press.

Huenemann, Lynn. 1978. *Songs and Dances of Native America: A Resource Text for Teachers and Students*. Tsaile, AZ: Education House.

Isaacs, Tony. 2013. Extensive e-mail conversations, 30 January–8 August.

James, Davidson. 2004. "*Késhjéé'*: Shoegame." *Leading the Way* 2(12): 1, 8, 9 (December).

———. 2006. "How to Play the Shoegame." *Leading the Way* 4(1): 2, 3 (January).

"*Késhjéé'* in the Valley: Pictures from the Phoenix Indian Center Shoe Game, January 11." 2013. *Navajo Times*, 7 February: C-5.

Kluckhohn, Clyde. 1944. *Navaho Witchcraft*. Boston: Beacon Press.

Kruger, Char. 2013. "4th Annual *Késhjéé* Enjoyed by All." *Division of Natural Resources* 9(2): 1 (March).

Matthews, Washington. 1889. "Navajo Gambling Songs." *American Anthropologist* 2(1): 1–19.

McAllester, David P. 1954. *Enemyway Music*. Papers of the Peabody Museum of American Archaeology and Ethnology, Harvard University 41(3).

McAllester, David P., and Douglas F. Mitchell. 1983. "Navajo Music." In *Handbook of North American Indians, Volume 10: Southwest*, edited by Alfonso Ortiz, 605–23. Washington, DC: Smithsonian Institution.

McPherson, Robert S., Jim Dandy, and Sarah E. Burak. 2012. *Navajo Tradition, Mormon Life: The Autobiography and Teachings of Jim Dandy*. Salt Lake City: University of Utah Press.

Mose, Don, Jr. 2004. *The Moccasin Game: A Navajo Legend. Késhjéé' Baa Hané*. Illustrated by Baje Whitethorne, edited by Kathryn Hurst. Blanding: San Juan School District. Bilingual publication with compact disc.

Navajo Tribal Code. 1962. Volumes 1 and 2, Titles 1–22 with tables and index. Orford, NH: Equity Publishing Company.

Nelson, Leroy, Avery Denny, and Robert Johnson. 2010. "*Késhjéé'* (*Diné* Moccasin Game)." Unpublished handout.

Nettl, Bruno. 1956. *Music in Primitive Culture*. Cambridge, MA: Harvard University Press.

Nuss, Robert. 2013. Extensive telephone conversation about Moccasin Game Song recordings. 4 March.

O'Bryan, Aileen. 1956. *The Diné: Origin Myths of the Navaho Indians*. Bureau of American Ethnology Bulletin 163. Washington, DC: Smithsonian Institution.

Patterson, Jan-Mikael. 2009. "Chieftain Tracks Records Nabs 3 Nammy Nods." *Navajo Times*, 24 September: C-1.

Quintero, Donovan, photojournalist. 2014. "New Year's at the Shoe Game." *Navajo Times*, 9 January: A-8.

Reichard, Gladys. 1950. *Navaho Religion: A Study of Symbolism*. Pantheon: Bollingen Series 18. New York: Bollingen Foundation, Inc.

Roessel, Ruth. 2004. *Shoe Game-Késhijéé: A Game Played in the Winter Months*. Spiral bound, illustrations by Robert Johnson. Copy provided by Robert Johnson.

Scales, Christopher A. 2012. *Recording Culture: Powwow Music and the Aboriginal Recording Industry on the Northern Plains*. Durham, NC: Duke University Press.

Silversmith, Shondiin. 2013. "Shoe Game a Fun Way to Learn Traditional Songs, Stories." *Navajo Times*, 3 January: A-8.

Tsistł'ahnii Yázhí. 1974. *Késhjéé. Dinék'ehjí Naaltsoos Wólta'í* 29. Albuquerque: Navajo Reading Study, University of New Mexico for Rock Point Community School. [Volume is in Navajo; includes fifty-five Moccasin Game Song texts.]

CHAPTER THIRTY-TWO

Rise Up and Dream

New Work Songs for the New China

Frederick Lau

The second half of the twentieth century in China was marked by seismic socio-political transformations, beginning with the establishment of the People's Republic of China by the Chinese Communist Party in 1949. The ensuing nation-wide political campaigns and movements, such as the 1957 anti-rightist campaign, the Great Leap Forward (1958–1961), and the Cultural Revolution (1966–1976), brought devastating unrest and turmoil to the country. With the death of Mao Zedong (1893–1976) and the subsequent rise of Deng Xiaoping (1904–1997) as the de facto leader of the country, China was once again rocked by unprecedented waves of change that challenged the fundamental political ideology and tenets of Mao's China.

Since the late 1970s, Deng Xiaoping's open door policy has affected China in ways that were beyond imagination. Economic growth in the private sector and decentralization of resource distribution greatly reconfigured the socio-cultural order once tightly controlled by the central government. Gone were the days when state-owned enterprises, people's communes, government-sponsored production teams, and work units were the locus of everyday life. Replacing them was a form of capitalist economy practiced in newly designated special economic zones along the coastal regions in cities such as Guangzhou, Fuzhou, Shanghai, Zhejiang, Wenzhou, Dalian, Tianjin, and Qingdao, among others. In these regions, government-implemented flexible economic policies enticed transnational corporations to set up factories, regional headquarters, manufacturing operations, joint ventures between foreign and local businesses, financial investment offices, and trading companies, in order to grow the nation's economy. New special economic zones became centers of job opportunities, attracting millions of peasants and young people from China's hinterland to boomtowns in the coastal areas and urban centers in search of lucrative employment. This new form of state-sanctioned private ownership and market economy was often referred to euphemistically as socialism with Chinese characteristics.

The former communist paradigm of society, centered on three major proletariat classes—workers, peasants, and soldiers—was eradicated and exchanged for a social formation that emerged directly from a market-driven economy. Since the 1980s, the gap between rich and poor has widened. People care less about political and ideological concerns than about accumulating wealth, maintaining an affluent lifestyle, and living to realize what the general secretary of the Communist Party of China, Xi Jinping (b. 1953), called in 2013 "Chinese Dreams" [*Zhongguo meng*] (Zhao 1997; Rofel 2007).[1] This new social reality inevitably affects all facets of social and cultural life. In a few short decades, the once government-sanctioned cultural life gave way to a bustling contemporary urban culture with all the trappings of glamorous cosmopolitan and extravagant lifestyles. Revolutionary music, mass songs, and music with overt political messages, which had been important tools for ideological work and political propaganda (Perris 1983; McDougall 1984; Wong 1984), were on the wane, relegated to the dustbin of nostalgia and memory. In their place is an eclectic collection of entertainment music ranging from diverse traditional music genres and homegrown pop songs to pop music from Hong Kong, Taiwan, Korea, and the United States. This chapter examines an often ignored genre from this colorful soundscape known as "new work song" (*xindagong gequ*), a new grassroots (*caogen*) musical phenomenon that developed from the migrant labor cultural and social arena. I argue that the new work songs constitute a dissenting voice in China's push to create a "harmonious society," a political slogan that dominates national discourse in the new millennium. Central to my analysis is the question of agency and how workers define their trajectories in relation to an emerging modern nation obsessed with wealth, modernity, cosmopolitanism, and globalization on a grand scale.

Laborers, Migrants, and the New Work Song (*Dagong Gequ*)

In the heyday of the Chinese communist revolution, workers were glorified by the State and often displayed as heroes in propaganda, such as the images in the posters shown in figures 32.1 and 32.2. Songs with clear messages, such as "We Workers Have Power," "Work Song for Laborers," "Working Class

Figure 32.1. Propaganda poster from the Chinese communist revolution. ***Courtesy of chineseposters.net***

Figure 32.2. Propaganda poster from the Chinese communist revolution. *Courtesy of chineseposters.net*

Have Tough Bones," and "Workers' Four Seasons Song," praise workers for their contributions and social significance. These popular political work songs became iconic in the state-sponsored propaganda machine, but they receded from the limelight as social trends began to change in 1978, to be replaced initially by pop songs from Hong Kong and Taiwan, and later from the United States. With the post-Mao open door policy, China has become a global powerhouse in the manufacturing industry in less than three decades. Workers, who are now free agents not tied to any government work unit, have poured into factory towns and big cities searching for better jobs and incomes, but often at the risk of living without a proper local household (*hukou*) registration that guarantees them basic social welfare. Commonly known as *gongren*, *dagongzhe*, *nongmingong*, or simply *mingong*, many migrant workers were low-class villagers, farmers, or former farmers. They were attracted by better and more profitable income in industrial and construction work in urban centers across the country. According to the *Economist*, the floating population of migrant workers in 2010 reached 240 million, each taking home about RMB 1,400 per month, which is a mere $197 U.S. dollars.[2]

The media often portray migrant workers as people without quality or identity. They are viewed as squatters and as the dregs of modern society. Many media articles report on the harmful effects of migrant workers and the pressures they place "on urban infrastructure . . . [such as] urban planning, transport, housing, markets, security, the environment, hygiene, [and] birth control" (Florence 2008:101). Ironically, *Time* magazine named "The Chinese Worker" as the runner-up for the person of the year title in December 2009. The article asks, "Who deserves the credit? Above all, the tens of millions of workers who have left their homes, and often their families, to find work in the factories of China's booming coastal cities. . . . [We] found some of the people who are leading the world to economic recovery: Chinese men and women, their struggles in the past, their thoughts on the present and their eyes on the future."[3] One may ask why, in the post-Mao era, workers in China were once again spotlighted for their sacrifices, this time not by the communist state, but by Chinese grassroots nongovernmental organizations for workers and by the international media.

In this contradictory milieu, a new genre of work songs emerged, collectively known as dagong gequ (laborers' song or new work songs). New work songs usually feature memorable, colloquial language and catchy melodies borrowed or derived from regional folk tunes, familiar Chinese pop tunes, or Western folk or folk rock songs from the 1980s and 1990s. They articulate sentiments that capture the reality, hardships, dreams, frustrations, and alienation of contemporary migrant life, in stark contrast to the period in which workers were regarded as heroes and as the foundation of a classless society. These songs have circulated widely among workers through rallies, concerts, social media, downloadable mp3 files, and ringtones. Understanding this grassroots musical movement and the ubiquitous use of new technology offers insight into the fissure between modernity, globalization, and migration that ripples throughout the country. As products of turbulent moments in China's history, new work songs not only offer outlets for migrants; they also create "a structure of feelings" and "articulations of the presence" that sees cultural activity as a process providing the "specificity of present being . . . the personal: this, here, now, alive, active, 'subjective'" (Williams 1977:128). Dagong gequ are personalized songs that furnish a disenfranchised group with a temporal present and a voice to be heard, empowered, recognized, and validated, rather than being condemned to a receding and forgotten past. The case study provided here of three well-known new work songs reveals the underbelly of modernity in China and the state's attempt to create economic miracles in the post-Mao era.

A Study of Three New Work Songs

The closing lines of "Praise Song for Laborers" proudly proclaim that "workers created the world; workers are the most glorious." The lyrics of this song, written by Sun Heng, a laborer turned performer and songwriter, vividly capture the bitterness and difficult life that modern workers endure. His message is loud and clear. Armed with the education that qualified him to be an elementary schoolteacher, Sun, like many of his contemporaries, left his hometown in Henan Province and went to the capital, Beijing, in search of better employment.[4] Yet like many migrants, Sun's experience is light years away from the "Chinese Dream" that the current government attempts to promote. Since his arrival in Beijing in 1998, he has worked in several manual labor jobs and eventually decided to devote his time and energy to fight for workers' rights through music and the arts. On 1 May 2002, Sun and several volunteers formed the New Workers' Arts Troupe in Beijing, a nongovernmental organization founded by workers. Its mission is to provide social welfare services, education, and cultural service through performing arts for migrant workers' groups. Since its inception, the troupe has presented more than three hundred concerts at construction sites, factories, universities, businesses, schools, and workers' community centers.[5] In March 2009, Sun Heng and his troupe performed in the Beijing Chao Yang district as part of a May First Labor Day or International Workers' Day Celebration, an annual event that was considered a major festivity during the height of the revolutionary period.

"Praise Song for Laborers" is written in verse and chorus form with a chordal accompaniment and a simple, memorable refrain. Sun Heng wrote the song in 2007 with his New Workers' Arts Troupe. Curiously, he based it on a Korean song, "Nimul Wihan Haengjingok [Marching for Thee]," the title of which refers to the North Korean leader Kim Il Sung (1912–1994). The song was often used by leftists in South Korea during anti-government rallies. The style of Sun's song is reminiscent of the rousing marches and revolutionary songs of the 1960s and 1970s. The lyrics employ simple language, accompanied by guitars strumming simple chords, a drum set marking time, and an electronic keyboard that doubles the melody.[6] Since its release, the song has been widely circulated and used in many formal concerts, public rallies, and informal gatherings of workers.

In this song, Sun decries the pain and suffering of leaving his family and friends behind in the province. He addresses issues of self-esteem and asks migrant workers to be proud of their profession. Rallying against stereotypes and negative attitudes toward migrant workers, Sun reminds the audience that these workers are the people who further China's modernization projects by building roads, bridges, and urban high-rises. The lyrics highlight the achievements and sacrifices of migrant workers and encourage them to hold their heads high and to strive for happiness. It is with their bare hands that they build the modern world, despite the discrimination and hardships they

Table 32.1. "Praise Song for Laborers"

劳动者赞歌 *[Laodongzhe zangge]*	*"Praise Song for Laborers"*
离开了亲人和朋友，踏上了征战的路途	Left my family and friends to embark on a journey of struggle,
为了生活而奔波，为了理想而奋斗	To hustle for a living, to fight for an ideal.
我们不是一无所有，我们有智慧和双手	We are not without anything, we have a pair of hands and wisdom.
我们用智慧和双手，建起大街桥梁和高楼	We use our wisdom and hands to build wide roads, bridges, and high rises.
风里来，雨里走，一刻不停留。	We walk through winds and rains, but never stop.
汗也撒，泪也流，昂起头向前走。	We sweat, we cry, but we raise our heads high and move forward.
我们的幸福和权利，要靠我们自己去争取，	We have to fight for our own happiness and rights.
劳动者创造了这个世界，劳动者最光荣	Laborers created this world, laborers are glorious!

face. The issues of respect and self-esteem are recurring themes in many of Sun Heng's interviews and blogs.

The second song, "Laborers Are One Family" (2004), addresses community building and urges workers to unify themselves. In the video clip of a concert for workers, Sun Heng appears carrying a guitar and harmonica.[7] The reference to Bob Dylan is hard to miss. The musical style, vocal timbre, audience reception, performance setting, and quality of the music remind one of American folk music and concerts of the 1960s. This reference invokes the power of songs in raising people's awareness of the hardship and unjust social conditions of migrant workers. Although the context is different, the results are surprisingly similar. In discussing the concept of folk song in Western society, Nettl points out that this term has "strong emotional connotations," particularly in American society (2005:358). He suggests that American folk song "stands variously for class, political orientation, ethnicity, tradition, purity, social attitude, [and] environmental consciousness" (Nettl 2005). In a similar vein, new work songs rest heavily on their emotional appeal and symbolism to keep migrant workers together as a visible social group. The use of American folk music and its implied rebellious overtone is a perfect match, as Western music has had a long-lasting impact on Chinese society (Lau 2008). Modern Chinese music began with the adoption of European musical practices and aesthetics. Like musicians in other parts of the world who creatively adapted Western music as part of their modernization projects (Nettl 1985), Chinese composers have also adapted and transformed Western musical practices to fit local contexts and social conditions since the turn of the twentieth century. For example, in the 1930s, the composer He Lu Ting incorporated Chinese pentatonicism into his compositions, whereas the pop composer Li Jing Hui created a type of vernacular song and dance for China's emerging modernity. Following this trend, Sun Heng's choice of Dylan's style is no accident, because Dylan and American folk music of the 1960s are iconic of social protest. By singing like Dylan with easily understandable Chinese lyrics, Sun and other migrant singers were able to voice their suffering effectively through song and performance.

"Laborers Are One Family" was the title track on the first album released by the Young Worker Art Troupe, which in 2010 changed its name to New Workers Art Troupe (*Xingongren Yishutuan*).[8] The song lyrics remind workers to unite and treat each other as family, regardless of their place of origin. Whether they came from Sichuan, Henan, Dongbei, or Anhui, everyone is the same in that they have to rely on manual skills to make a living. The song decries their difficult working conditions and reminds workers that their common goal is to stay alive. The only way migrant workers can survive

Table 32.2. "Laborers Are One Family"

天下打工是一家 *[Tianxia Dagong Shiyijia]*	*"Laborers Are One Family"*
你来自四川，我来自河南	You came from Sichuan, I came from Henan.
你来自东北，他来自安徽	You came from the Northeast, he came from Anhui.
无论我们来自何方	It doesn't matter where you came from,
都一样的要靠打工为生	You have to be a laborer to make a living.
你来搞建筑，我来做家政	You work in construction, I work in housekeeping.
你来做小买卖，他来做服务生	You have a small business, he is a waiter.
无论我们从事着哪一行啊	It doesn't matter what profession you are in,
只为了求生存走到一起来	It is only to survive that we came together.

hardship and resolve the problems of daily life and discrimination is for them to join hands, link arms, and stay together. In the dagong world, they are all brothers and sisters.

The final song, "Why? [*Weishenme*]," is similar to Cui Jian's 1986 hit, "I Have Nothing [*Yiwu Suoyou*]." Like Cui's earlier hit, which galvanized student protestors during the 1989 Tiananmen incident, "Why?" poses a series of rhetorical questions outlining the lingering concerns caused by China's recent modernization and globalization projects. Based on the Western China Shanbei folk song "Hanging the Red Lantern [*Guahongdeng*]," this song is accompanied by simple guitar chords and a recurring two- or three-note interlude played on the harmonica. The song asks, buildings are getting higher and higher; how come those who build them can never own one? Medical standards are improving; how come the number of patients who can't afford modern health care is increasing? The issue of basic social rights had resurfaced after almost two decades of economic development. If our education system is on a par with international standards, how come our children cannot even go to school? Our technology has improved, but relationships between human beings are deteriorating. The song underscores the sacrifices that workers have made for China's economic development and modernization projects.

Conclusions

The genre of dagong gequ constitutes a unique mode of cultural expression in China's engagement with the global economy. Like migrant workers everywhere in the world, mingongs have to rely on cultural resources to

Table 32.3. "Why"

为什么 *[Weishenme]*	*"Why"*
Verse 1	
为什么高楼越来越高	Why are buildings getting higher and higher,
盖楼的人一辈子连个房子都买不到	But those who built them could never afford them?
为什么医疗水平越来越高	Why are the standards of health care improving,
进不起医院看不起病的人越来越多了	But those who cannot afford the hospital are on the rise?
Chorus	
哎呀为什么？为呀为什么？	Aiya, why? Aiya, why?
为什么呀为什么？为呀为什么？	Why? Why?
Verse 2	
为什么教育都和世界接轨了	Education is reaching world standard,
孩子们上学却越来越难了	But it is harder for children to go to school.
为什么科技越来越发达了	Technology is becoming more developed;
人和人的关系却越来越糟糕	Relationships between people are getting worse.
Chorus	
Verse 3	
为什么物价不停在上涨	Why are prices constantly rising?
可怜我口袋里的工资却永远也赶不上	Poor me, my income could never catch up.
为什么经济飞速地增长了	Why is the economy constantly growing,
贫富之间的差距却越来越大	But the gap between the rich and poor is getting bigger?
Chorus	
Verse 4	
为什么穷人越来越穷了	Why are people getting poorer and poorer,
有钱的人有闲的人越来越麻木了	But people who have money and time have become numb?
为什么物质生活越来越好了	Why is it that when material life is getting better,
我们的精神和内心却越来越空虚了	Our hearts and spirits are becoming empty and lonely?
Chorus	

make their lives livable and meaningful. As Thomas Turino remarks, "In the city, [migrant workers] draw on ideas and styles of behavior learned from a multitude of heterogeneous sources. . . . They adapt, alter, combine, and create cultural resources in unique ways . . . the search for security, feelings of self-worth, and some kind of livable space not least among them" (Turino 1993:3). The new work songs outline various struggles and hardships that mingongs have to endure and negotiate, such as living at the bottom of a social, political, and economic reality without any help from the government.

Different in values and intent from work songs of the Maoist period, dagong gequ are symbolic resources that provide an outlet of relief for workers. They give voice to a collective aspiration to question authority and the imbalance between the state, social equity, and the market economy.

Wang Xu and Liu Gang, former migrant workers and street musicians who became the vocal duo *Xuri Yanggang*, state that it is the singing of dagong songs that relieved them of pain and suffering in their lives as mingongs.[9] They used to sing privately to alleviate frustrations, and ironically, it was their emotional singing first on the street and later via the Internet that brought them fame and recognition. Like Wang and Liu, many other migrant singers who appeared in video clips on the migrant workers' website invariably comment that songs and lyrics are a powerful medium for articulating who they are, constructing a collective identity, bringing people together, making their lives meaningful, and drawing attention to their struggling existence.[10] Through their engagement with dagong songs, workers participate in what Lisa Rofel calls the "politics of desire" (2007:14), that is, the creation of post-Mao subjectivities and cosmopolitan citizenship through the production of various symbolic and materialistic desires. They construct what they want, imagine what is good, and convince themselves that what they desire is exactly that for which they should strive. No matter what they are called, gongren, nongmingong, mingong, or *xingongren*, their goal is to pursue their dreams and to counteract the negative characterization of them as hooligans who disrupt the stability of the city, a powerful trope in the government's control of population mobility and distribution of wealth and resources (Florence 2008:95). Songs render their self-representation, lived experience, and struggles for social recognition audible, since workers are now the underdogs rather than the heroes they were in the struggle for class liberation of the 1950s and 1960s. Unlike earlier work songs designed by the government to inculcate and solidify the masses, these new grassroots work songs come directly from workers' own lived experience. They constitute a counternarrative to the government's dominant discourse and parallel the widespread labor protests that have occurred in China in recent years. Songs can often fly under the radar and be perceived as harmless, and music has a certain pervasiveness that other kinds of dissenting materials lack, especially when social media are involved in their circulation.

Technology helps to disseminate new work songs, which are not only popular among workers, but also circulate among nongovernmental organizations, college students, and social groups in large manufacturing towns. Consuming dagong songs as downloads, as ringtones, on the Internet, or in formal and informal concerts has become a form of moral support (*shengyuan*) made public. The physical act of singing out offers shengyuan, a term that translates literally as "to voice" and "to assist," and is often used in association with the word *weiquan* (to protect one's rights) by social movements, in the press, and on *weibo*, China's equivalent of Twitter. Weiquan refers to any social movement related to defending all basic rights of any person or group. I suggest that circulating, downloading, sharing, singing, and tweeting dagong songs is a modern form of shengyuan. Uploading dagong gequ onto the Internet makes migrants' problems virtual and visible, drawing immediate support for mingong.

The website publicity promoting one of the concerts of the New Workers Art Troupe states that "workers have done so much to contribute to our nation and society, how come we cannot speak up, sing out loudly and tell the world our feelings and emotions from the perspective of a laborer and a human being. Tonight, let us all shout together and sing out at the top of our lungs."[11] Music carries ideas that can change people. Music can fight because it can communicate under the radar, which protests cannot do. In post-Mao China, songs give voice to voiceless urban dwellers. They have attracted increasing support and participation from workers. When concerts are performed in the open air, parks, and makeshift construction sites turned into concert venues, audiences hear the performers' collective criticism against exploitation, injustice, inequality, disparaging social treatment, and poverty. Robbie Lieberman (1995) and Noriko Manabe (2013) argue in their studies of protest songs that memorable songs and socially significant verses have become powerful and practical weapons through which the disenfranchised can fight back and draw public attention to their cause. It is not surprising that both Woody Guthrie and Pete Seeger emblazoned the slogan "This machine kills fascists" on their guitars and banjos.

In a personal blog posted after his trip to visit a group of local workers in Changsa on 9 July 2013, Sun Heng wrote that "as we encounter numerous social problems such as inequality, the rich and poor divide, the gap between cities and villages, environmental degradation, food safety, moral turpitude, [and] lack of faith, we need changes. The progress of any society requires the help of government, businesses, social organizations, and the active participation of all citizens. We need to face reality in order to realize our ideal. An even better society is possible if we focus our mind on the world and have our feet firmly planted on the ground."[12] Although Sun does not represent the majority voice, his optimistic tone and the untiring work of his troupe have gradually established a strong presence among university students and members of other Chinese nongovernmental organizations. Migrant workers now have their own website called *Dashengchang* (Singing Loudly), which contains links to its performing troupes, workers' museum, discussion column, media coverage, special exhibitions, performance schedule, workers' education, social welfare, and general education.[13] The first screen of the website has a list of songs available for download. What is most impressive about their music project is that they have produced a special album titled *Labor and Respect*, a collection of the best songs from the last decades. It is clear that new work songs have been effective tools for migrant workers and their struggle for survival.

This preliminary study raises a series of questions for further research. What is the role of the migrant worker in national discourse, as China changes her image as a progressive socialist country? How will the reemergence of class in a presumably classless society affect the dominance of the Communist Party? Can music, technology, and the politics of culture become the real superpower in creating and challenging Chinese cognitive habits and modes of consciousness in the coming decades? I close with a quote from the home page of the Migrant Workers' website: "No matter how noisy the surroundings are, only the sound that comes from the heart can impress other souls. We firmly believe that the voice from reality is the most pleasant to listen to, the feeling from real life is the most glorious."[14]

Acknowledgments

I presented an early version of this paper on 3 November 2012 at the Annual Meeting of the Society for Ethnomusicology on a panel titled "Music and Modern Life in Contemporary China." I would like to thank Eric Florence of the Centre for Ethnic and Migration Studies, Université de Liège, Belgium, for reading an early draft of this chapter, for sharing his research and publications on Chinese migrant workers, and above all, for his intellectual inspiration and friendship. Most importantly, I would like to take this opportunity to thank Bruno Nettl for his tutelage and care, and for accepting me as one of his advisees. It is he who taught me to hear and "see" music in a new light, and that it is always people and context that make music special and worth studying.

Notes

1. www.thechinastory.org/yearbooks/yearbook-2013/forum-dreams-and-power/chinese-dreams-zhongguo-meng%E4%B8%AD%E5%9B%BD%E6%A2%A6/.

2. ibtimes.com/china-now-has-more-260-million-migrant-workers-whose-average-monthly-salary-2290-yuan-37409-1271559.

3. www.scmp.com/article/701508/time-honours-chinese-worker (accessed 24 August 2013).

4. gdschina/org/UploadFile/20130708145123365 8.jpg.

5. baike.baidu.com/view/3338419.htm#2.
6. v.youku.com/v_show/id_XMTY2NjA0.html.
7. v.youku.com/v_show/id_XMTY2NjA0.html.
8. baike.baidu.com/view/3286663.htm.
9. zh.wikipedia.org/wiki/%E6%97%AD%E6%97%A5%E9%98%B3%E5%88%9A.
10. www.dashengchang.org.cn/.
11. daheng126.blog.163.com/blog/static/1016740152013612112843716/.
12. daheng126.blog.163.com/blog/static/1016740152013612112843716/.
13. www.dashengchang.org.cn/.
14. www.baike.com/wiki/%E6%89%93%E5%B7%A5%E9%9D%92%E5%B9%B4%E8%89%BA%E6%9C%AF%E5%9B%A2.

References

Florence, Eric. 2008. "Struggling around *Dagong*: Discourses about and by Migrant Workers in the Pearl River Delta." Unpublished paper.

Lau, Frederick. 2008. *Music in China: Experiencing Music, Expressing Culture*. New York: Oxford University Press.

Lieberman, Robbie. 1995. *My Song Is My Weapon: People's Songs, American Communism, and the Politics of Culture, 1930–50*. Urbana: University of Illinois Press.

Manabe, Noriko. 2013. "Music in Japanese Antinuclear Demonstrations: The Evolution of a Contentious Performance Model." *Asia-Pacific Journal: Japan Focus* 11(4). Published electronically japanfocus.org/-Noriko-MANABE/4015.

McDougall, Bonnie S., ed. 1984. *Popular Chinese Literature and Performing Arts in the People's Republic of China, 1949–1979*. Berkeley: University of California Press.

Nettl, Bruno. 1985. *The Western Impact on World Music: Change, Adaptation, and Survival*. New York: Schirmer Books.

———. 2005. *The Study of Ethnomusicology: Thirty-One Issues and Concepts*. Urbana: University of Illinois Press.

Perris, Arnold. 1983. "Music as Propaganda: Art at the Command of Doctrine in the People's Republic of China." *Ethnomusicology* 27(1): 1–28.

Rofel, Lisa. 2007. *Desiring China: Experiments in Neoliberalism, Sexuality, and Public Culture*. Durham, NC: Duke University Press.

Turino, Thomas. 1993. *Moving Away from Silence: Music of the Peruvian Altiplano and the Experience of Urban Migration*. Chicago: University of Chicago Press.

Williams, Raymond. 1977. *Marxism and Literature*. Oxford: Oxford University Press.

Wong, Isabel K. F. 1984. "*Geming Gequ*: Songs for the Education of the Masses." In *Popular Chinese Literature and Performing Arts in the People's Republic of China, 1949–1979*, edited by Bonnie S. McDougall, 112–43. Berkeley: University of California Press.

Zhao, Bin. 1997. "Consumerism, Confucianism, Communism: Making Sense of China Today." *New Left Review* 222: 45–59.

CHAPTER THIRTY-THREE

~

Fusion Music in South India

Terada Yoshitaka

The music culture of South India is undergoing a major transformation with globalization as its backdrop. At first glance, Karnatak (South Indian classical) music today may appear to be vibrant and flourishing. The famous December music season in Chennai (formerly Madras) is attracting ever-increasing numbers of people, including those from other urban centers in India as well as Non-Resident Indians (NRIs) and Sri Lankan Tamils based in North America and Europe. Performance tours of Karnatak musicians overseas have also dramatically increased since the 1980s, and many have migrated away from India, returning only for performances. This movement of people has had a grave impact on music culture as a whole, and many musicians and patrons (especially of older generations) lament that its old charm and classicism are disappearing all too rapidly.

The large-scale movement of people is one of the tangible effects of globalization. The migration of Indian people and their settlement in North America and Europe has increased sharply since the 1960s. As of 2000, the United States alone has more than 1.8 million people of Indian descent. The thirst for the music of their homeland in these communities created opportunities for many Indian musicians to perform and teach abroad. For such musicians, increasing contact with Western (and Westernized Indian) audiences has rattled the social hierarchy in music. While vocal music was not readily accessible without prior familiarity, the violin caught the attention of Western audiences for its unique holding position and playing technique, and the intricate rhythmic structure and virtuosity of percussionists received an enthusiastic reception. The accompanists often "stole the show" from the vocalist, but they were expected to remain subservient to soloists. This type of firsthand experience led accompanists to reconsider their position in the musical and social hierarchy. This changing awareness among classical musicians served, at least partially, as a background for the emergence of a new musical genre.

In 2000, Dreams Audio of Chennai, South India, started marketing a series of recordings labeled "fusion."[1] The term refers primarily to the style of music in which familiar compositions of Karnatak music are rendered by various combinations of Indian and Western instruments, or to new compositions based on modal principles of Karnatak music, frequently with a synthesized accompaniment. Conservative musicians and fans of classical music disregarded the merit of fusion music, or criticized the intent of producing such music, as cheapening or destroying the age-old tradition. Despite the criticism from classical music orthodoxy and initial skepticism from the music industry, however, these CDs and cassette tapes proved commercially successful. Although live performances were relatively infrequent, recorded fusion music rapidly replaced classical and film music as background music in hotels, restaurants, and shopping centers.

This chapter explores the emergence of this new category of music in the context of increasing globalization and the changing dynamics of music culture in South India. The thrust behind producing fusion music is not only the music industry's desire to create a profitable genre for domestic and potentially foreign markets, but also a manifestation of the musicians' shifting motivations and varying responses to globalizing society. I first describe the emergence of fusion music, then analyze the motivations of its producers and performers in relation to the changing dynamics of music culture that have served as a backdrop for the unexpected prominence of this new genre.

Fusion as a Marketing Category

In South India, the term "fusion" was used sporadically in the past, referring loosely to various styles that blend Karnatak music with genres from outside of South India. It was in 2000 that the term was used for the first time to market a specific type of music in South India, and within a short period of several years, many recordings were produced and distributed in that newly created category.

The person most responsible for the emergence of fusion music in South India is J. Muthukumar. In his teens and twenties, Muthukumar played the trap-set in a film and light classical music group at marriage receptions and private parties in Chennai. Friendly and dynamic, he made many friends among fellow musicians, and the network he established during these years became an indispensable asset when he started his career in the music business. The successful early fusion albums that Muthukumar produced were with his personal friends, such as Kadri Gopalnath and Rajesh Vaidhya. After working for a marketing firm, he joined HMV (His Master's Voice) in 1984, and served as its production manager for the southern region until 2000. HMV, established in 1905, had monopolized the music reproduction industry in South India until the 1980s when Sangeetha, the first label specializing in Karnatak music, was founded.

A concert by a *vīna* player inspired Muthukumar to market fusion music. Karnatak pieces were played in the first half, followed by film songs in the second. Sensing the audience's considerably greater enthusiasm toward the vīna player's rendition of film songs, Muthukumar conceived the idea of producing Karnatak music with filmic arrangement to reach a wider audience. While at HMV, he attempted several experimental projects, and in the mid-1980s he released a series of cassette tapes consisting of remakes of old film songs from the 1940s and 1950s. Much later, in 1996, he experimented again on film-music remakes and produced a cover version of two film songs. One of them was "Adaludan Padal," a hit song from *Kudiruntha Koil* (The Sacred Dwelling), starring M. G. Ramachandran, an icon of South Indian cinema from the 1950s through the 1970s. The cassette tape that included these songs, *Vaanavil: Tamil Pop Songs* (Rainbow), however, acquired virtually no media attention or commercial success and was soon discontinued.

Muthukumar also collaborated with a music film director, M. S. Viswanathan, and a prominent Karnatak vocalist, Maharajapuram Santhanam, to produce *Sangamam: Carnatic Krithis with Orchestra* (Coming Together), a cassette tape containing classical compositions arranged in a manner similar to film music; the composed, sung portion is executed in the style of classical music, whereas filmic orchestral music is added for the prelude and interludes. This recording received stiff criticism from conservative critics and fans of classical music alike, discouraging HMV from releasing similar recordings afterward. Increasingly frustrated with HMV's conservative approach to music, Muthukumar left the company in 2000 to establish his own company, Dreams Audio. Without the organizational restrictions, he released twelve CDs labeled fusion during the short period of two years. In 2002, Dreams Audio merged with the larger and financially more secure Kosmic Music, and Muthukumar became its production manager. The reproduction and distribution rights of the fusion CDs produced under Dreams Audio were transferred to Kosmic Music.

Performance Contexts and the Audience

The largest live event for fans of South Indian fusion music (and rock music) has been the annual cultural festival at the Indian Institute of Technology (IIT) Madras, one of the elite universities that trains IT engineers for the global market. It is not only the most prestigious venue for local amateur bands of rock and fusion music, but also for professional groups that are invited to the event. With generous funding from multinational corporations such as Sony and Levi's, the IIT festival has sponsored concerts by many prominent groups, including the internationally famous Shakti. At this festival, the majority of the audience consists of college students and other young people who are not satisfied with the two major categories of music in South India: classical and film music.

Whereas college students may be the most avid fans of fusion music, others also listen to it. At present, full-fledged concerts by fusion musicians are infrequent, and live performances are usually confined to wedding receptions. The context in which most people are exposed to fusion music includes hotel lobbies, restaurants, and shopping centers. Music store owners state that people who purchase fusion music are first exposed to it at such venues. Increasingly, TV stations invite fusion groups to appear on their programs. Music associations for Karnatak music also sponsor concerts of fusion music occasionally. In such concerts, the audience consists mainly of members of associations who tend to be enthusiastic fans of Karnatak music, typically gray-haired and clad in traditional attire such as *vēshti* (lower garment for men) and *sari*. Few youngsters in jeans and T-shirts who might flock to the IIT festivals can be found there. Even die-hard fans of Karnatak music may discreetly play fusion CDs while driving their cars.

One area in which a fusion band is employed for live performance is in the wedding receptions of high castes, particularly Brahmans, who have been the primary practitioners and patrons of Karnatak music since the early decades of the twentieth century. The liberalization of the economy in 1991 provided many opportunities for young people to land lucrative IT professions. Because they often have considerably more income than their parents, they are assertive with their preferences, which reflect their urban lifestyle and exposure to Western culture. Parents, for the same reasons, are more attentive to their children's cultural tastes. In the context of a wedding reception, fusion music serves as a convenient middle ground between young professionals, who enjoy eclectic styles of music, and their parents, who adhere to devotion-based Karnatak music (figure 33.1).

Figure 33.1. A fusion band at a wedding reception (in Chennai, 2006). ***Photo by Terada Yoshitaka***

Inspirations

Fusion music was not created out of thin air, and its major proponents tend to cite two particular individuals who served as a source of inspiration. John McLaughlin is a British guitarist most famous for his association with Miles Davis and known for his interest in Indian music and culture, which is evident in the names of his own ensembles, Mahavishnu Orchestra and Shakti. The latter, founded in 1975, remains the most influential band for fusion musicians in India. Apart from McLaughlin, the group included Zakir Hussein (*tabla* from North Indian classical music) and three musicians from South India: L. Shankar (violin), Ramnad Raghavan (*mridangam*), and T. H. Vikku Vinayakram (*ghatam*). McLaughlin was one of the top players in the category known as *jazz fusion* (or *jazz rock*) in the 1970s, and his fame certainly contributed to the group's success in the international market. Many young musicians in India were inspired by Shakti's acoustic fusion music, which demonstrated that Karnatak music can be fused with Western music, both artistically and commercially.

Another individual who inspired fusion musicians is Ilaiyaraja, a prolific composer and music director who dominated the film-music scene in South India between the mid-1970s and the 1990s. Since his debut in 1976, he has written more than four thousand songs for 750 films. Ilaiyaraja is also known for his exceptional ability to incorporate elements of Karnatak music into film music while making it readily accessible to film-music fans. The release of the *How To Name It?* album in 1986 is regarded by most fusion musicians as an epoch-making event in the history of South Indian music. The music of South India had been bifurcated between classical and film music, and before this album, there was no separate category of popular music unconnected to films. The album includes many compositions that refuse easy categorization, as its title implies: the melody with *gamaka* (characteristically South Indian melodic embellishment), for example, is supported by Western harmony. Song titles such as "Do Not Compare" and "Do Anything" not only express Ilaiyaraja's desire for artistic creativity, but also document the existence of the rigid categorization of music at the time of the album's release. Ilaiyaraja called the album "experimental," but never used the term "fusion" for his music. Still, he remains a pioneer for most fusion players today who describe the album as a classic masterpiece.

Performers' Motivations

Most performers of fusion music have strong backgrounds in Karnatak music, and many come from lineages of accomplished musicians. Typically, they began their studies and performance careers at an early age. The privilege of already being in the loop certainly enables those musicians to advance in music careers, because to study under a famous musician and to secure enough support to succeed in a music career requires familial or other personal connections. Why would someone from such a privileged position risk his or her own career in Karnatak music by being involved in fusion music, of which some conservative musicians and patrons are harshly critical?

To Attract Indian Youths

Virtually all fusion musicians believe that Karnatak music as performed today is too old-fashioned for young people, who are increasingly urban and global in lifestyle and sensibility. Manikanth Kadri, who produced the most successful series of fusion albums, *Dream Journey*, with his saxophonist father Kadri Gopalnath, finds it important to provide familiar Karnatak compositions in modern arrangements to reach a wide audience (figure 33.2). In his albums, Gopalnath's saxophone solos—played mostly in classical style—are furnished with digitally produced pop-oriented accompaniment. Highly innovative, Gopalnath is credited for his successful adoption of the saxophone into Karnatak music. His reputation in the Karnatak music circle is firmly established, and he frequently performs at prestigious venues as a top-ranking musician.

As in the case of the majority of fusion albums, the Dream Journey series mostly contains well-known Karnatak songs, such as "Vatapi Ganapatim"

Figure 33.2. *Dream Journey* (2000), produced by Kadri Gopalnath, the first successful fusion album. *Courtesy of Manikanth Kadri*

and "Raghuvamsa Sudha," but also features what is known as "English notes" (or *nōttusvara*), which are songs written by the nineteenth-century composer Muttusvami Diksitar in the style of Western marches.[2] A few devotional songs that became popular in films such as *Alai Payuthe* have also been selected to entice film-music fans into classical music. Manikanth even conducts market research as to what songs should be included in their future endeavors.[3]

Rajesh Vaidhya, a vīna player, argues that classical music is too slow in tempo to reach young people today, and that fusion music can play a major role in exposing them to classical music. An early exposure to Western music and the opportunities to work with some famous pop icons, such as Elton John and Queen, initiated his interest in fusion music. Vaidhya has been the most prolific exponent of fusion music, having released eight albums within three short years, including *7–11*, which has seven pieces in many different genres and is named after the American convenience-store chain. Vaidhya's recordings typically include popular Karnatak compositions, mostly in duple meter, arranged with filmic orchestral interludes and programmed percussion.

K. N. Shashikiran also believes it is important to provide opportunities for young people to listen to classical music. Born into a family of Karnatak musicians, he held his first concert at the age of nine. While performing classical music with his brother as Carnatica Brothers, in 1998 Shashikiran established Carnatica, an organization that supports a music school for children, a recording studio, and a research archive. Through education, research, and production of recordings, he aims to obliterate the stereotypical image of Karnatak music as conservative and unchanging. In order to help achieve his goals, Shashikiran produced *Carnatic PEP Album* in 2002. He asserts that the initial lessons in Karnatak music are given too mechanically and children easily lose interest. To sustain their interest, he seeks to provide rudimentary songs with Western arrangements to "pep up" the children studying Karnatak music. A contrasting rhythm or genre is selected for each piece of the album for variety, so that children with a short attention span can stick to the lesson.

Many fusion players also regard Karnatak music as too religiously exclusive and wish to create a new style of music based on the modal principles of classical music (*rāgam* and *tālam*) but without overt association with devotional Hinduism. While classical compositions with nondevotional content do exist, Karnatak music is described in the dominant discourse as a path to approach the divine and to reexperience devotion to a saint virtually, which is expressed in the compositions. The Karnatak composers are often described as "saint-composers," and the trope that deifies the three famed composers of the nineteenth century as the "Trinity" (*trimūrtti*) has been firmly established.

Ghatam Karthick questions why such saint-composers cannot be listened to simply as great composers. Karnatak music features exaggerated vocal interjections, facial expressions, and bodily movements, all of which express intoxication with the music on the part of performers and listeners. This has made the classical music circle more like a religious cult, thus alienating others. To create classical music without overt religious connotations, Karthick writes new songs based on the modal principles of classical music, instead of arranging preexisting Karnatak masterpieces imbued with strong Hindu devotion.

To Achieve Equality through Music

Through his fusion music, Karthick also challenges social inequality and discrimination in music culture. He argues that no Karnatak music concert is possible without accompanists, who spend as many years in training and hardship as soloists, but that discrimination is rampant and prevalent in the areas of performance fees and general treatment. Karthick asserts that Karnatak music has a pyramid-like hierarchical structure in which discriminatory practices exist not only between soloists and accompanists, but also between melodic and rhythmic accompanists; there is even discrimination among rhythmic accompanists, between primary (mridangam) and secondary (*kanjīra*, ghatam, etc.) accompanists. Karthick believes that even his guru, Vikku Vinayakram, would have been treated as a mere ghatam player if he had not acquired fame outside of India as a member of Shakti. He aims to raise the accompanist's status in Karnatak music by becoming successful with his own instrumental ensemble, HeArtbeat.

Karthick's attempt may be placed in the history of experimental instrumentations attempted by individual musicians within Karnatak music. Novel combinations of instruments that emerged since the 1960s can be construed as accompanists' efforts to dismantle a hierarchical social organization by attempting to acquire the privilege hitherto monopolized by vocalists. The Violin Trio, consisting of three talented brothers (L. Vaidhanathan, L. Subramaniam, and L. Shankar), became popular in the late 1960s. It was the idea of their violinist father, V. Lakshminarayana, who was discontented about the subordinate position of violin players in Karnatak music. In the 1970s, the Trio attempted another experiment by hiring a *tavil* player as a rhythmic accompanist instead of the conventional mridangam player for some of their performances. The tavil is a double-headed drum, primarily used to accompany *nāgasvaram* (oboe) for temple and life-cycle rituals, and performed exclusively by members of non-Brahman castes.

The Trio's success inspired many other musicians to try their hands at innovation. The violinist Lalgudi Jayaraman had established a reputation as a top-ranking accompanist and later soloist, but he also formed an ensemble featuring the three instruments (violin, flute, and vīna) with an equal share of solo opportunities. The unique combination of instruments made them popular. Kunnakudi Vaidyanathan, a violinist with wide appeal, has given many solo performances with a tavil player since the 1970s. Although the combination of violin and tavil was already employed by the Violin Trio, Vaidyanathan became famous for playing *mallāri*, an instrumental composition that was previously played only at the beginning of the deity's procession during temple festivals (Terada 2008b). Such incorporation of tavil into Karnatak music, though initiated by high-caste Brahman musicians, raised the status of its players in *periya mēlam* ritual music, in which tavil accompanists were subservient to nāgasvaram soloists, both musically and socially. In the late 1980s, the violinist A. Kanyakumari formed yet another instrumental ensemble called Vadya Lahari, combining the violin, vīna, and nāgasvaram, further experimenting with intergenre instrumentation. Orchestras with an enormous number of identical instruments have also been attempted, such as Chittibabu's recording with fifty vīna players.[4]

While Karthick aims to change inequalities among classical musicians, others, such as Paul Jacob, find in music a possibility of changing people's attitudes toward caste differences. Jacob was one of the central figures in the small but active community of rock musicians in Chennai in the 1980s. Deeply influenced by Euro-American rock music of the 1960s, Jacob started playing the bass guitar in a dance band at the age of eleven. The performance venue of his early career was an Anglo-Indian dance show that had its origin in the colonial period and was popular until the 1980s, when such shows were held weekly in Chennai. Throughout the 1980s, Jacob was a member of Nemesis Avenue, now a legendary rock band that also included many musicians who later became influential in film and fusion music, for example, A. R. Rahman and Suresh Peters.

In 1995, Jacob established Bhodi Productions to encourage and support creative music making in Chennai. He was particularly frustrated over the social bifurcation of musicians between classical and film music. As many non-Brahmans have pointed out, classical music has become the prominent cultural domain in which Brahmans can claim authority and ownership, and their determination to maintain the status quo is unwavering (Terada 2008a). In one example of how Jacob worked to challenge this, he organized a concert in which Brahman Karnatak musicians and *dalit* (low-caste) folk musicians were asked to share the stage, an unprecedented event that upset conservative Brahmans. According to Jacob, the superiority complex among high-caste Karnatak musicians and patrons has made it difficult to engage in intercaste collaboration or orientation toward new and experimental music.

Jacob himself had firsthand experience with its closed nature when he tried to find a teacher in Karnatak music.

To Reach a Global Audience

Fusion music of South India has been directed mostly to the domestic market, but some musicians, such as Rangaswamy Parthasarathy, a veteran producer and composer of Tamil films, sees its potential for export. Through his New York–based Oriental Records, he produces and distributes recordings of Indian music for Indians in North America and others interested in Indian music. In 2000, he released *Resonance* by the Madras String Quartet, which has eight Karnatak compositions arranged for string quartet, merging Western and South Indian traditions of classical music. The CD is notable because it contains compositions and *rāgams* considered difficult for Western-style harmonization and slow tempo pieces that are rare in fusion music.[5] The CD jacket juxtaposes the four instruments of the string quartet against the background of a huge Hindu temple. Such strategic juxtaposition is obviously meant to lure those in the West who are interested in Indian or world music.

The leader of the quartet, V. S. Narasimhan, began his study in Karnatak music with his father at the age of five. Because he often played for films, Narasimhan also entered the film-music profession, which has been his primary source of income until today. A chance meeting with the American sociologist Adrian L'Armand, also a violin player, initiated his interest in Western classical music. After studying privately with L'Armand, he joined the Madras Chamber Orchestra (established in 1975), performing in concerts and interacting with visiting non-Indian musicians. In formulating an idea for playing Karnatak compositions in a string-quartet format, Narasimhan was inspired by the *Turtle Island String Quartet*, an American-based ensemble specializing in incorporating popular-music genres into the string-quartet format.[6]

Some musicians comment on the limitation of current fusion music, for it is only a merger of Indian and Western music. They want to show the wider potential of fusion music by incorporating traditions from other regions. M. Lalitha and M. Nandini, two sisters who are classically trained in violin, released the fusion CD *Revelation*, with Kosmic Music, in which they tried to use elements of Hungarian, Egyptian, and Japanese music.[7] They call their music "transglobal fusion music" to distinguish it from other types of fusion music in South India.

Their interest in diverse musical genres derived partly from their uncle, L. Vaidhanathan, a member of the Violin Trio mentioned above. He was interested in composition and the music of other countries early on, and in 1960 he formed a group called *LV's Band* (after his own name and Elvis Presley's) consisting of top players of film music to perform experimental music. For the LV's Band, he arranged existing Karnatak compositions and performed them on Western instruments, calling the style "global fusion," a precursor of the fusion music that emerged after 2000. Unable to find a sponsor, the group was forced to disband, and none of their recordings were released. As fusion became a commercially viable category in the 2000s, however, he released a few CDs with established Karnatak musicians, such as N. Ramani (flute) and E. Gayathri (vīna), before his death in 2007. He also wrote music for "Indian Orchestra" in Singapore using aspects of Chinese, Malay, and Indian music.

Conclusions

The emergence of fusion music since 2000 expresses the ambivalence, and perhaps even insecurity, among musicians trained in Karnatak music, the majority of whom live and work in an increasingly modern, urban, and global society. Whereas they stress the centrality and universality of their musical tradition, Karnatak musicians are concerned about its reception outside of South India. Some have been found modifying their repertory or manner of performance to ensure a positive response when touring abroad, whereas others proudly announce their successful collaboration with non-Indian musicians. Although Karnatak music has always been supported by a relatively small group of patrons and fans, musicians today are increasingly concerned about the validity and relevance of classical music to younger audiences. A similar uncertainty looms behind the emergence of fusion music.

It is also significant that fusion music is primarily instrumental. Supported by its popularity in the wider segments of society, fusion music offers musicians a venue for negotiating their position in the traditional hierarchy between soloists and accompanists, and for challenging caste-based divisions. The desire to challenge the status quo had already been expressed within the framework of Karnatak music through various instrumental ensembles since the 1960s, and many ideas behind the post-2000 fusion music had already been formulated. As such, fusion music is a recent manifestation of Karnatak musicians' strategies for survival in the highly competitive music profession, as well as for securing freedom for musical creativity.

The unexpected prominence of fusion music in the 2000s accompanies the changing dynamics of classical music and the resulting ambivalence of its practitioners. The popularity of fusion music brings aspects of Karnatak music to the wider public while it may significantly alter the social organization of the musicians who have sustained it.

Notes

1. The data for this chapter were collected mainly in 2003–2004. I am grateful to the Japanese Ministry of Education Grant-in-Aid for Scientific Research for providing funds for research in India. I acknowledge here with appreciation the assistance rendered by Raman Unni, my trusted colleague and friend in Chennai. The idea for this chapter was first presented in 2004 at the Ninth Annual Conference of the Asia Pacific Society for Ethnomusicology.

2. English notes are considered less serious, miscellaneous pieces, and therefore do not constitute the core repertory of Karnatak music, but are frequently taken up by fusion musicians due to the underlying similarity.

3. Historically, the incorporation of Western musical traditions was initiated by courtly kings, such as Saraboji II (1798–1832) of Tanjavur and Krishnaraja Wodeyar IV (1884–1940) of Mysore, who were eager to learn Western culture, including music (Seetha 1981; Vedavalli 1992). Western instruments were first introduced to India in ceremonial and military bands at royal courts, and were gradually adapted into vernacular traditions. Many Western instruments have penetrated deeply into classical music, and an instrument like the violin has become so prevalent that some may even think it is of Indian origin. Today, it is not rare to witness a concert featuring a saxophone, clarinet, mandolin, or guitar. Each time a Western instrument was introduced to India, its adaptability to Karnatak music was questioned (Iyer 1948; Vasudevan 1965), and subsequently, the instrument was physically modified (e.g., some keys of the clarinet and saxophone have been removed) or a new playing posture or technique was invented (e.g., the way the violin is positioned) to produce melodic embellishments known as *gamaka*.

4. Listen to *Serenade: An Extravaganza of 50 Veenas*. Similar examples include Kanyakumari's *Kanya: Virtual Virgo 27 Violins*.

5. For examples, listen to *Amba Kamakshi* (in *Bhairavi* rāgam) and *Moksham* (in *Saramadi* rāgam) respectively.

6. Narasimhan is frequently featured in Ilaiyaraja's music, including the path-breaking album *How To Name It?*

7. M. Lalitha and her sister Nandini are unique in Karnatak music in that they perform only as a violin duo (soloists), having never played as accompanists for others. In playing fusion music, they perform in a standing position like Western violinists, in contrast to the sitting position for classical music.

References

Iyer, C. S. 1948. "The Clarinet and Classical Carnatic Music." *Journal of Music Academy* 19: 51–57.

Rajagopalan, N. 1990. *A Garland: Biographical Dictionary of Carnatic Composers and Musicians, Book I*. Bombay: Bharatiya Vidya Bhavan.

Seetha, S. 1981. *Tanjore as a Seat of Music*. Madras: University of Madras.

Terada, Yoshitaka. 2008a. "*Tamil Isai* as a Challenge to Brahmanical Music Culture in South India." In *Music and Society in South Asia: Perspectives from Japan*, edited by Yoshitaka Terada, 203–26. Osaka: National Museum of Ethnology.

———. 2008b. "Temple Music Traditions in Hindu South India: *Periya Melam* and Its Performance Practice." *Asian Music* 39(2): 108–51.

Vasudevan, D. V. 1965. "Able Exponent of the Clarionet." *Hindu* (14 January).

Vedavalli, M. B. 1992. *Mysore as a Seat of Music*. Trivandrum: CBH Publications.

Interviews Conducted in Chennai, India

Lalitha Vaidyanathan: 2 March 2003.
N. Ramanathan: 10 March 2003.
Mandolin U. Rajesh: 11 March 2003.
G. S. Mani: 15 March 2003.
Manikant Kadri: 16 March 2003.
Rangasami Parthasarathy: 18 March 2003.
K. N. Shashikiran: 19 March 2003.
M. Lalitha: 21 March 2003.
Paul Jacob: 22 March 2003.
L. Vaidyanathan: 24 March 2003.
V. S. Narasimhan: 25 March 2003.
Prasanna: 22 December 2003.
Radhakrishna Dasa: 25 December 2003.
J. Muthukumar: 27 December 2003; 5 January 2004.
Baskar Mudhra: 29 December 2003.
Rajesh Vaidhya: 31 December 2003.
Ghatam Kartick: 1 January 2004.

CHAPTER THIRTY-FOUR

~

The Urge to Merge

Are Cross-Cultural Collaborations Destroying Hindustani Music?

Stephen Slawek

Bruno Nettl has noted that, in the history of ethnomusicology, scholars moved from a pursuit of salvaging the music of cultures presumed to have remained unchanged for much of their past to a realization that the only real continuity in culture is change (2005:272–75). Cultures, moreover, differ in their stance toward change in music, and even within a single society different musical styles and genres are permitted varying degrees of acceptable change. Typically, genres of popular music are expected to change their content and style relatively quickly, primarily to maintain commercial appeal, but also to demonstrate a certain vitality of creative expression that helps to validate the music. In contrast, much music associated with religious rituals that are expected to persist unchanged in perpetuity tends toward stability. Some examples from the music culture of India that exemplify these different rates of musical change would be the *filmi git* of Bollywood movies and the Brahmanic chanting of the Vedas. Attitudes regarding change in the art-music traditions of North and South India fall somewhere between these extremes, but, at least among musicians, there is consensus that central features of the traditions should remain essentially intact, and musicians generally regard change of the magnitude of what John Blacking would have called true musical change (1978), where there is a change in the system, as damaging to the tradition. Since the late 1960s, there has been a growing trend, typically called fusion, of Hindustani and Karnatak musicians engaging in cross-cultural musical collaborations. Whereas initial forays in this activity, for the most part, upheld the musical concepts and behavior expected of Indian classical musicians, more recent collaborations have strayed quite dramatically in both domains of the culture of Indian classical music. In this chapter, I address the implications of these projects in the context of Hindustani music, with respect to their potential impact on that tradition.

Niko Higgins, in his recent study exploring fusion in Karnatak music, notes that fusion resists easy definition. He states that in South India, musicians engaging in fusion exist between three musical practices—Karnatak, Western, and Indian film music. Additionally, to be fusion, the musical style requires displays of virtuosity and must eschew suggestions of spiritual associations (Higgins 2013:5).[1] Musicians rarely devote their entire musical lives to fusion, most continuing to perform traditional Karnatak renditions of *rāgas* and *tālas* while expending a portion of their musical energy on fusion projects. Of the theories addressing cultural mixing that have crossed ethnomusicology's path—from Herskovits's nuanced elaborations of acculturation (1958) and syncretism (1966) to Bhabha's concept of hybridity (1994) and Appadurai's concept of fractal cultures (1996)—most pertinent is the recognition of fusion as a means of expressing cosmopolitanism (Higgins 2013:25–29). It is this notion of cosmopolitanism that I also see as most salient in the current work of Hindustani musicians embracing fusion. However, I also see this as an adaptive response motivated by economic pressures.

While fusion is currently the in-thing among the younger generation of Indian musicians, such musical mixing was actually quite readily available in the late 1960s and early 1970s. From Ravi Shankar's *East Meets West* albums with Yehudi Menuhin and, later, Jean-Pierre Rampal, to his 1971 *Concerto No. 1 for Sitar and Orchestra*, to Ali Akbar Khan's recording *Karuna Supreme* with jazz saxophonist John Handy, to Ali Akbar's eldest son's experiments fusing rock with Hindustani music in his band Shanti, to the emergence of Shakti, mixing jazz-rock with North and South Indian music, the notion of cultural mixing through music was very much on the scene in the early 1970s.

Whereas countless musicians in India, including those teaching at institutions, have a direct investment in maintaining the integrity of the tradition of Hindustani music, the reality of musical life in India is that inexorable forces are at work and are causing musical experimentations and behaviors that transgress traditional norms in ways that far exceed the aforementioned examples from the 1970s. As an example of a late-1960s transgression of acceptable norms in Hindustani music culture, we might compare what appears today as a relatively innocuous album cover on the Capitol Records release of Jnan Prakash Ghosh's *Drums of India, Volume 1*, with the cover of the original 1968 EMI Gramophone release in India, which portrayed drawings of the drums heard on the recording being played in somewhat traditional contexts.[2] At the time of the Capitol Records release, I was privileged to attend classes that Ghosh taught at the University of Pennsylvania in 1969. After the album's release, a rumor quickly spread that Ghosh was very upset that the record label chose to market the album in the United States with pictures of an attractive young woman in a sari as the cover design. Presumably, the alignment of Hindustani music with feminine beauty was contrary to prevailing ideals of the spiritual nature of the music. Beyond that, the album cover might have caused memories to surface of past connections between percussion accompanists and courtesan culture.

Another example of transgression during the 1970s of Hindustani music's code of proper behavior comes from the early career of Ananda Shankar, the son of Uday Shankar, who received his initial training on the sitar from his uncle, Ravi Shankar. His 1970 release by Reprise Records of the self-titled album *Ananda Shankar* reflected the young Shankar's desire to connect with American fans of popular music, particularly those of the younger generation constituting the counterculture. Termed the breakout album of the new raga-rock fusion genre, Ananda covered songs like the Rolling Stones' "Jumpin' Jack Flash" and The Doors' "Light My Fire" on the album.[3] His uncle had already been angered by the young Shankar's alleged sitar performance in a Greenwich Village coffeehouse. Ravi Shankar was, in fact, angered to the point of refusing to continue teaching him, causing Ananda's father to ask Lalmani Misra at the Banaras Hindu University to accept his son as a student. The 1970 album, as far as I can remember, was viewed as a one-off novelty item confined to the youth market in the United States, a bit too far out to leave a lasting impact on the more staid world of Hindustani music. Ravi Shankar, of course, had already weathered severe criticism at home for playing classical rāgas in popular-music venues, such as Monterey and Woodstock. However, he consistently defended himself on the grounds that he had maintained the classical purity of the actual music in those performances.

From these two examples we see the importance placed on drawing boundaries of image, venue, and genre in Hindustani music during the early 1970s. The custodians of the culture of Hindustani music dictated an avoidance of association with popular music, promoted the association of spirituality with the music, and demanded proper physical performance spaces, such as university music departments and respectable auditoriums. Coffeehouses, clubs, and bars were forbidden territory for upholders of the tradition, whose manner of stage presentation typically evoked either the grandeur of a princely court or the solemnity of a Hindu temple. While these boundaries continue to exist within the insular world of Indian classical music, in the twenty-first century they have come to be transgressed more frequently and brazenly by young classical musicians engaging in fusion experiments. The exuberance with which musicians like Niladri Kumar, the son of Ravi Shankar's senior disciple Kartick Kumar, and Anoushka Shankar, Ravi Shankar's daughter, flaunt their transgression of these boundaries raises the question of whether a paradigm shift might be under way that will eventually alter fundamental concepts of rāga and tāla, the very basis of the musical tradition. In the remainder of this chapter, I use concepts of meaning creation drawn from Peircean semiotics to support this argument.

The semiotic process, as elaborated by Peirce and articulated by Thomas Turino (1999, 2014), involves the interaction of the object, a sign that stands for the object, and the interpretant, the reconstruction of the object by the perceiver on the basis of what is understood from the sign. As anyone who has attempted to grapple with Peirce's theory of the semiotic knows, this initial model of meaning creation rapidly evolves into a cumbersome model involving ten sign types that may further split into sixty-six classes (Atkin 2010). Thus, a sign may signify a defining quality, in which case it is termed a qualisign, or it may create meaning through physical existence, the sinsign, or it may create meaning by way of convention, the legisign. Similarly, signs relate to the objects for which they stand either as icons, indexes, or symbols. An iconic sign reflects some actual qualitative features of the object (a portrait is a good example); an indexical sign has a relationship of existential or physical co-occurrence between the sign and object in actual experience; a sign that successfully stands for something else by using a convention or some social rule or law is a symbol. A single sign is not limited to carrying only one of these relations. Similarly, signs and interpretants are related by the means whereby the sign, as a representation of its object, causes the interpretant to be formed. If it is through focusing on qualities, it is termed a rheme; if through existential features, it is a dicent; or if through focusing our understanding on some convention or rule, it is an argument.

Before looking at examples of musical collaborations that create confusion in determining boundaries of authenticity in Hindustani music, I briefly comment on a work of collaboration that did not create such confusion. Ravi Shankar's *Concerto No. 1 for Sitar and Orchestra* is a work commissioned by the London Philharmonic Orchestra and first performed in 1971. Puzzling out the numerous dicentic indexical sinsigns and legisigns by which the concerto creates a semiotic process that results in an interpretant that places the work within the realm of Indian music is not a simple task.[4] Given the density of sinsigns, for example, when the sitar plays ālāp, *joṛ*, *gats*, and *tihāīs*; the iconic signification of a tabla by the mimetic playing of the bongo; and legisigns such as actual rāgas and tālas in the composition,[5] I would argue that the piece, while representing a certain degree of musical mixing, does not represent a severe transgression of the tradition. In his own performances of the concerto, Shankar dressed as an Indian classical musician and performed with the same dignified countenance one would experience in his classical Indian concerts. The concerto, nonetheless, failed to win the favor of Indian musicians and was viewed as a problematic development for Hindustani music, particularly the limited scope for improvisation in the performance. The late Ustad Ali Akbar Khan once remarked to me that he sometimes even heard extracts from Ravi Shankar's composed works surfacing in Shankar's traditional sitar performances. Western composers and music theorists sometimes noted the scant use of harmony and counterpoint and the resulting thin textures in the piece, citing such weaknesses as a misuse of the orchestra.

Critics have also noted that the first concerto is based almost exclusively in Indian classical music. In his review of a 1998 performance of the piece, the *Los Angeles Times* music critic Mark Swed states:

> Shankar's concerto is a compelling, almost textbook-ideal adaptation of one musical tradition into another. Its melodies and rhythms come from raga, and the techniques of development also rely on Indian tradition, including sections for improvisation by the soloist. But Shankar uses the Western orchestra with imagination. Sometimes he looks for equivalents: Bongos serve as tabla; two harps play scales, echoing the sitar; the strings fill in the tambura's drone. Sometimes he creates new effects, as in a stunning lyrical horn solo or the wonderful wind and percussion writing. The blend of sitar (lightly amplified) and the orchestra sounds effortless. (articles.latimes.com/1998/dec/14/entertainment/ca-53840; accessed 11 February 2014)

Whereas such views of this work as a misuse of the Western orchestra, Indian classical music with Western instruments, or an imaginative use of the Western orchestra in adapting Indian music to Western music reveal that music often means different things to different people, they also illustrate Peirce's process of semiosis. The overall judgment of both the composer and his reviewers appears to accept the first concerto as authentically Indian at its core.

The next example comes from the relatively well-known collaboration between the Indian slide guitarist Pandit Vishwa Mohan Bhatt and the American guitarist Ry Cooder in the 1993 album *A Meeting by the River*. This particular musical experiment is notable as one of the few such ventures to capture a Grammy Award for Best World Music Album (in 1994). That Vishwa Mohan Bhatt placed great value in this award is evident in his continuing practice of including a piece from the album in performances as late as 2012, introducing the item as from his "Grammy Award–winning album." The track from the album on which I comment here is titled "Ganges Delta Blues." The performance uses what would be regarded as the African American minor pentatonic scale, a five-note scale associated with the American genre of the blues. The Hindustani rāga *Dhānī* shares this same scale, but the aesthetic of the piece, as indicated by the title, refers to the blues, for the most part, consistently from beginning to end. Whereas Vishwa Mohan Bhatt draws on idiomatic gestures of melody and ornamentation such as *gamak* and *mīṇḍ* in his playing, there is no clear expression of specifically rāga form.

How then do we characterize this example? Is it truly a fusion, as suggested by the piece's title, substituting the Ganges Delta for the Mississippi Delta, a region associated with the origin of the so-called Down Home, Delta, or Deep Blues style of acoustic guitar-based blues? Given the ubiquitous modality of the minor pentatonic in the blues, the piece would stand out as indexically suggesting it is a type of strange blues piece, not an Indian improvisation in a rāga. The so-called *mohan vīṇā*, the name Bhatt bestowed on his modified guitar, is also not a traditional Indian instrument; having its Indianized timbre interrupted frequently by Ry Cooder's rougher American sounding slide-guitar style reduces its potential to evoke some sense of Indian identity from a traditional Indian audience. The sign language of this piece falls heavily on the side of the blues, but not an authentic blues. Depending on the listener, this piece could variously be perceived as a free-form jam in what is essentially a blues idiom, with sprinklings of Indianisms throughout; a failed attempt at the blues by an Indian musician who destroys the blues with melodic runs and gamaks that have nothing to do with a deep-blues aesthetic; or a loosely conceived, diluted form of rāga Dhānī subjected to an uneasy alliance with an American performer of the blues with no knowledge of Hindustani *saṅgīta*. As each musician brings his own expertise to the venture, we might say the piece represents an authentically inauthentic work. From the Peircean semiotic perspective, I would judge that each musician brought great potential to the experiment in the form of rhematic indexical and symbolic legisigns, but because the piece fails to satisfy either a blues aesthetic nor a Hindustani aesthetic of rāga development, those signs do not become realized in the final analysis, at least for me as a listener.

The next example is the title track from Anoushka Shankar's *Traveller*, a CD that reached number one on the world music chart of Europe soon after its release in October 2011. The theme of the CD is the fusion of flamenco and Indian elements, supposedly facilitated by a very tenuous, if not historically fictitious, connection between the two traditions.[6] While this particular track is based in rāga *Bhupāl Toḍī* (1–flat-2–flat-3–5–flat-6), several other tracks on the CD are devoid of melodic material that can be traced to a rāga. Beyond these aspects of musical material that are clearly apparent in the individual creations, the CD is replete with musical signs indicating a rich variety of meanings, several of which have little connection to the classical traditions of India, but also some referring either to the Hindustani or to the Karnatak system of music (such as the inclusion of the South Indian double-headed *mridangam*). In this excerpt, the inclusion of the *morchang* (Jew's harp) suggests an allusion to the flamenco-Indian music connection via the Roma, thought to have originated in India, from which they migrated to various areas in Europe and North Africa. The morchang is an instrument commonly associated with Rajasthani folk music, and the original Roma are thought to have emigrated from the general area of northwest India. In this instance, the instrument is functioning as a rhematic index, suggesting a qualitative compatibility of Hindustani saṅgīta and flamenco. In doing so, the music is also suggesting the possibility of a transnational identity, or actually a supernational identity that spans two continents. Anoushka overdubs the melody, adding a melodic line in parallel intervals to the first melodic line, referring both to Western popular recording methods of overdubbing and to the Western penchant for harmonizing a melodic line. Providing each of the tracks of the CD with a song-like title also defines this CD as a work that resides more in popular music and less in classical music.

In this CD release and earlier ones, Anoushka Shankar is projecting not just a cosmopolitan identity, but a complicated person of several simultaneous cultures. I suspect that she would have a difficult time defending her musical creativity as springing forth solely from an authentically Indian base, a characterization more appropriate for her father's experimental creations. Anoushka's musicality is representative of her transnational, cosmopolitan persona, an identity that has been used in image form in the marketing of her commercially released recordings.[7] Indeed, her recently released album, *Traces of You*, marketed as progressive world music, displays Anoushka fully decked out in Western dress. Her tour to promote the album is taking her to venues such as the City Winery in Chicago, a restaurant-cum-performance venue, where Anoushka and her band of supporting musicians play to an audience satisfying their interest in cosmopolitan styles of world music. I might note that during her tour supporting her *Traveller* CD, she performed at the City Winery in New York City.[8] If her music is embraced in India as the wave of the future for Hindustani saṅgīta, there is no doubt that new standards of authenticity will surely develop. Anoushka delineated the qualitative difference between what she is doing and what her father had done a few decades ago in an interview conducted by Arun Rath for the PBS Soundtrack Quick Hits series:

> **Arun Rath**: When your father first started to, you know, experiment with other forms of music, with Western music, he got a lot of grief about that from purists in India. I'm wondering, have things changed much, or do you get a hard time at all from purists in the Indian tradition?
> **Anoushka Shankar**: There are some purists who probably write me off and don't think much of me, but for the most part, I mean, Indian classical music is thriving within the classical communities, but in the grand scheme of the Indian market it's not doing too well because it has to compete with the juggernaut of Bollywood music. And so practically any classical musician who wants to make a living ends up doing these kinds of fusion concerts and crossover things. You know, it's like, when it is genuine, that's great, and if it is something people have to do in order to do well, that's a real shame. But you were right to mention my father. When he did it, he was the first person to do it. And it was decades ahead of anyone else; so, at that point [in time] it was unheard of and it was very shocking, and it was very controversial. And it's funny, because if you look back, what he was doing was so different from crossover today. What he was doing was sort of spreading Indian music around the world. And so, where he would work with Western musicians or Western orchestras, if you look at the music, it is actually purely Indian music being played by different musicians and different instruments, whereas today it is more about a two-way dialogue. It is funny to look back and think that that was so pioneering and undone at the time. (www.pbs.org/arts/exhibit/quick-hits-anoushka-shankar/; accessed 30 June 2014)

One final example comes from Niladri Kumar who, until just a few years ago, was regarded as a quickly rising virtuoso sitarist performing in a strictly classical style. The devotional nature of the stage persona he maintained in his earlier incarnation is evident in a popular YouTube posting of his performance of rāga *Basant Mukhārī*. That Niladri appears not to exist any longer, as a more recent YouTube posting of a fusion performance by Niladri Kumar—best characterized as reinvented raga-rock shred style—makes clear (www.youtube.com/watch?v=HvZgMHQbXEQ). Niladri's rock-style sitar playing, nonetheless, still manages to draw on some traditional features: *savāl javāb* and a devotional song that was a favorite of Gandhi's, "Raghupatī Rāghava Rāja Rām." The video of this event reveals a seated Niladri wearing the kurta-pajama outfit associated with traditional sitarists, but the rest of the stage is hopping in the high-energy movement of a rock concert. Niladri's studio sitar,[9] an instrument that has become popular in the past six years, is plugged into an amplifier with a formidable array of effects over which Niladri demonstrates considerable command. Virtuosity is clearly on display as Niladri plays an extended figuration using only his left hand while resting his head on his right palm, throwing in a swooping descent in rock-guitar fashion to launch into the next section. The semiotics of this event are too complex to tease out in full here. From the fuzz timbre of a distorted rock-guitar sound to the quote of "Raghupatī Rāghava Rāja Rām," this item mixes up Bollywood filmī gīt with a popular bhajan, shred-guitar virtuosity, and driving rhythms. The only aspect of the performance that could be related to classical music is the *pajāmā-kurtā* Niladri is wearing. Just how much his dalliances with this hard-edged version of fusion might eventually creep into his classical performance style remains to be seen, assuming he even plans to continue performing in an accepted classical style. I did witness Viswa Mohan Bhatt incorporating electronic sound effects in his classical slide-guitar performance in Agra in February 2012, so Niladri's experimentation with effects may already have influenced at least one top-tier classical musician.

In both the Anoushka Shankar example and the Niladri Kumar example, the most telling evidence that these musical pieces have entered a cultural arena that has little to do with traditional Indian classical music is the energetic interpretants evidenced by the music's players and audiences. In other words, the body language of people responding to the music is that of popular Western culture—knees bending, hips swinging, shoulders moving in alternation, necks bending to the rhythm. One has to wonder what effect the burgeoning dalliance with fusion music is going to have on the classical tradition. While the late Ustad Ali Akbar Khan mischievously labeled this music as "confusion," in this chapter I go even further, arguing that it is fair to question whether these musical ventures might be bringing irreversible change to Hindustani saṅgīta, lessening its so-called classicism and turning the music in the direction of a popular idiom.

Notes

1. Whereas Higgins states that Karnatak musicians eschew associations with spirituality in their attempts at fusion, I do not see this occurring consistently among Hindustani musicians' fusion attempts. Anoushka Shankar, for example, continues to present the trope of spirituality infusing her fusion experiments both in her stage mannerisms, displaying deep introspection, and in promotional material advertising her CD releases.

2. Images of the two *Drums of India* album covers can be found through a Google search for "Jnan Prakash Ghosh *Drums of India* album covers."

3. All of the musical examples presented in this chapter can be found on YouTube. Rather than providing bibliographic information for original long-playing records, the format on which some of these examples were first released, I include below a URL for each of the musical excerpts so that the reader can find the example on the Internet.

4. For a detailed explication of Peircean terms for the various types of signs as they relate specifically to Indian classical music, see Martinez 2001:69–79.

5. The original score for Shankar's *Concerto No. 1 for Sitar and Orchestra* includes the rāga name of each movement in its title and also labels sections such as ālāp, joṛ, gat, and so forth, within movements.

6. For an extensive discussion of the progression from Romani culture to imaginary "gypsies" that took place over the centuries of Romani migration from South Asia to Europe and northern Africa, see Malvinni 2004:203–16. He does an excellent job of demonstrating that the presumed connection of Indian music to flamenco is a recent invention, one that serves well as a marketing ploy.

7. Numerous promotional photos of Anoushka Shankar may be viewed at www.anoushkashankar.com/galleries/ (accessed 30 June 2014).

8. Whereas the City Winery is a legitimate venue for presenting performances of world music, the presence of alcoholic beverages in a concert venue is strongly discouraged by musicians of Indian classical music. In addition to recalling the debasing treatment many musicians suffered under patronage in the princely states during the British Raj, where alcoholic beverages were often in abundant supply during musical soirees, for an audience to indulge in worldly vices in the midst of a performance of music detracts from the image of spiritual purity that the music is to promote. The reader might recall Ravi Shankar's lecturing young American listeners not to smoke during his performances in the late 1960s. I was very surprised to see members of the sponsoring corporation of a Ravi Shankar concert in Delhi in 1992 distributing glasses of whiskey at the back of the auditorium. When I commented on this to Ravi Shankar, he was mortified and lodged a strong protest with the sponsor of the event.

9. Whereas Niladri refers to this electrified, all-wooden sitar as a zitar, I am fairly certain that this variety of sitar was first created by the Rikhi Ram company of New Delhi around 2005 and was termed "studio sitar" by then-proprietor Bishan Dass Sharma (Bishan Dass Sharma, personal communication, 7 January 2006). Since then, the instrument has spread rapidly, the design being adopted by other instrument makers in Kolkata and in Miraj, a town in the western Indian province of Maharashtra known especially for the *tānpurās* manufactured there.

References

Appadurai, Arjun. 1996. *Modernity at Large: Cultural Dimensions of Globalization.* Minneapolis: University of Minnesota Press.

Atkin, Albert. 2010. "Peirce's Theory of Signs." *Stanford Encyclopedia of Philosophy*. plato.stanford.edu/entries/peirce-semiotics/.

Bendix, Regina. 1997. *In Search of Authenticity: The Formation of Folklore Studies*. Madison: University of Wisconsin Press.

Bhabha, Homi K. 1994. *The Location of Culture*. London: Routledge.

Blacking, John. 1978. "Some Problems of Theory and Method in the Study of Musical Change." *Yearbook of the International Folk Music Council* 9: 1–26.

Herskovits, Melville. 1958. *Acculturation: The Study of Culture Contact*. Gloucester, MA: Peter Smith.

———. 1966. *The New World Negro: Selected Papers in Afroamerican Studies*. Bloomington: Indiana University Press.

Higgins, Niko. 2013. "Confusion in the Karnatik Capital: Fusion in Chennai, India." Ph.D. Dissertation, Columbia University.

Malvinni, David. 2004. *The Gypsy Caravan: From Real Roma to Imaginary Gypsies in Western Music and Film*. New York: Routledge.

Martinez, José Luis. 2001. *Semiosis in Hindustani Music*. Delhi: Motilal Banarsidass.

Nettl, Bruno. 2005. *The Study of Ethnomusicology: Thirty-One Issues and Concepts*. Urbana: University of Illinois Press.

Rath, Arun. N.d. "Anoushka Shankar." PBS Soundtracks: Music Without Borders, Quick Hits. www.pbs.org/arts/exhibit/quick-hits-anoushka-shankar/ (accessed 30 June 2014).

Turino, Thomas. 1999. "Signs of Imagination, Identity, and Experience: A Peircian Semiotic Theory for Music." *Ethnomusicology* 43(2): 22–55.

———. 2014. "Peircean Thought as Core Theory for a Phenomenological Ethnomusicology." *Ethnomusicology* 58(2): 185–221.

Internet Sites for Musical Examples

Bhatt, Vishwa Mohan, and Ry Cooder. "Ganges Blues," from *Meeting by the River*. www.youtube.com/watch?v=Og5PdU2V7cA (accessed 30 June 2014).

Kumar, Niladri. www.youtube.com/watch?v=HvZgMHQbXEQ (accessed 30 June 2014).

Shankar, Anand. "Light My Fire" from *Anand Shankar*. www.youtube.com/watch?v=JpW8643S7Wk (accessed 30 June 2014).

Shankar, Anoushka. *Traveller*. www.anoushkashankar.com/ (accessed 30 June 2014).

Shankar, Ravi. *Concerto No. 1 for Sitar and Orchestra*. www.youtube.com/watch?v=O0OWmUyhBR0 (accessed 30 June 2014).

CHAPTER THIRTY-FIVE

~

Regional Songs in Local and Translocal Spaces

The Duck Dance Revisited

Victoria Lindsay Levine

> *Through most of the history of ethnomusicology, the most important factor in providing information has been 'location, location, location.' . . . And once location was established, we searched for reasons for the geographic distribution of a phenomenon, and went on to speculate about what this might tell us about its history.*
>
> —Bruno Nettl, *The Study of Ethnomusicology* (2005)

Bruno Nettl launched his career in 1954 with research on musical geography, tracing the distribution of style traits among Native North Americans in order to map music areas and to shed light on music history and musical change (Nettl 1954). He found that style traits clearly define some Native American music areas, but others are harder to delineate due to internal stylistic heterogeneity (Nettl 1969). Part of Nettl's scholarly practice is to revisit and revise his earlier work, and ultimately, he proposed that some music areas might best be defined by the distribution of individual songs, quipping that songs have the tendency to be "constantly on the move" (Nettl 2005:334). As Nettl's student, I share his interest in the movement of songs through space, time, and place. My research focuses on Native music cultures of the Eastern Woodlands, which is an especially heterogeneous music area. Because of the complexity of this region, I began tracing the distribution of individual songs in an effort to untangle the historical, social, and geographic processes that shaped Woodlands music cultures. Following Nettl's lead, this chapter revisits some of my earlier work, presenting new information on the distribution of one particular song, the Duck Dance, through the lens of contemporary geographic perspectives. I ask how one song came to be performed so widely among diverse Woodlands peoples, and argue that whereas individual songs play an important role in defining the Woodlands music area, they also play complementary roles in the formation of local and translocal musical identities.

The Duck Dance Song on the Move

I first heard the Duck Dance song in 1982 on recordings made by Choctaw singers from Mississippi, Louisiana, and Oklahoma. The Choctaw communities had become separated geographically during the removals of the nineteenth and early twentieth centuries, when the U.S. government forced most members of the southern tribes to relocate in the Indian Territory, which became the state of Oklahoma in 1907. I analyzed renditions of the song from each location, concluding that the Duck Dance performed by a Louisiana Choctaw singer was unrelated to the Mississippi and Oklahoma versions, and suggesting that the musical differences reflected divergent histories and concepts of identity (Levine 1985). I later learned that the Louisiana Choctaw song represented a multi-tribal musical repertory that developed in Louisiana during the late nineteenth century (Levine 1991). Collaborative research with the folklorist Jason Baird Jackson, beginning in 1998, uncovered connections between the multi-tribal Louisiana repertory and twenty-first-century Woodlands music and dance in Oklahoma. Through research on individual songs (cf. Jackson and Levine 2002), we found that the Duck Dance is the most widely distributed song in the Woodlands region. It is now, or has been in the past, performed by at least thirteen tribes, including the Alabama, Biloxi, Caddo, Chickasaw, Choctaw, Coushatta, Delaware, Euchee (Yuchi), Haudenosaunee (Iroquois), Muscogee (Creek), Ofo, Seminole, and Tunica. Many of these groups are subdivided into smaller local communities, and songs such as the Duck Dance may be known by different names. For example, the Sac and Fox perform a Swan Dance, which features one of the Duck Dance songs heard among Woodlands peoples, and the Shawnee also performed the Swan Dance in the past. This suggests that the song's distribution is even more complicated than the above list indicates (cf. Jackson and Levine 2002:293), and that its dissemination has occurred over a long time period, probably centuries.

The Duck Dance song belongs to a repertory referred to in English as Social Dances; I use this term for convenience, although Beverley Diamond has pointed out that "the 'social dance song' label is not entirely satisfactory, since there is a purpose and a meaning to each dance that blurs the boundary between what is sacred and what is secular" (Diamond 2008:104). In Oklahoma, Woodlands peoples perform Social Dances during the nighttime portion of ceremonial events, when the members of a local ceremonial ground are joined by visitors from other ceremonial grounds with whom they have reciprocal social relationships. Together, members of the local ceremonial ground and visitors perform collective dances from about midnight until about seven or eight o'clock in the morning. Depending upon the ceremony and local tradition, nighttime dances may include both stomp dances and what some Native people refer to as specialty dances, such as the Duck Dance. One particular Duck Dance song has been documented in scores of archival and commercial recordings. It was first recorded by Frank Speck in 1905 during his research with Muscogee and Euchee people in what was then still the Indian Territory. Other versions of this song were recorded in the 1930s by Frances Densmore, W. E. S. Folsom-Dickerson, and Mary Haas; in the 1940s and 1950s by Willard Rhodes and Karl Schmidt; in the 1960s and 1970s by Dorothy Gaus, James Howard, Claude Medford, and Jim Rementer; by me beginning in the 1980s; and by Jackson beginning in the 1990s. Commercial recordings of this Duck Dance song have been produced by American Indian Sound Chiefs, Canyon Records, the Library of Congress Music Division, Iroqrafts, the Mississippi Band of Choctaw Indians, the Choctaw-Chickasaw Heritage Committee of Oklahoma, and the Chickasaw Nation Dance Troupe. More recently, it was included on an album of Native rock music produced by Robbie Robertson. Clearly, this song has been on the move, raising questions about the regional processes that triggered its widespread diffusion.

Some answers may be found by considering the historical, geographic, and social forces that shaped Woodlands cultures. Woodlands peoples are the descendants of earlier Indigenous civilizations that archaeologists refer to as the Mound Builders. The Mound Builders constructed massive earthworks, including flat-topped pyramids and mounds they may have used in public rituals and ceremonies. The Mound Builders exerted a strong influence on many other Native North Americans through trade and cultural exchange; their interaction sphere focused east of the Mississippi River, extending from the Great Lakes to the Gulf Coast. The concept of interaction spheres was defined by the archaeologist Joseph Caldwell as "the areal matrices of regular and institutionally maintained intersocietal articulation" (cited in Binford 1965:208). Charles Mann further explains that "both less and more than a nation, an interaction sphere is a region in which one society disseminates its symbols, values, and inventions to others" (Mann 2005:257–58). It seems reasonable to assume that aspects of musical culture, including specific songs, were among the inventions that circulated within the Mound Builder interaction sphere. Beginning in the Mississippian period (ca. 700–1550 CE), "there is abundant evidence—including the testimony of contemporary Native people from the region—documenting the centrality of dance to the social and religious life" of Woodlands communities (Jackson 2014:122). It is not possible to determine precisely when the Duck Dance song began to circulate, but its unusually wide geographic dissemination suggests that it has been on the move through the Woodlands musical landscape since at least the late Mississippian period.

A system of rivers and streams winds its way through the Woodlands homeland. Because they were navigable by canoes, these bodies of water helped to connect Woodlands peoples throughout the area, serving as both conduits *and* sites for cultural interaction. River travel facilitated the maintenance of political, trade, and ceremonial alliances. Many Native languages were and are spoken by Woodlands peoples, and therefore a trade language known as the Mobilian jargon became integral to diplomacy and economic exchange in the southern part of the area (cf. Crawford 1978). The ethnic diversity of the area required Woodlands peoples to become adept at operating effectively within multiple communities and involved the cultivation of personal relationships, extended family networks, and clan connections. Songs and dances performed collectively must have played a significant role in mediating these social relationships. Furthermore, narratives written by European and Euramerican travelers and missionaries during the nineteenth century document the shape and content of Woodlands musical repertories as well as the custom of ceremonial ground visiting between Woodlands communities, and a nineteenth-century Choctaw song text also implies this practice (cf. Levine 1997). It is thus possible to conceptualize individual songs, such as the Duck Dance, as mobilizing agents within this cultural landscape.

In the nineteenth century, the U.S. federal government forced most Woodlands peoples to relocate; many of the southern tribes were removed to what is now Oklahoma, where their heritage remains vibrant in the twenty-first century. Throughout the summer months, Woodlands peoples in eastern Oklahoma perform ceremonies to give thanks to the Creator for the agricultural season, to honor the spirits of the plants and animals that sustain human life, and to celebrate their ongoing relationships with their ancestors and with one another (Jackson 2003:241–42). These events take place at outdoor ceremonial grounds located on private or tribally owned land. Ceremonial events generally begin on Friday afternoon and continue through sunrise on Sunday morning. Reciprocal visiting among ceremonial grounds remains vitally important in Woodlands ceremonialism. Whenever the members of a given ceremonial ground are not conducting their own ceremonies, they send delegations to participate in those being held by other communities. Visitors arrive at the ceremonial ground in time for an evening feast and participate in Social Dances throughout the night. In the early twenty-first century, then, songs such as the Duck Dance continue to mobilize Woodlands peoples through a continuum of collective performance that binds community to community and generation to generation across space and time.

The Duck Dance Song in Local Spaces

The Duck Dance song transcribed in figure 35.1 is recognizable wherever and whenever it is sung, no matter how far removed its singers are spatially or culturally. This version was performed by Newman Littlebear during an interview with Jason Jackson and me in 1998. Littlebear (Euchee/Shawnee) served for many years as the orator at the Euchee ceremonial grounds and is a respected song leader and authority on Euchee music, dance, and ritual (cf. Jackson 2003). He sings with an open and relaxed method of vocal production, and the song text consists entirely of vocables. In Littlebear's performance, the scale features five tones with intervals of a major second or minor third, the song has a range of a minor seventh, and the melody employs undulating, stepwise motion with an overall descending inflection. Four rhythmic patterns predominate and the underlying beat group changes for measure three. The song is in strophic form; the transcription shows one

Figure 35.1. "Duck Dance Song" performed by Newman Littlebear (Euchee/Shawnee)

strophe, which would be repeated several times. The end of the strophe is articulated by a brief call and response. Since Littlebear recorded this version outside of a ceremonial context, it differs somewhat from the way he usually performs the Duck Dance song. At Euchee ceremonial grounds, the Duck Dance is sung either as a solo by the leader or in unison by two leaders, and it is introduced by call and response whoops. The leader accompanies the song with a handheld container rattle made from a coconut shell, and the women dancers also keep the beat with leg rattles made of terrapin shells or evaporated milk cans. At a certain point in the choreography, the leader begins a second strophic-form song that contrasts with the song shown here in melody, rhythm, and vocables, and the second song is repeated until the dance ends. At their ceremonial grounds, the Euchee follow the Duck Dance with a set of stomp dances.

Euchee history and culture may be encapsulated as follows (after Jackson 2003). At the time of their initial contact with Europeans, the Euchee lived on the west side of the Appalachian Mountains in what is now Tennessee. They were incorporated into the Creek Confederacy during the late eighteenth century and were removed to the Indian Territory beginning in 1825, where they settled south of Tulsa. They represent a minority enclave within the Muscogee Nation; whereas the Euchee and Muscogee languages are not related (Euchee is a language isolate) and their origin narratives differ markedly, their music and ceremonial practices are similar. About three thousand people currently identity themselves as Euchee; they maintain three outdoor ceremonial grounds, known by the names of the creeks near which they are situated: Duck Creek, Polecat, and Sand Creek. The Duck Dance is one of five specialty dances the Euchee claim as their own; it is performed at night during the annual Soup Dance ceremony, which follows the summer Green Corn ceremony. The main focus of the Soup Dance is the "on-going relationship between the present-day Yuchi [Euchee] and the ancestors who passed Yuchi culture and identity down to them," and thus the Soup Dance serves to "focus attention more generally on the persistence of Yuchi culture through time" (Jackson 2003:241–42). It stands to reason, then, that the Euchee do not compose new specialty songs today; they have handed down this repertory across the generations and believe that it was given to them by the Creator at the time of creation.

Other Woodlands peoples also claim the Duck Dance as their own, though they may perform it in different social contexts and ascribe different meanings to it. Local variants exhibit differences in style, performance practice, instrumentation, and choreography, differences that range from subtle to striking. For example, a Seminole rendition of the Duck Dance song found on the recording *Indian Songs of Today* (Rhodes 1954) is a concert version, performed in unison by a children's choir. The phrasing differs slightly, the strophe is shorter, and there is no instrumental accompaniment, but the melody, rhythm, vocables, and form of the Seminole Duck Dance song are almost the same as the Euchee version. The Seminole are near neighbors of the Euchee geographically, culturally, and musically. In Oklahoma, members of the two tribes regularly visit each other's ceremonial grounds; therefore, the close resemblance of the two songs is not surprising, despite the fact that the recordings took place more than forty years apart and under very different circumstances. As would be expected, the Muscogee Duck Dance song is also quite similar to the Euchee and Seminole versions.

A Caddo Duck Dance song heard on the recording *Songs of the Caddo: Ceremonial and Social Dance Music* (Boley 1976) differs in several ways from the Euchee, Seminole, and Muscogee renditions, which is not surprising given that the Caddo are somewhat farther afield geographically, culturally, and musically. The Caddo version is accompanied by several singers all playing a powwow drum, although until the early twentieth century, it would have been accompanied by a water drum, as in Delaware and Shawnee practice. It includes six strophic-form songs, each of which is repeated several times before the singers move on to the next song. The second song in the series uses the melody shown in figure 35.1. The first song in the series is sung in unison; thereafter, the leader sings the first line of each strophe as a solo, and then the other singers repeat the first line together and sing the remainder of the strophe in unison. The Caddo singers use greater vocal tension than do Euchee, Seminole, or Muscogee singers, which makes sense given their historic proximity to Plains peoples. The Delaware Duck Dance song is close to the Caddo version, reflecting the historical connections between these two groups.

The recording *Choctaw-Chickasaw Dance Songs, Volume 1* (Ned and McCoy 1977) includes a Choctaw version of the Duck Dance song. This rendition features a duck call to humorous effect, but male dancers from other Woodlands communities also make quacking sounds in some Duck Dance recordings. I have not heard dancers "quack" during a ceremonial ground performance of the Duck Dance, but humor is integral to ceremonial ground life; by using the duck call on their recording, the Choctaw referenced this practice. The Choctaw song begins with an introduction that is reminiscent of the first Caddo song. Then the Choctaw sing a strophic-form song whose melody, rhythm, vocal production, phrasing, and vocables are similar to the Euchee version. The Choctaw have just one Duck Dance song, and they repeat the strophe as many times as necessary for the dancers to complete a full circuit of the dance area. On this recording, the song was accompanied by a handheld, double-headed drum, but until the mid-twentieth century, they would have accompanied this song with a pair of striking sticks. The male dancers attached sleigh bells to their regalia, which jingled as they danced. The Chickasaw Duck Dance song, available on *Chickasaw Social Songs and Stomp Dances* (White Deer 1994), strongly resembles the Choctaw version, which is to be expected because of the long history of interaction and exchange between these two groups (cf. Levine 2014). The Choctaw and Chickasaw discontinued ritual performances at ceremonial grounds by 1940, but since the 1970s, they have performed their dances to express their distinctive ethnic identities during folkloric exhibitions for educational purposes as well as during internal tribal events.

An archival recording of the Alabama (Alibamu) version of the Duck Dance song represents the multi-tribal repertory that flourished in western Louisiana in the nineteenth and early twentieth centuries. This song is similar to the Caddo version; the recording features two songs connected by a transition, which involves vocalization on a sustained tone accompanied by a rapid drum roll. The use of a transition to articulate strophic-form songs within a set is not uncommon in Woodlands Social Dance songs, but this is the only recording of a Duck Dance song that employs this performance practice. The Alabama evidently put this particular song to sleep, meaning that they stopped performing it because it was connected to a ritual that was unsustainable under colonization (cf. Jackson 2004; Levine 2014; Swan 1998). By the mid-twentieth century, they began to focus their cultural performances on fiddle dances as well as the powwow repertory.

Another archival recording features a Haudenosaunee version of the Duck Dance from the Six Nations Reserve in Ontario, Canada. The performance style differs markedly in terms of vocal production and instrumental accompaniment, which is not surprising given their geographic distance from the other peoples mentioned here. However, the song bears a strong resemblance to the first song in the Caddo Duck Dance series; the musical links may be traced through historical networks connecting the Haudenosaunee and Caddo via the Delaware and Shawnee. The Haudenosaunee singers accompany themselves with a water drum and a handheld container rattle made from a section of cow horn. Diamond notes that the Haudenosaunee associate the Duck Dance song with the spring, and that it "always evokes laughter" (Diamond 2008:110). She describes the choreography as follows: "A double line of men move forward to meet a double line of women. They 'push' the women backwards by walking toward them as the current might push a duck on the water. At a certain point, the men raise their arms and the women duck underneath. But those arms quite often fall again and 'capture' a pair of women" (Diamond 2008:110). Although it does not completely match this description, the Euchee, Muscogee, and Seminole Duck Dance features a similar choreography, in which "the men with their handkerchiefs create something like waves on a stream, with the women ducks swimming upstream and diving under the waves" (Jackson, personal communication, 4 November 2014).

These Duck Dance songs are in many ways similar to one another, yet in important ways, each one is unique, whether that stems from differences in performance context, instrumental accompaniment, methods of vocal production, performance in unison as opposed to call and response, or details of form and design. The members of each community that sings this song have adapted it to local spaces of performance and identity. Therefore, the comparison indicates relationships through time, while underscoring "the capacity of communities to consciously maintain distinctive local practices in interactionally complex settings" (Jackson and Levine 2002:302). In the culturally diverse world of Woodlands peoples, songs such as the Duck Dance express discrete identities within a larger regional system. Local communities, ceremonial grounds, and ethnic identities remain important because they provide the infrastructure for the preservation of traditional music and dance within the Woodlands musical landscape.

The Duck Dance Song in Translocal Spaces

Woodlands peoples found themselves at a critical juncture in the second half of the twentieth century, and since the 1970s, they have worked hard to reclaim traditional language and culture through community-based education and research programs. During this period, audio recordings have facilitated access to traditional music for Woodlands peoples without diminishing the centrality of direct participation in ceremonial ground life or other local performance venues. At the same time, Woodlands musicians have been reinterpreting their cultural heritage with translocal audiences in mind, by which I mean listeners who may or may not have connections to specific Woodlands communities. Popular music figures prominently in this work, since it accommodates creative adaptations of Social Dance songs and can communicate with listeners who are unfamiliar with the Indigenous histories, musical styles, or performance contexts being referenced. Several singer-songwriters with Woodlands ancestry have become prominent in popular music, including Pura Fé, Joy Harjo, Jim Pepper, Robbie Robertson, Joanne

Shenandoah, and the vocal trio Ulali. Generally these artists write songs that address aspects of Indigenous experience and incorporate components of Woodlands musical style without actually quoting traditional melodies. However, perhaps because it has circulated so widely in Woodlands musical culture, the Duck Dance song made its way into a popular music remix at the end of the twentieth century.

In 1998, the Canadian guitarist and songwriter Robbie Robertson published a concept album titled *Contact from the Underworld of Redboy*. Robertson is a member of the Mohawk Nation and has family ties to Six Nations Reserve. This album explores his First Nations ancestry, and the song "Stomp Dance (Unity)," which he wrote with Jim Wilson, pays homage to the Woodlands regional music culture as adapted to translocal performance spaces. The song is accompanied by programmed keyboards, guitar, bass, and percussion, bypassing instruments that would suggest a specific local identity such as leg rattles, handheld container rattles, or a powwow drum. Similarly, the song lyrics evoke nighttime Social Dances at ceremonial grounds in Oklahoma, but also refer to Six Nations Reserve. One couplet links communal dancing to the survival of First Nations peoples, which resonates with the Euchee concepts mentioned above regarding the ceremonial context in which they perform the Duck Dance. The refrain in Robertson's song connects feelings about community and place with collective performance:

Beating hearts, beating hearts
Come as one, come as one.
This is Indian Country,
This is Indian Country. (Robertson 1998)

Layered into this song is a rendition of the "Unity Stomp Dance" performed by the Six Nations Women Singers in call and response. The "Unity Stomp Dance" most likely originated in the 1960s or 1970s; it combines the Duck Dance song shown in figure 35.1 with stomp dance songs often heard at Woodlands ceremonial grounds. Its compositional process therefore expressed the concept of working together to achieve unity among Woodlands peoples. In most Woodlands performance venues, only men lead Social Dance songs; by choosing to sample a performance by female singers, Robertson spotlights a well-known ensemble from his home community while acknowledging the innovative role of women in Native music. Sadie Buck sings the lead in this Duck Dance; her powerful vocal resonance, distinctive timbre, sharply accented attacks, and subtle rhythmic nuances embody the Woodlands sound. Near the end of the song, the words "Oklahoma" and "intertribal," voiced by Robertson, float above the Duck Dance melody. Robertson's adaptation of the Duck Dance song in "Stomp Dance (Unity)" illustrates some of the ways contemporary Woodlands musicians circulate traditional songs in translocal spaces of performance, and in doing so, they further transform the landscape of Woodlands music culture. Perhaps most important, this song demonstrates that for Woodlands peoples, living within one's community of origin does not imply isolation from global culture, nor does participation in global culture imply a loss of either local or regional identity.

Conclusions

This chapter has attempted to show that the circulation of an individual song across the Woodlands region can indeed help to define a heterogeneous music area, as Bruno Nettl suggested in 2005. Untangling the historical, social, and geographic processes of the region enables us to imagine the Duck Dance song moving through the Mound Builder interaction sphere as Woodlands peoples established and cultivated far-reaching interethnic social networks. As the song was shared, the members of diverse local communities made it their own, adapting it to their musical preferences, performance practices, aesthetic values, and systems of meaning. Contemporary musicians working in the domain of popular music remixed the song, transforming Woodlands spaces of performance to encompass translocal audiences. There is good reason for optimism that songs will continue to mobilize social networks among Woodlands peoples, ensuring their cultural survival while redefining the Woodlands cultural landscape for the twenty-first century and beyond.

Acknowledgments

I presented an early version of this paper at the 2009 meetings of the Society for American Music; generous funding for this phase of my research was provided by Colorado College and by the National Endowment for the Humanities. This work builds on research begun by Charlotte Heth (Cherokee), James Howard, Gertrude Kurath, Claude Medford (Choctaw), Jim Rementer, and Gary White Deer (Choctaw). I am grateful to Charlotte J. Frisbie for her helpful feedback on an early draft of this paper. My understanding of Woodlands geographic, historical, and social processes owes much to Jason Jackson and draws heavily on his vast knowledge of the region, his many publications, and his sensitivity and skill as an ethnographer; it is a privilege to work with him. I have also been privileged to visit several Woodlands ceremonial grounds in Oklahoma, and to work closely with members of the Choctaw and Chickasaw Nations (especially Buster Ned, Adam Sampson, and Claude Medford) and members of the Euchee Tribe (especially Chief James Brown Jr., Chief Simon Harry, Newman Littlebear, Elenora Powell, Tribal Chairman Andrew Skeeter, and all members of the Skeeter Camp at Duck Creek ceremonial ground). Without their abundant hospitality and friendship, this work would be impossible; any errors or omissions are my own.

References

Binford, Lewis R. 1965. "Archaeological Systematics and the Study of Culture Process." *American Antiquity* 31(2): 203–10.

Boley, Raymond, producer. 1976. *Songs of the Caddo: Ceremonial and Social Dance Music, Volume 2*. Phoenix: Canyon Records.

Crawford, James M. 1978. *The Mobilian Trade Language*. Knoxville: University of Tennessee Press.

Diamond, Beverley. 2008. *Native American Music in Eastern North America: Experiencing Music, Expressing Culture*. New York: Oxford University Press.

Jackson, Jason Baird. 2003. *Yuchi Ceremonial Life: Performance, Meaning, and Tradition in a Contemporary American Indian Community*. Lincoln: University of Nebraska Press.

———. 2004. "Recontextualizing Revitalization: Cosmology and Cultural Stability in the Adoption of Peyotism among the Yuchi." In *Reassessing Revitalization Movements: Perspectives from North America and the Pacific Islands*, edited by Michael E. Harkin, 183–205. Lincoln: University of Nebraska Press.

———. 2014. "Seminole Histories of the Calusa: Dance, Narrative, and Historical Consciousness." *Native South* 7: 122–42.

Jackson, Jason Baird, and Victoria Lindsay Levine. 2002. "Singing for Garfish: Music and Woodland Communities in Eastern Oklahoma." *Ethnomusicology* 46(2): 284–306.

Levine, Victoria Lindsay. 1985. "Duck Dance." In *The Western Impact on World Music: Change, Adaptation, and Survival*, by Bruno Nettl, 139–41. New York: Schirmer Books.

———. 1991. "Arzelie Langley and a Lost Pantribal Tradition." In *Ethnomusicology and Modern Music History*, edited by Stephen Blum, Philip V. Bohlman, and Daniel M. Neuman, 190–206. Urbana: University of Illinois Press.

———. 1997. "Text and Context in Choctaw Social Dance Songs." *Florida Anthropologist* 50(4): 183–87.

———. 2014. "Reclaiming Choctaw and Chickasaw Cultural Identity through Music Revival." In *The Oxford Handbook of Music Revival*, edited by Caroline Bithell and Juniper Hill, 300–322. New York: Oxford University Press.

Mann, Charles C. 2005. *1491: New Revelations of the Americas before Columbus*. New York: Knopf.

Ned, Buster, and Dale McCoy. 1977. *Choctaw-Chickasaw Dance Songs, Volume 1*. Oklahoma City: Sweetland Productions.

Nettl, Bruno. 1954. *North American Indian Musical Styles*. Memoirs of the American Folklore Society, Volume 45. Philadelphia: American Folklore Society.

———. 1969. "Musical Areas Reconsidered: A Critique of North American Indian Research." In *Essays in Musicology in Honor of Dragan Plamenac*, edited by Gustave Reese and Robert J. Snow, 181–89. Pittsburgh: University of Pittsburgh Press.

———. 2005. *The Study of Ethnomusicology: Thirty-one Issues and Concepts*, new edition. Urbana: University of Illinois Press.

Rhodes, Willard. 1954. *Indian Songs of Today*. Washington, DC: Library of Congress, Music Division.

Robertson, Robbie. 1998. *Contact from the Underworld of Redboy*. Hollywood: Capitol Records, Inc.

Swan, Daniel C. 1998. "Early Osage Peyotism." *Plains Anthropologist* 43(163): 51–71.

White Deer, Gary, director. 1994. *Chickasaw Social Songs and Stomp Dances*. Oklahoma City: Ojas Studio.

~

Index

About the Editors and Contributors

Victoria Lindsay Levine is professor of music at Colorado College. She researches Native American and performs with *Gamelan Tunjung Sari*, which she founded in 1993. She is the author, co-author, or editor of numerous publications, including *Writing American Indian Music: Historic Transcriptions, Notations, and Arrangements* (2002). Her interests include musical revitalization, historical ethnomusicology, regional music culture, and Indigenous modernity. She has received fellowships from the American Council of Learned Societies, the National Endowment for the Humanities, and the Society for Ethnomusicology, as well as endowed professorships from Colorado College.

Philip V. Bohlman is the Mary Werkman Distinguished Service Professor of Music and Humanities at the University of Chicago, and Honorarprofessor at the Hochshule für Musik, Theater und Medien Hannover. With Bruno Nettl, he founded the series Chicago Studies in Ethnomusicology. Most recently, he is the author of *Wie sängen wir Seinen Gesang auf dem Boden der Fremde! Jüdische Musik zwischen Aschkenas und Moderne*. He serves as artistic director of the cabaret New Budapest Orpheum Society, whose CD, *As Dreams Fall Apart: The Golden Age of Jewish Film Music, 1925–1955*, appeared in 2014.

Theresa Allison, who is both a physician and an ethnomusicologist, is an associate professor of medicine and family and community medicine at the University of California, San Francisco Division of Geriatrics. She works mainly as the medical director of the home-based primary care intensive care management program at the San Francisco Veteran's Administration Medical Center. Her research involves the roles of music in nursing home daily life. She is currently exploring what it means to sing when one can no longer speak because of neurodegenerative disease.

Samuel Araújo is an associate professor of ethnomusicology at the School of Music of the Federal University of Rio de Janeiro and has served as the Tinker Visiting Professor in the Music Department at the University of Chicago. His research on the political and aesthetic dimensions of music and sound praxis has emphasized the role of academic research in the public sphere and has been published in numerous periodicals and books released in Brazil and abroad. He has developed participatory research initiatives integrating academic and non-academic collaborators, involving activist groups and non-governmental and governmental institutions in Brazil, Portugal, and Colombia.

Stephen Blum has taught since 1987 in the music Ph.D. programs at the City University of New York Graduate Center, where he initiated the concentration in ethnomusicology. After completing a dissertation on music of northeastern Iran at the University of Illinois, as Bruno Nettl's first doctoral student, he taught at Western Illinois University, the University of Illinois, and York University, where he was the founding director of the M.F.A. program in musicology of contemporary cultures. He has published numerous articles on the music of Iran, as well as studies of general topics such as music composition, improvisation, ethnomusicological analysis, and modern music history.

Patricia Shehan Campbell is the Donald E. Peterson Professor of Music at the University of Washington, where she teaches music education and ethnomusicology. She is the author of *Lessons from the World* (1991), *Music in Cultural Context* (1996), *Songs in Their Heads* (1998, 2010), *Teaching Music Globally* (2004), *Music and Teacher* (2008), and the co-author of *Music in Childhood* (2013, fourth edition). She is the co-editor of the *Oxford Handbook on Children's Musical Cultures* (2013) and of Oxford's Global Music Series. In 2012, she received the Taiji Prize, with Ravi Shankar and Bruno Nettl, for the preservation of traditional music.

Charles Capwell taught music appreciation, musicology, and ethnomusicology in the School of Music at the University of Illinois at Urbana-Champaign, where as a professor of music, he was Bruno Nettl's colleague for thirty years. Capwell was also affiliated with the Anthropology Department and the Center for East Asian and Pacific Studies. He edited the journal *Ethnomusicology* and produced numerous publications, including *The Music of the Bauls of Bengal* (1986). In addition to the music of Bengal, his research interests include colonialism and musical life in nineteenth-century Calcutta, popular and Islamic music of Indonesia, and the music of Asian Americans.

Martha Ellen Davis is an anthropologist and ethnomusicologist specializing in the musical culture of the Dominican Republic. She has also conducted research in Puerto Rico, Spain (León and the Canary Islands), Brazil, Trinidad, and Peru. She is affiliate professor of the University of Florida and coordinator of the Social Science Commission, Academy of Sciences, Dominican Republic. She received the Charles Seeger Prize (Society for Ethnomusicology, 1970), the Chicago Folklore Prize (honorable mention, 1976), and the Dominican National Essay Award for *La otra ciencia: El vodú dominicano como religion y medicina populares* (1987).

Beverley Diamond is the Canada Research Chair in Ethnomusicology at Memorial University of Newfoundland, where she established the Research Centre for the Study of Music, Media, and Place. She is known for her research on gender issues, Canadian historiography, and Indigenous music cultures. She co-edited *Aboriginal Music in Contemporary Canada: Echoes and Exchanges* (2012). Among her other publications are *Native American Music in Eastern North America* (2008) and *Music and Gender* (2000). She was elected to the Royal Society of Canada in 2008, served as a Trudeau Fellow (2009–2012), and is a member of the Order of Canada (2013).

Stefan Fiol is an assistant professor of ethnomusicology in the College-Conservatory of Music at the University of Cincinnati. He is currently completing a monograph that explores the production of folk music in the Indian Himalayas. His research has been published in the journals *Ethnomusicology*, *Ethnomusicology Forum*, *Asian Music*, *Journal of Asian Studies*, *South Asian Popular Culture*, and *Yearbook for Traditional Music*. He previously taught at the University of Illinois (2001–2003), the University of Notre Dame (2005–2006), and the Eastman School of Music (2008–2010).

Charlotte J. Frisbie is professor of anthropology emerita at Southern Illinois University, Edwardsville. A past president of the Society for Ethnomusicology and co-founder of the Navajo Studies Conference, Inc., she continues anthropological and ethnomusicological research and writing. Current Navajo work focuses on ethnohistory, historic preservation and restoration, traditional foods, Indigenous knowledge, responses to NAGPRA, and autobiographies. Other interests include Indigenous peoples of the Southwestern United States, gender studies, ritual drama, language and culture, action anthropology, collaborative ethnography, SEM's history and the early women in it, and the history of the southern Illinois farming community where she lives.

Robert Garfias serves on the faculty of the Department of Anthropology at the University of California, Irvine. His research has included the music of Japan, Romania, Turkey, Korea, and the Philippines, among other topics. He has served on the National Council of the Arts of the National Endowment for the Arts, the council of the Smithsonian Institution, and the Orange County Arts Alliance. He is a former president of the Society for Ethnomusicology. In 2005, Garfias was awarded the Order of the Rising Sun by the emperor of Japan, the highest honor that can be bestowed on a non-Japanese citizen.

Chris Goertzen teaches music history and world music at the University of Southern Mississippi. He is the author of *Fiddling for Norway: Revival and Identity* (1997), *Southern Fiddlers and Fiddle Contests* (2008), *Made in Mexico: Tradition, Tourism, and Political Ferment in Oaxaca* (2010); co-author of *Alice Person: Good Medicine and Good Music* (with David Hursh, 2009); and co-editor of *Routes and Roots: Fiddle and Dance Studies from Around the North Atlantic 4* (with Ian Russell, 2012) and the *Europe* volume of *The Garland Encyclopedia of World Music* (with Tim Rice and James Porter, 2000). He re-shingled the roof of Bruno and Wanda Nettl's house in the summer of 1981.

J. Richard Haefer is professor of music in the Emeritus College at Arizona State University. His research interests include theory and concepts of music in North American Indian cultures, Gregorian chant, the music of Mexico, and musical instruments. He is the director of the professional ensemble *Mariachi Corazón de Phoenix*, Precentor of *Schola Cantorum Sanctæ Crucis*, and area editor for North and South America for *The Grove Dictionary of Musical Instruments*, second edition.

Orin Hatton earned a B.Mus. at the University of Illinois at Urbana-Champaign and an M.A. at the Catholic University of America. He retired from the United States Navy Band and now serves as a program analyst with the United States Department of Veterans' Affairs. His article "Grass Dance Musical Style and Female Pow-wow Singers" received the 1986 Jaap Kunst Prize from the Society for Ethnomusicology. His other publications include *Power and Performance in Gros Ventre War Expedition Songs* (1990). As a member of the Saskatchewan Archaeological Society, he participated in a site survey in 2012 at Cabri Lake, Saskatchewan.

Zuzana Jurková studied ethnology and musicology at the Philosophical Faculty of Charles University and the music conservatory in Brno. She currently serves as professor and head of the Institute for Ethnomusicology at the Faculty of Humanities of Charles University. Her research focuses mainly on the musics of minorities, including Romani music. She also studies the history of Czech ethnomusicology and, more recently, urban ethnomusicology. She is the author of numerous publications, including *Voices of the Weak* (2009), *Sounds from the Margins* (2013), and *Prague Soundscapes* (2013). She has received grants and awards from the Open Society Fund, Fulbright, and other organizations.

William Kinderman is the author of *Beethoven's Diabelli Variations*; *Artaria 195: Beethoven's Sketchbook for the Missa Solemnis*; *The Piano Sonata in E Major, Opus 109*; *The String Quartets of Beethoven*; *Mozart's Piano Music*; *Genetic Criticism and the Creative Process*; *Beethoven*; *The Creative Process in Music from Mozart to Kurtág*; and *Wagner's Parsifal*. An accomplished pianist, he has recorded Beethoven's last sonatas and the *Diabelli Variations*. Kinderman is a professor at the University of Illinois at Urbana-Champaign and has been a guest professor at the University of Munich. In 2010, he received a research prize for lifetime achievement from the Humboldt Foundation.

Lars-Christian Koch is head of the Department of Ethnomusicology and the Berlin Phonogram Archive at the Museum of Ethnology in Berlin. He also serves as professor of ethnomusicology at the University of Cologne and honorary professor of ethnomusicology at the University of the Arts in Berlin. He has taught at the University of Vienna and the University of Chicago. Koch has conducted fieldwork in India and South Korea. His research interests include the theory and practice of North Indian rāga music, organology (especially instrument manufacturing), Buddhist music, popular music and urban culture, historical recordings, and music archaeology.

Frederick Lau teaches ethnomusicology and Chinese Studies at the University of Hawai'i, Manoa. His scholarly interests include a broad range of topics in Chinese, Western, and Asian music and cultures. He has published widely on traditional Chinese music, music and politics, music and nationalism, Chinese music in the diaspora, and issues related to twentieth-century Western avant-garde music. He is author of *Music in China* (2008) and co-editor of *Locating East Asia in Western Art Music* (2004) as well as *Vocal Music and Cultural Identity in Contemporary Music: Unlimited Voices in East Asia and the West* (2013).

Harry Liebersohn teaches history at the University of Illinois at Urbana-Champaign. He is the author of numerous books and articles including *The Traveler's World: Europe to the Pacific* (2006) and *The Return of the Gift: European History of a Global Idea* (2011). He was a fellow at the Institute for Advanced Study in Princeton, New Jersey, in 1996–1997 and at the Wissenschaftskolleg zu Berlin (Institute for Advanced Study, Berlin) in 2006–2007. In 2014–2015, he served as co-director of an interdisciplinary initiative titled "Dissonance: Music and Globalization since Edison's Phonograph," through the Center for Advanced Study, University of Illinois.

Daniel M. Neuman is the author of *The Life of Music in North India* and co-editor of *Ethnomusicology and Modern Music History* and *Bards, Ballads, and Boundaries: An Ethnographic Atlas of Musical Cultures in West Rajasthan.* He served for ten years as director of the School of Music at the University of Washington, Seattle before serving as dean of the School of the Arts and Architecture and executive vice chancellor and provost at the University of California, Los Angeles. He currently holds the Sambhi Chair in Indian Music at UCLA, where he is a professor of ethnomusicology.

A. J. Racy is a professor of ethnomusicology at the University of California, Los Angeles. He has published numerous works on music and musical cultures of the Middle East, including his award-winning *Making Music in the Arab World: The Culture and Artistry of Ṭarab* (2003). Born in Lebanon, Racy is a well-known composer, recording artist, and multi-instrumentalist who has performed and lectured widely in the United States and abroad.

Melinda Russell is professor of music and co-chair of the Music Department at Carleton College. She has published articles on the reception of reggae, the Macarena craze, oral/aural folk songs in modern American culture, the unsingability of the "Star-Spangled Banner," and classroom partnerships between part-time and tenure-track music faculty. Her current research focuses on the Minneapolis folk revival of the 1960s and on the folk musician and educator Charity Bailey.

Margaret Sarkissian serves as professor of music and chair of the Music Department at Smith College. She is the author of *D'Albuquerque's Children: Performing Tradition in Malaysia's Portuguese Settlement* (2000), *Kantiga di Padri să Chang* (1998), and many articles on the music and dance of the Portuguese and Straits Chinese communities in Malacca, Malaysia, where she has conducted extensive research since 1990.

Albrecht Schneider studied musicology and biology at the Universities of Bonn and Cologne, Germany. He served as professor of systematic musicology at the University of Hamburg from 1983 until he retired in 2012; he was also a Dozent at Comenius-University, Bratislava and a visiting professor at the University of California, Los Angeles. He is the author or co-author of numerous publications, including *Tonhöhe—Skala—Klang: Akustische, tonometrische und psychoakustische Untersuchungen auf vergleichender Grundlage* (1997), and he co-edited the journal *Systematische Musikwissenschaft/Systematic Musicology/Musicologie systématique*.

Anna Schultz is an assistant professor of music at Stanford University. Her first book, *Singing a Hindu Nation*, was published in 2013. Her second book, on Bene Israel devotional song and cultural translation, is being supported by a fellowship from the American Council of Learned Societies. Her other publications discuss South Asian popular song, Marathi and Indo-Caribbean Hindu devotional music, American country music, nationalism, the aesthetics of suffering, new media, recording technology, patronage, liveness, and diaspora.

Anthony Seeger is distinguished professor of ethnomusicology, emeritus, at the University of California, Los Angeles and director emeritus of Smithsonian Folkways Recordings. He has published three books, co-edited three others, and written numerous articles and book chapters on subjects including Indigenous peoples of Brazil, ethnomusicology, intellectual property, intangible cultural heritage, and audiovisual archiving. Beyond teaching, research, archiving, and record production, he has been president of the Society for Ethnomusicology and president and secretary general of the International Council for Traditional Music and served on many advisory and executive boards. He is a fellow of the American Academy of Arts and Sciences.

Amnon Shiloah (1928–2014) was professor of musicology at the Hebrew University of Jerusalem. His research and publication ranged widely across many areas of ethnomusicology, and he incorporated historical studies with ethnographic and anthropological approaches. His philological and exegetical studies of manuscripts in the history of Islam, especially in the two volumes of *The Theory of Music in Arab Writings (c. 900–1900)*, are the standard reference works in the field. His studies of music in modern Jewish communities, such as *Jewish Musical Traditions*, are foundational for modern Jewish music scholarship. Amnon Shiloah passed away as this volume was going to press.

Stephen Slawek is professor of ethnomusicology at the University of Texas at Austin. His research has focused on the music of India and on American popular music. He has served on the executive boards of the Society for Ethnomusicology and the Society for Asian Music, as editor of *Asian Music*, and as chair of the ethnomusicology committee for the American Institute of Indian Studies. He performs extensively on the Indian sitar, having given recitals on four continents. He has also directed the Butler School of Music's Javanese gamelan ensemble since 2012.

Gabriel Solis is associate professor of music, anthropology, and African American studies at the University of Illinois at Urbana-Champaign. He is the author of *Monk's Music: Thelonious Monk and Jazz History in the Making* (2008) and *Thelonious Monk Quartet with John Coltrane at Carnegie Hall* (2014). He co-edited *Musical Improvisation: Art, Education, and Society* with Bruno Nettl (2009), and his articles have appeared in journals such as *Ethnomusicology*, *The Journal of Popular Music Studies*, *Popular Music and Society*, *Current Sociology*, and *The Musical Quarterly*.

Marcello Sorce Keller produced a lot of musical pollution as a young man, when he worked as a pop music pianist and arranger. He later repented and studied musicology at the University of Illinois at Urbana-Champaign. After teaching in the United States, Italy, and Switzerland, he is now retired in Lugano, and keeps in touch with academe as a research fellow at the Institut für Musikwissenschaft of the University of Berne. His latest book, co-edited with Linda Barwick, is titled *Italy in Australia's Musical Landscape* (2012).

Gordon Thompson is professor of music and chair of the Music Department at Skidmore College, where he teaches popular music, South Asian music, and other courses in ethnomusicology. He is the author of numerous publications, including *Please Please Me: Sixties British Pop, Inside Out* (2008), which examines the social intersections between the music and recording industries in London between 1956 and 1968. Thompson is also a performer and composer who has written music for films and concerts. He is a frequent radio and television interviewee and contributes regularly to an Oxford Blog on the Beatles and British pop in the 1960s.

Thomas Turino is professor emeritus of musicology and anthropology at the University of Illinois at Urbana-Champaign. He has written on mestizo, Indigenous, and urban popular music of Peru; on nationalism, cosmopolitanism, and popular music in Zimbabwe; and on various theoretical topics including music in political movements and Peircean semiotics and phenomenology. He has also studied and taught courses on North American string band and early country music and is a performer on the five-string banjo, Cajun accordion, and occasionally the fiddle.

Philip Yampolsky recorded, edited, and annotated the twenty-volume audio CD series *Music of Indonesia* (Smithsonian Folkways Recordings) and was the founding director of the Robert E. Brown Center for World Music at the University of Illinois at Urbana-Champaign. He is an ethnomusicologist who has studied the music of Indonesia and its neighbors (especially now East Timor) for more than forty years. He lived in Indonesia for fifteen years. One of his many research interests is the worldwide gramophone industry prior to World War II. He is currently preparing a discography of commercial recordings made in Indonesia, Malaysia, and Singapore from 1903 to 1942.

Terada Yoshitaka serves as professor in the Department of Advanced Studies in Anthropology at the National Museum of Ethnology in Osaka, Japan. His primary areas of research are India, the Philippines, Japan, and Asian North America. His publications include the edited collection *Music and Society in South Asia: Perspectives from Japan* (2008). For the past fifteen years, he has experimented with filmmaking methods and has produced more than thirty films on musical traditions from diverse locations.